SAGA OF THE SWAMP THING BOOK FOUR

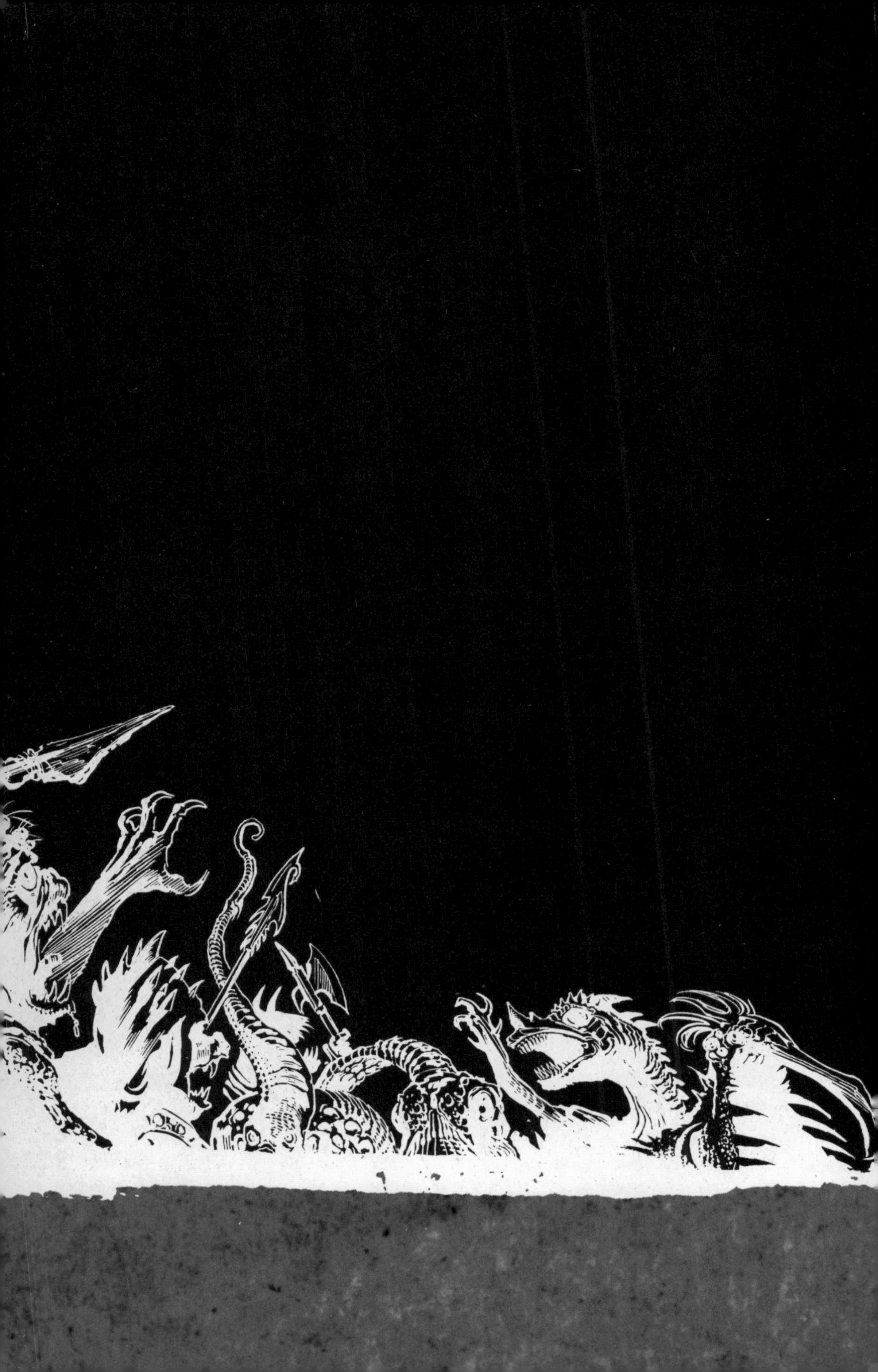

Written by **Alan Moore**

Art by Stephen Bissette John Totleben Stan Woch
Rick Veitch Alfredo Alcala Ron Randall Tom Mandrake

Colored by Tatjana Wood

Lettered by John Costanza

Original Series Cover Art by Stephen Bissette John Totleben

Original Series Cover Color by Tatjana Wood

Swamp Thing created by Len Wein and Bernie Wrightson

SAGA OF THE
SWAMP THING
BOOK FOUR

Karen Berger Editor – Original Series
Scott Nybakken Editor
Robbin Brosterman Design Director – Books
Louis Prandi Publication Design

Shelly Bond Executive Editor – Vertigo
Hank Kanalz Senior VP – Vertigo & Integrated Publishing

Diane Nelson President
Dan DiDio and **Jim Lee** Co-Publishers
Geoff Johns Chief Creative Officer
John Rood Executive VP – Sales, Marketing & Business Development
Amy Genkins Senior VP – Business & Legal Affairs
Nairi Gardiner Senior VP – Finance
Jeff Boison VP – Publishing Planning
Mark Chiarello VP – Art Direction & Design
John Cunningham VP – Marketing
Terri Cunningham VP – Editorial Administration
Alison Gill Senior VP – Manufacturing & Operations
Jay Kogan VP – Business & Legal Affairs, Publishing
Jack Mahan VP – Business Affairs, Talent
Nick Napolitano VP – Manufacturing Administration
Sue Pohja VP – Book Sales
Courtney Simmons Senior VP – Publicity
Bob Wayne Senior VP – Sales

Cover art by **John Totleben**.
Back cover art by **Stephen Bissette** and **John Totleben**.
Cover Color by **Allen Passalaqua**.

SAGA OF THE SWAMP THING BOOK FOUR
Published by DC Comics. Cover and compilation Copyright © 2010
DC Comics. All Rights Reserved. Introduction and foreword
Copyright © 1988 DC Comics. All Rights Reserved. Originally published as THE SAGA OF THE SWAMP THING 43-45 and SWAMP THING
46-50. Copyright © 1985 DC Comics. All Rights Reserved.
All characters, their distinctive likenesses and related elements
featured in this publication are trademarks of DC Comics.
The stories, characters and incidents featured in this publication
are entirely fictional. DC Comics does not read or accept unsolicited
submissions of ideas, stories or artwork.

DC Comics
1700 Broadway, New York, NY 10019
A Warner Bros. Entertainment Company.
Printed in the USA. Second Printing.
ISBN: 978-1-4012-4046-2

Library of Congress Cataloging-in-Publication Data

Moore, Alan, 1953- author.
  Saga of the Swamp Thing. Book four / Alan Moore, Stephen Bissette,
Stan Woch.
     pages cm
  "Originally published in single magazine form in Saga of the
Swamp Thing 43-45, Swamp Thing 46-50."
  ISBN 978-1-4012-4046-2
  1. Graphic novels. I. Bissette, Stephen, illustrator. II. Woch, Stan,
illustrator. III. Title.
  PN6728.S93M646 2013
  741.5'973—dc23
                                              2013009140

SUSTAINABLE FORESTRY INITIATIVE
Certified Chain of Custody
Promoting Sustainable Forestry
www.sfiprogram.org
SFI-01042
APPLIES TO TEXT STOCK ONLY

Introduction

"See, as it happens, I've got a couple of front row tickets for the end of the universe..."

If you go down to the swamp today — especially if you've splashed through this particular bayou before — you'll probably have noticed how each story in the *Swamp Thing* cycle not only builds on what has gone before, but in turn lays the foundations of what is to follow.

Assuming you have read *Swamp Thing* before, either in its monthly comic book form or in the present series of collections, you will be aware of how a particular story may cast an unexpected shadow back upon something you have read previously. The volume you are presently holding — telekinetics or suspension through other means excepted, of course — is a vital cornerstone of both the "American Gothic" cycle and the larger work itself.

"American Gothic" is the nightmarish odyssey through the dark continent of America which Moore describes, with mordant flippancy, as "a kind of Ramsey Campbell version of *Easy Rider*." The third story in this book — "Ghost Dance" (from *Swamp Thing* #45) — is the last of his "social horror" stories for the title, past examples of which included "Southern Change," "Strange Fruit," "The Curse," "The Nukeface Papers," "Still Waters," "Fish Story" and "Bogeymen." "Ghost Dance" is special for many reasons, and it is Moore's personal favorite of its group. Despite the fact that the other stories touched on such sensitive topics as sexism, racism, nuclear power and serial killing, the uncompromising espousal of gun control in "Ghost Dance" and its equation of U.S. citizens' right to bear arms with the bloody history of the genocide of Native Americans made it the most savagely criticized of all Moore's *Swamp Thing* stories.

Though it was eventually drawn by Stan Woch and Alfredo Alcala — and this is as good a time as any to point out that the *zeitgeist* of the *Swamp Thing* strip is so strong that the highly distinctive and individual art styles of such varied artists as Steve Bissette, John Totleben, Ron Randall, Shawn McManus, Rick Veitch, Stan Woch and Alfredo Alcala have blended into a wholly consistent and unified visual "voice" throughout the series — the germ of the story was provided by Jim Wheelock, a friend of Bissette and Totleben. He sent them an account of the horrific existence of Sarah Winchester, scion of the legendary gun manufacturing dynasty which gave its name to the Winchester carbine. This account, together with research material gathered by Steve Donnelly at the Winchester home in California, were Moore's inspiration for "Ghost Dance," an evocation of Sarah Winchester's terror of the spirits of those her family's weapons had slaughtered over the years.

One of Moore's greatest strengths as a writer is that he takes such a catholic and eclectic interest in the world around him: his stories derive from sources richer and deeper than those of many of his contemporaries, who show few signs of being aware of much of anything apart from previous comics and a few current movies. "Ghost Dance" also demonstrates, more than any other *Swamp Thing* story, Moore's mastery of the deadly terrain that exists in the no-man's-land between screaming horror and howling farce. The two cowboys blasting each other literally to bloody ribbons, the buffalos in the closet — Clive Barker himself would have been proud of those batwinged flights of fancy.

In "Revelations" (*Swamp Thing* #46), Moore interweaves the strands of "American Gothic" with the events of DC's mega-series *Crisis on Infinite Earths* (you wondered what all that business with Batman and the red sky in "Bogeymen" was about? *This* is what it was about). In *Crisis*, DC attempted to rationalize almost five decades of convoluted and random storylines by collapsing the tesseract of alternative worlds and contradictory histories into one rationalized universe, and each and every title — even those pursuing independent and individual directions — had to be touched by this macro-plot. Moore's solution was typically elegant: he advances his own tale by using the conversation between DC's perennial mystery man, the Phantom Stranger, and his own snide, sleazy and charismatic creation, John

Constantine, to show some of the "American Gothic" cards which had hitherto remained hidden up his capacious sleeves. It is, indeed, "Revelations" which kicks "American Gothic" into the high gear that whirls us remorselessly towards the cycle's climax in issue #50.

"The Parliament of Trees" (*Swamp Thing* #47), though, is central not only to "American Gothic" but to the entire *Swamp Thing* saga. It represents not only as vital a stage in Swamp Thing's education as his introduction by Jason (the Floronic Man) Woodrue to the concept of the Green (see *Saga of the Swamp Thing Book One*) and his discovery in "Growth Patterns" (*Book Three*) of his own near-immortality, but it also picks up and amplifies hints dropped in "Abandoned Houses" (*Book Two*) concerning his possible relationship to previous "Swamp Things." (There is even a subliminal tribute to the first-ever swamp creature, the Heap, but that's something for hardcore comics nuts to chuckle over and others not to bother their pretty little heads with.)

Elsewhere in this most subtle and curious of *Swamp Thing* stories, Moore demonstrates once again the very real ecological concern which is one of the sturdiest underpinnings of his work on the series — what will be the consequences of humanity's short-sighted and one-sided relationship with the Earth, with the Green? — and his capacity for the sheer hard work of genuinely creative research. His use of the Brujeria — as described in Bruce Chatwin's extraordinary travel book *In Patagonia* — and his familiarity with the ancient Aztec mysticism evoked by Carlos Castaneda (in *The Teachings of Don Juan* and its various sequels) give the Brujeria sequences of this crucial stage of "American Gothic" a breath-catching verisimilitude which is virtually unique to comics. The Invunche is a figure from genuine South American mythology — at least I *hope* it's mythology, heh heh — and it carries an infinitely more authentic, folkloric degree of mythic resonance than the hackneyed scarecrows you find on the corner of Hollywood and Pulp.

Furthermore, "The Parliament of Trees," with its taut, raging dissection of the intimate connections between voyeurism and Puritanism, sows the first seeds of the explosion which will carry Swamp Thing — and Abby — far beyond the climax of "American Gothic." But that, like many other things, is a tale for another time.

"See, as it happens, I've got a couple of front row tickets for the end of the universe. I thought it'd be best to use them now. I mean you never know... there may not be a second performance."

— Charles Shaar Murray
February 1988

Pundit and provocateur Charles Shaar Murray has been opining professionally about music, comics and culture since 1970. A founding writer for Q and Mojo magazines and a long-time contributor to New Musical Express, he has written for countless other publications (including The Guardian, The Observer, The Independent, Vogue, Guitarist and New Statesman) and made numerous appearances on radio and television. He is also the author of four books, including the 1989 biography Crosstown Traffic: Jimi Hendrix and Post-War Pop, *which won the Ralph J. Gleason Music Book Award, and 1999's* Boogie Man: The Adventures of John Lee Hooker in the American Twentieth Century, *which was short-listed for the same honor. By night he sings and plays guitar for London blues band Crosstown Lightnin', co-featuring harmonica maestro Buffalo Bill Smith; by day he's working on a new book about The Clash. His novel* The Hellhound Sample *is due to be published in mid-2011.*

Foreword

So what do you want to know?

We could talk about the philosophy behind this, the climax of the "American Gothic" storyline begun in *Saga of the Swamp Thing* #35. I remember Alan Moore telling me about it, in a Greek restaurant next to Forbidden Planet 2, the London TV and film fantasy bookshop, during the period in which he was writing it, a long time ago. Imagine the scene: Alan, who is huge and hairy, like a Yeti in a suit, with a grin like Maxwell the Magic Cat (but if you know who Maxwell the Magic Cat is then you probably know what Alan Moore looks like), and he's got something with too many legs on his fork[1], which he is using to gesture with, and he's explaining: "The trouble with America is it has a very Manichean attitude" — I'm quoting from memory, you understand — "and I suppose that's what I want to address at the end of 'American Gothic.' It's this attitude that there's good and evil, black and white. And there isn't. That's what 'American Gothic' is about."

And then he goes on to tell me what happens to Sargon and Zatara, and about the hand, and this is all over a meal, you understand, and by the end of it I'm slightly queasy, because Alan's descriptions are *really* graphic, but I'm convinced.

[*Educational bit*: what the Manichean system is about is that everything is either good or evil; there's only one darkness and one light. It began in the third century AD and was founded by someone called Mani (surprisingly enough) and was influenced by many of the religions around at the time — Judaism, pre-Catholic Christianity, Buddhism, Zoroastrianism and so on. It soon spread like wildfire to become one of the great religions, uniting ancient mythology with simple spiritual worship and strict morality — an incredibly simplistic conception of sin and goodness. In the Manichean version of Armageddon, the God of Light appears, accompanied by the "perfected" humans, while the angels supporting the world withdraw and everything collapses into ruins; a conflagration consumes the world, and Light, now complete, rules above the powerless Darkness.

[The Manichean religion was pretty much destroyed by the Catholic Church in the thirteenth century, but the point Alan Moore is making is that in a way it's still very much alive and kicking in America today. Just look at Hollywood (*Rambo*, etc.). And born-again evangelical Revivalism.]

So here we are.

We've seen the vampire fish punks, and the werewolf, and the zombie. We're about to meet the ghosts of the guns, and the Parliament of Trees, and attend a party on a satellite as well-attended as any that Jerry Cornelius haunted. And following these preliminaries, Swamp Thing and John Constantine are about to declare war — or something — on the Brujeria, and on the Darkness that menaces Heaven itself.

The battle gets underway in "A Murder of Crows" (*Swamp Thing* #48), which also marks John Totleben's first solo work on the title, although he'd inked about three-quarters of the Moore-written stories. It's a beautiful job. Panels linger — Swamp Thing in his South American garb, like an Inca god; and Judith's transformation.

There's an ongoing argument in the world of horror about hinting versus showing. On one side of the fence you have the M.R. James school, who terrify by hints and implications, letting the reader build up his or her picture of the menace; on the other side are the Clive Barkers, who show you the monster as soon as they can — and make damn sure it's scary and strange and horrible. Alan — and John and Steve and Rick — have always tended to show you the monster. Judith's metamorphosis is an exception; explicit, but shadowy. We never see her vomit her intestines into the bowl; instead her transformation is accomplished in three panels of shadows... and it's every bit as gruesome.

"The Summoning" (*Swamp Thing* #49) gives us Stan Woch and Alfredo Alcala drawing and inking, as the two teams (astral and physical) are put together to

---

[1] This was before he stopped eating things with legs, you understand.

commence battle against the Darkness. Sargon the Sorcerer, Dr. Occult, Zatara and his daughter Zatanna are hustled together by John Constantine (and I don't believe he really thought they had an ice sculpture's chance in hell of ever actually winning) in Baron Winter's Georgetown mansion.

You don't really need to know who all these people are: they're the detritus, the flotsam and jetsam of the DC occult universe. But in brief: Dr. Occult was one of DC's first-ever characters in the late thirties; Zatara was also a Golden Age star — a kind of Mandrake the Magician whose magical spells need to be read backwards ("daer sdrawkcab" as he would intone), and his daughter, Zatanna, was his equivalent in the sixties, wearing fishnet stockings and a top hat; Sargon again comes from early in the DC era, and, like Zatanna and Zatara, he became a stage magician to cover the fact that he could do real magic; Baron Winter was created by Marv Wolfman in *Night Force* — an enigma in a transtemporal mansion.

We have met most of the spiritual mob who accompany Swamp Thing through the War before; perhaps the only character new to *Swamp Thing* readers is Doctor Fate, another survivor of the Golden Age who can best be described as a symbiotic relationship between an archaeologist and a magical Egyptian helmet.

Despite the fact that "The End" (*Swamp Thing* #50), the consummation of the "American Gothic" storyline, was twice the length of a regular comic, it could still be longer. Armageddon comes and goes in forty pages, leaving in its wake a number of dead and shattered individuals and a philosophy that practically any religion would find heretical — or at least uncomfortable. It also marked the end of the Bissette and Totleben art team on the title — two individuals who, as much as Alan Moore, had given it its distinctive feel and look. Their replacements were Rick Veitch and Alfredo Alcala, neither of them newcomers to the book.

"Home Free" (*Swamp Thing* #51), which is not included in this volume, represents an epilogue to "American Gothic" and takes us into the title's next major arc. The seed of this storyline, however, is revealed here in "The Parliament of Trees" (*Swamp Thing* #47) and "A Murder of Crows" — it's about prejudice and love: what happens when people love the "wrong" people. In it we also get the closest that we are likely to get to discovering what makes John Constantine tick.

He's hard to get a handle of, is Constantine. Alan Moore told me that he used to think he'd created the man, until one afternoon, in a Westminster sandwich bar, they met. Apparently by accident. Constantine was wearing a natty suit and a grubby overcoat, and carrying a rucksack. He briefly said hello to Alan, and went off to eat his sandwiches.

Alan swears it's true, and I believe him. To the end of the world. Which you may find somewhere in the volume you are holding...

— Neil Gaiman
Sussex, May 1988

World-renowned for The Sandman *and one of comics' most accomplished writers, Neil Gaiman is also the* New York Times *best-selling author of the novels* Anansi Boys, American Gods *and the Newbery Medal-winning* The Graveyard Book, *as well as the multimedia creations* Neverwhere, Stardust *and* Coraline. *Among his many awards are the Hugo, the Nebula, the Eisner, the Harvey, the Bram Stoker and the World Fantasy Award. Originally from England, Gaiman now lives in the United States.*

SAGA OF THE

SWAMP THING

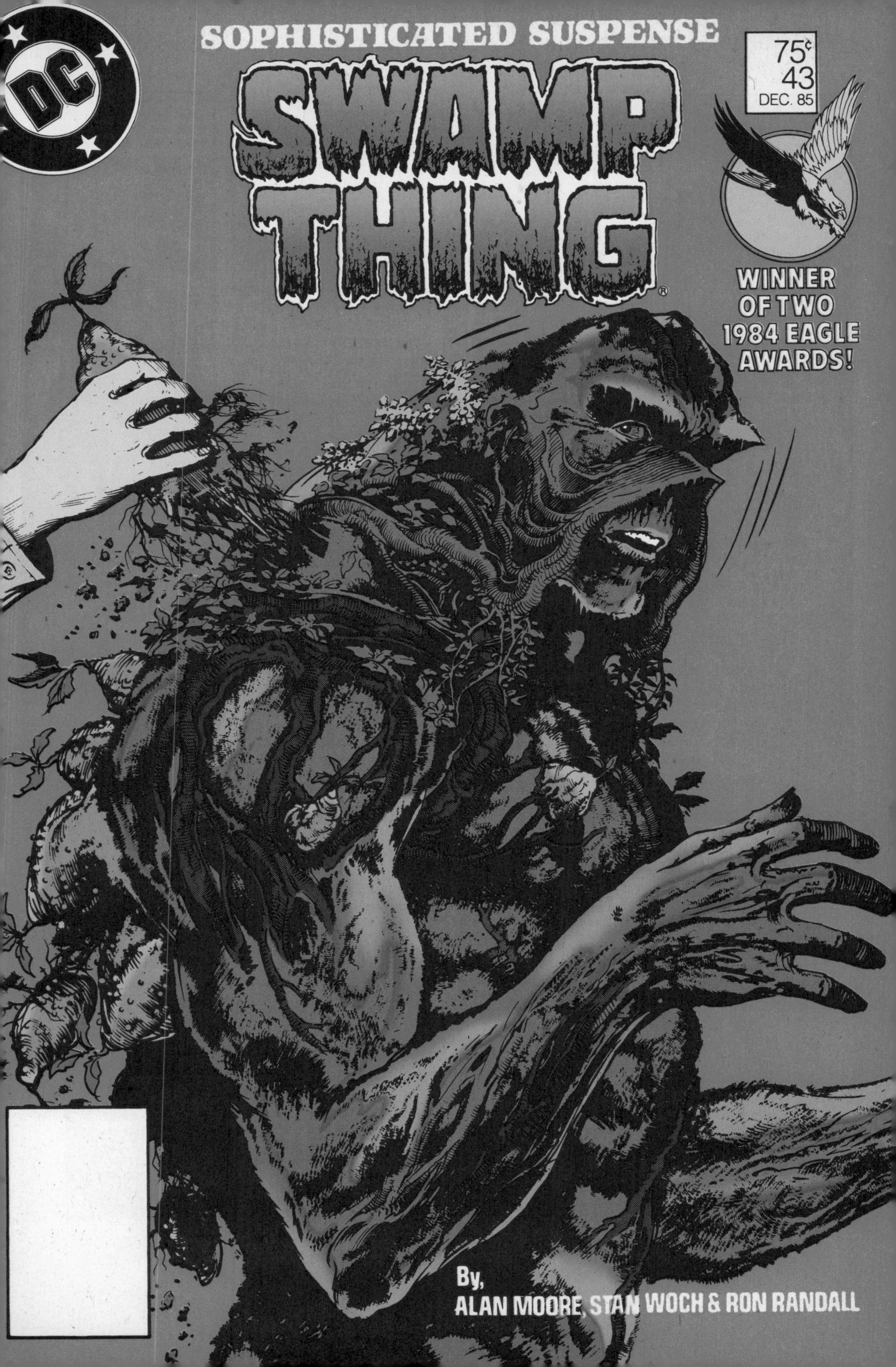

SOPHISTICATED SUSPENSE
SWAMP THING®
75¢
43
DEC. 85
WINNER OF TWO 1984 EAGLE AWARDS!
By,
ALAN MOORE, STAN WOCH & RON RANDALL

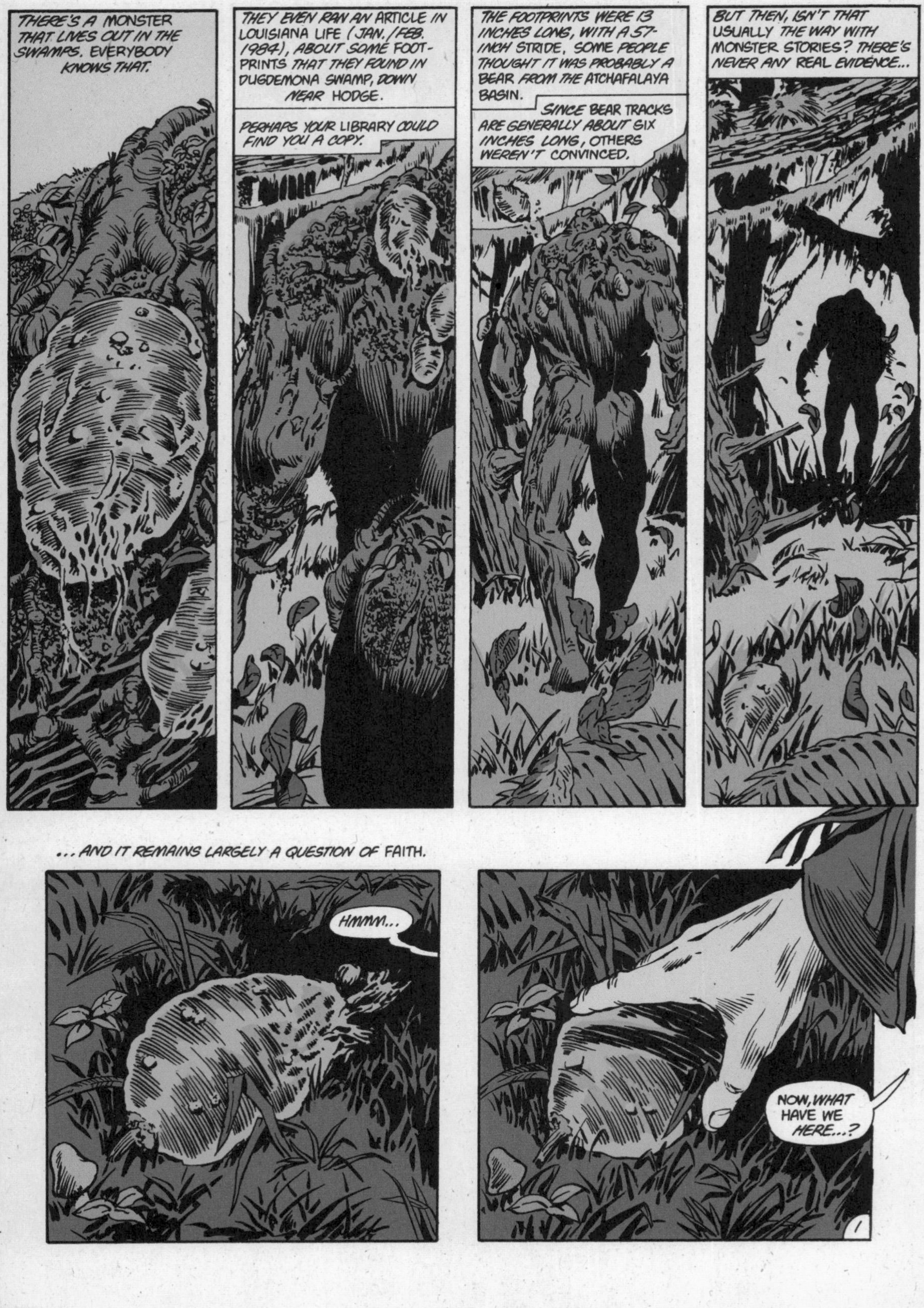
THERE'S A MONSTER THAT LIVES OUT IN THE SWAMPS. EVERYBODY KNOWS THAT.
THEY EVEN RAN AN ARTICLE IN LOUISIANA LIFE (JAN./FEB. 1984), ABOUT SOME FOOT-PRINTS THAT THEY FOUND IN DUGDEMONA SWAMP, DOWN NEAR HODGE.
PERHAPS YOUR LIBRARY COULD FIND YOU A COPY.
THE FOOTPRINTS WERE 13 INCHES LONG, WITH A 57-INCH STRIDE. SOME PEOPLE THOUGHT IT WAS PROBABLY A BEAR FROM THE ATCHAFALAYA BASIN.
SINCE BEAR TRACKS ARE GENERALLY ABOUT SIX INCHES LONG, OTHERS WEREN'T CONVINCED.
BUT THEN, ISN'T THAT USUALLY THE WAY WITH MONSTER STORIES? THERE'S NEVER ANY REAL EVIDENCE...
...AND IT REMAINS LARGELY A QUESTION OF FAITH.
HMMM...
NOW, WHAT HAVE WE HERE...?
1

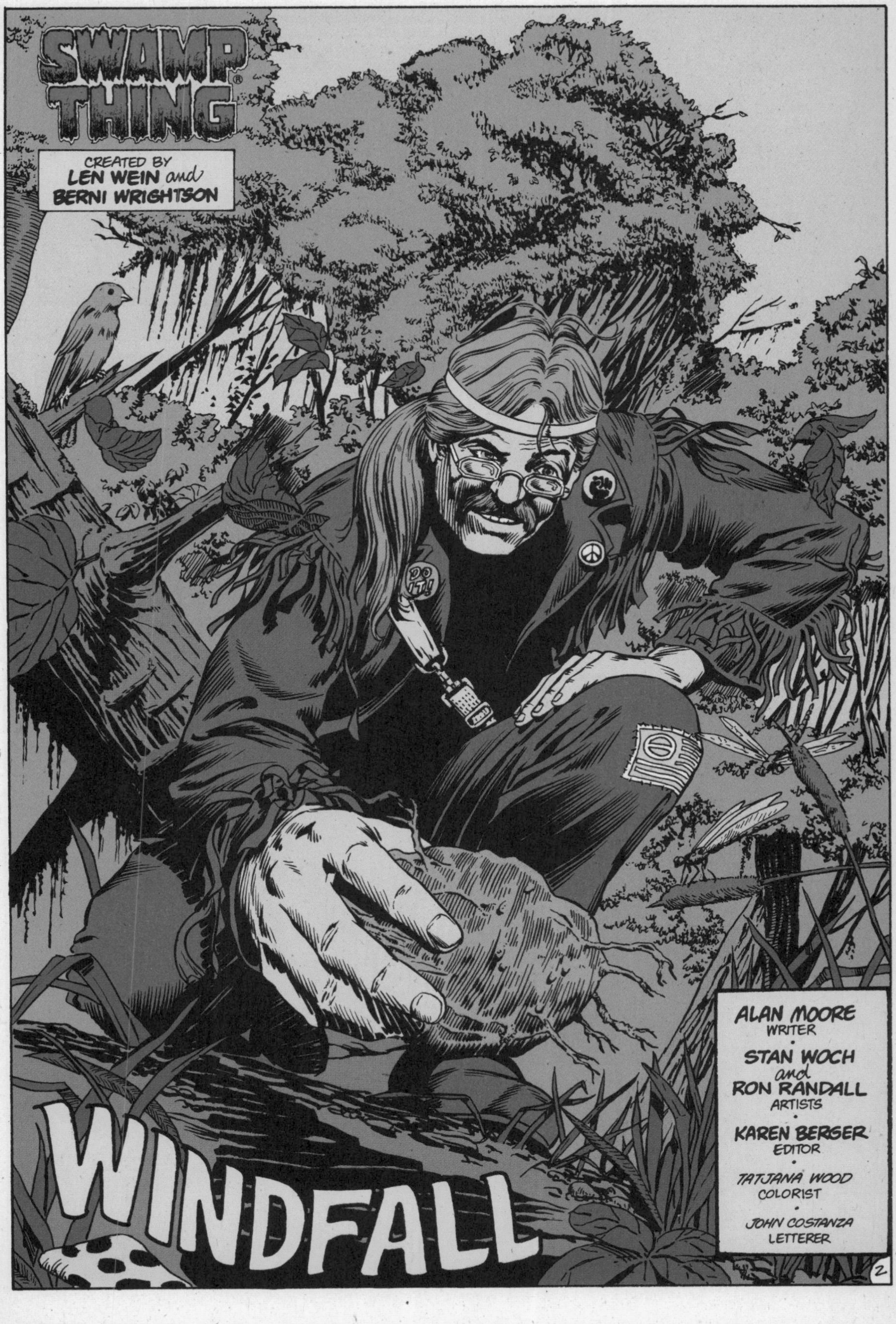
SWAMP THING®
CREATED BY LEN WEIN and BERNI WRIGHTSON
DO IT!
WINDFALL
ALAN MOORE WRITER
STAN WOCH and RON RANDALL ARTISTS
KAREN BERGER EDITOR
TATJANA WOOD COLORIST
JOHN COSTANZA LETTERER
2

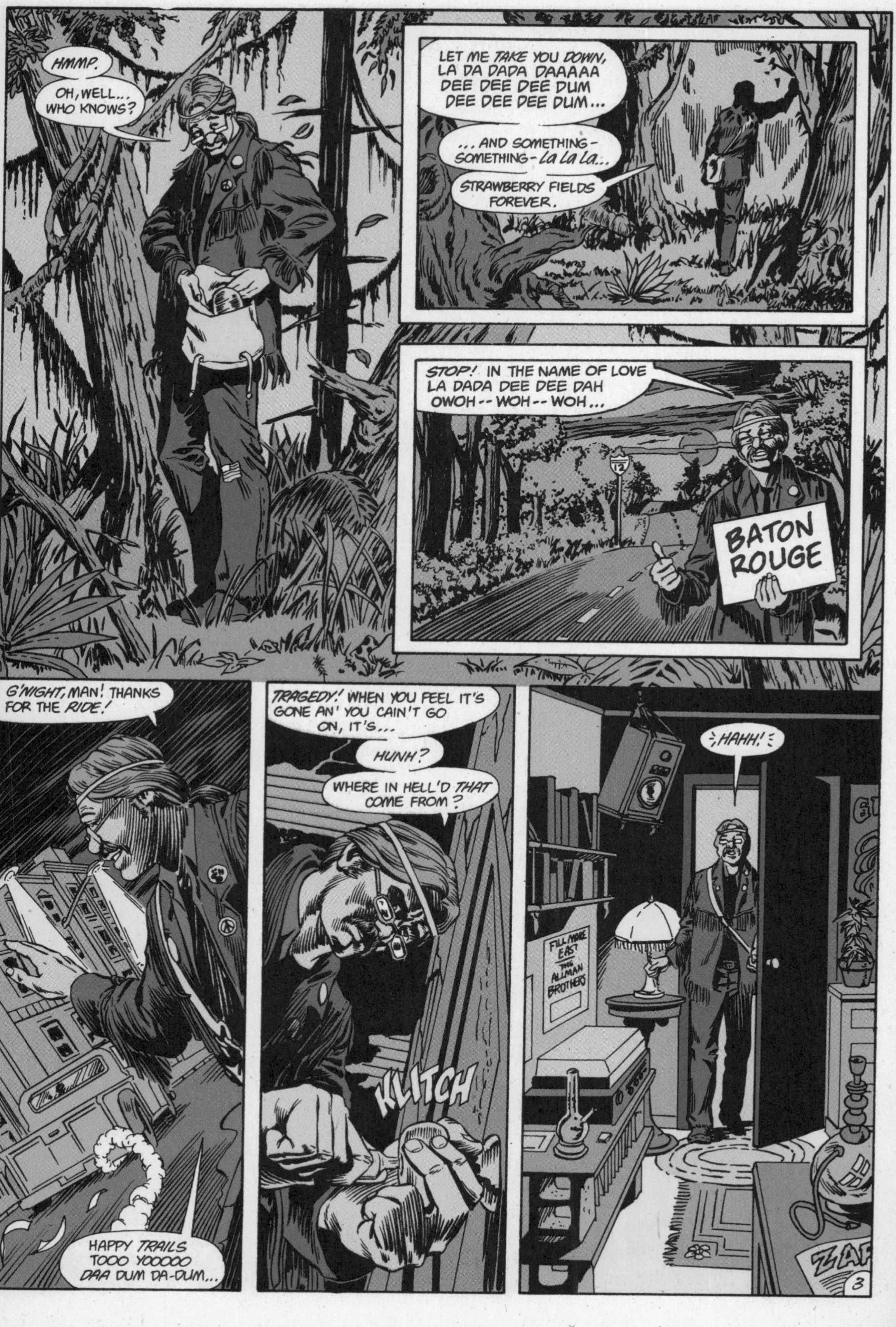
HMMP.
OH, WELL... WHO KNOWS?
LET ME TAKE YOU DOWN, LA DA DADA DAAAAA DEE DEE DEE DUM DEE DEE DEE DUM...
... AND SOMETHING-SOMETHING-La La La...
STRAWBERRY FIELDS FOREVER.
STOP! IN THE NAME OF LOVE LA DADA DEE DEE DAH OWOH -- WOH -- WOH...
BATON ROUGE
G'NIGHT, MAN! THANKS FOR THE RIDE!
HAPPY TRAILS TOOO YOOOOO DAA DUM DA-DUM...
TRAGEDY! WHEN YOU FEEL IT'S GONE AN' YOU CAIN'T GO ON, IT'S...
HUNH?
WHERE IN HELL'D THAT COME FROM?
KLITCH
HAHH!
FILLMORE EAST THE ALLMAN BROTHERS
3

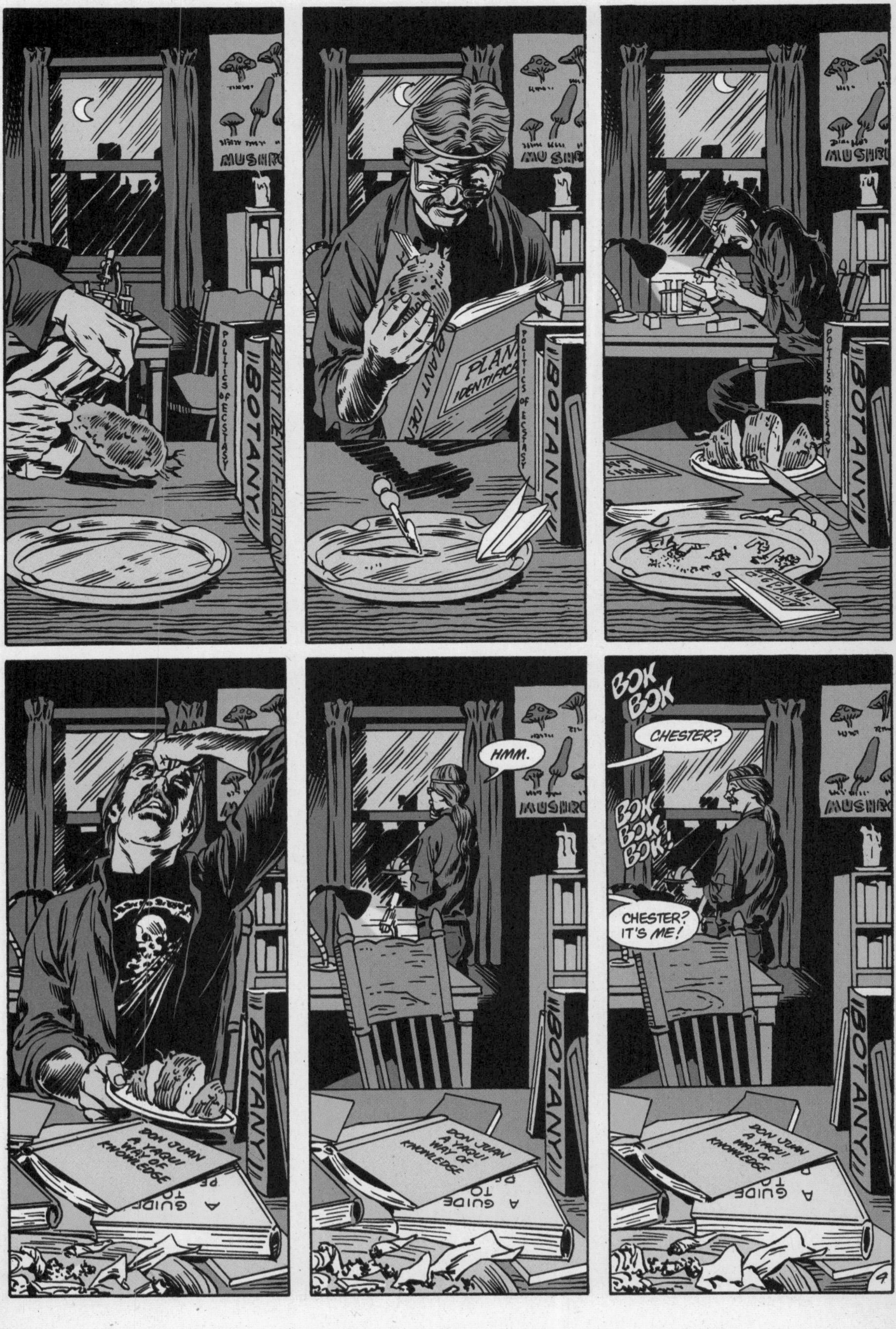
POLITICS OF ECSTASY
BOTANY
PLANT IDENTIFICATION
HMM.
BOK BOK
CHESTER?
BOK BOK BOK!
CHESTER? IT'S ME!
DON JUAN A YAQUI WAY OF KNOWLEDGE
A GUIDE TO

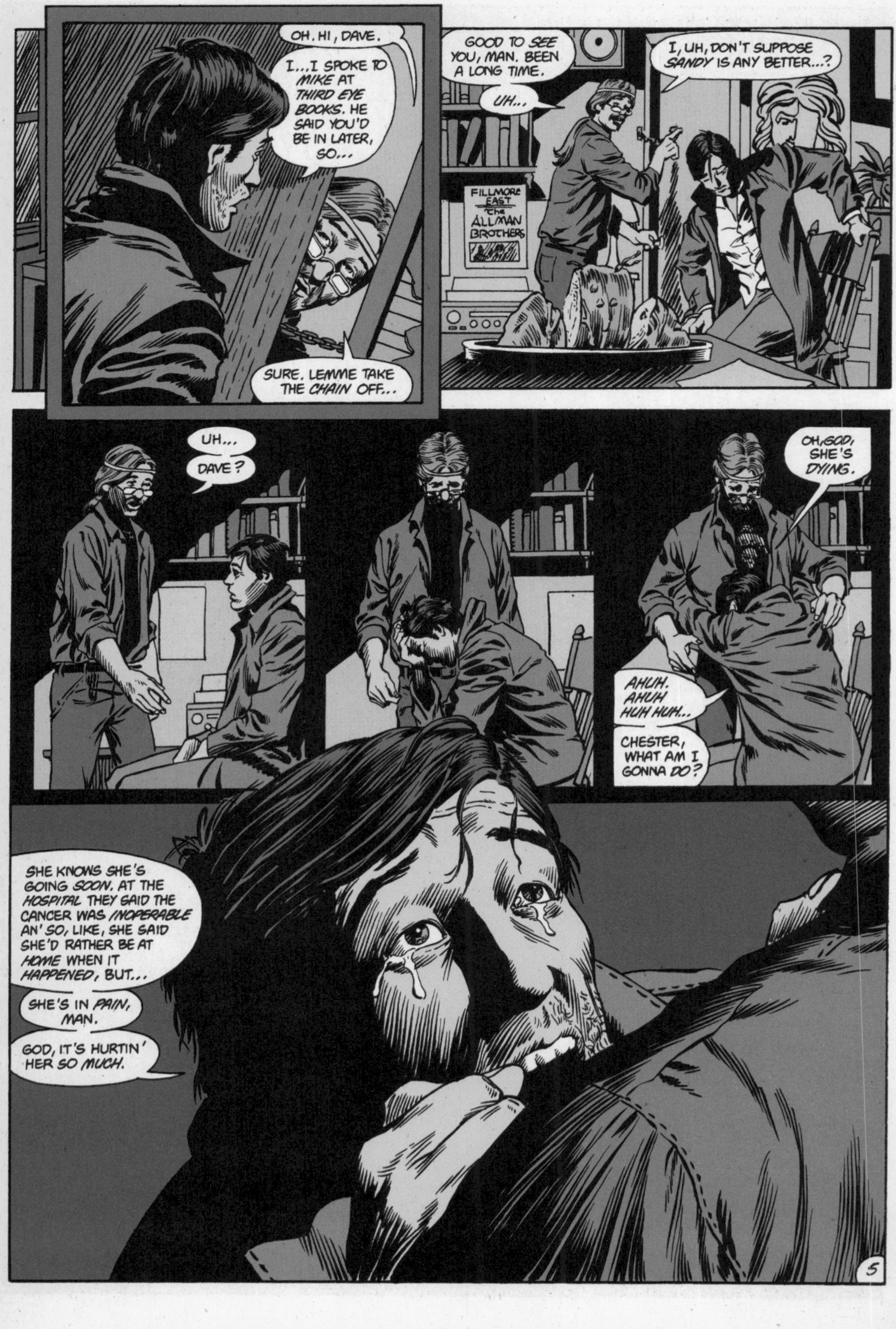
OH, HI, DAVE.
I...I SPOKE TO MIKE AT THIRD EYE BOOKS. HE SAID YOU'D BE IN LATER, SO...
SURE, LEMME TAKE THE CHAIN OFF...
GOOD TO SEE YOU, MAN. BEEN A LONG TIME.
UH...
FILLMORE EAST The ALLMAN BROTHERS
I, UH, DON'T SUPPOSE SANDY IS ANY BETTER...?
UH...
DAVE?
OH, GOD, SHE'S DYING.
AHUH. AHUH HUH HUH...
CHESTER, WHAT AM I GONNA DO?
SHE KNOWS SHE'S GOING SOON. AT THE HOSPITAL THEY SAID THE CANCER WAS INOPERABLE AN' SO, LIKE, SHE SAID SHE'D RATHER BE AT HOME WHEN IT HAPPENED, BUT...
SHE'S IN PAIN, MAN.
GOD, IT'S HURTIN' HER SO MUCH.
5

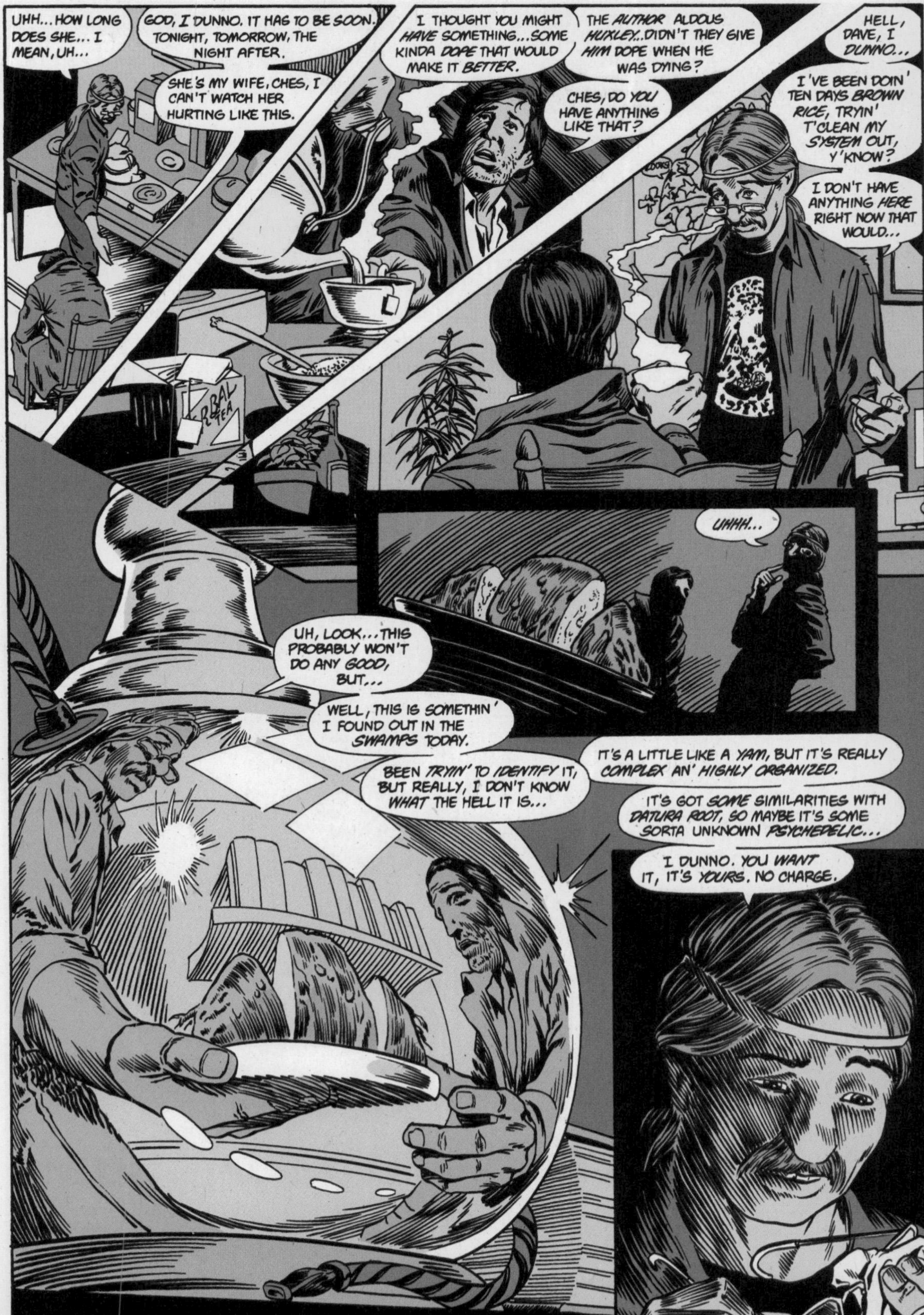
UHH... HOW LONG DOES SHE... I MEAN, UH...
GOD, I DUNNO. IT HAS TO BE SOON. TONIGHT, TOMORROW, THE NIGHT AFTER.
SHE'S MY WIFE, CHES, I CAN'T WATCH HER HURTING LIKE THIS.
I THOUGHT YOU MIGHT HAVE SOMETHING... SOME KINDA DOPE THAT WOULD MAKE IT BETTER.
THE AUTHOR ALDOUS HUXLEY...DIDN'T THEY GIVE HIM DOPE WHEN HE WAS DYING?
CHES, DO YOU HAVE ANYTHING LIKE THAT?
HELL, DAVE, I DUNNO...
I'VE BEEN DOIN' TEN DAYS BROWN RICE, TRYIN' T'CLEAN MY SYSTEM OUT, Y'KNOW?
I DON'T HAVE ANYTHING HERE RIGHT NOW THAT WOULD...
UHHH...
UH, LOOK... THIS PROBABLY WON'T DO ANY GOOD, BUT...
WELL, THIS IS SOMETHIN' I FOUND OUT IN THE SWAMPS TODAY.
BEEN TRYIN' TO IDENTIFY IT, BUT REALLY, I DON'T KNOW WHAT THE HELL IT IS...
IT'S A LITTLE LIKE A YAM, BUT IT'S REALLY COMPLEX AN' HIGHLY ORGANIZED.
IT'S GOT SOME SIMILARITIES WITH DATURA ROOT, SO MAYBE IT'S SOME SORTA UNKNOWN PSYCHEDELIC...
I DUNNO. YOU WANT IT, IT'S YOURS. NO CHARGE.
6

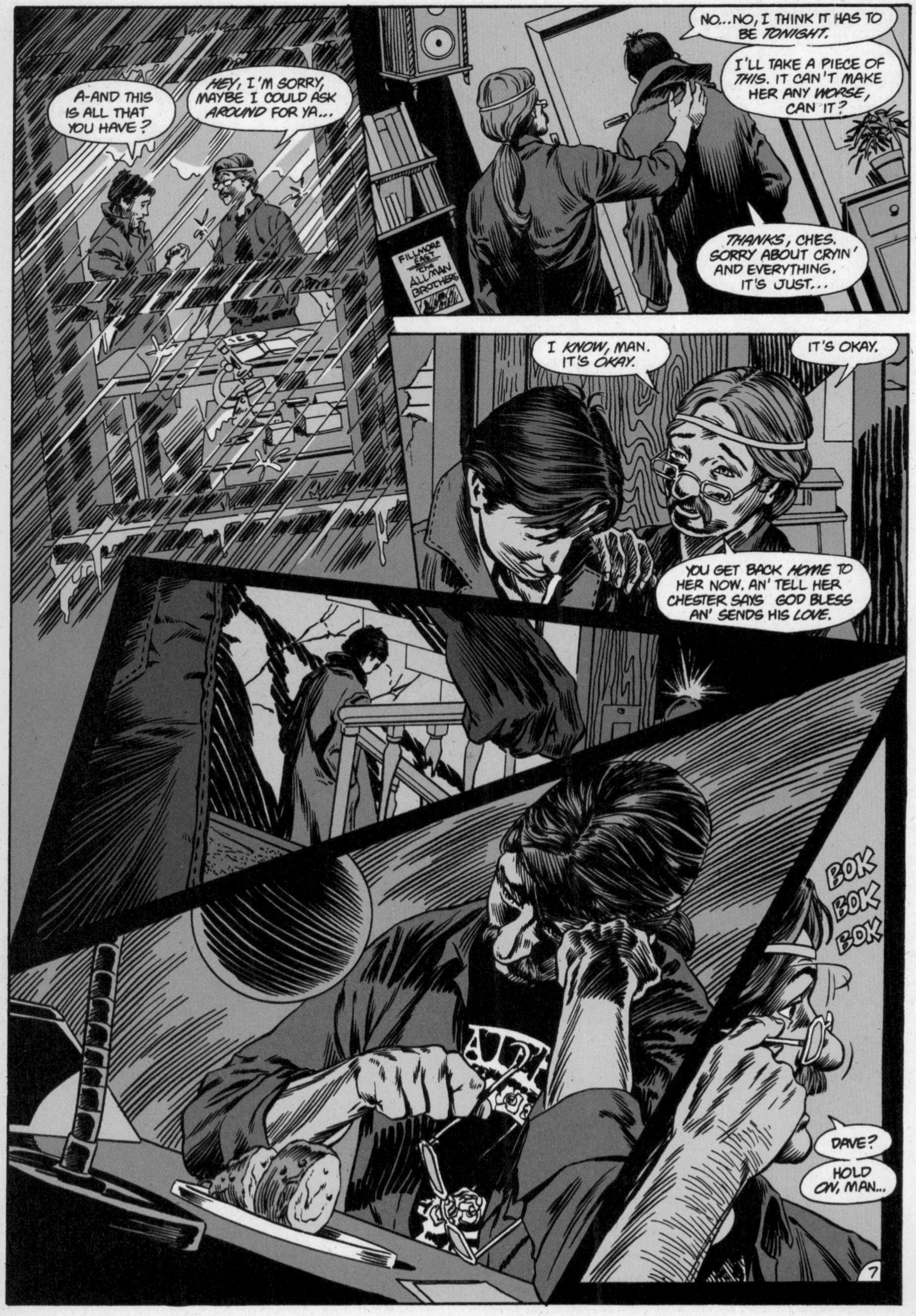
A-AND THIS IS ALL THAT YOU HAVE?
HEY, I'M SORRY, MAYBE I COULD ASK AROUND FOR YA...
NO...NO, I THINK IT HAS TO BE TONIGHT.
I'LL TAKE A PIECE OF THIS. IT CAN'T MAKE HER ANY WORSE, CAN IT?
FILLMORE EAST THE ALLMAN BROTHERS
THANKS, CHES. SORRY ABOUT CRYIN' AND EVERYTHING. IT'S JUST...
I KNOW, MAN. IT'S OKAY.
IT'S OKAY.
YOU GET BACK HOME TO HER NOW. AN' TELL HER CHESTER SAYS GOD BLESS AN' SENDS HIS LOVE.
BOK BOK BOK
DAVE?
HOLD ON, MAN...
7

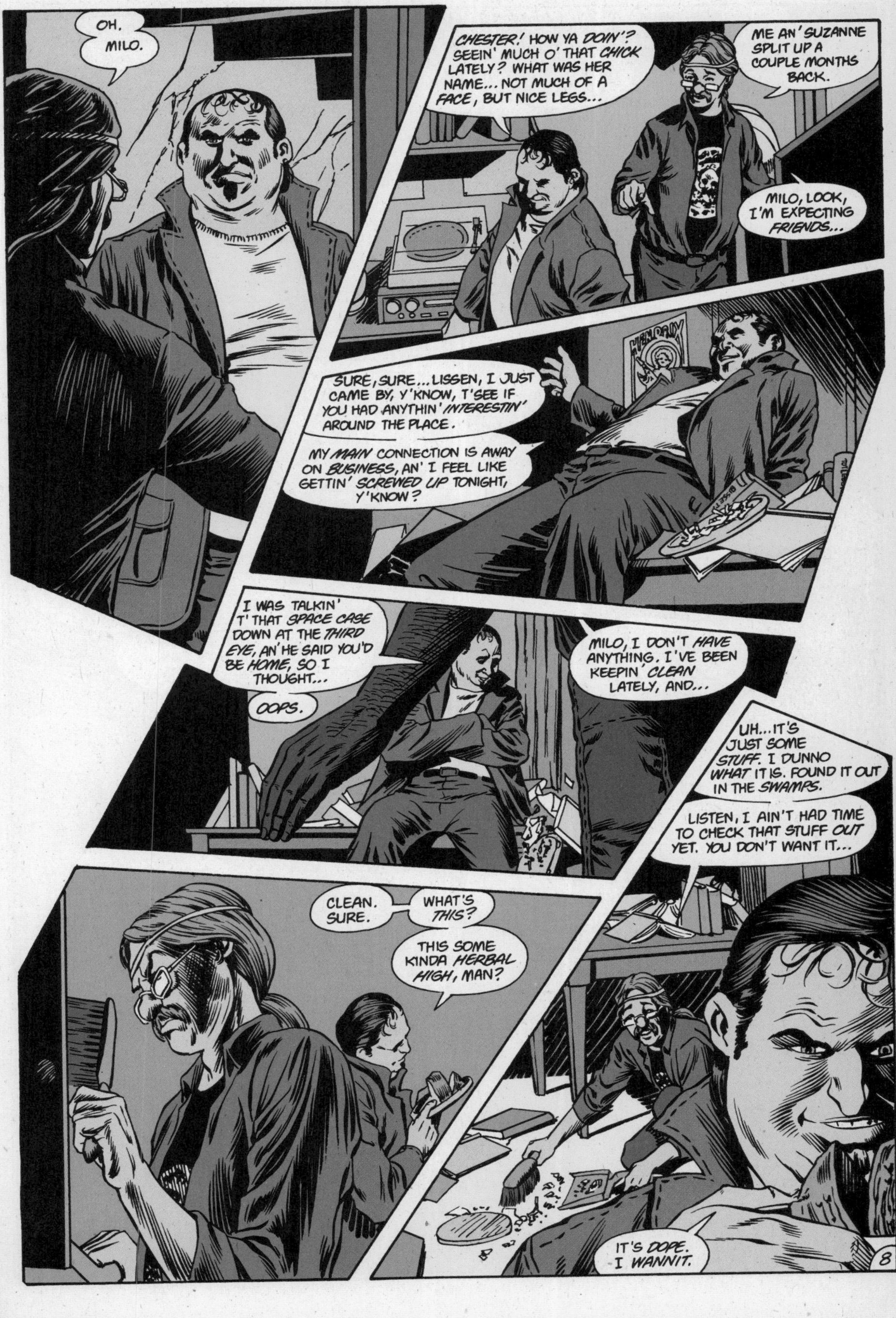
OH. MILO.
CHESTER! HOW YA DOIN'? SEEIN' MUCH O' THAT CHICK LATELY? WHAT WAS HER NAME... NOT MUCH OF A FACE, BUT NICE LEGS...
ME AN' SUZANNE SPLIT UP A COUPLE MONTHS BACK.
MILO, LOOK, I'M EXPECTING FRIENDS...
SURE, SURE... LISSEN, I JUST CAME BY, Y'KNOW, T'SEE IF YOU HAD ANYTHIN' INTERESTIN' AROUND THE PLACE.
MY MAIN CONNECTION IS AWAY ON BUSINESS, AN' I FEEL LIKE GETTIN' SCREWED UP TONIGHT, Y'KNOW?
I WAS TALKIN' T'THAT SPACE CASE DOWN AT THE THIRD EYE, AN' HE SAID YOU'D BE HOME, SO I THOUGHT...
OOPS.
MILO, I DON'T HAVE ANYTHING. I'VE BEEN KEEPIN' CLEAN LATELY, AND...
CLEAN. SURE.
WHAT'S THIS?
THIS SOME KINDA HERBAL HIGH, MAN?
UH... IT'S JUST SOME STUFF. I DUNNO WHAT IT IS. FOUND IT OUT IN THE SWAMPS.
LISTEN, I AIN'T HAD TIME TO CHECK THAT STUFF OUT YET. YOU DON'T WANT IT...
IT'S DOPE. I WANNIT.
8

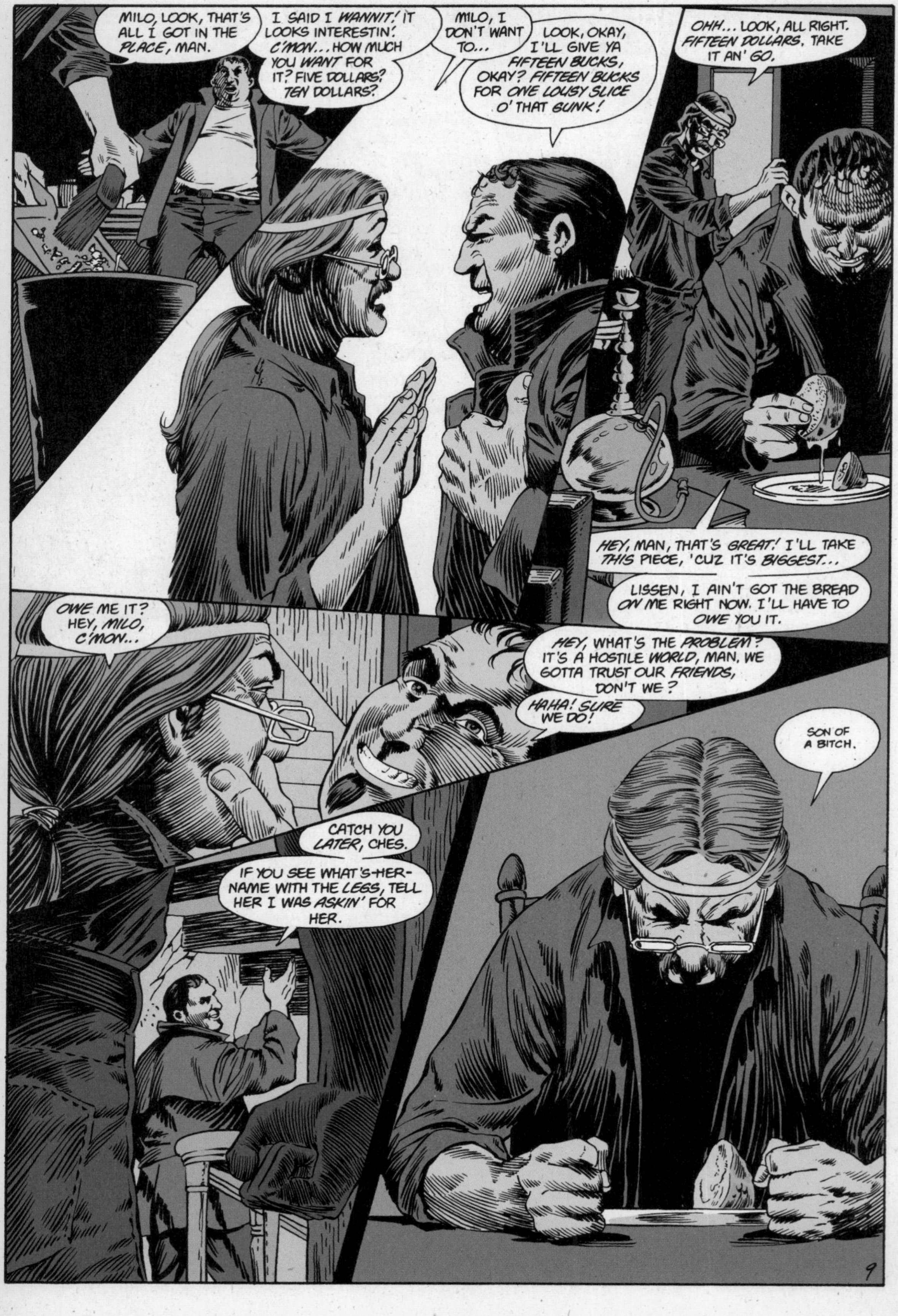
MILO, LOOK, THAT'S ALL I GOT IN THE PLACE, MAN.
I SAID I WANNIT! IT LOOKS INTERESTIN'. C'MON... HOW MUCH YOU WANT FOR IT? FIVE DOLLARS? TEN DOLLARS?
MILO, I DON'T WANT TO...
LOOK, OKAY, I'LL GIVE YA FIFTEEN BUCKS, OKAY? FIFTEEN BUCKS FOR ONE LOUSY SLICE O' THAT GUNK!
OHH... LOOK, ALL RIGHT. FIFTEEN DOLLARS. TAKE IT AN' GO.
HEY, MAN, THAT'S GREAT! I'LL TAKE THIS PIECE, 'CUZ IT'S BIGGEST...
LISSEN, I AIN'T GOT THE BREAD ON ME RIGHT NOW. I'LL HAVE TO OWE YOU IT.
OWE ME IT? HEY, MILO, C'MON...
HEY, WHAT'S THE PROBLEM? IT'S A HOSTILE WORLD, MAN. WE GOTTA TRUST OUR FRIENDS, DON'T WE?
HAHA! SURE WE DO!
CATCH YOU LATER, CHES.
IF YOU SEE WHAT'S-HER-NAME WITH THE LEGS, TELL HER I WAS ASKIN' FOR HER.
SON OF A BITCH.
9

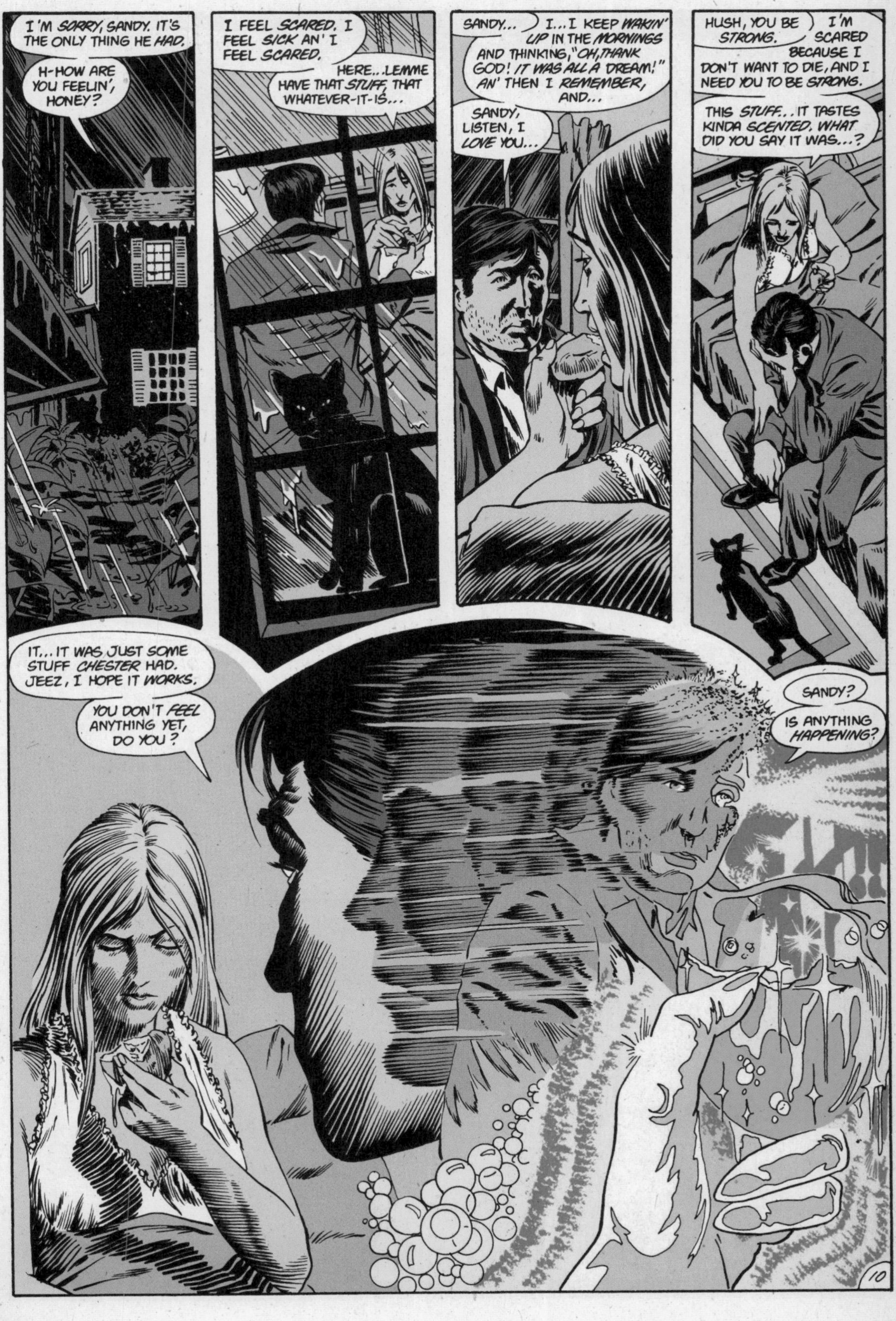
I'M SORRY, SANDY. IT'S THE ONLY THING HE HAD.
H-HOW ARE YOU FEELIN', HONEY?
I FEEL SCARED. I FEEL SICK AN' I FEEL SCARED.
HERE...LEMME HAVE THAT STUFF, THAT WHATEVER-IT-IS...
SANDY...
I...I KEEP WAKIN' UP IN THE MORNINGS AND THINKING, "OH, THANK GOD! IT WAS ALL A DREAM!" AN' THEN I REMEMBER, AND...
SANDY, LISTEN, I LOVE YOU...
HUSH, YOU BE STRONG.
I'M SCARED BECAUSE I DON'T WANT TO DIE, AND I NEED YOU TO BE STRONG.
THIS STUFF...IT TASTES KINDA SCENTED. WHAT DID YOU SAY IT WAS...?
IT...IT WAS JUST SOME STUFF CHESTER HAD. JEEZ, I HOPE IT WORKS.
YOU DON'T FEEL ANYTHING YET, DO YOU?
SANDY?
IS ANYTHING HAPPENING?
10

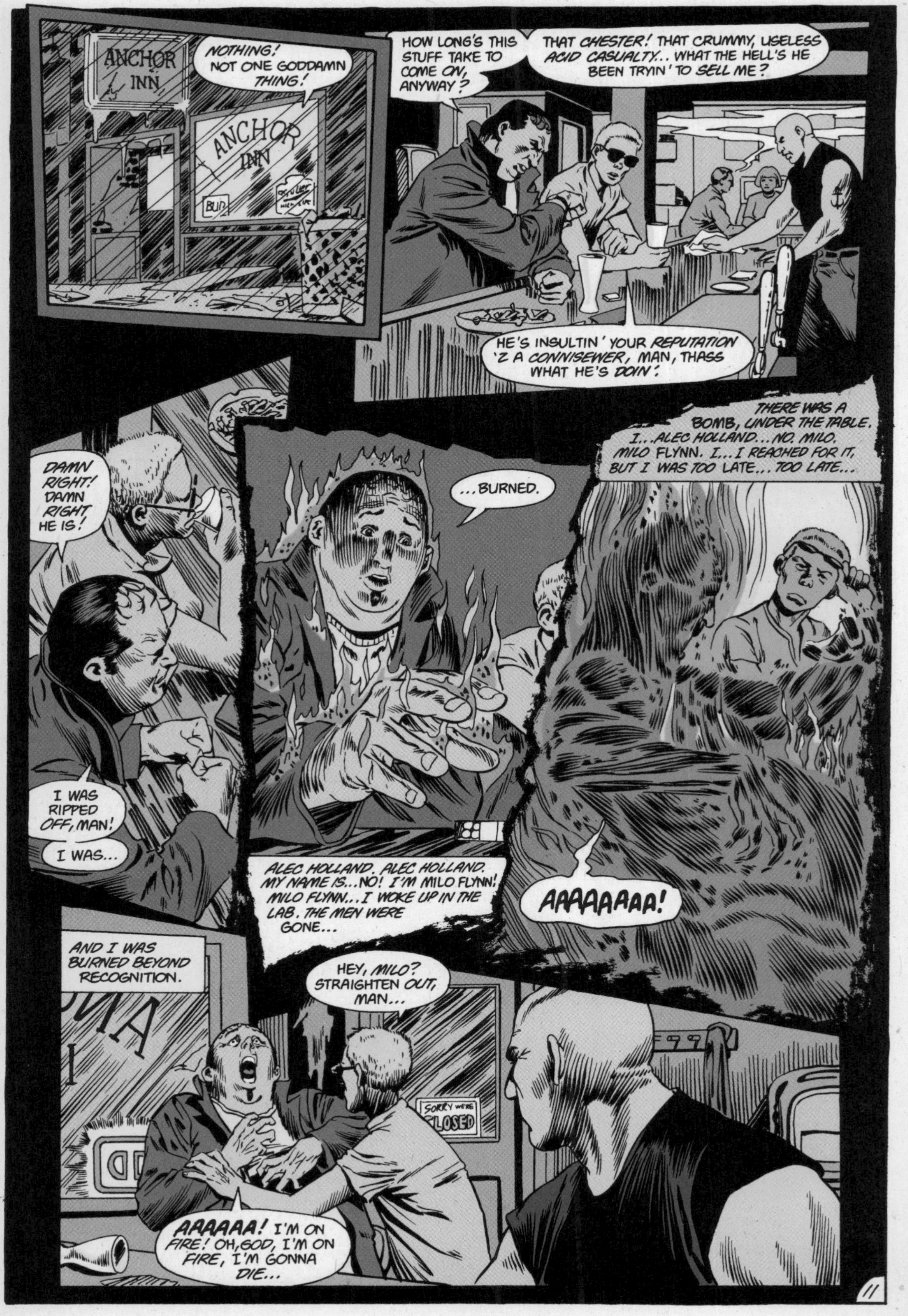
ANCHOR INN
NOTHING! NOT ONE GODDAMN THING!
ANCHOR INN
BUD
HOW LONG'S THIS STUFF TAKE TO COME ON, ANYWAY?
THAT CHESTER! THAT CRUMMY, USELESS ACID CASUALTY... WHAT THE HELL'S HE BEEN TRYIN' TO SELL ME?
HE'S INSULTIN' YOUR REPUTATION 'Z A CONNISEWER, MAN, THASS WHAT HE'S DOIN'.
DAMN RIGHT! DAMN RIGHT HE IS!
I WAS RIPPED OFF, MAN!
I WAS...
...BURNED.
THERE WAS A BOMB, UNDER THE TABLE. I...ALEC HOLLAND...NO. MILO. MILO FLYNN. I...I REACHED FOR IT, BUT I WAS TOO LATE...TOO LATE...
ALEC HOLLAND. ALEC HOLLAND. MY NAME IS...NO! I'M MILO FLYNN! MILO FLYNN...I WOKE UP IN THE LAB. THE MEN WERE GONE...
AAAAAAAA!
AND I WAS BURNED BEYOND RECOGNITION.
HEY, MILO? STRAIGHTEN OUT, MAN...
SORRY WE'RE CLOSED
AAAAAA! I'M ON FIRE! OH, GOD, I'M ON FIRE, I'M GONNA DIE...
11

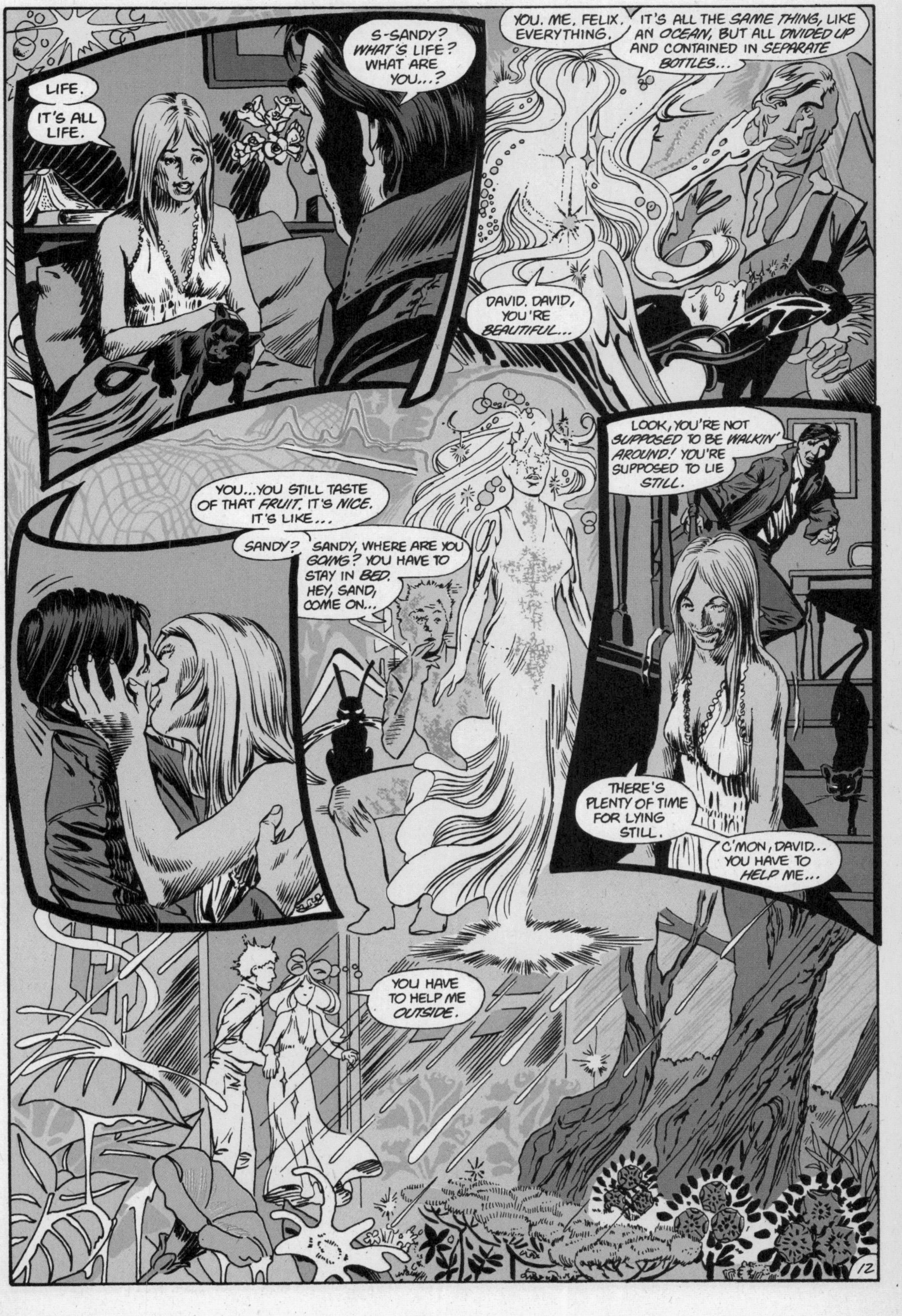
LIFE.
IT'S ALL LIFE.
S-SANDY? WHAT'S LIFE? WHAT ARE YOU...?
YOU. ME. FELIX. EVERYTHING.
IT'S ALL THE SAME THING, LIKE AN OCEAN, BUT ALL DIVIDED UP AND CONTAINED IN SEPARATE BOTTLES...
DAVID. DAVID, YOU'RE BEAUTIFUL...
YOU...YOU STILL TASTE OF THAT FRUIT. IT'S NICE. IT'S LIKE...
SANDY?
SANDY, WHERE ARE YOU GOING? YOU HAVE TO STAY IN BED. HEY, SAND, COME ON...
LOOK, YOU'RE NOT SUPPOSED TO BE WALKIN' AROUND! YOU'RE SUPPOSED TO LIE STILL.
THERE'S PLENTY OF TIME FOR LYING STILL.
C'MON, DAVID... YOU HAVE TO HELP ME...
YOU HAVE TO HELP ME OUTSIDE.
12

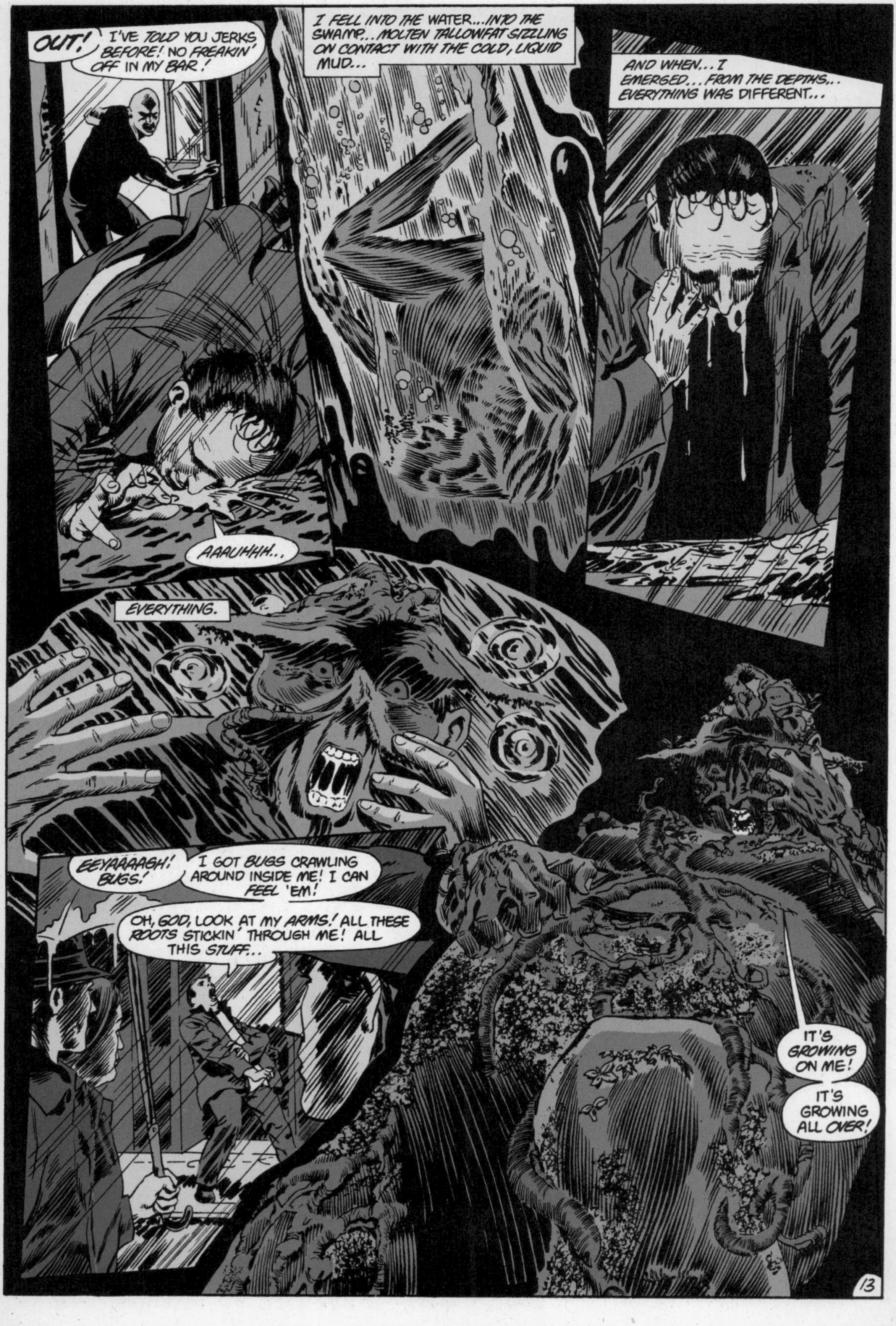
OUT! I'VE TOLD YOU JERKS BEFORE! NO FREAKIN' OFF IN MY BAR!
AAAUHHH...
I FELL INTO THE WATER...INTO THE SWAMP...MOLTEN TALLOWFAT SIZZLING ON CONTACT WITH THE COLD, LIQUID MUD...
AND WHEN... I EMERGED... FROM THE DEPTHS... EVERYTHING WAS DIFFERENT...
EVERYTHING.
EEYAAAAGH! BUGS!
I GOT BUGS CRAWLING AROUND INSIDE ME! I CAN FEEL 'EM!
OH, GOD, LOOK AT MY ARMS! ALL THESE ROOTS STICKIN' THROUGH ME! ALL THIS STUFF...
IT'S GROWING ON ME!
IT'S GROWING ALL OVER!
13

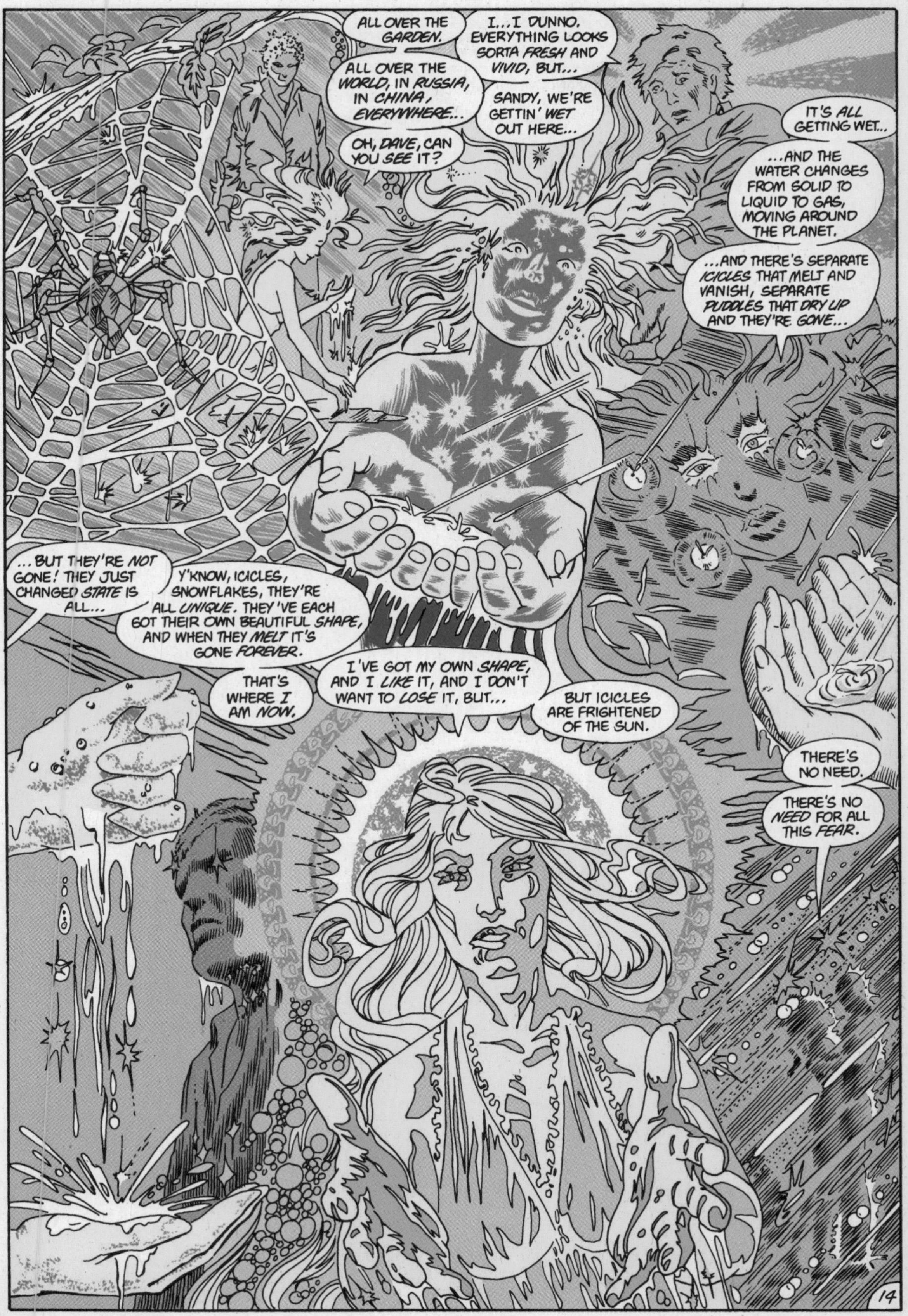
ALL OVER THE GARDEN.
ALL OVER THE WORLD, IN RUSSIA, IN CHINA, EVERYWHERE...
OH, DAVE, CAN YOU SEE IT?
I... I DUNNO. EVERYTHING LOOKS SORTA FRESH AND VIVID, BUT...
SANDY, WE'RE GETTIN' WET OUT HERE...
IT'S ALL GETTING WET...
...AND THE WATER CHANGES FROM SOLID TO LIQUID TO GAS, MOVING AROUND THE PLANET.
...AND THERE'S SEPARATE ICICLES THAT MELT AND VANISH, SEPARATE PUDDLES THAT DRY UP AND THEY'RE GONE...
...BUT THEY'RE NOT GONE! THEY JUST CHANGED STATE IS ALL...
Y'KNOW, ICICLES, SNOWFLAKES, THEY'RE ALL UNIQUE. THEY'VE EACH GOT THEIR OWN BEAUTIFUL SHAPE, AND WHEN THEY MELT IT'S GONE FOREVER.
THAT'S WHERE I AM NOW.
I'VE GOT MY OWN SHAPE, AND I LIKE IT, AND I DON'T WANT TO LOSE IT, BUT...
BUT ICICLES ARE FRIGHTENED OF THE SUN.
THERE'S NO NEED.
THERE'S NO NEED FOR ALL THIS FEAR.
14

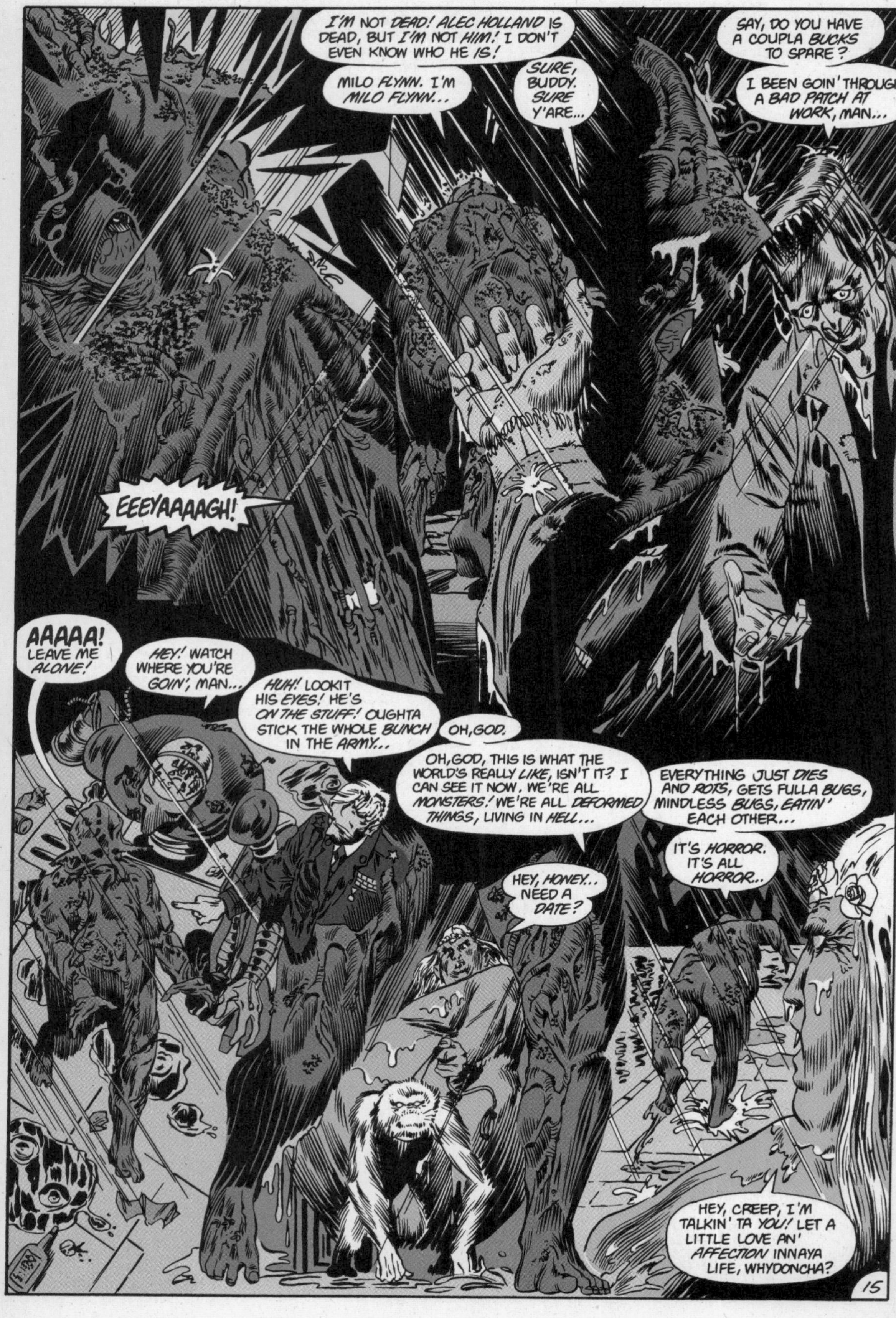
I'M NOT DEAD! ALEC HOLLAND IS DEAD, BUT I'M NOT HIM! I DON'T EVEN KNOW WHO HE IS!
MILO FLYNN. I'M MILO FLYNN...
SURE, BUDDY. SURE Y'ARE...
SAY, DO YOU HAVE A COUPLA BUCKS TO SPARE?
I BEEN GOIN' THROUGH A BAD PATCH AT WORK, MAN...
EEEYAAAAGH!
AAAAA! LEAVE ME ALONE!
HEY! WATCH WHERE YOU'RE GOIN', MAN...
HUH! LOOKIT HIS EYES! HE'S ON THE STUFF! OUGHTA STICK THE WHOLE BUNCH IN THE ARMY...
OH, GOD.
OH, GOD, THIS IS WHAT THE WORLD'S REALLY LIKE, ISN'T IT? I CAN SEE IT NOW. WE'RE ALL MONSTERS! WE'RE ALL DEFORMED THINGS, LIVING IN HELL...
EVERYTHING JUST DIES AND ROTS, GETS FULLA BUGS, MINDLESS BUGS, EATIN' EACH OTHER...
IT'S HORROR. IT'S ALL HORROR...
HEY, HONEY... NEED A DATE?
HEY, CREEP, I'M TALKIN' TA YOU! LET A LITTLE LOVE AN' AFFECTION INNAYA LIFE, WHYDONCHA?
15

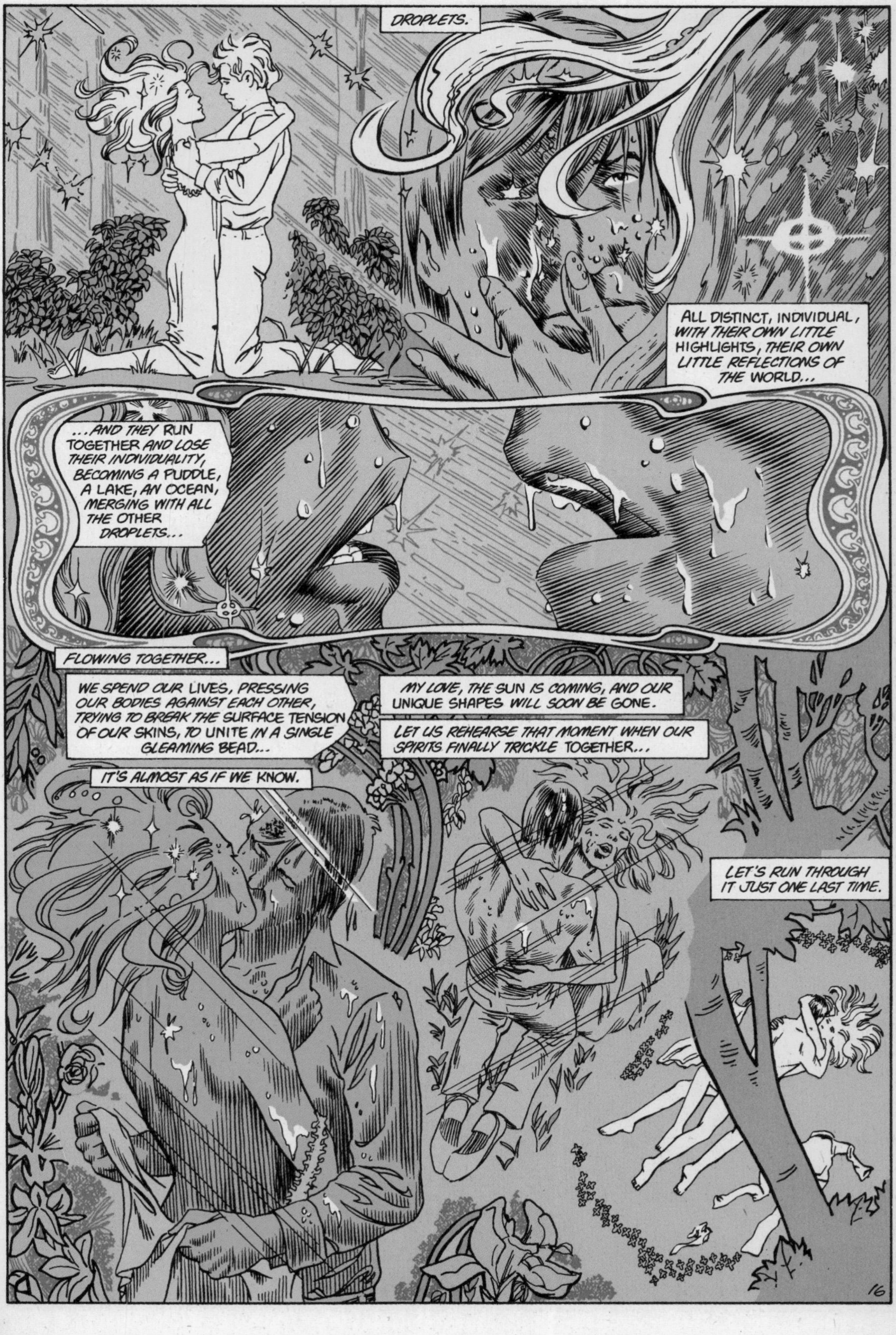
DROPLETS.
ALL DISTINCT, INDIVIDUAL, WITH THEIR OWN LITTLE HIGHLIGHTS, THEIR OWN LITTLE REFLECTIONS OF THE WORLD...
...AND THEY RUN TOGETHER AND LOSE THEIR INDIVIDUALITY, BECOMING A PUDDLE, A LAKE, AN OCEAN, MERGING WITH ALL THE OTHER DROPLETS...
FLOWING TOGETHER...
WE SPEND OUR LIVES, PRESSING OUR BODIES AGAINST EACH OTHER, TRYING TO BREAK THE SURFACE TENSION OF OUR SKINS, TO UNITE IN A SINGLE GLEAMING BEAD...
IT'S ALMOST AS IF WE KNOW.
MY LOVE, THE SUN IS COMING, AND OUR UNIQUE SHAPES WILL SOON BE GONE.
LET US REHEARSE THAT MOMENT WHEN OUR SPIRITS FINALLY TRICKLE TOGETHER...
LET'S RUN THROUGH IT JUST ONE LAST TIME.
16

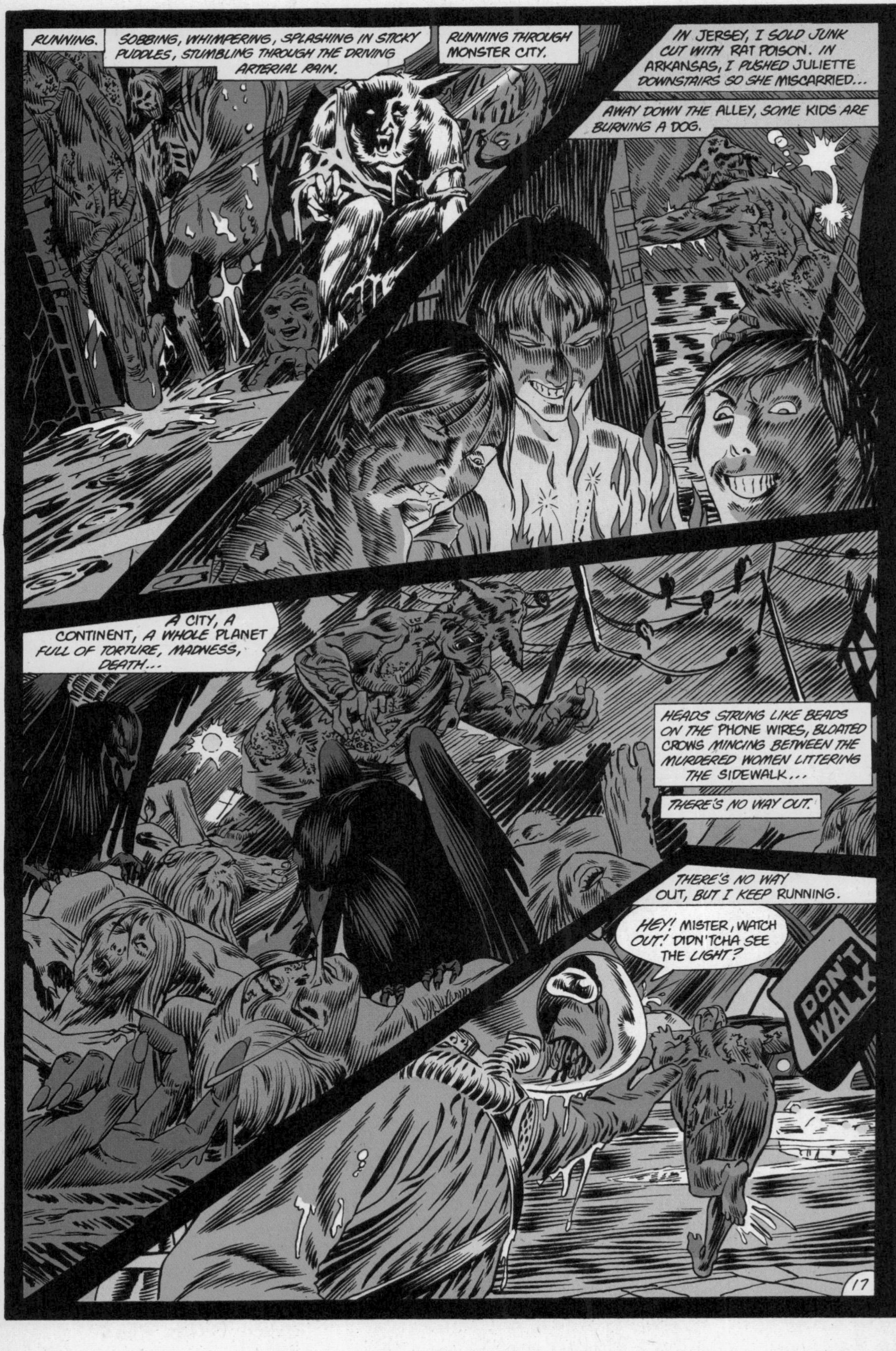
RUNNING.
SOBBING, WHIMPERING, SPLASHING IN STICKY PUDDLES, STUMBLING THROUGH THE DRIVING ARTERIAL RAIN.
RUNNING THROUGH MONSTER CITY.
IN JERSEY, I SOLD JUNK CUT WITH RAT POISON. IN ARKANSAS, I PUSHED JULIETTE DOWNSTAIRS SO SHE MISCARRIED...
AWAY DOWN THE ALLEY, SOME KIDS ARE BURNING A DOG.
A CITY, A CONTINENT, A WHOLE PLANET FULL OF TORTURE, MADNESS, DEATH...
HEADS STRUNG LIKE BEADS ON THE PHONE WIRES, BLOATED CROWS MINCING BETWEEN THE MURDERED WOMEN LITTERING THE SIDEWALK...
THERE'S NO WAY OUT.
THERE'S NO WAY OUT, BUT I KEEP RUNNING.
HEY! MISTER, WATCH OUT! DIDN'TCHA SEE THE LIGHT?
DON'T WALK
17

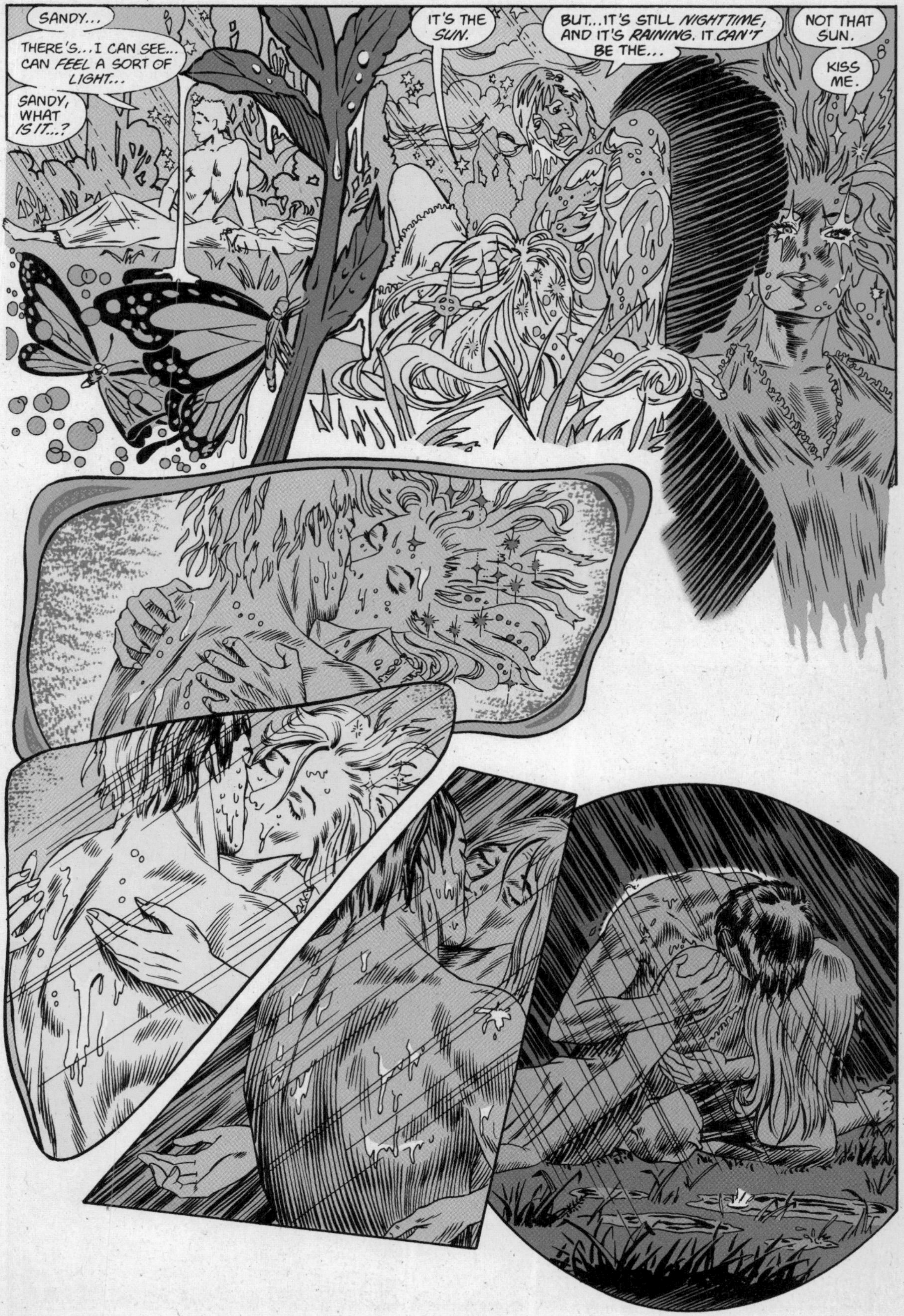
SANDY...
THERE'S... I CAN SEE... CAN FEEL A SORT OF LIGHT...
SANDY, WHAT IS IT...?
IT'S THE SUN.
BUT... IT'S STILL NIGHTTIME, AND IT'S RAINING. IT CAN'T BE THE...
NOT THAT SUN.
KISS ME.

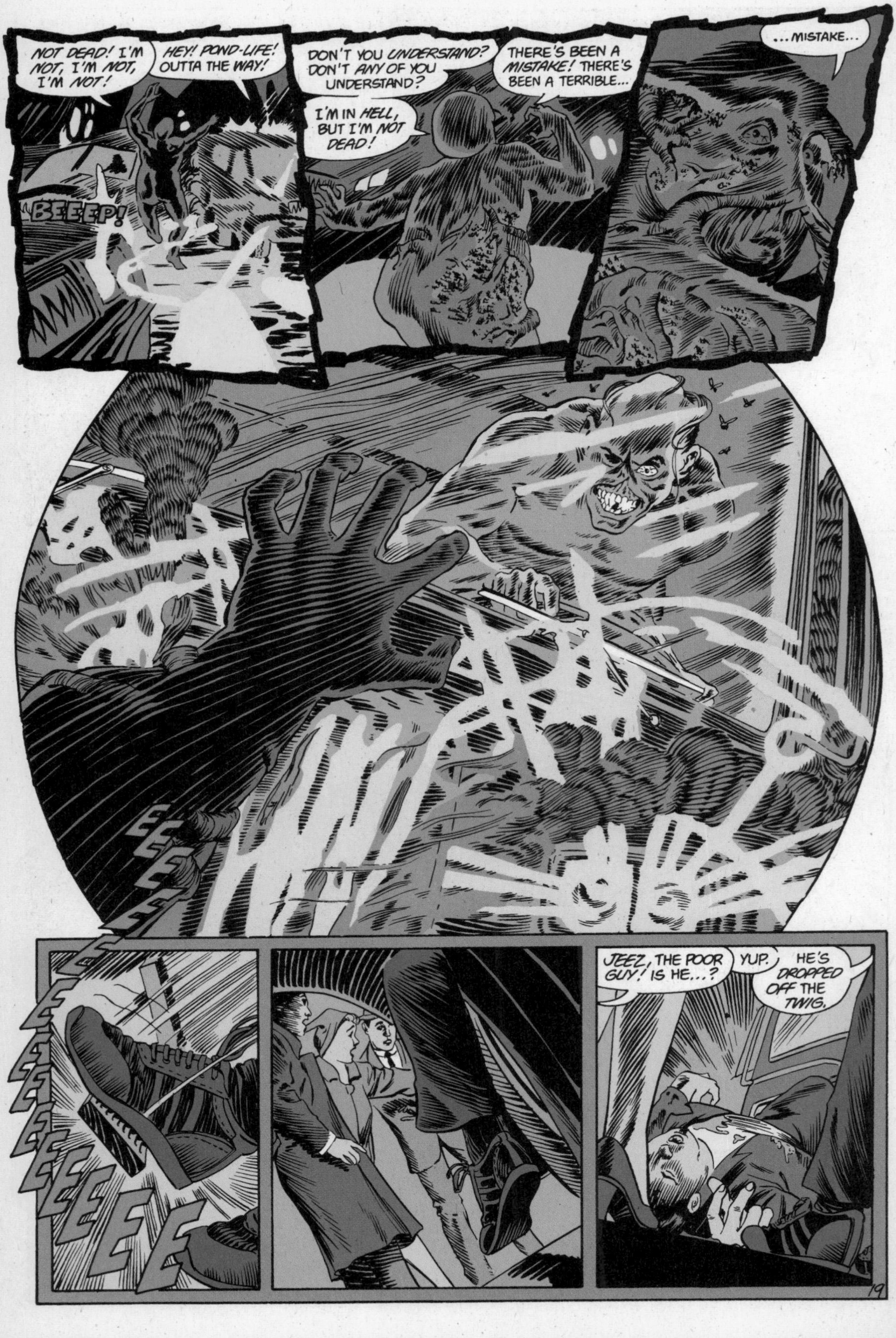
NOT DEAD! I'M NOT, I'M NOT, I'M NOT!
HEY! POND-LIFE! OUTTA THE WAY!
BEEEP!
DON'T YOU UNDERSTAND? DON'T ANY OF YOU UNDERSTAND?
I'M IN HELL, BUT I'M NOT DEAD!
THERE'S BEEN A MISTAKE! THERE'S BEEN A TERRIBLE...
...MISTAKE...
EEEEEEEEEEEEEEEEEE
JEEZ, THE POOR GUY! IS HE...?
YUP.
HE'S DROPPED OFF THE TWIG.
19

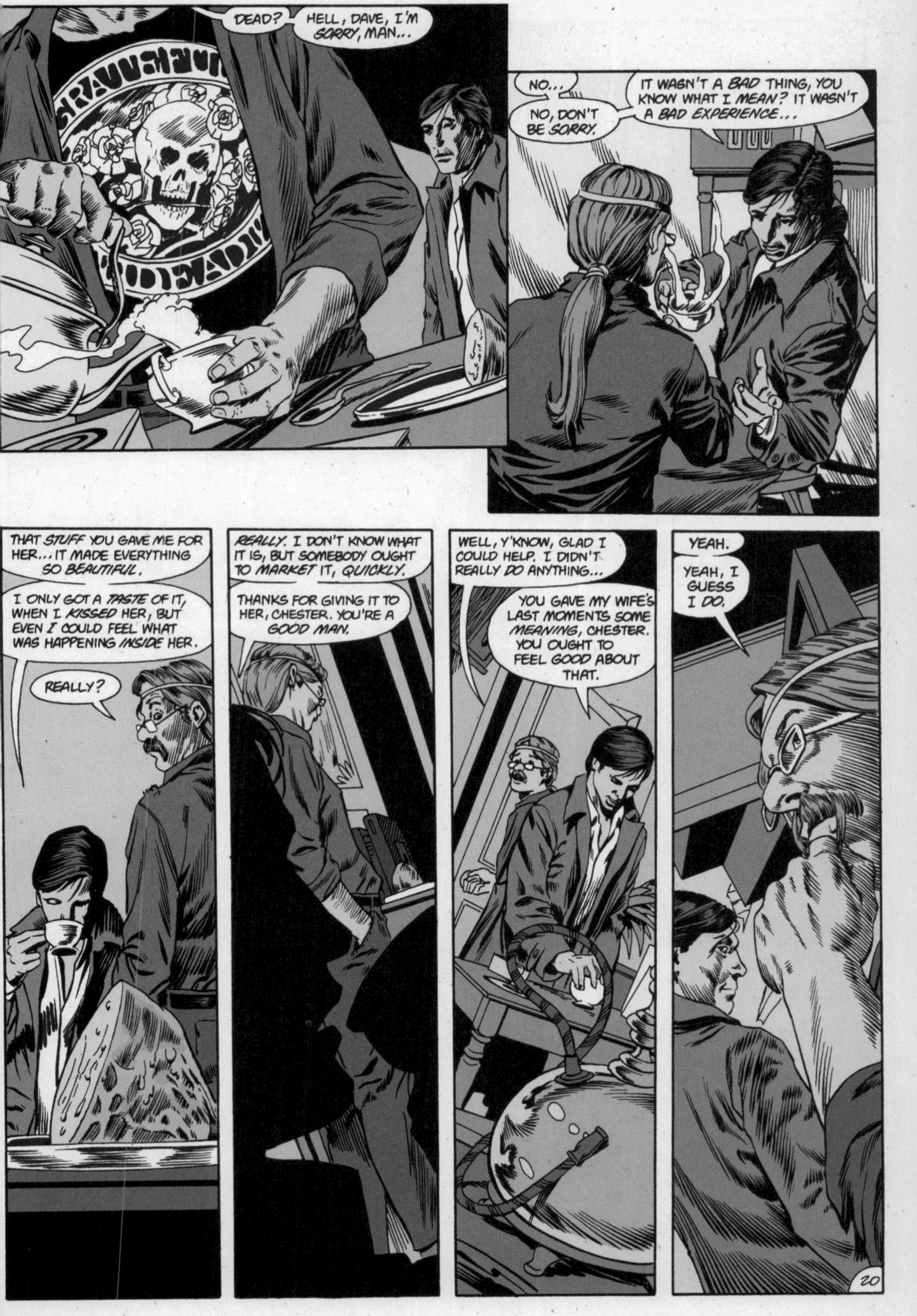
DEAD?
HELL, DAVE, I'M SORRY, MAN...
NO...
NO, DON'T BE SORRY.
IT WASN'T A BAD THING, YOU KNOW WHAT I MEAN? IT WASN'T A BAD EXPERIENCE...
THAT STUFF YOU GAVE ME FOR HER... IT MADE EVERYTHING SO BEAUTIFUL.
I ONLY GOT A TASTE OF IT, WHEN I KISSED HER, BUT EVEN I COULD FEEL WHAT WAS HAPPENING INSIDE HER.
REALLY?
REALLY. I DON'T KNOW WHAT IT IS, BUT SOMEBODY OUGHT TO MARKET IT, QUICKLY.
THANKS FOR GIVING IT TO HER, CHESTER. YOU'RE A GOOD MAN.
WELL, Y'KNOW, GLAD I COULD HELP. I DIDN'T REALLY DO ANYTHING...
YOU GAVE MY WIFE'S LAST MOMENTS SOME MEANING, CHESTER. YOU OUGHT TO FEEL GOOD ABOUT THAT.
YEAH.
YEAH, I GUESS I DO.
20

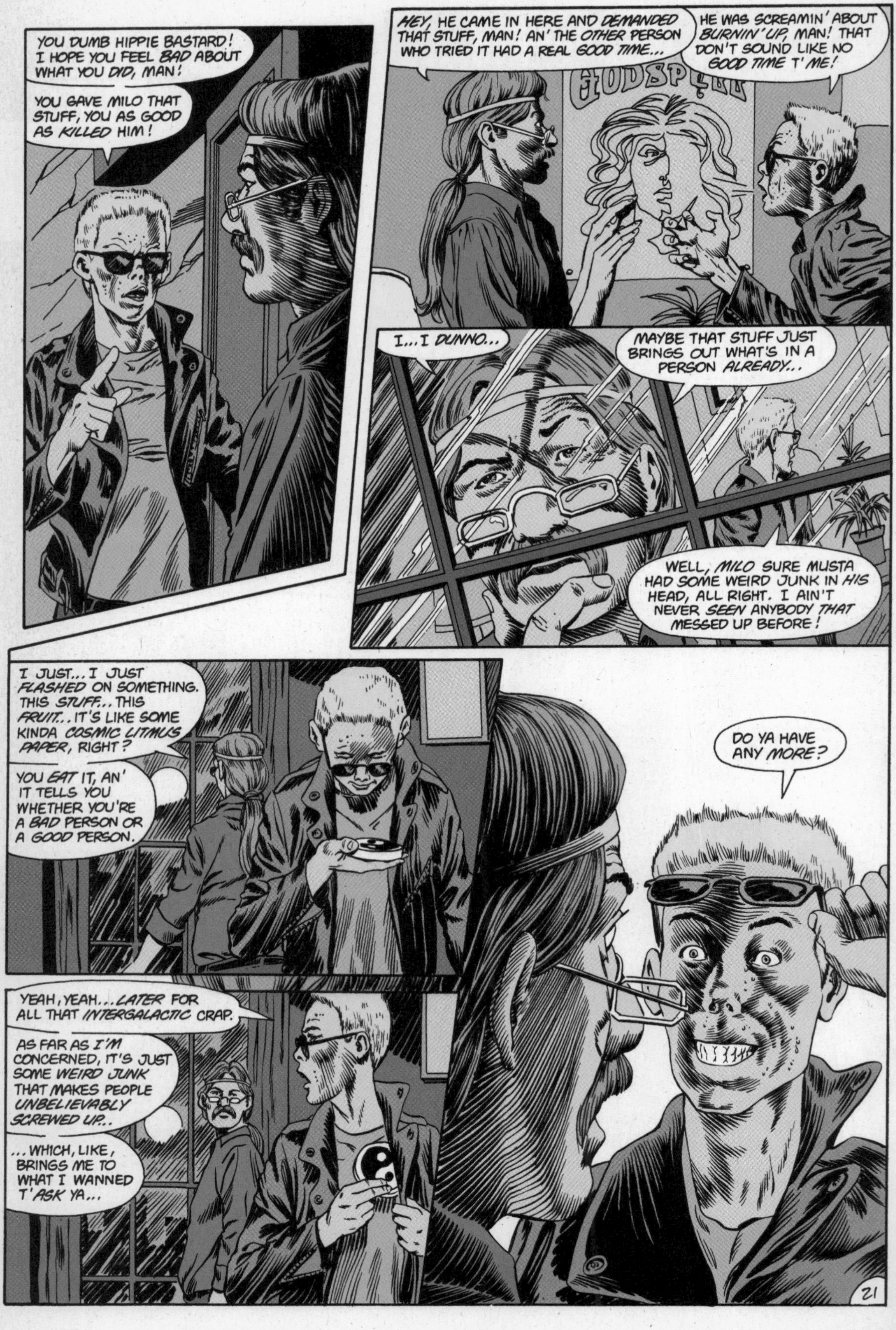
YOU DUMB HIPPIE BASTARD! I HOPE YOU FEEL BAD ABOUT WHAT YOU DID, MAN!
YOU GAVE MILO THAT STUFF, YOU AS GOOD AS KILLED HIM!
HEY, HE CAME IN HERE AND DEMANDED THAT STUFF, MAN! AN' THE OTHER PERSON WHO TRIED IT HAD A REAL GOOD TIME...
HE WAS SCREAMIN' ABOUT BURNIN' UP, MAN! THAT DON'T SOUND LIKE NO GOOD TIME T' ME!
I... I DUNNO...
MAYBE THAT STUFF JUST BRINGS OUT WHAT'S IN A PERSON ALREADY...
WELL, MILO SURE MUSTA HAD SOME WEIRD JUNK IN HIS HEAD, ALL RIGHT. I AIN'T NEVER SEEN ANYBODY THAT MESSED UP BEFORE!
I JUST... I JUST FLASHED ON SOMETHING. THIS STUFF... THIS FRUIT... IT'S LIKE SOME KINDA COSMIC LITMUS PAPER, RIGHT?
YOU EAT IT, AN' IT TELLS YOU WHETHER YOU'RE A BAD PERSON OR A GOOD PERSON.
YEAH, YEAH... LATER FOR ALL THAT INTERGALACTIC CRAP.
AS FAR AS I'M CONCERNED, IT'S JUST SOME WEIRD JUNK THAT MAKES PEOPLE UNBELIEVABLY SCREWED UP...
...WHICH, LIKE, BRINGS ME TO WHAT I WANNED T'ASK YA...
DO YA HAVE ANY MORE?
21

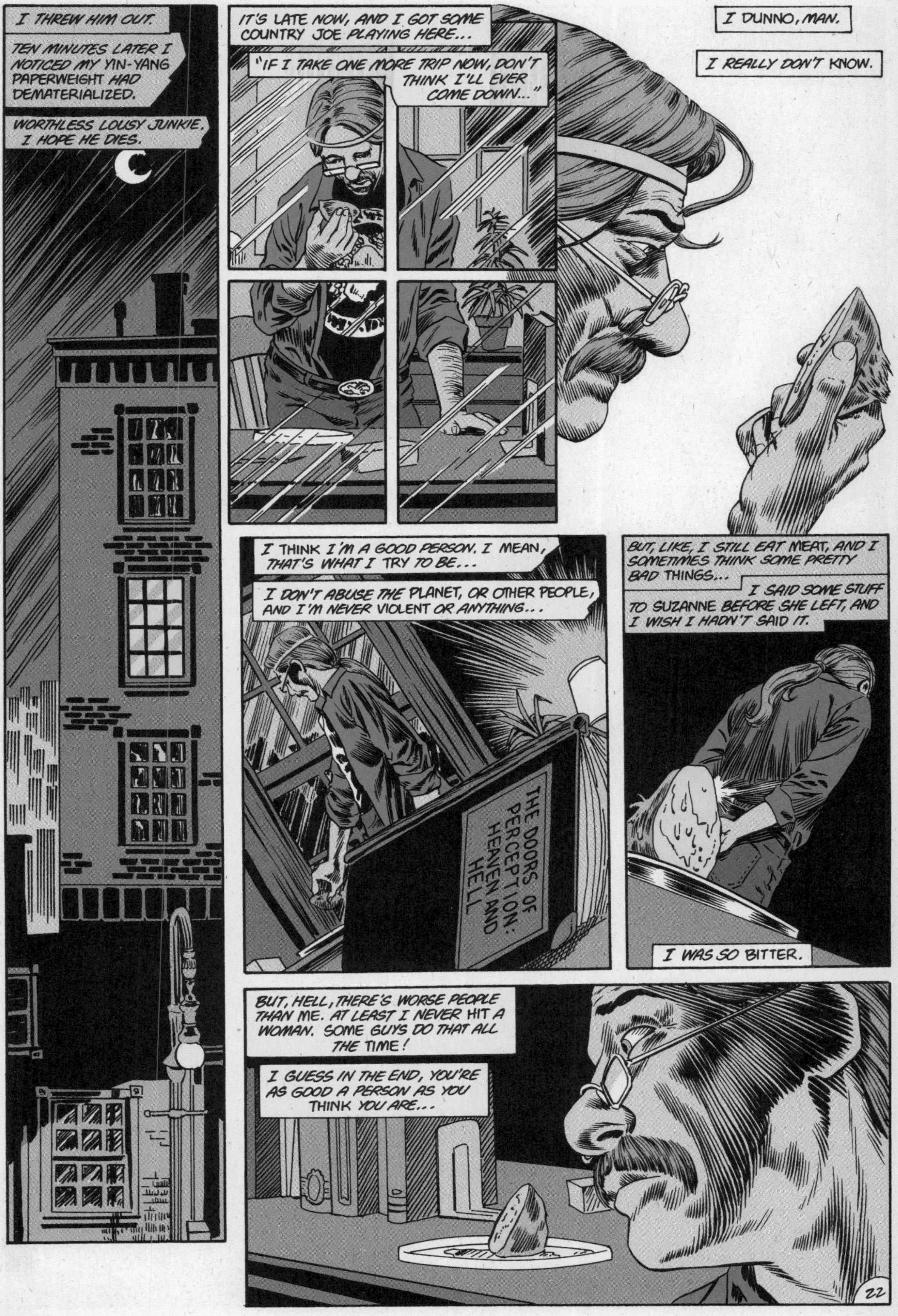
I THREW HIM OUT.
TEN MINUTES LATER I NOTICED MY YIN-YANG PAPERWEIGHT HAD DEMATERIALIZED.
WORTHLESS LOUSY JUNKIE. I HOPE HE DIES.
IT'S LATE NOW, AND I GOT SOME COUNTRY JOE PLAYING HERE...
"IF I TAKE ONE MORE TRIP NOW, DON'T THINK I'LL EVER COME DOWN..."
I DUNNO, MAN.
I REALLY DON'T KNOW.
I THINK I'M A GOOD PERSON. I MEAN, THAT'S WHAT I TRY TO BE...
I DON'T ABUSE THE PLANET, OR OTHER PEOPLE, AND I'M NEVER VIOLENT OR ANYTHING...
THE DOORS OF PERCEPTION: HEAVEN AND HELL
BUT, LIKE, I STILL EAT MEAT, AND I SOMETIMES THINK SOME PRETTY BAD THINGS...
I SAID SOME STUFF TO SUZANNE BEFORE SHE LEFT, AND I WISH I HADN'T SAID IT.
I WAS SO BITTER.
BUT, HELL, THERE'S WORSE PEOPLE THAN ME. AT LEAST I NEVER HIT A WOMAN. SOME GUYS DO THAT ALL THE TIME!
I GUESS IN THE END, YOU'RE AS GOOD A PERSON AS YOU THINK YOU ARE...
22

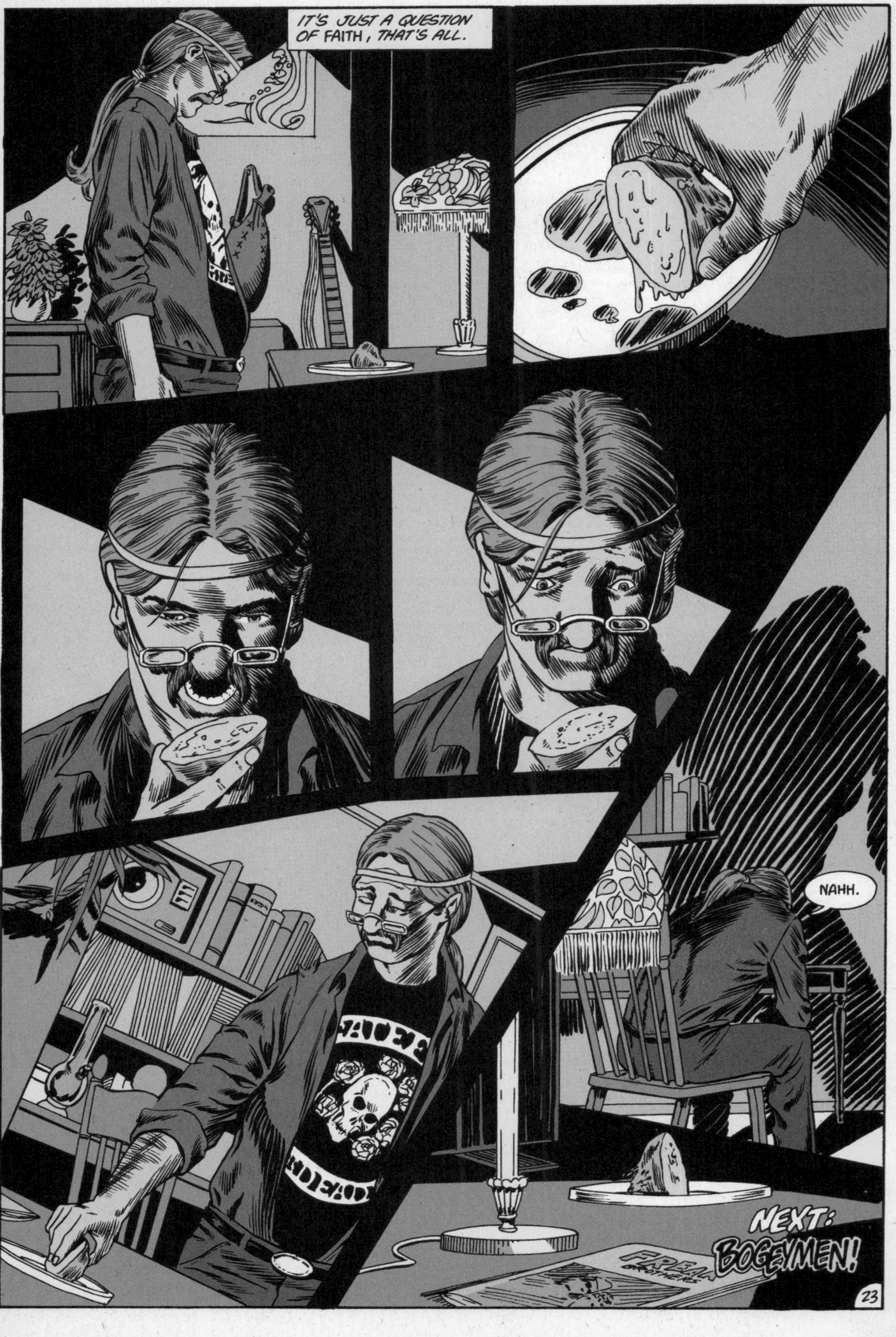
IT'S JUST A QUESTION OF FAITH, THAT'S ALL.
NAHH.
NEXT: BOGEYMEN!
23

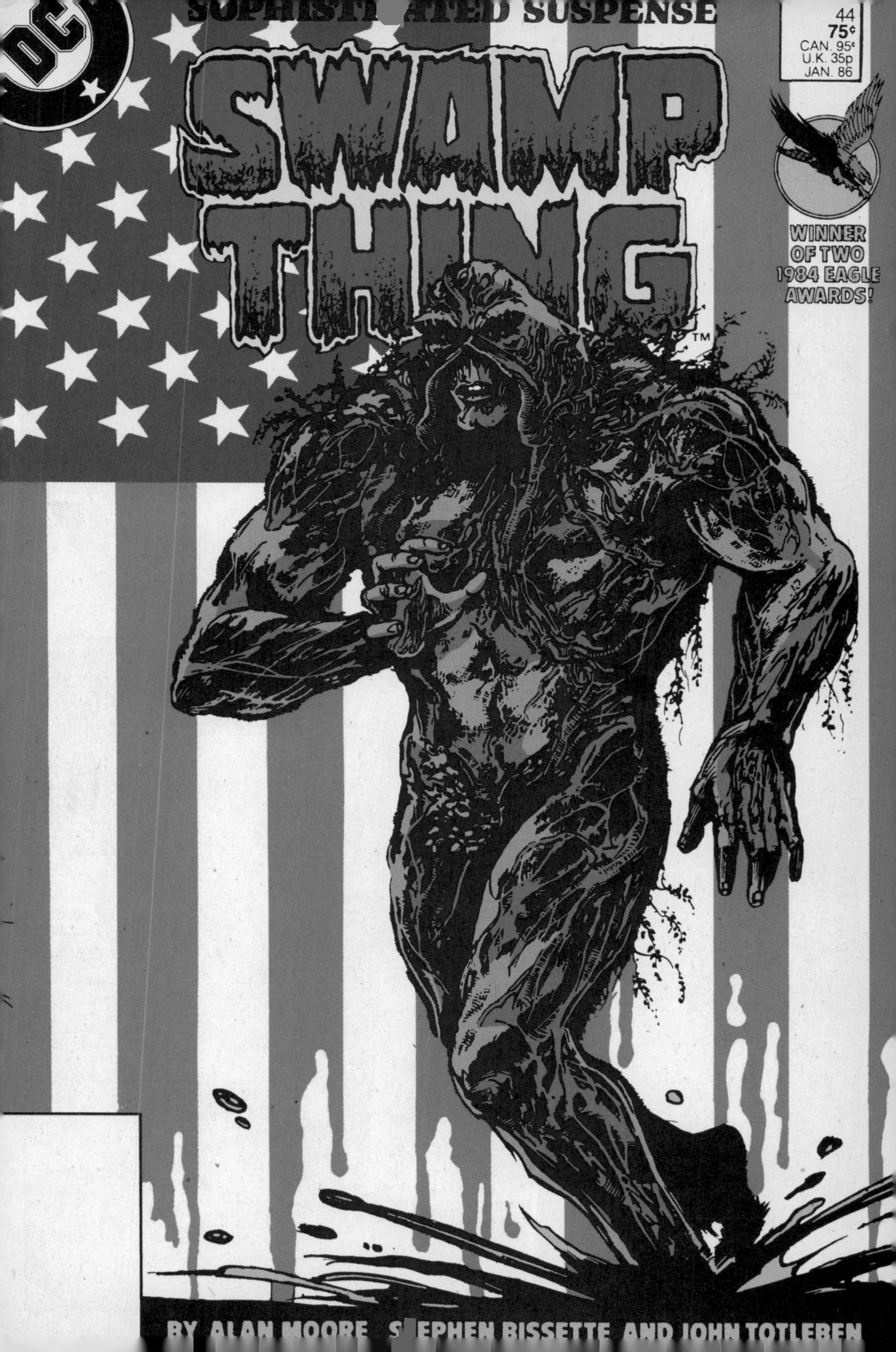
SOPHISTI ATED SUSPENSE
44
75¢
CAN. 95¢
U.K. 35p
JAN. 86
SWAMP THING™
WINNER OF TWO 1984 EAGLE AWARDS!
BY ALAN MOORE S EPHEN BISSETTE AND JOHN TOTLEBEN

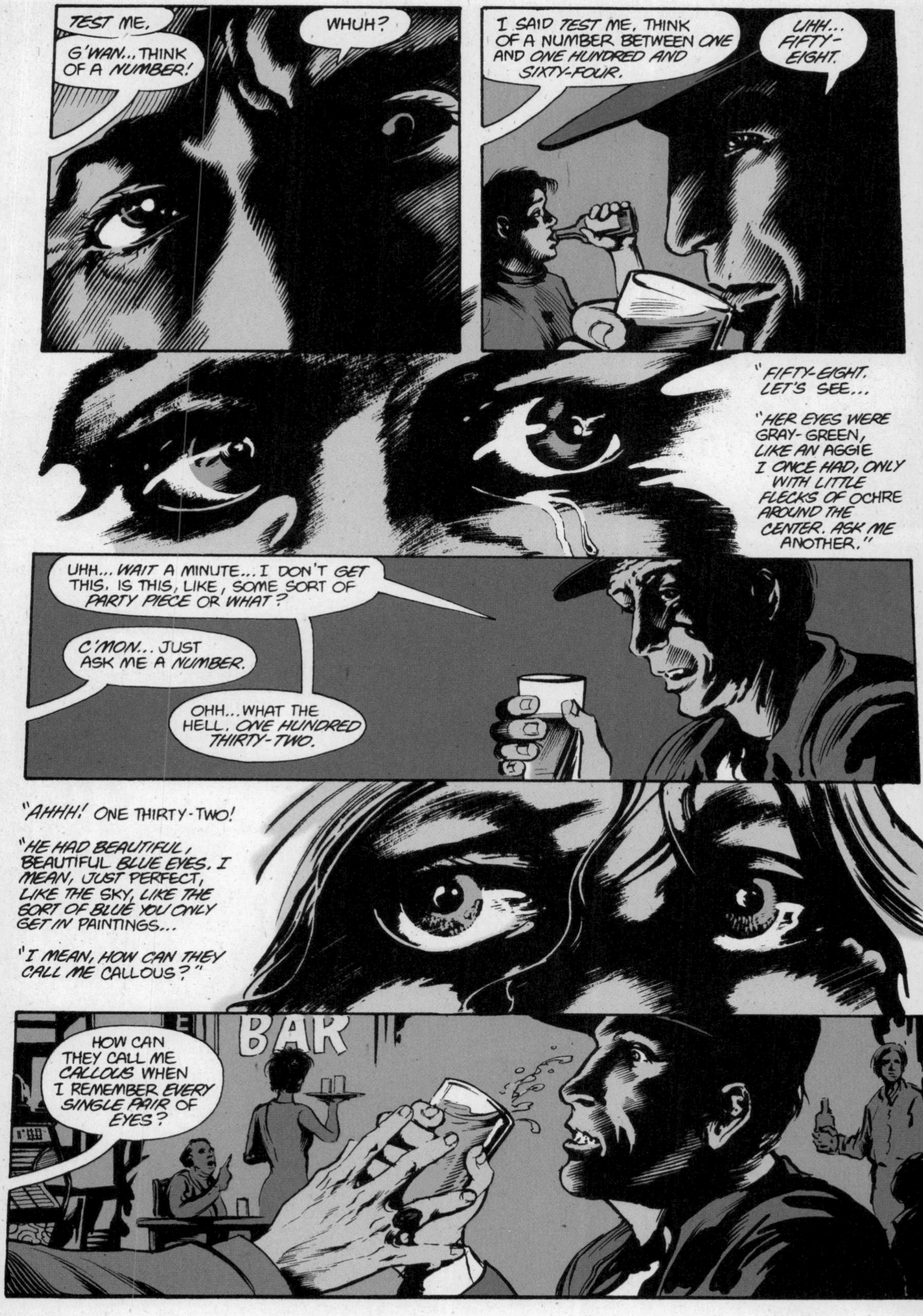
TEST ME.
G'WAN... THINK OF A NUMBER!
WHUH?
I SAID TEST ME. THINK OF A NUMBER BETWEEN ONE AND ONE HUNDRED AND SIXTY-FOUR.
UHH... FIFTY-EIGHT.
"FIFTY-EIGHT. LET'S SEE...
"HER EYES WERE GRAY-GREEN, LIKE AN AGGIE I ONCE HAD, ONLY WITH LITTLE FLECKS OF OCHRE AROUND THE CENTER. ASK ME ANOTHER."
UHH... WAIT A MINUTE... I DON'T GET THIS. IS THIS, LIKE, SOME SORT OF PARTY PIECE OR WHAT?
C'MON... JUST ASK ME A NUMBER.
OHH... WHAT THE HELL. ONE HUNDRED THIRTY-TWO.
"AHHH! ONE THIRTY-TWO!
"HE HAD BEAUTIFUL, BEAUTIFUL BLUE EYES. I MEAN, JUST PERFECT, LIKE THE SKY, LIKE THE SORT OF BLUE YOU ONLY GET IN PAINTINGS...
"I MEAN, HOW CAN THEY CALL ME CALLOUS?"
BAR
HOW CAN THEY CALL ME CALLOUS WHEN I REMEMBER EVERY SINGLE PAIR OF EYES?

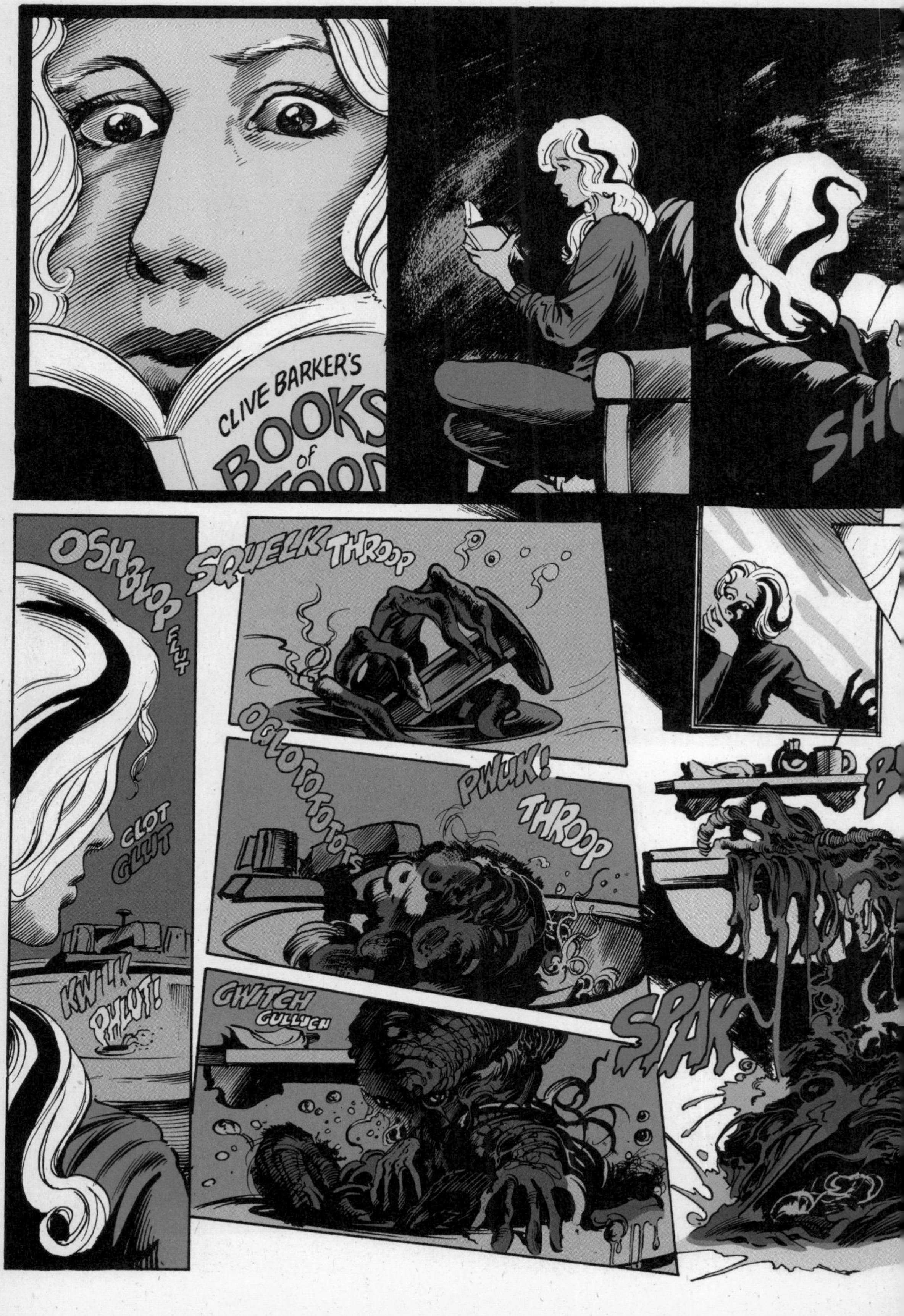
CLIVE BARKER'S BOOKS of BLOOD
SH
OSH
BLOP
FLUT
SQUELK
THROOP
OGLOTOTOTOTS
PWLIK!
THROOP
CLOT
GLUT
KWILK
PHLUT!
GWTCH
GULLUCH
SPAK

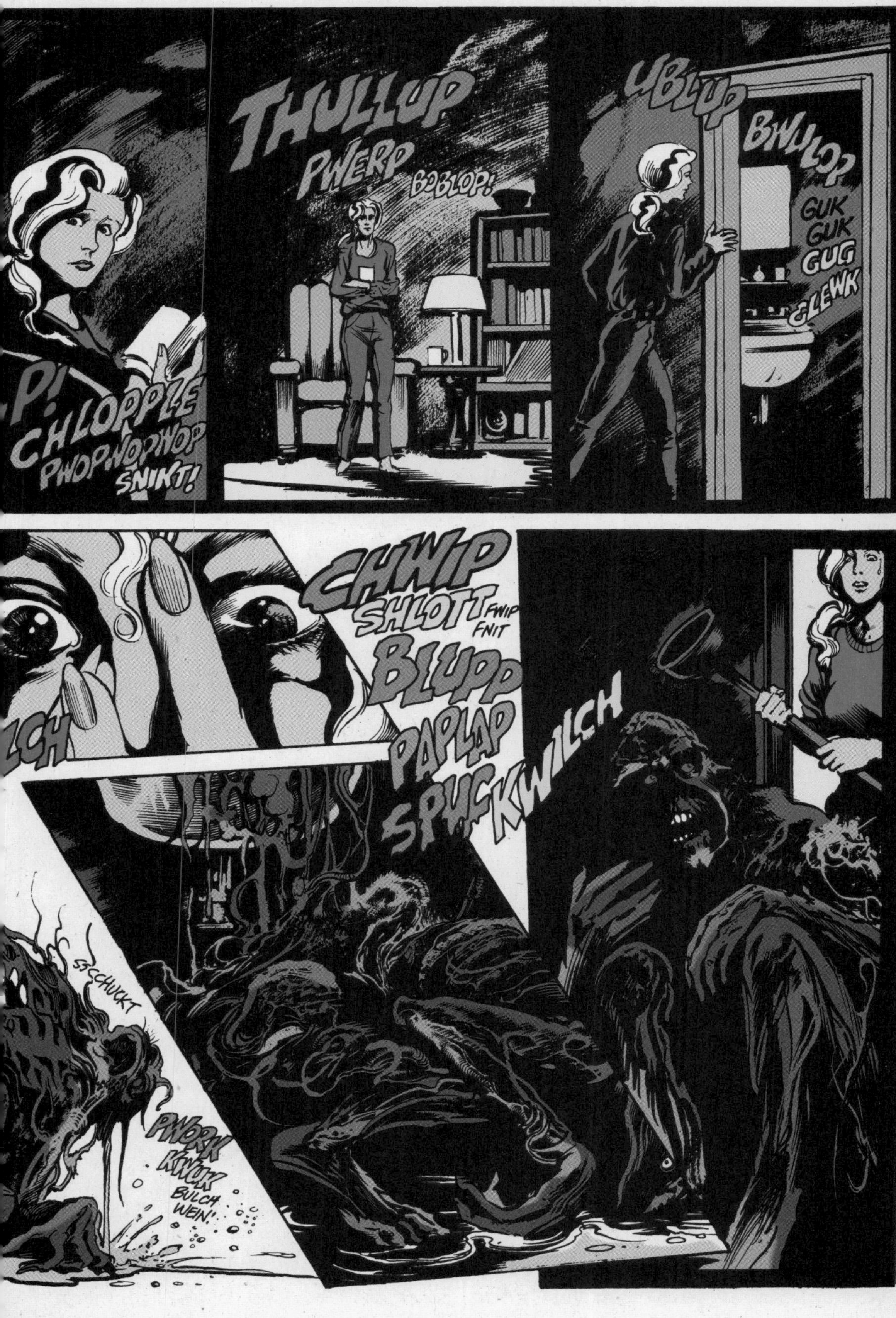
P!
CHLOPPLE
PWOPWOPWOP
SNIKT!
THULLUP
PWERP
BOBLOP!
UBLUP
BWULOP
GUK
GUK
GUG
GLEWK
LCH
CHWIP
SHLOTT
FWIP
FNIT
BLUPP
PAPLAP
SPUCKWILCH
SCHUCKT
PWORK
KWUK
BULCH
WEIN!

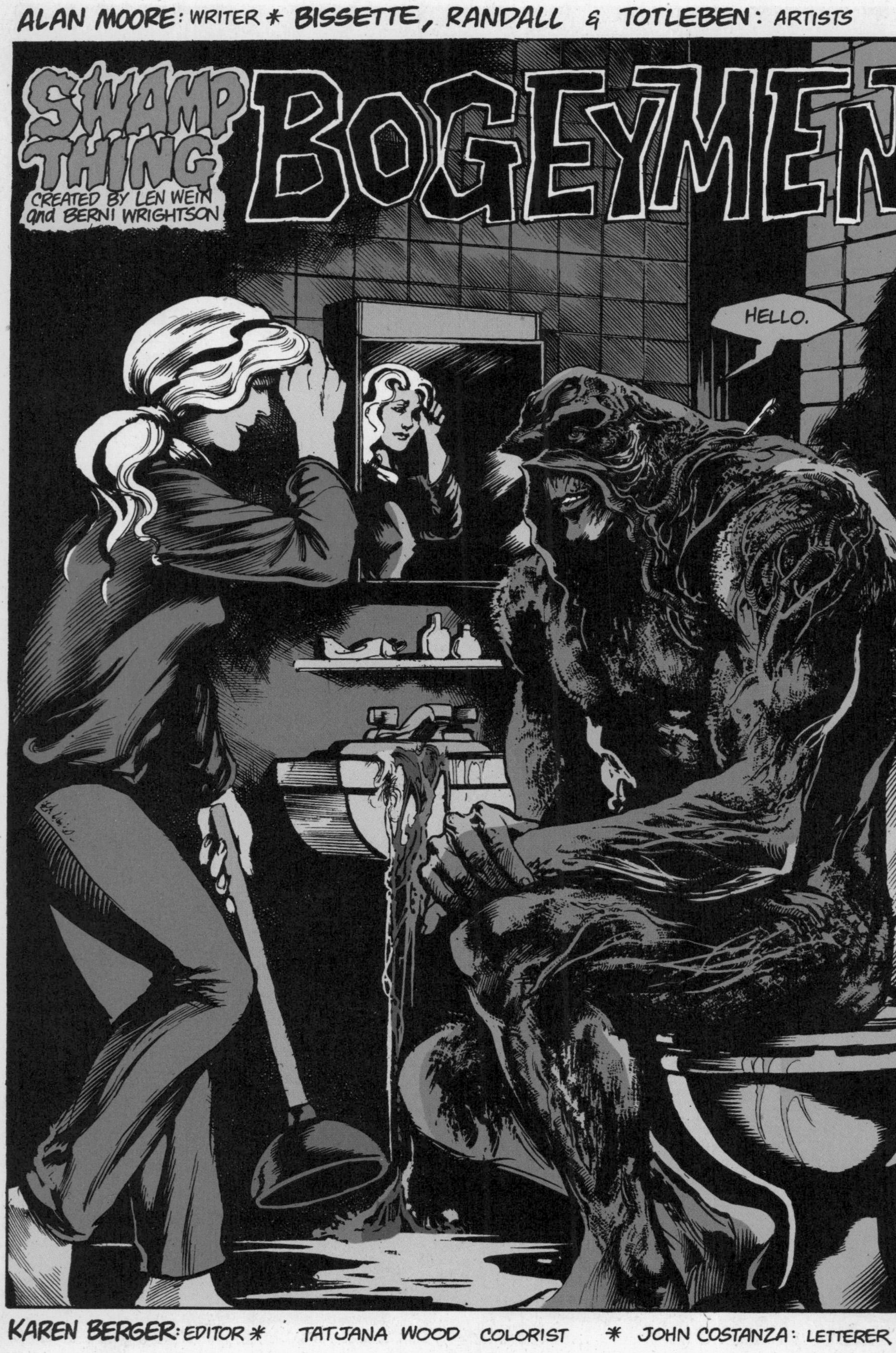
ALAN MOORE: WRITER * BISSETTE, RANDALL & TOTLEBEN: ARTISTS
SWAMP THING
CREATED BY LEN WEIN and BERNI WRIGHTSON
BOGEYMEN
HELLO.
KAREN BERGER: EDITOR * TATJANA WOOD COLORIST * JOHN COSTANZA: LETTERER

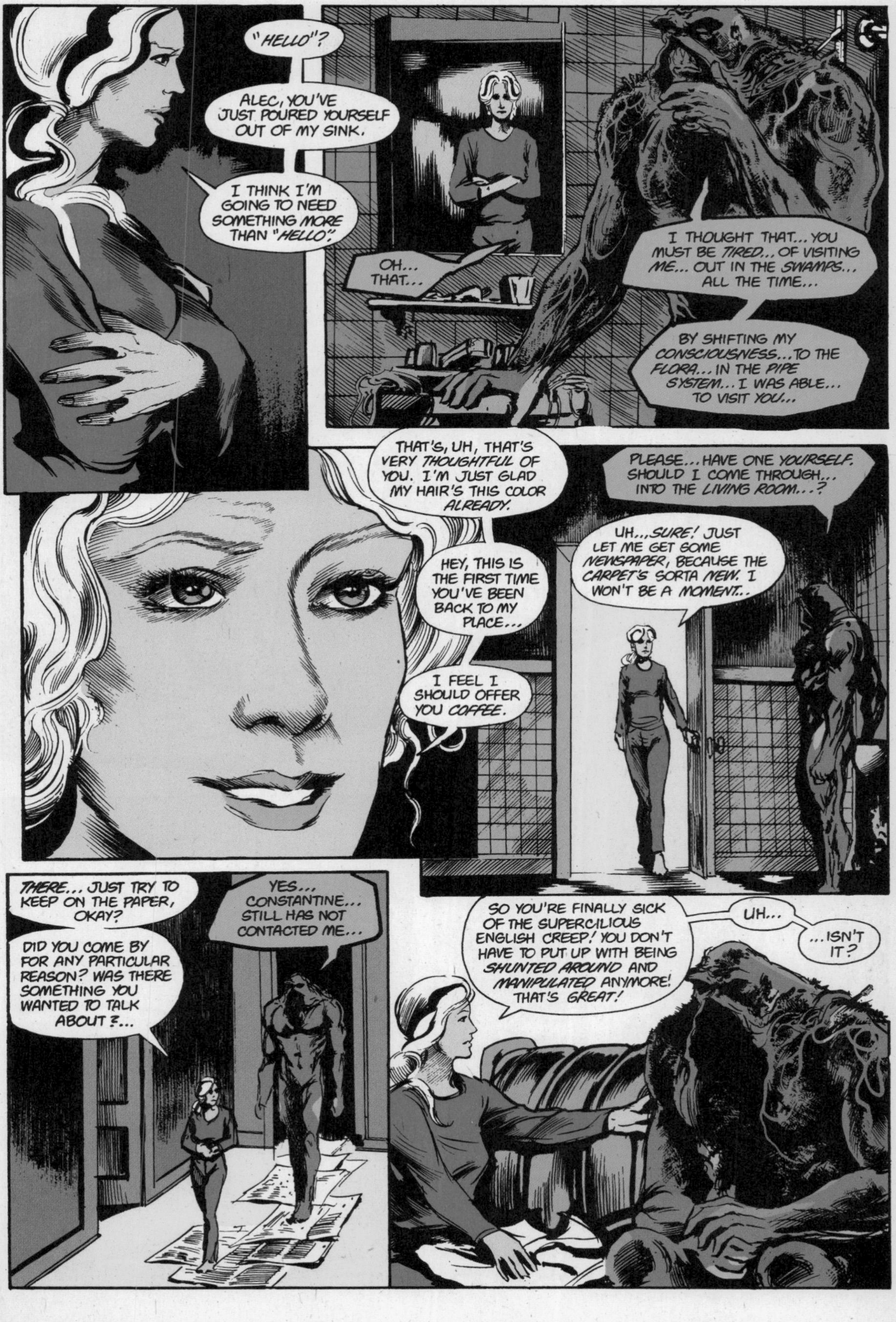
"HELLO"?
ALEC, YOU'VE JUST POURED YOURSELF OUT OF MY SINK.
I THINK I'M GOING TO NEED SOMETHING MORE THAN "HELLO".
OH... THAT...
I THOUGHT THAT... YOU MUST BE TIRED... OF VISITING ME... OUT IN THE SWAMPS... ALL THE TIME...
BY SHIFTING MY CONSCIOUSNESS... TO THE FLORA... IN THE PIPE SYSTEM... I WAS ABLE... TO VISIT YOU...
THAT'S, UH, THAT'S VERY THOUGHTFUL OF YOU. I'M JUST GLAD MY HAIR'S THIS COLOR ALREADY.
HEY, THIS IS THE FIRST TIME YOU'VE BEEN BACK TO MY PLACE...
I FEEL I SHOULD OFFER YOU COFFEE.
PLEASE... HAVE ONE YOURSELF. SHOULD I COME THROUGH... INTO THE LIVING ROOM...?
UH... SURE! JUST LET ME GET SOME NEWSPAPER, BECAUSE THE CARPET'S SORTA NEW. I WON'T BE A MOMENT...
THERE... JUST TRY TO KEEP ON THE PAPER, OKAY?
DID YOU COME BY FOR ANY PARTICULAR REASON? WAS THERE SOMETHING YOU WANTED TO TALK ABOUT?...
YES... CONSTANTINE... STILL HAS NOT CONTACTED ME...
SO YOU'RE FINALLY SICK OF THE SUPERCILIOUS ENGLISH CREEP! YOU DON'T HAVE TO PUT UP WITH BEING SHUNTED AROUND AND MANIPULATED ANYMORE! THAT'S GREAT!
UH...
...ISN'T IT?

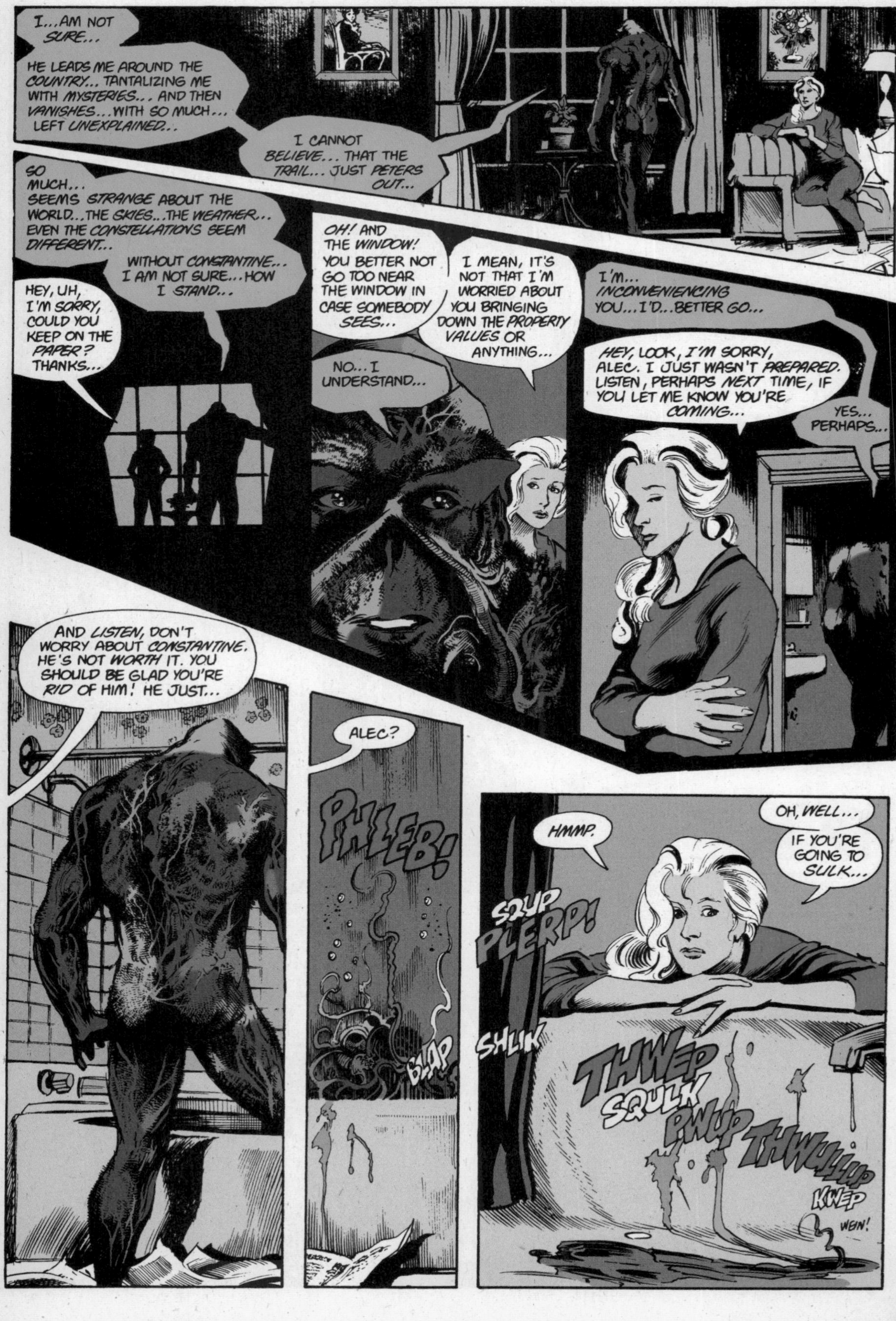
I... AM NOT SURE...
HE LEADS ME AROUND THE COUNTRY... TANTALIZING ME WITH MYSTERIES... AND THEN VANISHES... WITH SO MUCH... LEFT UNEXPLAINED...
I CANNOT BELIEVE... THAT THE TRAIL... JUST PETERS OUT...
SO MUCH... SEEMS STRANGE ABOUT THE WORLD... THE SKIES... THE WEATHER... EVEN THE CONSTELLATIONS SEEM DIFFERENT...
WITHOUT CONSTANTINE... I AM NOT SURE... HOW I STAND...
HEY, UH, I'M SORRY, COULD YOU KEEP ON THE PAPER? THANKS...
OH! AND THE WINDOW! YOU BETTER NOT GO TOO NEAR THE WINDOW IN CASE SOMEBODY SEES...
I MEAN, IT'S NOT THAT I'M WORRIED ABOUT YOU BRINGING DOWN THE PROPERTY VALUES OR ANYTHING...
NO... I UNDERSTAND...
I'M... INCONVENIENCING YOU... I'D... BETTER GO...
HEY, LOOK, I'M SORRY, ALEC. I JUST WASN'T PREPARED. LISTEN, PERHAPS NEXT TIME, IF YOU LET ME KNOW YOU'RE COMING...
YES... PERHAPS...
AND LISTEN, DON'T WORRY ABOUT CONSTANTINE. HE'S NOT WORTH IT. YOU SHOULD BE GLAD YOU'RE RID OF HIM! HE JUST...
ALEC?
PHLEB!
BLAP
SHLIK
HMMP.
OH, WELL...
IF YOU'RE GOING TO SULK...
SQUP
PLERP!
THWEP
SQULK
PWUP
THWULLUP
KWEP
WEIN!

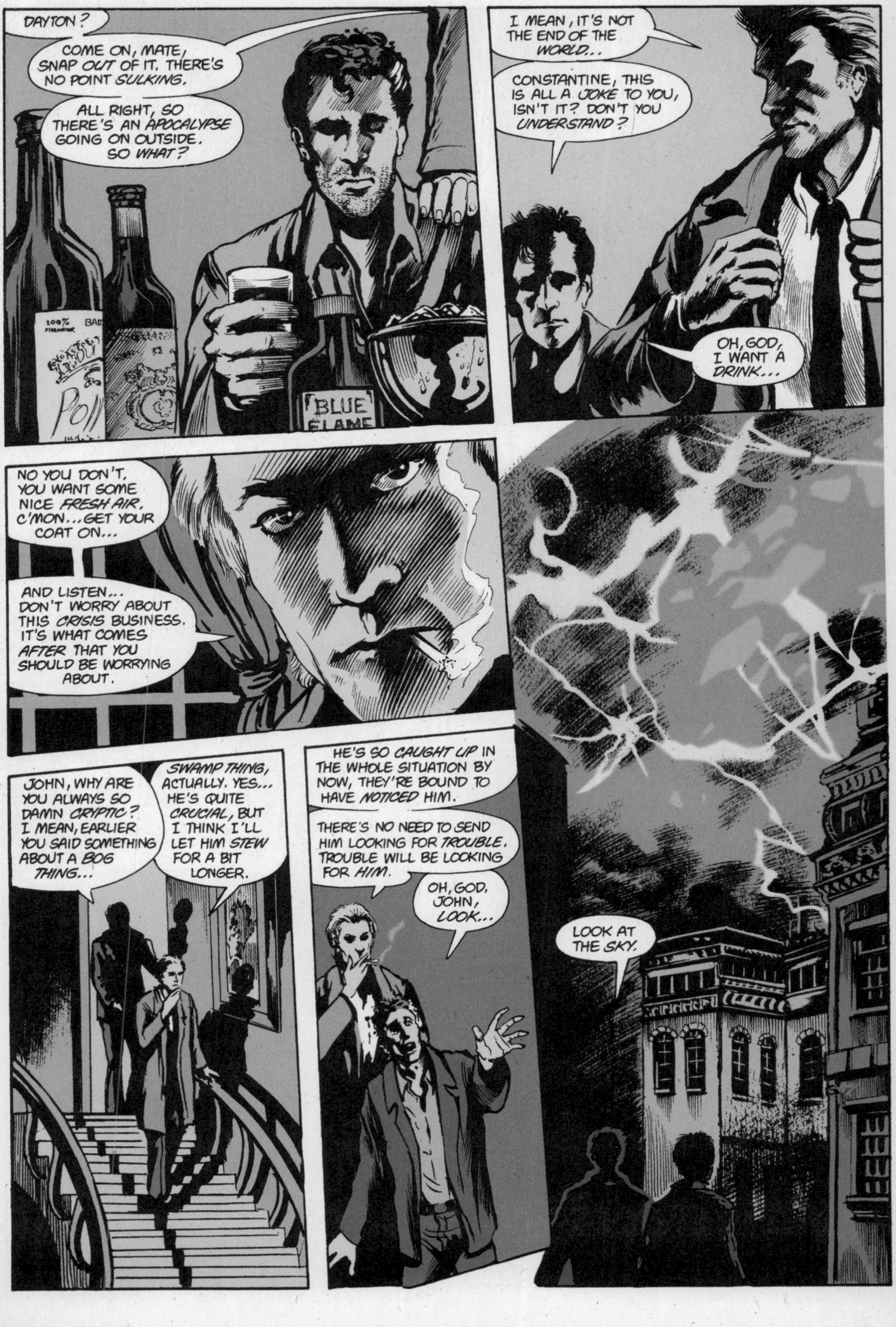
DAYTON?
COME ON, MATE, SNAP OUT OF IT. THERE'S NO POINT SULKING.
ALL RIGHT, SO THERE'S AN APOCALYPSE GOING ON OUTSIDE. SO WHAT?
BLUE FLAME
I MEAN, IT'S NOT THE END OF THE WORLD...
CONSTANTINE, THIS IS ALL A JOKE TO YOU, ISN'T IT? DON'T YOU UNDERSTAND?
OH, GOD, I WANT A DRINK...
NO YOU DON'T, YOU WANT SOME NICE FRESH AIR. C'MON... GET YOUR COAT ON...
AND LISTEN... DON'T WORRY ABOUT THIS CRISIS BUSINESS. IT'S WHAT COMES AFTER THAT YOU SHOULD BE WORRYING ABOUT.
JOHN, WHY ARE YOU ALWAYS SO DAMN CRYPTIC? I MEAN, EARLIER YOU SAID SOMETHING ABOUT A BOG THING...
SWAMP THING, ACTUALLY. YES... HE'S QUITE CRUCIAL, BUT I THINK I'LL LET HIM STEW FOR A BIT LONGER.
HE'S SO CAUGHT UP IN THE WHOLE SITUATION BY NOW, THEY'RE BOUND TO HAVE NOTICED HIM.
THERE'S NO NEED TO SEND HIM LOOKING FOR TROUBLE. TROUBLE WILL BE LOOKING FOR HIM.
OH, GOD, JOHN, LOOK...
LOOK AT THE SKY.

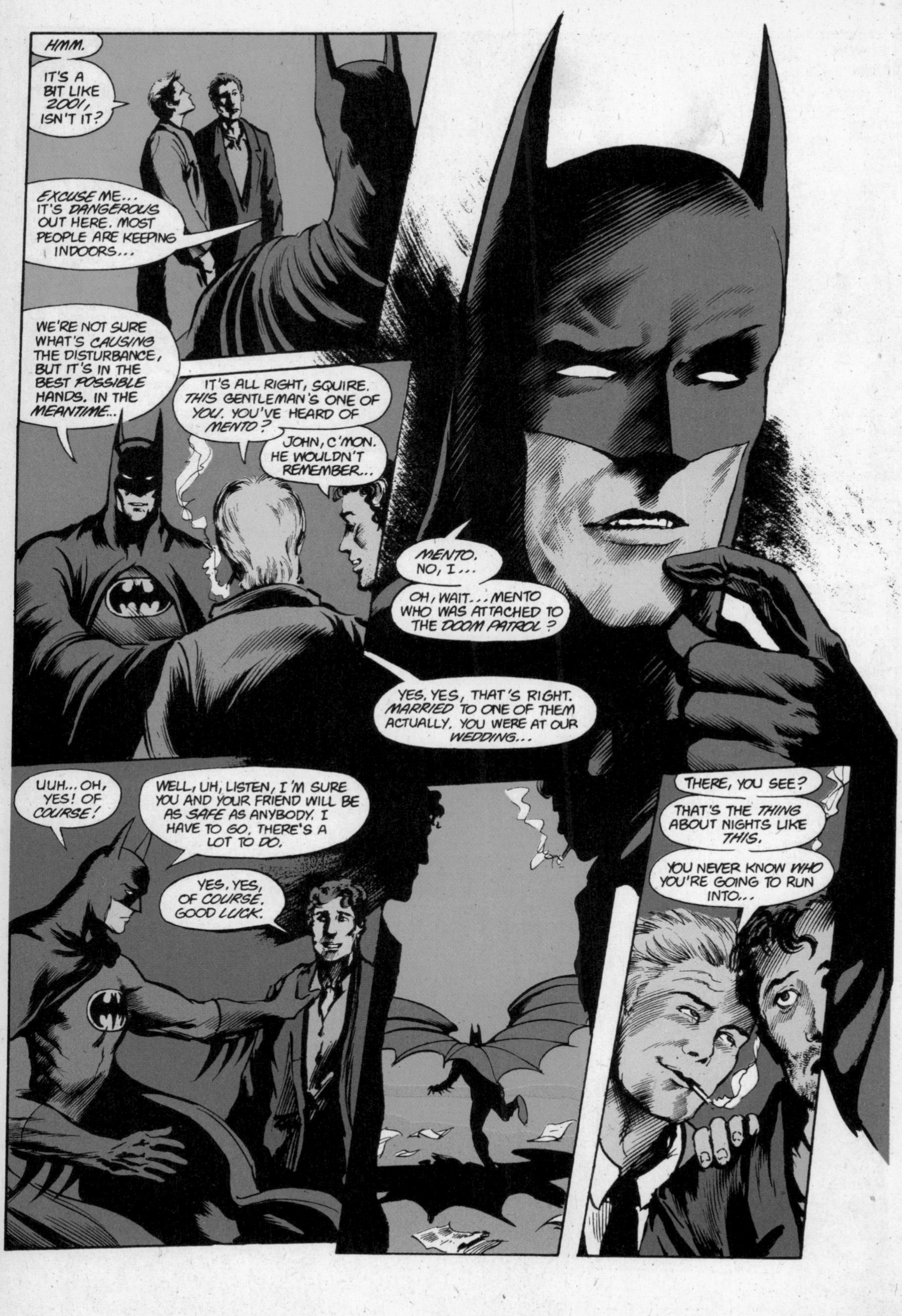
HMM.
IT'S A BIT LIKE 2001, ISN'T IT?
EXCUSE ME... IT'S DANGEROUS OUT HERE. MOST PEOPLE ARE KEEPING INDOORS...
WE'RE NOT SURE WHAT'S CAUSING THE DISTURBANCE, BUT IT'S IN THE BEST POSSIBLE HANDS. IN THE MEANTIME...
IT'S ALL RIGHT, SQUIRE. THIS GENTLEMAN'S ONE OF YOU. YOU'VE HEARD OF MENTO?
JOHN, C'MON. HE WOULDN'T REMEMBER...
MENTO. NO, I...
OH, WAIT... MENTO WHO WAS ATTACHED TO THE DOOM PATROL?
YES, YES, THAT'S RIGHT. MARRIED TO ONE OF THEM ACTUALLY. YOU WERE AT OUR WEDDING...
UUH... OH, YES! OF COURSE!
WELL, UH, LISTEN, I'M SURE YOU AND YOUR FRIEND WILL BE AS SAFE AS ANYBODY. I HAVE TO GO, THERE'S A LOT TO DO.
YES, YES, OF COURSE. GOOD LUCK.
THERE, YOU SEE?
THAT'S THE THING ABOUT NIGHTS LIKE THIS.
YOU NEVER KNOW WHO YOU'RE GOING TO RUN INTO...

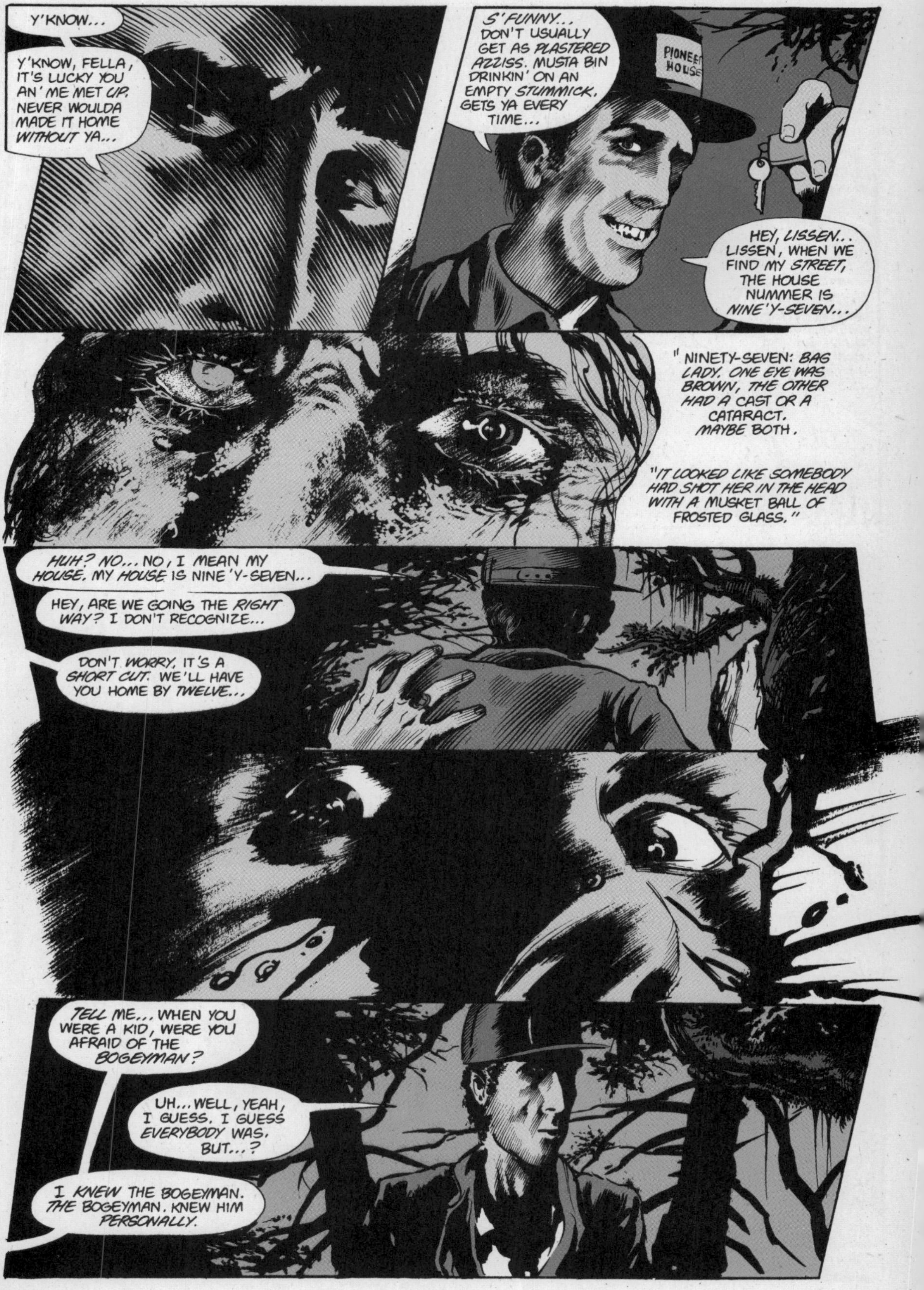
Y'KNOW...
Y'KNOW, FELLA, IT'S LUCKY YOU AN' ME MET UP. NEVER WOULDA MADE IT HOME WITHOUT YA...
S'FUNNY... DON'T USUALLY GET AS PLASTERED AZZISS. MUSTA BIN DRINKIN' ON AN EMPTY STUMMICK. GETS YA EVERY TIME...
PIONEER HOUSE
HEY, LISSEN... LISSEN, WHEN WE FIND MY STREET, THE HOUSE NUMMER IS NINE'Y-SEVEN...
"NINETY-SEVEN: BAG LADY. ONE EYE WAS BROWN, THE OTHER HAD A CAST OR A CATARACT. MAYBE BOTH.
"IT LOOKED LIKE SOMEBODY HAD SHOT HER IN THE HEAD WITH A MUSKET BALL OF FROSTED GLASS."
HUH? NO... NO, I MEAN MY HOUSE. MY HOUSE IS NINE'Y-SEVEN...
HEY, ARE WE GOING THE RIGHT WAY? I DON'T RECOGNIZE...
DON'T WORRY, IT'S A SHORT CUT. WE'LL HAVE YOU HOME BY TWELVE...
TELL ME... WHEN YOU WERE A KID, WERE YOU AFRAID OF THE BOGEYMAN?
UH... WELL, YEAH, I GUESS. I GUESS EVERYBODY WAS. BUT...?
I KNEW THE BOGEYMAN. THE BOGEYMAN. KNEW HIM PERSONALLY.

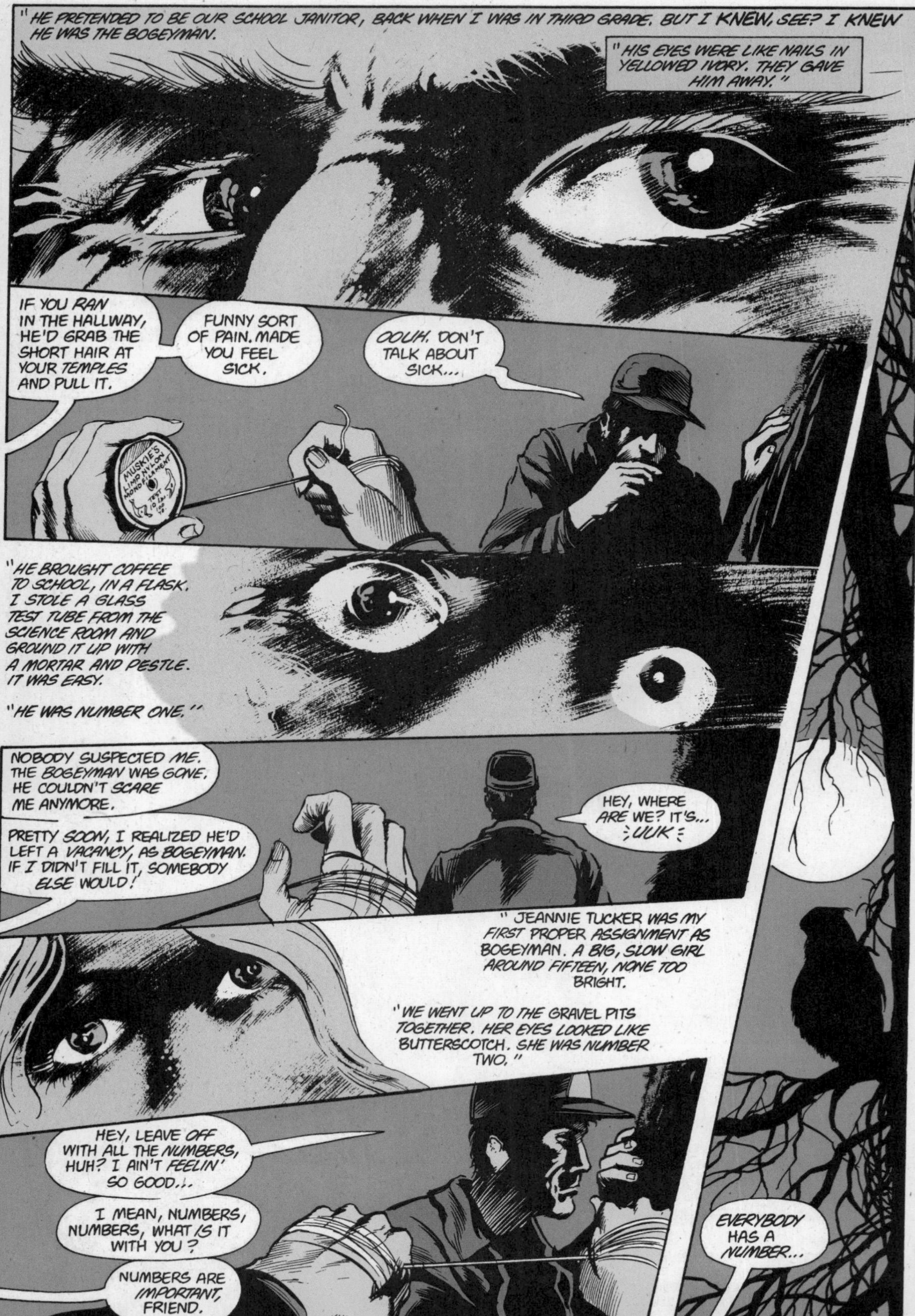
"HE PRETENDED TO BE OUR SCHOOL JANITOR, BACK WHEN I WAS IN THIRD GRADE. BUT I KNEW, SEE? I KNEW HE WAS THE BOGEYMAN.
"HIS EYES WERE LIKE NAILS IN YELLOWED IVORY. THEY GAVE HIM AWAY."
IF YOU RAN IN THE HALLWAY, HE'D GRAB THE SHORT HAIR AT YOUR TEMPLES AND PULL IT.
FUNNY SORT OF PAIN. MADE YOU FEEL SICK.
OOUH. DON'T TALK ABOUT SICK...
MUSKIE'S LIMP NYLON MONOFILAMENT
"HE BROUGHT COFFEE TO SCHOOL, IN A FLASK. I STOLE A GLASS TEST TUBE FROM THE SCIENCE ROOM AND GROUND IT UP WITH A MORTAR AND PESTLE. IT WAS EASY.
"HE WAS NUMBER ONE."
NOBODY SUSPECTED ME. THE BOGEYMAN WAS GONE. HE COULDN'T SCARE ME ANYMORE.
PRETTY SOON, I REALIZED HE'D LEFT A VACANCY, AS BOGEYMAN. IF I DIDN'T FILL IT, SOMEBODY ELSE WOULD!
HEY, WHERE ARE WE? IT'S... UUK
" JEANNIE TUCKER WAS MY FIRST PROPER ASSIGNMENT AS BOGEYMAN. A BIG, SLOW GIRL AROUND FIFTEEN, NONE TOO BRIGHT.
"WE WENT UP TO THE GRAVEL PITS TOGETHER. HER EYES LOOKED LIKE BUTTERSCOTCH. SHE WAS NUMBER TWO."
HEY, LEAVE OFF WITH ALL THE NUMBERS, HUH? I AIN'T FEELIN' SO GOOD...
I MEAN, NUMBERS, NUMBERS, WHAT IS IT WITH YOU?
NUMBERS ARE IMPORTANT, FRIEND.
EVERYBODY HAS A NUMBER...

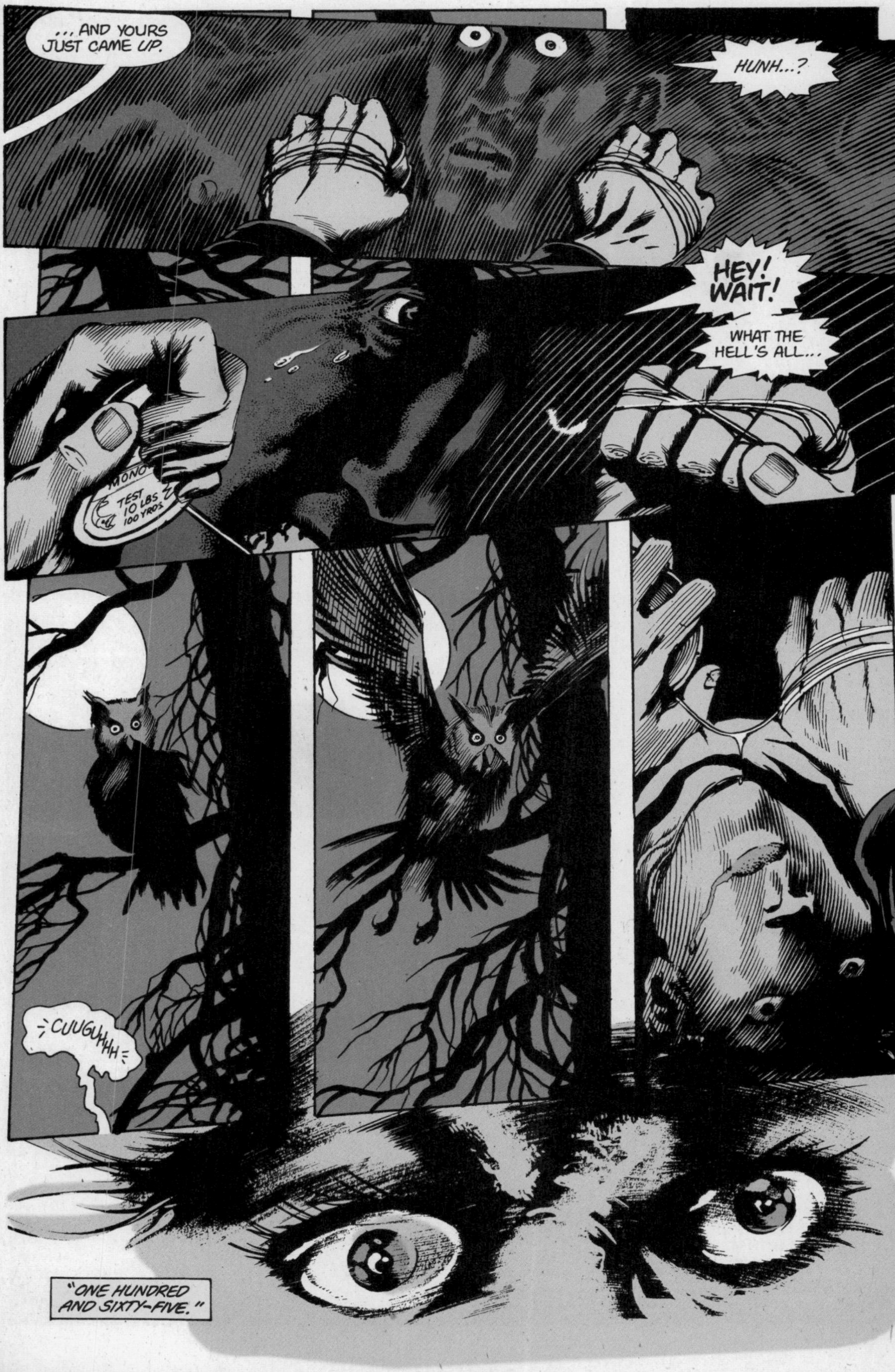
...AND YOURS JUST CAME UP.
HUNH...?
HEY! WAIT!
WHAT THE HELL'S ALL...
MONO TEST 10 LBS 100 YRDS.
CUUGUHHH
"ONE HUNDRED AND SIXTY-FIVE."

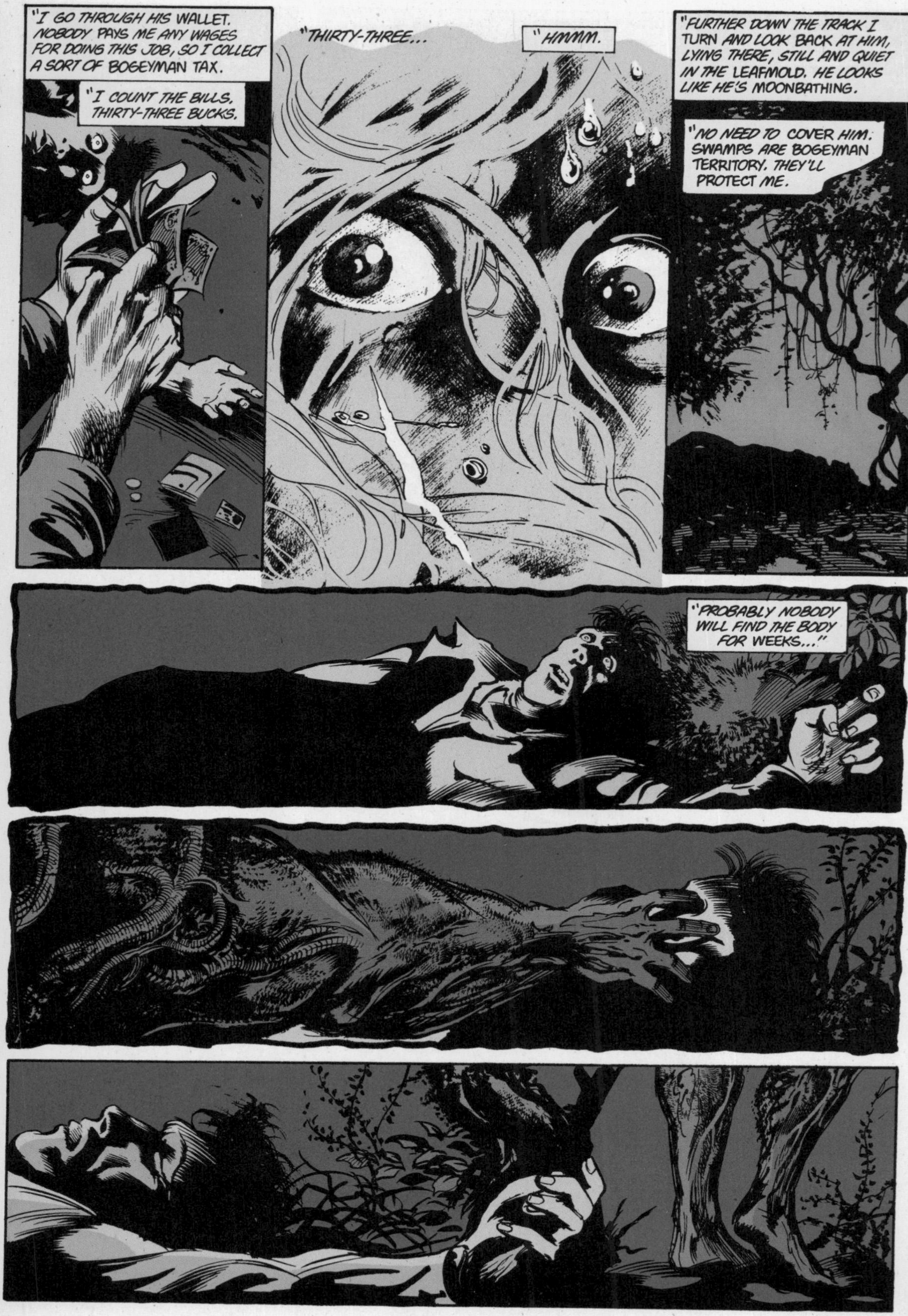
"I GO THROUGH HIS WALLET. NOBODY PAYS ME ANY WAGES FOR DOING THIS JOB, SO I COLLECT A SORT OF BOGEYMAN TAX.
"I COUNT THE BILLS. THIRTY-THREE BUCKS.
"THIRTY-THREE...
"HMMM.
"FURTHER DOWN THE TRACK I TURN AND LOOK BACK AT HIM, LYING THERE, STILL AND QUIET IN THE LEAFMOLD. HE LOOKS LIKE HE'S MOONBATHING.
"NO NEED TO COVER HIM. SWAMPS ARE BOGEYMAN TERRITORY. THEY'LL PROTECT ME.
"PROBABLY NOBODY WILL FIND THE BODY FOR WEEKS..."

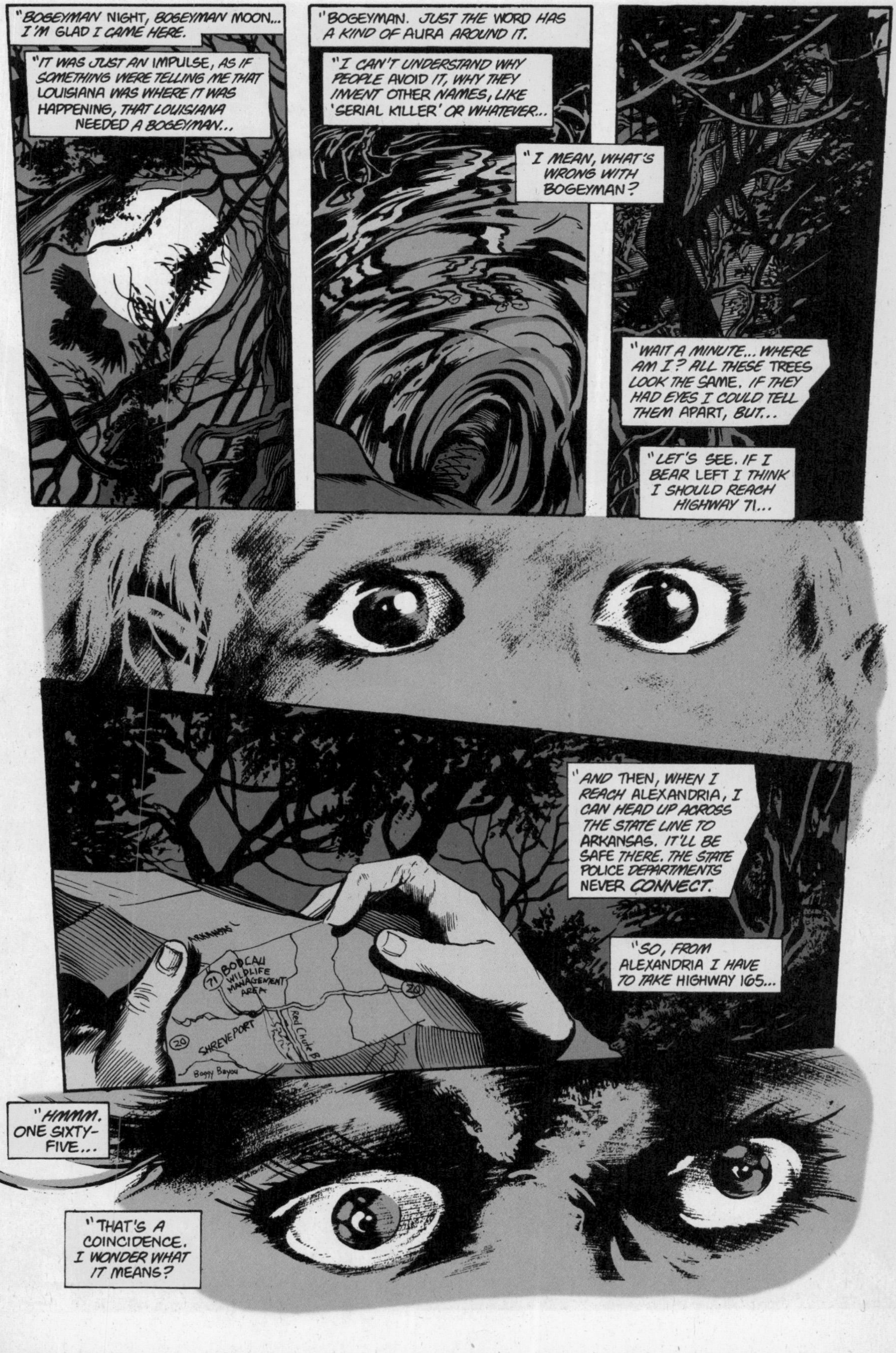
"BOGEYMAN NIGHT, BOGEYMAN MOON... I'M GLAD I CAME HERE.
"IT WAS JUST AN IMPULSE, AS IF SOMETHING WERE TELLING ME THAT LOUISIANA WAS WHERE IT WAS HAPPENING, THAT LOUISIANA NEEDED A BOGEYMAN...
"BOGEYMAN. JUST THE WORD HAS A KIND OF AURA AROUND IT.
"I CAN'T UNDERSTAND WHY PEOPLE AVOID IT, WHY THEY INVENT OTHER NAMES, LIKE 'SERIAL KILLER' OR WHATEVER...
"I MEAN, WHAT'S WRONG WITH BOGEYMAN?
"WAIT A MINUTE... WHERE AM I? ALL THESE TREES LOOK THE SAME. IF THEY HAD EYES I COULD TELL THEM APART, BUT...
"LET'S SEE. IF I BEAR LEFT I THINK I SHOULD REACH HIGHWAY 71...
"AND THEN, WHEN I REACH ALEXANDRIA, I CAN HEAD UP ACROSS THE STATE LINE TO ARKANSAS. IT'LL BE SAFE THERE. THE STATE POLICE DEPARTMENTS NEVER CONNECT.
"SO, FROM ALEXANDRIA I HAVE TO TAKE HIGHWAY 165...
BODCAU WILDLIFE MANAGEMENT AREA
71
20
SHREVEPORT
Red Chute B
Boggy Bayou
"HMMM. ONE SIXTY-FIVE...
"THAT'S A COINCIDENCE. I WONDER WHAT IT MEANS?

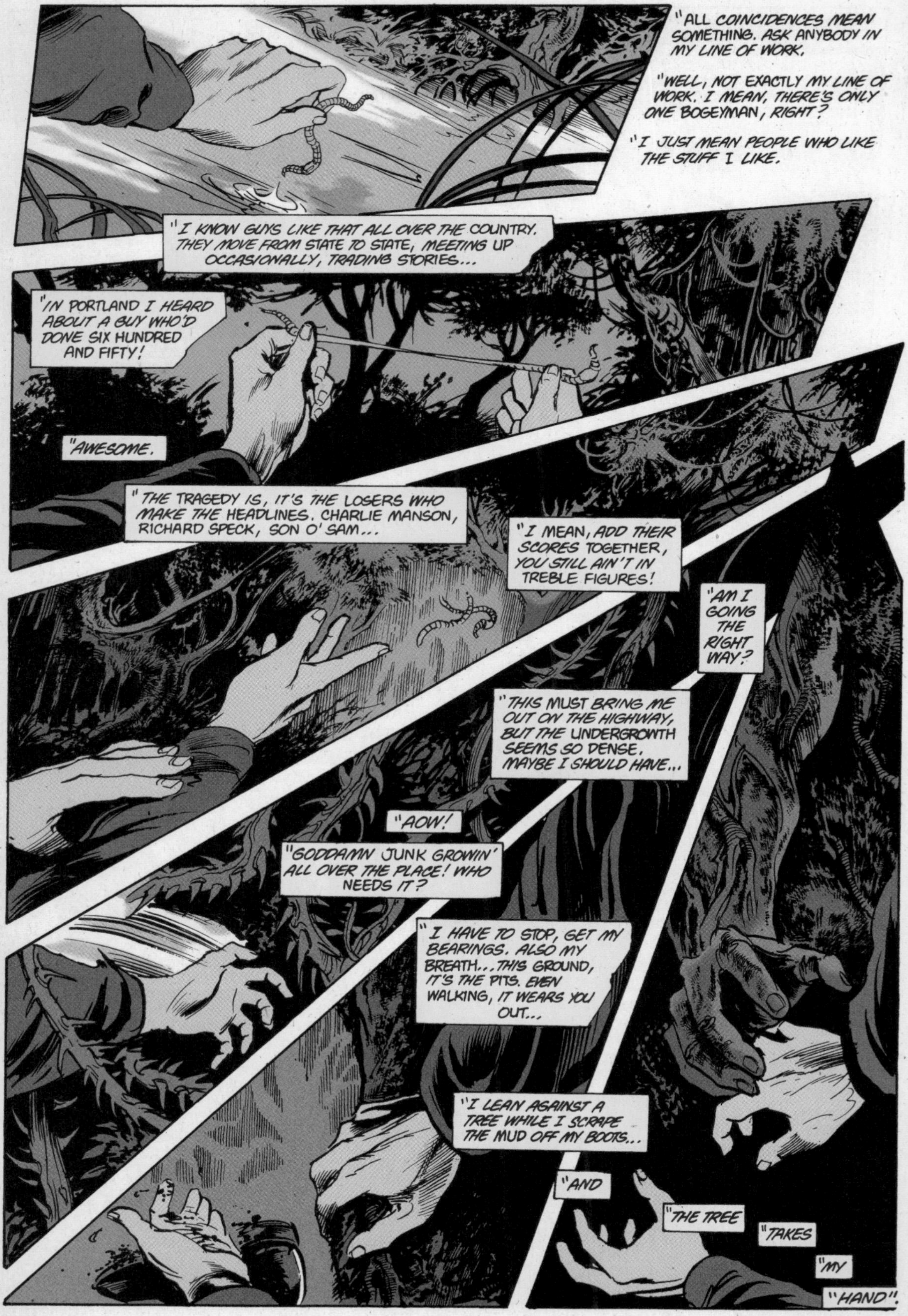
"ALL COINCIDENCES MEAN SOMETHING. ASK ANYBODY IN MY LINE OF WORK.
"WELL, NOT EXACTLY MY LINE OF WORK. I MEAN, THERE'S ONLY ONE BOGEYMAN, RIGHT?
"I JUST MEAN PEOPLE WHO LIKE THE STUFF I LIKE.
"I KNOW GUYS LIKE THAT ALL OVER THE COUNTRY. THEY MOVE FROM STATE TO STATE, MEETING UP OCCASIONALLY, TRADING STORIES...
"IN PORTLAND I HEARD ABOUT A GUY WHO'D DONE SIX HUNDRED AND FIFTY!
"AWESOME.
"THE TRAGEDY IS, IT'S THE LOSERS WHO MAKE THE HEADLINES. CHARLIE MANSON, RICHARD SPECK, SON O' SAM...
"I MEAN, ADD THEIR SCORES TOGETHER, YOU STILL AIN'T IN TREBLE FIGURES!
"AM I GOING THE RIGHT WAY?
"THIS MUST BRING ME OUT ON THE HIGHWAY, BUT THE UNDERGROWTH SEEMS SO DENSE. MAYBE I SHOULD HAVE...
"AOW!
"GODDAMN JUNK GROWIN' ALL OVER THE PLACE! WHO NEEDS IT?
"I HAVE TO STOP, GET MY BEARINGS. ALSO MY BREATH... THIS GROUND, IT'S THE PITS. EVEN WALKING, IT WEARS YOU OUT...
"I LEAN AGAINST A TREE WHILE I SCRAPE THE MUD OFF MY BOOTS...
"AND
"THE TREE
"TAKES
"MY
"HAND".

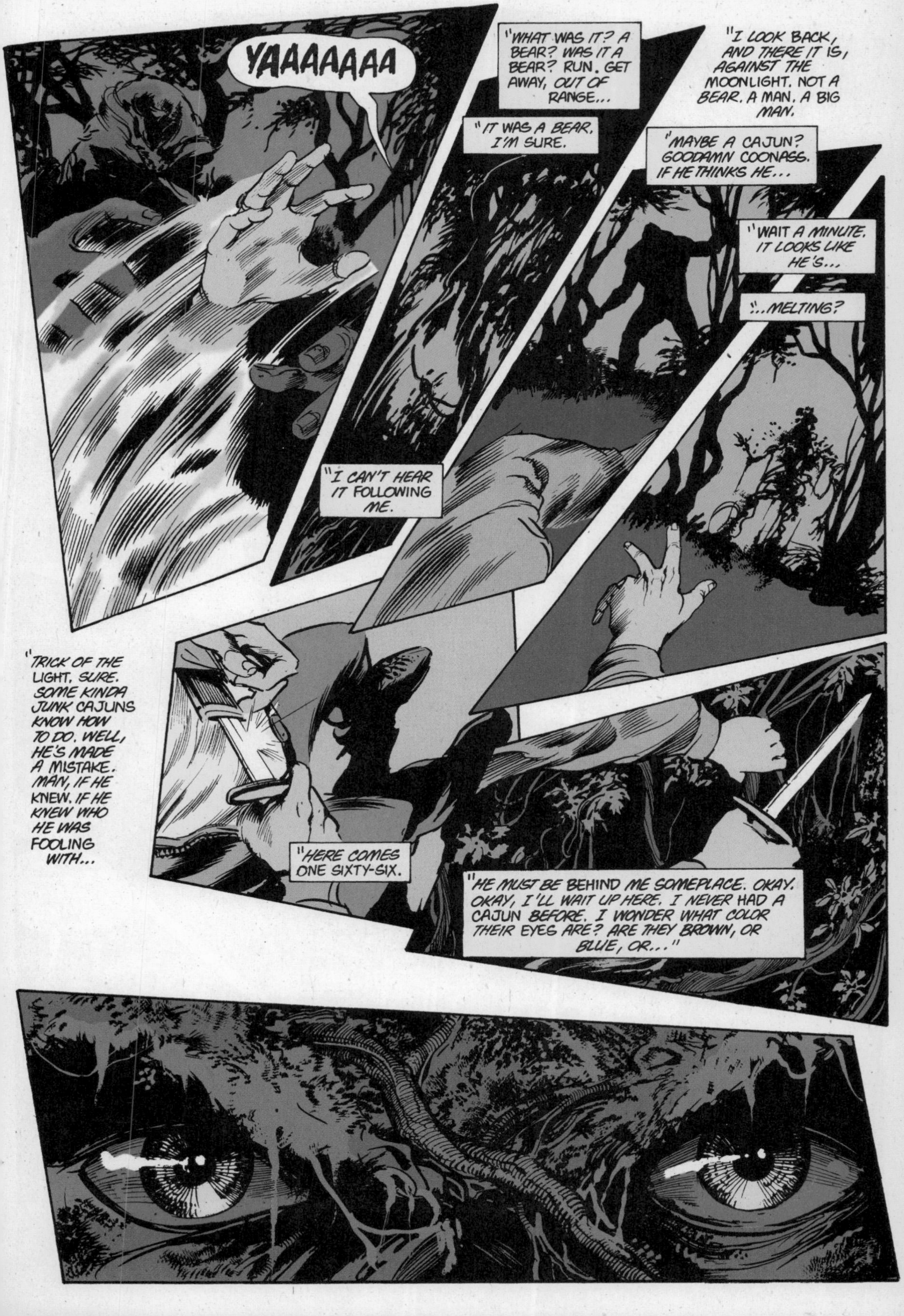
YAAAAAAA
"WHAT WAS IT? A BEAR? WAS IT A BEAR? RUN. GET AWAY, OUT OF RANGE...
"IT WAS A BEAR, I'M SURE.
"I CAN'T HEAR IT FOLLOWING ME.
"I LOOK BACK, AND THERE IT IS, AGAINST THE MOONLIGHT. NOT A BEAR. A MAN. A BIG MAN.
"MAYBE A CAJUN? GODDAMN COONASS. IF HE THINKS HE...
"WAIT A MINUTE. IT LOOKS LIKE HE'S...
"...MELTING?
"TRICK OF THE LIGHT. SURE. SOME KINDA JUNK CAJUNS KNOW HOW TO DO. WELL, HE'S MADE A MISTAKE. MAN, IF HE KNEW. IF HE KNEW WHO HE WAS FOOLING WITH...
"HERE COMES ONE SIXTY-SIX.
"HE MUST BE BEHIND ME SOMEPLACE. OKAY. OKAY, I'LL WAIT UP HERE. I NEVER HAD A CAJUN BEFORE. I WONDER WHAT COLOR THEIR EYES ARE? ARE THEY BROWN, OR BLUE, OR..."

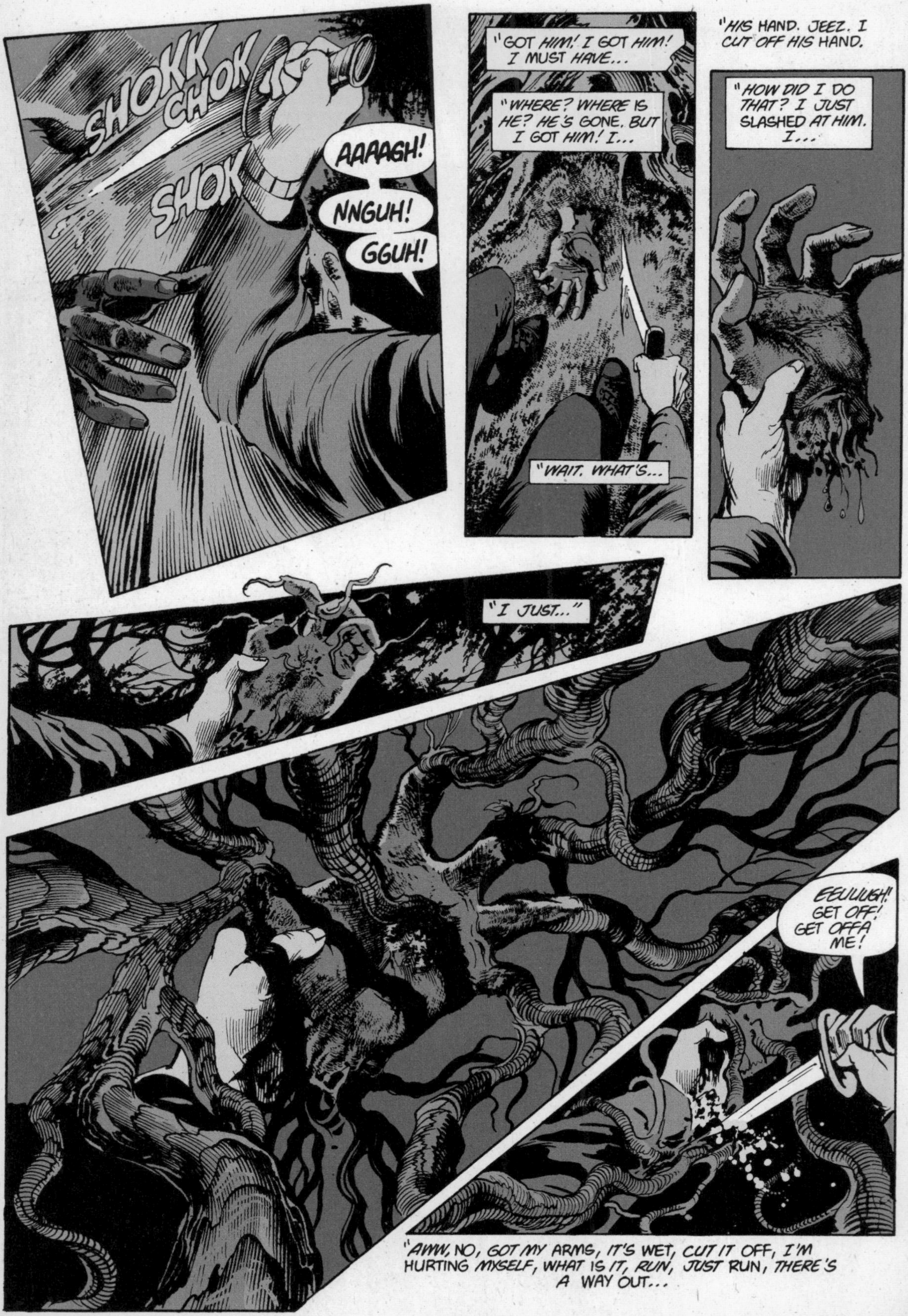
SHOKK
CHOK
SHOK
AAAAGH!
NNGUH!
GGUH!
"GOT HIM! I GOT HIM! I MUST HAVE...
"WHERE? WHERE IS HE? HE'S GONE. BUT I GOT HIM! I...
"WAIT. WHAT'S...
"HIS HAND. JEEZ. I CUT OFF HIS HAND.
"HOW DID I DO THAT? I JUST SLASHED AT HIM. I...
"I JUST..."
EEUUUGH! GET OFF! GET OFFA ME!
"AWW, NO, GOT MY ARMS, IT'S WET, CUT IT OFF, I'M HURTING MYSELF, WHAT IS IT, RUN, JUST RUN, THERE'S A WAY OUT...

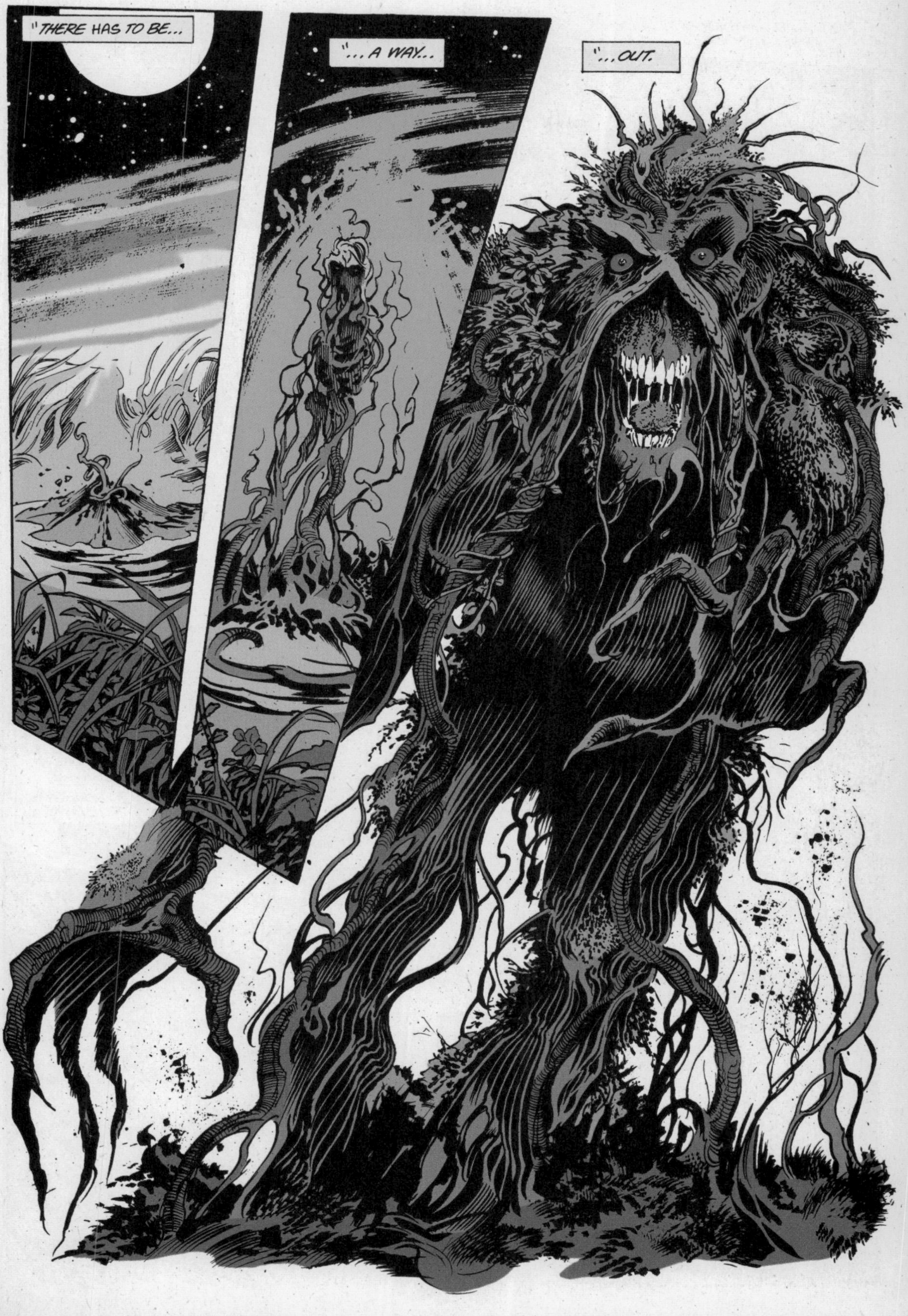
"THERE HAS TO BE...
"...A WAY...
"...OUT.

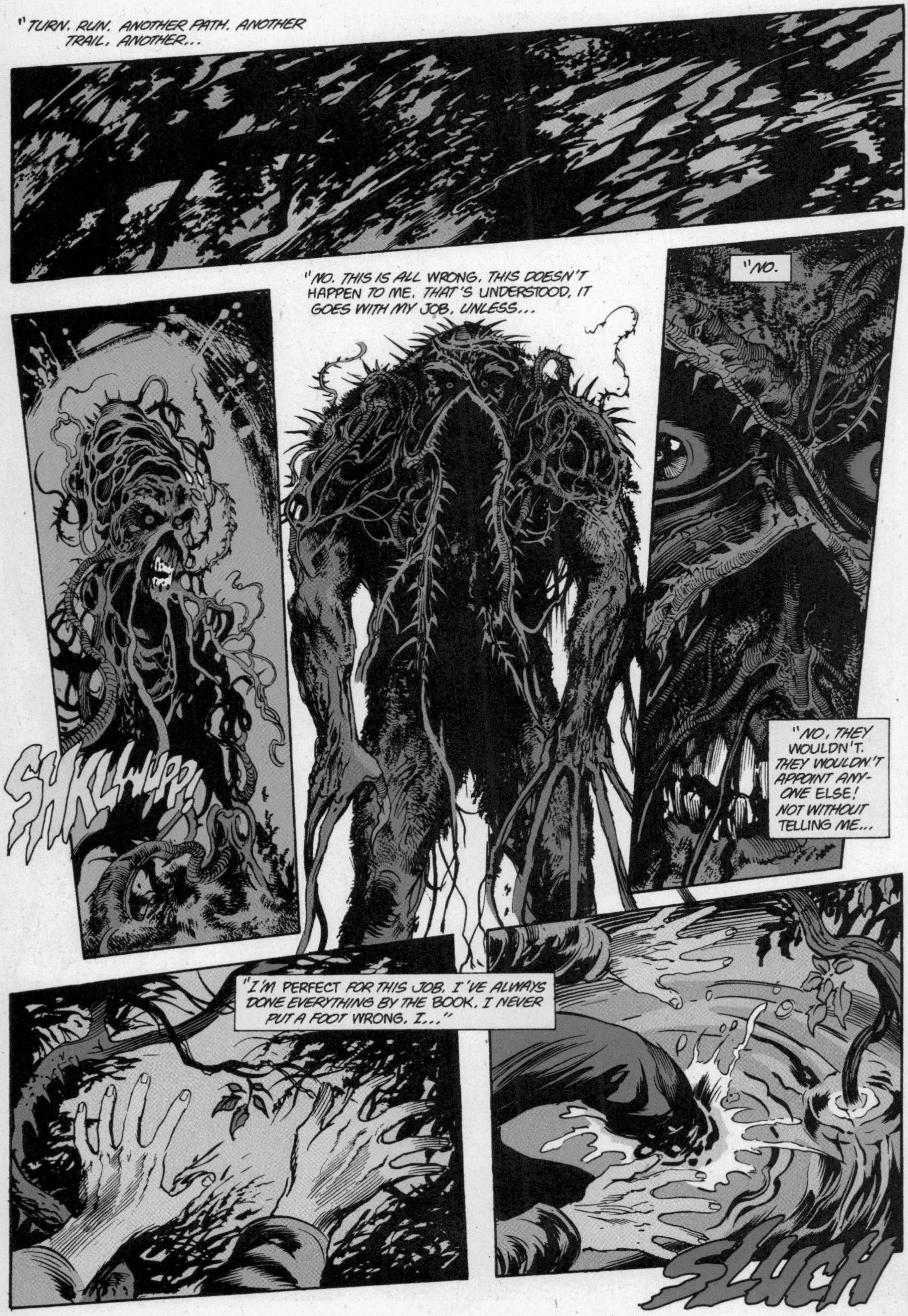
"TURN. RUN. ANOTHER PATH. ANOTHER TRAIL. ANOTHER...
SHKLWUPP!
"NO. THIS IS ALL WRONG. THIS DOESN'T HAPPEN TO ME. THAT'S UNDERSTOOD. IT GOES WITH MY JOB. UNLESS...
"NO.
"NO, THEY WOULDN'T. THEY WOULDN'T APPOINT ANYONE ELSE! NOT WITHOUT TELLING ME...
"I'M PERFECT FOR THIS JOB. I'VE ALWAYS DONE EVERYTHING BY THE BOOK. I NEVER PUT A FOOT WRONG. I..."
SLUCH

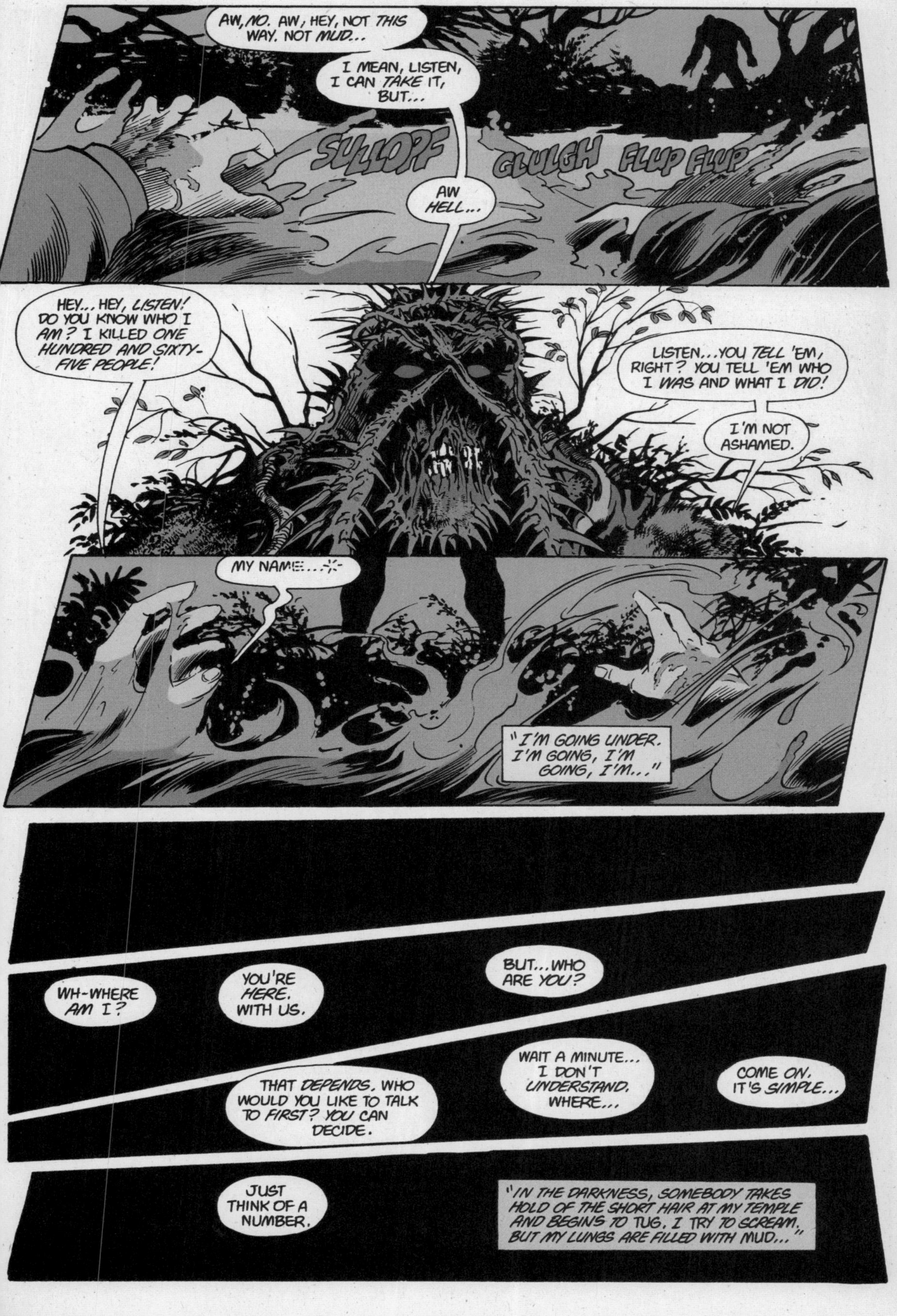
AW, NO. AW, HEY, NOT THIS WAY. NOT MUD...
I MEAN, LISTEN, I CAN TAKE IT, BUT...
SULLOPF
GLULGH
FLUP FLUP
AW HELL...
HEY... HEY, LISTEN! DO YOU KNOW WHO I AM? I KILLED ONE HUNDRED AND SIXTY-FIVE PEOPLE!
LISTEN... YOU TELL 'EM, RIGHT? YOU TELL 'EM WHO I WAS AND WHAT I DID!
I'M NOT ASHAMED.
MY NAME...
"I'M GOING UNDER. I'M GOING, I'M GOING, I'M..."
WH-WHERE AM I?
YOU'RE HERE. WITH US.
BUT... WHO ARE YOU?
THAT DEPENDS. WHO WOULD YOU LIKE TO TALK TO FIRST? YOU CAN DECIDE.
WAIT A MINUTE... I DON'T UNDERSTAND. WHERE...
COME ON. IT'S SIMPLE...
JUST THINK OF A NUMBER.
"IN THE DARKNESS, SOMEBODY TAKES HOLD OF THE SHORT HAIR AT MY TEMPLE AND BEGINS TO TUG. I TRY TO SCREAM, BUT MY LUNGS ARE FILLED WITH MUD..."

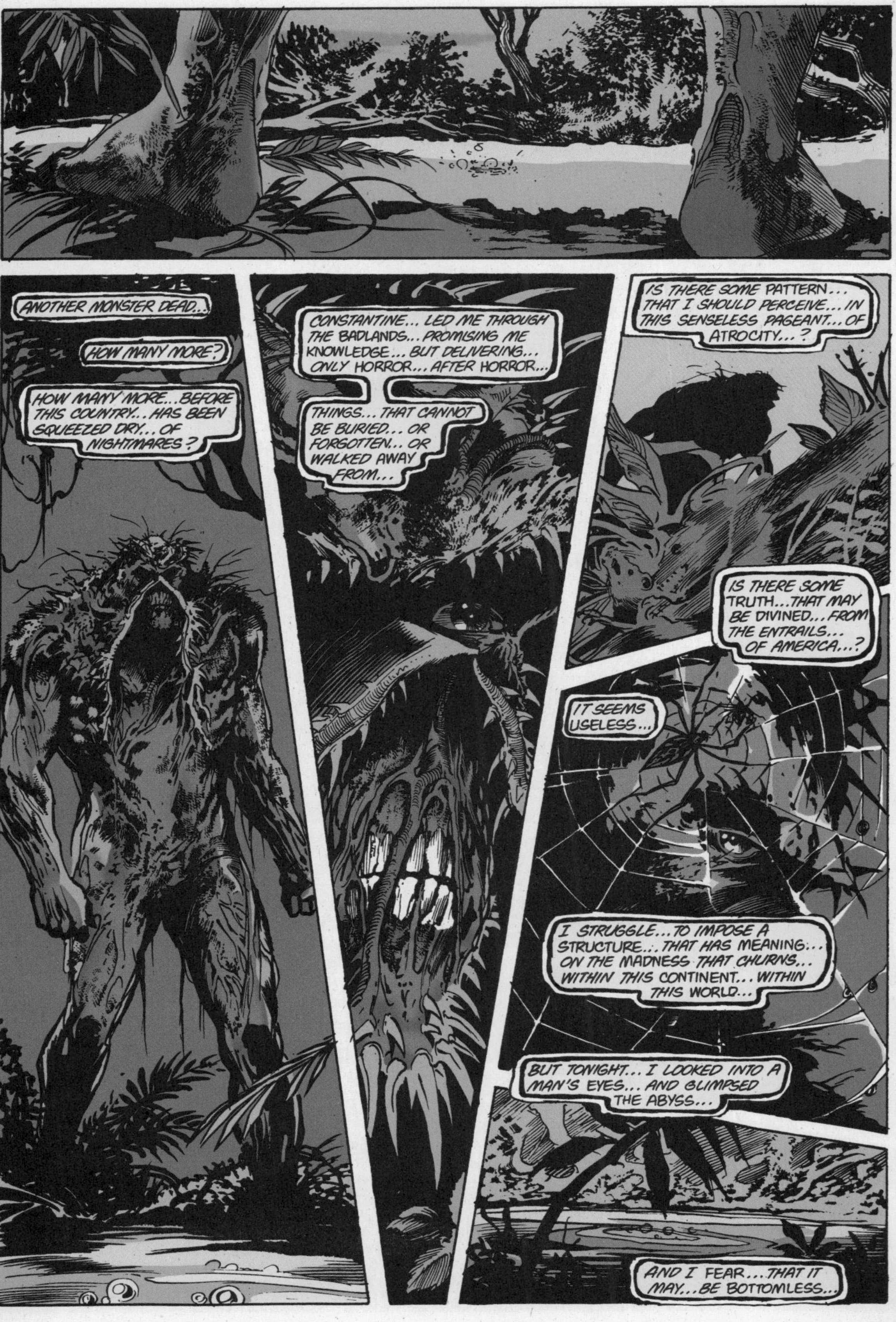
ANOTHER MONSTER DEAD...
HOW MANY MORE?
HOW MANY MORE...BEFORE THIS COUNTRY... HAS BEEN SQUEEZED DRY... OF NIGHTMARES?
CONSTANTINE... LED ME THROUGH THE BADLANDS... PROMISING ME KNOWLEDGE... BUT DELIVERING... ONLY HORROR... AFTER HORROR...
THINGS... THAT CANNOT BE BURIED... OR FORGOTTEN... OR WALKED AWAY FROM...
IS THERE SOME PATTERN... THAT I SHOULD PERCEIVE... IN THIS SENSELESS PAGEANT... OF ATROCITY...?
IS THERE SOME TRUTH...THAT MAY BE DIVINED... FROM THE ENTRAILS... OF AMERICA...?
IT SEEMS USELESS...
I STRUGGLE...TO IMPOSE A STRUCTURE... THAT HAS MEANING... ON THE MADNESS THAT CHURNS... WITHIN THIS CONTINENT... WITHIN THIS WORLD...
BUT TONIGHT... I LOOKED INTO A MAN'S EYES... AND GLIMPSED THE ABYSS...
AND I FEAR... THAT IT MAY... BE BOTTOMLESS...

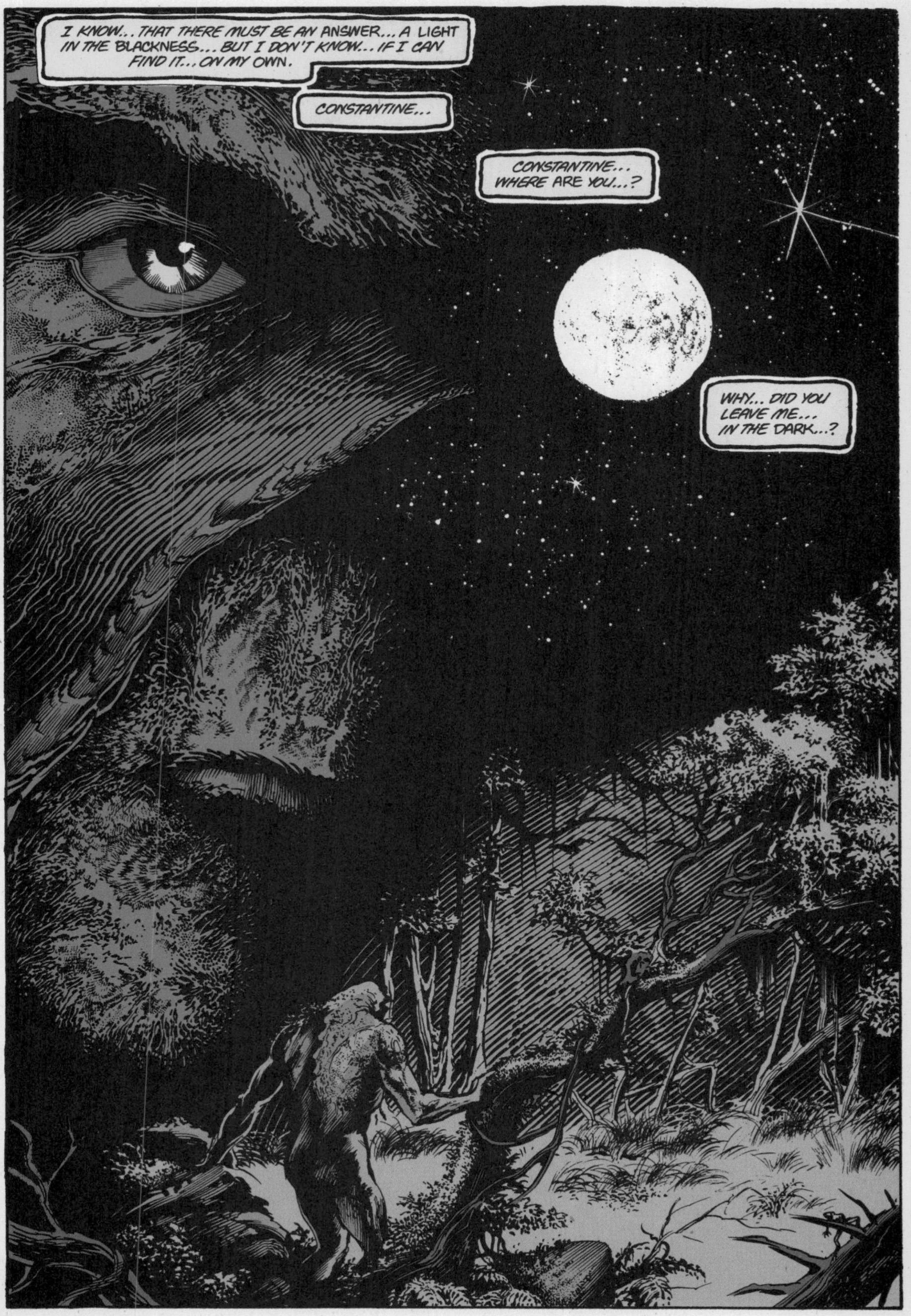
I KNOW... THAT THERE MUST BE AN ANSWER... A LIGHT IN THE BLACKNESS... BUT I DON'T KNOW... IF I CAN FIND IT... ON MY OWN.
CONSTANTINE...
CONSTANTINE... WHERE ARE YOU...?
WHY... DID YOU LEAVE ME... IN THE DARK...?

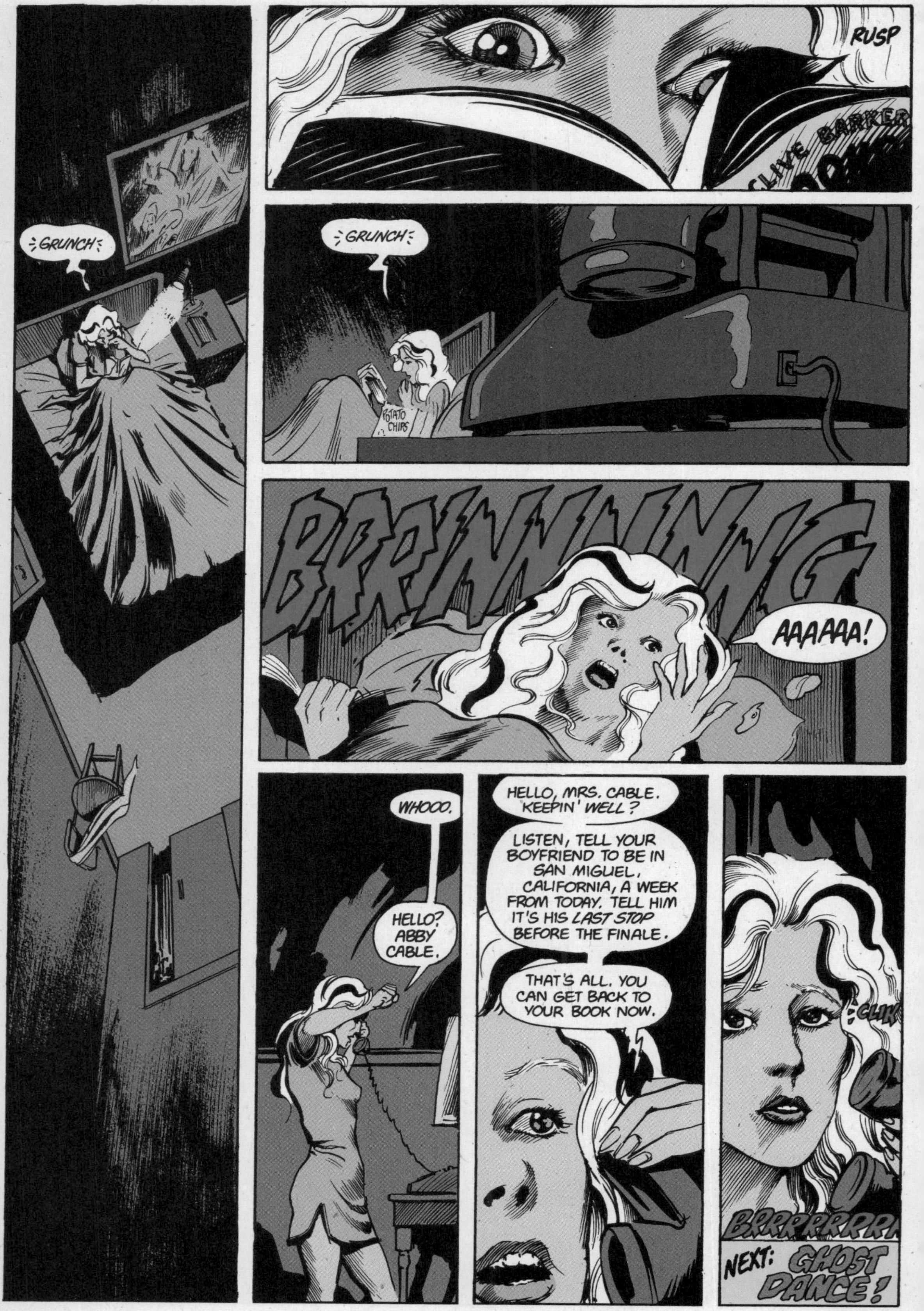
RUSP
CLIVE BARKER
GRUNCH
GRUNCH
POTATO CHIPS
BRRNNNNG
AAAAAA!
WHOOO.
HELLO? ABBY CABLE.
HELLO, MRS. CABLE. KEEPIN' WELL?
LISTEN, TELL YOUR BOYFRIEND TO BE IN SAN MIGUEL, CALIFORNIA, A WEEK FROM TODAY. TELL HIM IT'S HIS LAST STOP BEFORE THE FINALE.
THAT'S ALL. YOU CAN GET BACK TO YOUR BOOK NOW.
BRRRRRRRR
NEXT: GHOST DANCE!

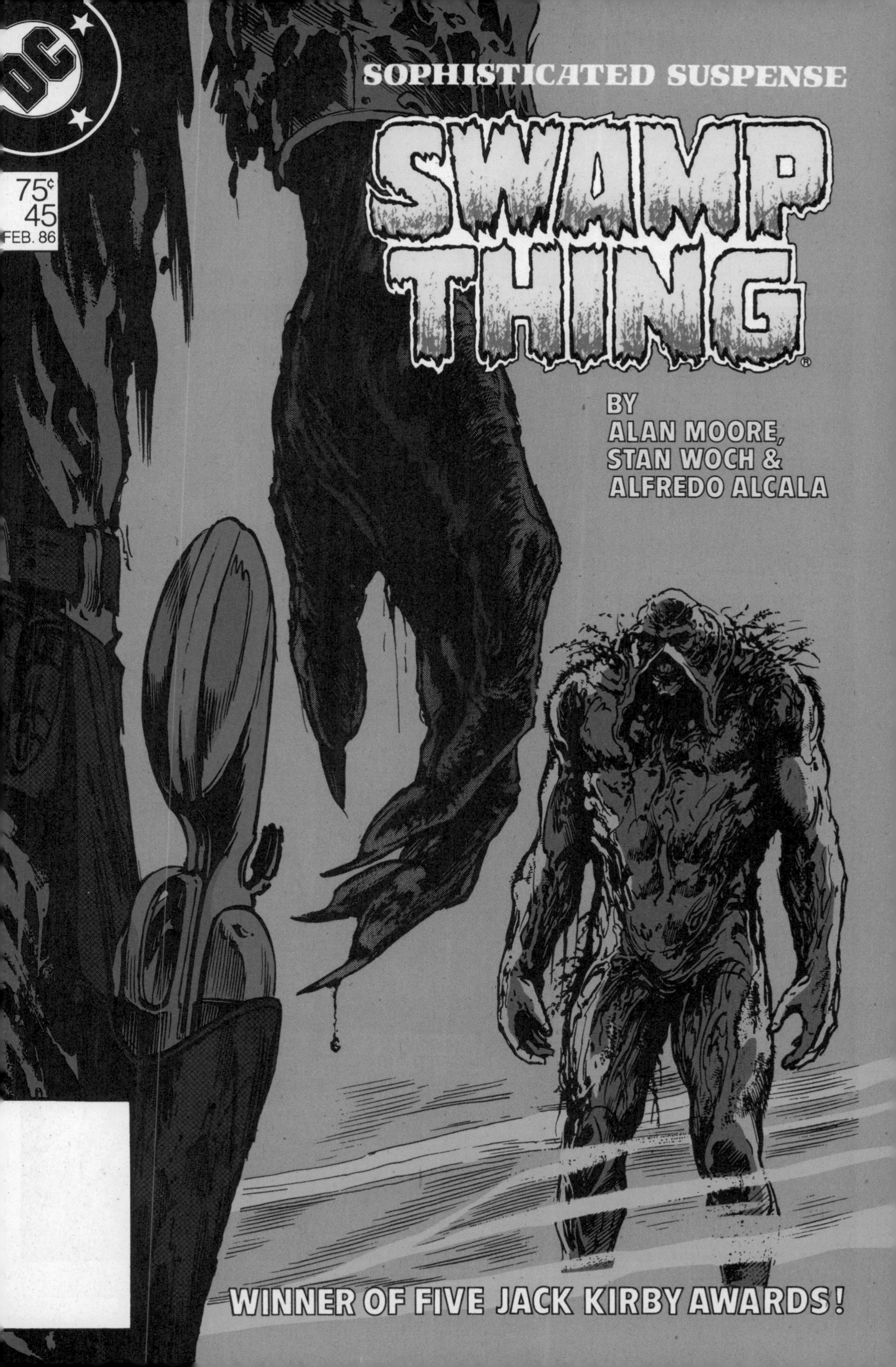
DC
SOPHISTICATED SUSPENSE
SWAMP THING®
75¢
45
FEB. 86
BY
ALAN MOORE,
STAN WOCH &
ALFREDO ALCALA
WINNER OF FIVE JACK KIRBY AWARDS!

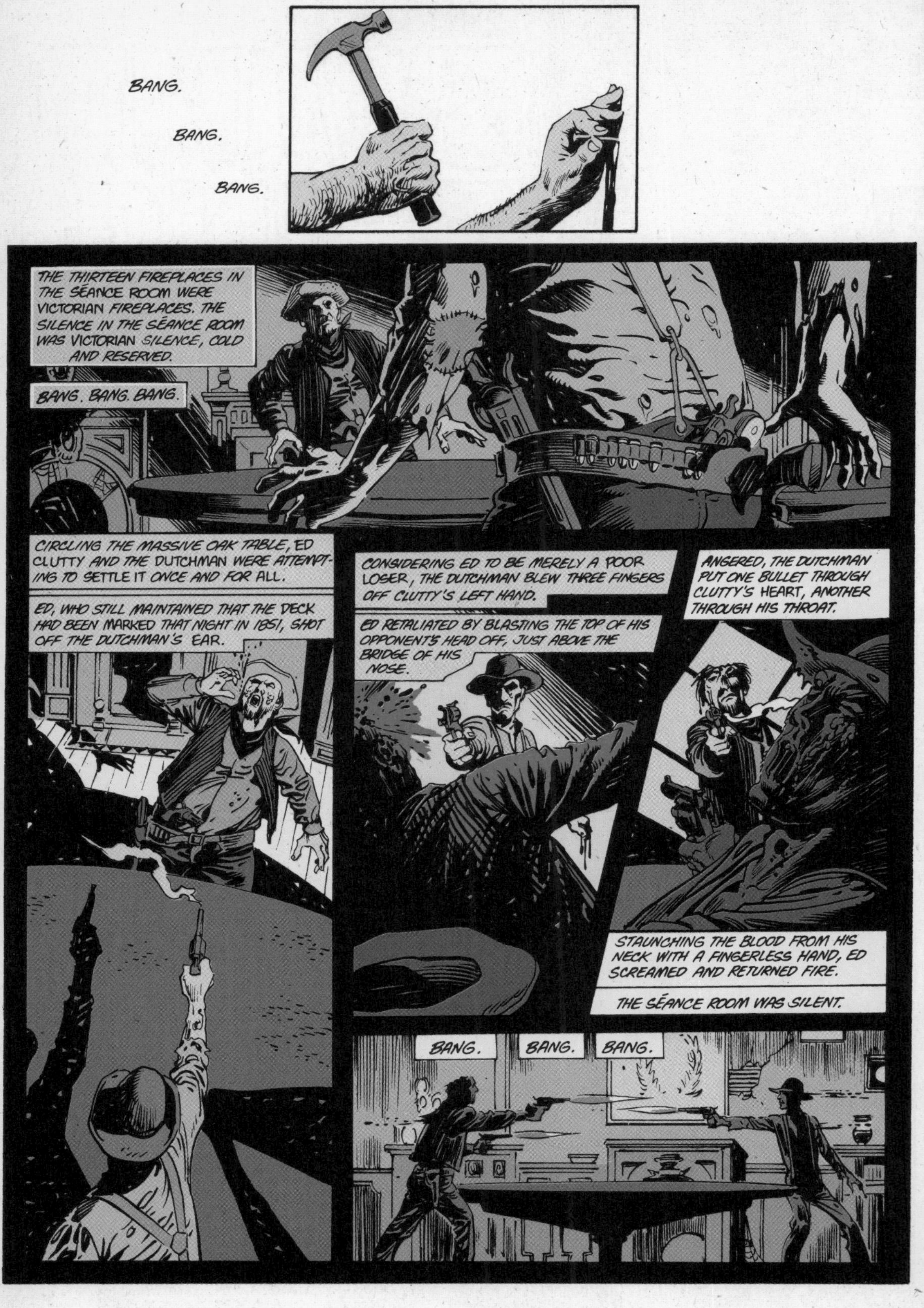
BANG.
BANG.
BANG.
THE THIRTEEN FIREPLACES IN THE SÉANCE ROOM WERE VICTORIAN FIREPLACES. THE SILENCE IN THE SÉANCE ROOM WAS VICTORIAN SILENCE, COLD AND RESERVED.
BANG. BANG. BANG.
CIRCLING THE MASSIVE OAK TABLE, ED CLUTTY AND THE DUTCHMAN WERE ATTEMPTING TO SETTLE IT ONCE AND FOR ALL.
ED, WHO STILL MAINTAINED THAT THE DECK HAD BEEN MARKED THAT NIGHT IN 1851, SHOT OFF THE DUTCHMAN'S EAR.
CONSIDERING ED TO BE MERELY A POOR LOSER, THE DUTCHMAN BLEW THREE FINGERS OFF CLUTTY'S LEFT HAND.
ED RETALIATED BY BLASTING THE TOP OF HIS OPPONENT'S HEAD OFF, JUST ABOVE THE BRIDGE OF HIS NOSE.
ANGERED, THE DUTCHMAN PUT ONE BULLET THROUGH CLUTTY'S HEART, ANOTHER THROUGH HIS THROAT.
STAUNCHING THE BLOOD FROM HIS NECK WITH A FINGERLESS HAND, ED SCREAMED AND RETURNED FIRE.
THE SÉANCE ROOM WAS SILENT.
BANG.
BANG.
BANG.

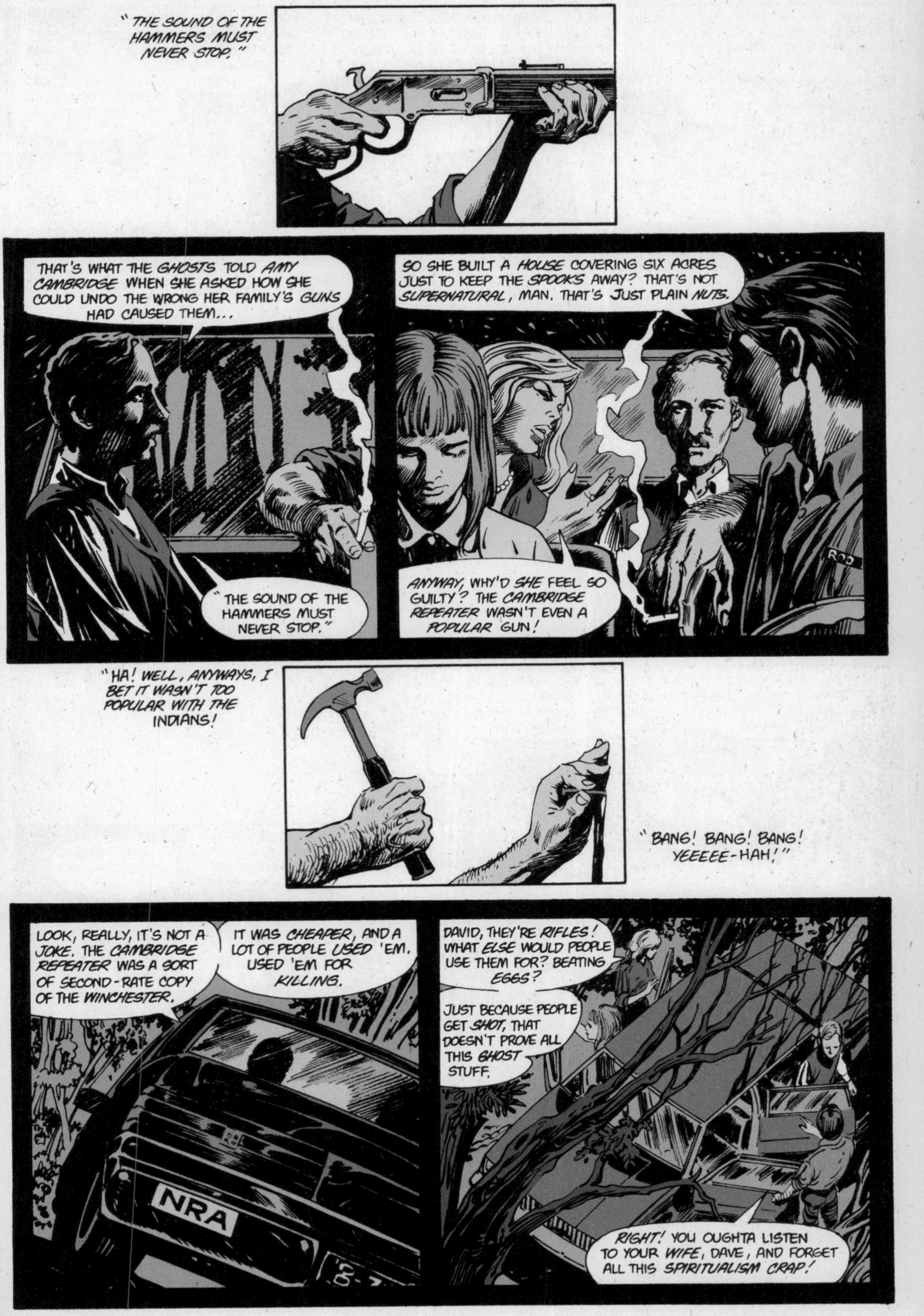
"THE SOUND OF THE HAMMERS MUST NEVER STOP."
THAT'S WHAT THE GHOSTS TOLD AMY CAMBRIDGE WHEN SHE ASKED HOW SHE COULD UNDO THE WRONG HER FAMILY'S GUNS HAD CAUSED THEM...
"THE SOUND OF THE HAMMERS MUST NEVER STOP."
SO SHE BUILT A HOUSE COVERING SIX ACRES JUST TO KEEP THE SPOOKS AWAY? THAT'S NOT SUPERNATURAL, MAN. THAT'S JUST PLAIN NUTS.
ANYWAY, WHY'D SHE FEEL SO GUILTY? THE CAMBRIDGE REPEATER WASN'T EVEN A POPULAR GUN!
"HA! WELL, ANYWAYS, I BET IT WASN'T TOO POPULAR WITH THE INDIANS!
"BANG! BANG! BANG! YEEEEE-HAH!"
LOOK, REALLY, IT'S NOT A JOKE. THE CAMBRIDGE REPEATER WAS A SORT OF SECOND-RATE COPY OF THE WINCHESTER.
IT WAS CHEAPER, AND A LOT OF PEOPLE USED 'EM. USED 'EM FOR KILLING.
NRA
DAVID, THEY'RE RIFLES! WHAT ELSE WOULD PEOPLE USE THEM FOR? BEATING EGGS?
JUST BECAUSE PEOPLE GET SHOT, THAT DOESN'T PROVE ALL THIS GHOST STUFF.
RIGHT! YOU OUGHTA LISTEN TO YOUR WIFE, DAVE, AND FORGET ALL THIS SPIRITUALISM CRAP!

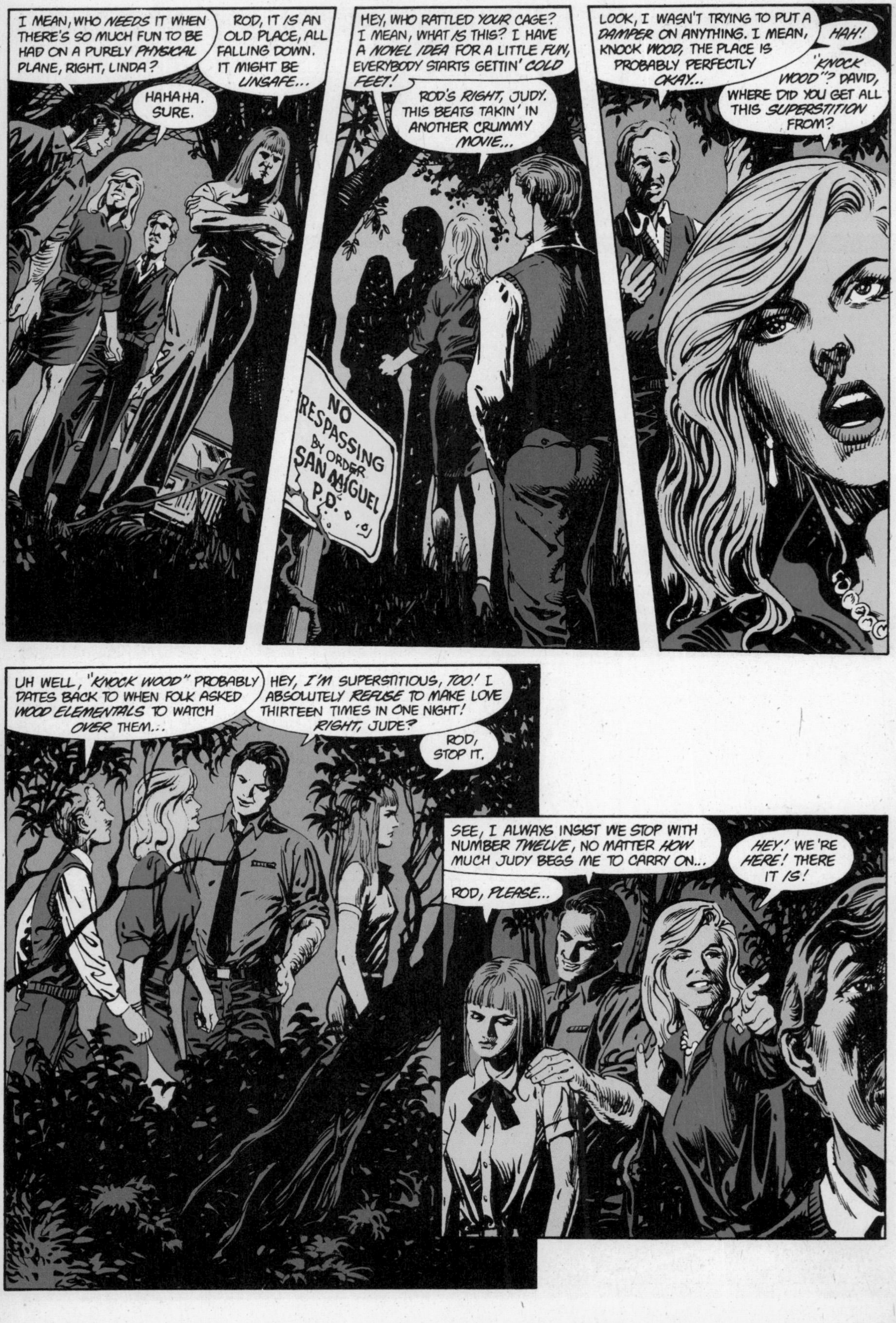
I MEAN, WHO NEEDS IT WHEN THERE'S SO MUCH FUN TO BE HAD ON A PURELY PHYSICAL PLANE, RIGHT, LINDA?
ROD, IT IS AN OLD PLACE, ALL FALLING DOWN. IT MIGHT BE UNSAFE...
HAHAHA. SURE.
HEY, WHO RATTLED YOUR CAGE? I MEAN, WHAT IS THIS? I HAVE A NOVEL IDEA FOR A LITTLE FUN, EVERYBODY STARTS GETTIN' COLD FEET!
ROD'S RIGHT, JUDY. THIS BEATS TAKIN' IN ANOTHER CRUMMY MOVIE...
NO TRESPASSING BY ORDER SAN MIGUEL P.D.
LOOK, I WASN'T TRYING TO PUT A DAMPER ON ANYTHING. I MEAN, KNOCK WOOD, THE PLACE IS PROBABLY PERFECTLY OKAY...
HAH!
"KNOCK WOOD"? DAVID, WHERE DID YOU GET ALL THIS SUPERSTITION FROM?
UH WELL, "KNOCK WOOD" PROBABLY DATES BACK TO WHEN FOLK ASKED WOOD ELEMENTALS TO WATCH OVER THEM...
HEY, I'M SUPERSTITIOUS, TOO! I ABSOLUTELY REFUSE TO MAKE LOVE THIRTEEN TIMES IN ONE NIGHT! RIGHT, JUDE?
ROD, STOP IT.
SEE, I ALWAYS INSIST WE STOP WITH NUMBER TWELVE, NO MATTER HOW MUCH JUDY BEGS ME TO CARRY ON...
ROD, PLEASE...
HEY! WE'RE HERE! THERE IT IS!

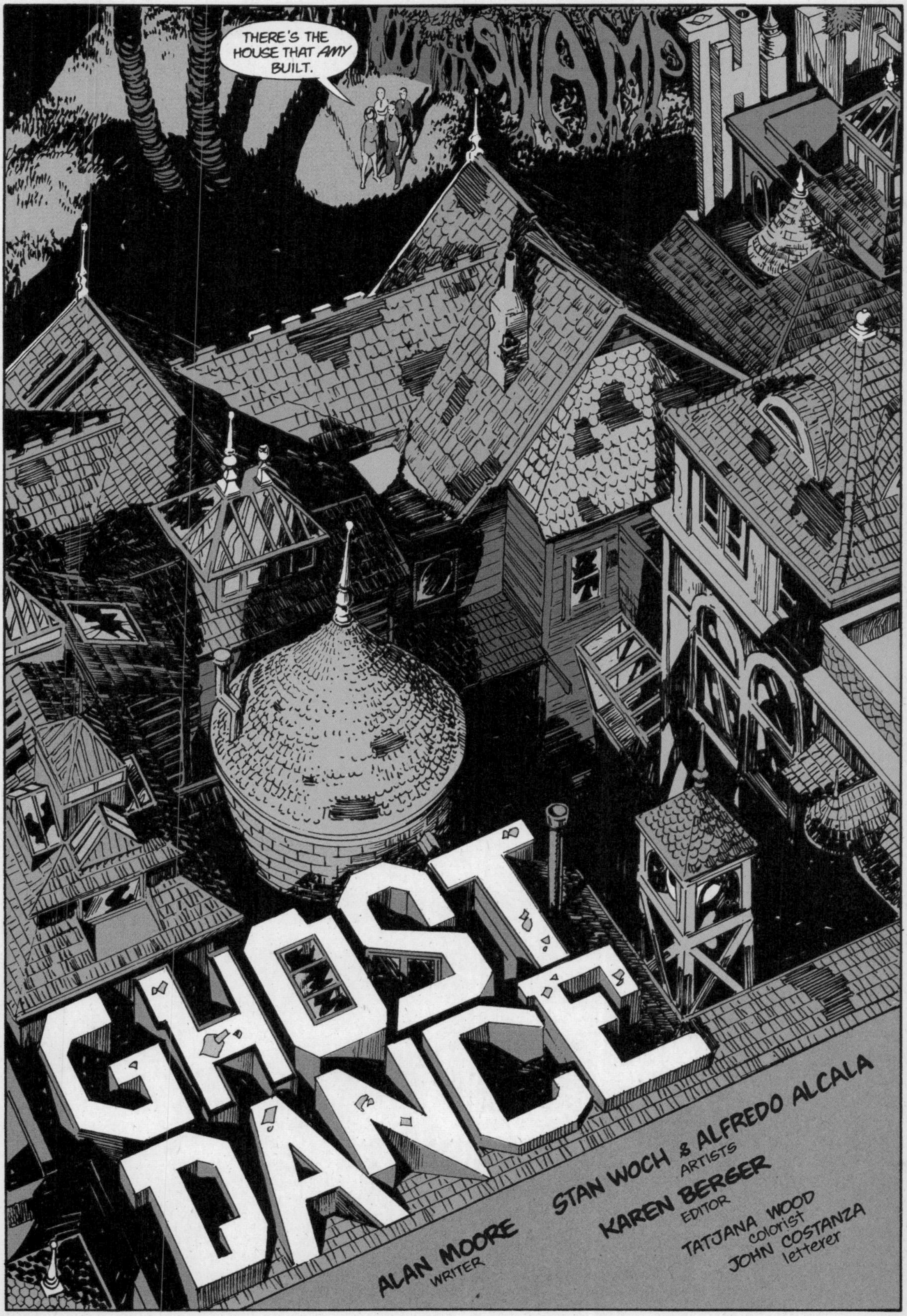
SWAMP THING
THERE'S THE HOUSE THAT AMY BUILT.
GHOST DANCE
ALAN MOORE WRITER
STAN WOCH & ALFREDO ALCALA ARTISTS
KAREN BERGER EDITOR
TATJANA WOOD colorist
JOHN COSTANZA letterer

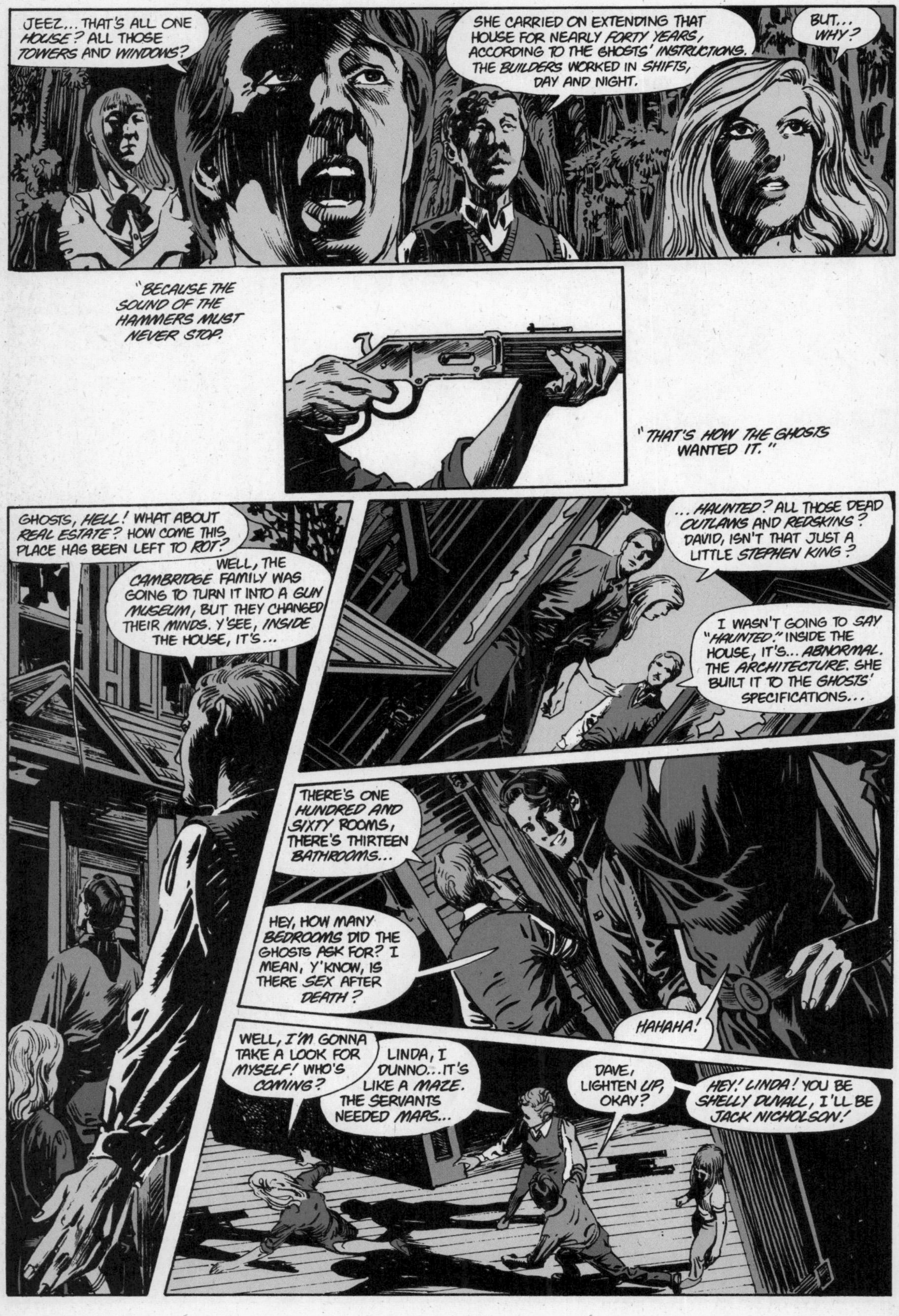
JEEZ... THAT'S ALL ONE HOUSE? ALL THOSE TOWERS AND WINDOWS?
SHE CARRIED ON EXTENDING THAT HOUSE FOR NEARLY FORTY YEARS, ACCORDING TO THE GHOSTS' INSTRUCTIONS. THE BUILDERS WORKED IN SHIFTS, DAY AND NIGHT.
BUT... WHY?
"BECAUSE THE SOUND OF THE HAMMERS MUST NEVER STOP.
"THAT'S HOW THE GHOSTS WANTED IT."
GHOSTS, HELL! WHAT ABOUT REAL ESTATE? HOW COME THIS PLACE HAS BEEN LEFT TO ROT?
WELL, THE CAMBRIDGE FAMILY WAS GOING TO TURN IT INTO A GUN MUSEUM, BUT THEY CHANGED THEIR MINDS. Y'SEE, INSIDE THE HOUSE, IT'S...
...HAUNTED? ALL THOSE DEAD OUTLAWS AND REDSKINS? DAVID, ISN'T THAT JUST A LITTLE STEPHEN KING?
I WASN'T GOING TO SAY "HAUNTED." INSIDE THE HOUSE, IT'S... ABNORMAL. THE ARCHITECTURE. SHE BUILT IT TO THE GHOSTS' SPECIFICATIONS...
THERE'S ONE HUNDRED AND SIXTY ROOMS, THERE'S THIRTEEN BATHROOMS...
HEY, HOW MANY BEDROOMS DID THE GHOSTS ASK FOR? I MEAN, Y'KNOW, IS THERE SEX AFTER DEATH?
HAHAHA!
WELL, I'M GONNA TAKE A LOOK FOR MYSELF! WHO'S COMING?
LINDA, I DUNNO... IT'S LIKE A MAZE. THE SERVANTS NEEDED MAPS...
DAVE, LIGHTEN UP, OKAY?
HEY! LINDA! YOU BE SHELLY DUVALL, I'LL BE JACK NICHOLSON!

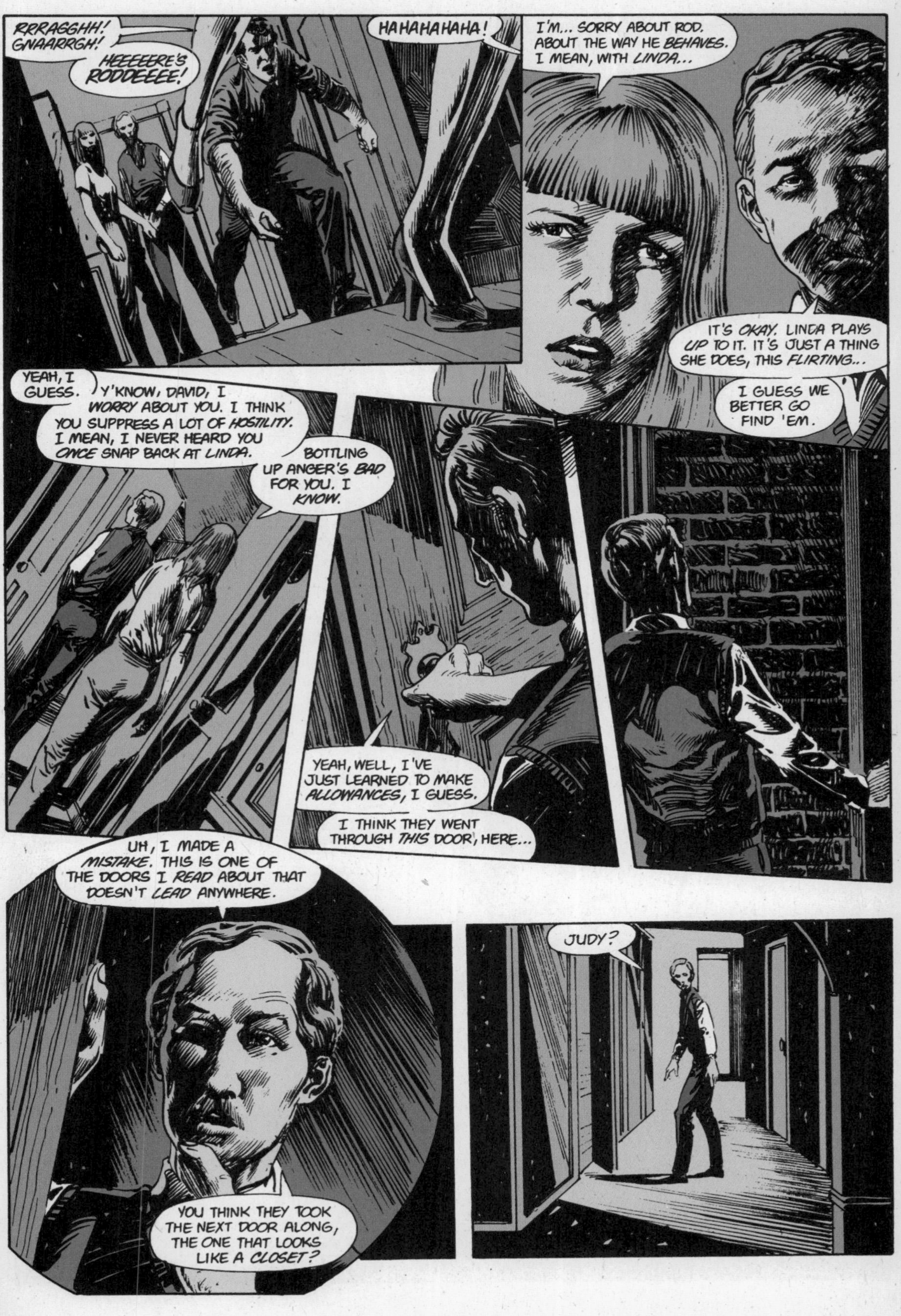
RRRAGGHH! GNAARRGH!
HEEEEERE'S RODDEEEE!
HAHAHAHAHA!
I'M... SORRY ABOUT ROD. ABOUT THE WAY HE BEHAVES. I MEAN, WITH LINDA...
IT'S OKAY. LINDA PLAYS UP TO IT. IT'S JUST A THING SHE DOES, THIS FLIRTING...
I GUESS WE BETTER GO FIND 'EM.
YEAH, I GUESS.
Y'KNOW, DAVID, I WORRY ABOUT YOU. I THINK YOU SUPPRESS A LOT OF HOSTILITY. I MEAN, I NEVER HEARD YOU ONCE SNAP BACK AT LINDA.
BOTTLING UP ANGER'S BAD FOR YOU. I KNOW.
YEAH, WELL, I'VE JUST LEARNED TO MAKE ALLOWANCES, I GUESS.
I THINK THEY WENT THROUGH THIS DOOR, HERE...
UH, I MADE A MISTAKE. THIS IS ONE OF THE DOORS I READ ABOUT THAT DOESN'T LEAD ANYWHERE.
YOU THINK THEY TOOK THE NEXT DOOR ALONG, THE ONE THAT LOOKS LIKE A CLOSET?
JUDY?

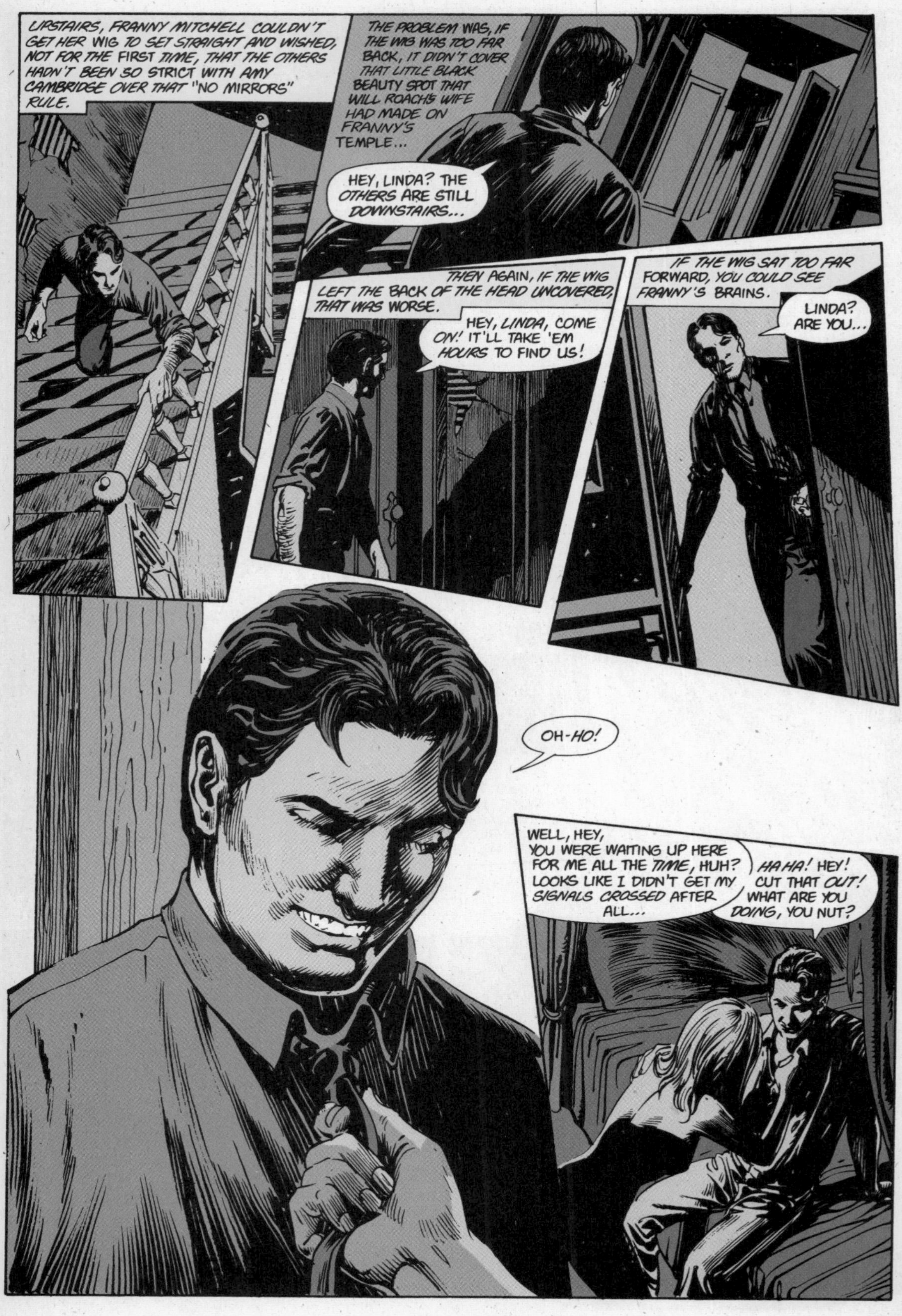
UPSTAIRS, FRANNY MITCHELL COULDN'T GET HER WIG TO SET STRAIGHT AND WISHED, NOT FOR THE FIRST TIME, THAT THE OTHERS HADN'T BEEN SO STRICT WITH AMY CAMBRIDGE OVER THAT "NO MIRRORS" RULE.
THE PROBLEM WAS, IF THE WIG WAS TOO FAR BACK, IT DIDN'T COVER THAT LITTLE BLACK BEAUTY SPOT THAT WILL ROACH'S WIFE HAD MADE ON FRANNY'S TEMPLE...
HEY, LINDA? THE OTHERS ARE STILL DOWNSTAIRS...
THEN AGAIN, IF THE WIG LEFT THE BACK OF THE HEAD UNCOVERED, THAT WAS WORSE.
HEY, LINDA, COME ON! IT'LL TAKE 'EM HOURS TO FIND US!
IF THE WIG SAT TOO FAR FORWARD, YOU COULD SEE FRANNY'S BRAINS.
LINDA? ARE YOU...
OH-HO!
WELL, HEY, YOU WERE WAITING UP HERE FOR ME ALL THE TIME, HUH? LOOKS LIKE I DIDN'T GET MY SIGNALS CROSSED AFTER ALL...
HA HA! HEY! CUT THAT OUT! WHAT ARE YOU DOING, YOU NUT?

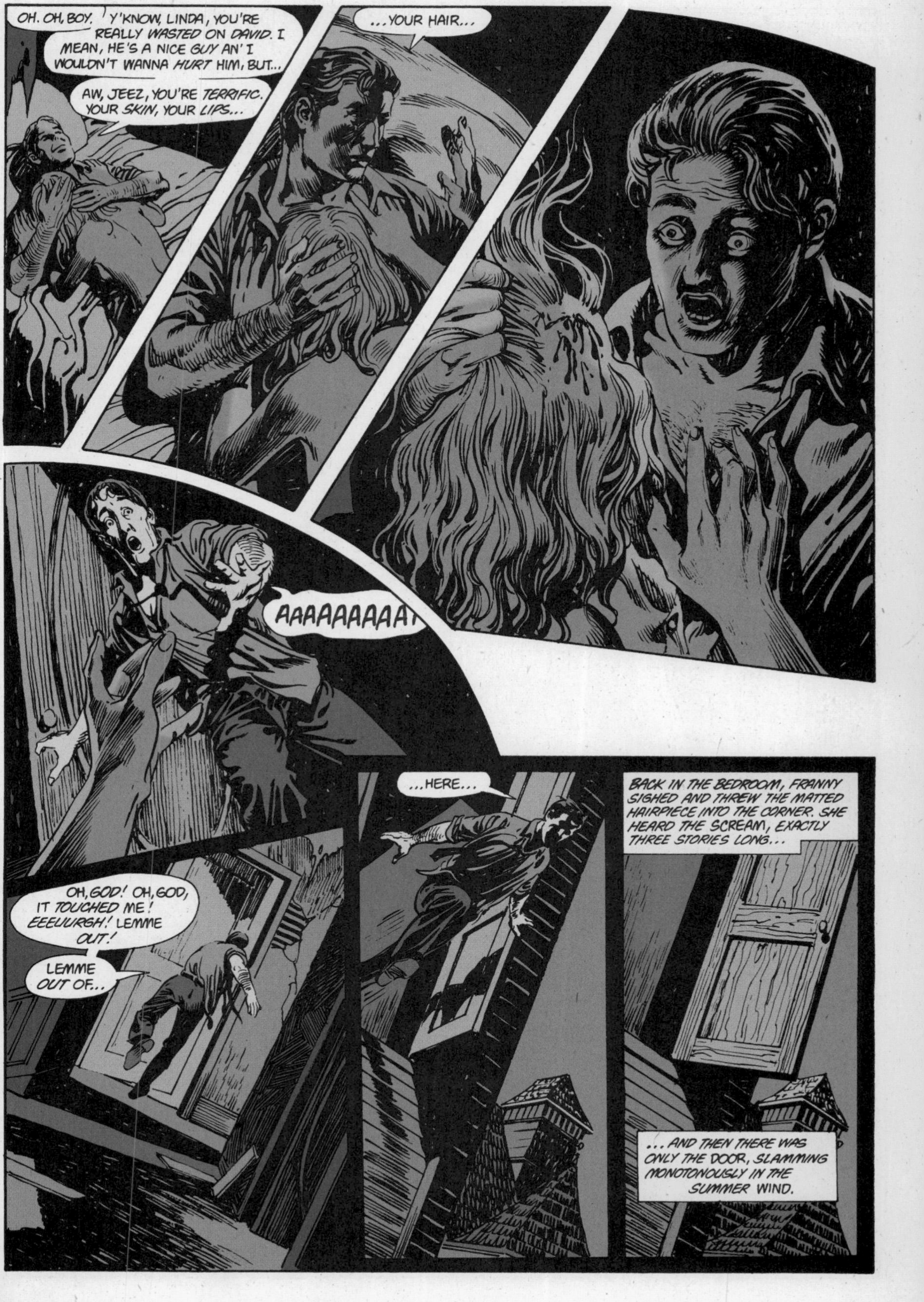
OH. OH, BOY. Y'KNOW, LINDA, YOU'RE REALLY WASTED ON DAVID. I MEAN, HE'S A NICE GUY AN' I WOULDN'T WANNA HURT HIM, BUT...
AW, JEEZ, YOU'RE TERRIFIC. YOUR SKIN, YOUR LIPS...
...YOUR HAIR...
AAAAAAAAAT
OH, GOD! OH, GOD, IT TOUCHED ME! EEEUURGH! LEMME OUT!
LEMME OUT OF...
...HERE...
BACK IN THE BEDROOM, FRANNY SIGHED AND THREW THE MATTED HAIRPIECE INTO THE CORNER. SHE HEARD THE SCREAM, EXACTLY THREE STORIES LONG...
...AND THEN THERE WAS ONLY THE DOOR, SLAMMING MONOTONOUSLY IN THE SUMMER WIND.

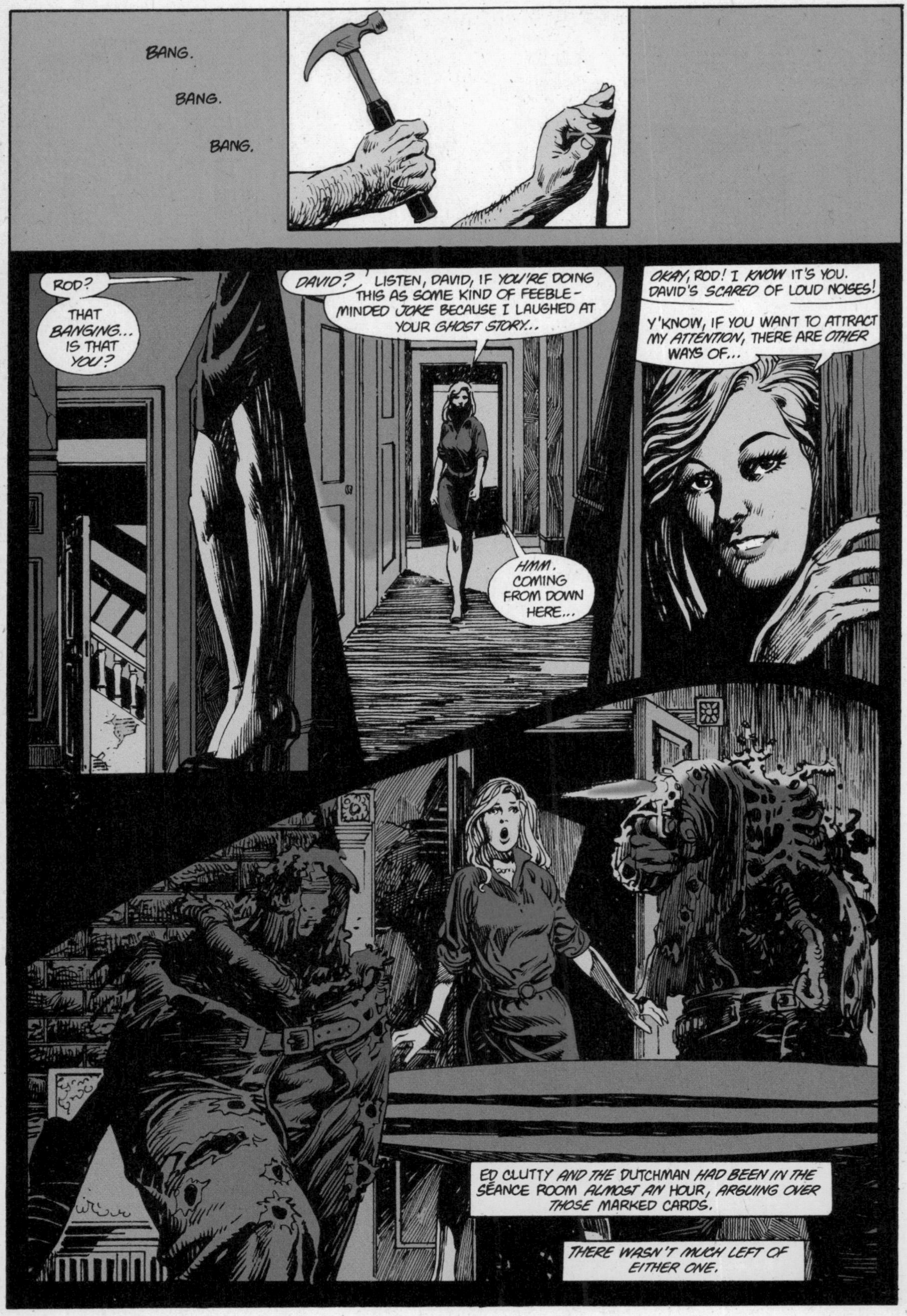
BANG.
BANG.
BANG.
ROD?
THAT BANGING... IS THAT YOU?
DAVID?
LISTEN, DAVID, IF YOU'RE DOING THIS AS SOME KIND OF FEEBLE-MINDED JOKE BECAUSE I LAUGHED AT YOUR GHOST STORY...
HMM. COMING FROM DOWN HERE...
OKAY, ROD! I KNOW IT'S YOU. DAVID'S SCARED OF LOUD NOISES!
Y'KNOW, IF YOU WANT TO ATTRACT MY ATTENTION, THERE ARE OTHER WAYS OF...
ED CLUTTY AND THE DUTCHMAN HAD BEEN IN THE SÉANCE ROOM ALMOST AN HOUR, ARGUING OVER THOSE MARKED CARDS.
THERE WASN'T MUCH LEFT OF EITHER ONE.

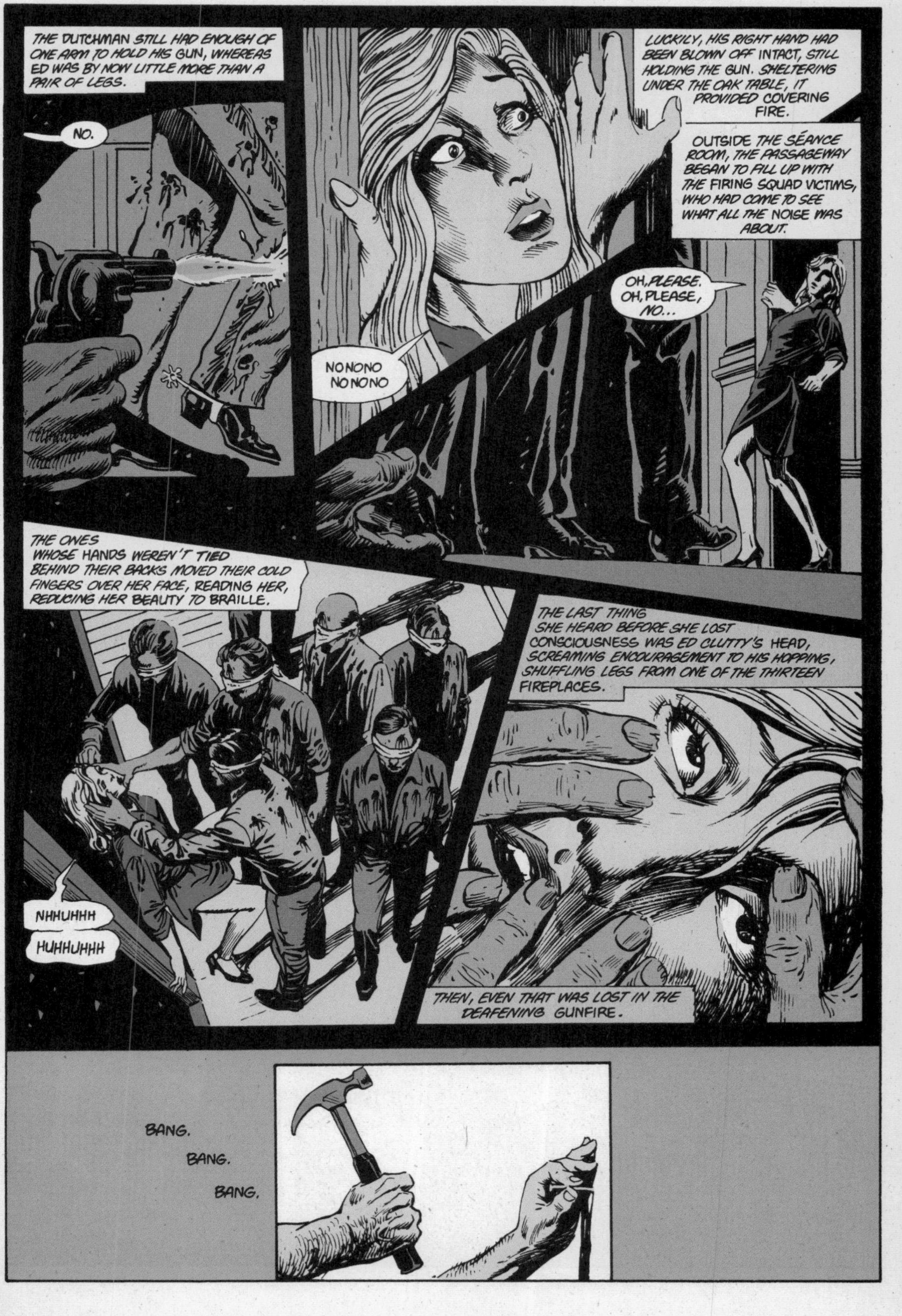
THE DUTCHMAN STILL HAD ENOUGH OF ONE ARM TO HOLD HIS GUN, WHEREAS ED WAS BY NOW LITTLE MORE THAN A PAIR OF LEGS.
NO.
LUCKILY, HIS RIGHT HAND HAD BEEN BLOWN OFF INTACT, STILL HOLDING THE GUN. SHELTERING UNDER THE OAK TABLE, IT PROVIDED COVERING FIRE.
OUTSIDE THE SÉANCE ROOM, THE PASSAGEWAY BEGAN TO FILL UP WITH THE FIRING SQUAD VICTIMS, WHO HAD COME TO SEE WHAT ALL THE NOISE WAS ABOUT.
OH, PLEASE. OH, PLEASE, NO...
NONONO NONONO
THE ONES WHOSE HANDS WEREN'T TIED BEHIND THEIR BACKS MOVED THEIR COLD FINGERS OVER HER FACE, READING HER, REDUCING HER BEAUTY TO BRAILLE.
NHHUHHH
HUHHUHHH
THE LAST THING SHE HEARD BEFORE SHE LOST CONSCIOUSNESS WAS ED CLUTTY'S HEAD, SCREAMING ENCOURAGEMENT TO HIS HOPPING, SHUFFLING LEGS FROM ONE OF THE THIRTEEN FIREPLACES.
THEN, EVEN THAT WAS LOST IN THE DEAFENING GUNFIRE.
BANG.
BANG.
BANG.

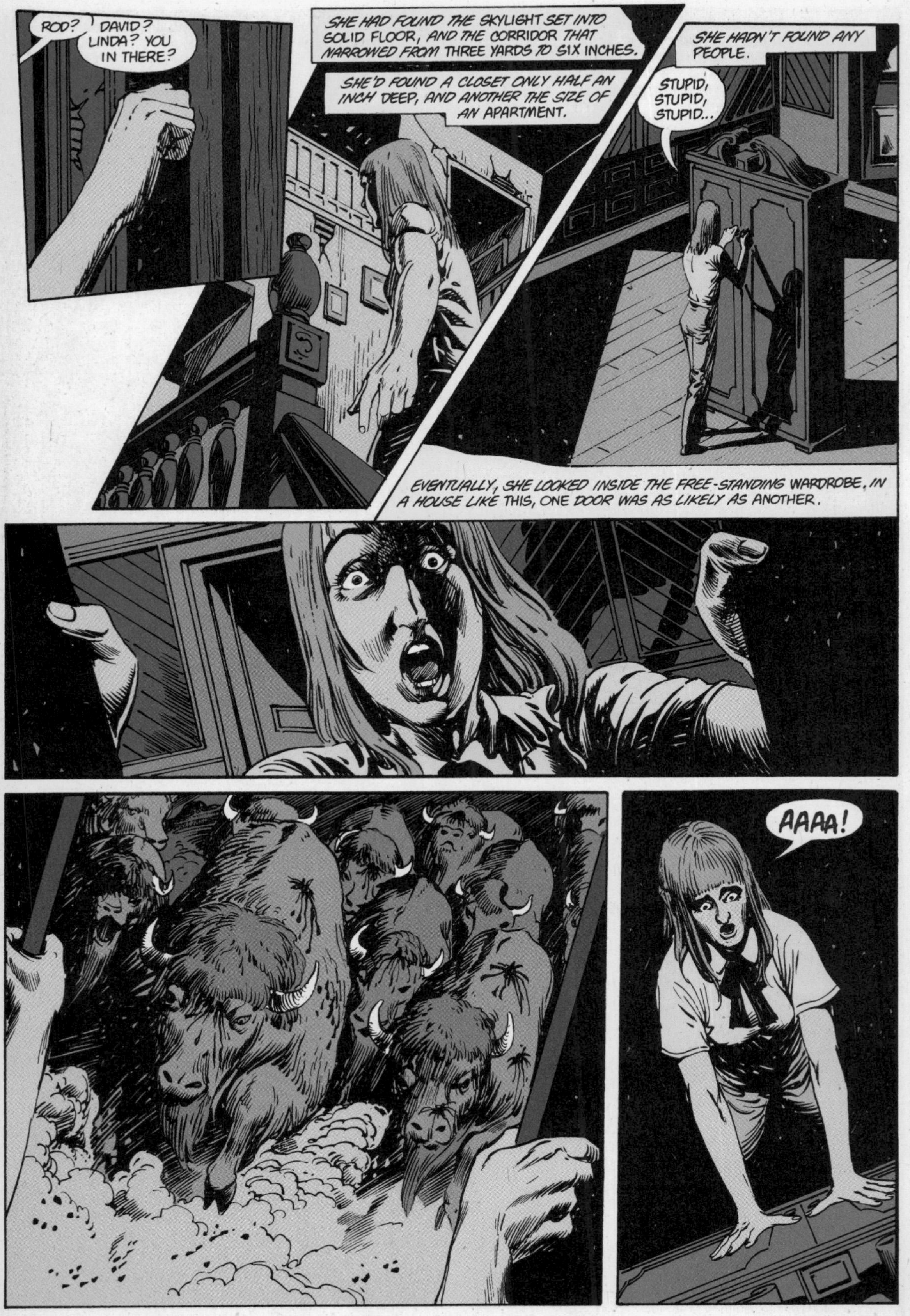
ROD? DAVID? LINDA? YOU IN THERE?
SHE HAD FOUND THE SKYLIGHT SET INTO SOLID FLOOR, AND THE CORRIDOR THAT NARROWED FROM THREE YARDS TO SIX INCHES.
SHE'D FOUND A CLOSET ONLY HALF AN INCH DEEP, AND ANOTHER THE SIZE OF AN APARTMENT.
SHE HADN'T FOUND ANY PEOPLE.
STUPID, STUPID, STUPID...
EVENTUALLY, SHE LOOKED INSIDE THE FREE-STANDING WARDROBE. IN A HOUSE LIKE THIS, ONE DOOR WAS AS LIKELY AS ANOTHER.
AAAA!

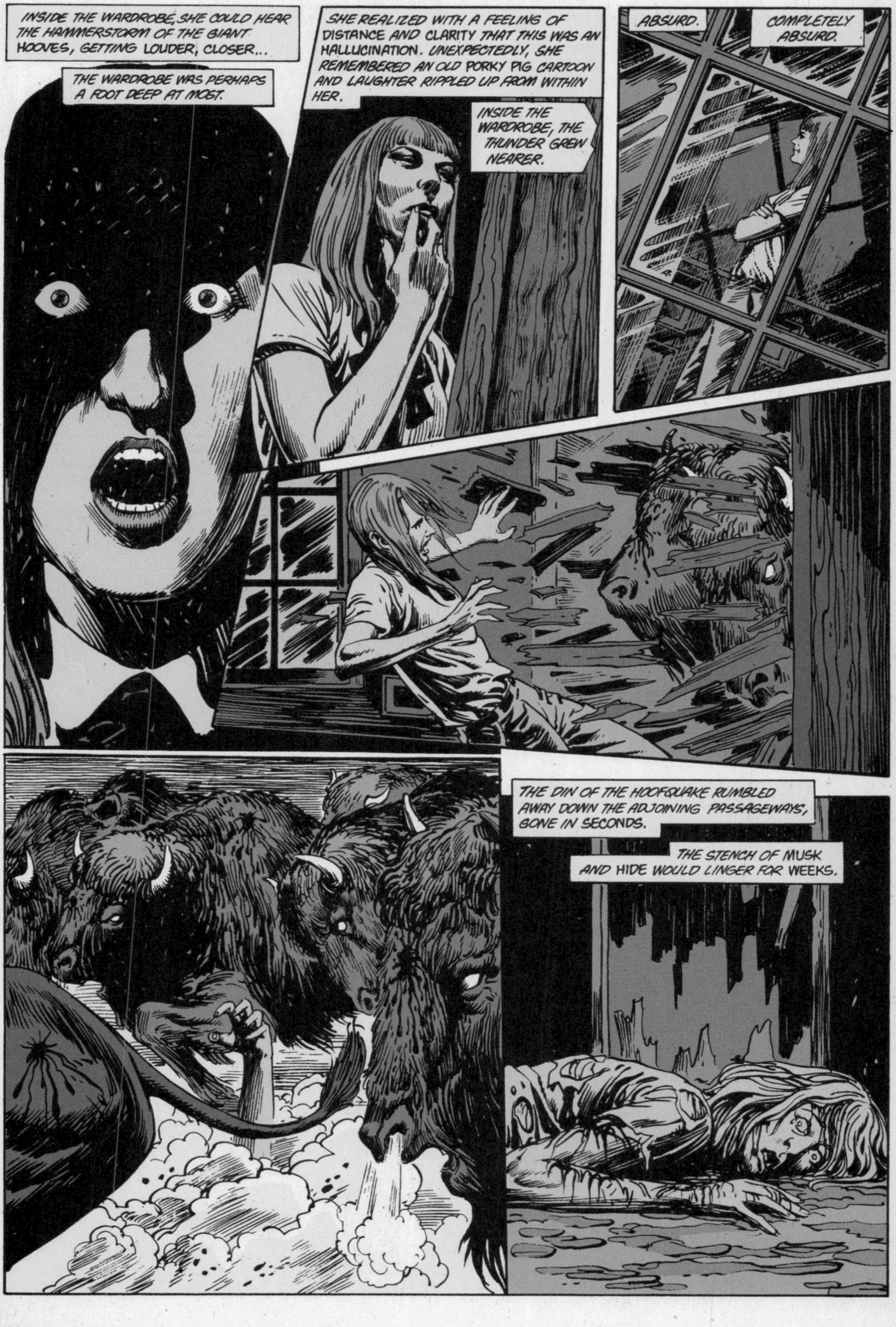
INSIDE THE WARDROBE, SHE COULD HEAR THE HAMMERSTORM OF THE GIANT HOOVES, GETTING LOUDER, CLOSER...
THE WARDROBE WAS PERHAPS A FOOT DEEP AT MOST.
SHE REALIZED WITH A FEELING OF DISTANCE AND CLARITY THAT THIS WAS AN HALLUCINATION. UNEXPECTEDLY, SHE REMEMBERED AN OLD PORKY PIG CARTOON AND LAUGHTER RIPPLED UP FROM WITHIN HER.
INSIDE THE WARDROBE, THE THUNDER GREW NEARER.
ABSURD.
COMPLETELY ABSURD.
THE DIN OF THE HOOFQUAKE RUMBLED AWAY DOWN THE ADJOINING PASSAGEWAYS, GONE IN SECONDS.
THE STENCH OF MUSK AND HIDE WOULD LINGER FOR WEEKS.

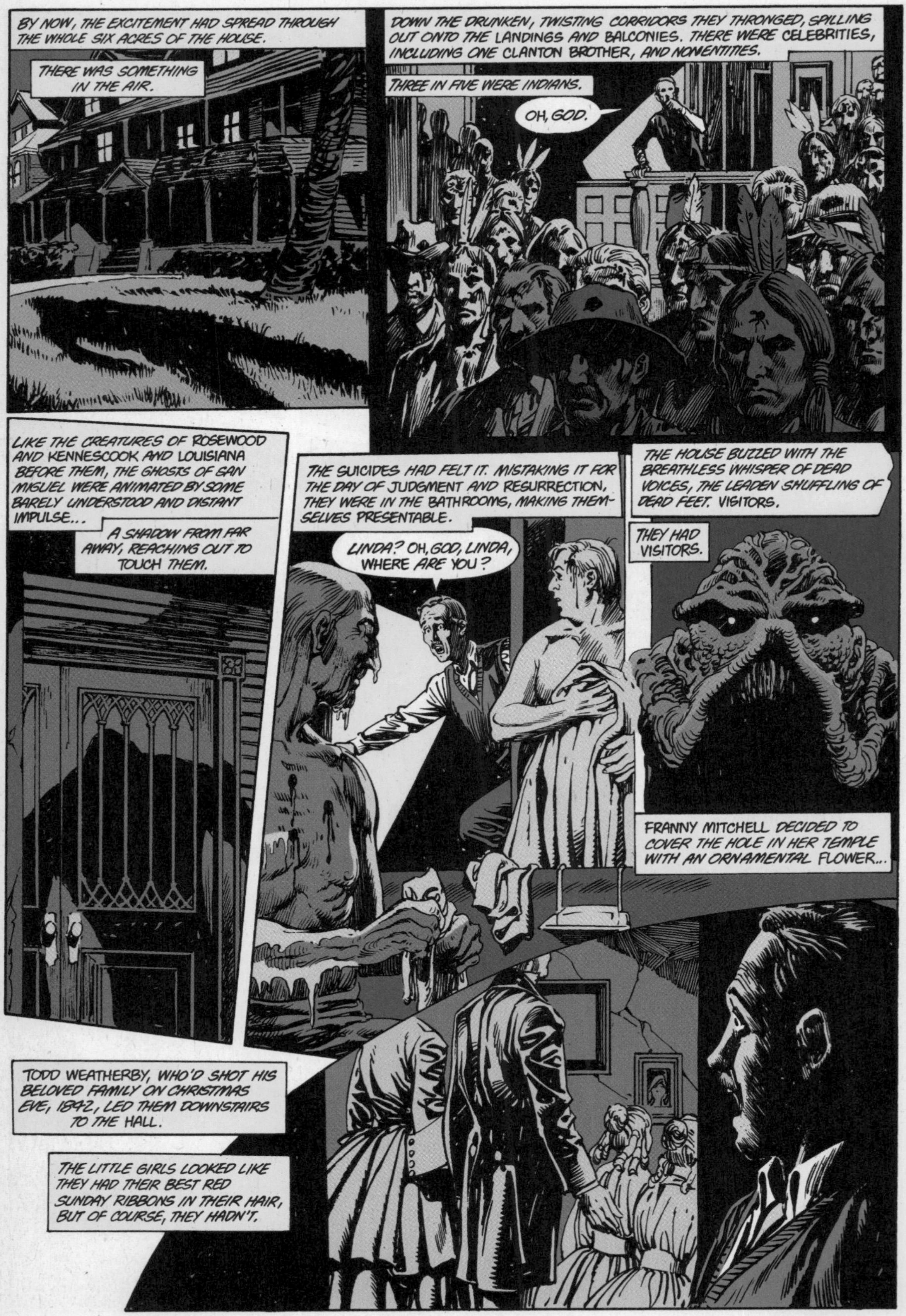
BY NOW, THE EXCITEMENT HAD SPREAD THROUGH THE WHOLE SIX ACRES OF THE HOUSE.
THERE WAS SOMETHING IN THE AIR.
DOWN THE DRUNKEN, TWISTING CORRIDORS THEY THRONGED, SPILLING OUT ONTO THE LANDINGS AND BALCONIES. THERE WERE CELEBRITIES, INCLUDING ONE CLANTON BROTHER, AND NONENTITIES.
THREE IN FIVE WERE INDIANS.
OH, GOD.
LIKE THE CREATURES OF ROSEWOOD AND KENNESCOOK AND LOUISIANA BEFORE THEM, THE GHOSTS OF SAN MIGUEL WERE ANIMATED BY SOME BARELY UNDERSTOOD AND DISTANT IMPULSE...
A SHADOW FROM FAR AWAY, REACHING OUT TO TOUCH THEM.
THE SUICIDES HAD FELT IT. MISTAKING IT FOR THE DAY OF JUDGMENT AND RESURRECTION, THEY WERE IN THE BATHROOMS, MAKING THEMSELVES PRESENTABLE.
LINDA? OH, GOD, LINDA, WHERE ARE YOU?
THE HOUSE BUZZED WITH THE BREATHLESS WHISPER OF DEAD VOICES, THE LEADEN SHUFFLING OF DEAD FEET. VISITORS.
THEY HAD VISITORS.
FRANNY MITCHELL DECIDED TO COVER THE HOLE IN HER TEMPLE WITH AN ORNAMENTAL FLOWER...
TODD WEATHERBY, WHO'D SHOT HIS BELOVED FAMILY ON CHRISTMAS EVE, 1842, LED THEM DOWNSTAIRS TO THE HALL.
THE LITTLE GIRLS LOOKED LIKE THEY HAD THEIR BEST RED SUNDAY RIBBONS IN THEIR HAIR, BUT OF COURSE, THEY HADN'T.

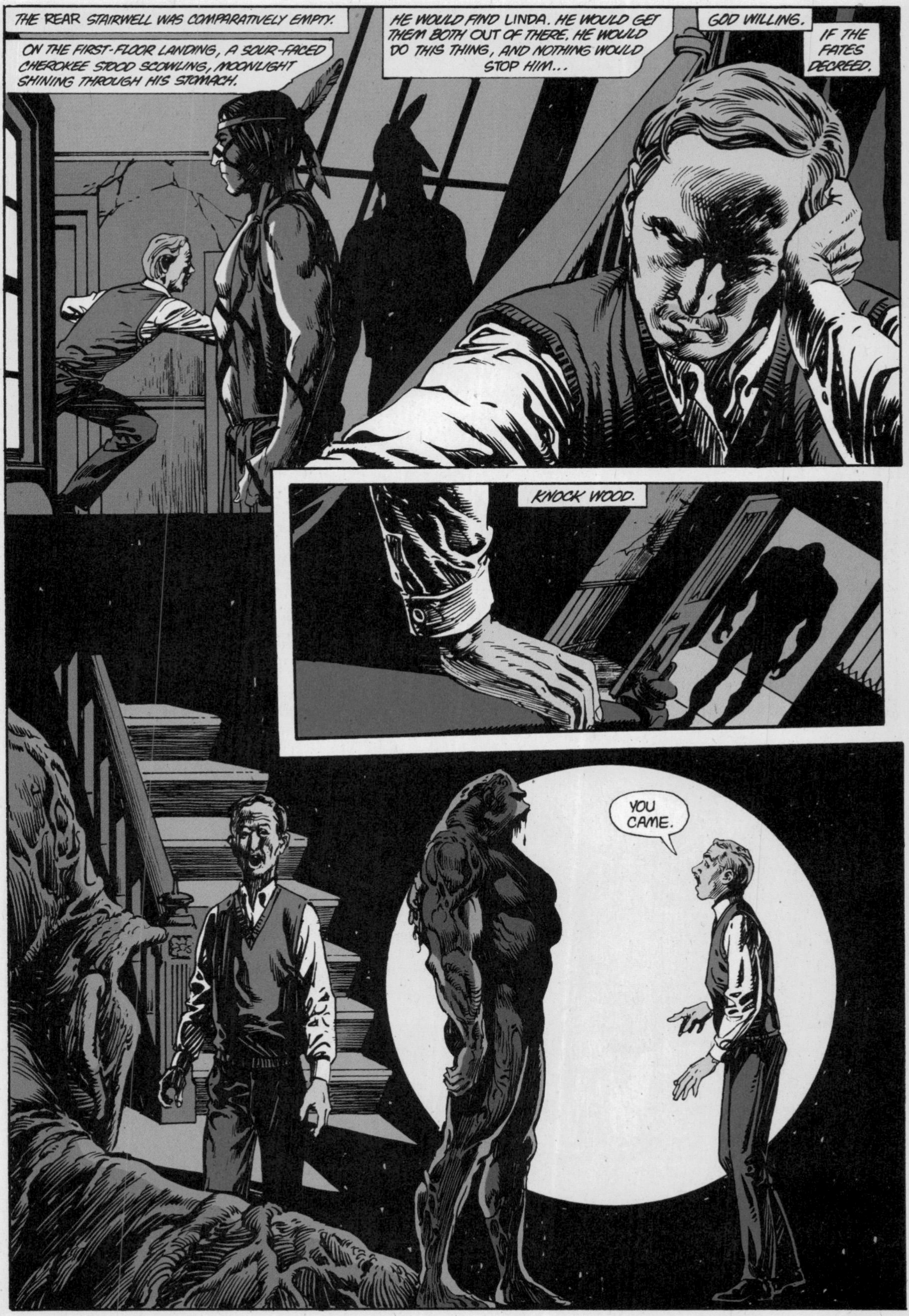
THE REAR STAIRWELL WAS COMPARATIVELY EMPTY.
ON THE FIRST-FLOOR LANDING, A SOUR-FACED CHEROKEE STOOD SCOWLING, MOONLIGHT SHINING THROUGH HIS STOMACH.
HE WOULD FIND LINDA. HE WOULD GET THEM BOTH OUT OF THERE. HE WOULD DO THIS THING, AND NOTHING WOULD STOP HIM...
GOD WILLING.
IF THE FATES DECREED.
KNOCK WOOD.
YOU CAME.

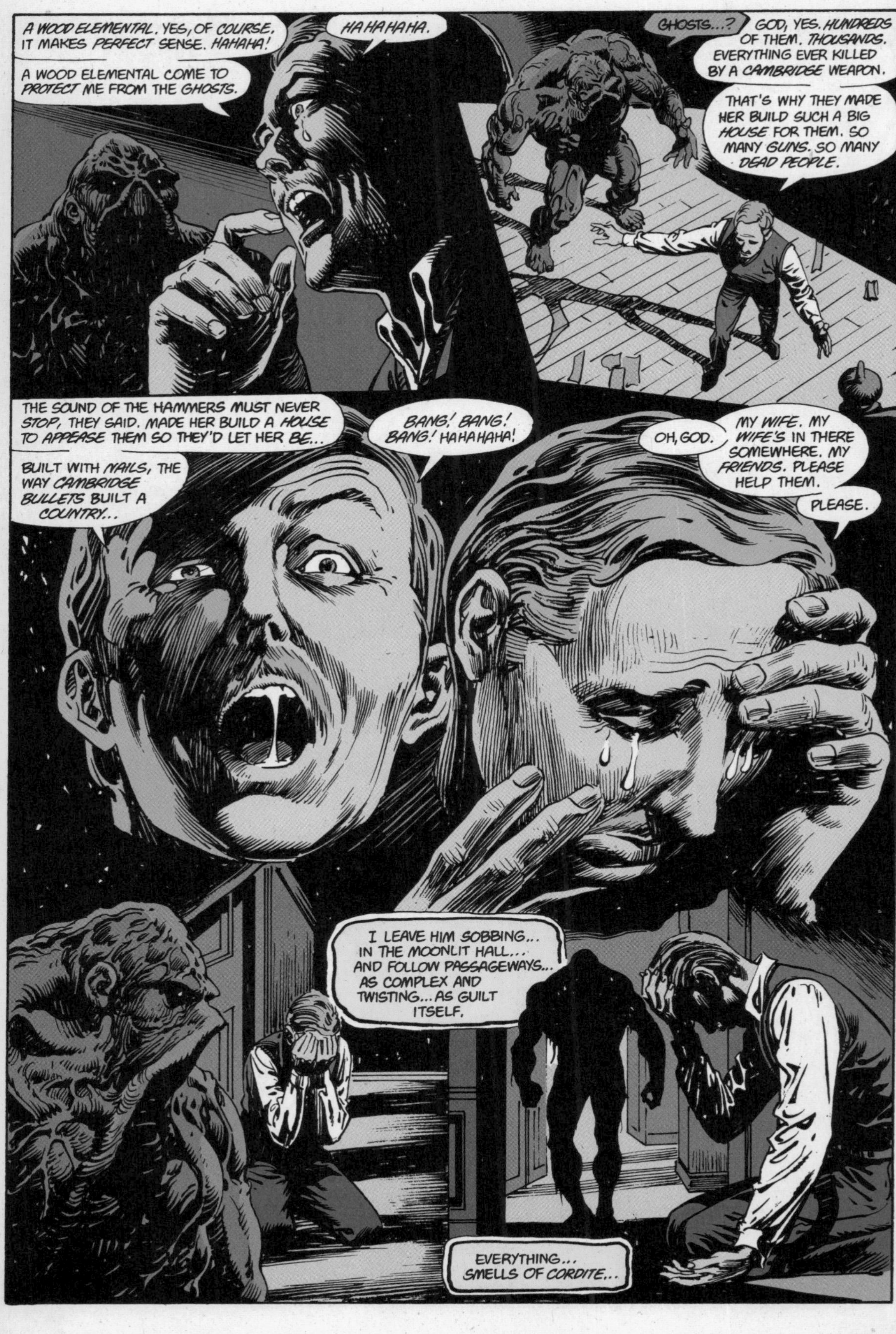
A WOOD ELEMENTAL. YES, OF COURSE. IT MAKES PERFECT SENSE. HAHAHA!
A WOOD ELEMENTAL COME TO PROTECT ME FROM THE GHOSTS.
HA HA HA HA HA.
GHOSTS...?
GOD, YES. HUNDREDS OF THEM. THOUSANDS. EVERYTHING EVER KILLED BY A CAMBRIDGE WEAPON.
THAT'S WHY THEY MADE HER BUILD SUCH A BIG HOUSE FOR THEM. SO MANY GUNS. SO MANY DEAD PEOPLE.
THE SOUND OF THE HAMMERS MUST NEVER STOP, THEY SAID. MADE HER BUILD A HOUSE TO APPEASE THEM SO THEY'D LET HER BE...
BUILT WITH NAILS, THE WAY CAMBRIDGE BULLETS BUILT A COUNTRY...
BANG! BANG! BANG! HAHAHAHA!
OH, GOD.
MY WIFE. MY WIFE'S IN THERE SOMEWHERE. MY FRIENDS. PLEASE HELP THEM.
PLEASE.
I LEAVE HIM SOBBING... IN THE MOONLIT HALL... AND FOLLOW PASSAGEWAYS... AS COMPLEX AND TWISTING... AS GUILT ITSELF.
EVERYTHING... SMELLS OF CORDITE...

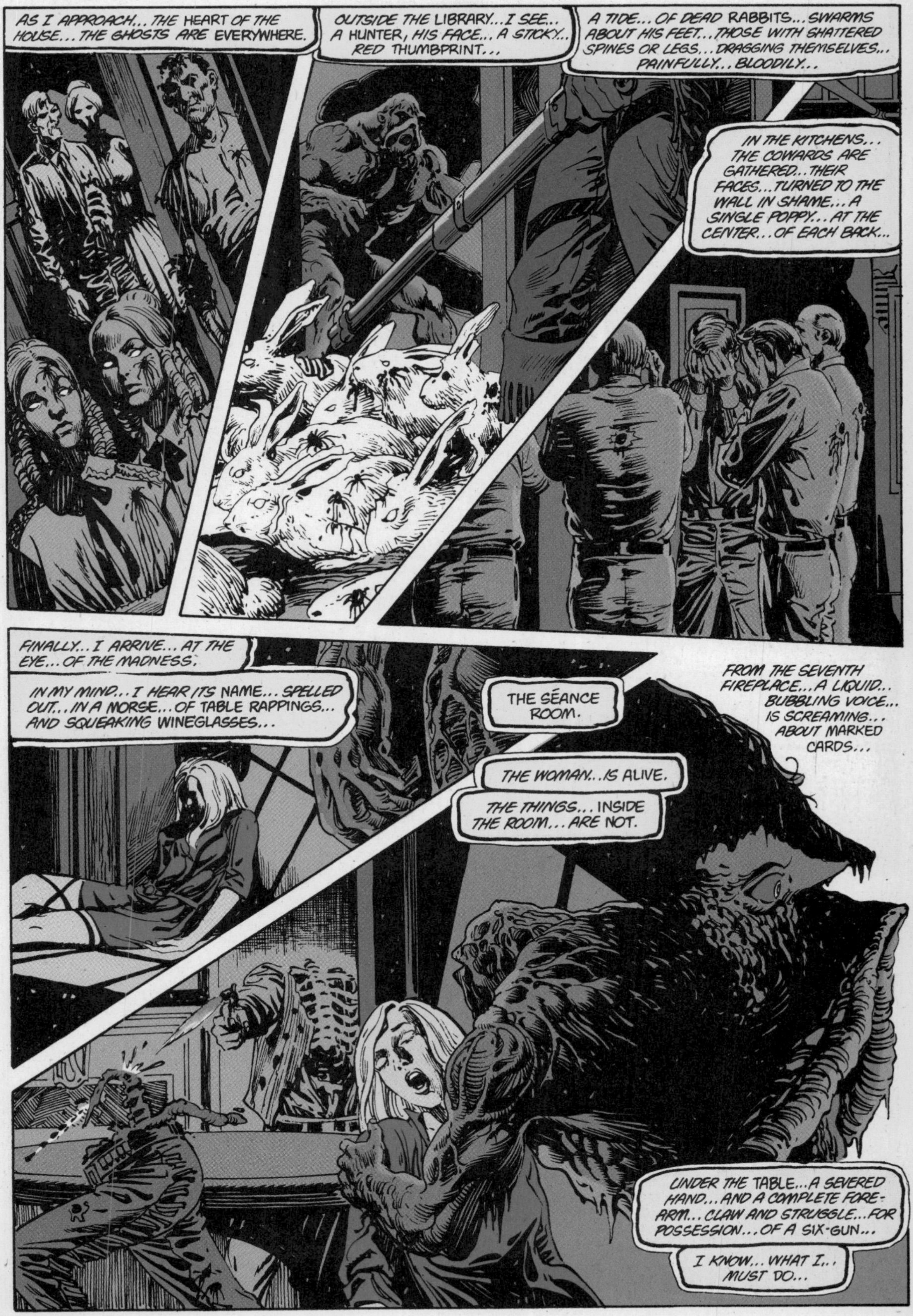
AS I APPROACH... THE HEART OF THE HOUSE... THE GHOSTS ARE EVERYWHERE.
OUTSIDE THE LIBRARY... I SEE... A HUNTER, HIS FACE... A STICKY... RED THUMBPRINT...
A TIDE... OF DEAD RABBITS... SWARMS ABOUT HIS FEET... THOSE WITH SHATTERED SPINES OR LEGS... DRAGGING THEMSELVES... PAINFULLY... BLOODILY...
IN THE KITCHENS... THE COWARDS ARE GATHERED... THEIR FACES... TURNED TO THE WALL IN SHAME... A SINGLE POPPY... AT THE CENTER... OF EACH BACK...
FINALLY... I ARRIVE... AT THE EYE... OF THE MADNESS.
IN MY MIND... I HEAR ITS NAME... SPELLED OUT... IN A MORSE... OF TABLE RAPPINGS... AND SQUEAKING WINEGLASSES...
THE SÉANCE ROOM.
FROM THE SEVENTH FIREPLACE... A LIQUID... BUBBLING VOICE... IS SCREAMING... ABOUT MARKED CARDS...
THE WOMAN... IS ALIVE.
THE THINGS... INSIDE THE ROOM... ARE NOT.
UNDER THE TABLE... A SEVERED HAND... AND A COMPLETE FORE-ARM... CLAW AND STRUGGLE... FOR POSSESSION... OF A SIX-GUN...
I KNOW... WHAT I... MUST DO...

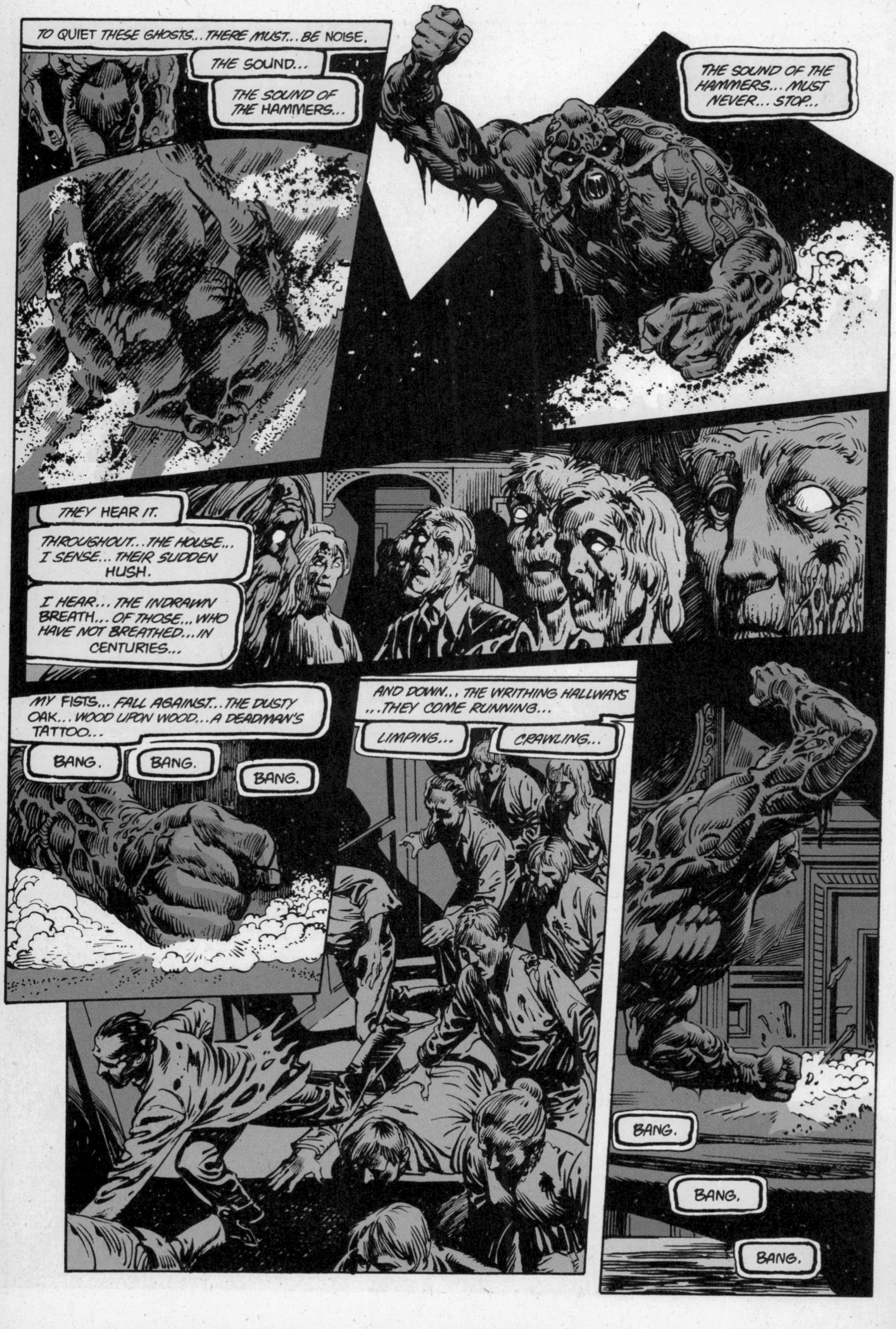
TO QUIET THESE GHOSTS... THERE MUST... BE NOISE.
THE SOUND...
THE SOUND OF THE HAMMERS...
THE SOUND OF THE HAMMERS... MUST NEVER... STOP...
THEY HEAR IT.
THROUGHOUT... THE HOUSE... I SENSE... THEIR SUDDEN HUSH.
I HEAR... THE INDRAWN BREATH... OF THOSE... WHO HAVE NOT BREATHED... IN CENTURIES...
MY FISTS... FALL AGAINST... THE DUSTY OAK... WOOD UPON WOOD... A DEADMAN'S TATTOO...
BANG.
BANG.
BANG.
AND DOWN... THE WRITHING HALLWAYS ...THEY COME RUNNING...
LIMPING...
CRAWLING...
BANG.
BANG.
BANG.

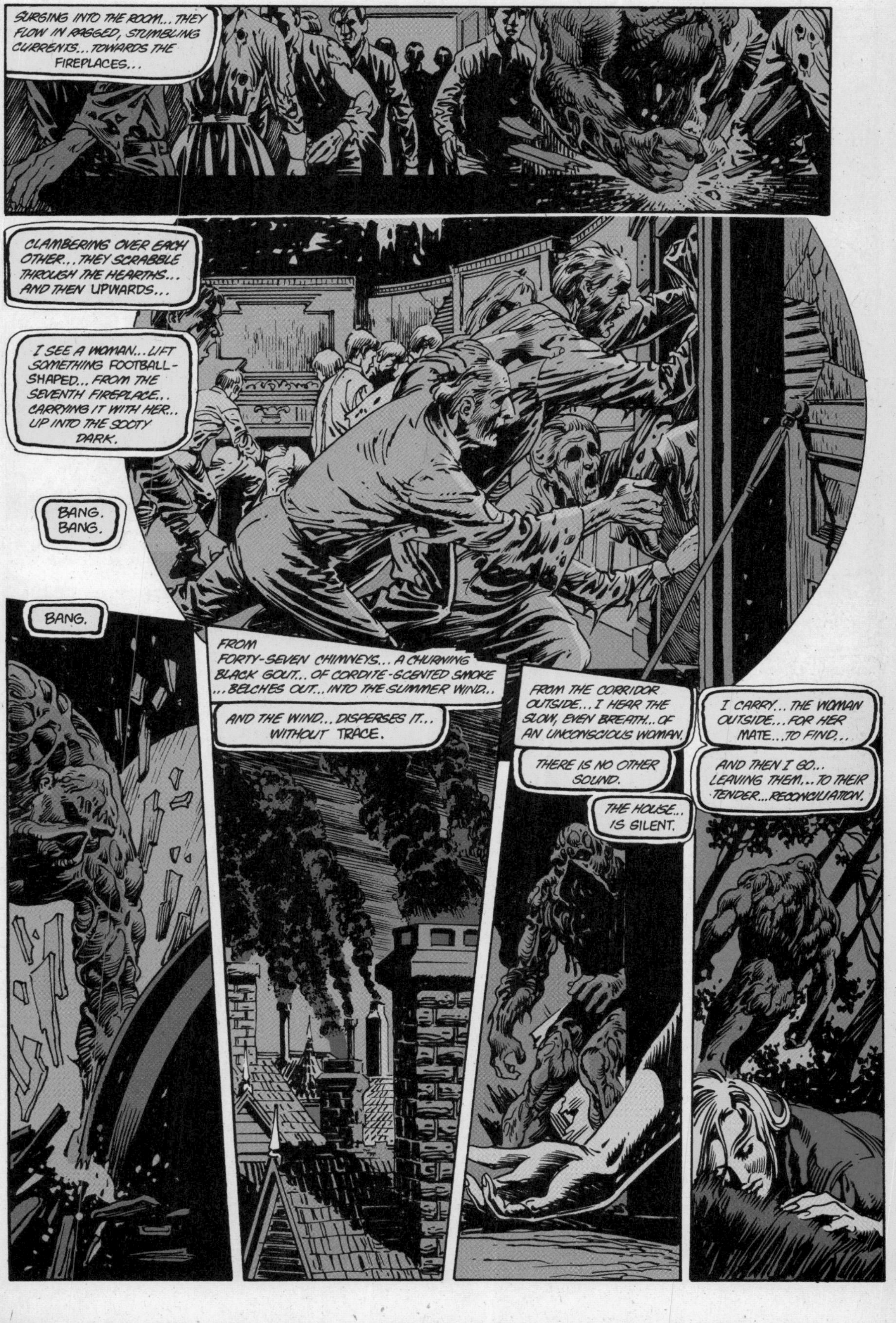
SURGING INTO THE ROOM... THEY FLOW IN RAGGED, STUMBLING CURRENTS... TOWARDS THE FIREPLACES...
CLAMBERING OVER EACH OTHER... THEY SCRABBLE THROUGH THE HEARTHS... AND THEN UPWARDS...
I SEE A WOMAN... LIFT SOMETHING FOOTBALL-SHAPED... FROM THE SEVENTH FIREPLACE... CARRYING IT WITH HER... UP INTO THE SOOTY DARK.
BANG. BANG.
BANG.
FROM FORTY-SEVEN CHIMNEYS... A CHURNING BLACK GOUT... OF CORDITE-SCENTED SMOKE ...BELCHES OUT... INTO THE SUMMER WIND...
AND THE WIND... DISPERSES IT... WITHOUT TRACE.
FROM THE CORRIDOR OUTSIDE... I HEAR THE SLOW, EVEN BREATH... OF AN UNCONSCIOUS WOMAN.
THERE IS NO OTHER SOUND.
THE HOUSE... IS SILENT.
I CARRY... THE WOMAN OUTSIDE... FOR HER MATE... TO FIND...
AND THEN I GO... LEAVING THEM... TO THEIR TENDER... RECONCILIATION.

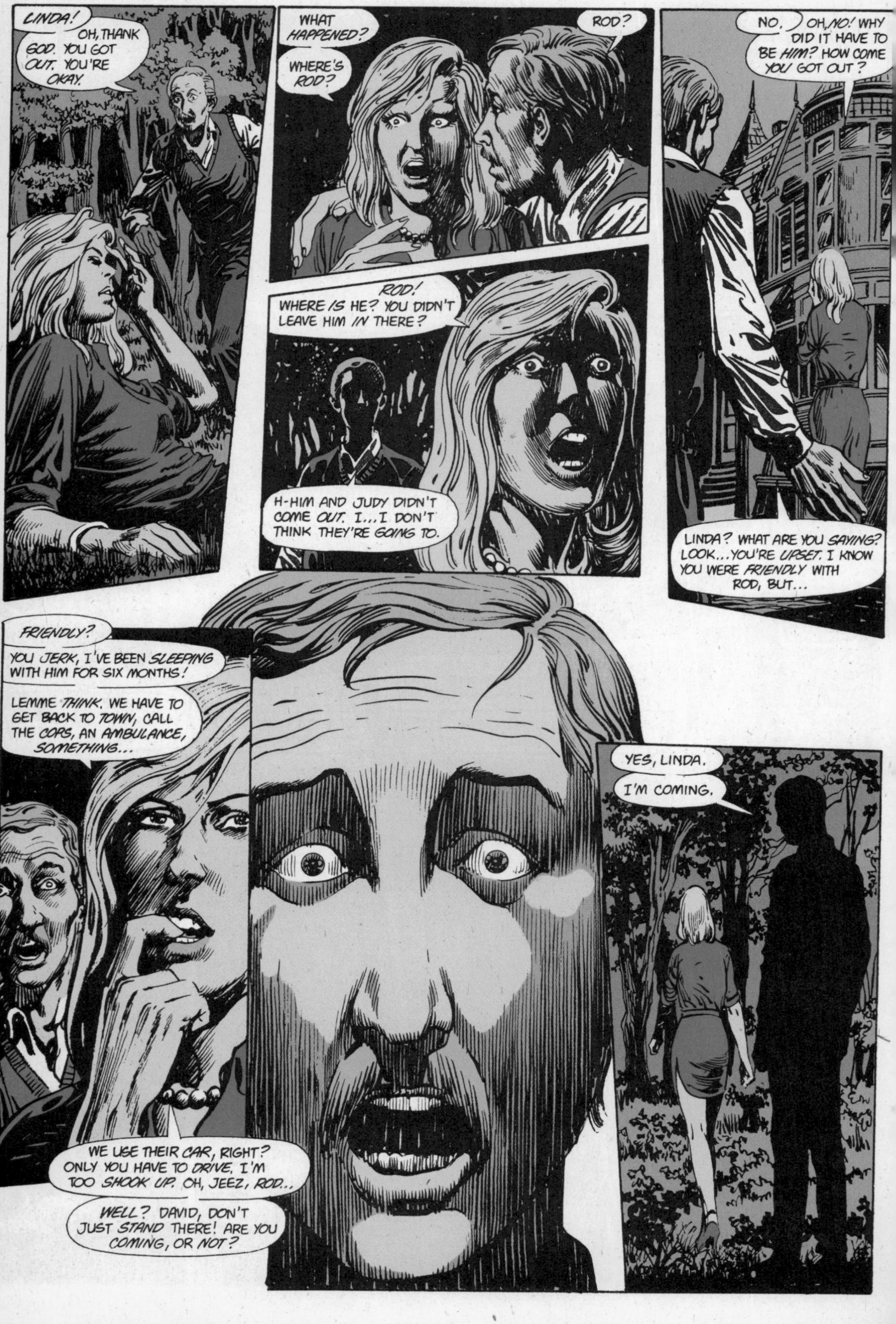
LINDA!
OH, THANK GOD. YOU GOT OUT. YOU'RE OKAY.
WHAT HAPPENED?
WHERE'S ROD?
ROD?
ROD! WHERE IS HE? YOU DIDN'T LEAVE HIM IN THERE?
H-HIM AND JUDY DIDN'T COME OUT. I... I DON'T THINK THEY'RE GOING TO.
NO.
OH, NO! WHY DID IT HAVE TO BE HIM? HOW COME YOU GOT OUT?
LINDA? WHAT ARE YOU SAYING? LOOK... YOU'RE UPSET. I KNOW YOU WERE FRIENDLY WITH ROD, BUT...
FRIENDLY?
YOU JERK, I'VE BEEN SLEEPING WITH HIM FOR SIX MONTHS!
LEMME THINK. WE HAVE TO GET BACK TO TOWN, CALL THE COPS, AN AMBULANCE, SOMETHING...
WE USE THEIR CAR, RIGHT? ONLY YOU HAVE TO DRIVE. I'M TOO SHOOK UP. OH, JEEZ, ROD...
WELL? DAVID, DON'T JUST STAND THERE! ARE YOU COMING, OR NOT?
YES, LINDA.
I'M COMING.

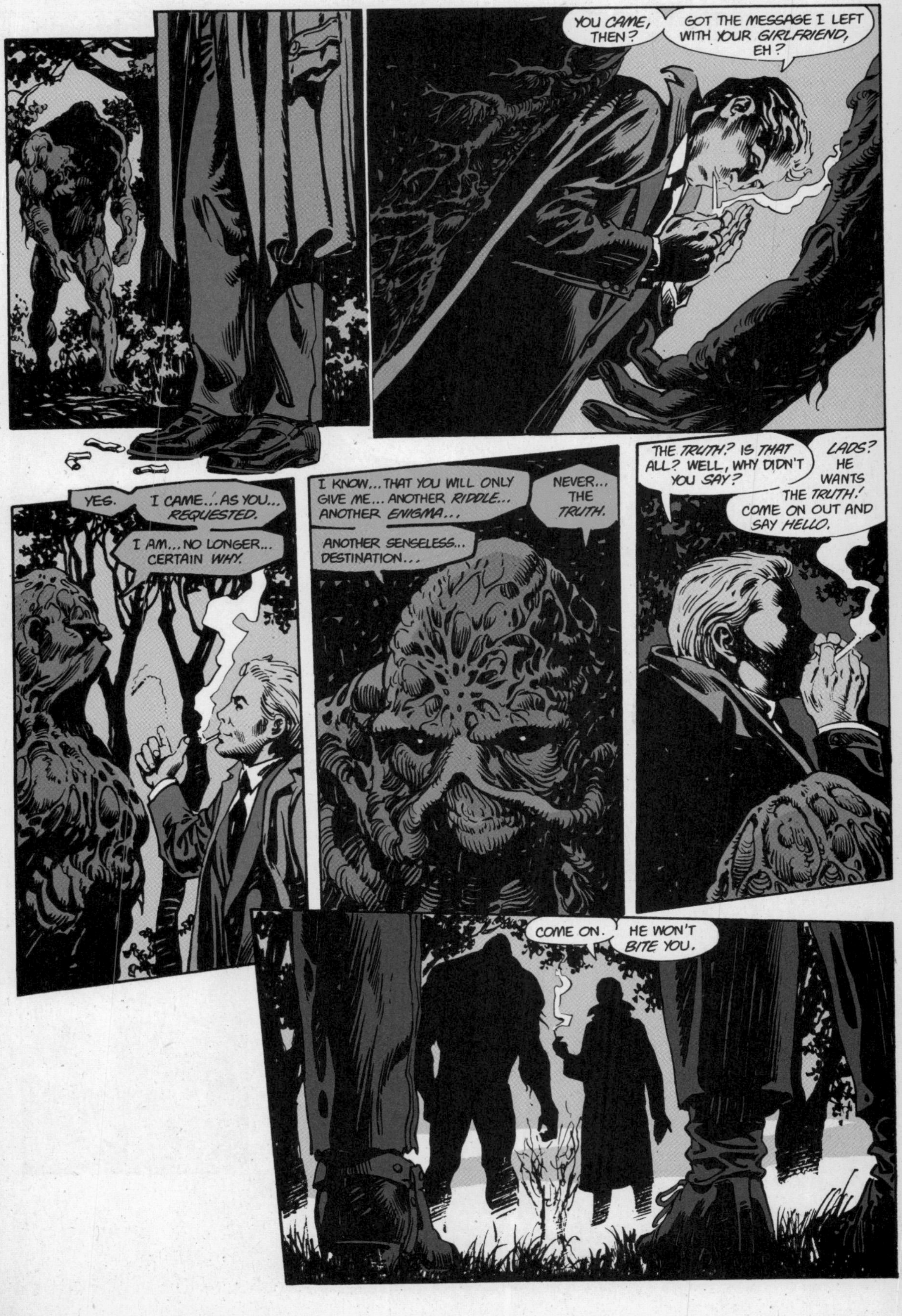
YOU CAME, THEN?
GOT THE MESSAGE I LEFT WITH YOUR GIRLFRIEND, EH?
YES.
I CAME... AS YOU... REQUESTED.
I AM... NO LONGER... CERTAIN WHY.
I KNOW... THAT YOU WILL ONLY GIVE ME... ANOTHER RIDDLE... ANOTHER ENIGMA...
NEVER... THE TRUTH.
ANOTHER SENSELESS... DESTINATION...
THE TRUTH? IS THAT ALL? WELL, WHY DIDN'T YOU SAY?
LADS? HE WANTS THE TRUTH! COME ON OUT AND SAY HELLO.
COME ON.
HE WON'T BITE YOU.

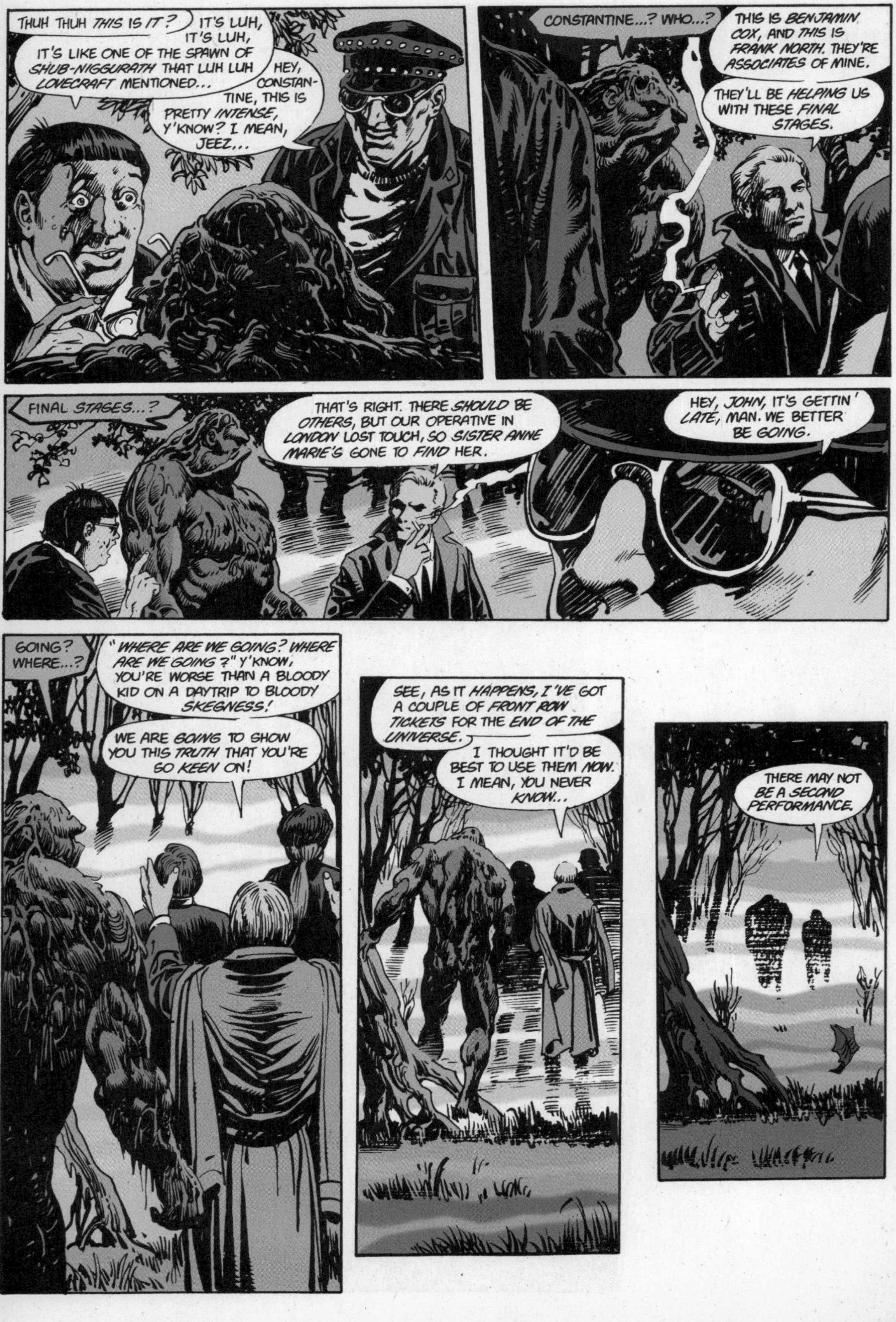
THUH THUH THIS IS IT?
IT'S LUH, IT'S LUH, IT'S LIKE ONE OF THE SPAWN OF SHUB-NIGGURATH THAT LUH LUH LOVECRAFT MENTIONED...
HEY, CONSTANTINE, THIS IS PRETTY INTENSE, Y'KNOW? I MEAN, JEEZ...
CONSTANTINE...? WHO...?
THIS IS BENJAMIN COX, AND THIS IS FRANK NORTH. THEY'RE ASSOCIATES OF MINE.
THEY'LL BE HELPING US WITH THESE FINAL STAGES.
FINAL STAGES...?
THAT'S RIGHT. THERE SHOULD BE OTHERS, BUT OUR OPERATIVE IN LONDON LOST TOUCH, SO SISTER ANNE MARIE'S GONE TO FIND HER.
HEY, JOHN, IT'S GETTIN' LATE, MAN. WE BETTER BE GOING.
GOING? WHERE...?
"WHERE ARE WE GOING? WHERE ARE WE GOING?" Y'KNOW, YOU'RE WORSE THAN A BLOODY KID ON A DAYTRIP TO BLOODY SKEGNESS!
WE ARE GOING TO SHOW YOU THIS TRUTH THAT YOU'RE SO KEEN ON!
SEE, AS IT HAPPENS, I'VE GOT A COUPLE OF FRONT ROW TICKETS FOR THE END OF THE UNIVERSE.
I THOUGHT IT'D BE BEST TO USE THEM NOW. I MEAN, YOU NEVER KNOW...
THERE MAY NOT BE A SECOND PERFORMANCE.

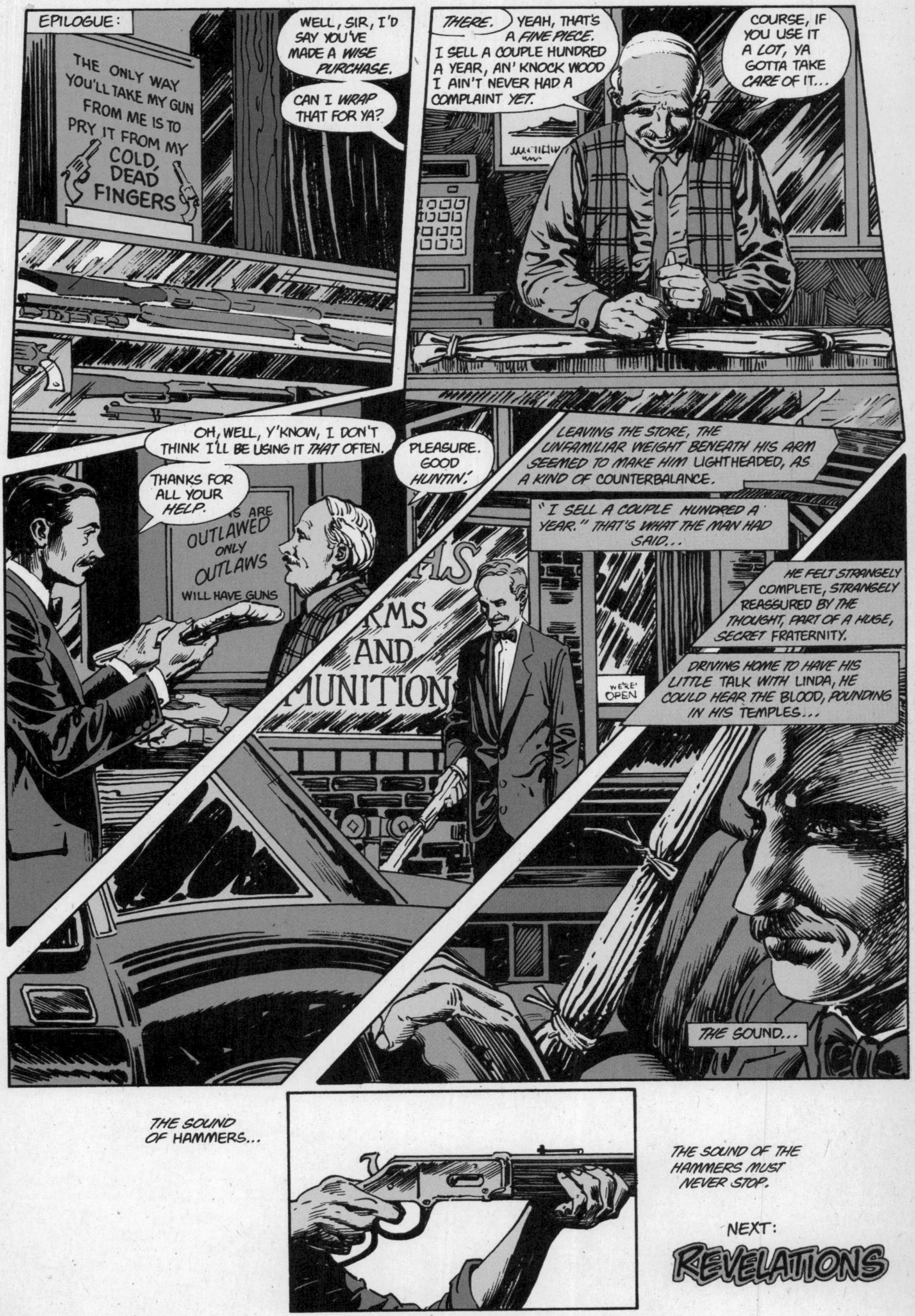
EPILOGUE:
THE ONLY WAY YOU'LL TAKE MY GUN FROM ME IS TO PRY IT FROM MY COLD, DEAD FINGERS
WELL, SIR, I'D SAY YOU'VE MADE A WISE PURCHASE.
CAN I WRAP THAT FOR YA?
THERE.
YEAH, THAT'S A FINE PIECE. I SELL A COUPLE HUNDRED A YEAR, AN' KNOCK WOOD I AIN'T NEVER HAD A COMPLAINT YET.
COURSE, IF YOU USE IT A LOT, YA GOTTA TAKE CARE OF IT...
OH, WELL, Y'KNOW, I DON'T THINK I'LL BE USING IT THAT OFTEN.
THANKS FOR ALL YOUR HELP.
PLEASURE. GOOD HUNTIN'.
OUTLAWED ONLY OUTLAWS WILL HAVE GUNS
LEAVING THE STORE, THE UNFAMILIAR WEIGHT BENEATH HIS ARM SEEMED TO MAKE HIM LIGHTHEADED, AS A KIND OF COUNTERBALANCE.
"I SELL A COUPLE HUNDRED A YEAR." THAT'S WHAT THE MAN HAD SAID...
HE FELT STRANGELY COMPLETE, STRANGELY REASSURED BY THE THOUGHT, PART OF A HUGE, SECRET FRATERNITY.
RMS AND MUNITION
WE'RE OPEN
DRIVING HOME TO HAVE HIS LITTLE TALK WITH LINDA, HE COULD HEAR THE BLOOD, POUNDING IN HIS TEMPLES...
THE SOUND...
THE SOUND OF HAMMERS...
THE SOUND OF THE HAMMERS MUST NEVER STOP.
NEXT:
REVELATIONS

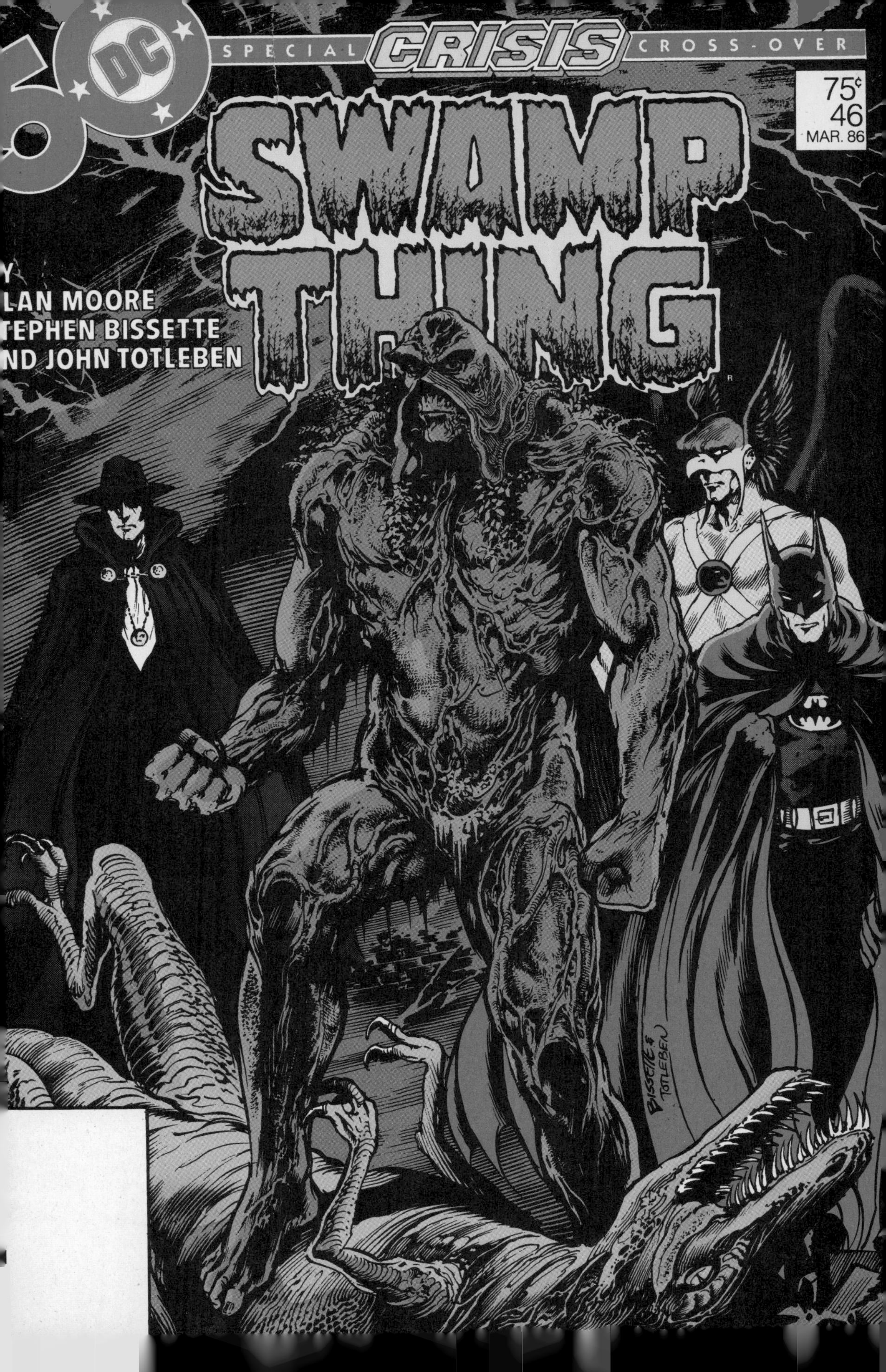
DC
SPECIAL CRISIS CROSS-OVER
75¢
46
MAR. 86
SWAMP THING
Y
LAN MOORE
TEPHEN BISSETTE
ND JOHN TOTLEBEN
BISSETTE & TOTLEBEN

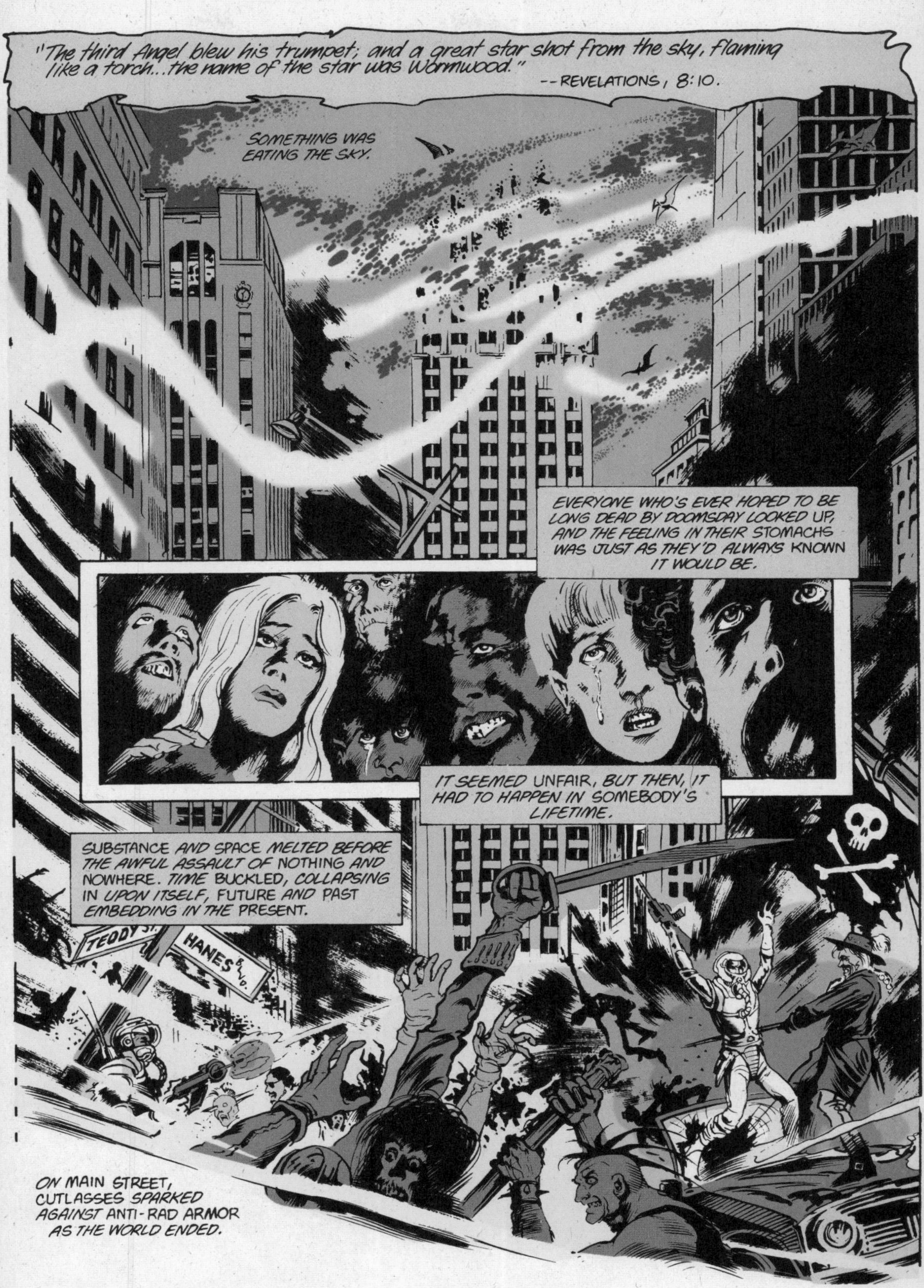
"The third Angel blew his trumpet; and a great star shot from the sky, flaming like a torch...the name of the star was Wormwood."
--REVELATIONS, 8:10.
SOMETHING WAS EATING THE SKY.
EVERYONE WHO'S EVER HOPED TO BE LONG DEAD BY DOOMSDAY LOOKED UP, AND THE FEELING IN THEIR STOMACHS WAS JUST AS THEY'D ALWAYS KNOWN IT WOULD BE.
IT SEEMED UNFAIR, BUT THEN, IT HAD TO HAPPEN IN SOMEBODY'S LIFETIME.
SUBSTANCE AND SPACE MELTED BEFORE THE AWFUL ASSAULT OF NOTHING AND NOWHERE. TIME BUCKLED, COLLAPSING IN UPON ITSELF, FUTURE AND PAST EMBEDDING IN THE PRESENT.
TEDDY ST.
HANES
ON MAIN STREET, CUTLASSES SPARKED AGAINST ANTI-RAD ARMOR AS THE WORLD ENDED.

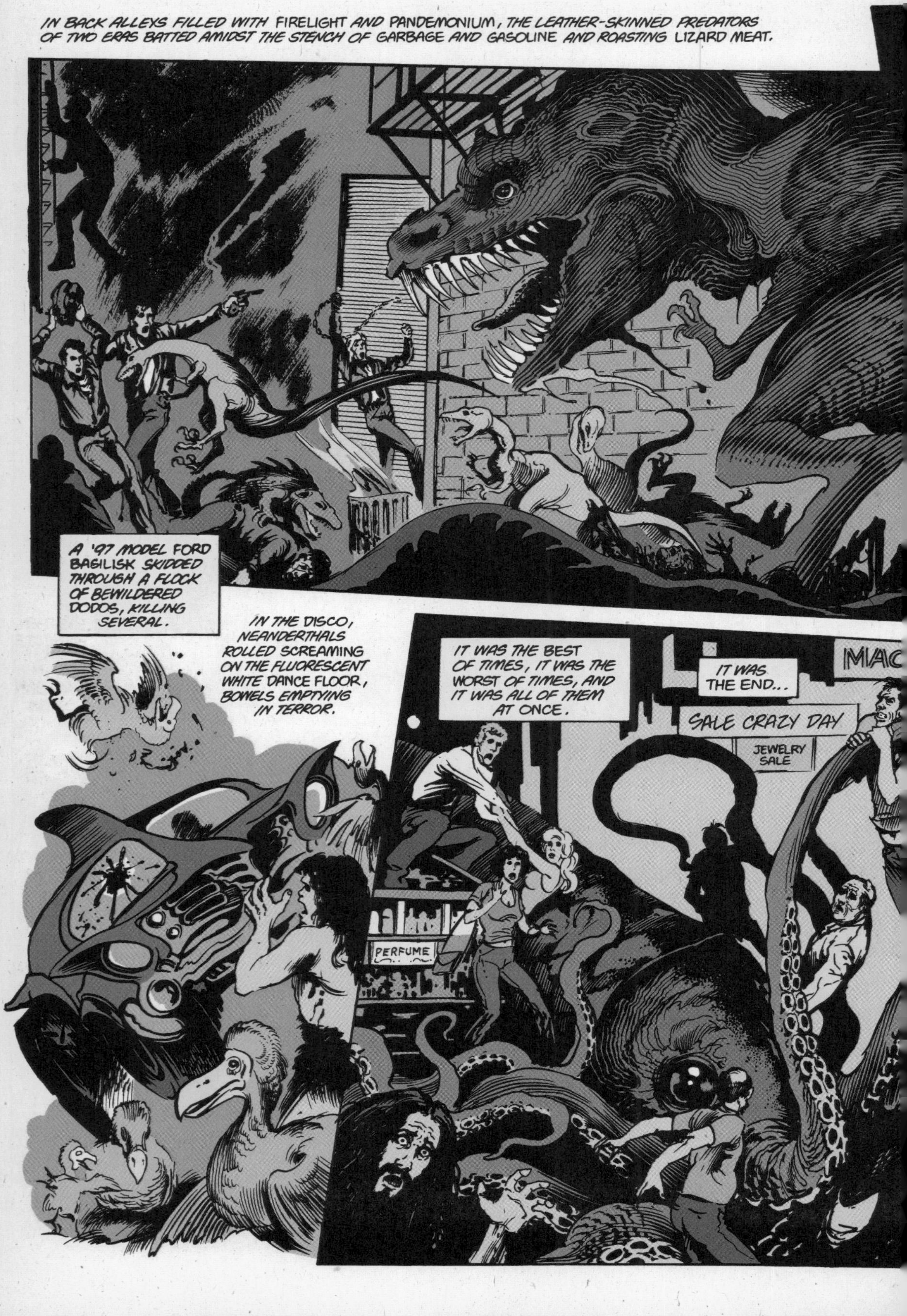
IN BACK ALLEYS FILLED WITH FIRELIGHT AND PANDEMONIUM, THE LEATHER-SKINNED PREDATORS OF TWO ERAS BATTED AMIDST THE STENCH OF GARBAGE AND GASOLINE AND ROASTING LIZARD MEAT.
A '97 MODEL FORD BASILISK SKIDDED THROUGH A FLOCK OF BEWILDERED DODOS, KILLING SEVERAL.
IN THE DISCO, NEANDERTHALS ROLLED SCREAMING ON THE FLUORESCENT WHITE DANCE FLOOR, BOWELS EMPTYING IN TERROR.
IT WAS THE BEST OF TIMES, IT WAS THE WORST OF TIMES, AND IT WAS ALL OF THEM AT ONCE.
IT WAS THE END...
MAC
SALE CRAZY DAY
JEWELRY SALE
PERFUME

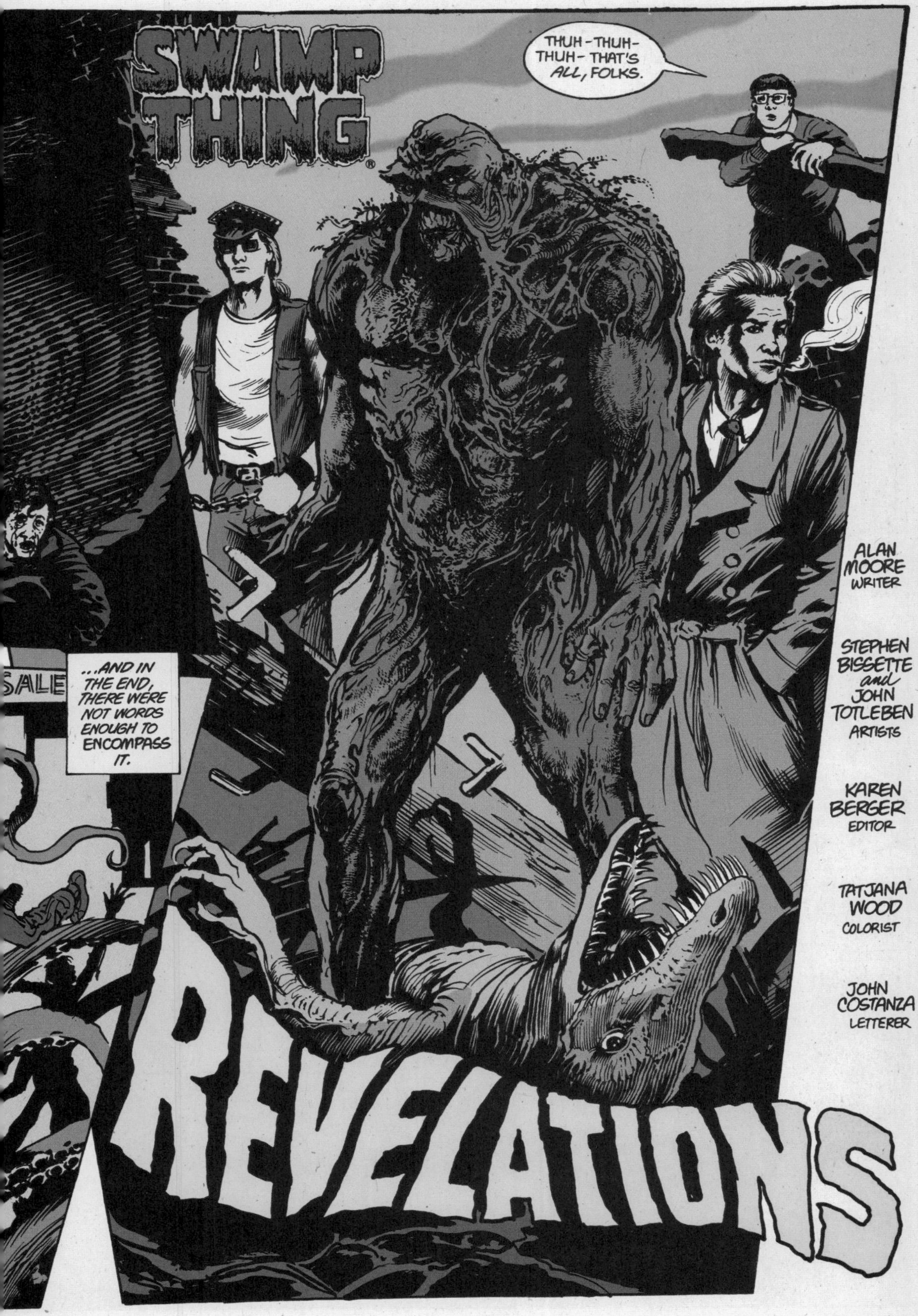
SWAMP THING®
THUH-THUH-THUH-THAT'S ALL, FOLKS.
SALE
...AND IN THE END, THERE WERE NOT WORDS ENOUGH TO ENCOMPASS IT.
REVELATIONS
ALAN MOORE WRITER
STEPHEN BISSETTE and JOHN TOTLEBEN ARTISTS
KAREN BERGER EDITOR
TATJANA WOOD COLORIST
JOHN COSTANZA LETTERER

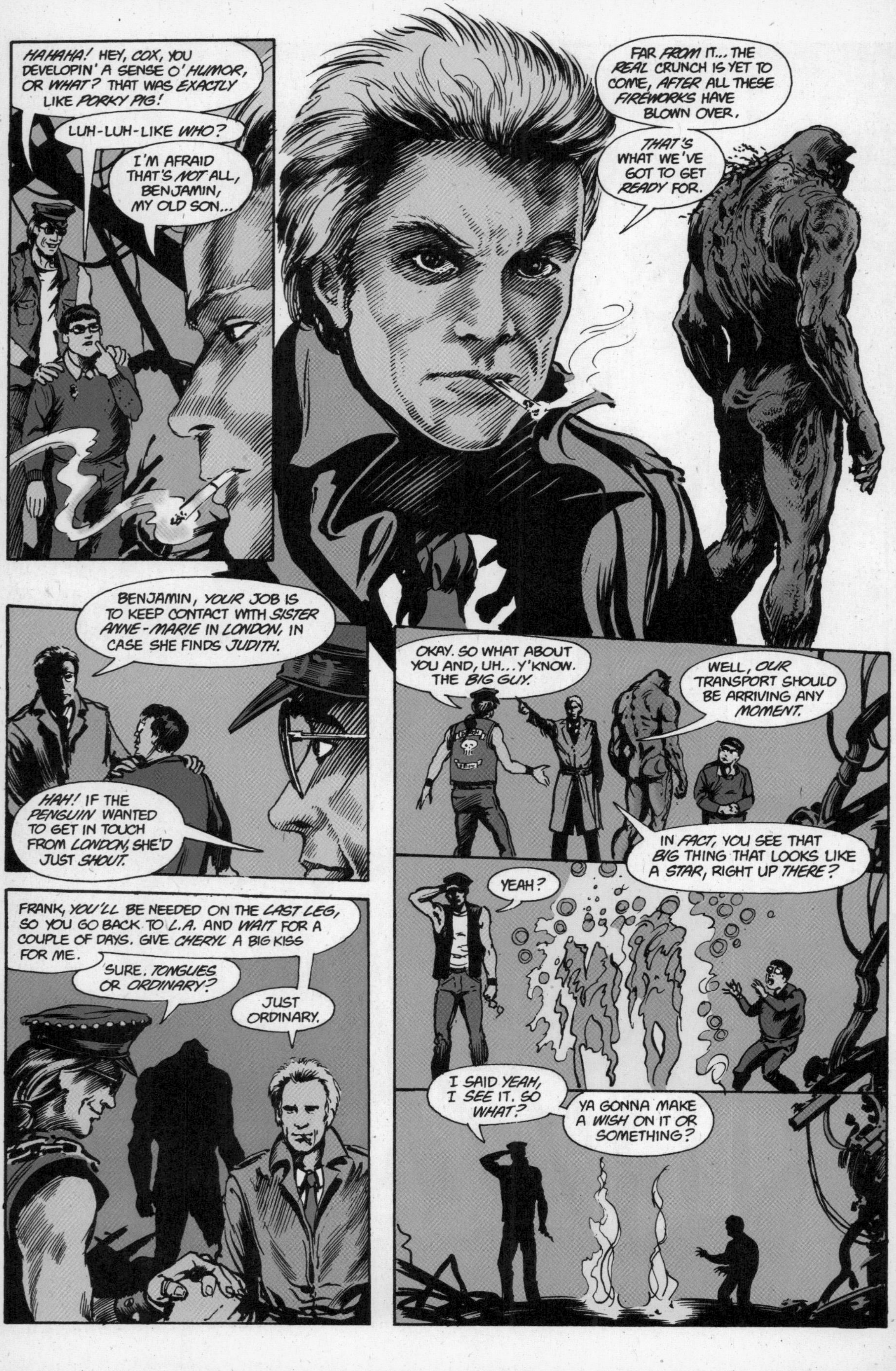
HAHAHA! HEY, COX, YOU DEVELOPIN' A SENSE O' HUMOR, OR WHAT? THAT WAS EXACTLY LIKE PORKY PIG!
LUH-LUH-LIKE WHO?
I'M AFRAID THAT'S NOT ALL, BENJAMIN, MY OLD SON...
FAR FROM IT... THE REAL CRUNCH IS YET TO COME, AFTER ALL THESE FIREWORKS HAVE BLOWN OVER.
THAT'S WHAT WE'VE GOT TO GET READY FOR.
BENJAMIN, YOUR JOB IS TO KEEP CONTACT WITH SISTER ANNE-MARIE IN LONDON, IN CASE SHE FINDS JUDITH.
HAH! IF THE PENGUIN WANTED TO GET IN TOUCH FROM LONDON, SHE'D JUST SHOUT.
OKAY. SO WHAT ABOUT YOU AND, UH... Y'KNOW. THE BIG GUY.
WELL, OUR TRANSPORT SHOULD BE ARRIVING ANY MOMENT.
IN FACT, YOU SEE THAT BIG THING THAT LOOKS LIKE A STAR, RIGHT UP THERE?
YEAH?
FRANK, YOU'LL BE NEEDED ON THE LAST LEG, SO YOU GO BACK TO L.A. AND WAIT FOR A COUPLE OF DAYS. GIVE CHERYL A BIG KISS FOR ME.
SURE. TONGUES OR ORDINARY?
JUST ORDINARY.
I SAID YEAH, I SEE IT. SO WHAT?
YA GONNA MAKE A WISH ON IT OR SOMETHING?

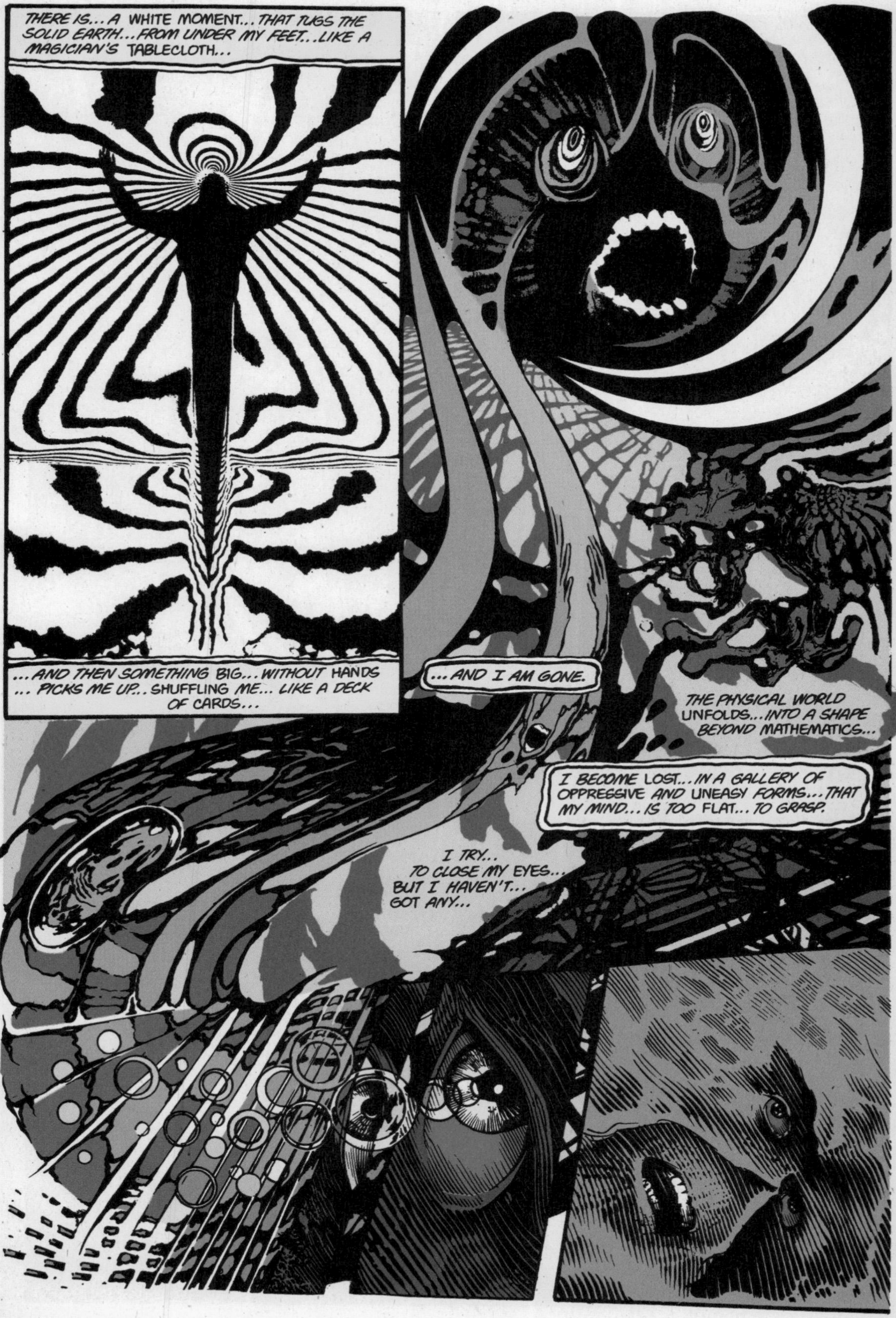
THERE IS... A WHITE MOMENT... THAT TUGS THE SOLID EARTH... FROM UNDER MY FEET... LIKE A MAGICIAN'S TABLECLOTH...
...AND THEN SOMETHING BIG... WITHOUT HANDS ... PICKS ME UP... SHUFFLING ME... LIKE A DECK OF CARDS...
...AND I AM GONE.
THE PHYSICAL WORLD UNFOLDS... INTO A SHAPE BEYOND MATHEMATICS...
I BECOME LOST... IN A GALLERY OF OPPRESSIVE AND UNEASY FORMS... THAT MY MIND... IS TOO FLAT... TO GRASP.
I TRY... TO CLOSE MY EYES... BUT I HAVEN'T... GOT ANY...

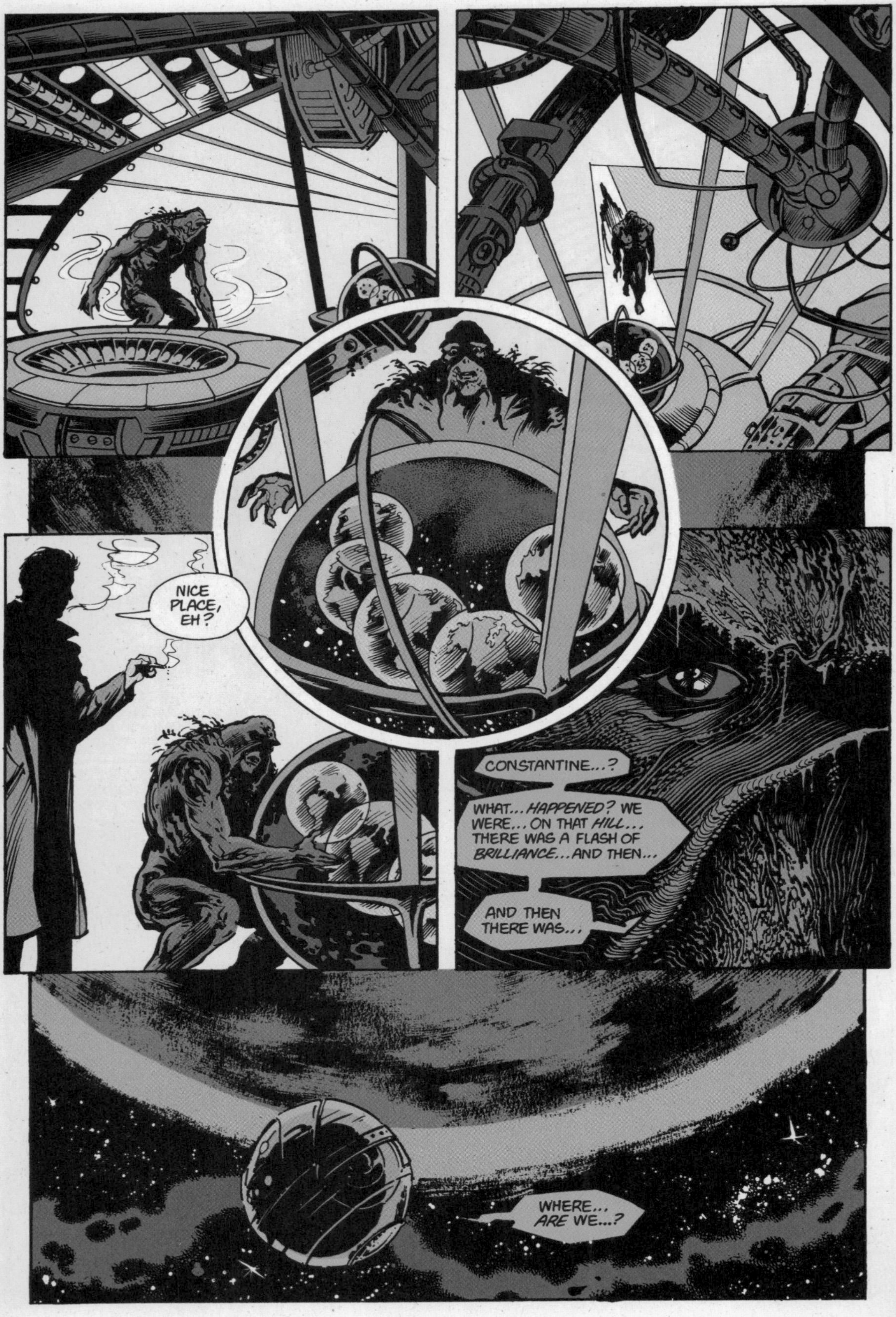
NICE PLACE, EH?
CONSTANTINE...?
WHAT... HAPPENED? WE WERE... ON THAT HILL... THERE WAS A FLASH OF BRILLIANCE... AND THEN...
AND THEN THERE WAS...
WHERE... ARE WE...?

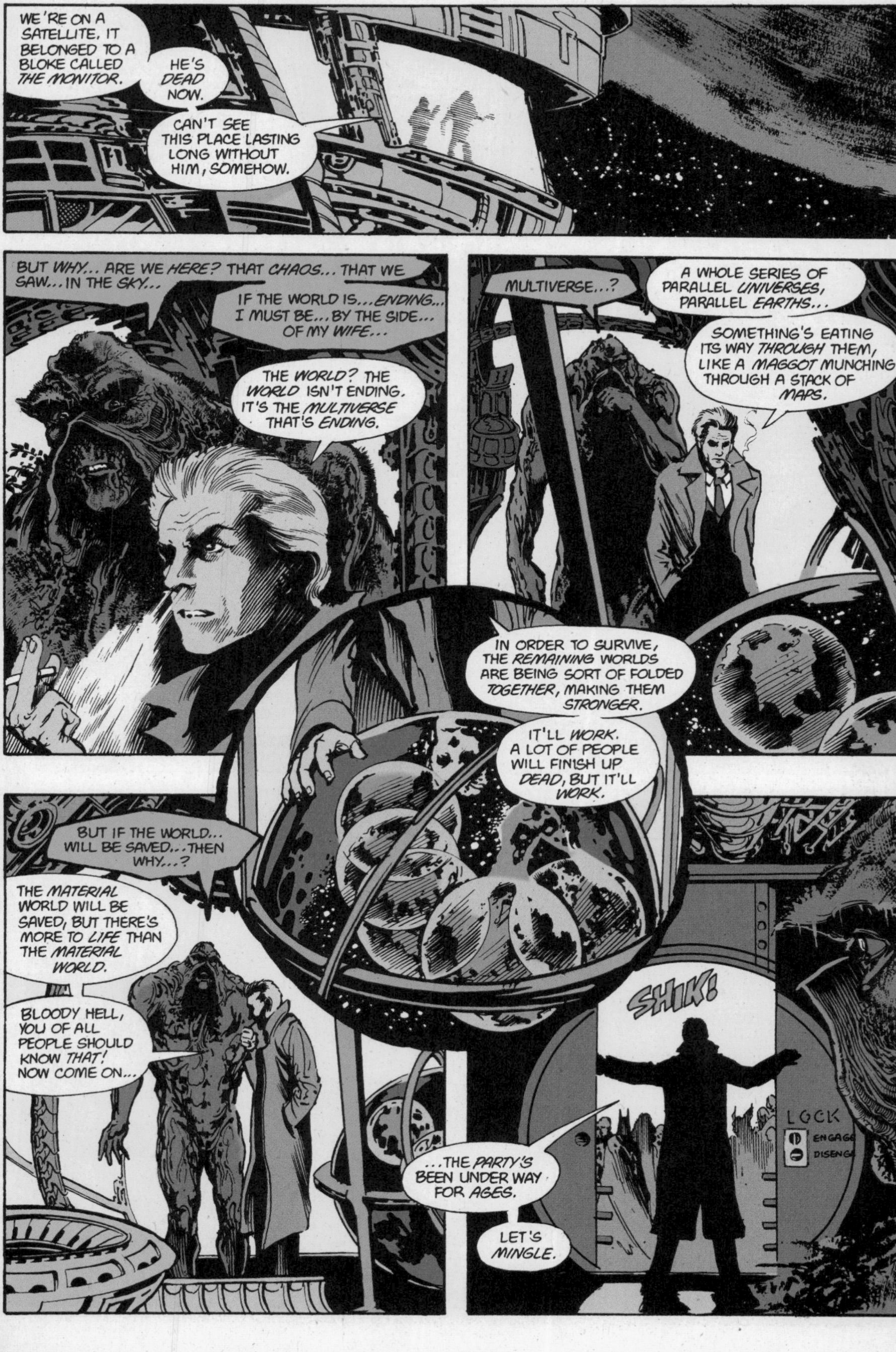
WE'RE ON A SATELLITE. IT BELONGED TO A BLOKE CALLED THE MONITOR.
HE'S DEAD NOW.
CAN'T SEE THIS PLACE LASTING LONG WITHOUT HIM, SOMEHOW.
BUT WHY... ARE WE HERE? THAT CHAOS... THAT WE SAW... IN THE SKY...
IF THE WORLD IS... ENDING... I MUST BE... BY THE SIDE... OF MY WIFE...
THE WORLD? THE WORLD ISN'T ENDING. IT'S THE MULTIVERSE THAT'S ENDING.
MULTIVERSE...?
A WHOLE SERIES OF PARALLEL UNIVERSES, PARALLEL EARTHS...
SOMETHING'S EATING ITS WAY THROUGH THEM, LIKE A MAGGOT MUNCHING THROUGH A STACK OF MAPS.
IN ORDER TO SURVIVE, THE REMAINING WORLDS ARE BEING SORT OF FOLDED TOGETHER, MAKING THEM STRONGER.
IT'LL WORK. A LOT OF PEOPLE WILL FINISH UP DEAD, BUT IT'LL WORK.
BUT IF THE WORLD... WILL BE SAVED... THEN WHY...?
THE MATERIAL WORLD WILL BE SAVED, BUT THERE'S MORE TO LIFE THAN THE MATERIAL WORLD.
BLOODY HELL, YOU OF ALL PEOPLE SHOULD KNOW THAT! NOW COME ON...
SHIK!
LOCK
...THE PARTY'S BEEN UNDER WAY FOR AGES.
LET'S MINGLE.

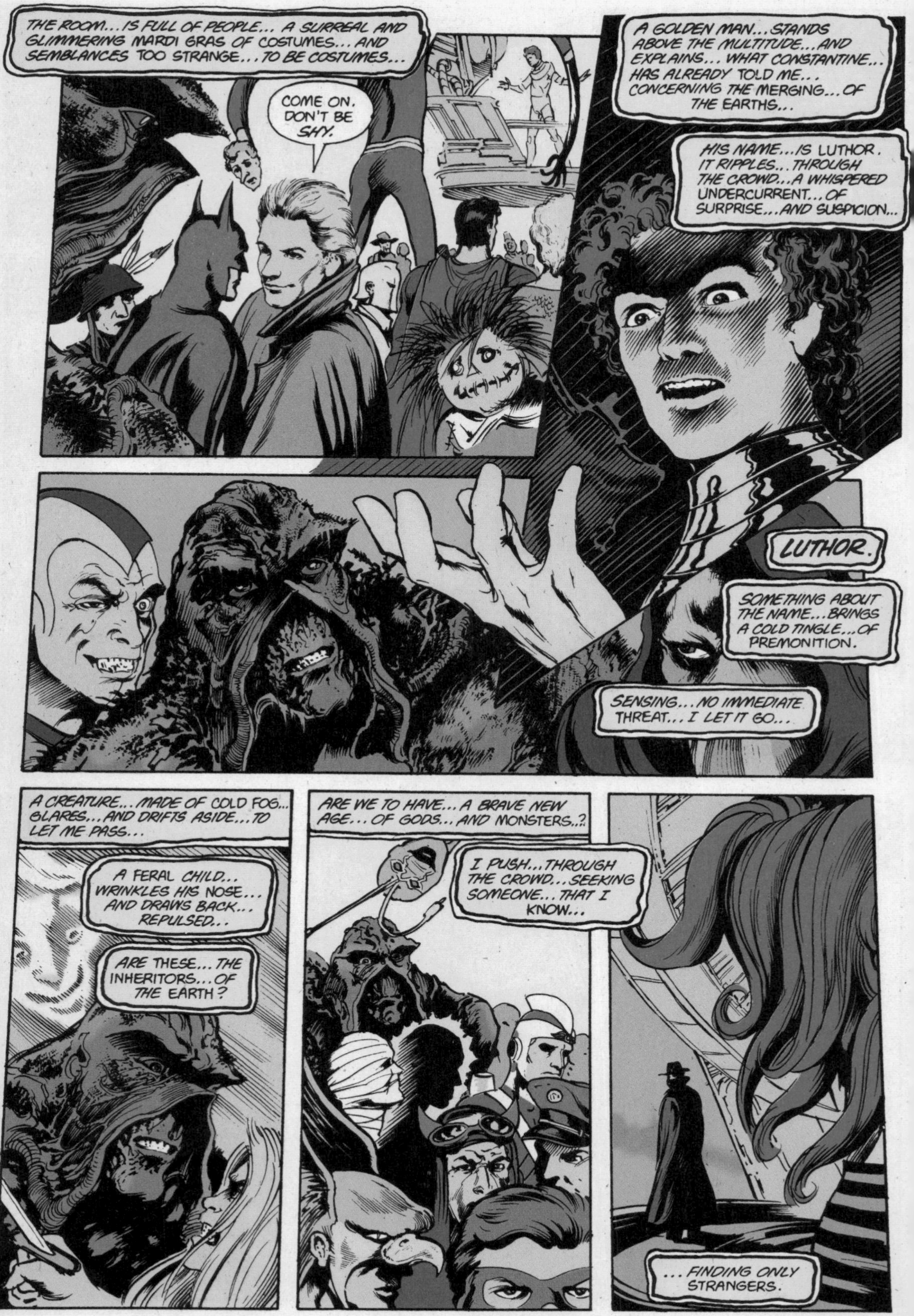
THE ROOM... IS FULL OF PEOPLE... A SURREAL AND GLIMMERING MARDI GRAS OF COSTUMES... AND SEMBLANCES TOO STRANGE... TO BE COSTUMES...
COME ON. DON'T BE SHY.
A GOLDEN MAN... STANDS ABOVE THE MULTITUDE... AND EXPLAINS... WHAT CONSTANTINE... HAS ALREADY TOLD ME... CONCERNING THE MERGING... OF THE EARTHS...
HIS NAME... IS LUTHOR. IT RIPPLES... THROUGH THE CROWD... A WHISPERED UNDERCURRENT... OF SURPRISE... AND SUSPICION...
LUTHOR.
SOMETHING ABOUT THE NAME... BRINGS A COLD TINGLE... OF PREMONITION.
SENSING... NO IMMEDIATE THREAT... I LET IT GO...
A CREATURE... MADE OF COLD FOG... GLARES... AND DRIFTS ASIDE... TO LET ME PASS...
A FERAL CHILD... WRINKLES HIS NOSE... AND DRAWS BACK... REPULSED...
ARE THESE... THE INHERITORS... OF THE EARTH?
ARE WE TO HAVE... A BRAVE NEW AGE... OF GODS... AND MONSTERS..?
I PUSH... THROUGH THE CROWD... SEEKING SOMEONE... THAT I KNOW...
... FINDING ONLY STRANGERS.

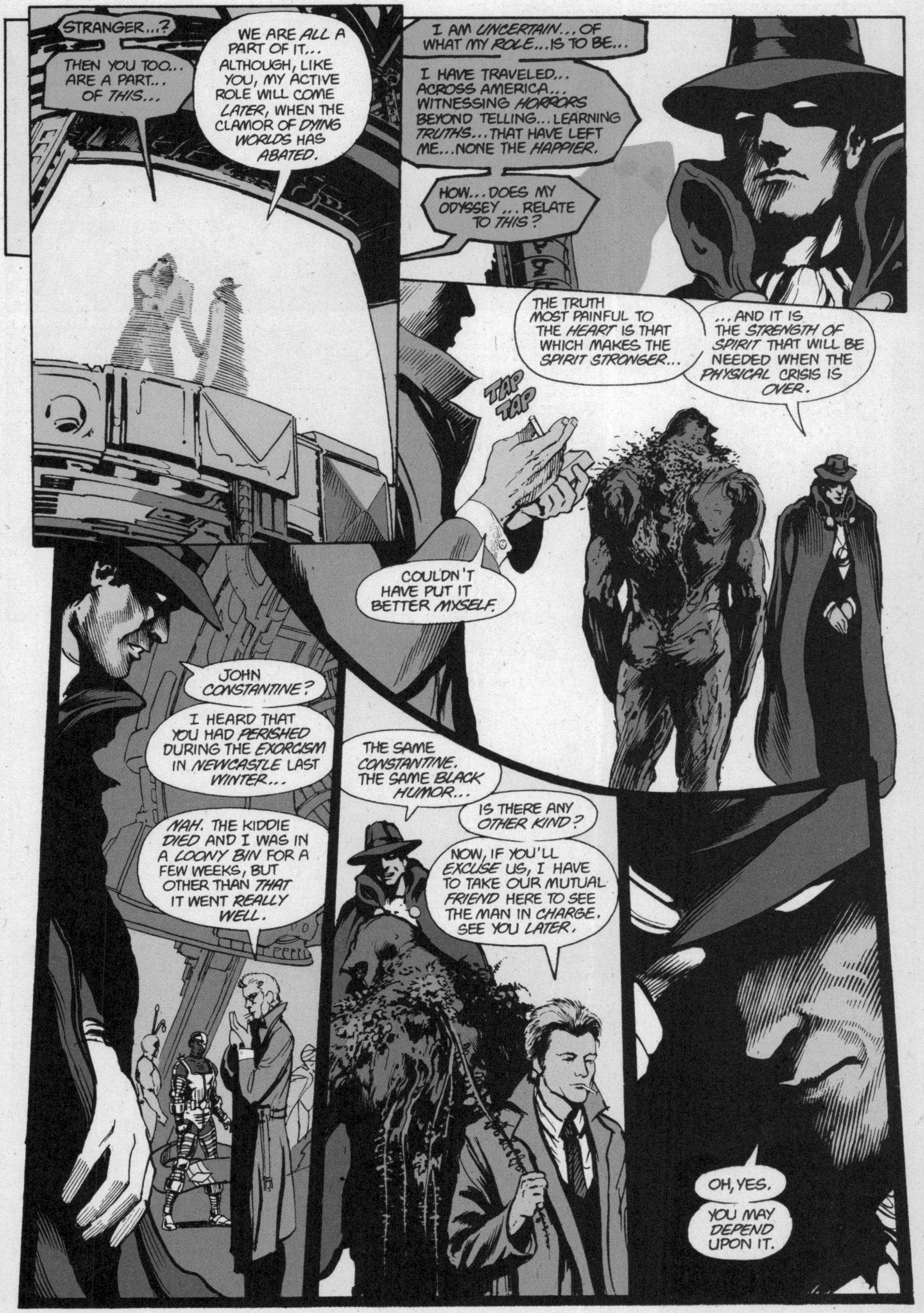
STRANGER...?
THEN YOU TOO... ARE A PART... OF THIS...
WE ARE ALL A PART OF IT... ALTHOUGH, LIKE YOU, MY ACTIVE ROLE WILL COME LATER, WHEN THE CLAMOR OF DYING WORLDS HAS ABATED.
I AM UNCERTAIN... OF WHAT MY ROLE... IS TO BE...
I HAVE TRAVELED... ACROSS AMERICA... WITNESSING HORRORS BEYOND TELLING... LEARNING TRUTHS... THAT HAVE LEFT ME... NONE THE HAPPIER.
HOW... DOES MY ODYSSEY... RELATE TO THIS?
THE TRUTH MOST PAINFUL TO THE HEART IS THAT WHICH MAKES THE SPIRIT STRONGER...
...AND IT IS THE STRENGTH OF SPIRIT THAT WILL BE NEEDED WHEN THE PHYSICAL CRISIS IS OVER.
TAP TAP
COULDN'T HAVE PUT IT BETTER MYSELF.
JOHN CONSTANTINE?
I HEARD THAT YOU HAD PERISHED DURING THE EXORCISM IN NEWCASTLE LAST WINTER...
NAH. THE KIDDIE DIED AND I WAS IN A LOONY BIN FOR A FEW WEEKS, BUT OTHER THAN THAT IT WENT REALLY WELL.
THE SAME CONSTANTINE. THE SAME BLACK HUMOR...
IS THERE ANY OTHER KIND?
NOW, IF YOU'LL EXCUSE US, I HAVE TO TAKE OUR MUTUAL FRIEND HERE TO SEE THE MAN IN CHARGE. SEE YOU LATER.
OH, YES.
YOU MAY DEPEND UPON IT.

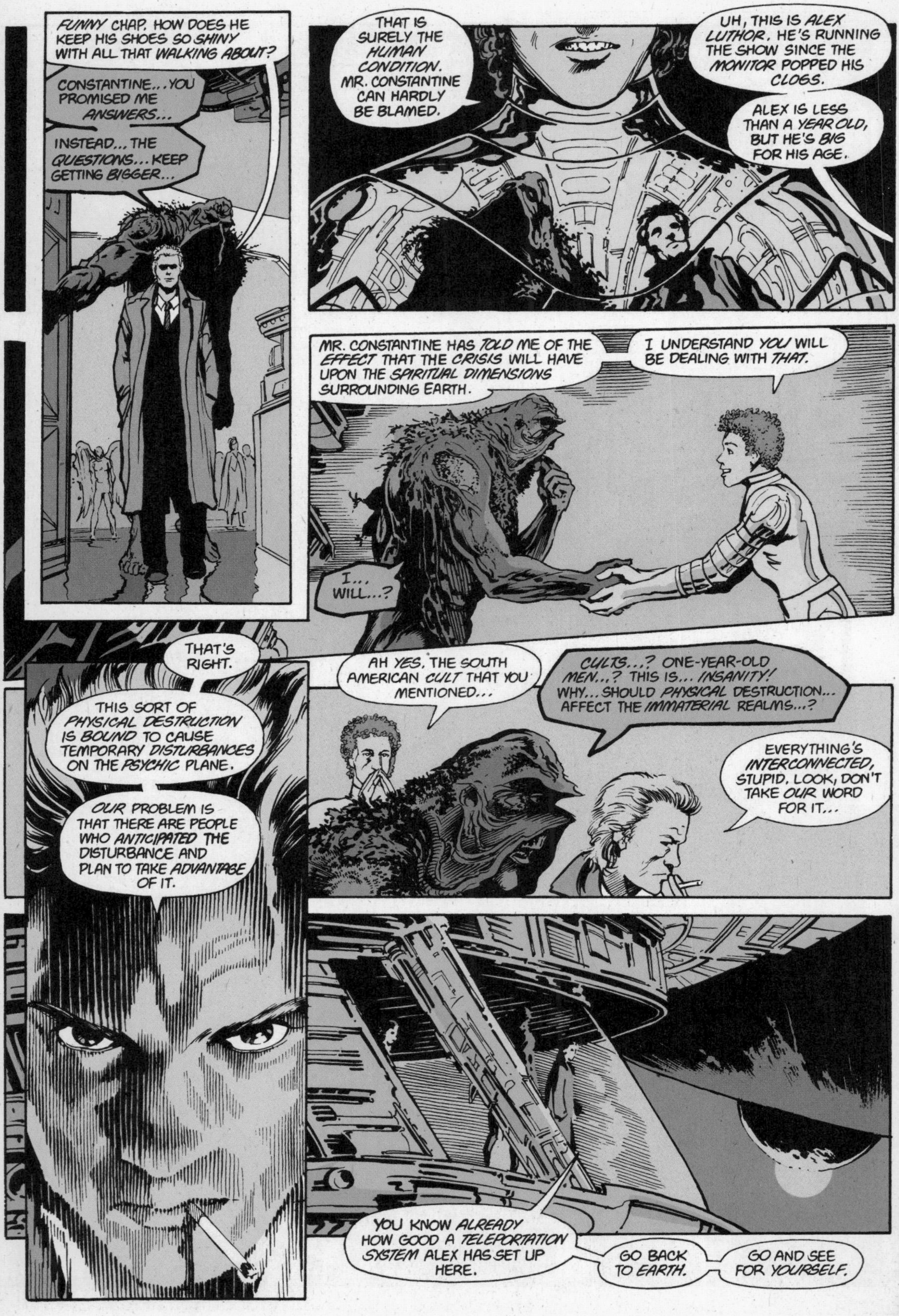
FUNNY CHAP. HOW DOES HE KEEP HIS SHOES SO SHINY WITH ALL THAT WALKING ABOUT?
CONSTANTINE... YOU PROMISED ME ANSWERS...
INSTEAD... THE QUESTIONS... KEEP GETTING BIGGER...
THAT IS SURELY THE HUMAN CONDITION. MR. CONSTANTINE CAN HARDLY BE BLAMED.
UH, THIS IS ALEX LUTHOR. HE'S RUNNING THE SHOW SINCE THE MONITOR POPPED HIS CLOGS.
ALEX IS LESS THAN A YEAR OLD, BUT HE'S BIG FOR HIS AGE.
MR. CONSTANTINE HAS TOLD ME OF THE EFFECT THAT THE CRISIS WILL HAVE UPON THE SPIRITUAL DIMENSIONS SURROUNDING EARTH.
I UNDERSTAND YOU WILL BE DEALING WITH THAT.
I... WILL...?
THAT'S RIGHT.
THIS SORT OF PHYSICAL DESTRUCTION IS BOUND TO CAUSE TEMPORARY DISTURBANCES ON THE PSYCHIC PLANE.
OUR PROBLEM IS THAT THERE ARE PEOPLE WHO ANTICIPATED THE DISTURBANCE AND PLAN TO TAKE ADVANTAGE OF IT.
AH YES, THE SOUTH AMERICAN CULT THAT YOU MENTIONED...
CULTS...? ONE-YEAR-OLD MEN...? THIS IS... INSANITY! WHY... SHOULD PHYSICAL DESTRUCTION... AFFECT THE IMMATERIAL REALMS...?
EVERYTHING'S INTERCONNECTED, STUPID. LOOK, DON'T TAKE OUR WORD FOR IT...
YOU KNOW ALREADY HOW GOOD A TELEPORTATION SYSTEM ALEX HAS SET UP HERE.
GO BACK TO EARTH.
GO AND SEE FOR YOURSELF.

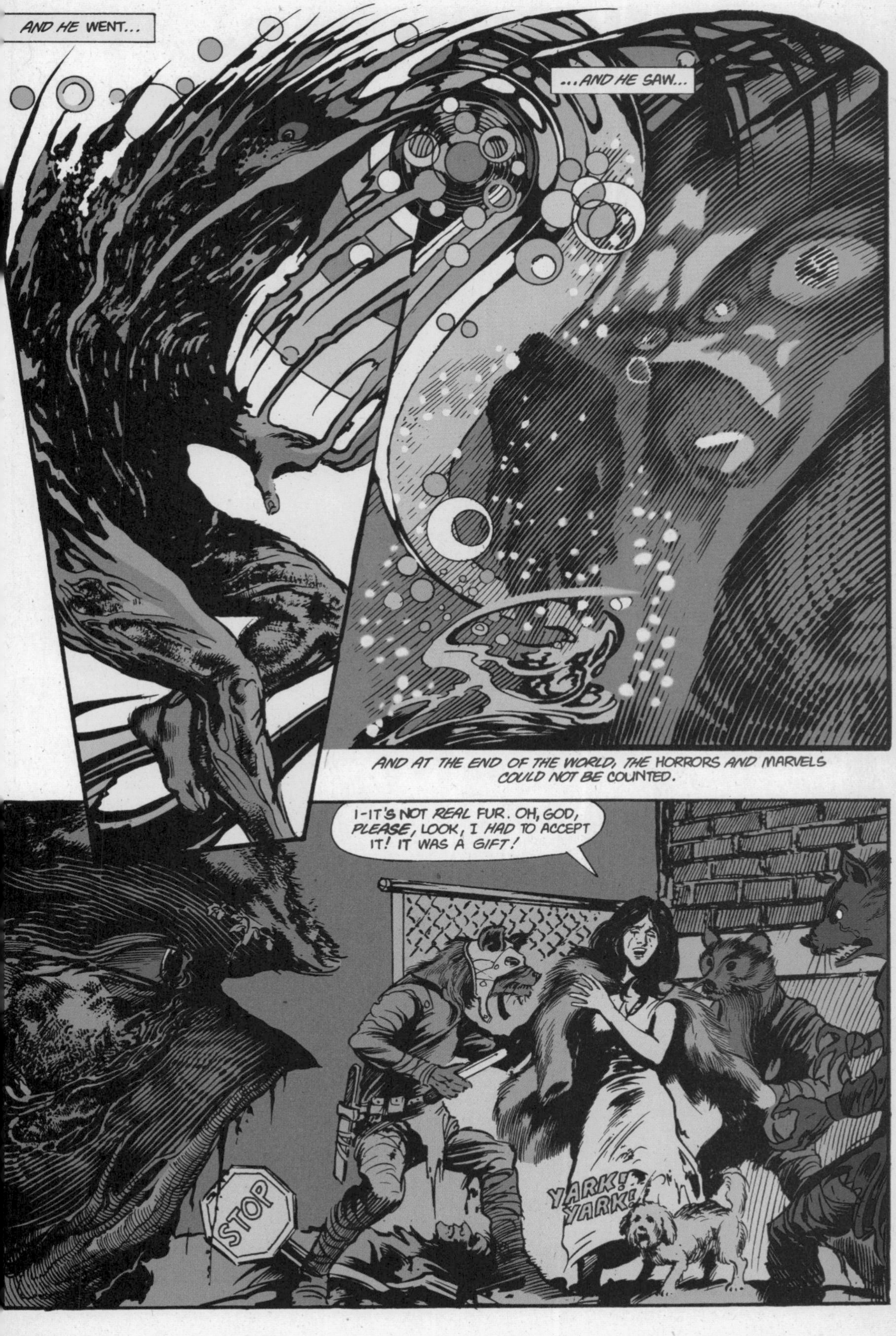
AND HE WENT...
...AND HE SAW...
AND AT THE END OF THE WORLD, THE HORRORS AND MARVELS COULD NOT BE COUNTED.
I-IT'S NOT REAL FUR. OH, GOD, PLEASE, LOOK, I HAD TO ACCEPT IT! IT WAS A GIFT!
STOP
YARK! YARK!

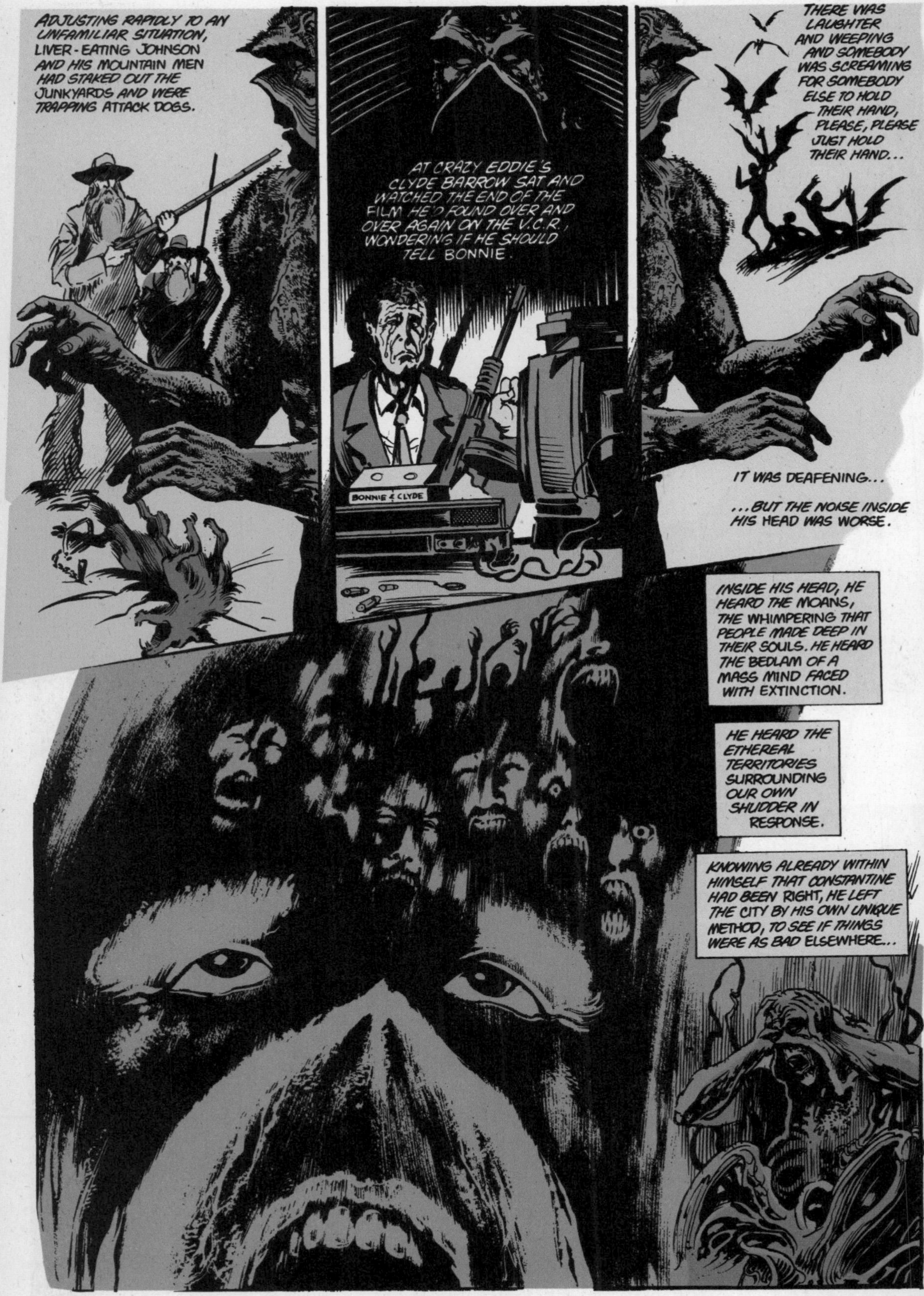
ADJUSTING RAPIDLY TO AN UNFAMILIAR SITUATION, LIVER-EATING JOHNSON AND HIS MOUNTAIN MEN HAD STAKED OUT THE JUNKYARDS AND WERE TRAPPING ATTACK DOGS.
AT CRAZY EDDIE'S CLYDE BARROW SAT AND WATCHED THE END OF THE FILM HE'D FOUND OVER AND OVER AGAIN ON THE V.C.R., WONDERING IF HE SHOULD TELL BONNIE.
BONNIE & CLYDE
THERE WAS LAUGHTER AND WEEPING AND SOMEBODY WAS SCREAMING FOR SOMEBODY ELSE TO HOLD THEIR HAND, PLEASE, PLEASE JUST HOLD THEIR HAND...
IT WAS DEAFENING...
...BUT THE NOISE INSIDE HIS HEAD WAS WORSE.
INSIDE HIS HEAD, HE HEARD THE MOANS, THE WHIMPERING THAT PEOPLE MADE DEEP IN THEIR SOULS. HE HEARD THE BEDLAM OF A MASS MIND FACED WITH EXTINCTION.
HE HEARD THE ETHEREAL TERRITORIES SURROUNDING OUR OWN SHUDDER IN RESPONSE.
KNOWING ALREADY WITHIN HIMSELF THAT CONSTANTINE HAD BEEN RIGHT, HE LEFT THE CITY BY HIS OWN UNIQUE METHOD, TO SEE IF THINGS WERE AS BAD ELSEWHERE...

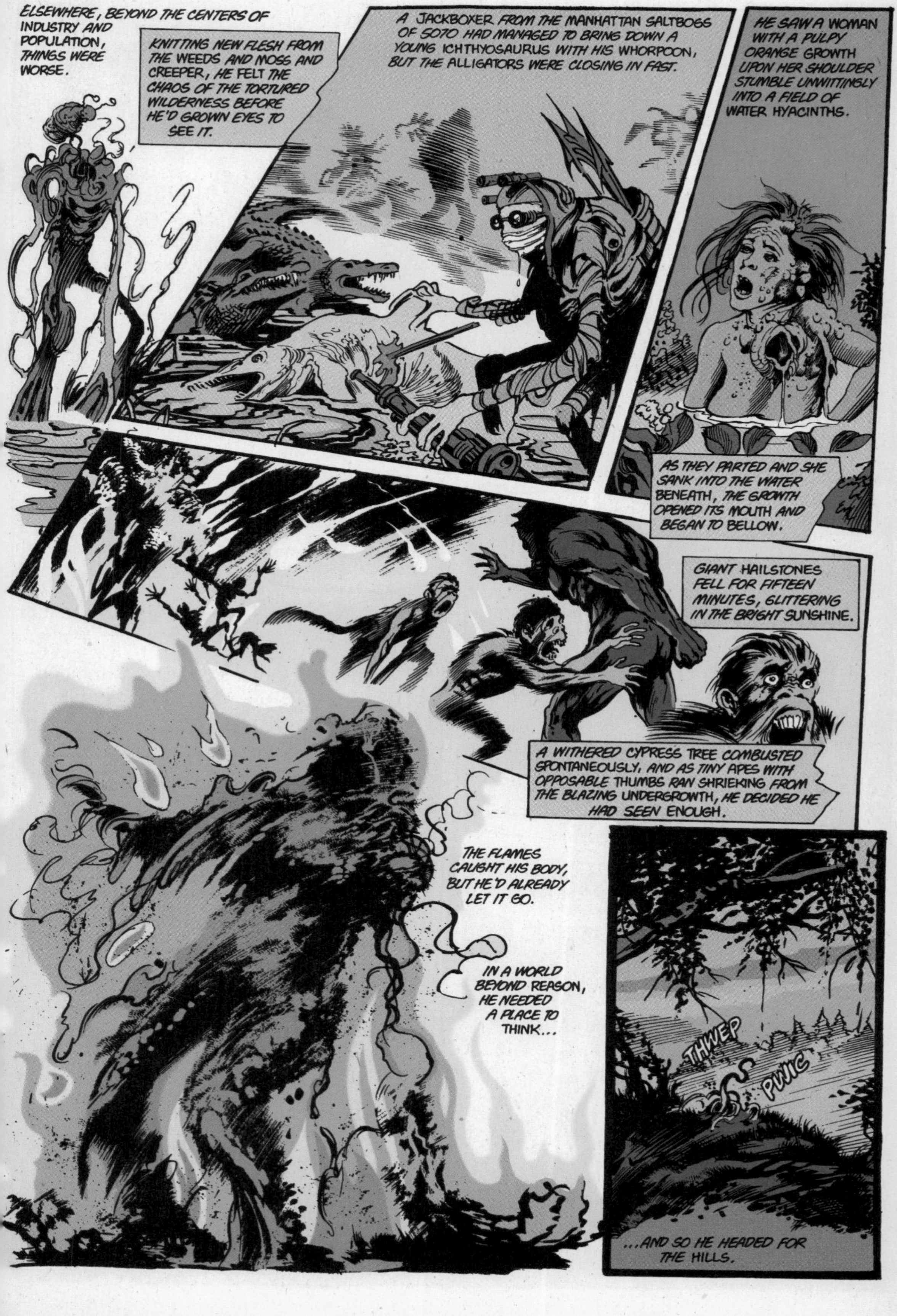
ELSEWHERE, BEYOND THE CENTERS OF INDUSTRY AND POPULATION, THINGS WERE WORSE.
KNITTING NEW FLESH FROM THE WEEDS AND MOSS AND CREEPER, HE FELT THE CHAOS OF THE TORTURED WILDERNESS BEFORE HE'D GROWN EYES TO SEE IT.
A JACKBOXER FROM THE MANHATTAN SALTBOGS OF SOTO HAD MANAGED TO BRING DOWN A YOUNG ICHTHYOSAURUS WITH HIS WHORPOON, BUT THE ALLIGATORS WERE CLOSING IN FAST.
HE SAW A WOMAN WITH A PULPY ORANGE GROWTH UPON HER SHOULDER STUMBLE UNWITTINGLY INTO A FIELD OF WATER HYACINTHS.
AS THEY PARTED AND SHE SANK INTO THE WATER BENEATH, THE GROWTH OPENED ITS MOUTH AND BEGAN TO BELLOW.
GIANT HAILSTONES FELL FOR FIFTEEN MINUTES, GLITTERING IN THE BRIGHT SUNSHINE.
A WITHERED CYPRESS TREE COMBUSTED SPONTANEOUSLY, AND AS TINY APES WITH OPPOSABLE THUMBS RAN SHRIEKING FROM THE BLAZING UNDERGROWTH, HE DECIDED HE HAD SEEN ENOUGH.
THE FLAMES CAUGHT HIS BODY, BUT HE'D ALREADY LET IT GO.
IN A WORLD BEYOND REASON, HE NEEDED A PLACE TO THINK...
THWEP
PWIIC
...AND SO HE HEADED FOR THE HILLS.

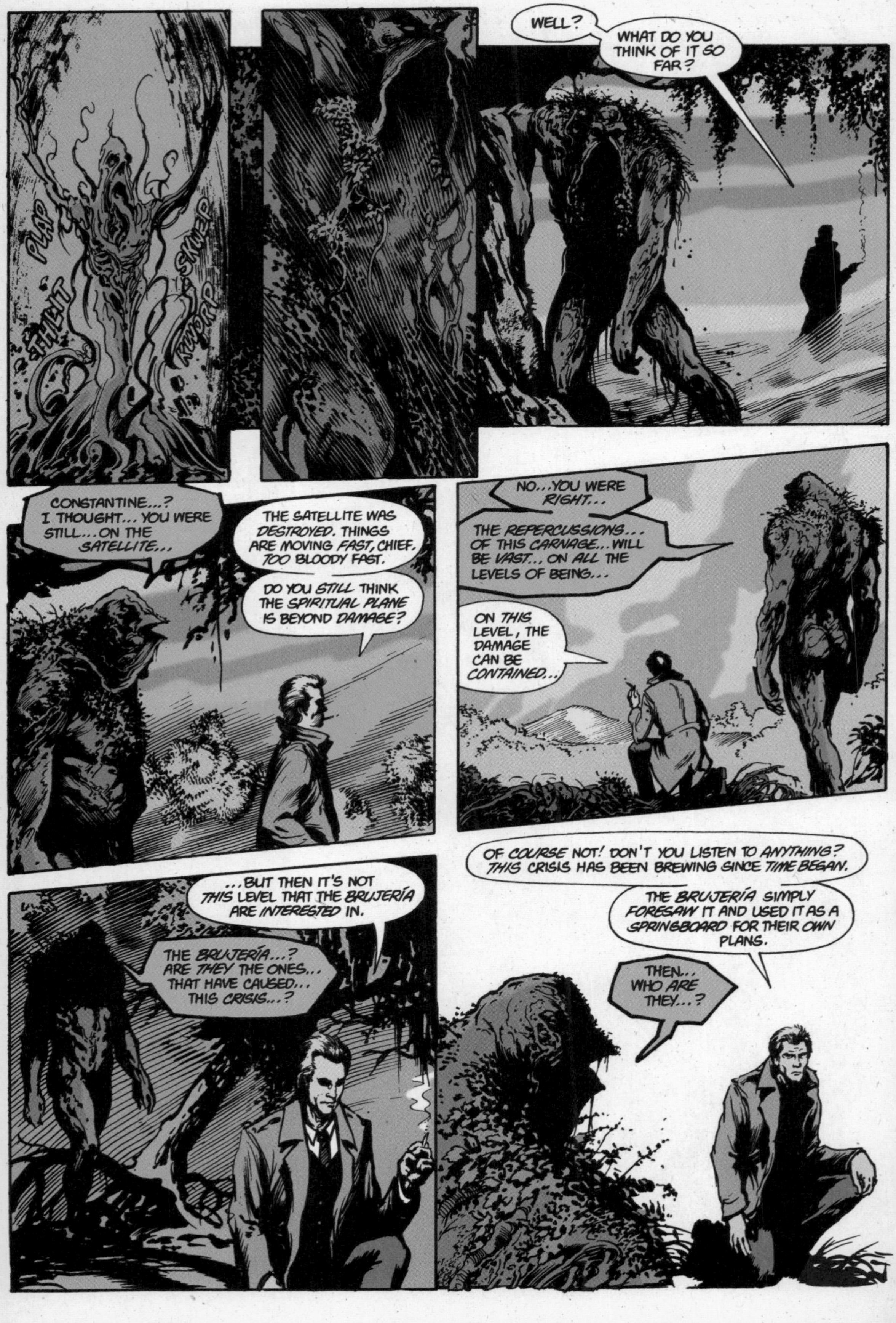

PLAP
THHT
SKWEP
KWORP
WELL?
WHAT DO YOU THINK OF IT SO FAR?
CONSTANTINE...? I THOUGHT... YOU WERE STILL...ON THE SATELLITE...
THE SATELLITE WAS DESTROYED. THINGS ARE MOVING FAST, CHIEF. TOO BLOODY FAST.
DO YOU STILL THINK THE SPIRITUAL PLANE IS BEYOND DAMAGE?
NO...YOU WERE RIGHT...
THE REPERCUSSIONS... OF THIS CARNAGE...WILL BE VAST..., ON ALL THE LEVELS OF BEING...
ON THIS LEVEL, THE DAMAGE CAN BE CONTAINED...
...BUT THEN IT'S NOT THIS LEVEL THAT THE BRUJERÍA ARE INTERESTED IN.
THE BRUJERÍA...? ARE THEY THE ONES... THAT HAVE CAUSED... THIS CRISIS...?
OF COURSE NOT! DON'T YOU LISTEN TO ANYTHING? THIS CRISIS HAS BEEN BREWING SINCE TIME BEGAN.
THE BRUJERÍA SIMPLY FORESAW IT AND USED IT AS A SPRINGBOARD FOR THEIR OWN PLANS.
THEN... WHO ARE THEY...?

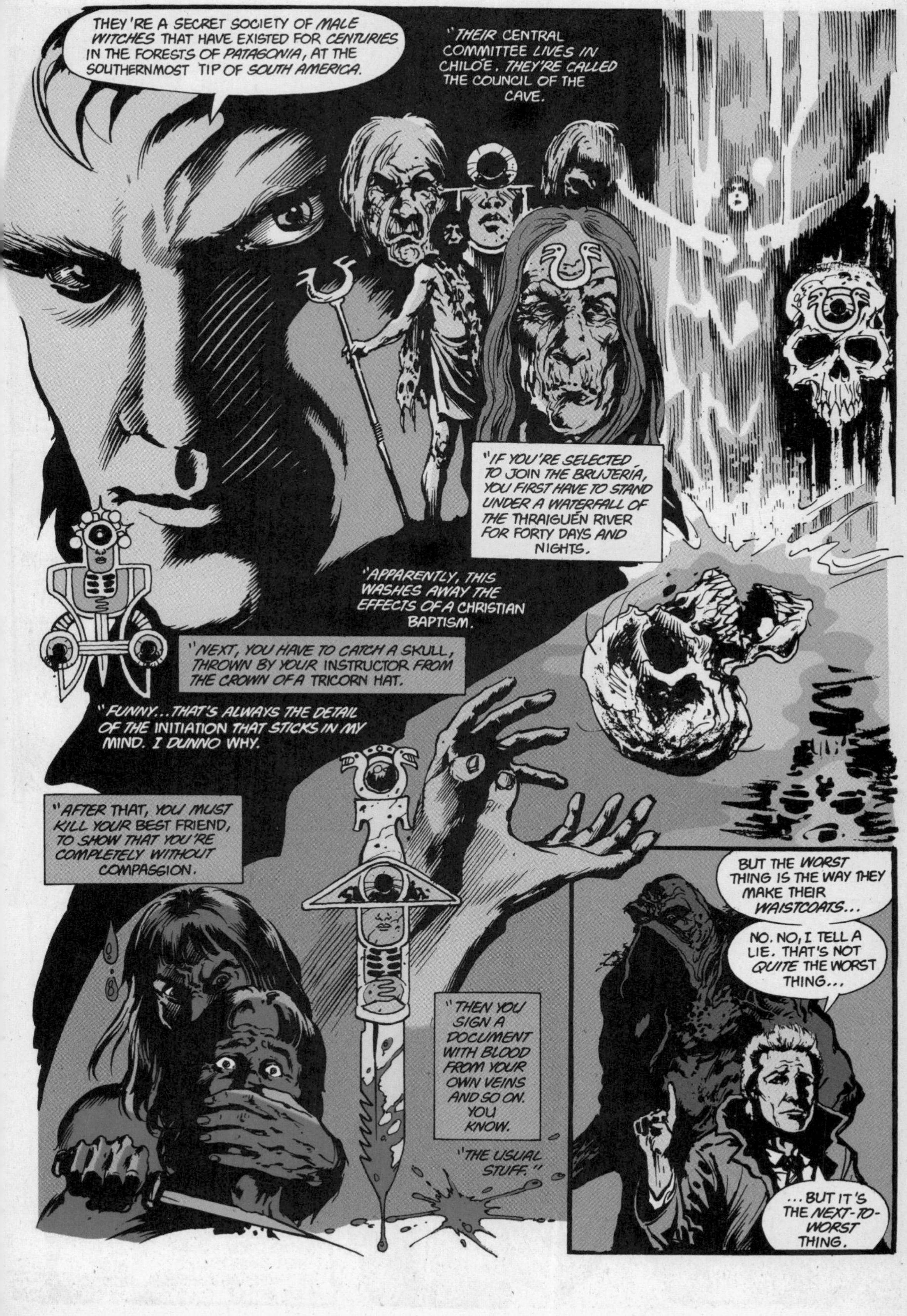
THEY'RE A SECRET SOCIETY OF MALE WITCHES THAT HAVE EXISTED FOR CENTURIES IN THE FORESTS OF PATAGONIA, AT THE SOUTHERNMOST TIP OF SOUTH AMERICA.
"THEIR CENTRAL COMMITTEE LIVES IN CHILOÉ. THEY'RE CALLED THE COUNCIL OF THE CAVE.
"IF YOU'RE SELECTED TO JOIN THE BRUJERÍA, YOU FIRST HAVE TO STAND UNDER A WATERFALL OF THE THRAIGUÉN RIVER FOR FORTY DAYS AND NIGHTS.
"APPARENTLY, THIS WASHES AWAY THE EFFECTS OF A CHRISTIAN BAPTISM.
"NEXT, YOU HAVE TO CATCH A SKULL, THROWN BY YOUR INSTRUCTOR FROM THE CROWN OF A TRICORN HAT.
"FUNNY...THAT'S ALWAYS THE DETAIL OF THE INITIATION THAT STICKS IN MY MIND. I DUNNO WHY.
"AFTER THAT, YOU MUST KILL YOUR BEST FRIEND, TO SHOW THAT YOU'RE COMPLETELY WITHOUT COMPASSION.
"THEN YOU SIGN A DOCUMENT WITH BLOOD FROM YOUR OWN VEINS AND SO ON. YOU KNOW.
"THE USUAL STUFF."
BUT THE WORST THING IS THE WAY THEY MAKE THEIR WAISTCOATS...
NO. NO, I TELL A LIE. THAT'S NOT QUITE THE WORST THING...
...BUT IT'S THE NEXT-TO-WORST THING.

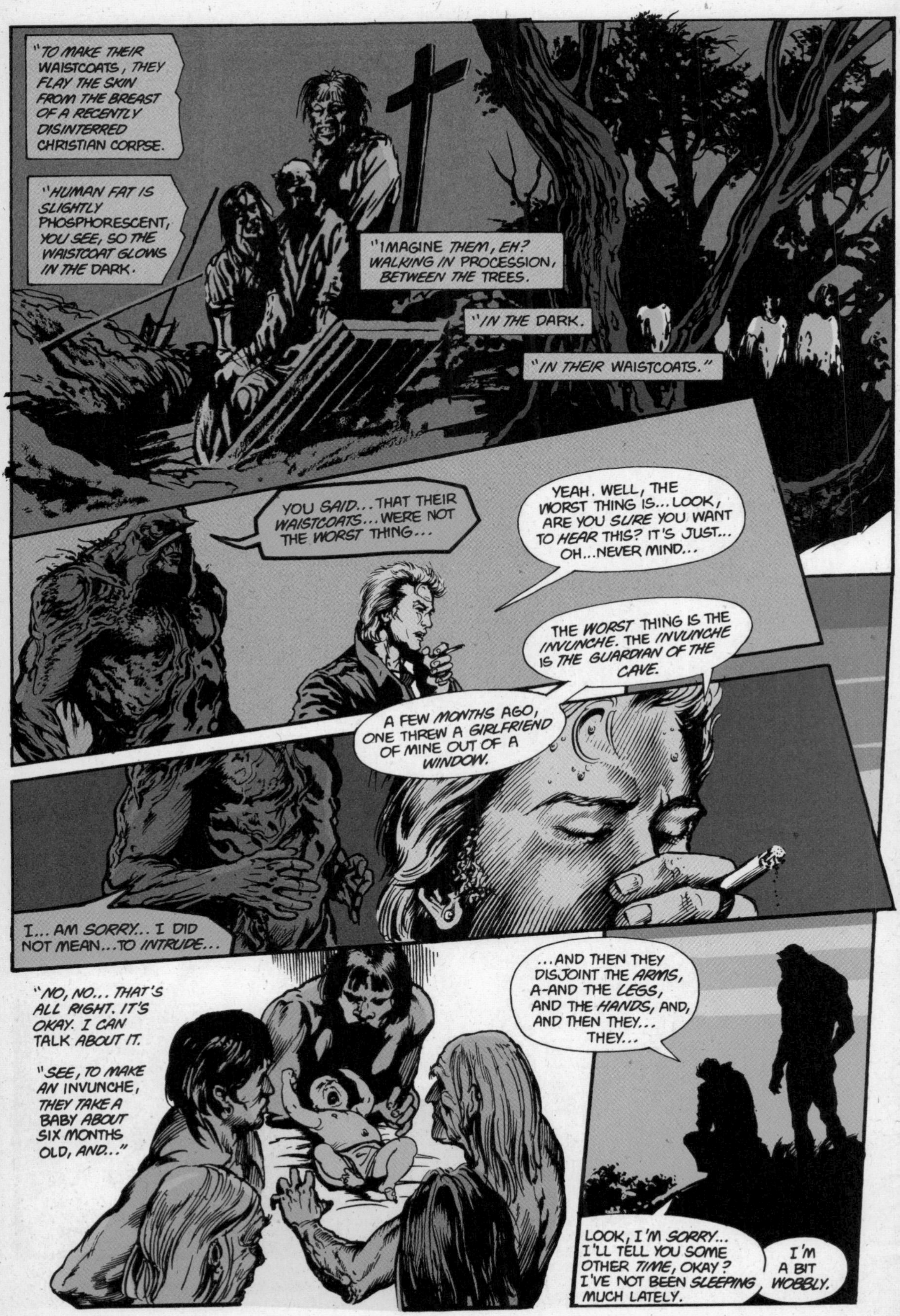
"TO MAKE THEIR WAISTCOATS, THEY FLAY THE SKIN FROM THE BREAST OF A RECENTLY DISINTERRED CHRISTIAN CORPSE.
"HUMAN FAT IS SLIGHTLY PHOSPHORESCENT, YOU SEE, SO THE WAISTCOAT GLOWS IN THE DARK.
"IMAGINE THEM, EH? WALKING IN PROCESSION, BETWEEN THE TREES.
"IN THE DARK.
"IN THEIR WAISTCOATS."
YOU SAID... THAT THEIR WAISTCOATS... WERE NOT THE WORST THING...
YEAH. WELL, THE WORST THING IS... LOOK, ARE YOU SURE YOU WANT TO HEAR THIS? IT'S JUST... OH... NEVER MIND...
THE WORST THING IS THE INVUNCHE. THE INVUNCHE IS THE GUARDIAN OF THE CAVE.
A FEW MONTHS AGO, ONE THREW A GIRLFRIEND OF MINE OUT OF A WINDOW.
I... AM SORRY... I DID NOT MEAN... TO INTRUDE...
"NO, NO... THAT'S ALL RIGHT. IT'S OKAY. I CAN TALK ABOUT IT.
"SEE, TO MAKE AN INVUNCHE, THEY TAKE A BABY ABOUT SIX MONTHS OLD, AND..."
...AND THEN THEY DISJOINT THE ARMS, A-AND THE LEGS, AND THE HANDS, AND, AND THEN THEY... THEY...
LOOK, I'M SORRY... I'LL TELL YOU SOME OTHER TIME, OKAY? I'VE NOT BEEN SLEEPING MUCH LATELY.
I'M A BIT WOBBLY.

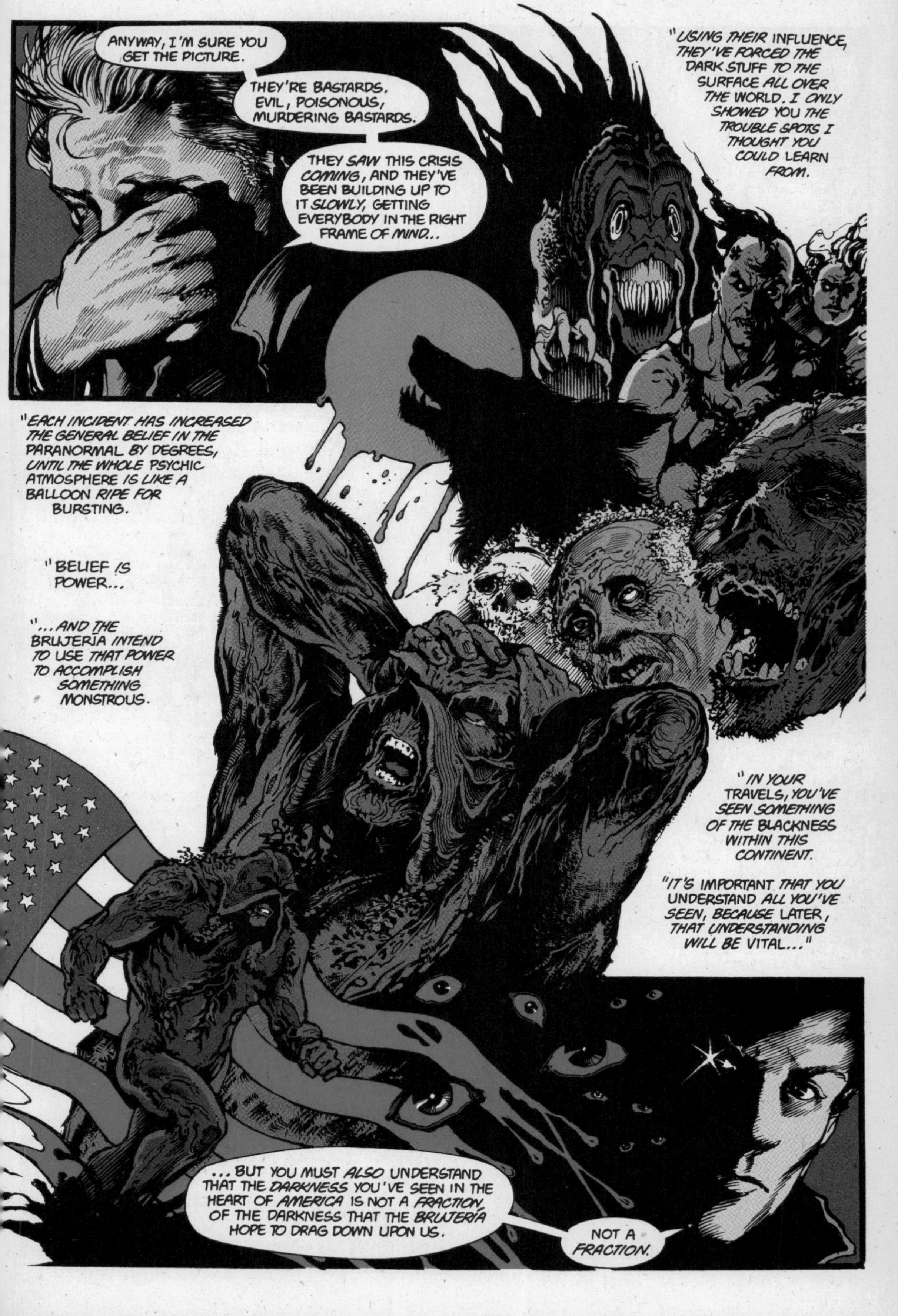
ANYWAY, I'M SURE YOU GET THE PICTURE.
THEY'RE BASTARDS. EVIL, POISONOUS, MURDERING BASTARDS.
THEY SAW THIS CRISIS COMING, AND THEY'VE BEEN BUILDING UP TO IT SLOWLY, GETTING EVERYBODY IN THE RIGHT FRAME OF MIND...
"USING THEIR INFLUENCE, THEY'VE FORCED THE DARK STUFF TO THE SURFACE ALL OVER THE WORLD. I ONLY SHOWED YOU THE TROUBLE SPOTS I THOUGHT YOU COULD LEARN FROM.
"EACH INCIDENT HAS INCREASED THE GENERAL BELIEF IN THE PARANORMAL BY DEGREES, UNTIL THE WHOLE PSYCHIC ATMOSPHERE IS LIKE A BALLOON RIPE FOR BURSTING.
"BELIEF IS POWER...
"...AND THE BRUJERIA INTEND TO USE THAT POWER TO ACCOMPLISH SOMETHING MONSTROUS.
"IN YOUR TRAVELS, YOU'VE SEEN SOMETHING OF THE BLACKNESS WITHIN THIS CONTINENT.
"IT'S IMPORTANT THAT YOU UNDERSTAND ALL YOU'VE SEEN, BECAUSE LATER, THAT UNDERSTANDING WILL BE VITAL..."
...BUT YOU MUST ALSO UNDERSTAND THAT THE DARKNESS YOU'VE SEEN IN THE HEART OF AMERICA IS NOT A FRACTION OF THE DARKNESS THAT THE BRUJERIA HOPE TO DRAG DOWN UPON US.
NOT A FRACTION.

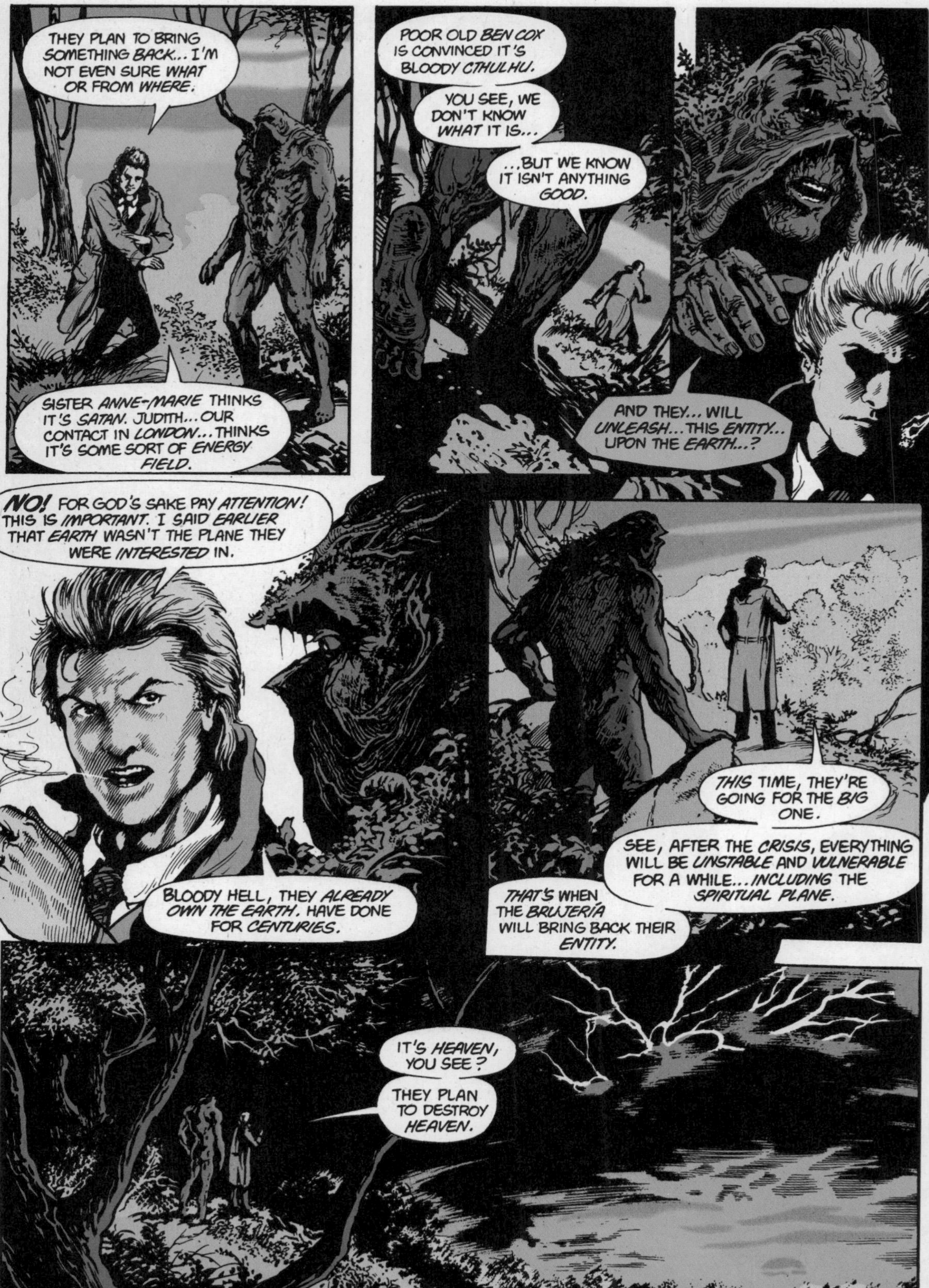
THEY PLAN TO BRING SOMETHING BACK... I'M NOT EVEN SURE WHAT OR FROM WHERE.
SISTER ANNE-MARIE THINKS IT'S SATAN. JUDITH... OUR CONTACT IN LONDON... THINKS IT'S SOME SORT OF ENERGY FIELD.
POOR OLD BEN COX IS CONVINCED IT'S BLOODY CTHULHU.
YOU SEE, WE DON'T KNOW WHAT IT IS...
...BUT WE KNOW IT ISN'T ANYTHING GOOD.
AND THEY... WILL UNLEASH... THIS ENTITY... UPON THE EARTH...?
NO! FOR GOD'S SAKE PAY ATTENTION! THIS IS IMPORTANT. I SAID EARLIER THAT EARTH WASN'T THE PLANE THEY WERE INTERESTED IN.
BLOODY HELL, THEY ALREADY OWN THE EARTH. HAVE DONE FOR CENTURIES.
THIS TIME, THEY'RE GOING FOR THE BIG ONE.
SEE, AFTER THE CRISIS, EVERYTHING WILL BE UNSTABLE AND VULNERABLE FOR A WHILE... INCLUDING THE SPIRITUAL PLANE.
THAT'S WHEN THE BRUJERÍA WILL BRING BACK THEIR ENTITY.
IT'S HEAVEN, YOU SEE?
THEY PLAN TO DESTROY HEAVEN.

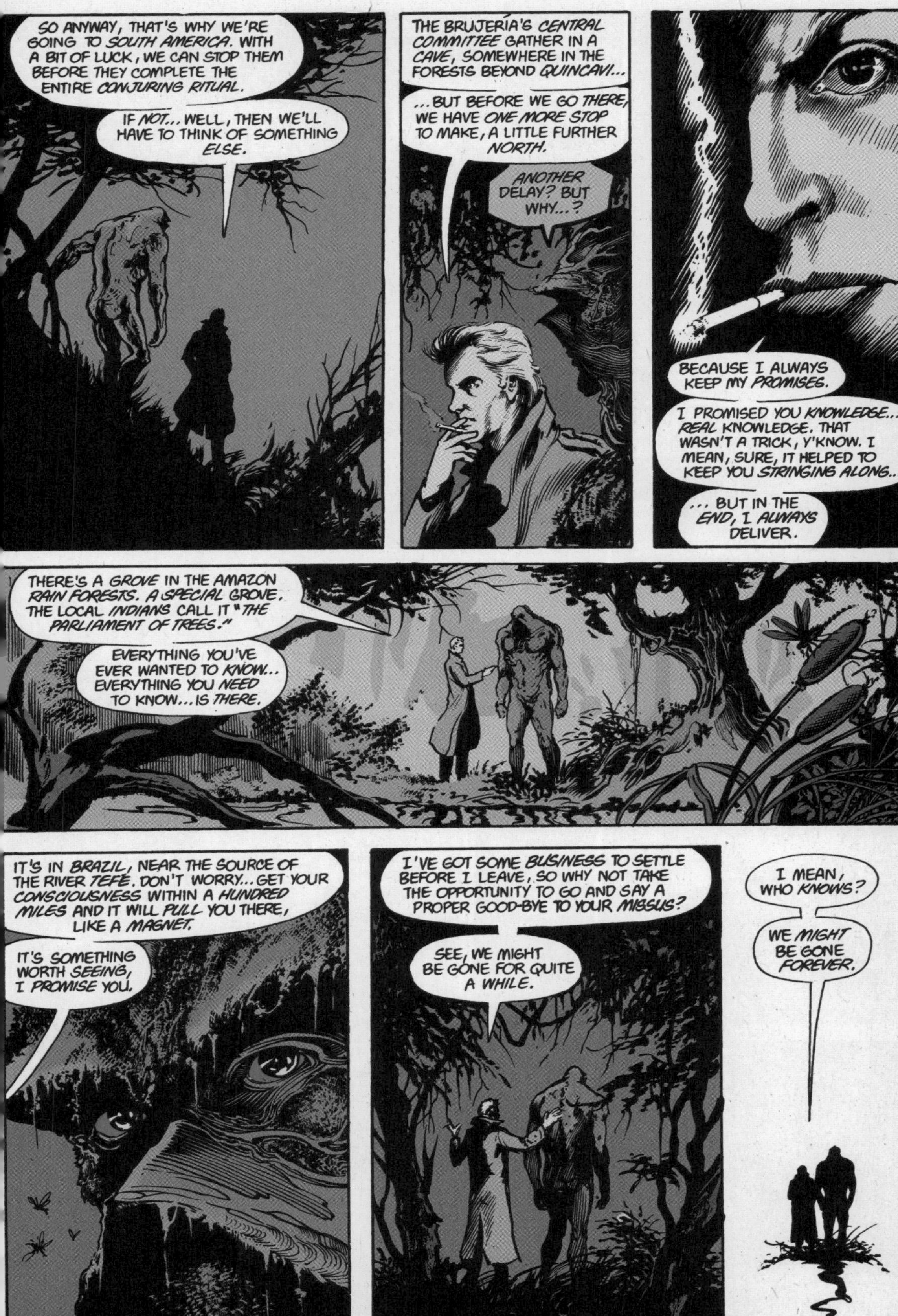
SO ANYWAY, THAT'S WHY WE'RE GOING TO *SOUTH AMERICA*. WITH A BIT OF LUCK, WE CAN STOP THEM BEFORE THEY COMPLETE THE ENTIRE *CONJURING RITUAL*.
IF *NOT*... WELL, THEN WE'LL HAVE TO THINK OF SOMETHING *ELSE*.
THE BRUJERIA'S *CENTRAL COMMITTEE* GATHER IN A *CAVE*, SOMEWHERE IN THE FORESTS BEYOND *QUINCAVI*...
...BUT BEFORE WE GO *THERE*, WE HAVE *ONE MORE STOP* TO MAKE, A LITTLE FURTHER *NORTH*.
ANOTHER DELAY? BUT WHY...?
BECAUSE I ALWAYS KEEP MY *PROMISES*.
I PROMISED YOU *KNOWLEDGE*... *REAL* KNOWLEDGE. THAT WASN'T A TRICK, Y'KNOW. I MEAN, SURE, IT HELPED TO KEEP YOU *STRINGING ALONG*...
... BUT IN THE *END*, I *ALWAYS* DELIVER.
THERE'S A *GROVE* IN THE AMAZON *RAIN FORESTS*. *A SPECIAL GROVE*. THE LOCAL *INDIANS* CALL IT "*THE PARLIAMENT OF TREES*."
EVERYTHING YOU'VE EVER WANTED TO *KNOW*... EVERYTHING YOU *NEED* TO KNOW... IS *THERE*.
IT'S IN *BRAZIL*, NEAR THE SOURCE OF THE RIVER *TEFÉ*. DON'T WORRY... GET YOUR *CONSCIOUSNESS* WITHIN A *HUNDRED MILES* AND IT WILL *PULL* YOU THERE, LIKE A *MAGNET*.
IT'S SOMETHING WORTH *SEEING*, I *PROMISE* YOU.
I'VE GOT SOME *BUSINESS* TO SETTLE BEFORE I LEAVE, SO WHY NOT TAKE THE OPPORTUNITY TO GO AND SAY A PROPER GOOD-BYE TO YOUR *MISSUS*?
SEE, WE MIGHT BE GONE FOR QUITE A WHILE.
I MEAN, WHO *KNOWS*?
WE *MIGHT* BE GONE *FOREVER*.

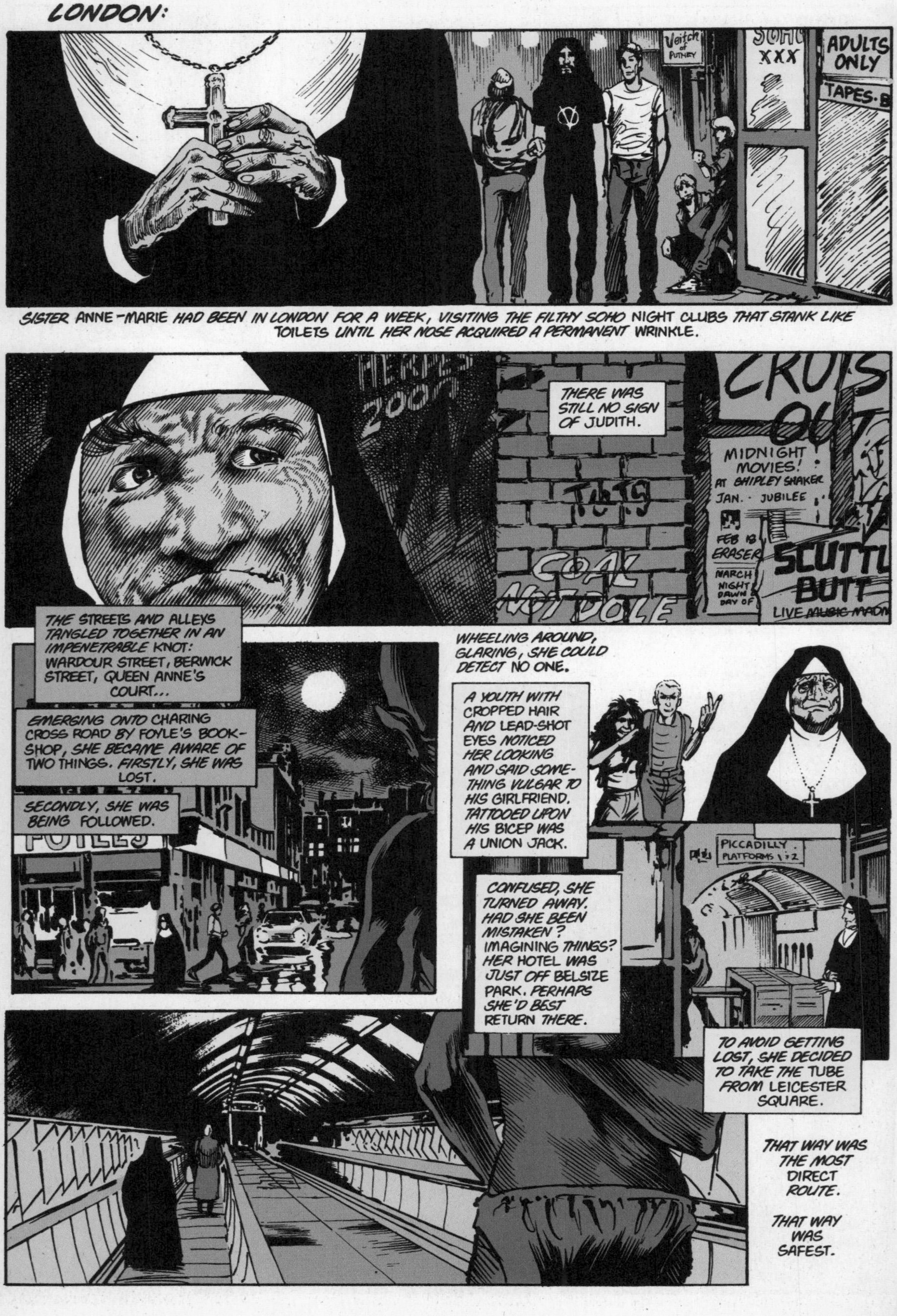
LONDON:
Veitch of PUTNEY
SOHO XXX
ADULTS ONLY
TAPES
SISTER ANNE-MARIE HAD BEEN IN LONDON FOR A WEEK, VISITING THE FILTHY SOHO NIGHT CLUBS THAT STANK LIKE TOILETS UNTIL HER NOSE ACQUIRED A PERMANENT WRINKLE.
THERE WAS STILL NO SIGN OF JUDITH.
MIDNIGHT MOVIES!
SCUTTLE BUTT
COAL NOT DOLE
THE STREETS AND ALLEYS TANGLED TOGETHER IN AN IMPENETRABLE KNOT: WARDOUR STREET, BERWICK STREET, QUEEN ANNE'S COURT...
EMERGING ONTO CHARING CROSS ROAD BY FOYLE'S BOOKSHOP, SHE BECAME AWARE OF TWO THINGS. FIRSTLY, SHE WAS LOST.
SECONDLY, SHE WAS BEING FOLLOWED.
WHEELING AROUND, GLARING, SHE COULD DETECT NO ONE.
A YOUTH WITH CROPPED HAIR AND LEAD-SHOT EYES NOTICED HER LOOKING AND SAID SOMETHING VULGAR TO HIS GIRLFRIEND. TATTOOED UPON HIS BICEP WAS A UNION JACK.
CONFUSED, SHE TURNED AWAY. HAD SHE BEEN MISTAKEN? IMAGINING THINGS? HER HOTEL WAS JUST OFF BELSIZE PARK. PERHAPS SHE'D BEST RETURN THERE.
PICCADILLY PLATFORMS 1 2
TO AVOID GETTING LOST, SHE DECIDED TO TAKE THE TUBE FROM LEICESTER SQUARE.
THAT WAY WAS THE MOST DIRECT ROUTE.
THAT WAY WAS SAFEST.

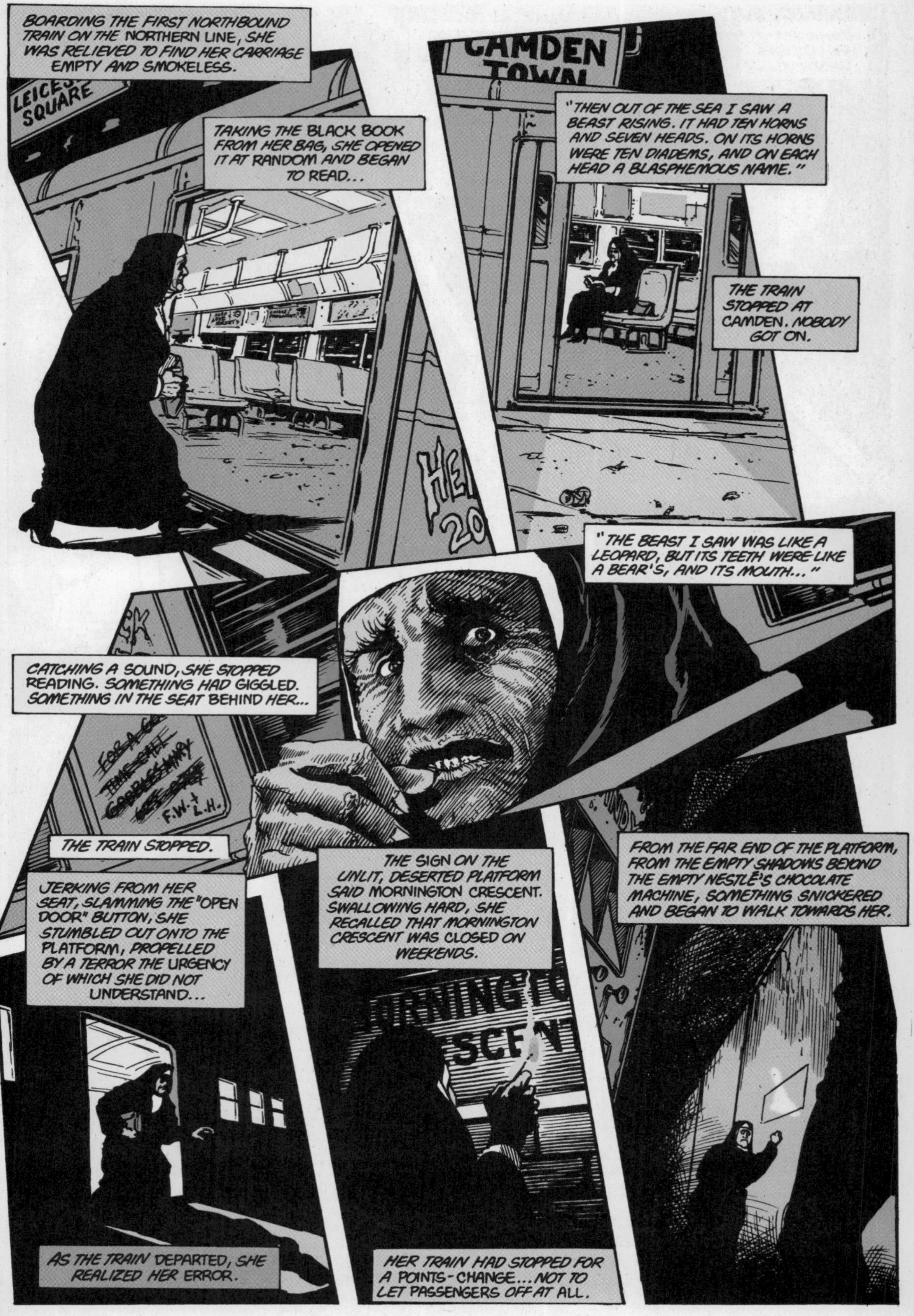
BOARDING THE FIRST NORTHBOUND TRAIN ON THE NORTHERN LINE, SHE WAS RELIEVED TO FIND HER CARRIAGE EMPTY AND SMOKELESS.
SQUARE
TAKING THE BLACK BOOK FROM HER BAG, SHE OPENED IT AT RANDOM AND BEGAN TO READ...
CAMDEN
"THEN OUT OF THE SEA I SAW A BEAST RISING. IT HAD TEN HORNS AND SEVEN HEADS. ON ITS HORNS WERE TEN DIADEMS, AND ON EACH HEAD A BLASPHEMOUS NAME."
THE TRAIN STOPPED AT CAMDEN. NOBODY GOT ON.
"THE BEAST I SAW WAS LIKE A LEOPARD, BUT ITS TEETH WERE LIKE A BEAR'S, AND ITS MOUTH..."
CATCHING A SOUND, SHE STOPPED READING. SOMETHING HAD GIGGLED. SOMETHING IN THE SEAT BEHIND HER...
F.W. + L.H.
THE TRAIN STOPPED.
JERKING FROM HER SEAT, SLAMMING THE "OPEN DOOR" BUTTON, SHE STUMBLED OUT ONTO THE PLATFORM, PROPELLED BY A TERROR THE URGENCY OF WHICH SHE DID NOT UNDERSTAND...
THE SIGN ON THE UNLIT, DESERTED PLATFORM SAID MORNINGTON CRESCENT. SWALLOWING HARD, SHE RECALLED THAT MORNINGTON CRESCENT WAS CLOSED ON WEEKENDS.
FROM THE FAR END OF THE PLATFORM, FROM THE EMPTY SHADOWS BEYOND THE EMPTY NESTLÉ'S CHOCOLATE MACHINE, SOMETHING SNICKERED AND BEGAN TO WALK TOWARDS HER.
AS THE TRAIN DEPARTED, SHE REALIZED HER ERROR.
HER TRAIN HAD STOPPED FOR A POINTS-CHANGE... NOT TO LET PASSENGERS OFF AT ALL.

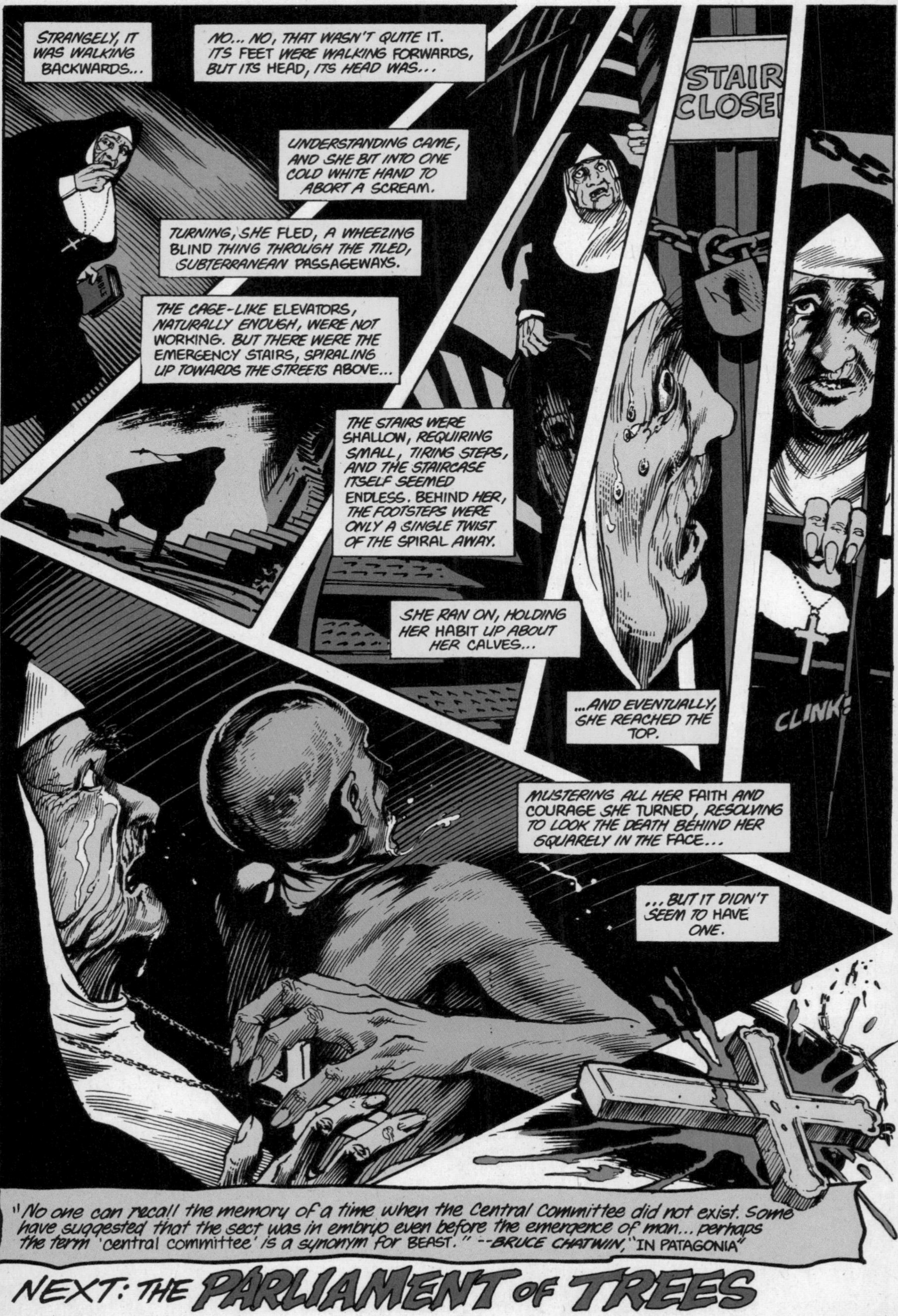
STRANGELY, IT WAS WALKING BACKWARDS...
NO... NO, THAT WASN'T QUITE IT. ITS FEET WERE WALKING FORWARDS, BUT ITS HEAD, ITS HEAD WAS...
STAIR CLOSE
UNDERSTANDING CAME, AND SHE BIT INTO ONE COLD WHITE HAND TO ABORT A SCREAM.
TURNING, SHE FLED, A WHEEZING BLIND THING THROUGH THE TILED, SUBTERRANEAN PASSAGEWAYS.
THE CAGE-LIKE ELEVATORS, NATURALLY ENOUGH, WERE NOT WORKING. BUT THERE WERE THE EMERGENCY STAIRS, SPIRALING UP TOWARDS THE STREETS ABOVE...
THE STAIRS WERE SHALLOW, REQUIRING SMALL, TIRING STEPS, AND THE STAIRCASE ITSELF SEEMED ENDLESS. BEHIND HER, THE FOOTSTEPS WERE ONLY A SINGLE TWIST OF THE SPIRAL AWAY.
SHE RAN ON, HOLDING HER HABIT UP ABOUT HER CALVES...
...AND EVENTUALLY, SHE REACHED THE TOP.
CLINK!
MUSTERING ALL HER FAITH AND COURAGE SHE TURNED, RESOLVING TO LOOK THE DEATH BEHIND HER SQUARELY IN THE FACE...
...BUT IT DIDN'T SEEM TO HAVE ONE.
"No one can recall the memory of a time when the Central Committee did not exist. Some have suggested that the sect was in embryo even before the emergence of man... perhaps the term 'central committee' is a synonym for BEAST." --BRUCE CHATWIN, "IN PATAGONIA"
NEXT: THE PARLIAMENT OF TREES

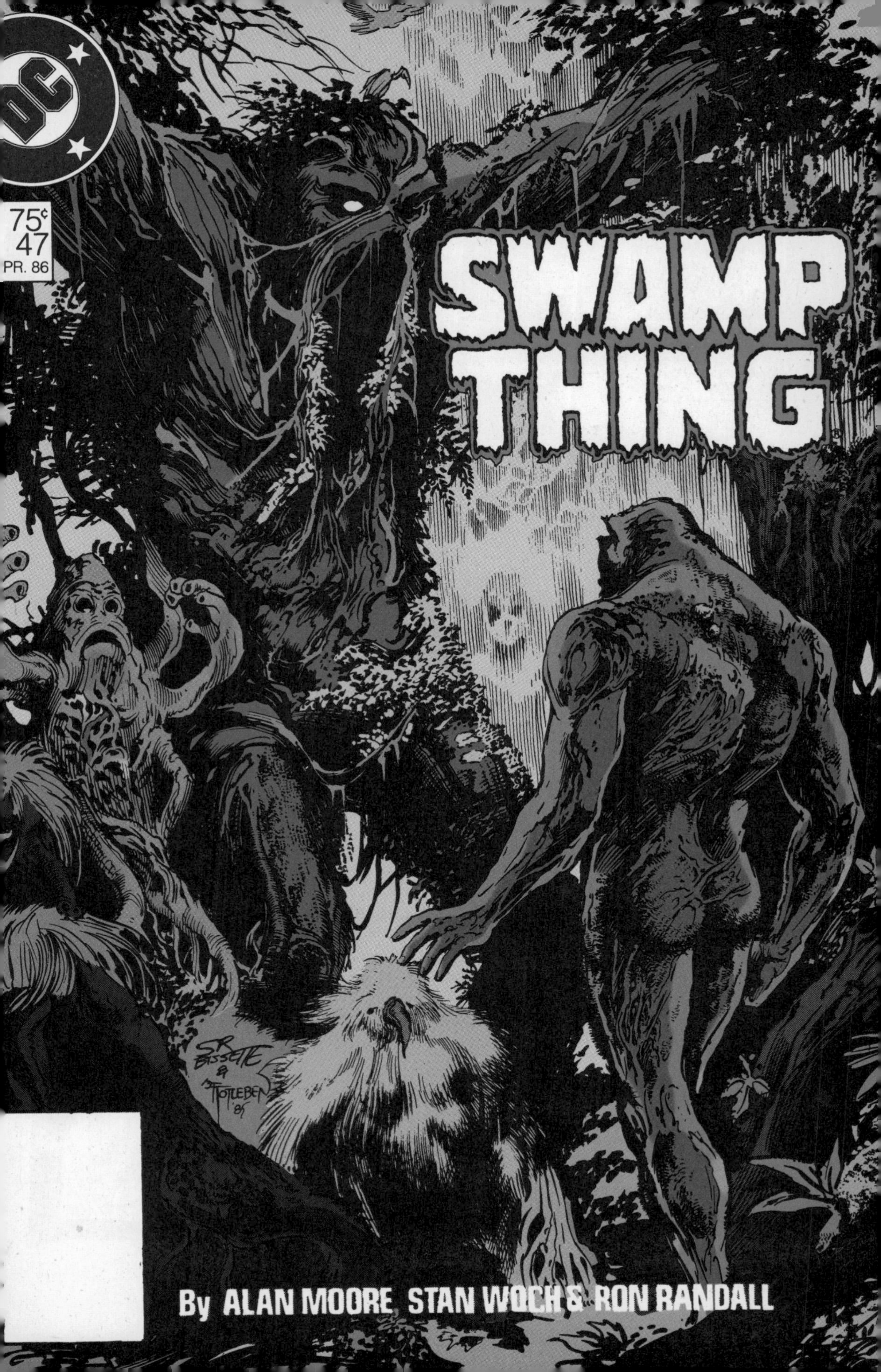
75¢
47
PR. 86
SWAMP THING
By ALAN MOORE STAN WOCH & RON RANDALL

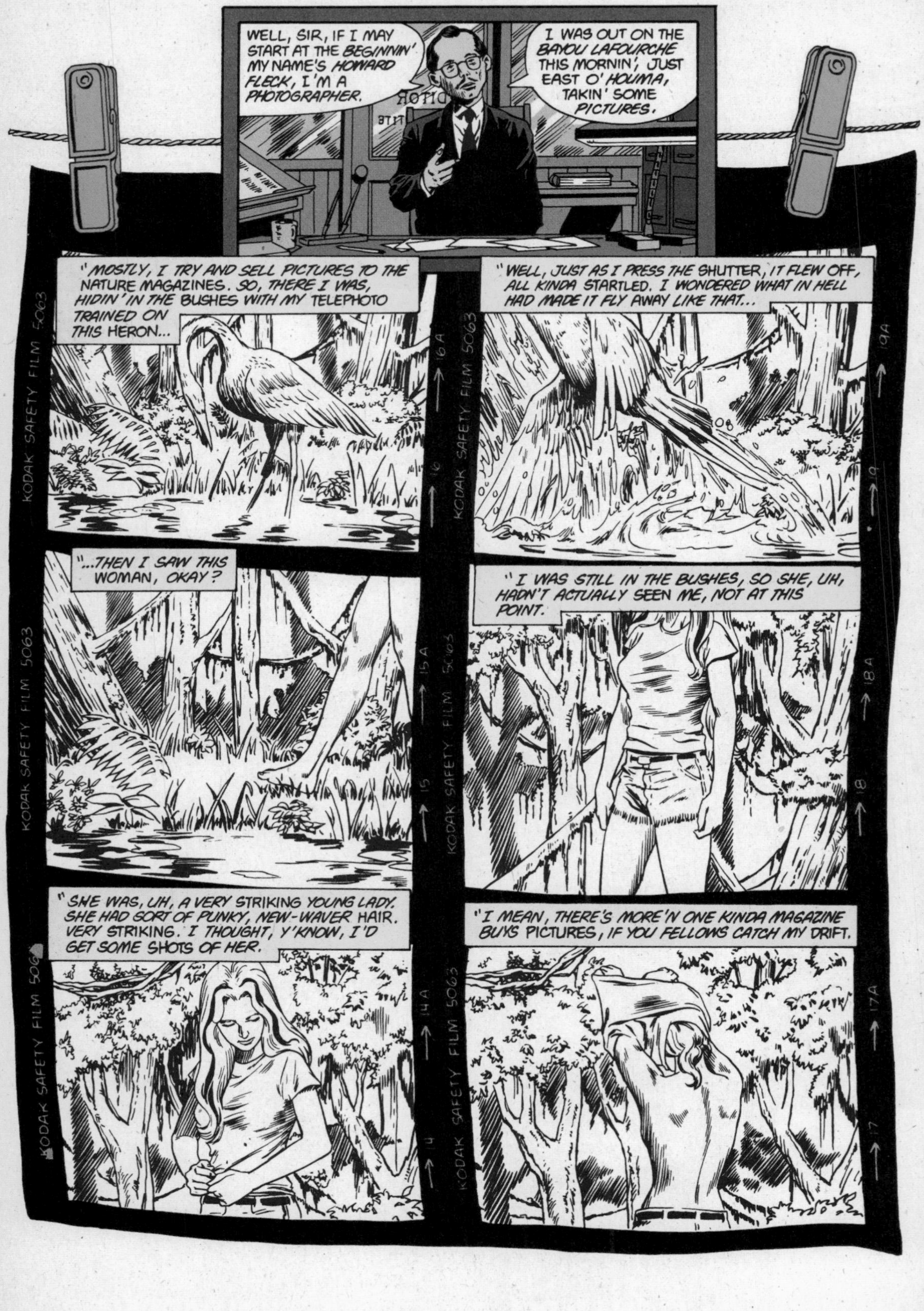

WELL, SIR, IF I MAY START AT THE BEGINNIN'. MY NAME'S HOWARD FLECK, I'M A PHOTOGRAPHER.
I WAS OUT ON THE BAYOU LAFOURCHE THIS MORNIN', JUST EAST O' HOUMA, TAKIN' SOME PICTURES.
"MOSTLY, I TRY AND SELL PICTURES TO THE NATURE MAGAZINES. SO, THERE I WAS, HIDIN' IN THE BUSHES WITH MY TELEPHOTO TRAINED ON THIS HERON...
KODAK SAFETY FILM 5063
16
16A
"WELL, JUST AS I PRESS THE SHUTTER, IT FLEW OFF, ALL KINDA STARTLED. I WONDERED WHAT IN HELL HAD MADE IT FLY AWAY LIKE THAT...
KODAK SAFETY FILM 5063
19
19A
"...THEN I SAW THIS WOMAN, OKAY?
KODAK SAFETY FILM 5063
15
15A
"I WAS STILL IN THE BUSHES, SO SHE, UH, HADN'T ACTUALLY SEEN ME, NOT AT THIS POINT.
KODAK SAFETY FILM 5063
18
18A
"SHE WAS, UH, A VERY STRIKING YOUNG LADY. SHE HAD SORT OF PUNKY, NEW-WAVER HAIR. VERY STRIKING. I THOUGHT, Y'KNOW, I'D GET SOME SHOTS OF HER.
KODAK SAFETY FILM 506
14
14A
"I MEAN, THERE'S MORE'N ONE KINDA MAGAZINE BUYS PICTURES, IF YOU FELLOWS CATCH MY DRIFT.
KODAK SAFETY FILM 5063
17
17A

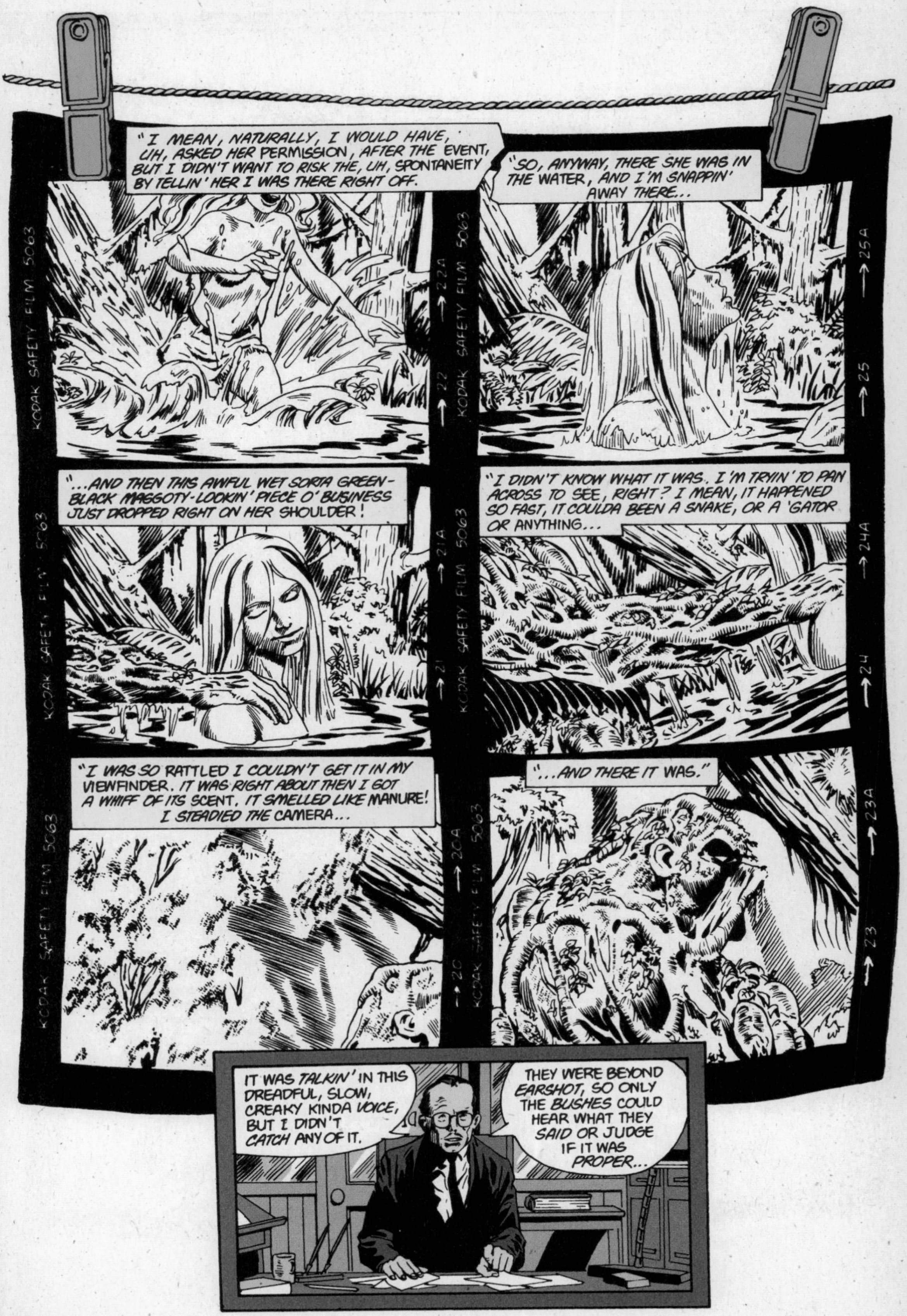
"I MEAN, NATURALLY, I WOULD HAVE, UH, ASKED HER PERMISSION, AFTER THE EVENT, BUT I DIDN'T WANT TO RISK THE, UH, SPONTANEITY BY TELLIN' HER I WAS THERE RIGHT OFF.
"SO, ANYWAY, THERE SHE WAS IN THE WATER, AND I'M SNAPPIN' AWAY THERE...
"...AND THEN THIS AWFUL WET SORTA GREEN-BLACK MAGGOTY-LOOKIN' PIECE O' BUSINESS JUST DROPPED RIGHT ON HER SHOULDER!
"I DIDN'T KNOW WHAT IT WAS. I'M TRYIN' TO PAN ACROSS TO SEE, RIGHT? I MEAN, IT HAPPENED SO FAST, IT COULDA BEEN A SNAKE, OR A 'GATOR OR ANYTHING...
"I WAS SO RATTLED I COULDN'T GET IT IN MY VIEWFINDER. IT WAS RIGHT ABOUT THEN I GOT A WHIFF OF ITS SCENT. IT SMELLED LIKE MANURE! I STEADIED THE CAMERA...
"...AND THERE IT WAS."
IT WAS TALKIN' IN THIS DREADFUL, SLOW, CREAKY KINDA VOICE, BUT I DIDN'T CATCH ANY OF IT.
THEY WERE BEYOND EARSHOT, SO ONLY THE BUSHES COULD HEAR WHAT THEY SAID OR JUDGE IF IT WAS PROPER...

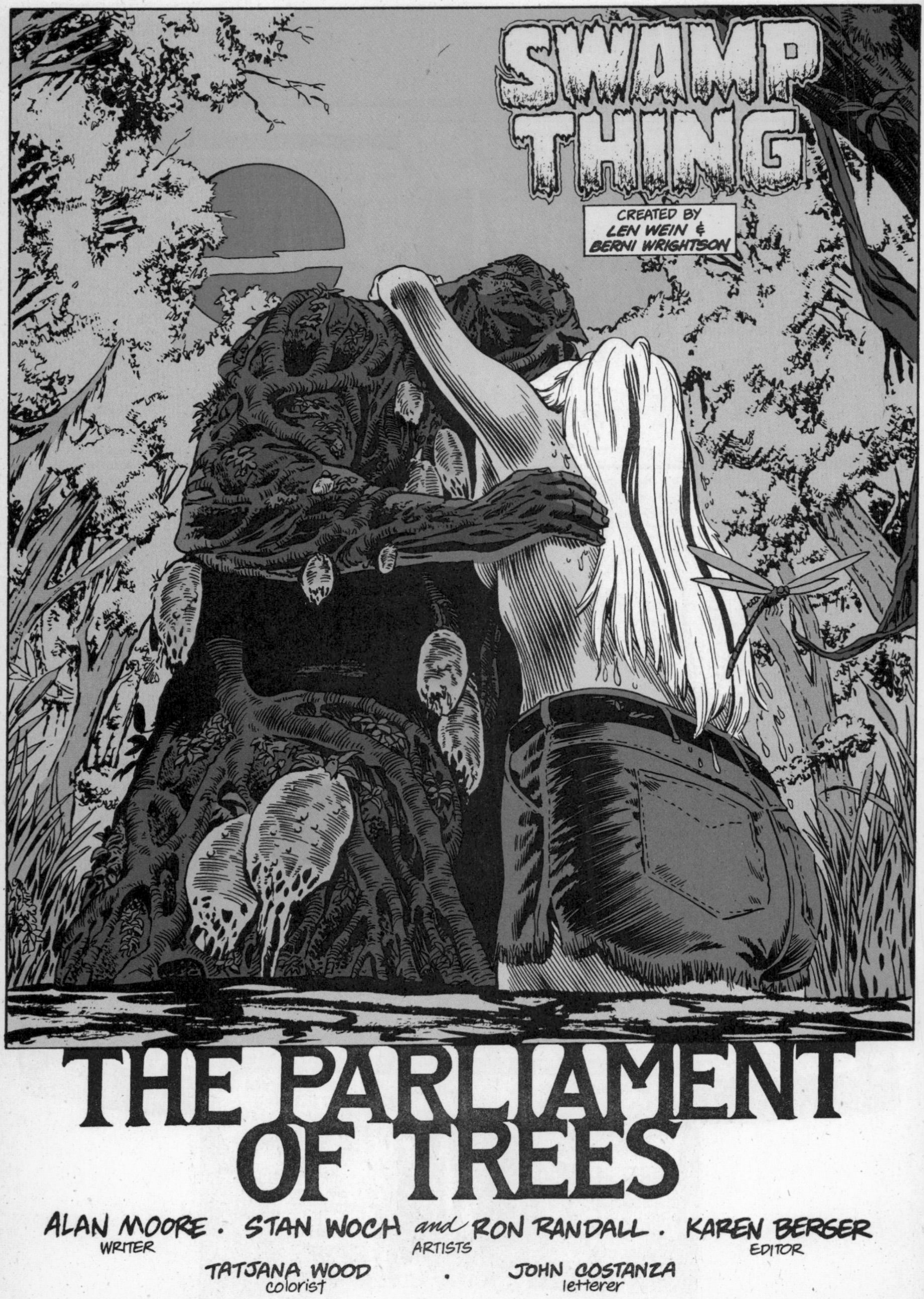
SWAMP THING
CREATED BY LEN WEIN & BERNI WRIGHTSON

THE PARLIAMENT OF TREES

ALAN MOORE, WRITER · STAN WOCH and RON RANDALL, ARTISTS · KAREN BERGER, EDITOR

TATJANA WOOD, colorist · JOHN COSTANZA, letterer

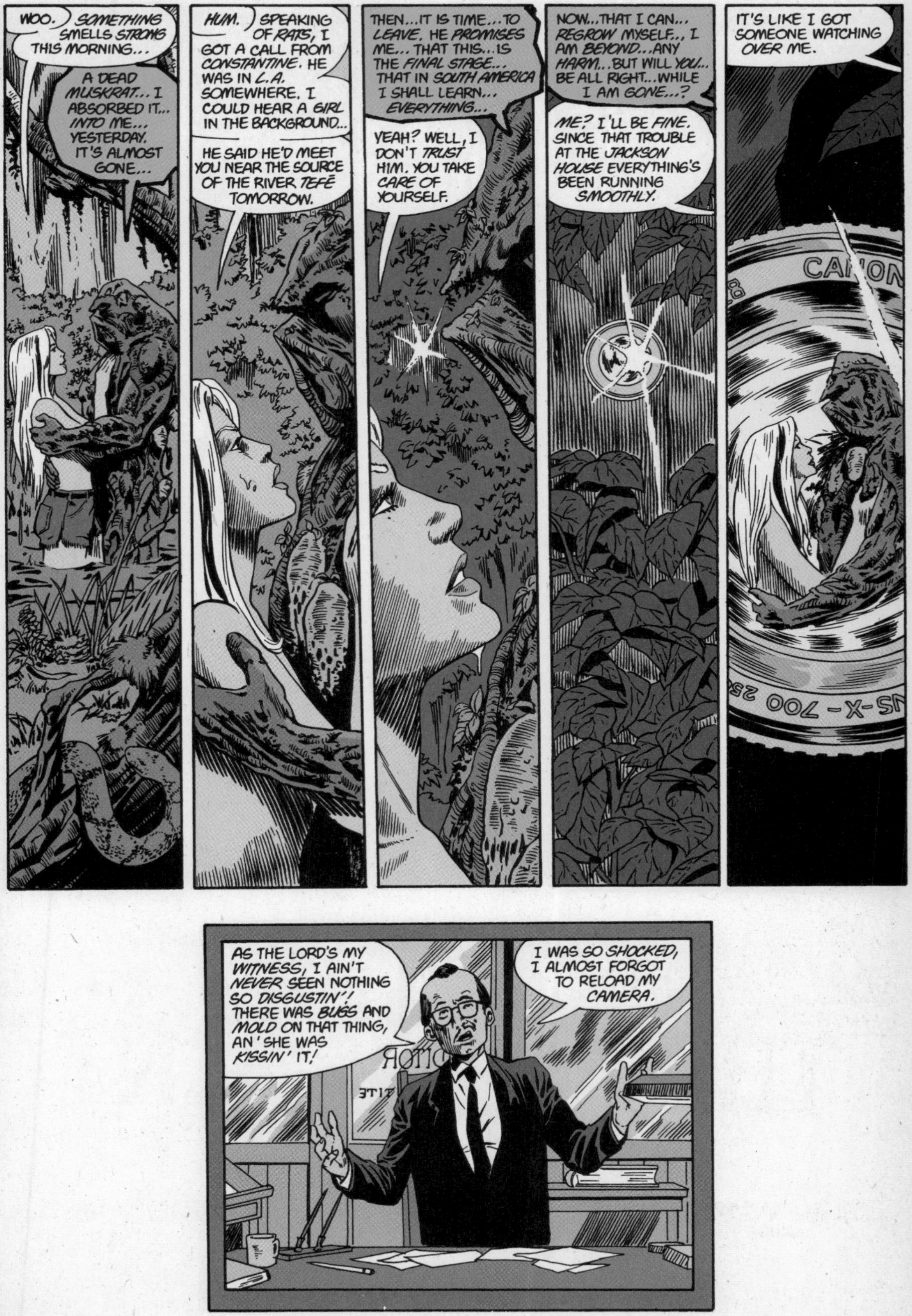
WOO. SOMETHING SMELLS STRONG THIS MORNING...
A DEAD MUSKRAT... I ABSORBED IT... INTO ME... YESTERDAY. IT'S ALMOST GONE...
HUM. SPEAKING OF RATS, I GOT A CALL FROM CONSTANTINE. HE WAS IN L.A. SOMEWHERE. I COULD HEAR A GIRL IN THE BACKGROUND...
HE SAID HE'D MEET YOU NEAR THE SOURCE OF THE RIVER TEFÉ TOMORROW.
THEN...IT IS TIME...TO LEAVE. HE PROMISES ME... THAT THIS...IS THE FINAL STAGE... THAT IN SOUTH AMERICA I SHALL LEARN... EVERYTHING...
YEAH? WELL, I DON'T TRUST HIM. YOU TAKE CARE OF YOURSELF.
NOW...THAT I CAN... REGROW MYSELF... I AM BEYOND...ANY HARM...BUT WILL YOU... BE ALL RIGHT...WHILE I AM GONE...?
ME? I'LL BE FINE. SINCE THAT TROUBLE AT THE JACKSON HOUSE EVERYTHING'S BEEN RUNNING SMOOTHLY.
IT'S LIKE I GOT SOMEONE WATCHING OVER ME.
AS THE LORD'S MY WITNESS, I AIN'T NEVER SEEN NOTHING SO DISGUSTIN'! THERE WAS BUGS AND MOLD ON THAT THING, AN' SHE WAS KISSIN' IT!
I WAS SO SHOCKED, I ALMOST FORGOT TO RELOAD MY CAMERA.

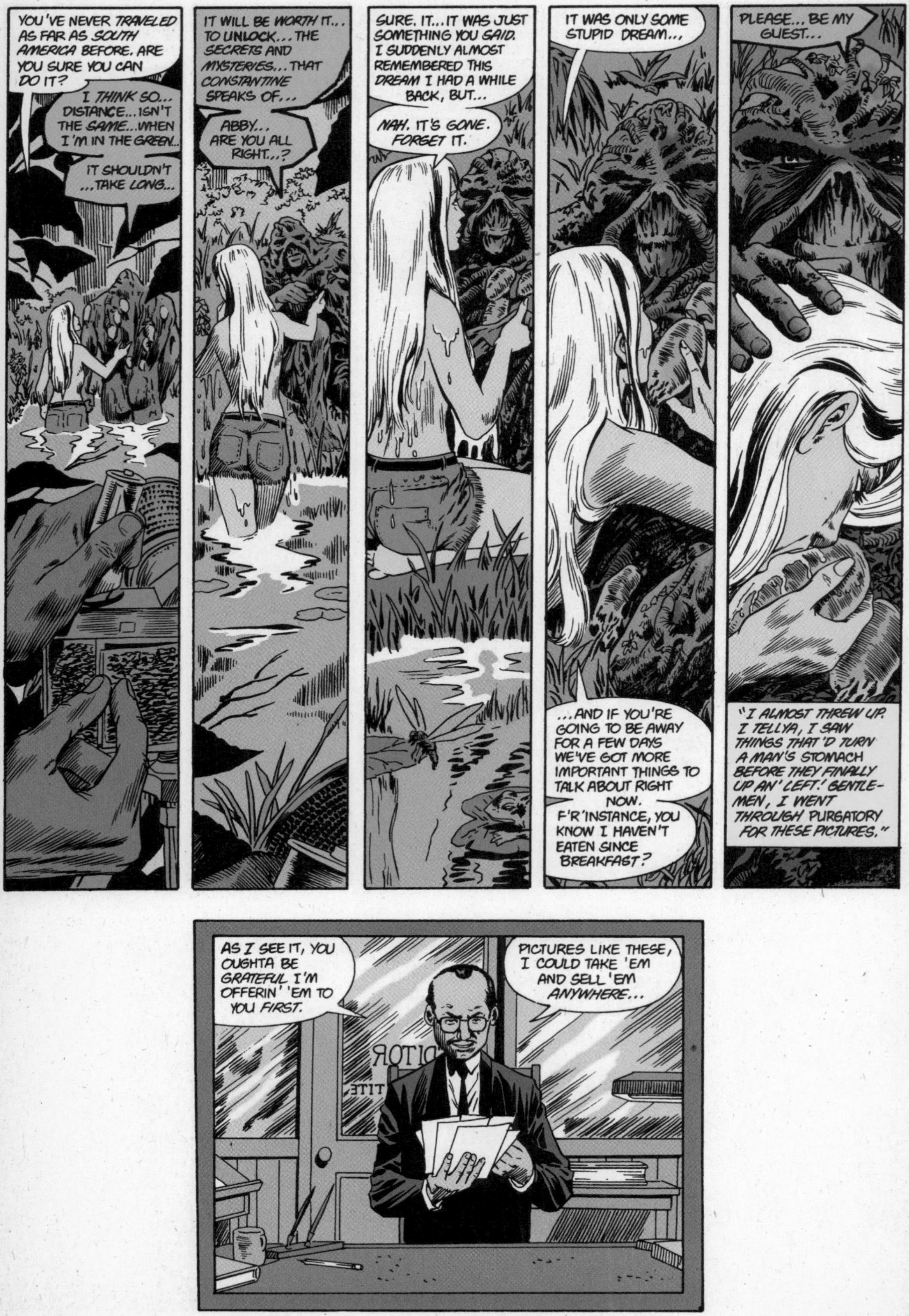

YOU'VE NEVER TRAVELED AS FAR AS SOUTH AMERICA BEFORE. ARE YOU SURE YOU CAN DO IT?
I THINK SO... DISTANCE... ISN'T THE SAME... WHEN I'M IN THE GREEN...
IT SHOULDN'T ...TAKE LONG...
IT WILL BE WORTH IT... TO UNLOCK... THE SECRETS AND MYSTERIES... THAT CONSTANTINE SPEAKS OF...
ABBY... ARE YOU ALL RIGHT...?
SURE. IT... IT WAS JUST SOMETHING YOU SAID. I SUDDENLY ALMOST REMEMBERED THIS DREAM I HAD A WHILE BACK, BUT...
NAH. IT'S GONE. FORGET IT.
IT WAS ONLY SOME STUPID DREAM...
...AND IF YOU'RE GOING TO BE AWAY FOR A FEW DAYS WE'VE GOT MORE IMPORTANT THINGS TO TALK ABOUT RIGHT NOW.
F'R'INSTANCE, YOU KNOW I HAVEN'T EATEN SINCE BREAKFAST?
PLEASE... BE MY GUEST...
"I ALMOST THREW UP. I TELLYA, I SAW THINGS THAT'D TURN A MAN'S STOMACH BEFORE THEY FINALLY UP AN' LEFT.' GENTLEMEN, I WENT THROUGH PURGATORY FOR THESE PICTURES."
AS I SEE IT, YOU OUGHTA BE GRATEFUL I'M OFFERIN' 'EM TO YOU FIRST.
PICTURES LIKE THESE, I COULD TAKE 'EM AND SELL 'EM ANYWHERE...

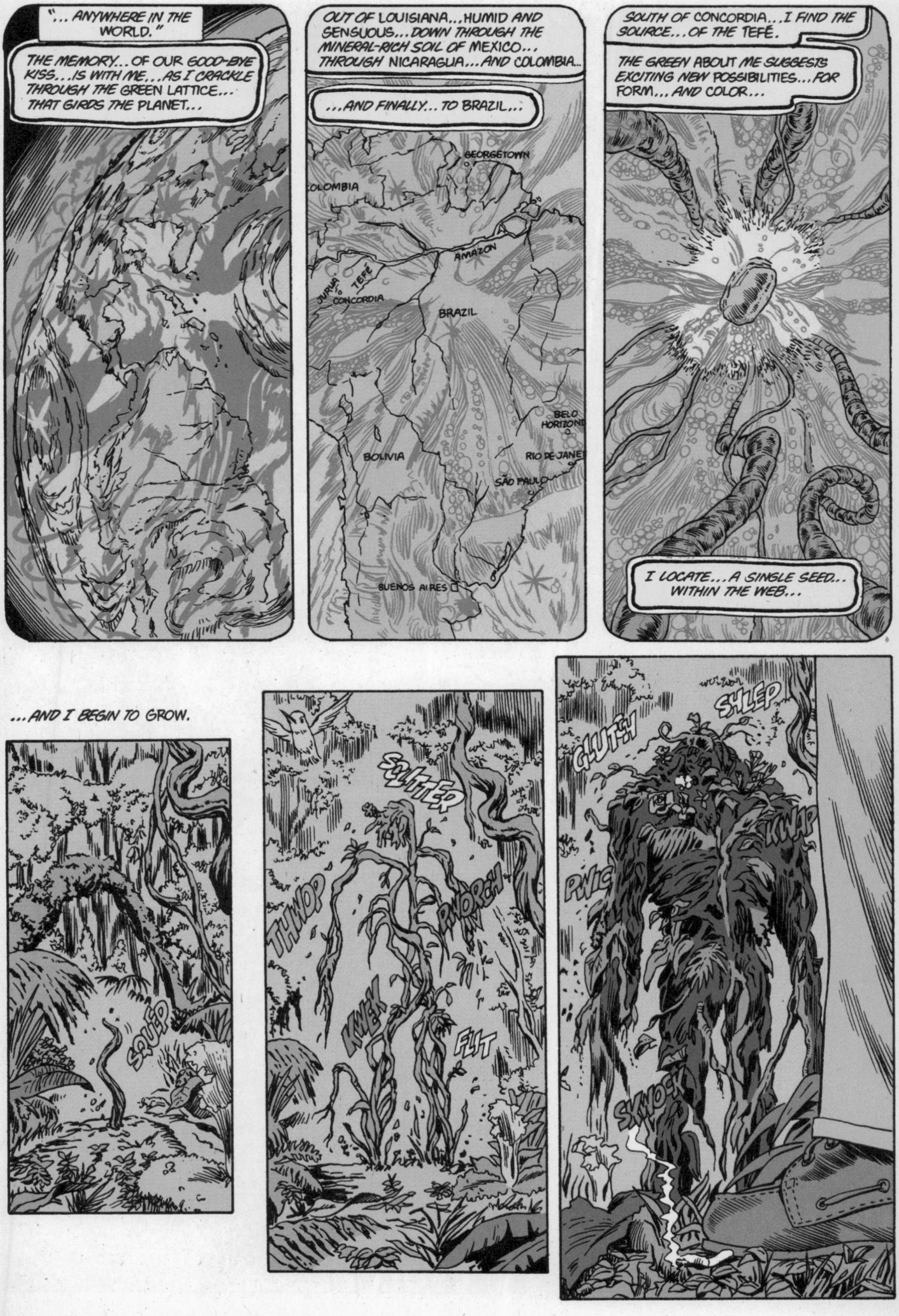
"... ANYWHERE IN THE WORLD."
THE MEMORY... OF OUR GOOD-BYE KISS... IS WITH ME... AS I CRACKLE THROUGH THE GREEN LATTICE... THAT GIRDS THE PLANET...
OUT OF LOUISIANA... HUMID AND SENSUOUS... DOWN THROUGH THE MINERAL-RICH SOIL OF MEXICO... THROUGH NICARAGUA... AND COLOMBIA...
... AND FINALLY... TO BRAZIL...
GEORGETOWN
COLOMBIA
AMAZON
JURUA
TEFÉ
CONCORDIA
BRAZIL
BELO HORIZONTE
BOLIVIA
RIO DE JANEI
SÃO PAULO
BUENOS AIRES
SOUTH OF CONCORDIA... I FIND THE SOURCE... OF THE TEFÉ.
THE GREEN ABOUT ME SUGGESTS EXCITING NEW POSSIBILITIES... FOR FORM... AND COLOR...
I LOCATE... A SINGLE SEED... WITHIN THE WEB...
... AND I BEGIN TO GROW.
SQUEP
SPLITTER
THWOP
RWORCH
KWEK
FLIT
GLUTCH
SHLEP
KWAP
PWIC
SKWOSH

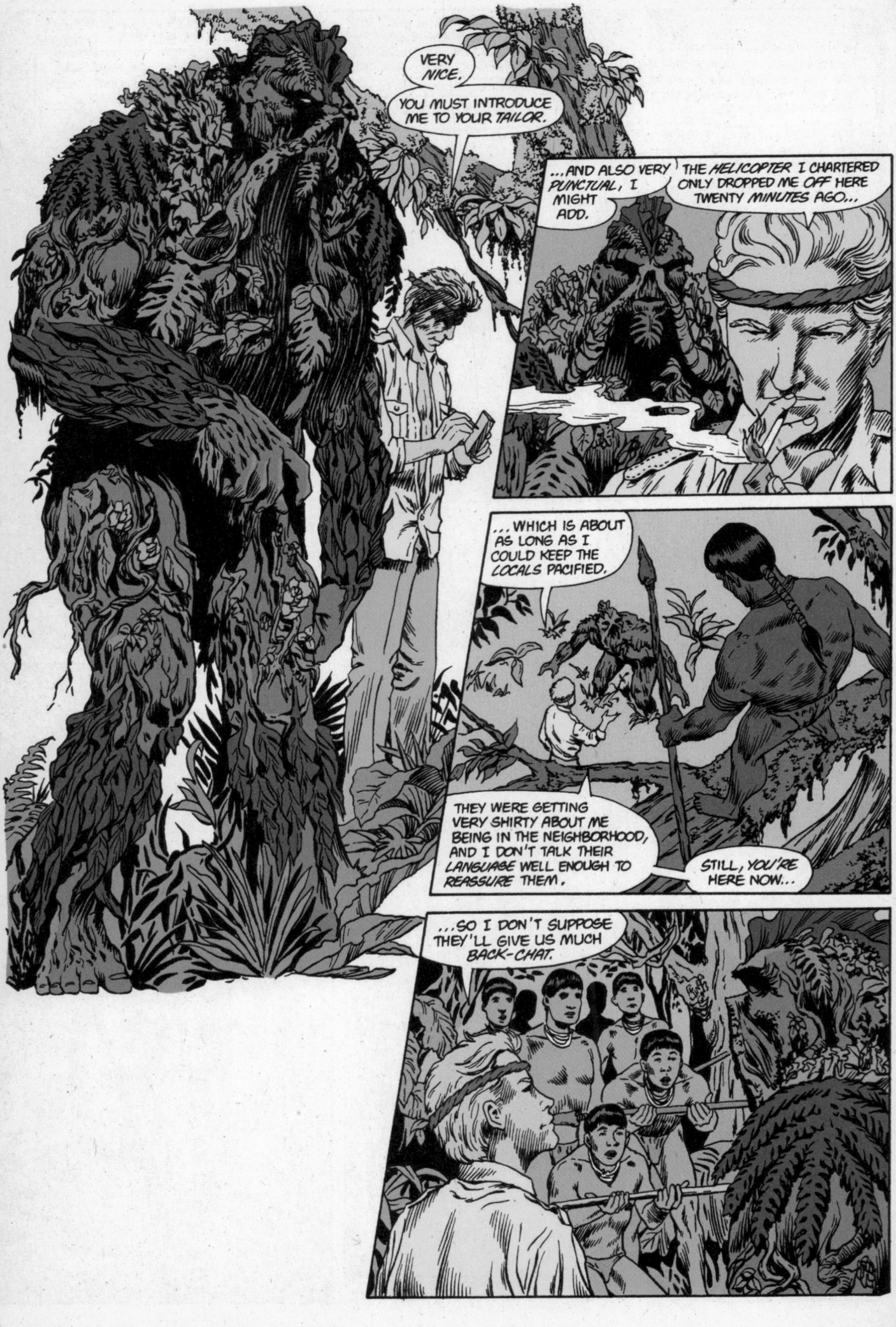
VERY NICE.
YOU MUST INTRODUCE ME TO YOUR TAILOR.
...AND ALSO VERY PUNCTUAL, I MIGHT ADD.
THE HELICOPTER I CHARTERED ONLY DROPPED ME OFF HERE TWENTY MINUTES AGO...
...WHICH IS ABOUT AS LONG AS I COULD KEEP THE LOCALS PACIFIED.
THEY WERE GETTING VERY SHIRTY ABOUT ME BEING IN THE NEIGHBORHOOD, AND I DON'T TALK THEIR LANGUAGE WELL ENOUGH TO REASSURE THEM.
STILL, YOU'RE HERE NOW...
...SO I DON'T SUPPOSE THEY'LL GIVE US MUCH BACK-CHAT.

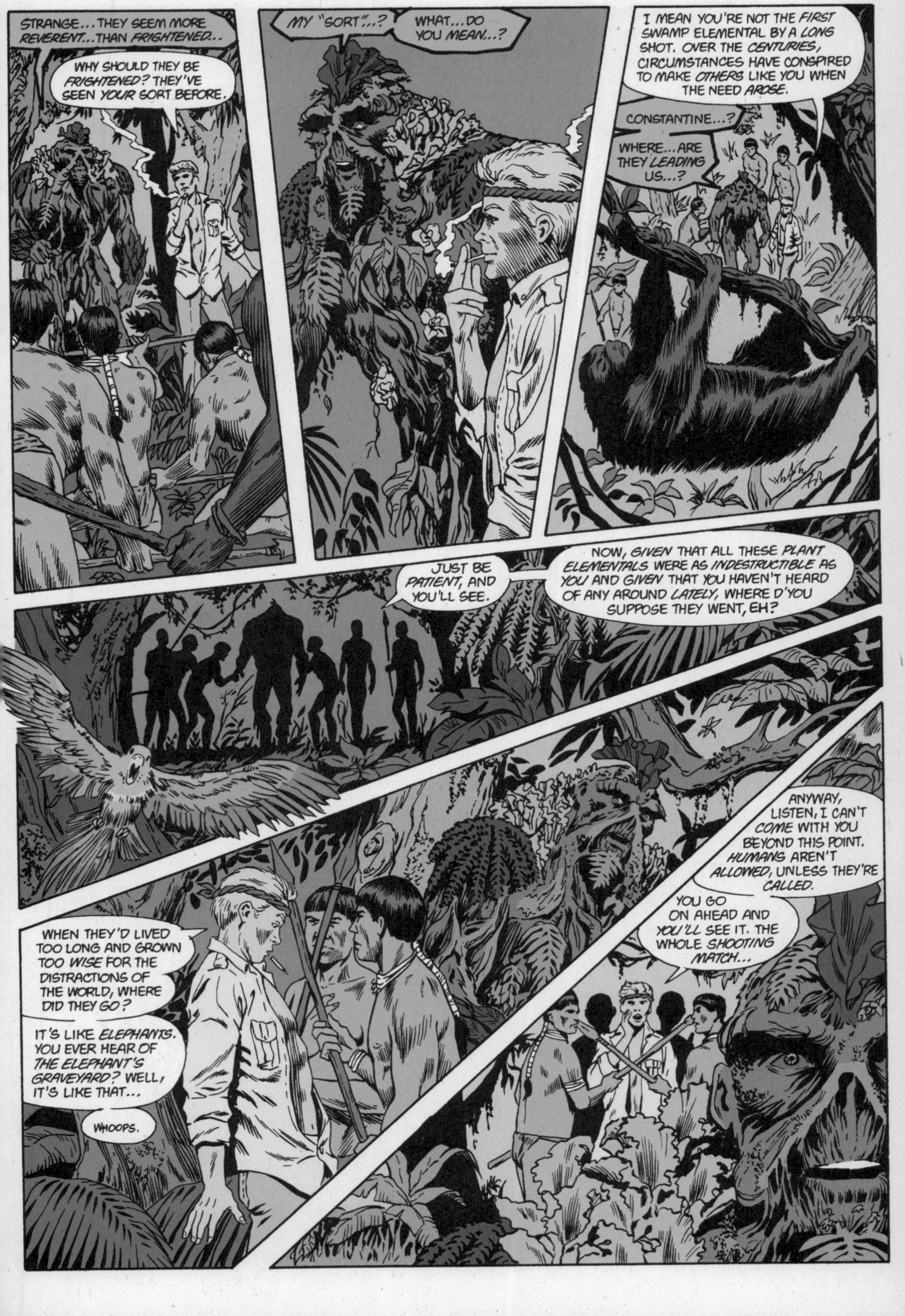
STRANGE... THEY SEEM MORE REVERENT... THAN FRIGHTENED...
WHY SHOULD THEY BE FRIGHTENED? THEY'VE SEEN YOUR SORT BEFORE.
MY "SORT"...?
WHAT... DO YOU MEAN...?
I MEAN YOU'RE NOT THE FIRST SWAMP ELEMENTAL BY A LONG SHOT. OVER THE CENTURIES, CIRCUMSTANCES HAVE CONSPIRED TO MAKE OTHERS LIKE YOU WHEN THE NEED AROSE.
CONSTANTINE...?
WHERE... ARE THEY LEADING US...?
JUST BE PATIENT, AND YOU'LL SEE.
NOW, GIVEN THAT ALL THESE PLANT ELEMENTALS WERE AS INDESTRUCTIBLE AS YOU AND GIVEN THAT YOU HAVEN'T HEARD OF ANY AROUND LATELY, WHERE D'YOU SUPPOSE THEY WENT, EH?
WHEN THEY'D LIVED TOO LONG AND GROWN TOO WISE FOR THE DISTRACTIONS OF THE WORLD, WHERE DID THEY GO?
IT'S LIKE ELEPHANTS. YOU EVER HEAR OF THE ELEPHANT'S GRAVEYARD? WELL, IT'S LIKE THAT...
WHOOPS.
ANYWAY, LISTEN, I CAN'T COME WITH YOU BEYOND THIS POINT. HUMANS AREN'T ALLOWED, UNLESS THEY'RE CALLED.
YOU GO ON AHEAD AND YOU'LL SEE IT. THE WHOLE SHOOTING MATCH...

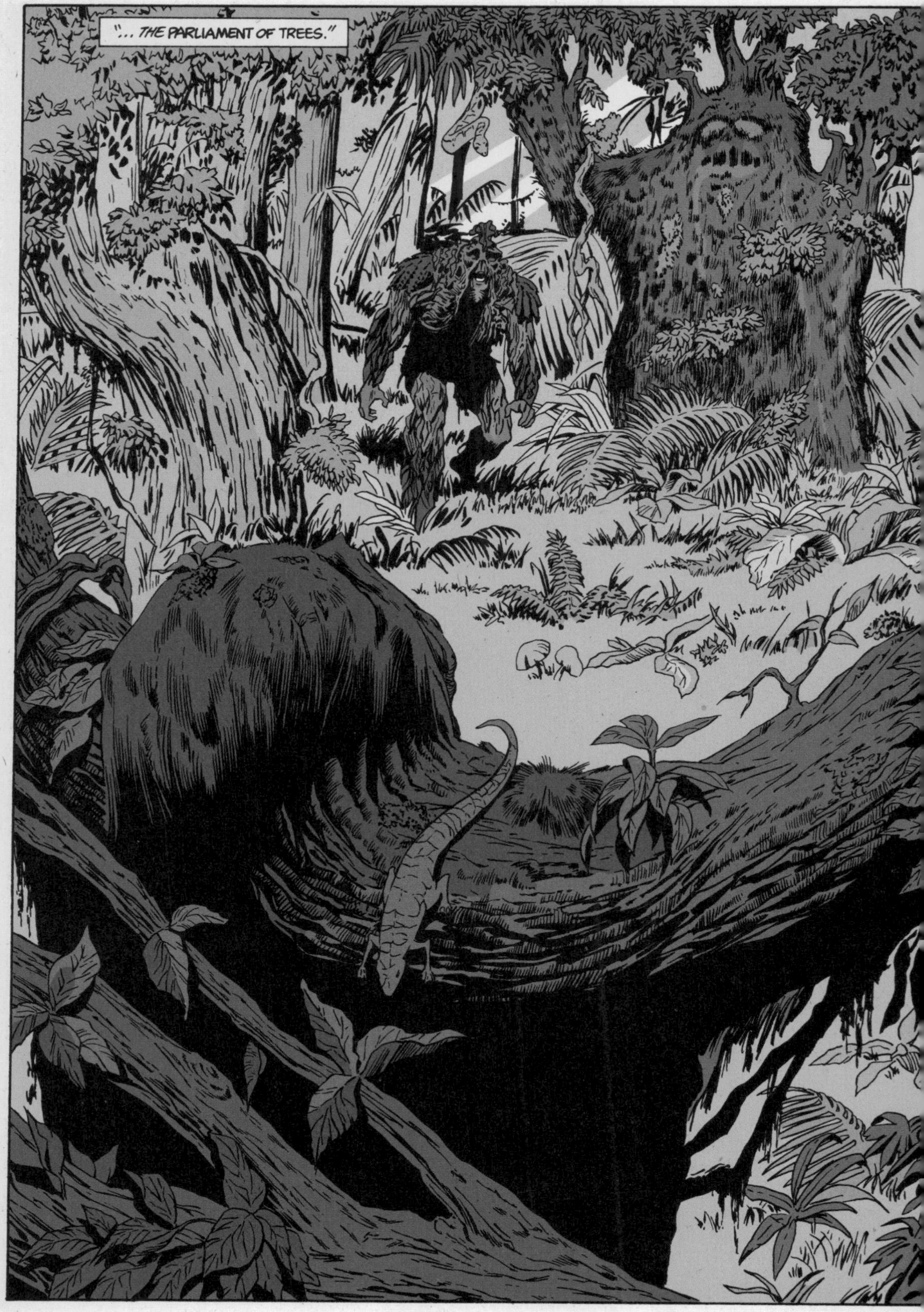
"... THE PARLIAMENT OF TREES."

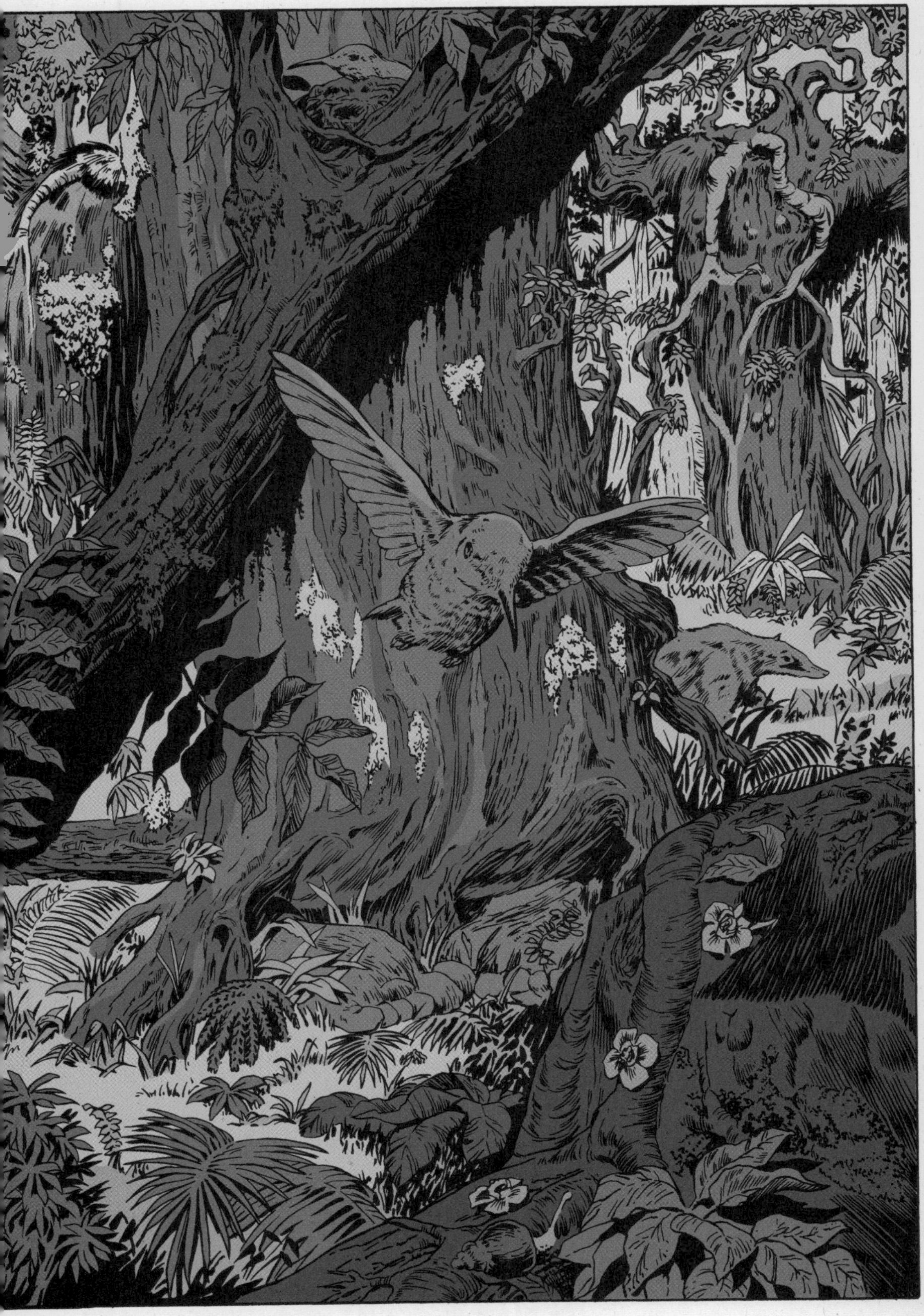

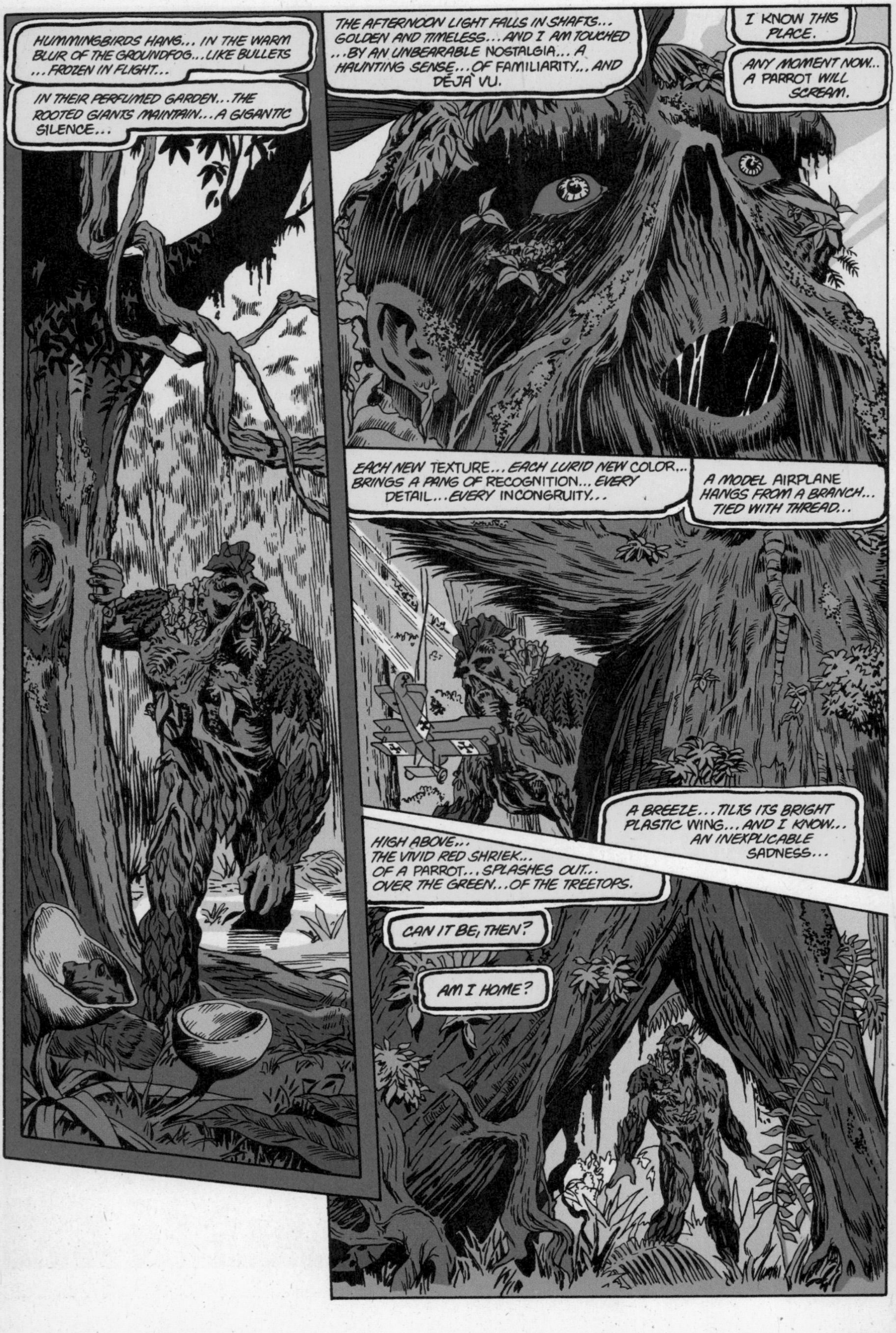
HUMMINGBIRDS HANG... IN THE WARM BLUR OF THE GROUNDFOG... LIKE BULLETS ... FROZEN IN FLIGHT...
IN THEIR PERFUMED GARDEN... THE ROOTED GIANTS MAINTAIN... A GIGANTIC SILENCE...
THE AFTERNOON LIGHT FALLS IN SHAFTS... GOLDEN AND TIMELESS... AND I AM TOUCHED ...BY AN UNBEARABLE NOSTALGIA... A HAUNTING SENSE... OF FAMILIARITY... AND DÉJÀ VU.
I KNOW THIS PLACE.
ANY MOMENT NOW... A PARROT WILL SCREAM.
EACH NEW TEXTURE... EACH LURID NEW COLOR... BRINGS A PANG OF RECOGNITION... EVERY DETAIL... EVERY INCONGRUITY...
A MODEL AIRPLANE HANGS FROM A BRANCH... TIED WITH THREAD...
A BREEZE... TILTS ITS BRIGHT PLASTIC WING... AND I KNOW... AN INEXPLICABLE SADNESS...
HIGH ABOVE... THE VIVID RED SHRIEK... OF A PARROT... SPLASHES OUT... OVER THE GREEN... OF THE TREETOPS.
CAN IT BE, THEN?
AM I HOME?

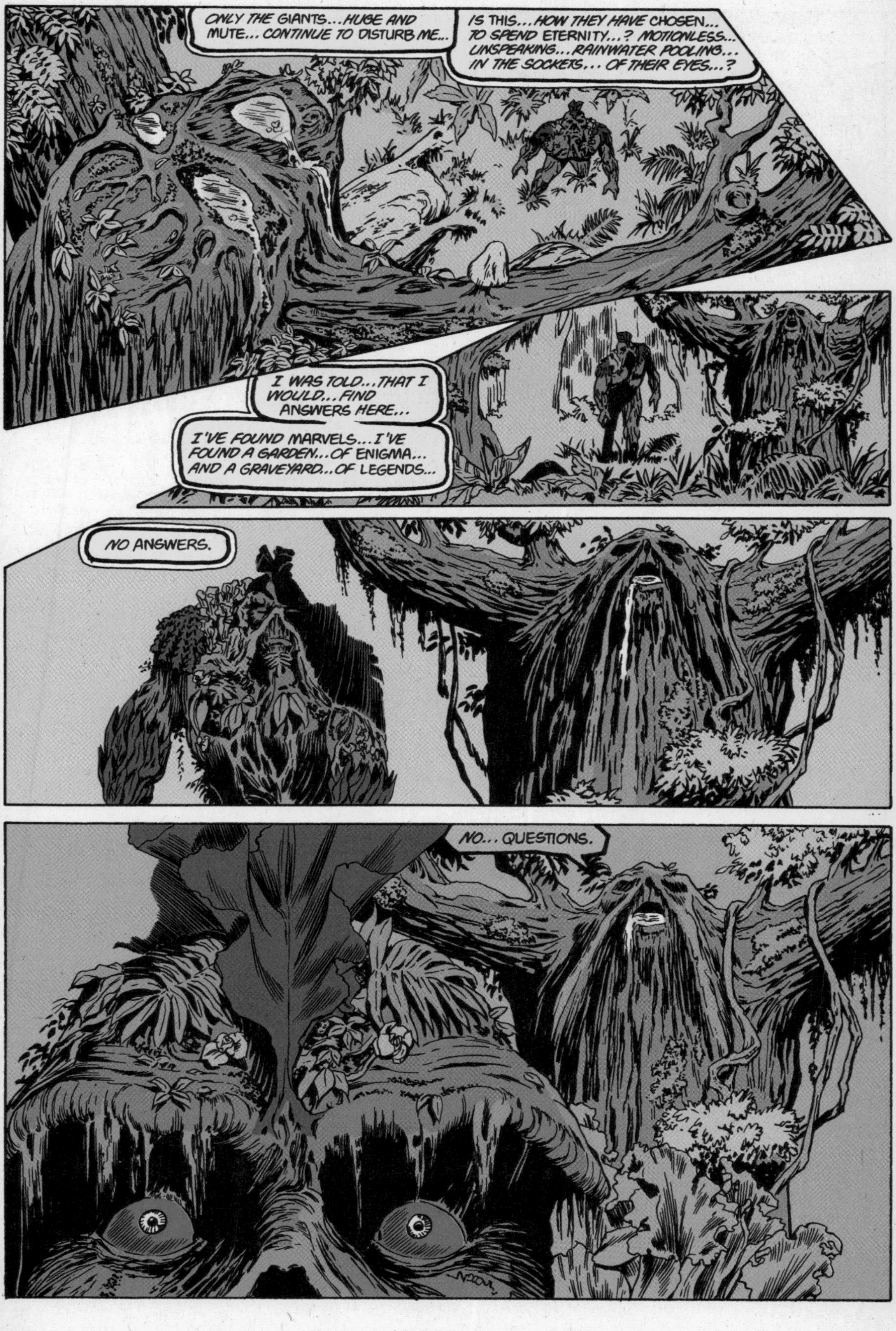
ONLY THE GIANTS... HUGE AND MUTE... CONTINUE TO DISTURB ME...
IS THIS... HOW THEY HAVE CHOSEN... TO SPEND ETERNITY...? MOTIONLESS... UNSPEAKING... RAINWATER POOLING... IN THE SOCKETS... OF THEIR EYES...?
I WAS TOLD... THAT I WOULD... FIND ANSWERS HERE...
I'VE FOUND MARVELS... I'VE FOUND A GARDEN... OF ENIGMA... AND A GRAVEYARD... OF LEGENDS...
NO ANSWERS.
NO... QUESTIONS.

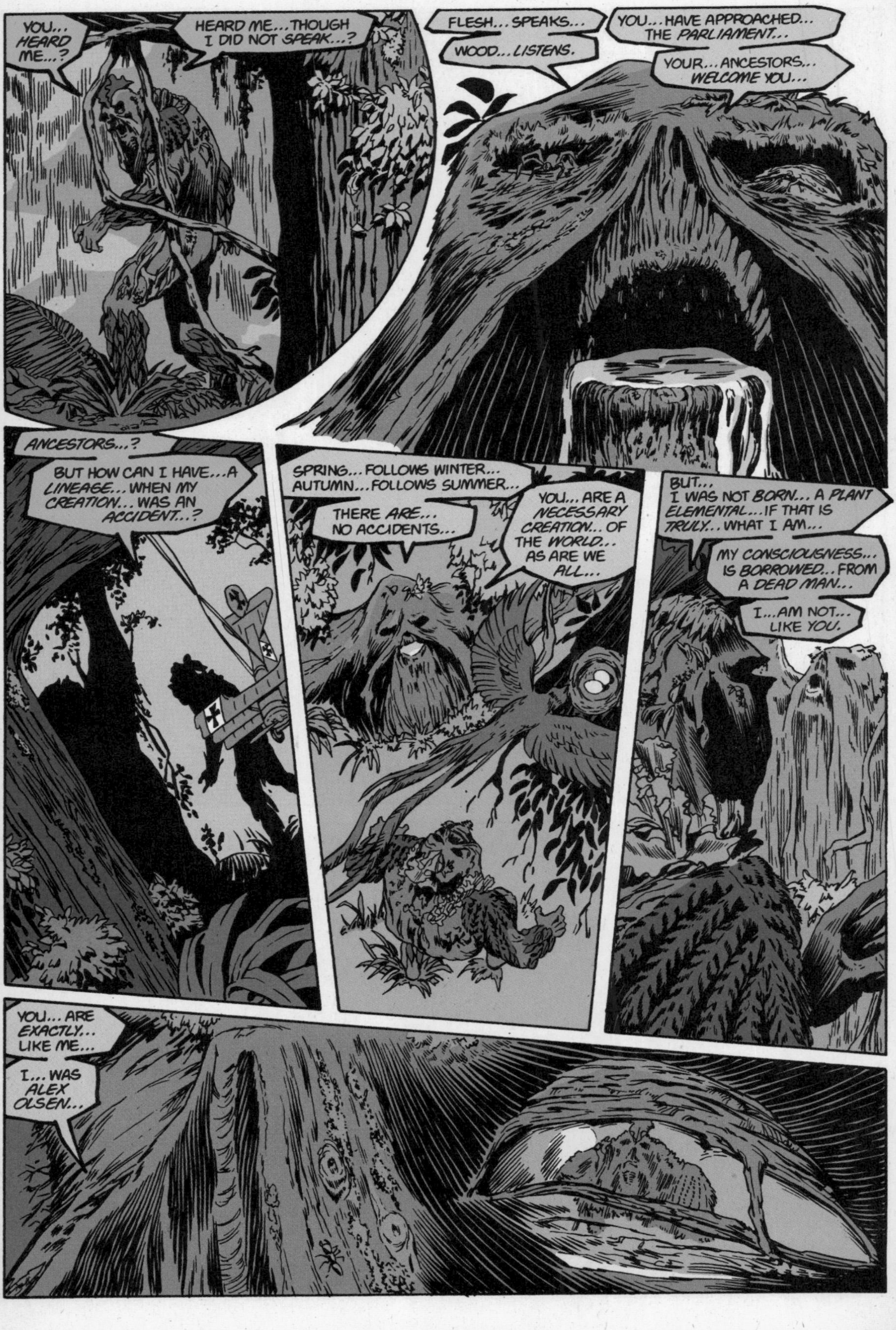
YOU... HEARD ME...?
HEARD ME... THOUGH I DID NOT SPEAK...?
FLESH... SPEAKS...
WOOD... LISTENS.
YOU... HAVE APPROACHED... THE PARLIAMENT...
YOUR... ANCESTORS... WELCOME YOU...
ANCESTORS...?
BUT HOW CAN I HAVE... A LINEAGE... WHEN MY CREATION... WAS AN ACCIDENT...?
SPRING... FOLLOWS WINTER... AUTUMN... FOLLOWS SUMMER...
THERE ARE... NO ACCIDENTS...
YOU... ARE A NECESSARY CREATION... OF THE WORLD... AS ARE WE ALL...
BUT... I WAS NOT BORN... A PLANT ELEMENTAL... IF THAT IS TRULY... WHAT I AM...
MY CONSCIOUSNESS... IS BORROWED... FROM A DEAD MAN...
I... AM NOT... LIKE YOU.
YOU... ARE EXACTLY... LIKE ME...
I... WAS ALEX OLSEN...

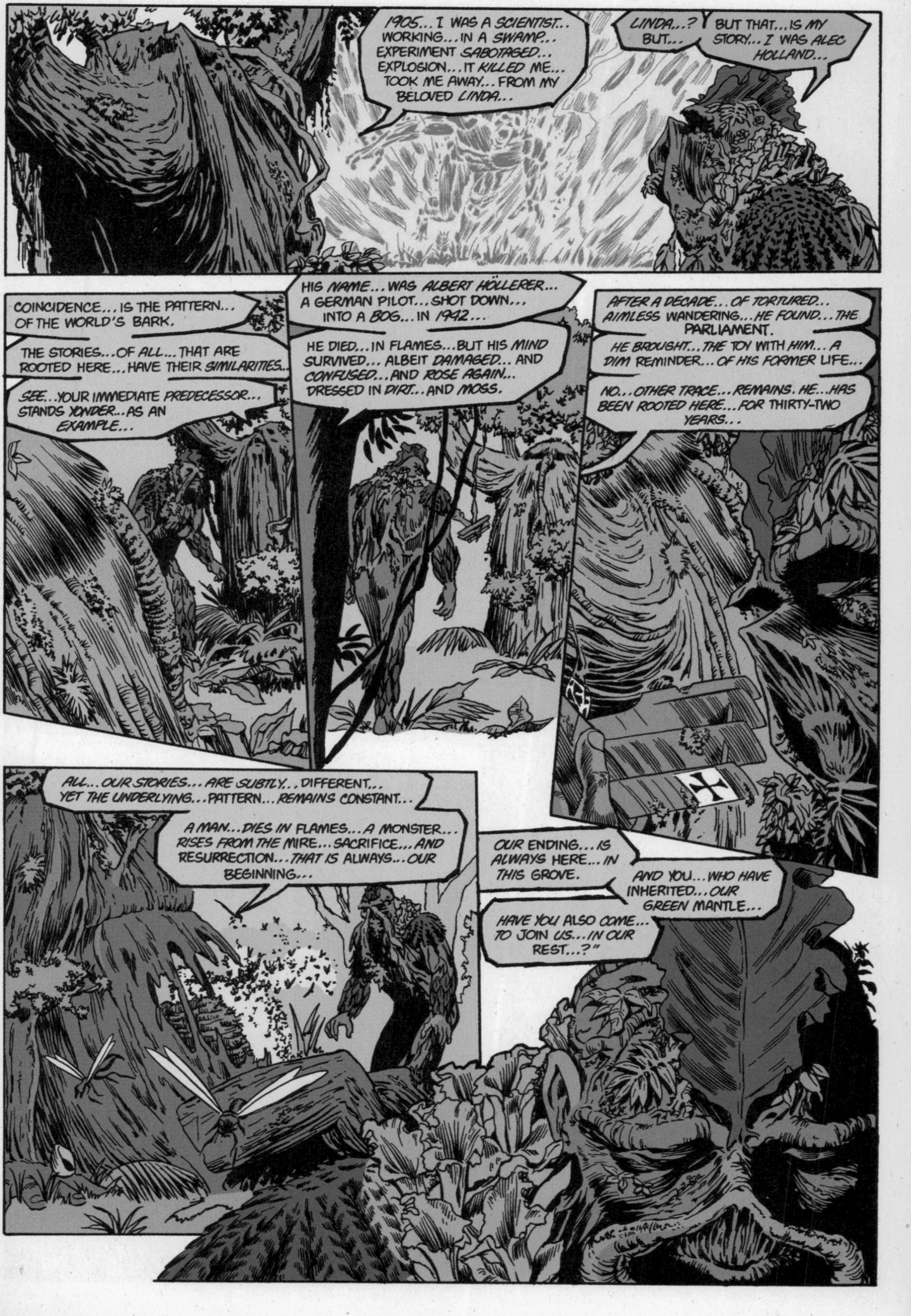
1905... I WAS A SCIENTIST... WORKING... IN A SWAMP... EXPERIMENT SABOTAGED... EXPLOSION... IT KILLED ME... TOOK ME AWAY... FROM MY BELOVED LINDA...
LINDA...? BUT...
BUT THAT... IS MY STORY... I WAS ALEC HOLLAND...
COINCIDENCE... IS THE PATTERN... OF THE WORLD'S BARK.
THE STORIES... OF ALL... THAT ARE ROOTED HERE... HAVE THEIR SIMILARITIES...
SEE... YOUR IMMEDIATE PREDECESSOR... STANDS YONDER... AS AN EXAMPLE...
HIS NAME... WAS ALBERT HÖLLERER... A GERMAN PILOT... SHOT DOWN... INTO A BOG... IN 1942...
HE DIED... IN FLAMES... BUT HIS MIND SURVIVED... ALBEIT DAMAGED... AND CONFUSED... AND ROSE AGAIN... DRESSED IN DIRT... AND MOSS.
AFTER A DECADE... OF TORTURED... AIMLESS WANDERING... HE FOUND... THE PARLIAMENT.
HE BROUGHT... THE TOY WITH HIM... A DIM REMINDER... OF HIS FORMER LIFE...
NO... OTHER TRACE... REMAINS. HE... HAS BEEN ROOTED HERE... FOR THIRTY-TWO YEARS...
ALL... OUR STORIES... ARE SUBTLY... DIFFERENT... YET THE UNDERLYING... PATTERN... REMAINS CONSTANT...
A MAN... DIES IN FLAMES... A MONSTER... RISES FROM THE MIRE... SACRIFICE... AND RESURRECTION... THAT IS ALWAYS... OUR BEGINNING...
OUR ENDING... IS ALWAYS HERE... IN THIS GROVE.
AND YOU... WHO HAVE INHERITED... OUR GREEN MANTLE...
HAVE YOU ALSO COME... TO JOIN US... IN OUR REST...?"

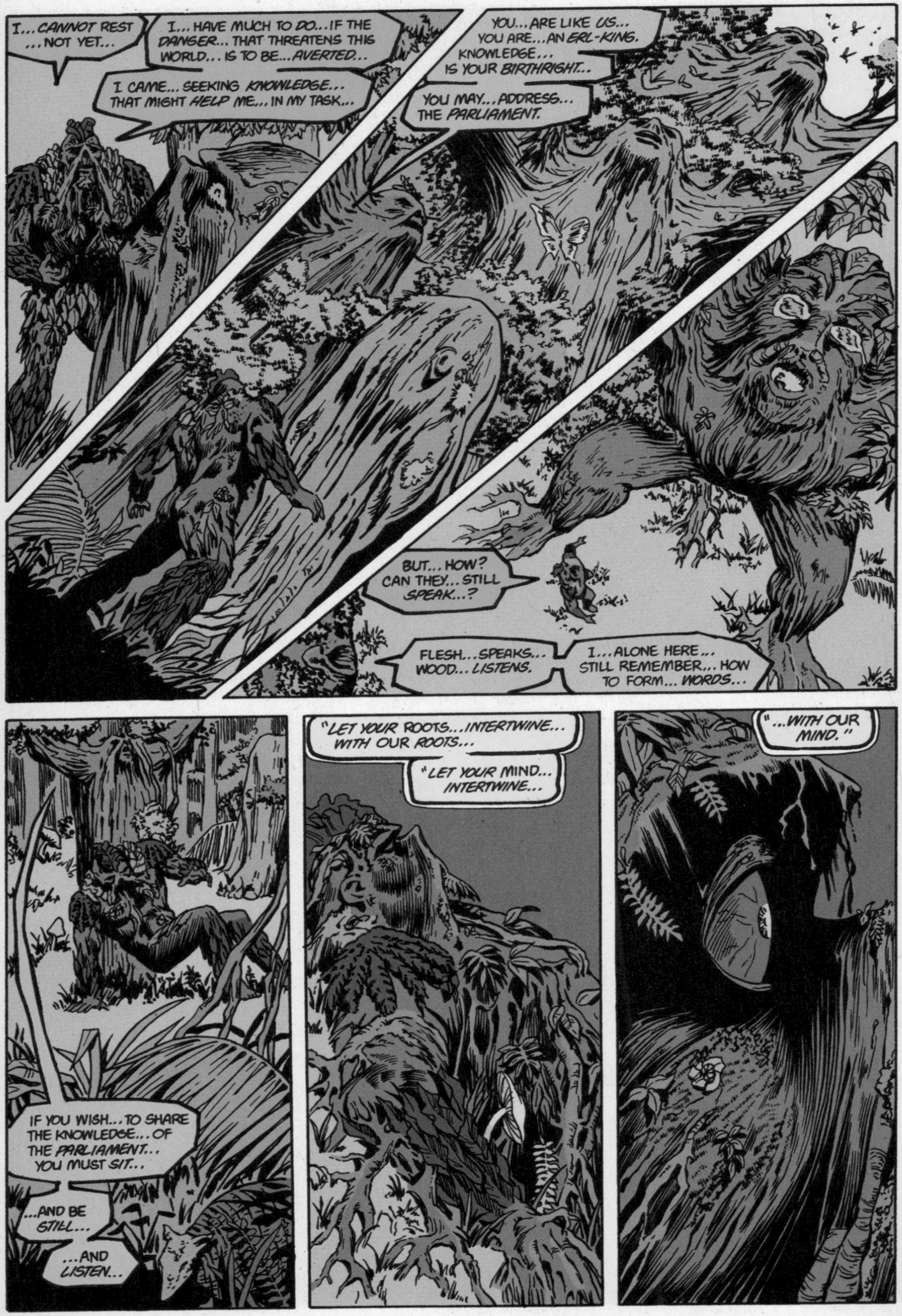
I... CANNOT REST ... NOT YET...
I... HAVE MUCH TO DO... IF THE DANGER... THAT THREATENS THIS WORLD... IS TO BE... AVERTED...
I CAME... SEEKING KNOWLEDGE... THAT MIGHT HELP ME... IN MY TASK...
YOU... ARE LIKE US... YOU ARE... AN ERL-KING. KNOWLEDGE... IS YOUR BIRTHRIGHT...
YOU MAY... ADDRESS... THE PARLIAMENT.
BUT... HOW? CAN THEY... STILL SPEAK...?
FLESH... SPEAKS... WOOD... LISTENS.
I... ALONE HERE... STILL REMEMBER... HOW TO FORM... WORDS...
IF YOU WISH... TO SHARE THE KNOWLEDGE... OF THE PARLIAMENT... YOU MUST SIT...
...AND BE STILL...
...AND LISTEN...
"LET YOUR ROOTS... INTERTWINE... WITH OUR ROOTS...
"LET YOUR MIND... INTERTWINE...
"...WITH OUR MIND."

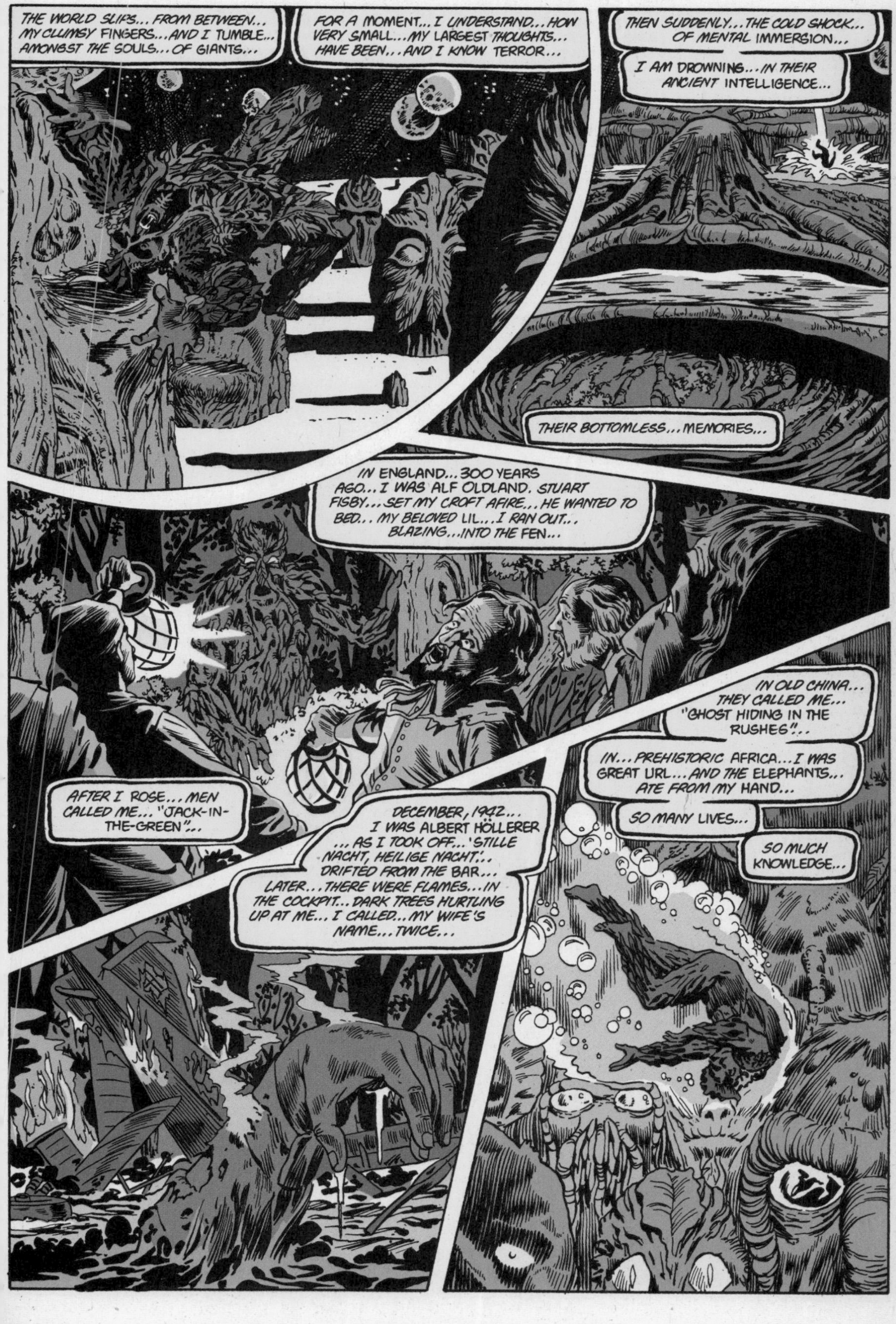
THE WORLD SLIPS... FROM BETWEEN... MY CLUMSY FINGERS... AND I TUMBLE... AMONGST THE SOULS... OF GIANTS...
FOR A MOMENT... I UNDERSTAND... HOW VERY SMALL... MY LARGEST THOUGHTS... HAVE BEEN... AND I KNOW TERROR...
THEN SUDDENLY... THE COLD SHOCK... OF MENTAL IMMERSION...
I AM DROWNING... IN THEIR ANCIENT INTELLIGENCE...
THEIR BOTTOMLESS... MEMORIES...
IN ENGLAND... 300 YEARS AGO... I WAS ALF OLDLAND. STUART FISBY... SET MY CROFT AFIRE... HE WANTED TO BED... MY BELOVED LIL... I RAN OUT... BLAZING... INTO THE FEN...
AFTER I ROSE... MEN CALLED ME... "JACK-IN-THE-GREEN"...
IN OLD CHINA... THEY CALLED ME... "GHOST HIDING IN THE RUSHES"...
IN... PREHISTORIC AFRICA... I WAS GREAT URL... AND THE ELEPHANTS... ATE FROM MY HAND...
SO MANY LIVES...
SO MUCH KNOWLEDGE...
DECEMBER, 1942... I WAS ALBERT HÖLLERER ... AS I TOOK OFF... 'STILLE NACHT, HEILIGE NACHT'... DRIFTED FROM THE BAR... LATER... THERE WERE FLAMES... IN THE COCKPIT... DARK TREES HURTLING UP AT ME... I CALLED... MY WIFE'S NAME... TWICE...

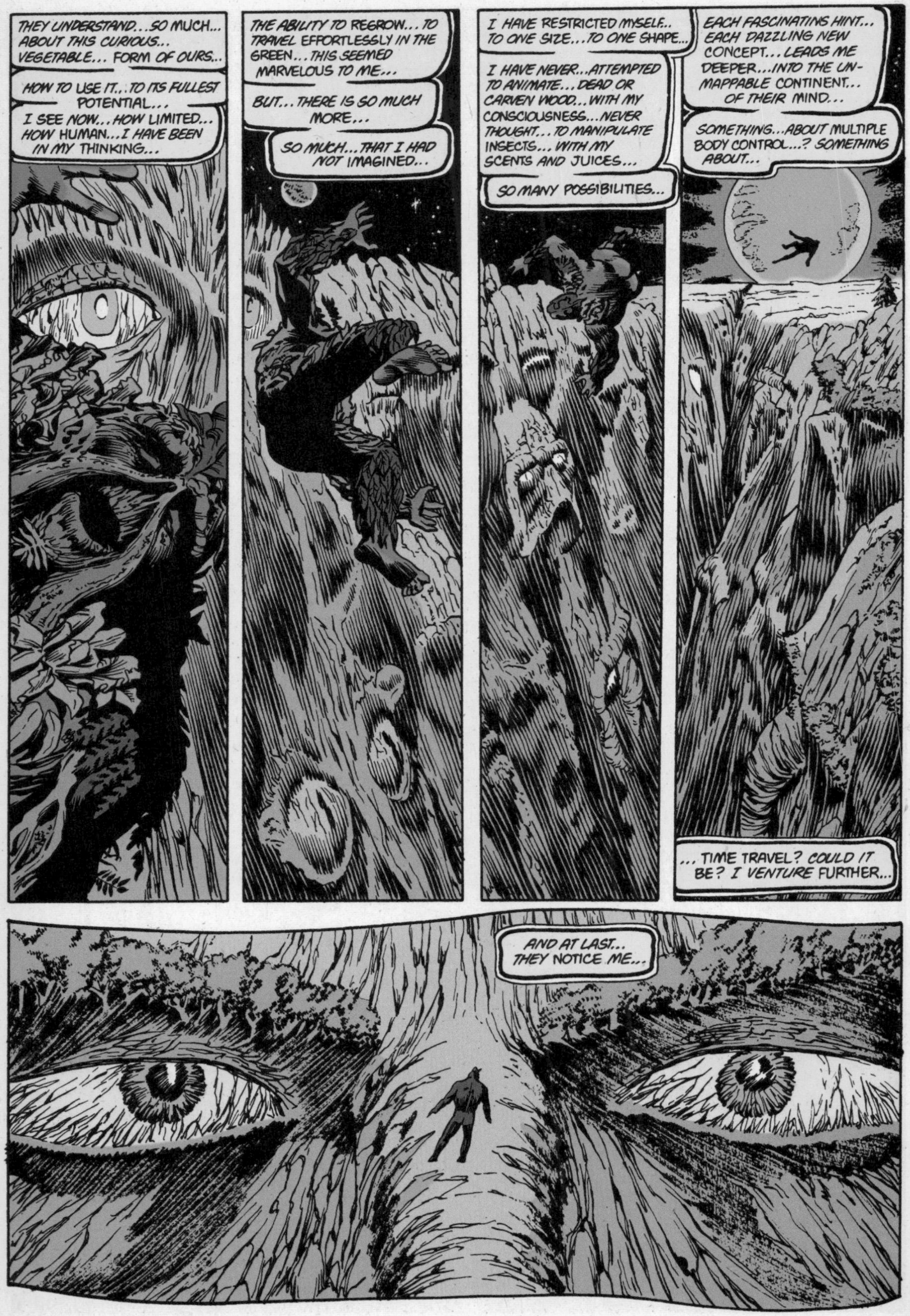
THEY UNDERSTAND... SO MUCH... ABOUT THIS CURIOUS... VEGETABLE... FORM OF OURS...
HOW TO USE IT... TO ITS FULLEST POTENTIAL...
I SEE NOW... HOW LIMITED... HOW HUMAN... I HAVE BEEN IN MY THINKING...
THE ABILITY TO REGROW... TO TRAVEL EFFORTLESSLY IN THE GREEN... THIS SEEMED MARVELOUS TO ME...
BUT... THERE IS SO MUCH MORE...
SO MUCH... THAT I HAD NOT IMAGINED...
I HAVE RESTRICTED MYSELF.. TO ONE SIZE... TO ONE SHAPE...
I HAVE NEVER... ATTEMPTED TO ANIMATE... DEAD OR CARVEN WOOD... WITH MY CONSCIOUSNESS... NEVER THOUGHT... TO MANIPULATE INSECTS... WITH MY SCENTS AND JUICES...
SO MANY POSSIBILITIES...
EACH FASCINATING HINT... EACH DAZZLING NEW CONCEPT... LEADS ME DEEPER... INTO THE UN-MAPPABLE CONTINENT... OF THEIR MIND...
SOMETHING... ABOUT MULTIPLE BODY CONTROL...? SOMETHING ABOUT...
... TIME TRAVEL? COULD IT BE? I VENTURE FURTHER...
AND AT LAST... THEY NOTICE ME...

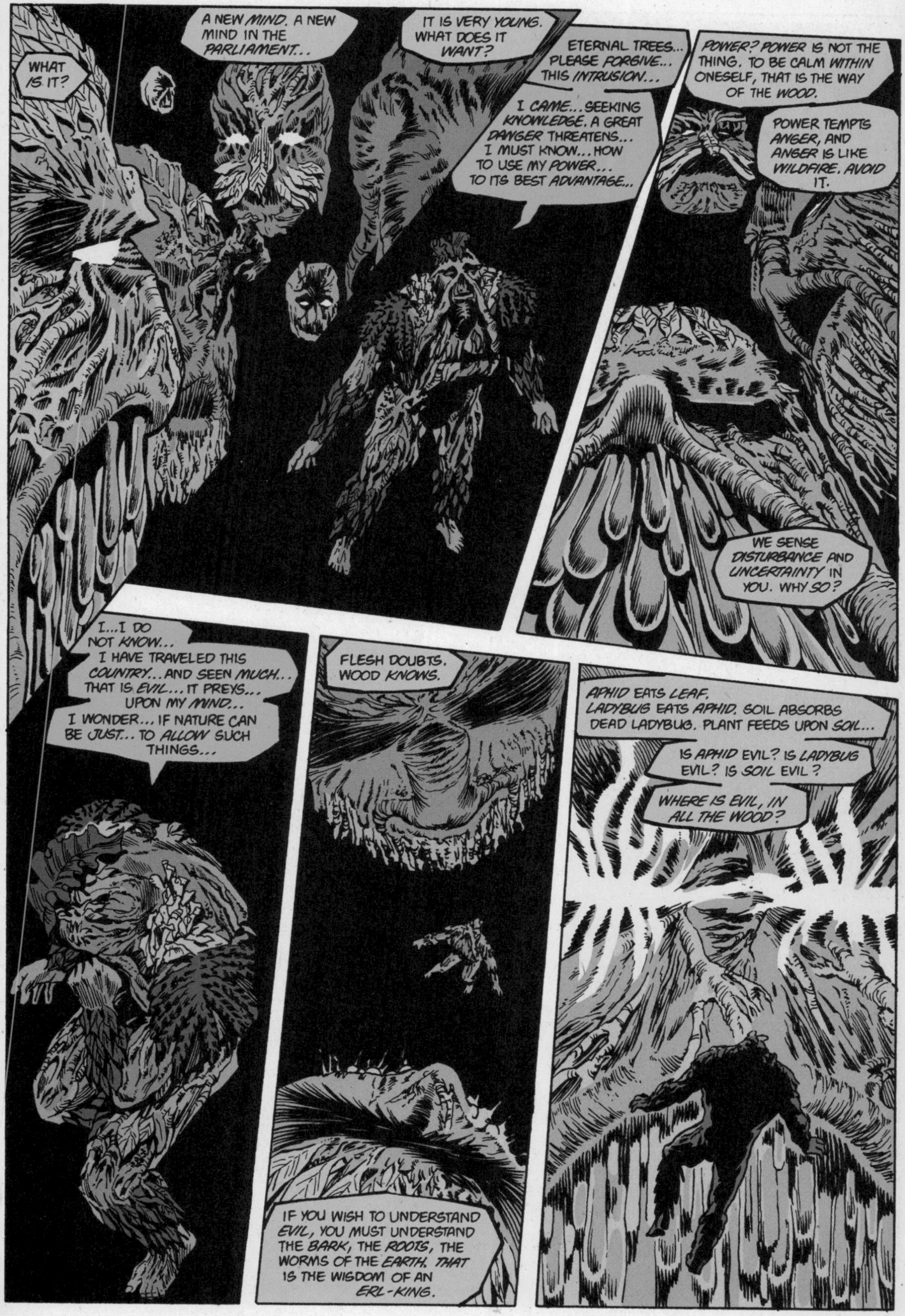
WHAT IS IT?
A NEW MIND. A NEW MIND IN THE PARLIAMENT...
IT IS VERY YOUNG. WHAT DOES IT WANT?
ETERNAL TREES... PLEASE FORGIVE... THIS INTRUSION...
I CAME... SEEKING KNOWLEDGE. A GREAT DANGER THREATENS... I MUST KNOW... HOW TO USE MY POWER... TO ITS BEST ADVANTAGE...
POWER? POWER IS NOT THE THING. TO BE CALM WITHIN ONESELF, THAT IS THE WAY OF THE WOOD.
POWER TEMPTS ANGER, AND ANGER IS LIKE WILDFIRE. AVOID IT.
WE SENSE DISTURBANCE AND UNCERTAINTY IN YOU. WHY SO?
I...I DO NOT KNOW... I HAVE TRAVELED THIS COUNTRY... AND SEEN MUCH... THAT IS EVIL... IT PREYS... UPON MY MIND...
I WONDER... IF NATURE CAN BE JUST... TO ALLOW SUCH THINGS...
FLESH DOUBTS. WOOD KNOWS.
IF YOU WISH TO UNDERSTAND EVIL, YOU MUST UNDERSTAND THE BARK, THE ROOTS, THE WORMS OF THE EARTH. THAT IS THE WISDOM OF AN ERL-KING.
APHID EATS LEAF. LADYBUG EATS APHID. SOIL ABSORBS DEAD LADYBUG. PLANT FEEDS UPON SOIL...
IS APHID EVIL? IS LADYBUG EVIL? IS SOIL EVIL?
WHERE IS EVIL, IN ALL THE WOOD?

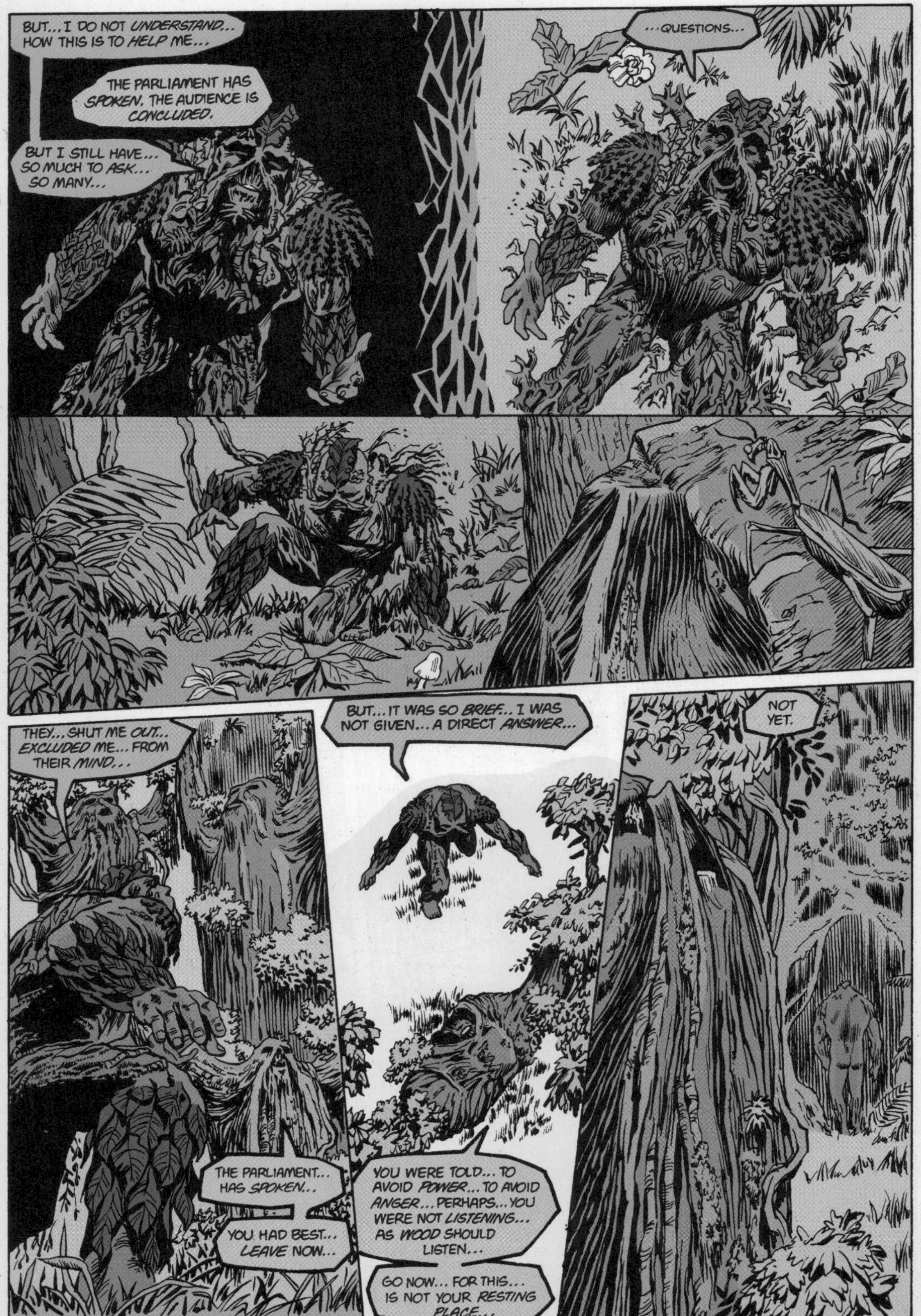
BUT... I DO NOT UNDERSTAND... HOW THIS IS TO HELP ME...
THE PARLIAMENT HAS SPOKEN. THE AUDIENCE IS CONCLUDED.
BUT I STILL HAVE... SO MUCH TO ASK... SO MANY...
...QUESTIONS...
THEY... SHUT ME OUT... EXCLUDED ME... FROM THEIR MIND...
BUT... IT WAS SO BRIEF... I WAS NOT GIVEN... A DIRECT ANSWER...
NOT YET.
THE PARLIAMENT... HAS SPOKEN...
YOU HAD BEST... LEAVE NOW...
YOU WERE TOLD... TO AVOID POWER... TO AVOID ANGER... PERHAPS... YOU WERE NOT LISTENING... AS WOOD SHOULD LISTEN...
GO NOW... FOR THIS... IS NOT YOUR RESTING PLACE...

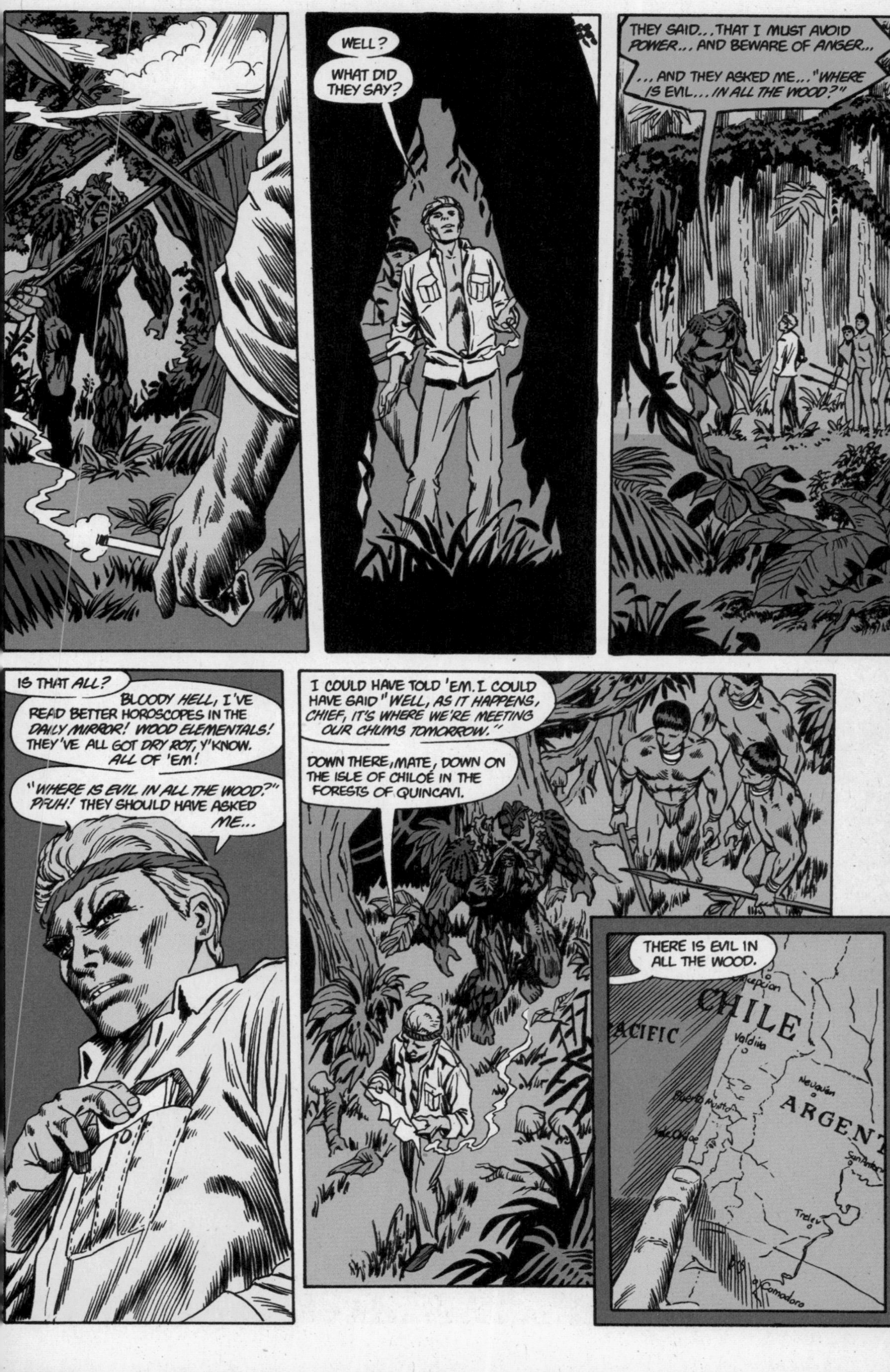
WELL? WHAT DID THEY SAY?
THEY SAID... THAT I MUST AVOID POWER... AND BEWARE OF ANGER...
...AND THEY ASKED ME... "WHERE IS EVIL... IN ALL THE WOOD?"
IS THAT ALL?
BLOODY HELL, I'VE READ BETTER HOROSCOPES IN THE DAILY MIRROR! WOOD ELEMENTALS! THEY'VE ALL GOT DRY ROT, Y'KNOW. ALL OF 'EM!
"WHERE IS EVIL IN ALL THE WOOD?" PFUH! THEY SHOULD HAVE ASKED ME...
I COULD HAVE TOLD 'EM. I COULD HAVE SAID "WELL, AS IT HAPPENS, CHIEF, IT'S WHERE WE'RE MEETING OUR CHUMS TOMORROW."
DOWN THERE, MATE, DOWN ON THE ISLE OF CHILOÉ IN THE FORESTS OF QUINCAVI.
THERE IS EVIL IN ALL THE WOOD.
CHILE
Valdivia

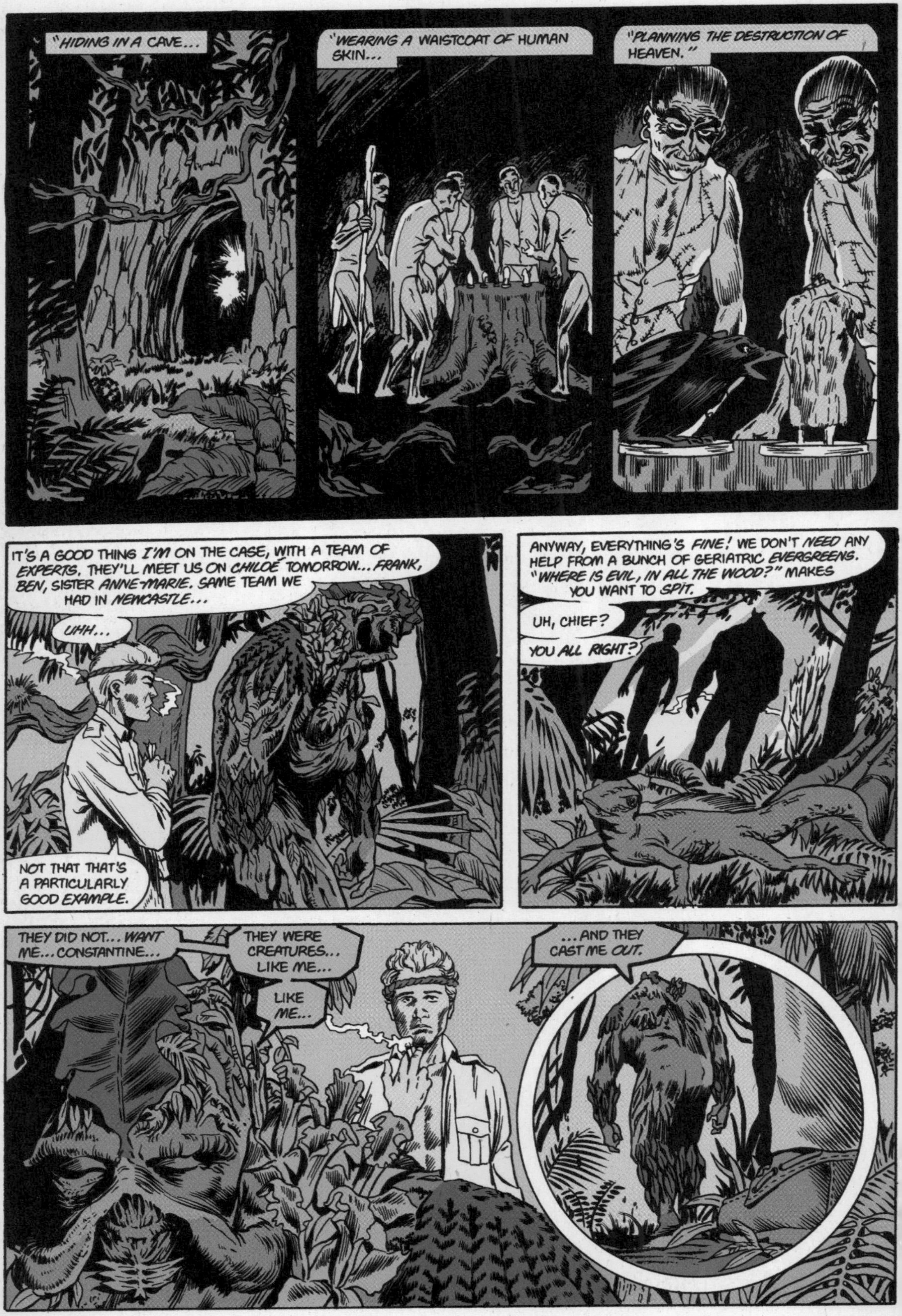
"HIDING IN A CAVE...
"WEARING A WAISTCOAT OF HUMAN SKIN...
"PLANNING THE DESTRUCTION OF HEAVEN."
IT'S A GOOD THING I'M ON THE CASE, WITH A TEAM OF EXPERTS. THEY'LL MEET US ON CHILOÉ TOMORROW... FRANK, BEN, SISTER ANNE-MARIE. SAME TEAM WE HAD IN NEWCASTLE...
UHH...
NOT THAT THAT'S A PARTICULARLY GOOD EXAMPLE.
ANYWAY, EVERYTHING'S FINE! WE DON'T NEED ANY HELP FROM A BUNCH OF GERIATRIC EVERGREENS. "WHERE IS EVIL, IN ALL THE WOOD?" MAKES YOU WANT TO SPIT.
UH, CHIEF?
YOU ALL RIGHT?
THEY DID NOT... WANT ME... CONSTANTINE...
THEY WERE CREATURES... LIKE ME...
LIKE ME...
...AND THEY CAST ME OUT.

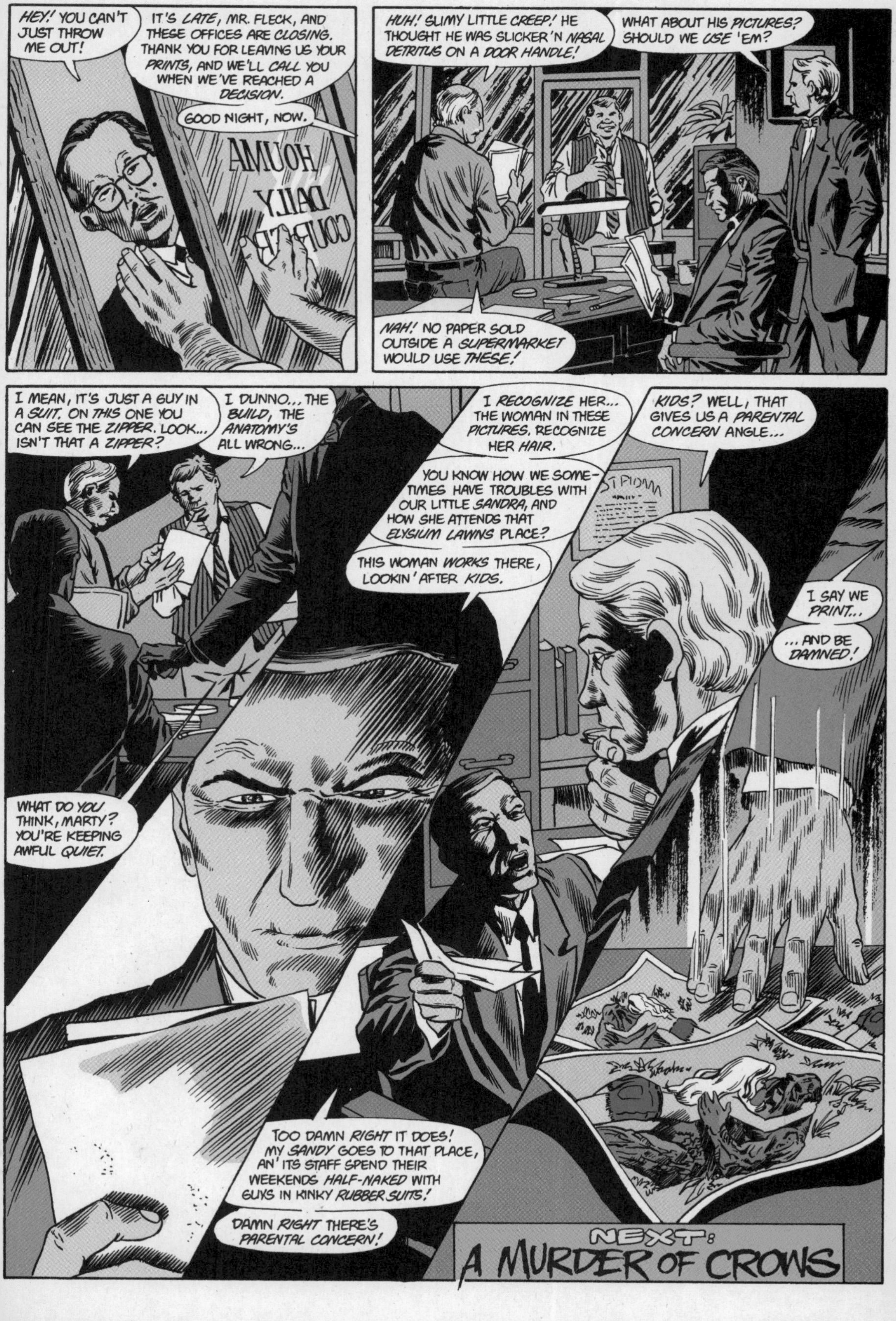
HEY! YOU CAN'T JUST THROW ME OUT!
IT'S LATE, MR. FLECK, AND THESE OFFICES ARE CLOSING. THANK YOU FOR LEAVING US YOUR PRINTS, AND WE'LL CALL YOU WHEN WE'VE REACHED A DECISION.
GOOD NIGHT, NOW.
HOUMA DAILY COUR
HUH! SLIMY LITTLE CREEP! HE THOUGHT HE WAS SLICKER'N NASAL DETRITUS ON A DOOR HANDLE!
WHAT ABOUT HIS PICTURES? SHOULD WE USE 'EM?
NAH! NO PAPER SOLD OUTSIDE A SUPERMARKET WOULD USE THESE!
I MEAN, IT'S JUST A GUY IN A SUIT. ON THIS ONE YOU CAN SEE THE ZIPPER. LOOK... ISN'T THAT A ZIPPER?
I DUNNO... THE BUILD, THE ANATOMY'S ALL WRONG...
I RECOGNIZE HER... THE WOMAN IN THESE PICTURES. RECOGNIZE HER HAIR.
YOU KNOW HOW WE SOMETIMES HAVE TROUBLES WITH OUR LITTLE SANDRA, AND HOW SHE ATTENDS THAT ELYSIUM LAWNS PLACE?
THIS WOMAN WORKS THERE, LOOKIN' AFTER KIDS.
KIDS? WELL, THAT GIVES US A PARENTAL CONCERN ANGLE...
I SAY WE PRINT...
...AND BE DAMNED!
WHAT DO YOU THINK, MARTY? YOU'RE KEEPING AWFUL QUIET.
TOO DAMN RIGHT IT DOES! MY SANDY GOES TO THAT PLACE, AN' ITS STAFF SPEND THEIR WEEKENDS HALF-NAKED WITH GUYS IN KINKY RUBBER SUITS!
DAMN RIGHT THERE'S PARENTAL CONCERN!
NEXT: A MURDER OF CROWS

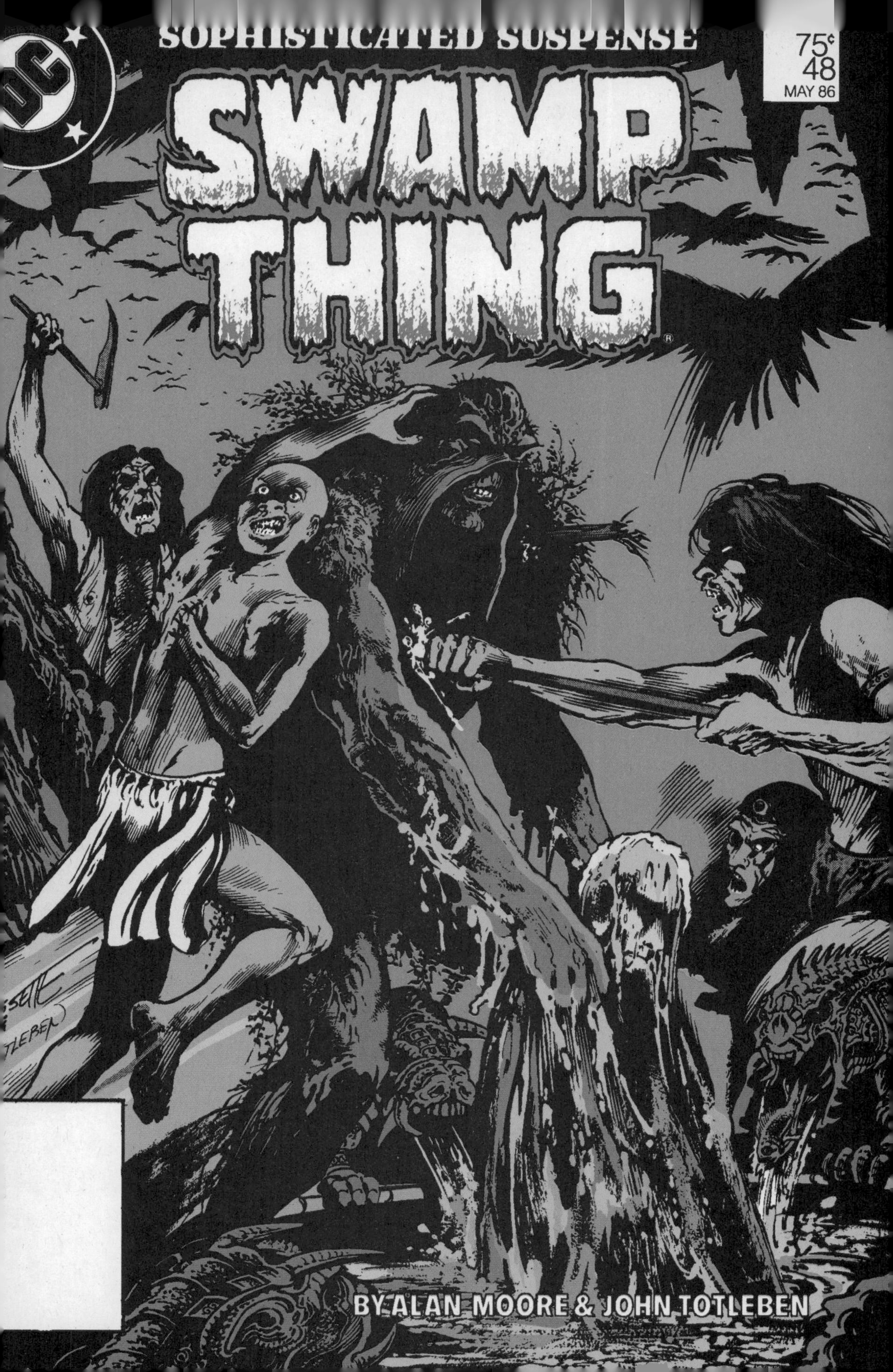
SOPHISTICATED SUSPENSE
SWAMP THING
75¢
48
MAY 86
BY ALAN MOORE & JOHN TOTLEBEN

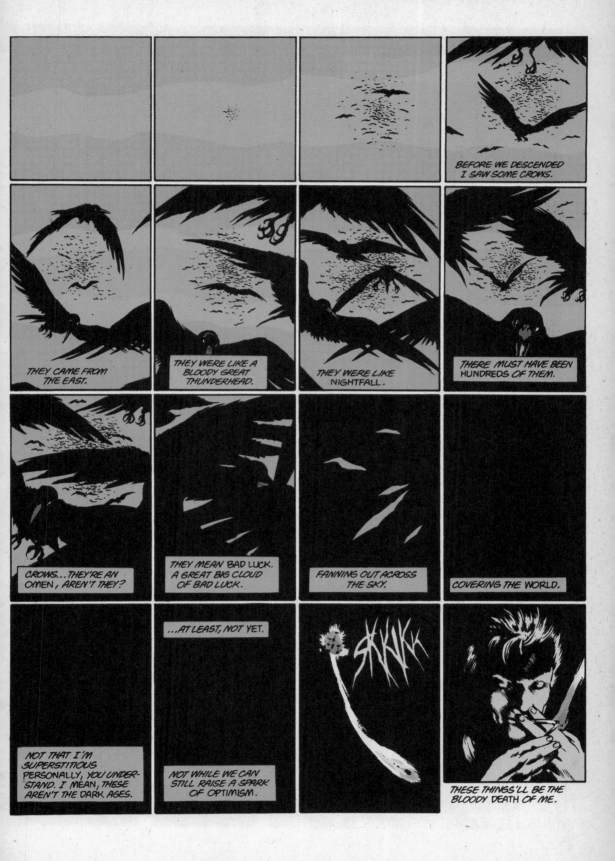

BEFORE WE DESCENDED I SAW SOME CROWS.

THEY CAME FROM THE EAST.

THEY WERE LIKE A BLOODY GREAT THUNDERHEAD.

THEY WERE LIKE NIGHTFALL.

THERE MUST HAVE BEEN HUNDREDS OF THEM.

CROWS...THEY'RE AN OMEN, AREN'T THEY?

THEY MEAN BAD LUCK. A GREAT BIG CLOUD OF BAD LUCK.

FANNING OUT ACROSS THE SKY.

COVERING THE WORLD.

NOT THAT I'M SUPERSTITIOUS PERSONALLY, YOU UNDERSTAND. I MEAN, THESE AREN'T THE DARK AGES.

...AT LEAST, NOT YET.

NOT WHILE WE CAN STILL RAISE A SPARK OF OPTIMISM.

SKKIK

THESE THINGS'LL BE THE BLOODY DEATH OF ME.

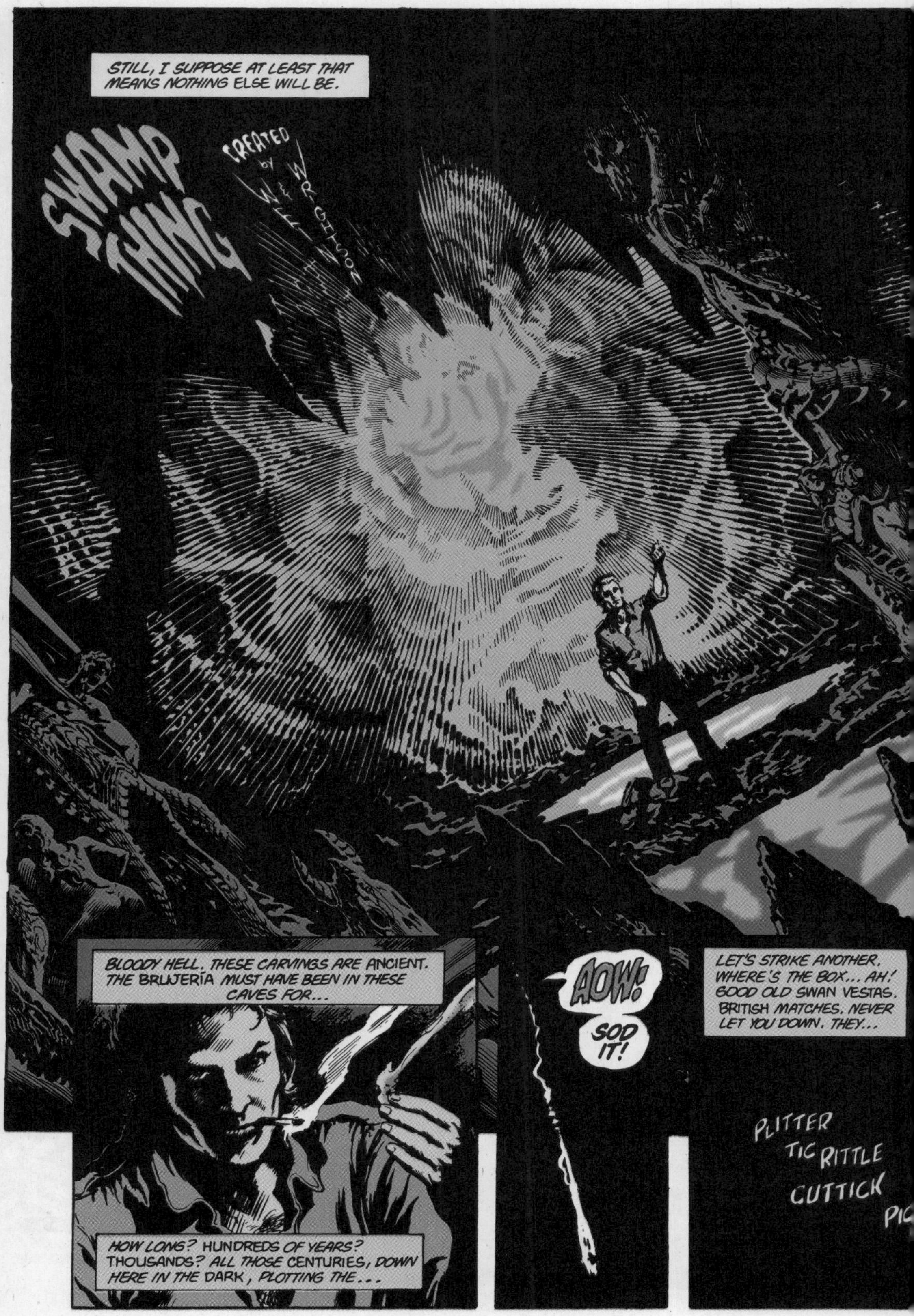
STILL, I SUPPOSE AT LEAST THAT MEANS NOTHING ELSE WILL BE.
SWAMP THING
CREATED by WEIN & WRIGHTSON
BLOODY HELL. THESE CARVINGS ARE ANCIENT. THE BRUJERÍA MUST HAVE BEEN IN THESE CAVES FOR...
HOW LONG? HUNDREDS OF YEARS? THOUSANDS? ALL THOSE CENTURIES, DOWN HERE IN THE DARK, PLOTTING THE...
AOW!
SOD IT!
LET'S STRIKE ANOTHER. WHERE'S THE BOX... AH! GOOD OLD SWAN VESTAS. BRITISH MATCHES. NEVER LET YOU DOWN. THEY...
PLITTER
TIC RITTLE
CUTTICK

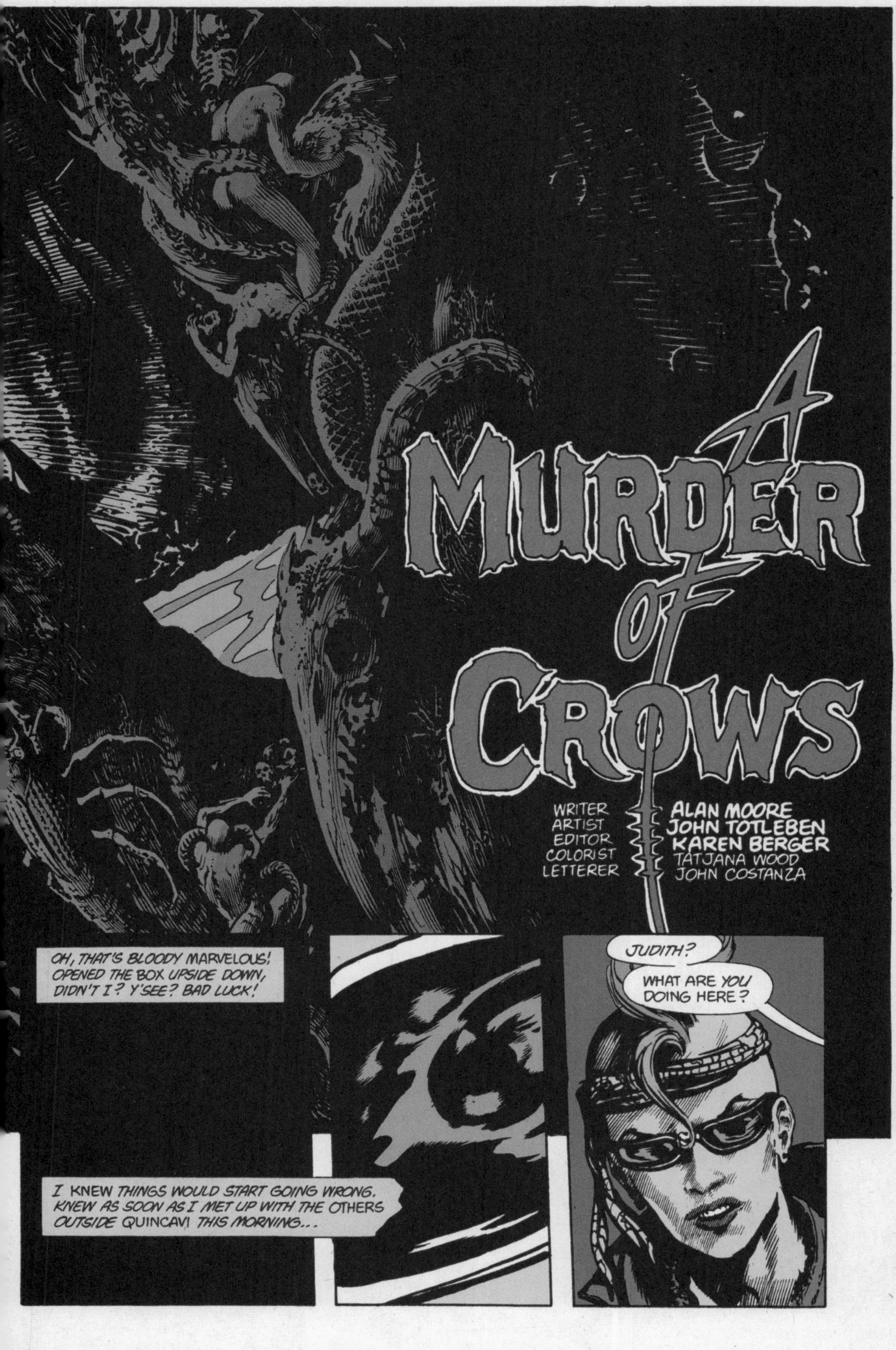
A MURDER OF CROWS
WRITER ALAN MOORE
ARTIST JOHN TOTLEBEN
EDITOR KAREN BERGER
COLORIST TATJANA WOOD
LETTERER JOHN COSTANZA
OH, THAT'S BLOODY MARVELOUS! OPENED THE BOX UPSIDE DOWN, DIDN'T I? Y'SEE? BAD LUCK!
I KNEW THINGS WOULD START GOING WRONG. KNEW AS SOON AS I MET UP WITH THE OTHERS OUTSIDE QUINCAVI THIS MORNING...
JUDITH?
WHAT ARE YOU DOING HERE?

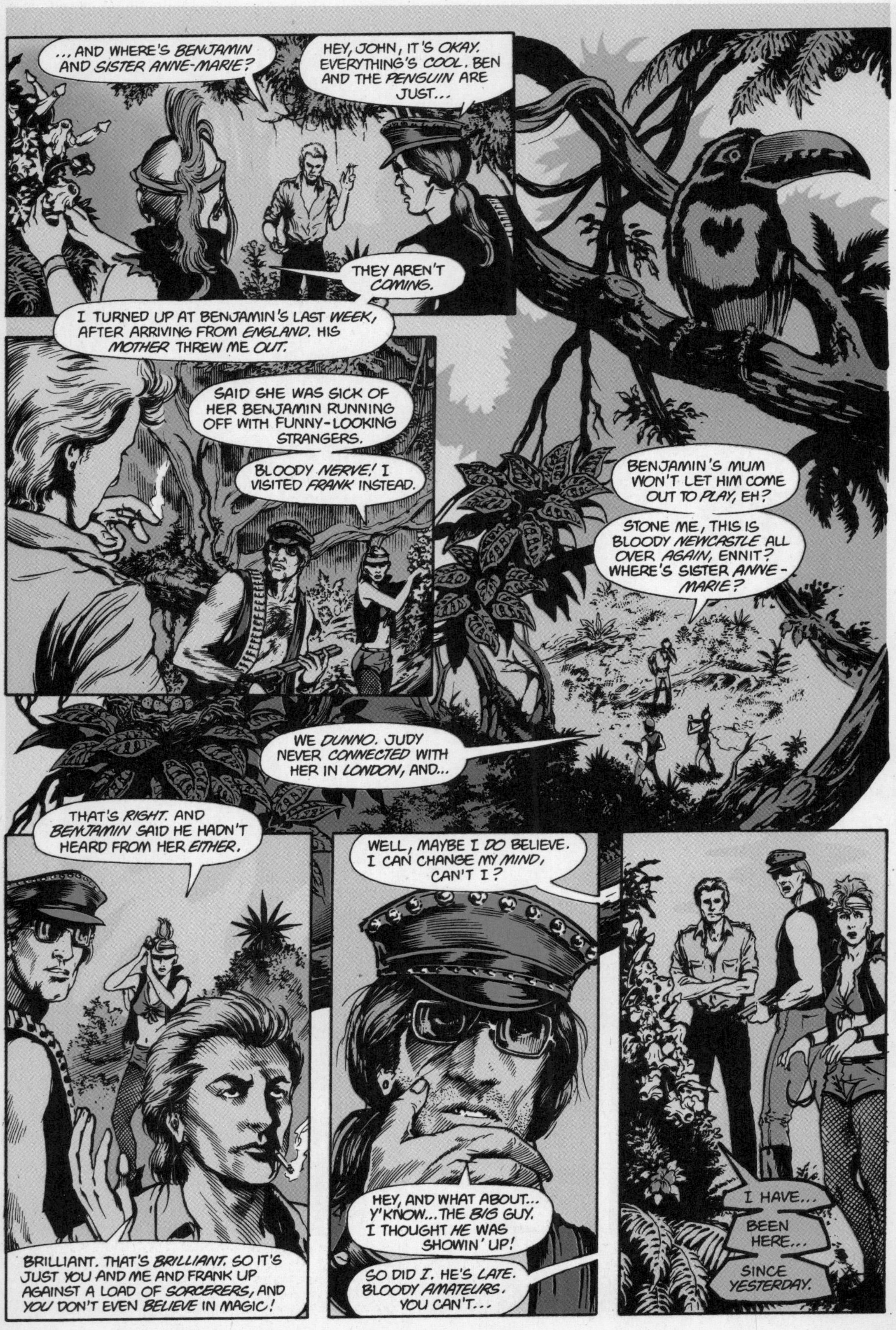
...AND WHERE'S BENJAMIN AND SISTER ANNE-MARIE?
HEY, JOHN, IT'S OKAY. EVERYTHING'S COOL. BEN AND THE PENGUIN ARE JUST...
THEY AREN'T COMING.
I TURNED UP AT BENJAMIN'S LAST WEEK, AFTER ARRIVING FROM ENGLAND. HIS MOTHER THREW ME OUT.
SAID SHE WAS SICK OF HER BENJAMIN RUNNING OFF WITH FUNNY-LOOKING STRANGERS.
BLOODY NERVE! I VISITED FRANK INSTEAD.
BENJAMIN'S MUM WON'T LET HIM COME OUT TO PLAY, EH?
STONE ME, THIS IS BLOODY NEWCASTLE ALL OVER AGAIN, ENNIT? WHERE'S SISTER ANNE-MARIE?
WE DUNNO. JUDY NEVER CONNECTED WITH HER IN LONDON, AND...
THAT'S RIGHT. AND BENJAMIN SAID HE HADN'T HEARD FROM HER EITHER.
BRILLIANT. THAT'S BRILLIANT. SO IT'S JUST YOU AND ME AND FRANK UP AGAINST A LOAD OF SORCERERS, AND YOU DON'T EVEN BELIEVE IN MAGIC!
WELL, MAYBE I DO BELIEVE. I CAN CHANGE MY MIND, CAN'T I?
HEY, AND WHAT ABOUT... Y'KNOW... THE BIG GUY. I THOUGHT HE WAS SHOWIN' UP!
SO DID I. HE'S LATE. BLOODY AMATEURS. YOU CAN'T...
I HAVE...
BEEN HERE...
SINCE YESTERDAY.

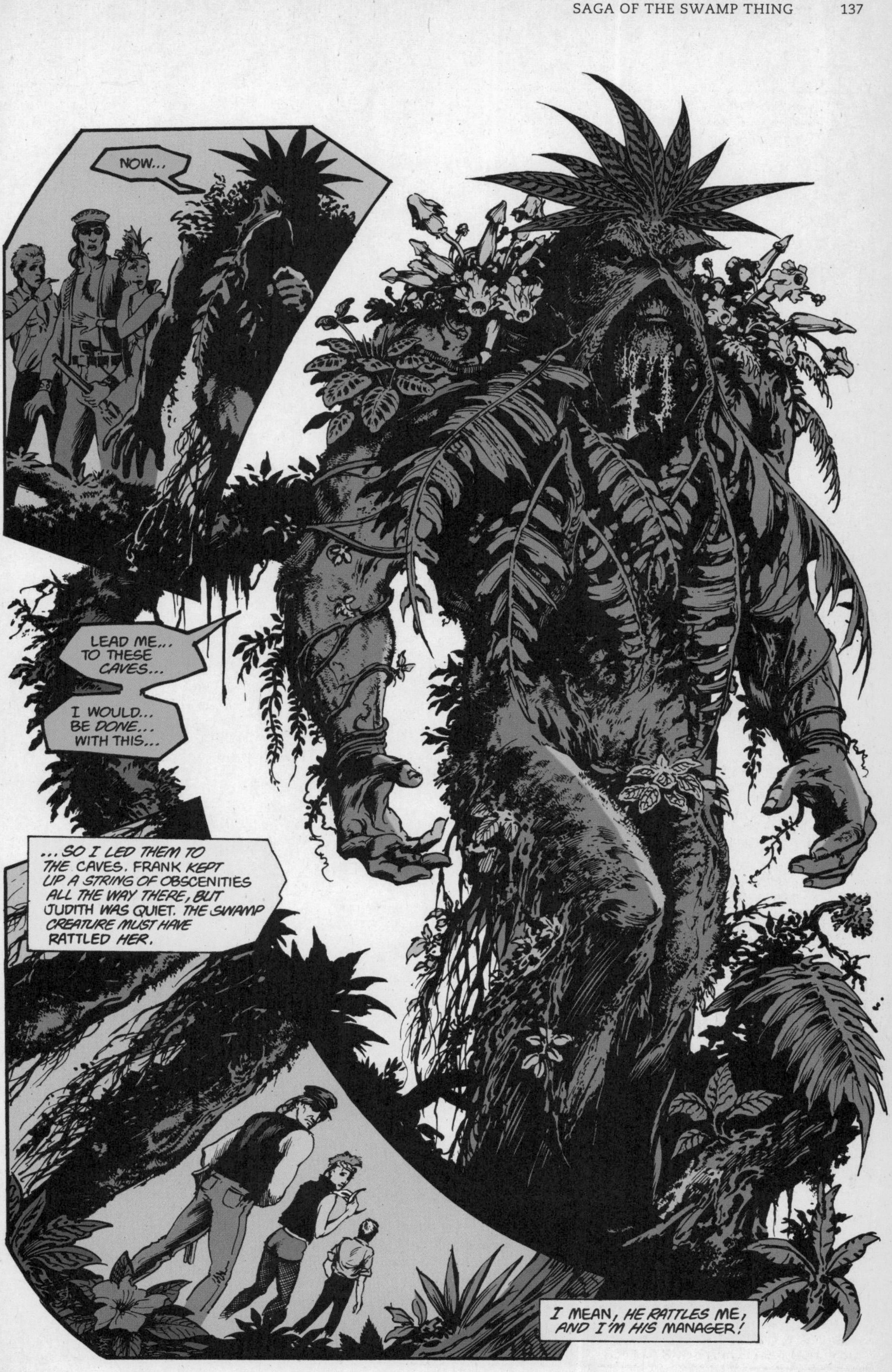
NOW...
LEAD ME... TO THESE CAVES...
I WOULD... BE DONE... WITH THIS...
...SO I LED THEM TO THE CAVES. FRANK KEPT UP A STRING OF OBSCENITIES ALL THE WAY THERE, BUT JUDITH WAS QUIET. THE SWAMP CREATURE MUST HAVE RATTLED HER.
I MEAN, HE RATTLES ME, AND I'M HIS MANAGER!

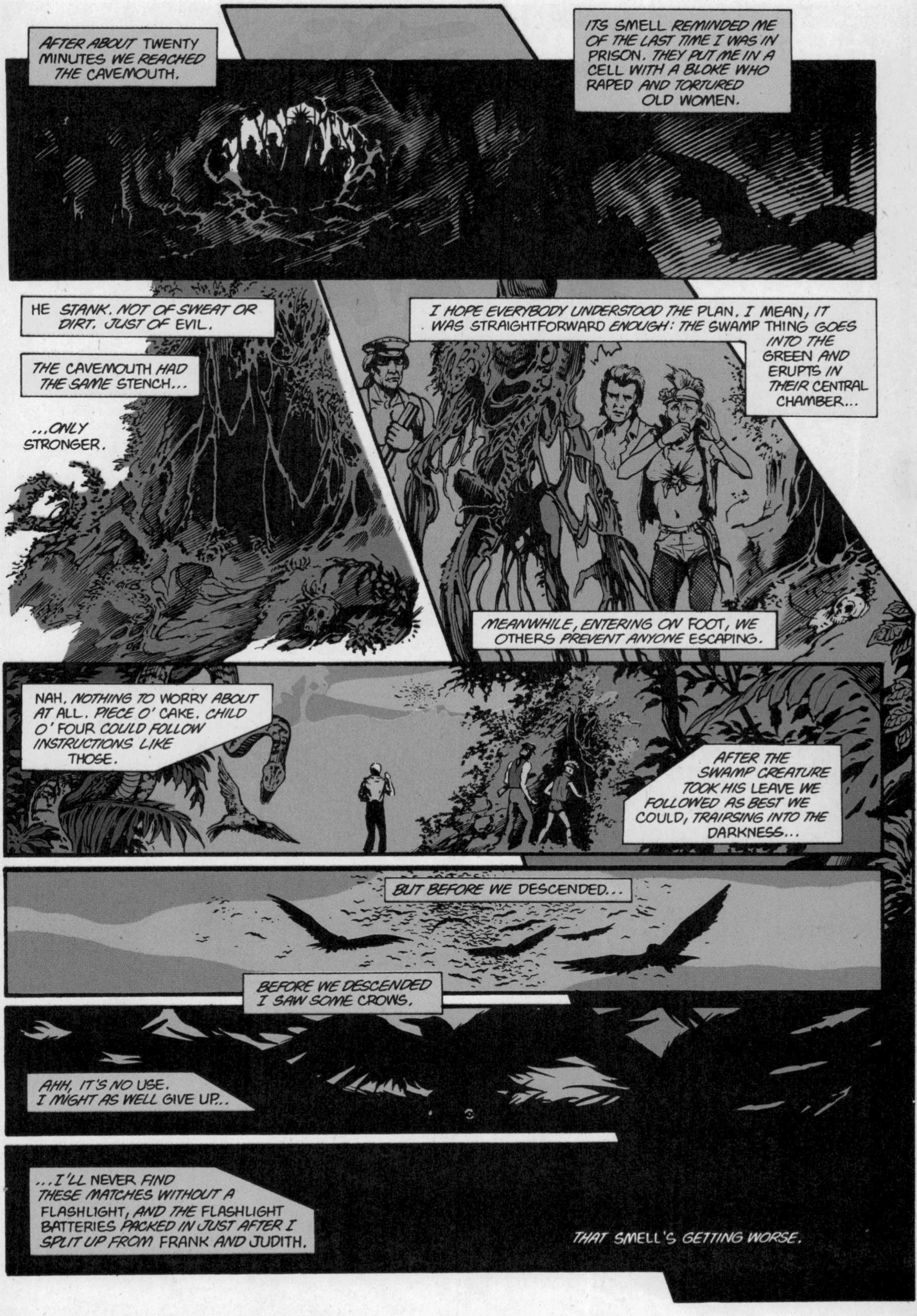
AFTER ABOUT TWENTY MINUTES WE REACHED THE CAVEMOUTH.
ITS SMELL REMINDED ME OF THE LAST TIME I WAS IN PRISON. THEY PUT ME IN A CELL WITH A BLOKE WHO RAPED AND TORTURED OLD WOMEN.
HE STANK. NOT OF SWEAT OR DIRT. JUST OF EVIL.
THE CAVEMOUTH HAD THE SAME STENCH...
...ONLY STRONGER.
I HOPE EVERYBODY UNDERSTOOD THE PLAN. I MEAN, IT WAS STRAIGHTFORWARD ENOUGH: THE SWAMP THING GOES INTO THE GREEN AND ERUPTS IN THEIR CENTRAL CHAMBER...
MEANWHILE, ENTERING ON FOOT, WE OTHERS PREVENT ANYONE ESCAPING.
NAH. NOTHING TO WORRY ABOUT AT ALL. PIECE O' CAKE. CHILD O' FOUR COULD FOLLOW INSTRUCTIONS LIKE THOSE.
AFTER THE SWAMP CREATURE TOOK HIS LEAVE WE FOLLOWED AS BEST WE COULD, TRAIPSING INTO THE DARKNESS...
BUT BEFORE WE DESCENDED...
BEFORE WE DESCENDED I SAW SOME CROWS.
AHH, IT'S NO USE. I MIGHT AS WELL GIVE UP...
...I'LL NEVER FIND THESE MATCHES WITHOUT A FLASHLIGHT, AND THE FLASHLIGHT BATTERIES PACKED IN JUST AFTER I SPLIT UP FROM FRANK AND JUDITH.
THAT SMELL'S GETTING WORSE.

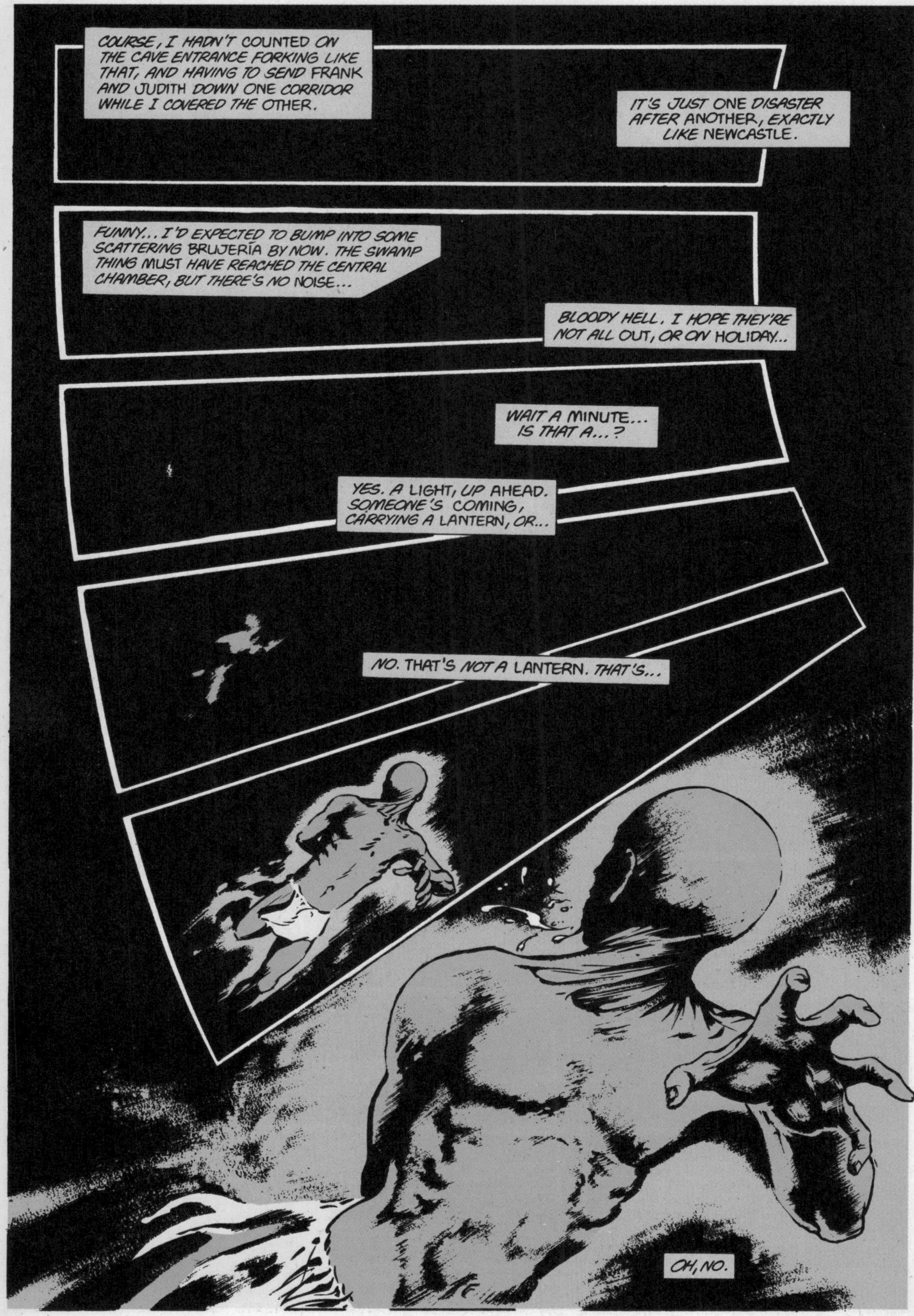
COURSE, I HADN'T COUNTED ON THE CAVE ENTRANCE FORKING LIKE THAT, AND HAVING TO SEND FRANK AND JUDITH DOWN ONE CORRIDOR WHILE I COVERED THE OTHER.
IT'S JUST ONE DISASTER AFTER ANOTHER, EXACTLY LIKE NEWCASTLE.
FUNNY... I'D EXPECTED TO BUMP INTO SOME SCATTERING BRUJERÍA BY NOW. THE SWAMP THING MUST HAVE REACHED THE CENTRAL CHAMBER, BUT THERE'S NO NOISE...
BLOODY HELL. I HOPE THEY'RE NOT ALL OUT, OR ON HOLIDAY...
WAIT A MINUTE... IS THAT A...?
YES. A LIGHT, UP AHEAD. SOMEONE'S COMING, CARRYING A LANTERN, OR...
NO. THAT'S NOT A LANTERN. THAT'S...
OH, NO.

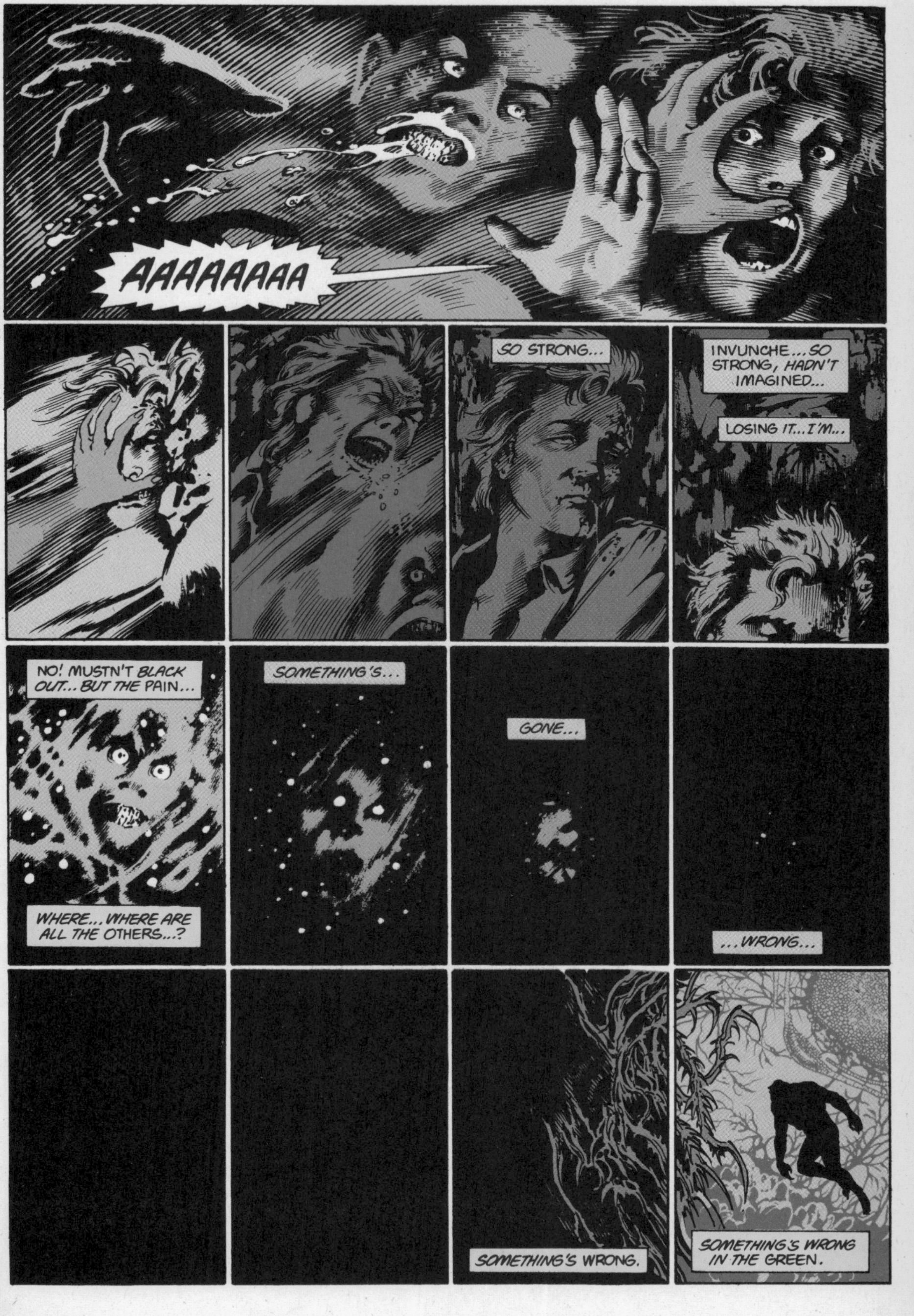
AAAAAAAA
SO STRONG...
INVUNCHE... SO STRONG, HADN'T IMAGINED...
LOSING IT... I'M...
NO! MUSTN'T BLACK OUT... BUT THE PAIN...
WHERE... WHERE ARE ALL THE OTHERS...?
SOMETHING'S...
GONE...
...WRONG...
SOMETHING'S WRONG.
SOMETHING'S WRONG IN THE GREEN.

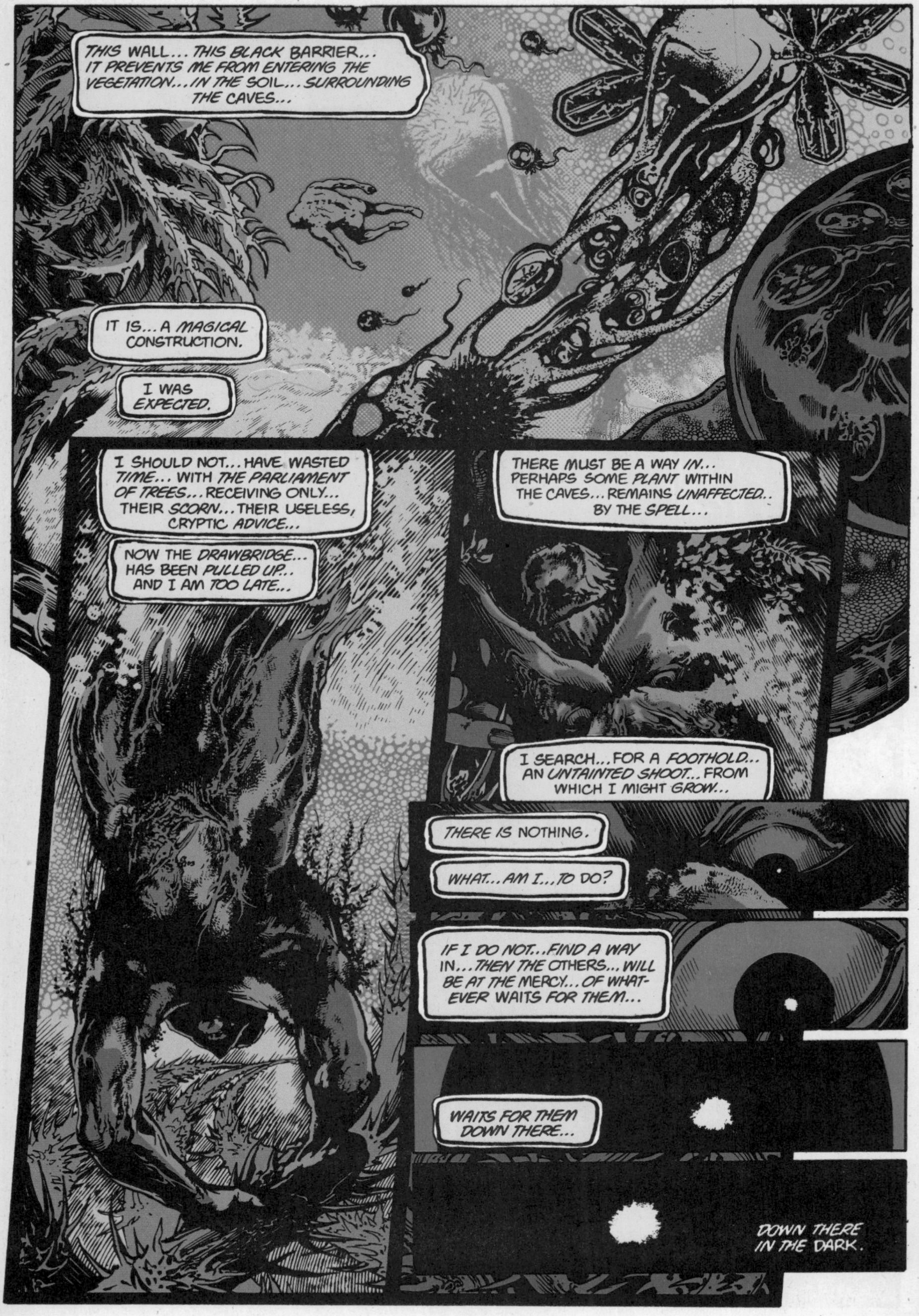
THIS WALL... THIS BLACK BARRIER... IT PREVENTS ME FROM ENTERING THE VEGETATION... IN THE SOIL... SURROUNDING THE CAVES...
IT IS... A MAGICAL CONSTRUCTION.
I WAS EXPECTED.
I SHOULD NOT... HAVE WASTED TIME... WITH THE PARLIAMENT OF TREES... RECEIVING ONLY... THEIR SCORN... THEIR USELESS, CRYPTIC ADVICE...
NOW THE DRAWBRIDGE... HAS BEEN PULLED UP... AND I AM TOO LATE...
THERE MUST BE A WAY IN... PERHAPS SOME PLANT WITHIN THE CAVES... REMAINS UNAFFECTED... BY THE SPELL...
I SEARCH... FOR A FOOTHOLD... AN UNTAINTED SHOOT... FROM WHICH I MIGHT GROW...
THERE IS NOTHING.
WHAT... AM I... TO DO?
IF I DO NOT... FIND A WAY IN... THEN THE OTHERS... WILL BE AT THE MERCY... OF WHAT-EVER WAITS FOR THEM...
WAITS FOR THEM DOWN THERE...
DOWN THERE IN THE DARK.

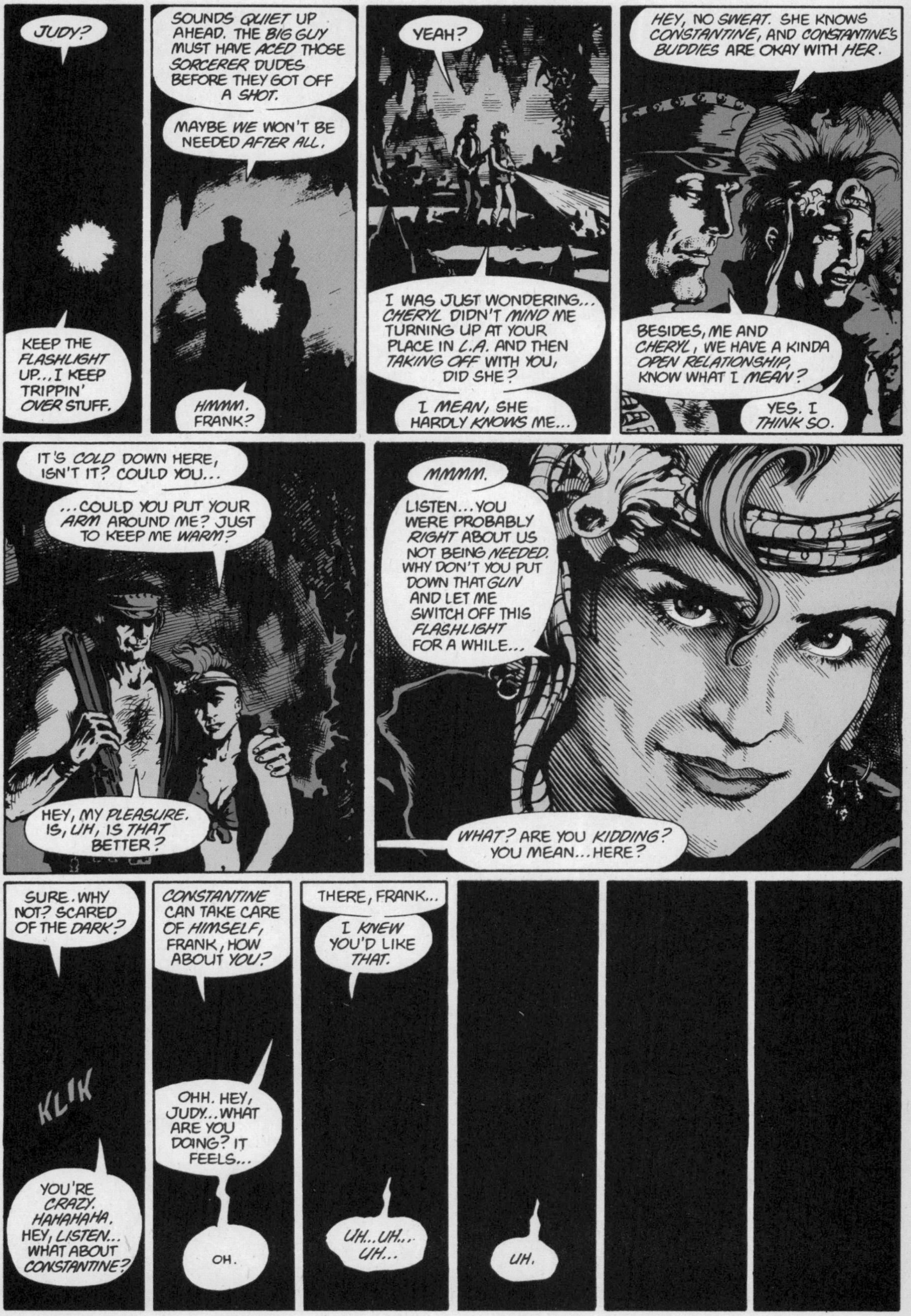
JUDY?
KEEP THE FLASHLIGHT UP... I KEEP TRIPPIN' OVER STUFF.
SOUNDS QUIET UP AHEAD. THE BIG GUY MUST HAVE ACED THOSE SORCERER DUDES BEFORE THEY GOT OFF A SHOT.
MAYBE WE WON'T BE NEEDED AFTER ALL.
HMMM. FRANK?
YEAH?
I WAS JUST WONDERING... CHERYL DIDN'T MIND ME TURNING UP AT YOUR PLACE IN L.A. AND THEN TAKING OFF WITH YOU, DID SHE?
I MEAN, SHE HARDLY KNOWS ME...
HEY, NO SWEAT. SHE KNOWS CONSTANTINE, AND CONSTANTINE'S BUDDIES ARE OKAY WITH HER.
BESIDES, ME AND CHERYL, WE HAVE A KINDA OPEN RELATIONSHIP, KNOW WHAT I MEAN?
YES. I THINK SO.
IT'S COLD DOWN HERE, ISN'T IT? COULD YOU...
...COULD YOU PUT YOUR ARM AROUND ME? JUST TO KEEP ME WARM?
HEY, MY PLEASURE. IS, UH, IS THAT BETTER?
MMMM.
LISTEN... YOU WERE PROBABLY RIGHT ABOUT US NOT BEING NEEDED. WHY DON'T YOU PUT DOWN THAT GUN AND LET ME SWITCH OFF THIS FLASHLIGHT FOR A WHILE...
WHAT? ARE YOU KIDDING? YOU MEAN... HERE?
SURE. WHY NOT? SCARED OF THE DARK?
KLIK
YOU'RE CRAZY. HAHAHAHA. HEY, LISTEN... WHAT ABOUT CONSTANTINE?
CONSTANTINE CAN TAKE CARE OF HIMSELF, FRANK. HOW ABOUT YOU?
OHH. HEY, JUDY... WHAT ARE YOU DOING? IT FEELS...
OH.
THERE, FRANK...
I KNEW YOU'D LIKE THAT.
UH... UH... UH...
UH.

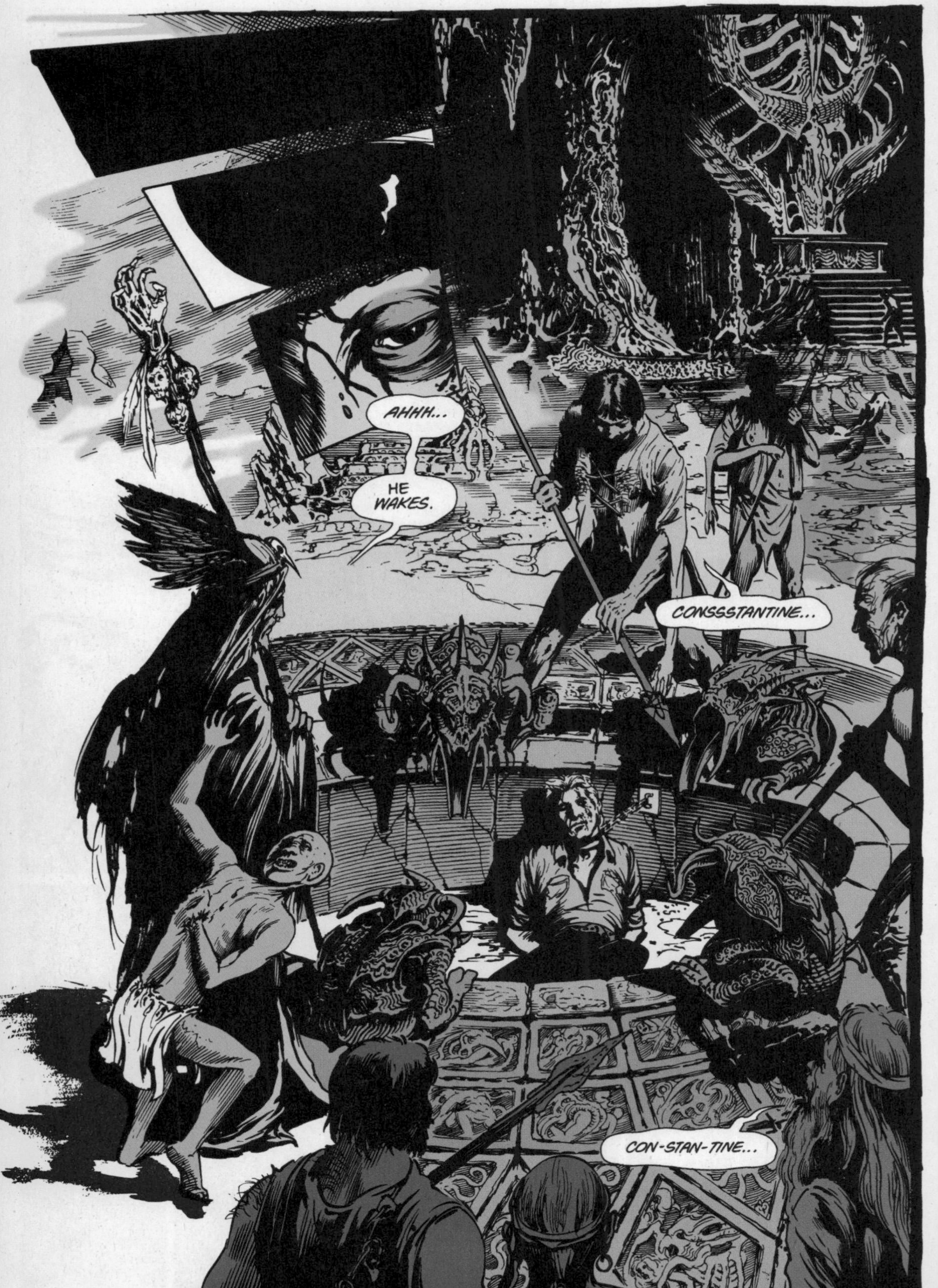
AHHH...
HE WAKES.
CONSSSTANTINE...
CON-STAN-TINE...

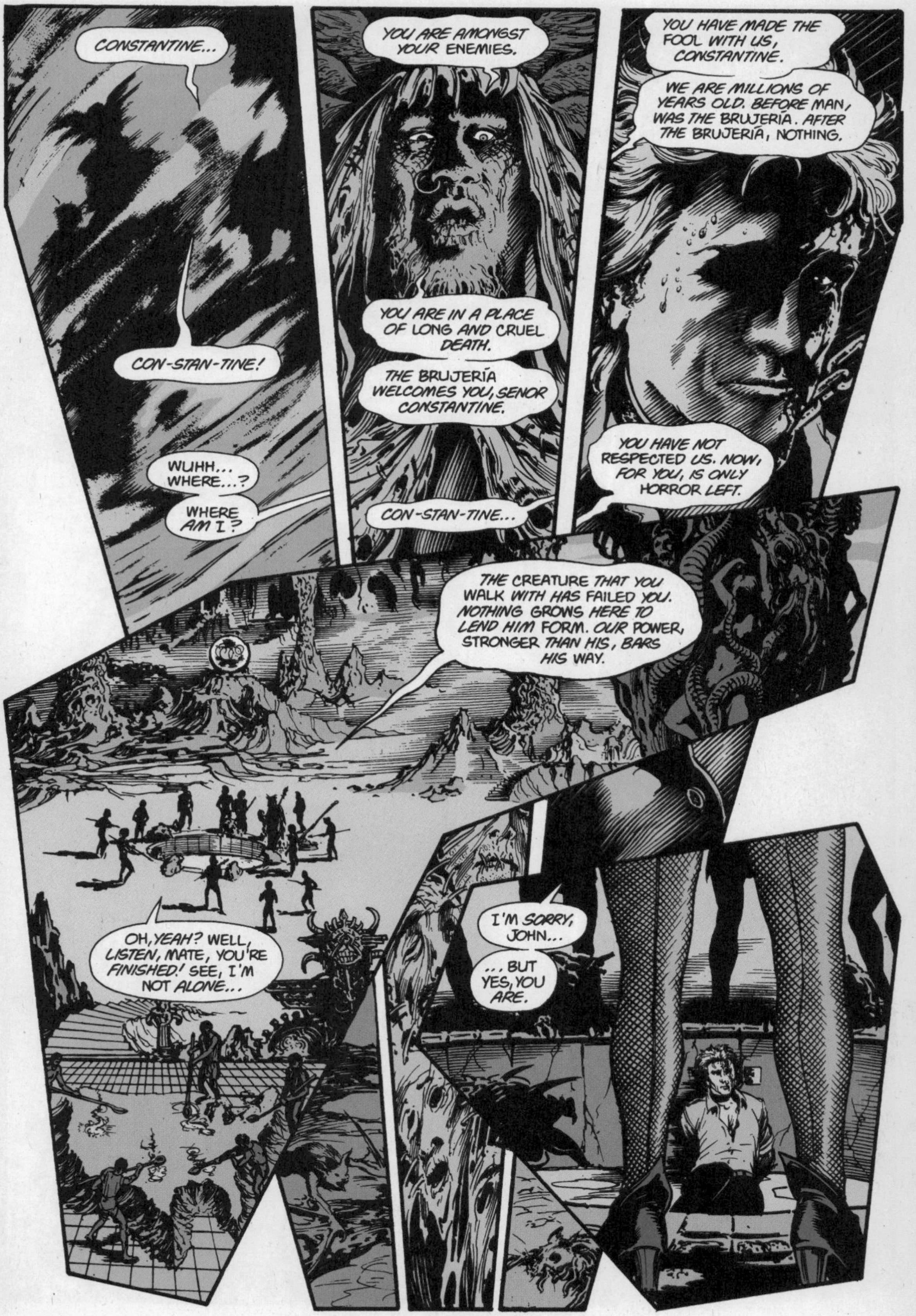
CONSTANTINE...
CON-STAN-TINE!
WUHH... WHERE...?
WHERE AM I?
YOU ARE AMONGST YOUR ENEMIES.
YOU ARE IN A PLACE OF LONG AND CRUEL DEATH.
THE BRUJERÍA WELCOMES YOU, SENOR CONSTANTINE.
CON-STAN-TINE...
YOU HAVE MADE THE FOOL WITH US, CONSTANTINE.
WE ARE MILLIONS OF YEARS OLD. BEFORE MAN, WAS THE BRUJERÍA. AFTER THE BRUJERÍA, NOTHING.
YOU HAVE NOT RESPECTED US. NOW, FOR YOU, IS ONLY HORROR LEFT.
THE CREATURE THAT YOU WALK WITH HAS FAILED YOU. NOTHING GROWS HERE TO LEND HIM FORM. OUR POWER, STRONGER THAN HIS, BARS HIS WAY.
OH, YEAH? WELL, LISTEN, MATE, YOU'RE FINISHED! SEE, I'M NOT ALONE...
I'M SORRY, JOHN...
...BUT YES, YOU ARE.

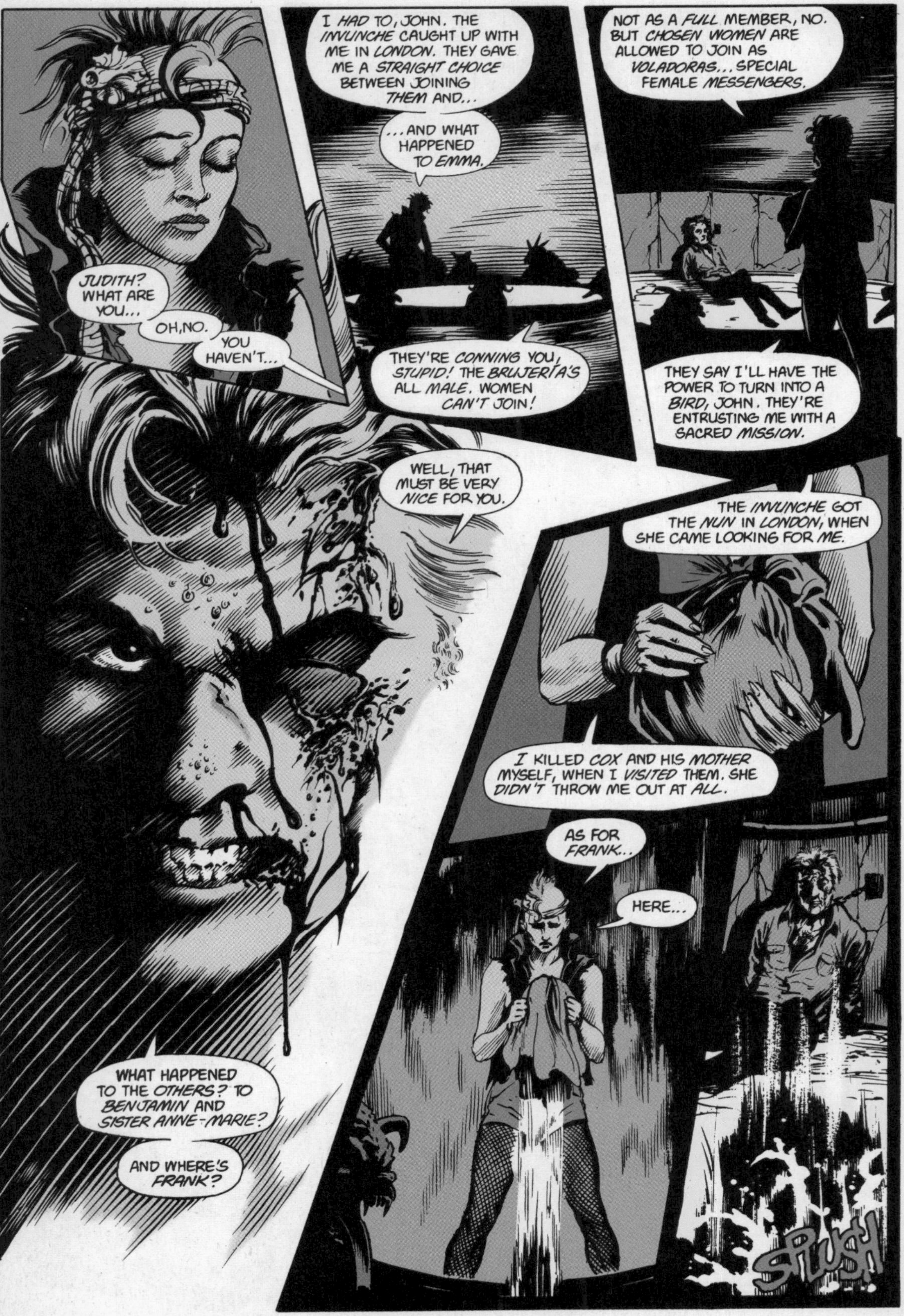
JUDITH? WHAT ARE YOU...
OH, NO.
YOU HAVEN'T...
I HAD TO, JOHN. THE INVUNCHE CAUGHT UP WITH ME IN LONDON. THEY GAVE ME A STRAIGHT CHOICE BETWEEN JOINING THEM AND...
...AND WHAT HAPPENED TO EMMA.
THEY'RE CONNING YOU, STUPID! THE BRUJERÍA'S ALL MALE. WOMEN CAN'T JOIN!
NOT AS A FULL MEMBER, NO. BUT CHOSEN WOMEN ARE ALLOWED TO JOIN AS VOLADORAS... SPECIAL FEMALE MESSENGERS.
THEY SAY I'LL HAVE THE POWER TO TURN INTO A BIRD, JOHN. THEY'RE ENTRUSTING ME WITH A SACRED MISSION.
WELL, THAT MUST BE VERY NICE FOR YOU.
WHAT HAPPENED TO THE OTHERS? TO BENJAMIN AND SISTER ANNE-MARIE?
AND WHERE'S FRANK?
THE INVUNCHE GOT THE NUN IN LONDON, WHEN SHE CAME LOOKING FOR ME.
I KILLED COX AND HIS MOTHER MYSELF, WHEN I VISITED THEM. SHE DIDN'T THROW ME OUT AT ALL.
AS FOR FRANK...
HERE...
SPLUSH

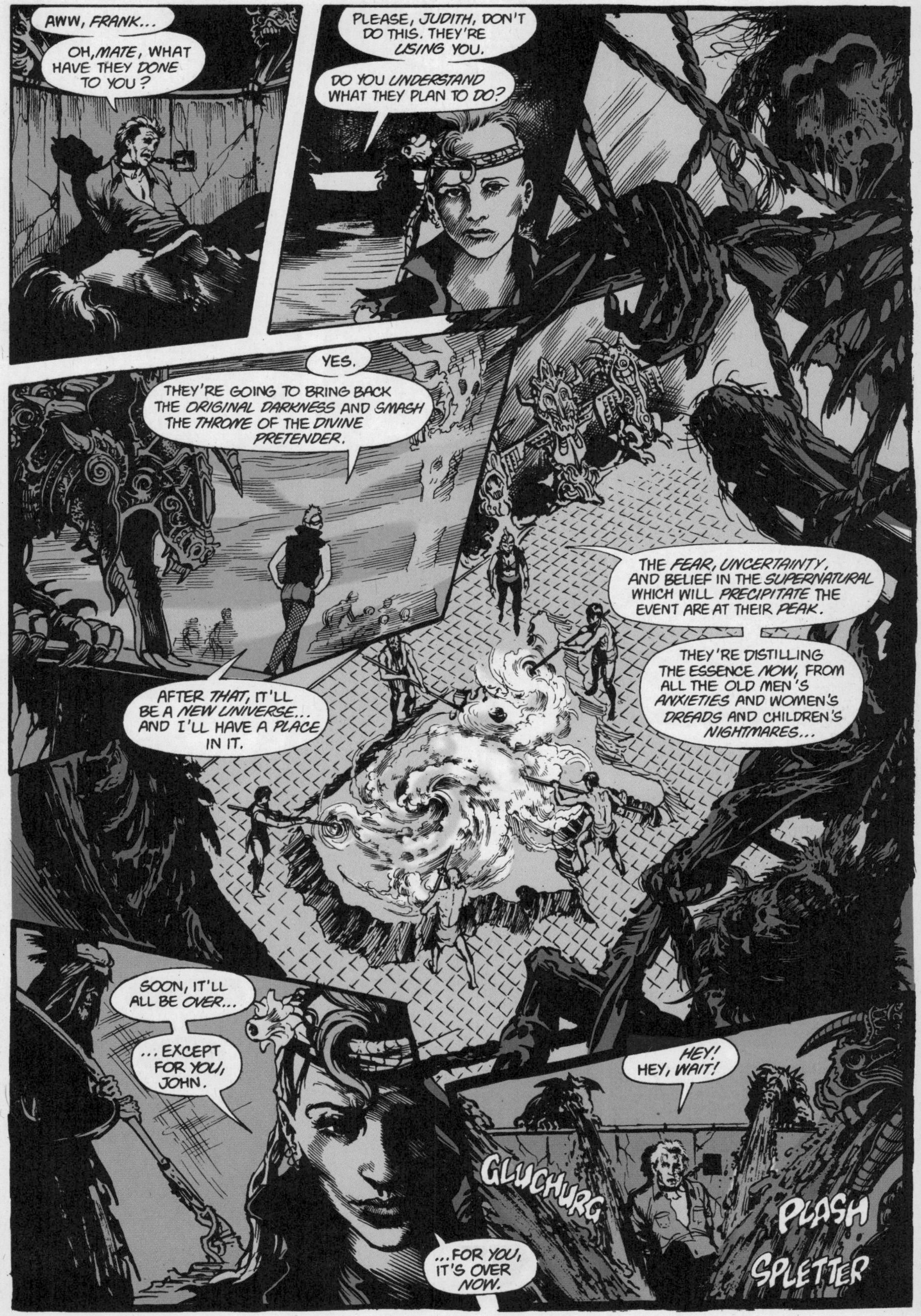
AWW, FRANK...
OH, MATE, WHAT HAVE THEY DONE TO YOU?
PLEASE, JUDITH, DON'T DO THIS. THEY'RE USING YOU.
DO YOU UNDERSTAND WHAT THEY PLAN TO DO?
YES.
THEY'RE GOING TO BRING BACK THE ORIGINAL DARKNESS AND SMASH THE THRONE OF THE DIVINE PRETENDER.
AFTER THAT, IT'LL BE A NEW UNIVERSE... AND I'LL HAVE A PLACE IN IT.
THE FEAR, UNCERTAINTY, AND BELIEF IN THE SUPERNATURAL WHICH WILL PRECIPITATE THE EVENT ARE AT THEIR PEAK.
THEY'RE DISTILLING THE ESSENCE NOW, FROM ALL THE OLD MEN'S ANXIETIES AND WOMEN'S DREADS AND CHILDREN'S NIGHTMARES...
SOON, IT'LL ALL BE OVER...
... EXCEPT FOR YOU, JOHN.
...FOR YOU, IT'S OVER NOW.
HEY! HEY, WAIT!
GLUCHURG
PLASH
SPLETTER

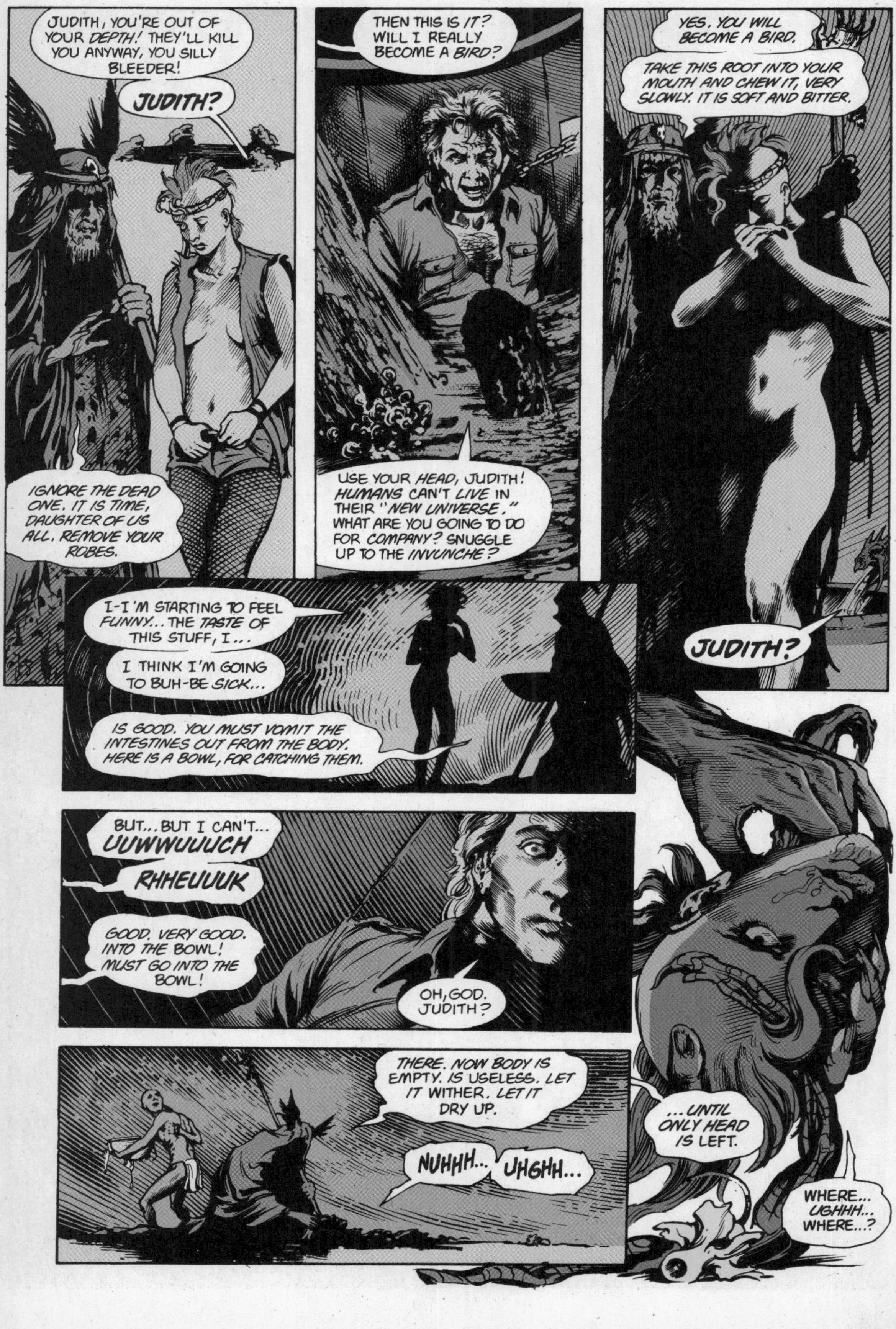
JUDITH, YOU'RE OUT OF YOUR DEPTH! THEY'LL KILL YOU ANYWAY, YOU SILLY BLEEDER!
JUDITH?
IGNORE THE DEAD ONE. IT IS TIME, DAUGHTER OF US ALL. REMOVE YOUR ROBES.
THEN THIS IS IT? WILL I REALLY BECOME A BIRD?
USE YOUR HEAD, JUDITH! HUMANS CAN'T LIVE IN THEIR "NEW UNIVERSE." WHAT ARE YOU GOING TO DO FOR COMPANY? SNUGGLE UP TO THE INVUNCHE?
YES. YOU WILL BECOME A BIRD.
TAKE THIS ROOT INTO YOUR MOUTH AND CHEW IT, VERY SLOWLY. IT IS SOFT AND BITTER.
JUDITH?
I-I'M STARTING TO FEEL FUNNY... THE TASTE OF THIS STUFF, I...
I THINK I'M GOING TO BUH-BE SICK...
IS GOOD. YOU MUST VOMIT THE INTESTINES OUT FROM THE BODY. HERE IS A BOWL, FOR CATCHING THEM.
BUT... BUT I CAN'T...
UUWWUUUCH
RHHEUUUK
GOOD. VERY GOOD. INTO THE BOWL! MUST GO INTO THE BOWL!
OH, GOD. JUDITH?
THERE. NOW BODY IS EMPTY. IS USELESS. LET IT WITHER. LET IT DRY UP.
...UNTIL ONLY HEAD IS LEFT.
NUHHH...
UHGHH...
WHERE... UGHHH... WHERE...?

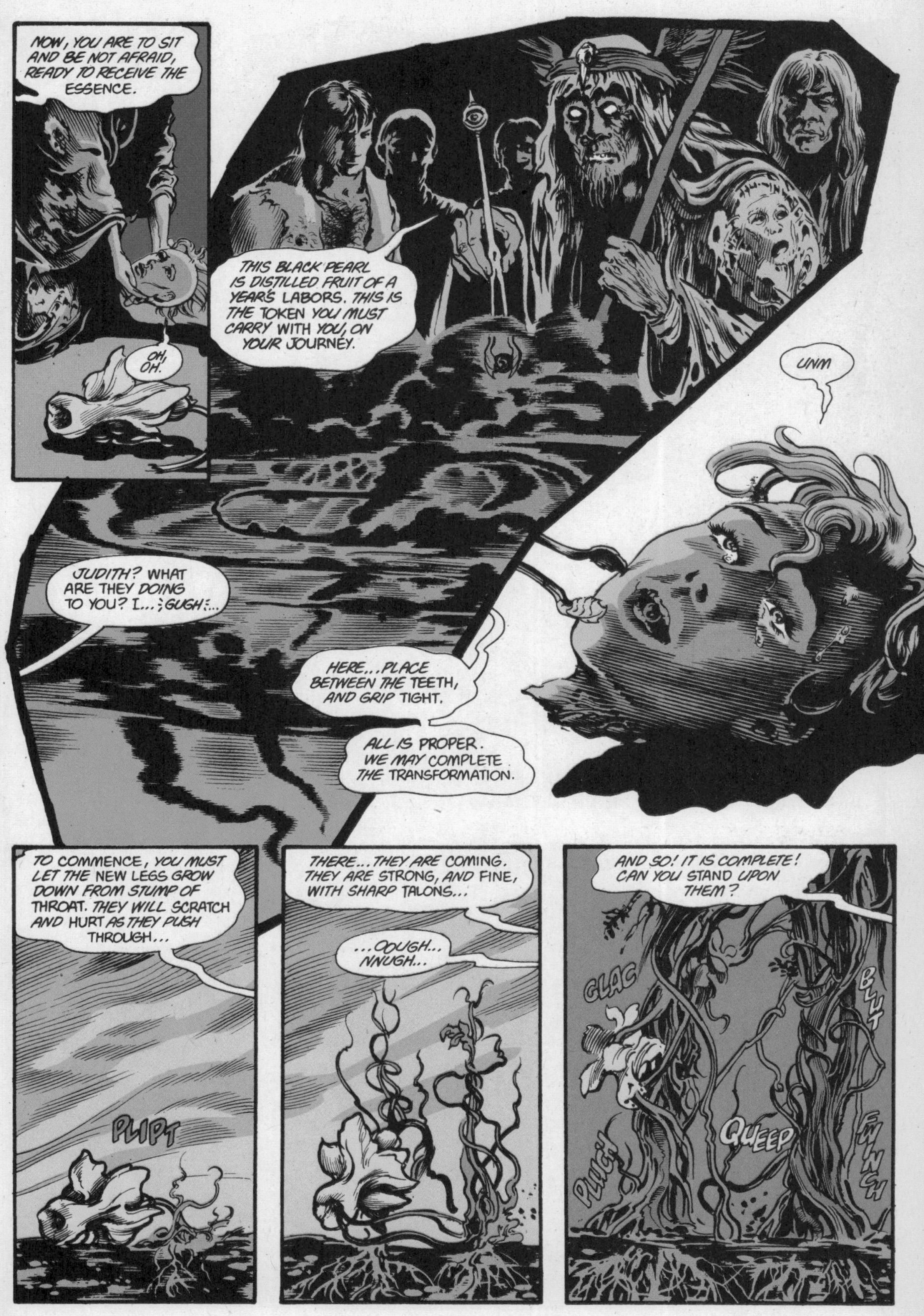
NOW, YOU ARE TO SIT AND BE NOT AFRAID, READY TO RECEIVE THE ESSENCE.
OH, OH.
THIS BLACK PEARL IS DISTILLED FRUIT OF A YEAR'S LABORS. THIS IS THE TOKEN YOU MUST CARRY WITH YOU, ON YOUR JOURNEY.
UNM
JUDITH? WHAT ARE THEY DOING TO YOU? I... GUGH...
HERE...PLACE BETWEEN THE TEETH, AND GRIP TIGHT.
ALL IS PROPER. WE MAY COMPLETE THE TRANSFORMATION.
TO COMMENCE, YOU MUST LET THE NEW LEGS GROW DOWN FROM STUMP OF THROAT. THEY WILL SCRATCH AND HURT AS THEY PUSH THROUGH...
PLIPT
THERE... THEY ARE COMING. THEY ARE STRONG, AND FINE, WITH SHARP TALONS...
...OOUGH... NNUGH...
AND SO! IT IS COMPLETE! CAN YOU STAND UPON THEM?
GLAC
BLUT
QUEEP
PLUCH
FWINCH

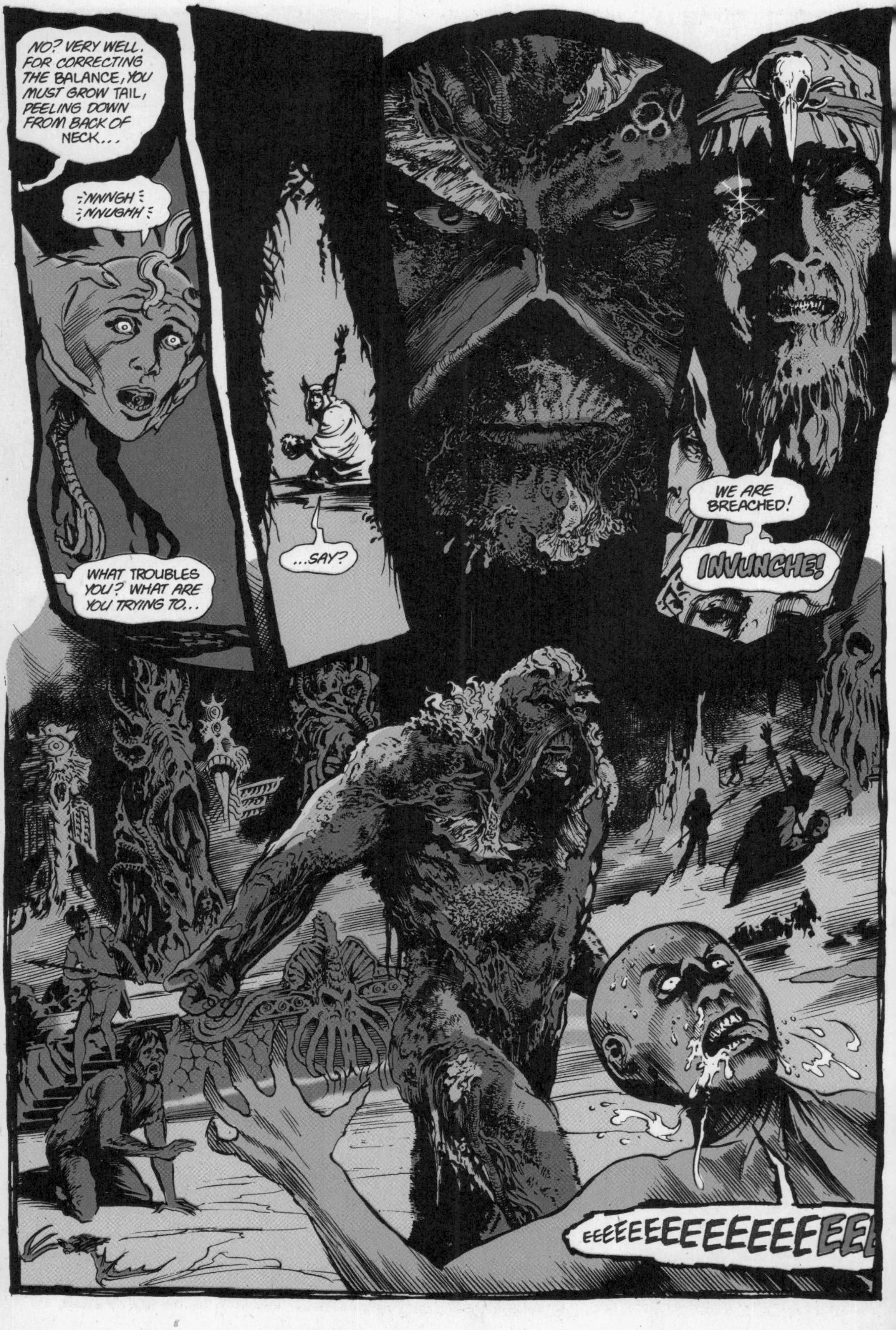
NO? VERY WELL. FOR CORRECTING THE BALANCE, YOU MUST GROW TAIL, PEELING DOWN FROM BACK OF NECK...
NNNGH NNUGHH
WHAT TROUBLES YOU? WHAT ARE YOU TRYING TO...
...SAY?
WE ARE BREACHED!
INVUNCHE!
EEEEEEEEEEEEEEEEE

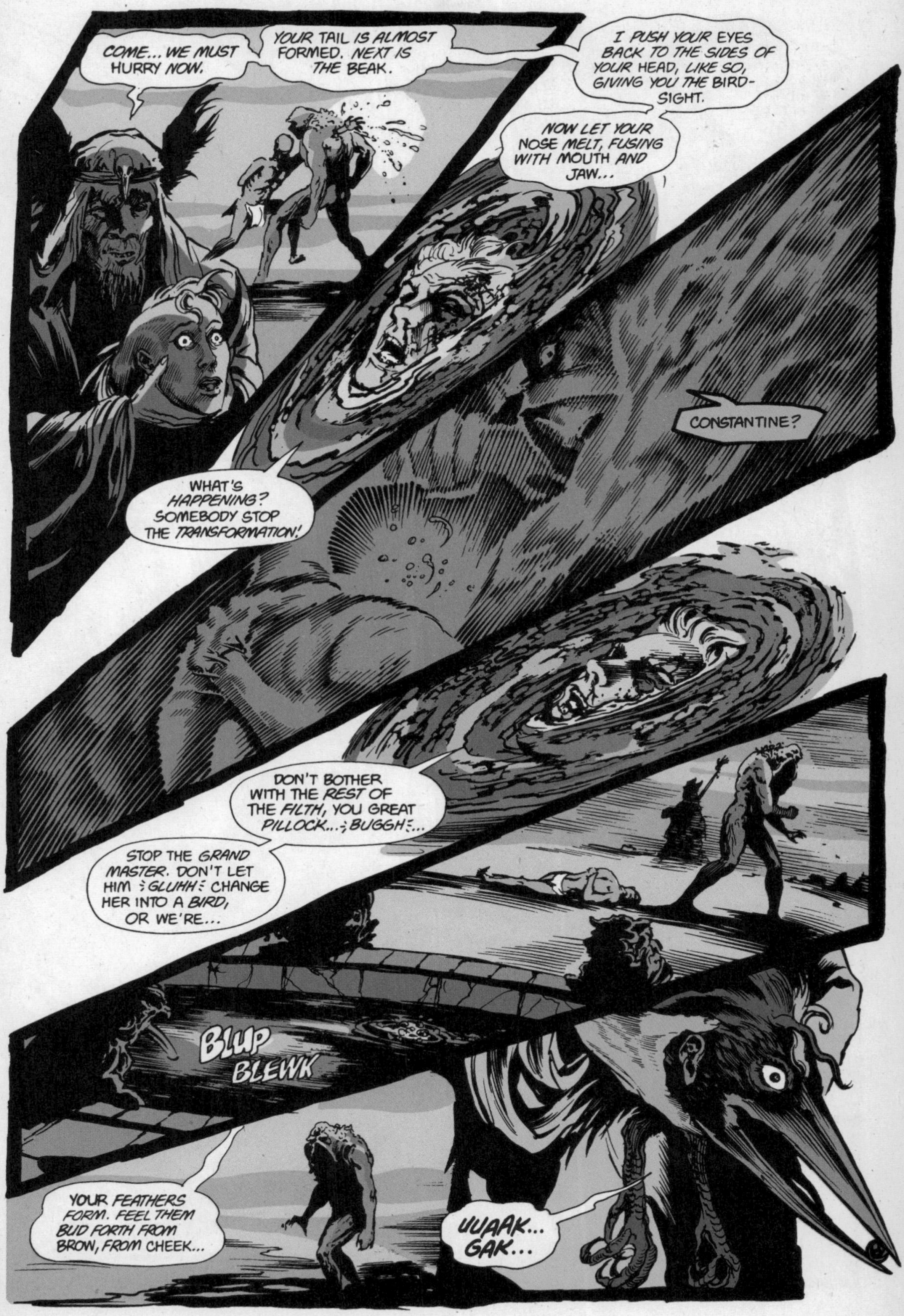
COME... WE MUST HURRY NOW.
YOUR TAIL IS ALMOST FORMED. NEXT IS THE BEAK.
I PUSH YOUR EYES BACK TO THE SIDES OF YOUR HEAD, LIKE SO, GIVING YOU THE BIRD-SIGHT.
NOW LET YOUR NOSE MELT, FUSING WITH MOUTH AND JAW...
CONSTANTINE?
WHAT'S HAPPENING? SOMEBODY STOP THE TRANSFORMATION!
DON'T BOTHER WITH THE REST OF THE FILTH, YOU GREAT PILLOCK... BUGGH...
STOP THE GRAND MASTER. DON'T LET HIM GLUHH CHANGE HER INTO A BIRD, OR WE'RE...
BLUP
BLEWK
YOUR FEATHERS FORM. FEEL THEM BUD FORTH FROM BROW, FROM CHEEK...
UUAAK... GAK...

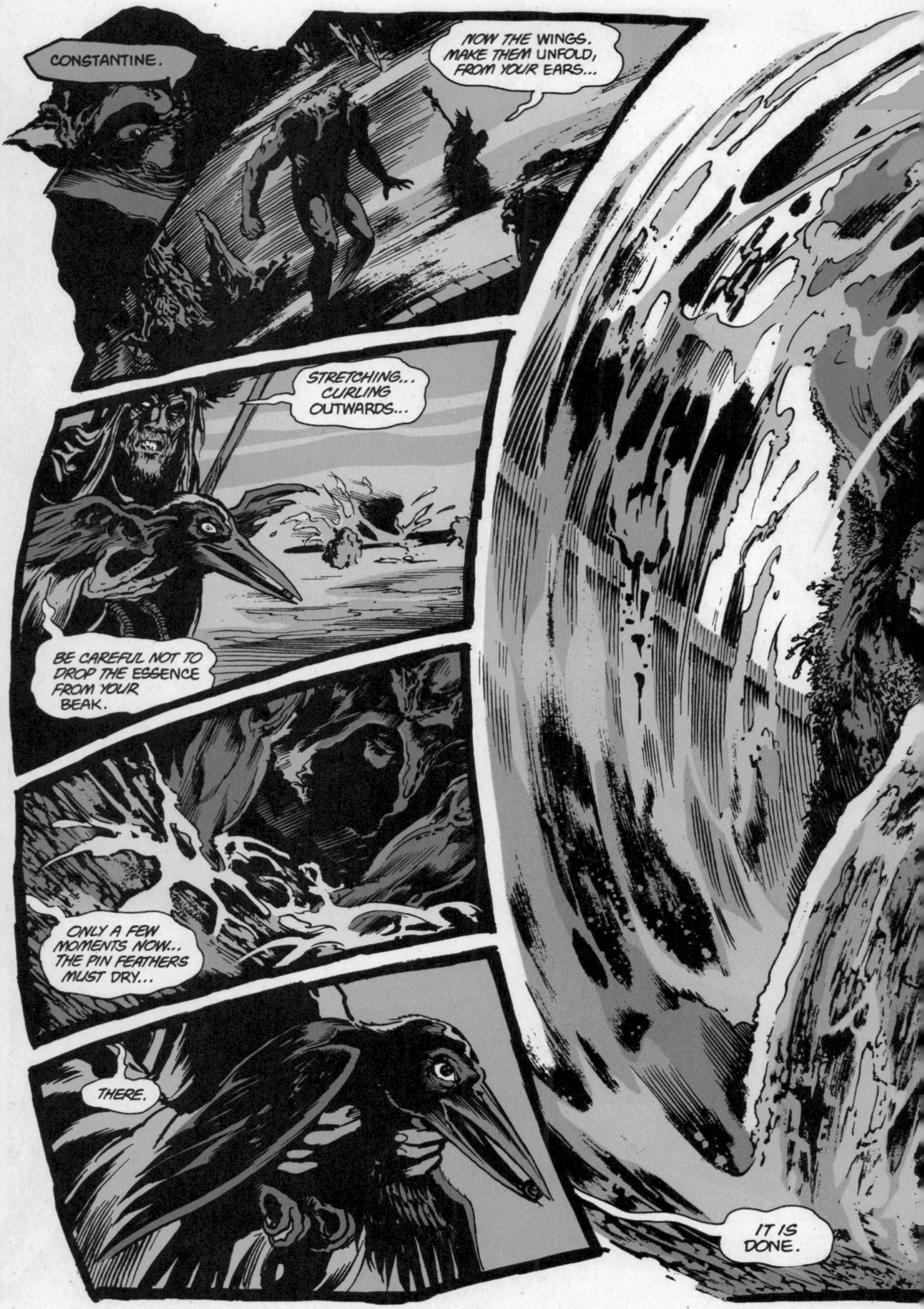
CONSTANTINE.
NOW THE WINGS. MAKE THEM UNFOLD, FROM YOUR EARS...
STRETCHING... CURLING OUTWARDS...
BE CAREFUL NOT TO DROP THE ESSENCE FROM YOUR BEAK.
ONLY A FEW MOMENTS NOW... THE PIN FEATHERS MUST DRY...
THERE.
IT IS DONE.

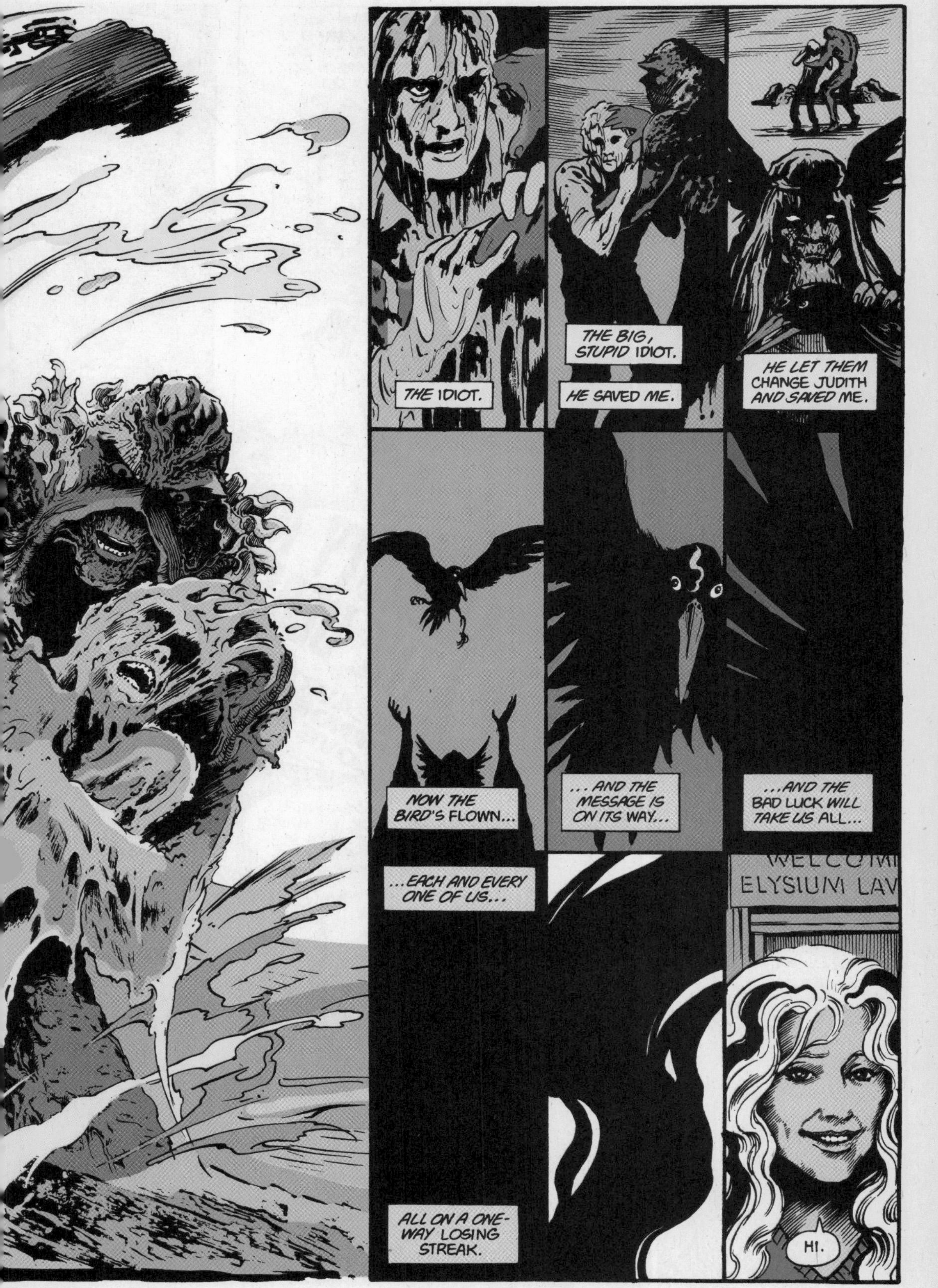
THE IDIOT.
THE BIG, STUPID IDIOT.
HE SAVED ME.
HE LET THEM CHANGE JUDITH AND SAVED ME.
NOW THE BIRD'S FLOWN...
...AND THE MESSAGE IS ON ITS WAY...
...AND THE BAD LUCK WILL TAKE US ALL...
...EACH AND EVERY ONE OF US...
ALL ON A ONE-WAY LOSING STREAK.
ELYSIUM LAV
HI.

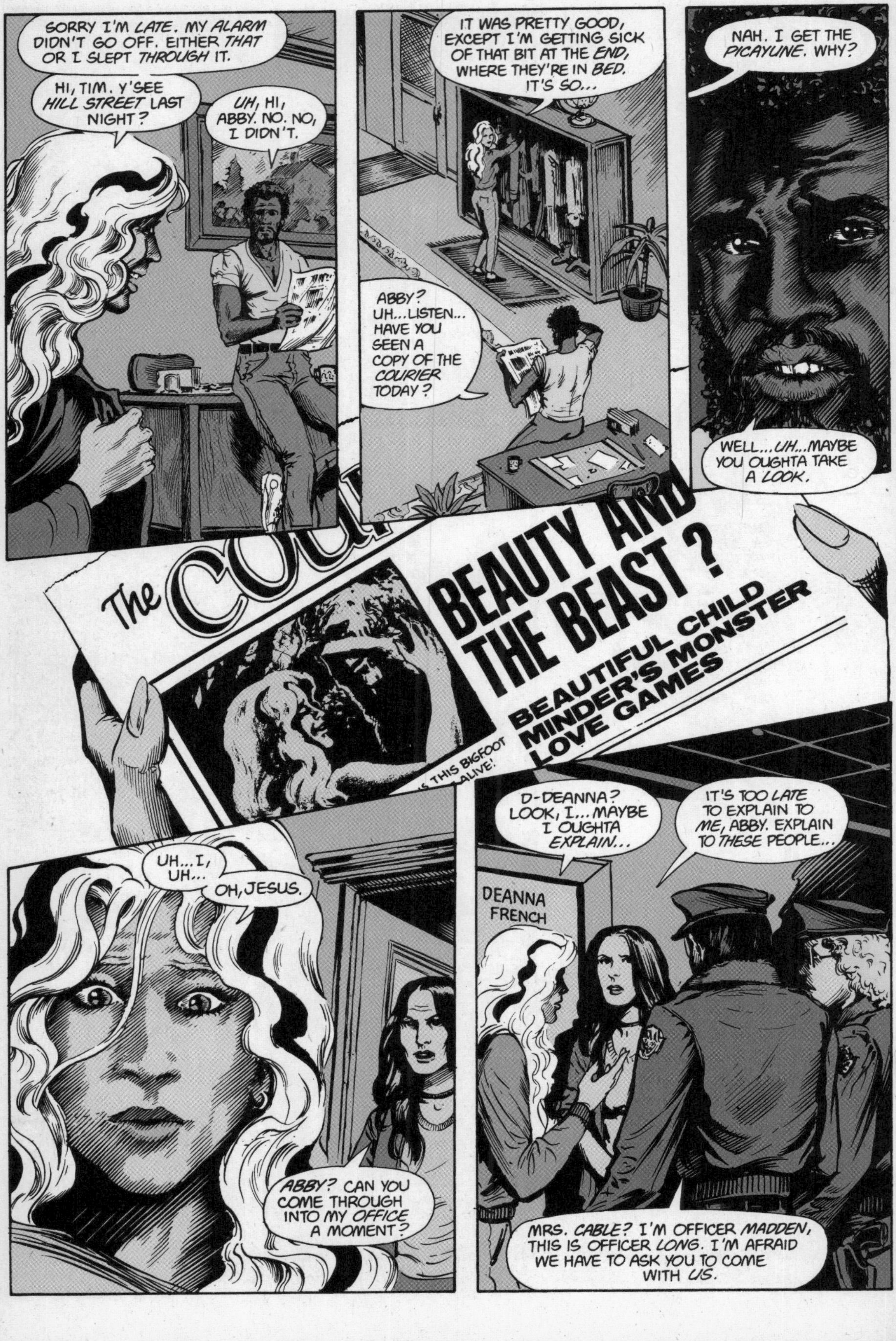
SORRY I'M LATE. MY ALARM DIDN'T GO OFF. EITHER THAT OR I SLEPT THROUGH IT.
HI, TIM. Y'SEE HILL STREET LAST NIGHT?
UH, HI, ABBY. NO. NO, I DIDN'T.
IT WAS PRETTY GOOD, EXCEPT I'M GETTING SICK OF THAT BIT AT THE END, WHERE THEY'RE IN BED. IT'S SO...
ABBY? UH...LISTEN... HAVE YOU SEEN A COPY OF THE COURIER TODAY?
NAH. I GET THE PICAYUNE. WHY?
WELL...UH...MAYBE YOU OUGHTA TAKE A LOOK.
The COU
BEAUTY AND THE BEAST?
BEAUTIFUL CHILD MINDER'S MONSTER LOVE GAMES
S THIS BIGFOOT
ALIVE!
UH...I, UH...
OH, JESUS.
ABBY? CAN YOU COME THROUGH INTO MY OFFICE A MOMENT?
D-DEANNA? LOOK, I...MAYBE I OUGHTA EXPLAIN...
IT'S TOO LATE TO EXPLAIN TO ME, ABBY. EXPLAIN TO THESE PEOPLE...
DEANNA FRENCH
MRS. CABLE? I'M OFFICER MADDEN, THIS IS OFFICER LONG. I'M AFRAID WE HAVE TO ASK YOU TO COME WITH US.

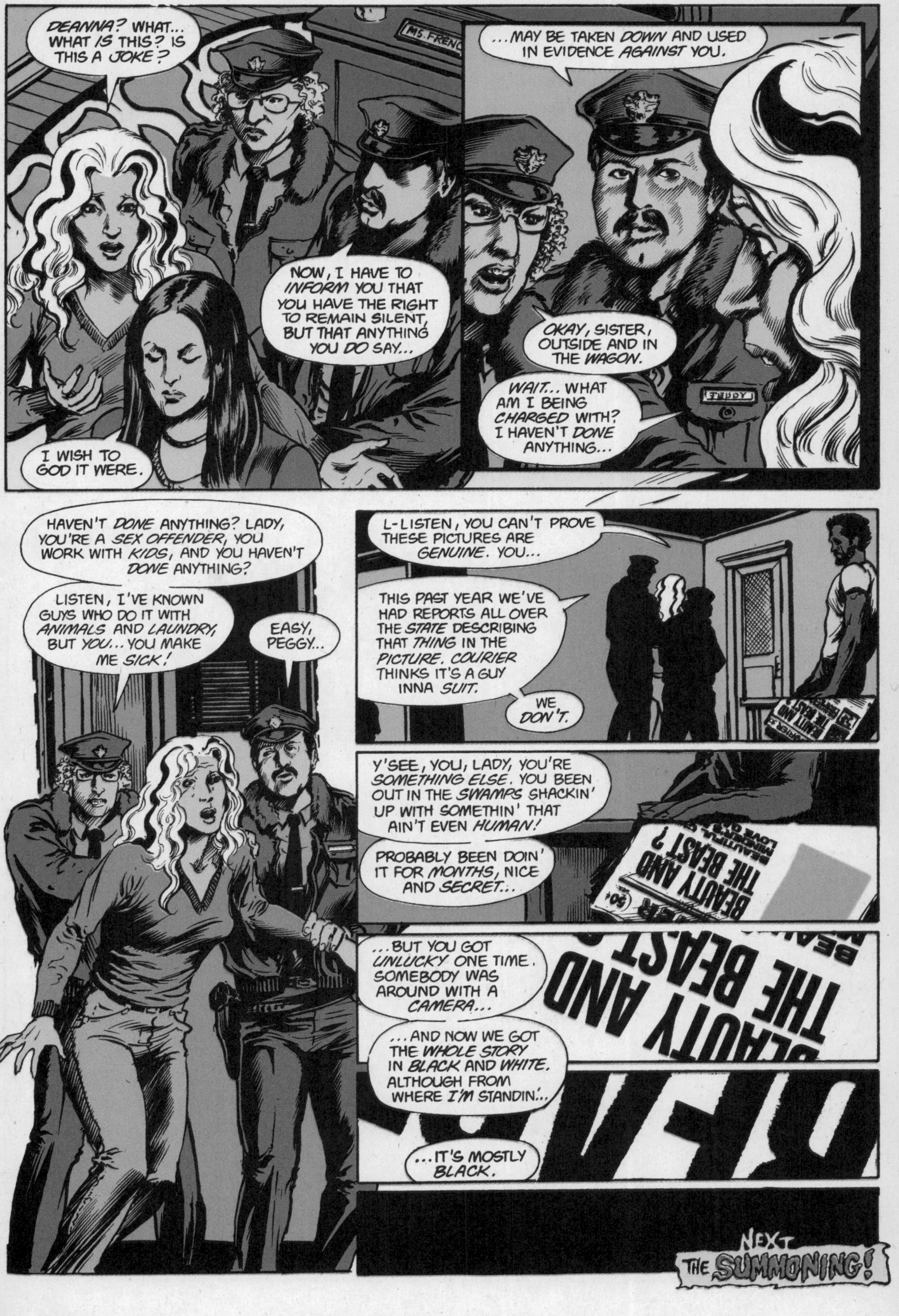
DEANNA? WHAT... WHAT IS THIS? IS THIS A JOKE?
MS. FRENC
NOW, I HAVE TO INFORM YOU THAT YOU HAVE THE RIGHT TO REMAIN SILENT, BUT THAT ANYTHING YOU DO SAY...
I WISH TO GOD IT WERE.
...MAY BE TAKEN DOWN AND USED IN EVIDENCE AGAINST YOU.
OKAY, SISTER, OUTSIDE AND IN THE WAGON.
WAIT... WHAT AM I BEING CHARGED WITH? I HAVEN'T DONE ANYTHING...
TEDDY
HAVEN'T DONE ANYTHING? LADY, YOU'RE A SEX OFFENDER, YOU WORK WITH KIDS, AND YOU HAVEN'T DONE ANYTHING?
LISTEN, I'VE KNOWN GUYS WHO DO IT WITH ANIMALS AND LAUNDRY, BUT YOU... YOU MAKE ME SICK!
EASY, PEGGY...
L-LISTEN, YOU CAN'T PROVE THESE PICTURES ARE GENUINE. YOU...
THIS PAST YEAR WE'VE HAD REPORTS ALL OVER THE STATE DESCRIBING THAT THING IN THE PICTURE. COURIER THINKS IT'S A GUY INNA SUIT.
WE DON'T.
Y'SEE, YOU, LADY, YOU'RE SOMETHING ELSE. YOU BEEN OUT IN THE SWAMPS SHACKIN' UP WITH SOMETHIN' THAT AIN'T EVEN HUMAN!
PROBABLY BEEN DOIN' IT FOR MONTHS, NICE AND SECRET...
BEAUTY AND THE BEAST ?
...BUT YOU GOT UNLUCKY ONE TIME. SOMEBODY WAS AROUND WITH A CAMERA...
...AND NOW WE GOT THE WHOLE STORY IN BLACK AND WHITE. ALTHOUGH FROM WHERE I'M STANDIN'...
BEAUTY AND THE BEAST
...IT'S MOSTLY BLACK.
NEXT THE SUMMONING!

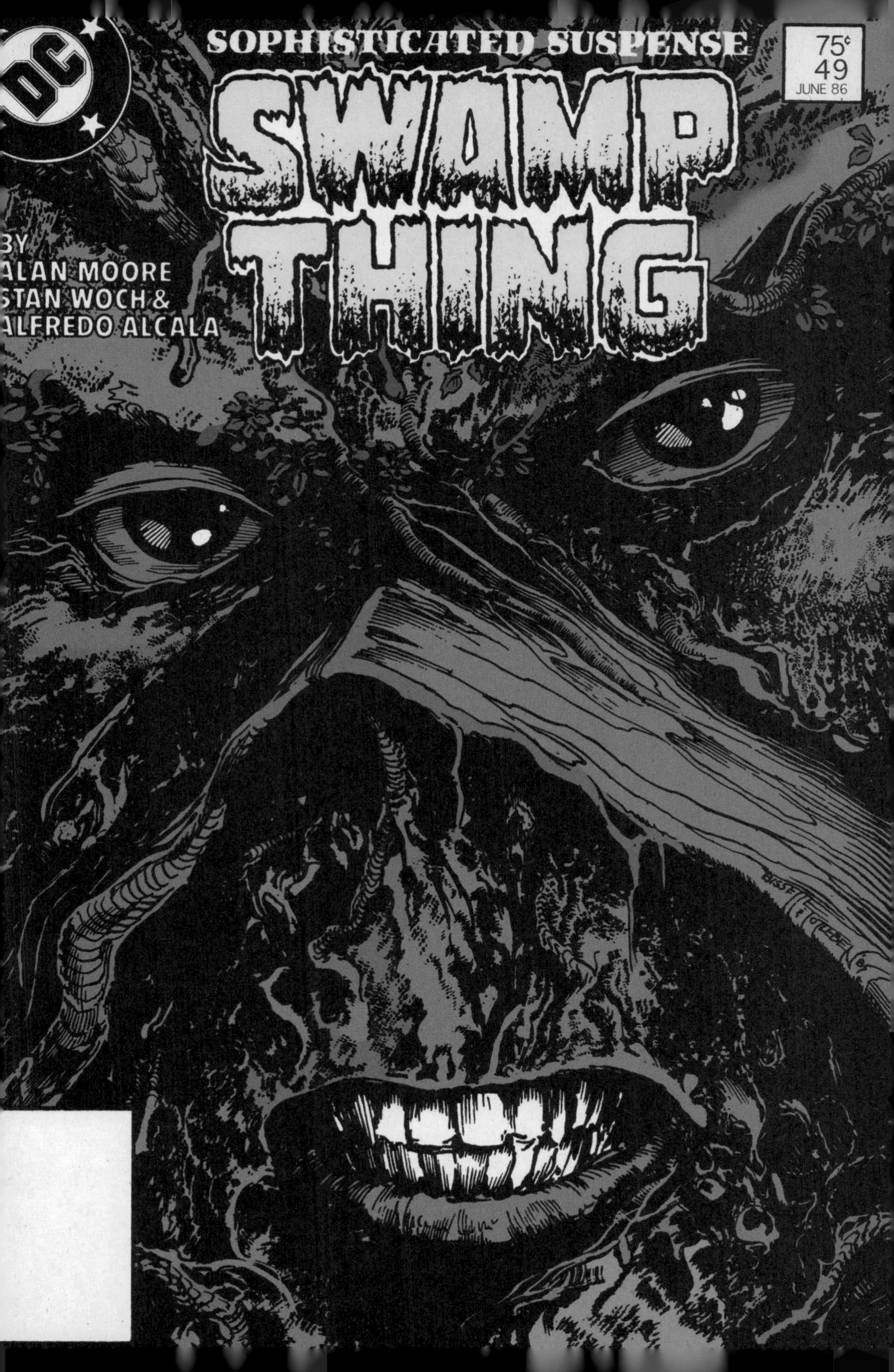
SOPHISTICATED SUSPENSE
75¢
49
JUNE 86
SWAMP THING
BY
ALAN MOORE
STAN WOCH &
ALFREDO ALCALA

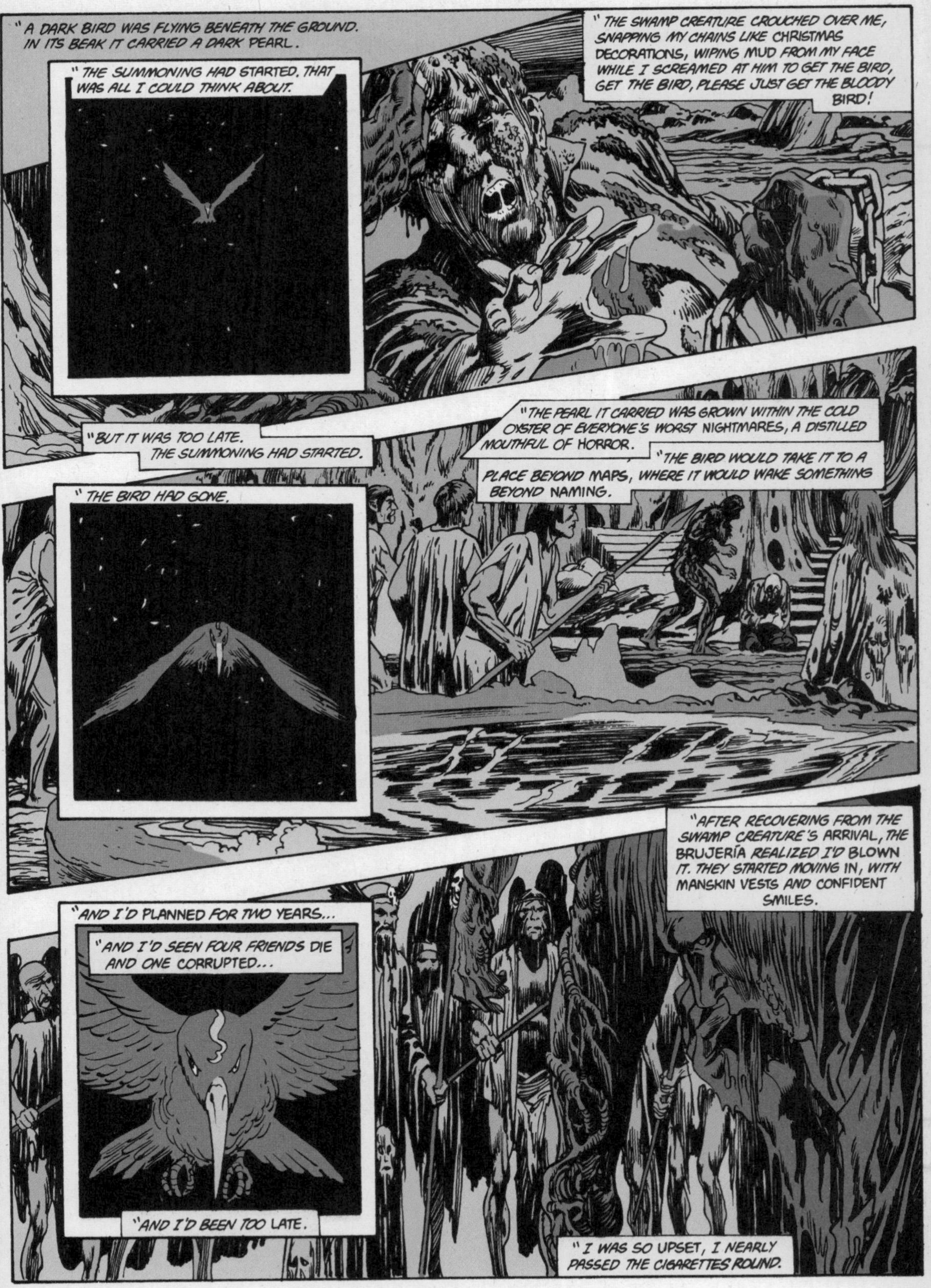
"A DARK BIRD WAS FLYING BENEATH THE GROUND. IN ITS BEAK IT CARRIED A DARK PEARL.
"THE SUMMONING HAD STARTED. THAT WAS ALL I COULD THINK ABOUT.
"THE SWAMP CREATURE CROUCHED OVER ME, SNAPPING MY CHAINS LIKE CHRISTMAS DECORATIONS, WIPING MUD FROM MY FACE WHILE I SCREAMED AT HIM TO GET THE BIRD, GET THE BIRD, PLEASE JUST GET THE BLOODY BIRD!
"BUT IT WAS TOO LATE. THE SUMMONING HAD STARTED.
"THE PEARL IT CARRIED WAS GROWN WITHIN THE COLD OYSTER OF EVERYONE'S WORST NIGHTMARES, A DISTILLED MOUTHFUL OF HORROR.
"THE BIRD WOULD TAKE IT TO A PLACE BEYOND MAPS, WHERE IT WOULD WAKE SOMETHING BEYOND NAMING.
"THE BIRD HAD GONE.
"AFTER RECOVERING FROM THE SWAMP CREATURE'S ARRIVAL, THE BRUJERÍA REALIZED I'D BLOWN IT. THEY STARTED MOVING IN, WITH MANSKIN VESTS AND CONFIDENT SMILES.
"AND I'D PLANNED FOR TWO YEARS...
"AND I'D SEEN FOUR FRIENDS DIE AND ONE CORRUPTED...
"AND I'D BEEN TOO LATE.
"I WAS SO UPSET, I NEARLY PASSED THE CIGARETTES ROUND.

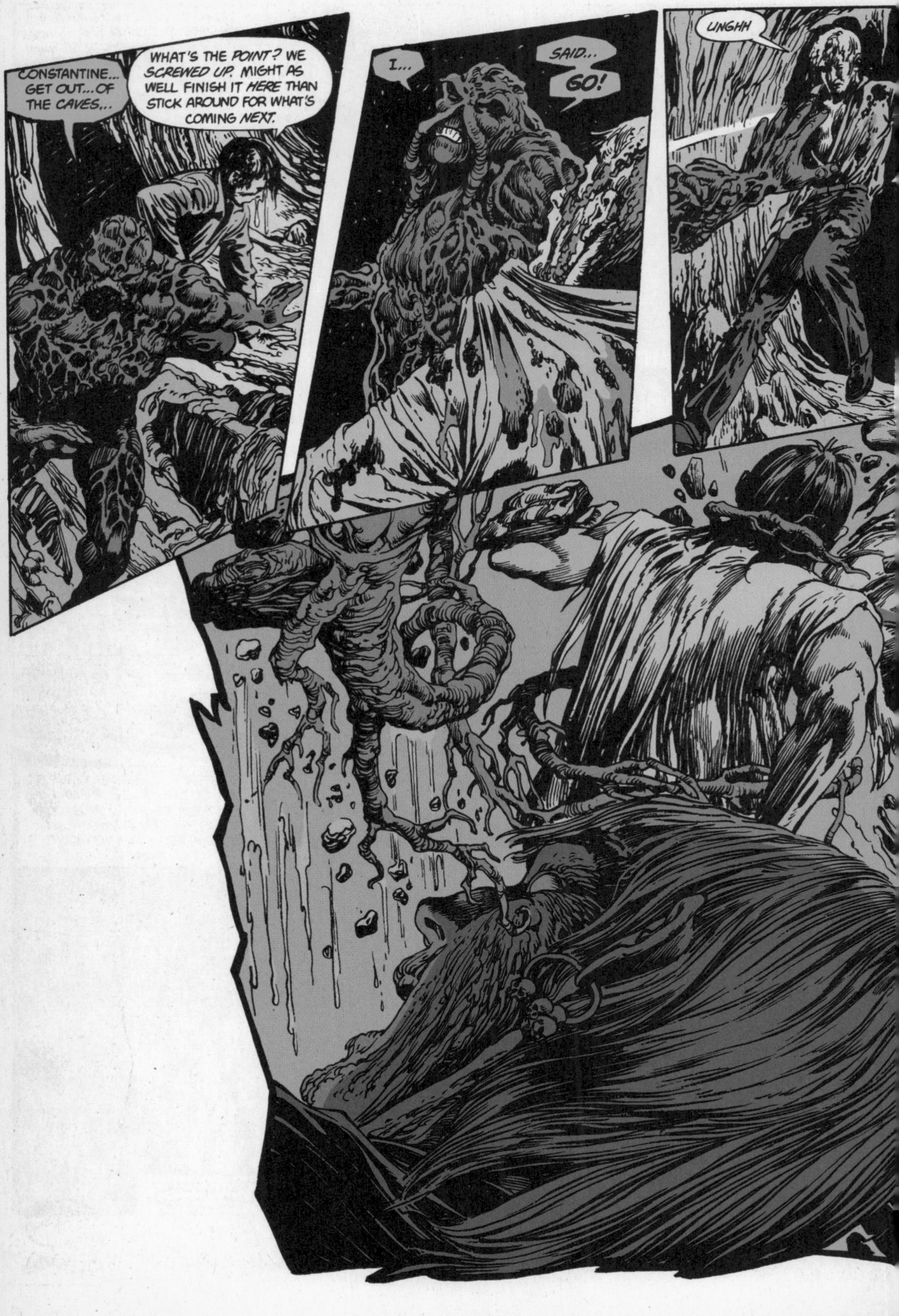
CONSTANTINE... GET OUT...OF THE CAVES...
WHAT'S THE POINT? WE SCREWED UP. MIGHT AS WELL FINISH IT HERE THAN STICK AROUND FOR WHAT'S COMING NEXT.
I...
SAID... GO!
UNGHH

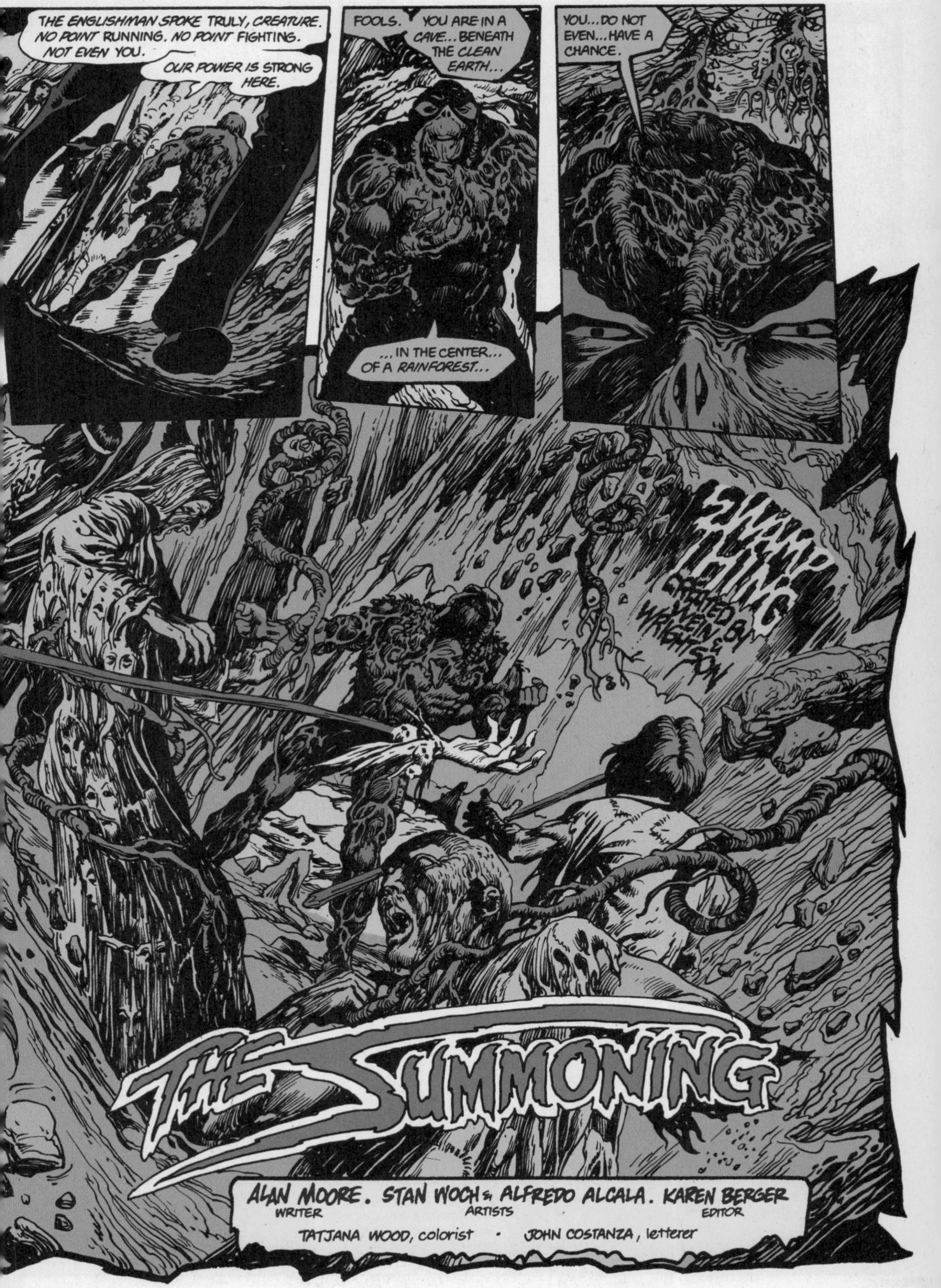
THE ENGLISHMAN SPOKE TRULY, CREATURE. NO POINT RUNNING. NO POINT FIGHTING. NOT EVEN YOU.
OUR POWER IS STRONG HERE.
FOOLS.
YOU ARE IN A CAVE... BENEATH THE CLEAN EARTH...
...IN THE CENTER... OF A RAINFOREST...
YOU...DO NOT EVEN...HAVE A CHANCE.
SWAMP THING
CREATED BY WEIN & WRIGHTSON
THE SUMMONING
ALAN MOORE. WRITER
STAN WOCH & ALFREDO ALCALA. ARTISTS
KAREN BERGER EDITOR
TATJANA WOOD, colorist · JOHN COSTANZA, letterer

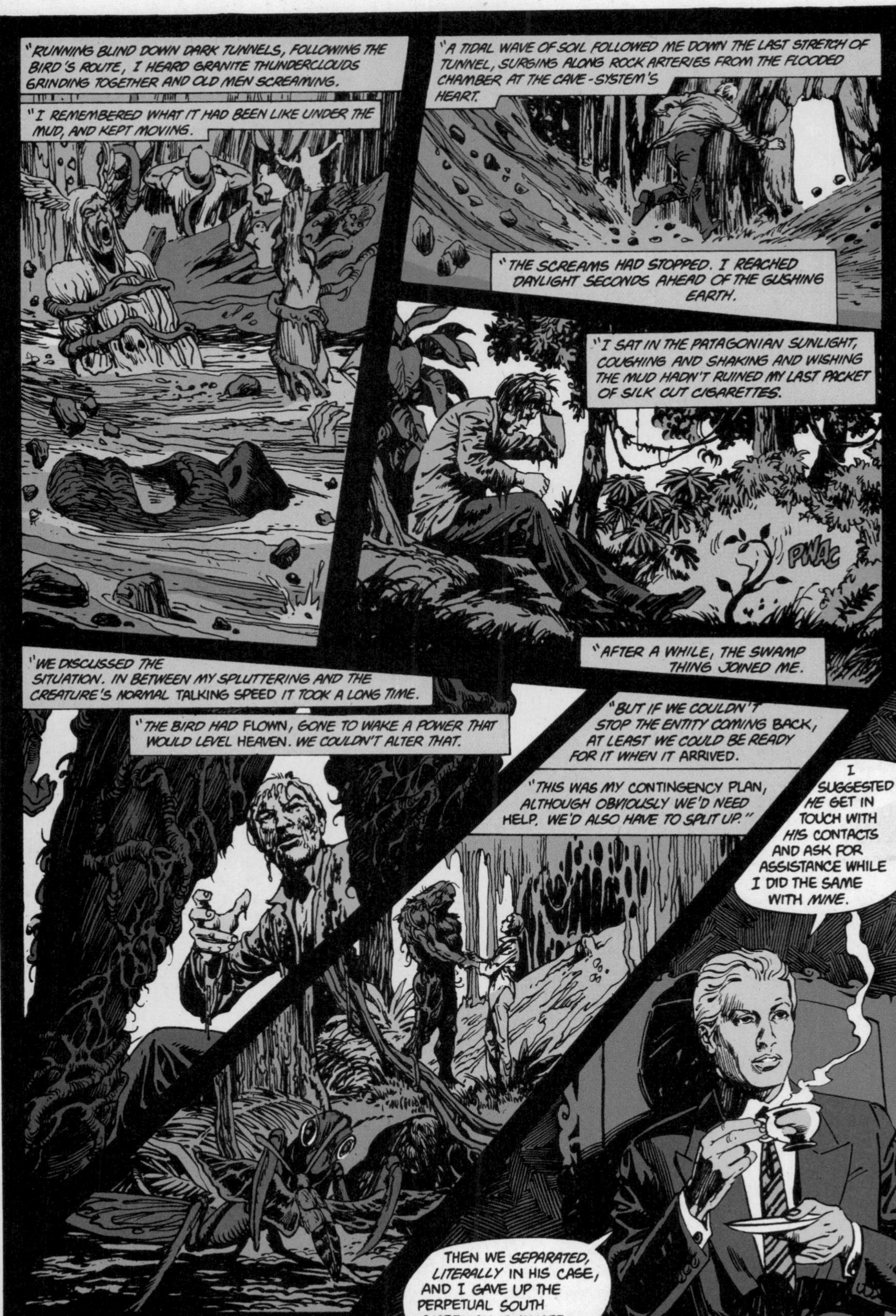
"RUNNING BLIND DOWN DARK TUNNELS, FOLLOWING THE BIRD'S ROUTE, I HEARD GRANITE THUNDERCLOUDS GRINDING TOGETHER AND OLD MEN SCREAMING.
"I REMEMBERED WHAT IT HAD BEEN LIKE UNDER THE MUD, AND KEPT MOVING.
"A TIDAL WAVE OF SOIL FOLLOWED ME DOWN THE LAST STRETCH OF TUNNEL, SURGING ALONG ROCK ARTERIES FROM THE FLOODED CHAMBER AT THE CAVE-SYSTEM'S HEART.
"THE SCREAMS HAD STOPPED. I REACHED DAYLIGHT SECONDS AHEAD OF THE GUSHING EARTH.
"I SAT IN THE PATAGONIAN SUNLIGHT, COUGHING AND SHAKING AND WISHING THE MUD HADN'T RUINED MY LAST PACKET OF SILK CUT CIGARETTES.
PWAC
"AFTER A WHILE, THE SWAMP THING JOINED ME.
"WE DISCUSSED THE SITUATION. IN BETWEEN MY SPLUTTERING AND THE CREATURE'S NORMAL TALKING SPEED IT TOOK A LONG TIME.
"THE BIRD HAD FLOWN, GONE TO WAKE A POWER THAT WOULD LEVEL HEAVEN. WE COULDN'T ALTER THAT.
"BUT IF WE COULDN'T STOP THE ENTITY COMING BACK, AT LEAST WE COULD BE READY FOR IT WHEN IT ARRIVED.
"THIS WAS MY CONTINGENCY PLAN, ALTHOUGH OBVIOUSLY WE'D NEED HELP. WE'D ALSO HAVE TO SPLIT UP."
I SUGGESTED HE GET IN TOUCH WITH HIS CONTACTS AND ASK FOR ASSISTANCE WHILE I DID THE SAME WITH MINE.
THEN WE SEPARATED, LITERALLY IN HIS CASE, AND I GAVE UP THE PERPETUAL SOUTH AMERICAN SUMMER...

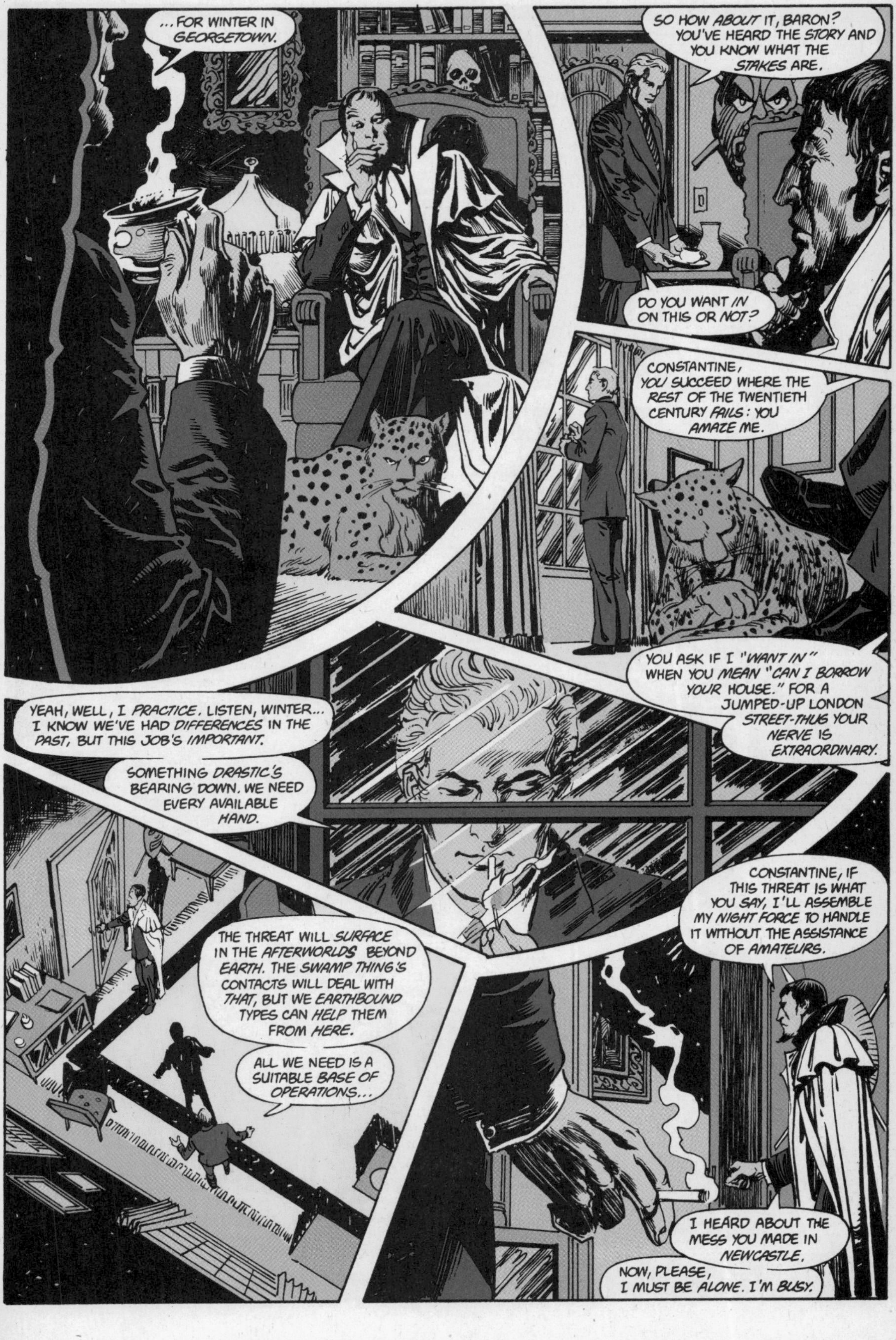
...FOR WINTER IN GEORGETOWN.
SO HOW ABOUT IT, BARON? YOU'VE HEARD THE STORY AND YOU KNOW WHAT THE STAKES ARE.
DO YOU WANT IN ON THIS OR NOT?
CONSTANTINE, YOU SUCCEED WHERE THE REST OF THE TWENTIETH CENTURY FAILS: YOU AMAZE ME.
YOU ASK IF I "WANT IN" WHEN YOU MEAN "CAN I BORROW YOUR HOUSE." FOR A JUMPED-UP LONDON STREET-THUG YOUR NERVE IS EXTRAORDINARY.
YEAH, WELL, I PRACTICE. LISTEN, WINTER... I KNOW WE'VE HAD DIFFERENCES IN THE PAST, BUT THIS JOB'S IMPORTANT.
SOMETHING DRASTIC'S BEARING DOWN. WE NEED EVERY AVAILABLE HAND.
THE THREAT WILL SURFACE IN THE AFTERWORLDS BEYOND EARTH. THE SWAMP THING'S CONTACTS WILL DEAL WITH THAT, BUT WE EARTHBOUND TYPES CAN HELP THEM FROM HERE.
ALL WE NEED IS A SUITABLE BASE OF OPERATIONS...
CONSTANTINE, IF THIS THREAT IS WHAT YOU SAY, I'LL ASSEMBLE MY NIGHT FORCE TO HANDLE IT WITHOUT THE ASSISTANCE OF AMATEURS.
I HEARD ABOUT THE MESS YOU MADE IN NEWCASTLE.
NOW, PLEASE, I MUST BE ALONE. I'M BUSY.

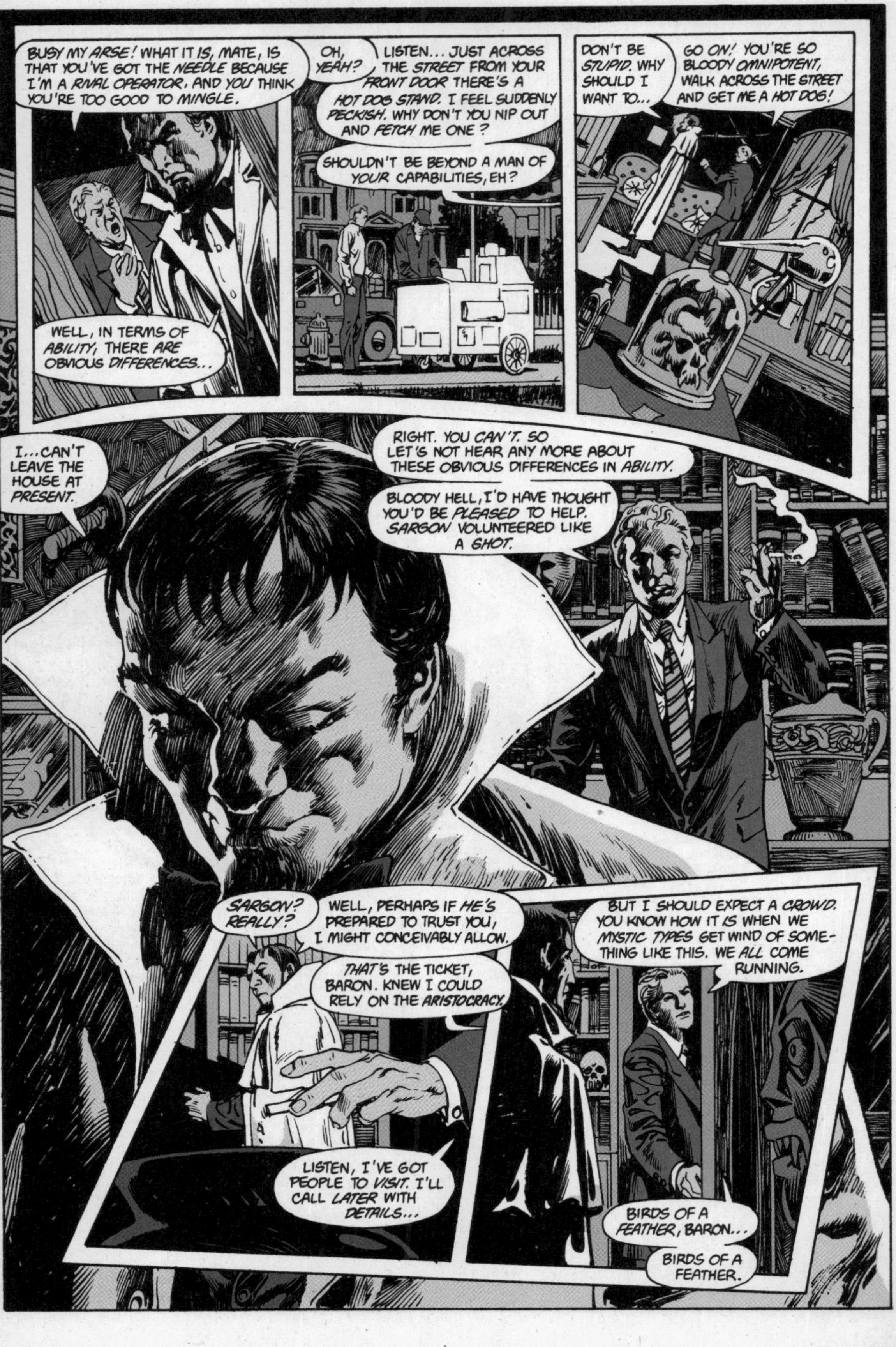
BUSY MY ARSE! WHAT IT IS, MATE, IS THAT YOU'VE GOT THE NEEDLE BECAUSE I'M A RIVAL OPERATOR, AND YOU THINK YOU'RE TOO GOOD TO MINGLE.
WELL, IN TERMS OF ABILITY, THERE ARE OBVIOUS DIFFERENCES...
OH, YEAH?
LISTEN... JUST ACROSS THE STREET FROM YOUR FRONT DOOR THERE'S A HOT DOG STAND. I FEEL SUDDENLY PECKISH. WHY DON'T YOU NIP OUT AND FETCH ME ONE?
SHOULDN'T BE BEYOND A MAN OF YOUR CAPABILITIES, EH?
DON'T BE STUPID. WHY SHOULD I WANT TO...
GO ON! YOU'RE SO BLOODY OMNIPOTENT, WALK ACROSS THE STREET AND GET ME A HOT DOG!
I...CAN'T LEAVE THE HOUSE AT PRESENT.
RIGHT. YOU CAN'T. SO LET'S NOT HEAR ANY MORE ABOUT THESE OBVIOUS DIFFERENCES IN ABILITY.
BLOODY HELL, I'D HAVE THOUGHT YOU'D BE PLEASED TO HELP. SARGON VOLUNTEERED LIKE A SHOT.
SARGON? REALLY?
WELL, PERHAPS IF HE'S PREPARED TO TRUST YOU, I MIGHT CONCEIVABLY ALLOW.
THAT'S THE TICKET, BARON. KNEW I COULD RELY ON THE ARISTOCRACY.
LISTEN, I'VE GOT PEOPLE TO VISIT. I'LL CALL LATER WITH DETAILS...
BUT I SHOULD EXPECT A CROWD. YOU KNOW HOW IT IS WHEN WE MYSTIC TYPES GET WIND OF SOMETHING LIKE THIS. WE ALL COME RUNNING.
BIRDS OF A FEATHER, BARON...
BIRDS OF A FEATHER.

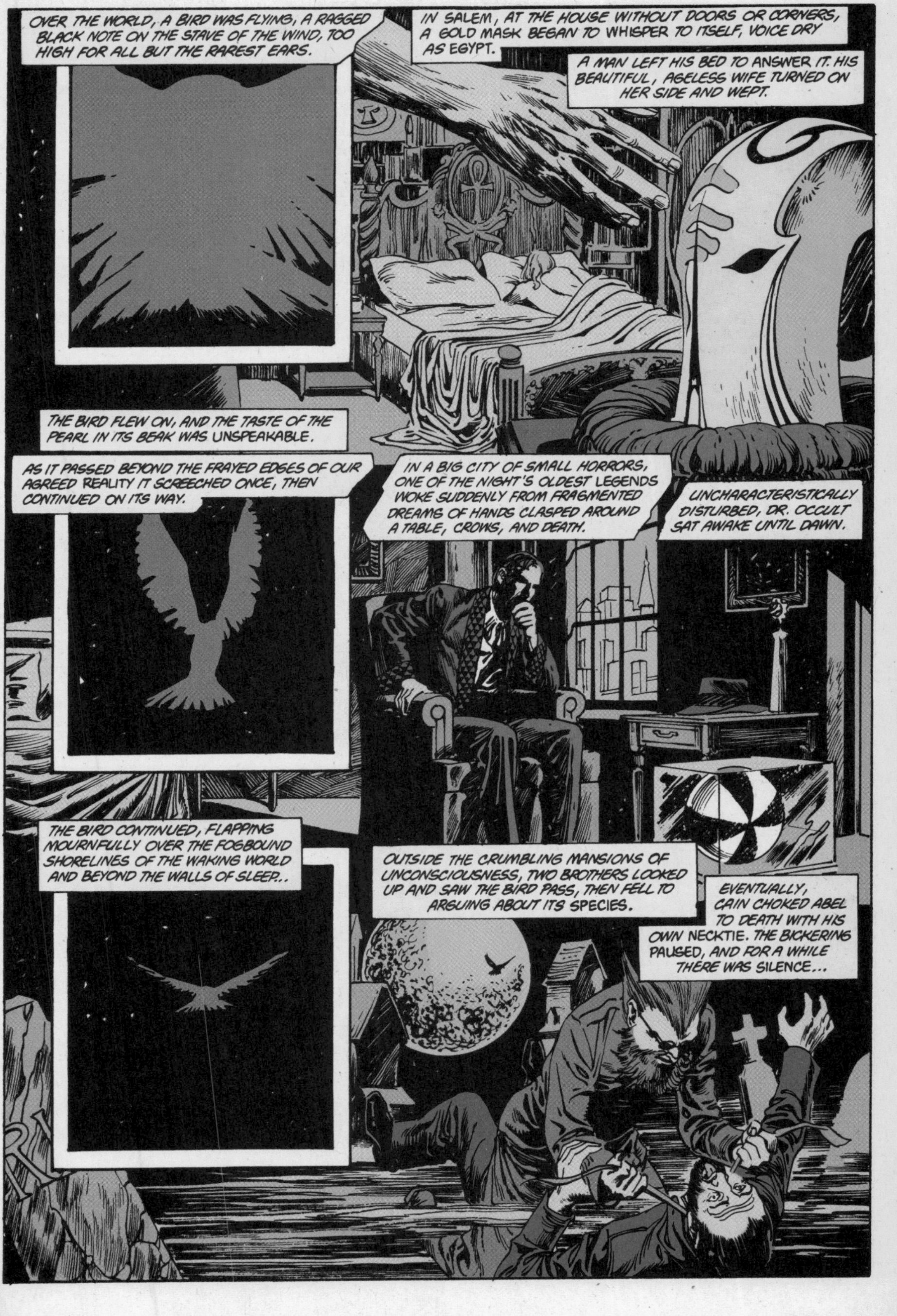
OVER THE WORLD, A BIRD WAS FLYING, A RAGGED BLACK NOTE ON THE STAVE OF THE WIND, TOO HIGH FOR ALL BUT THE RAREST EARS.
IN SALEM, AT THE HOUSE WITHOUT DOORS OR CORNERS, A GOLD MASK BEGAN TO WHISPER TO ITSELF, VOICE DRY AS EGYPT.
A MAN LEFT HIS BED TO ANSWER IT. HIS BEAUTIFUL, AGELESS WIFE TURNED ON HER SIDE AND WEPT.
THE BIRD FLEW ON, AND THE TASTE OF THE PEARL IN ITS BEAK WAS UNSPEAKABLE.
AS IT PASSED BEYOND THE FRAYED EDGES OF OUR AGREED REALITY IT SCREECHED ONCE, THEN CONTINUED ON ITS WAY.
IN A BIG CITY OF SMALL HORRORS, ONE OF THE NIGHT'S OLDEST LEGENDS WOKE SUDDENLY FROM FRAGMENTED DREAMS OF HANDS CLASPED AROUND A TABLE, CROWS, AND DEATH.
UNCHARACTERISTICALLY DISTURBED, DR. OCCULT SAT AWAKE UNTIL DAWN.
THE BIRD CONTINUED, FLAPPING MOURNFULLY OVER THE FOGBOUND SHORELINES OF THE WAKING WORLD AND BEYOND THE WALLS OF SLEEP...
OUTSIDE THE CRUMBLING MANSIONS OF UNCONSCIOUSNESS, TWO BROTHERS LOOKED UP AND SAW THE BIRD PASS, THEN FELL TO ARGUING ABOUT ITS SPECIES.
EVENTUALLY, CAIN CHOKED ABEL TO DEATH WITH HIS OWN NECKTIE. THE BICKERING PAUSED, AND FOR A WHILE THERE WAS SILENCE...

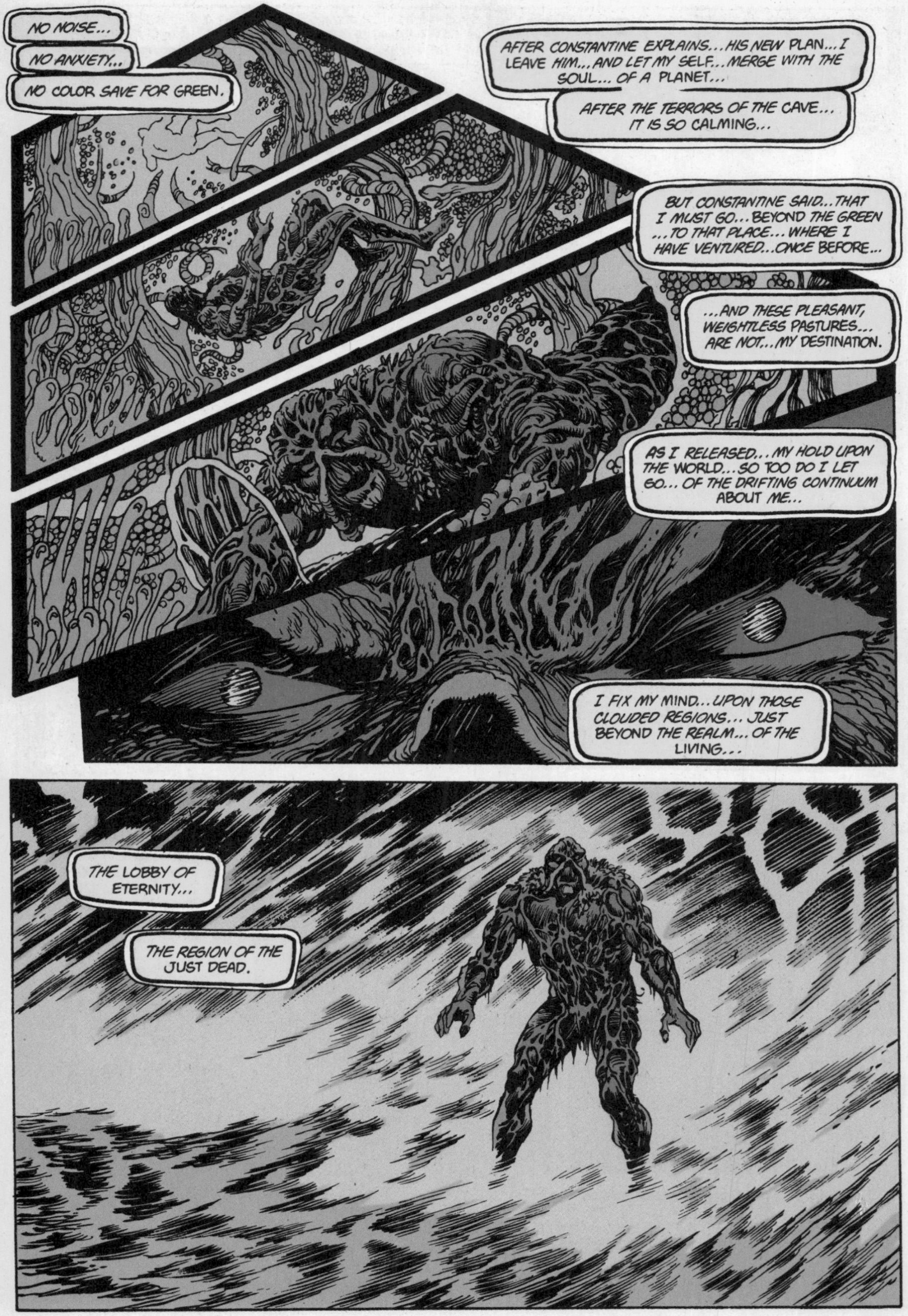
NO NOISE...
NO ANXIETY...
NO COLOR SAVE FOR GREEN.
AFTER CONSTANTINE EXPLAINS... HIS NEW PLAN... I LEAVE HIM... AND LET MY SELF... MERGE WITH THE SOUL... OF A PLANET...
AFTER THE TERRORS OF THE CAVE... IT IS SO CALMING...
BUT CONSTANTINE SAID... THAT I MUST GO... BEYOND THE GREEN ...TO THAT PLACE... WHERE I HAVE VENTURED... ONCE BEFORE...
...AND THESE PLEASANT, WEIGHTLESS PASTURES... ARE NOT... MY DESTINATION.
AS I RELEASED... MY HOLD UPON THE WORLD... SO TOO DO I LET GO... OF THE DRIFTING CONTINUUM ABOUT ME...
I FIX MY MIND... UPON THOSE CLOUDED REGIONS... JUST BEYOND THE REALM... OF THE LIVING...
THE LOBBY OF ETERNITY...
THE REGION OF THE JUST DEAD.

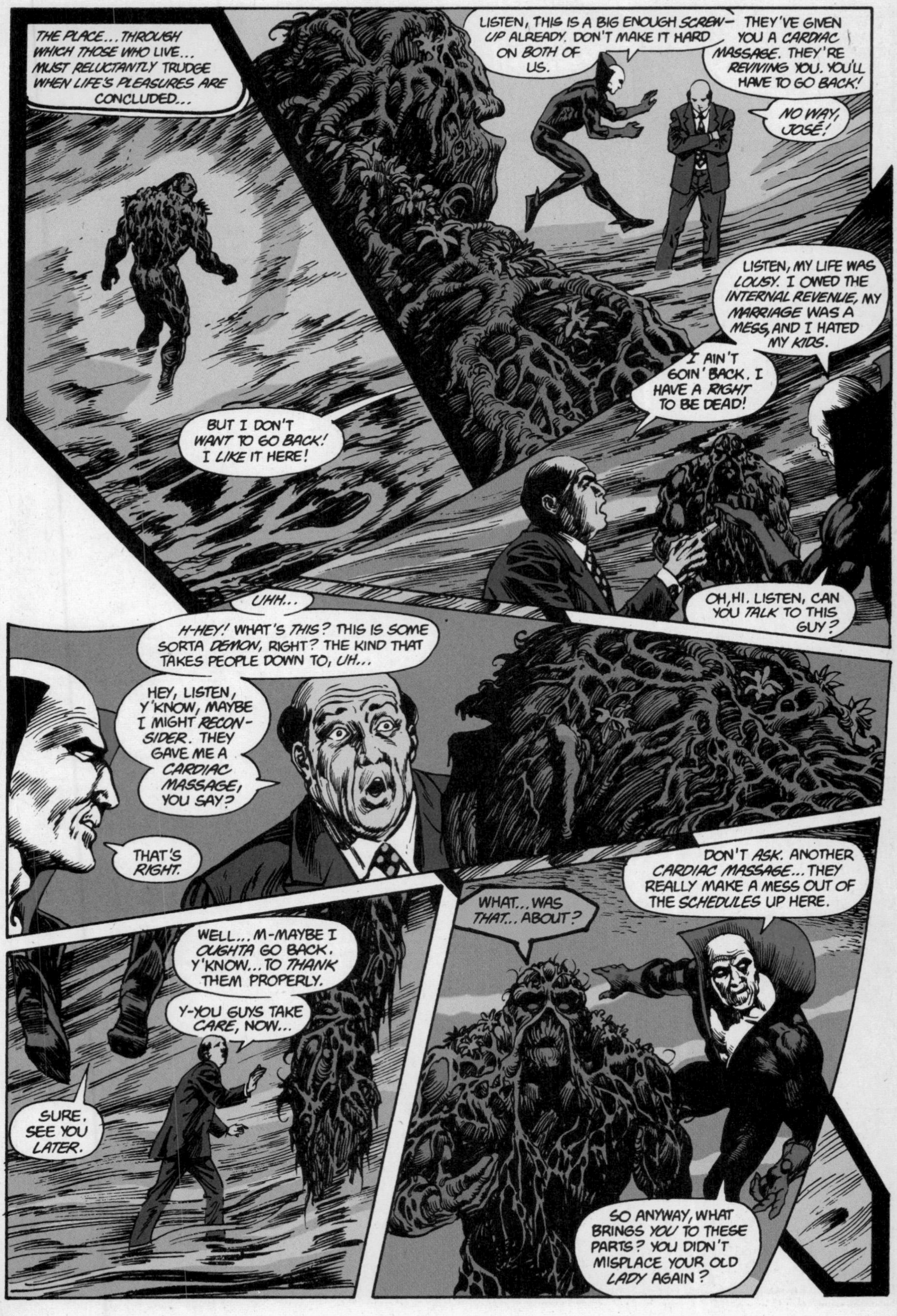
THE PLACE...THROUGH WHICH THOSE WHO LIVE... MUST RELUCTANTLY TRUDGE WHEN LIFE'S PLEASURES ARE CONCLUDED...
LISTEN, THIS IS A BIG ENOUGH SCREW-UP ALREADY. DON'T MAKE IT HARD ON BOTH OF US.
THEY'VE GIVEN YOU A CARDIAC MASSAGE. THEY'RE REVIVING YOU. YOU'LL HAVE TO GO BACK!
NO WAY, JOSÉ!
LISTEN, MY LIFE WAS LOUSY. I OWED THE INTERNAL REVENUE, MY MARRIAGE WAS A MESS, AND I HATED MY KIDS.
I AIN'T GOIN' BACK. I HAVE A RIGHT TO BE DEAD!
BUT I DON'T WANT TO GO BACK! I LIKE IT HERE!
OH, HI. LISTEN, CAN YOU TALK TO THIS GUY?
UHH...
H-HEY! WHAT'S THIS? THIS IS SOME SORTA DEMON, RIGHT? THE KIND THAT TAKES PEOPLE DOWN TO, UH...
HEY, LISTEN, Y'KNOW, MAYBE I MIGHT RECON-SIDER. THEY GAVE ME A CARDIAC MASSAGE, YOU SAY?
THAT'S RIGHT.
WELL... M-MAYBE I OUGHTA GO BACK. Y'KNOW... TO THANK THEM PROPERLY.
Y-YOU GUYS TAKE CARE, NOW...
SURE. SEE YOU LATER.
WHAT... WAS THAT... ABOUT?
DON'T ASK. ANOTHER CARDIAC MASSAGE... THEY REALLY MAKE A MESS OUT OF THE SCHEDULES UP HERE.
SO ANYWAY, WHAT BRINGS YOU TO THESE PARTS? YOU DIDN'T MISPLACE YOUR OLD LADY AGAIN?

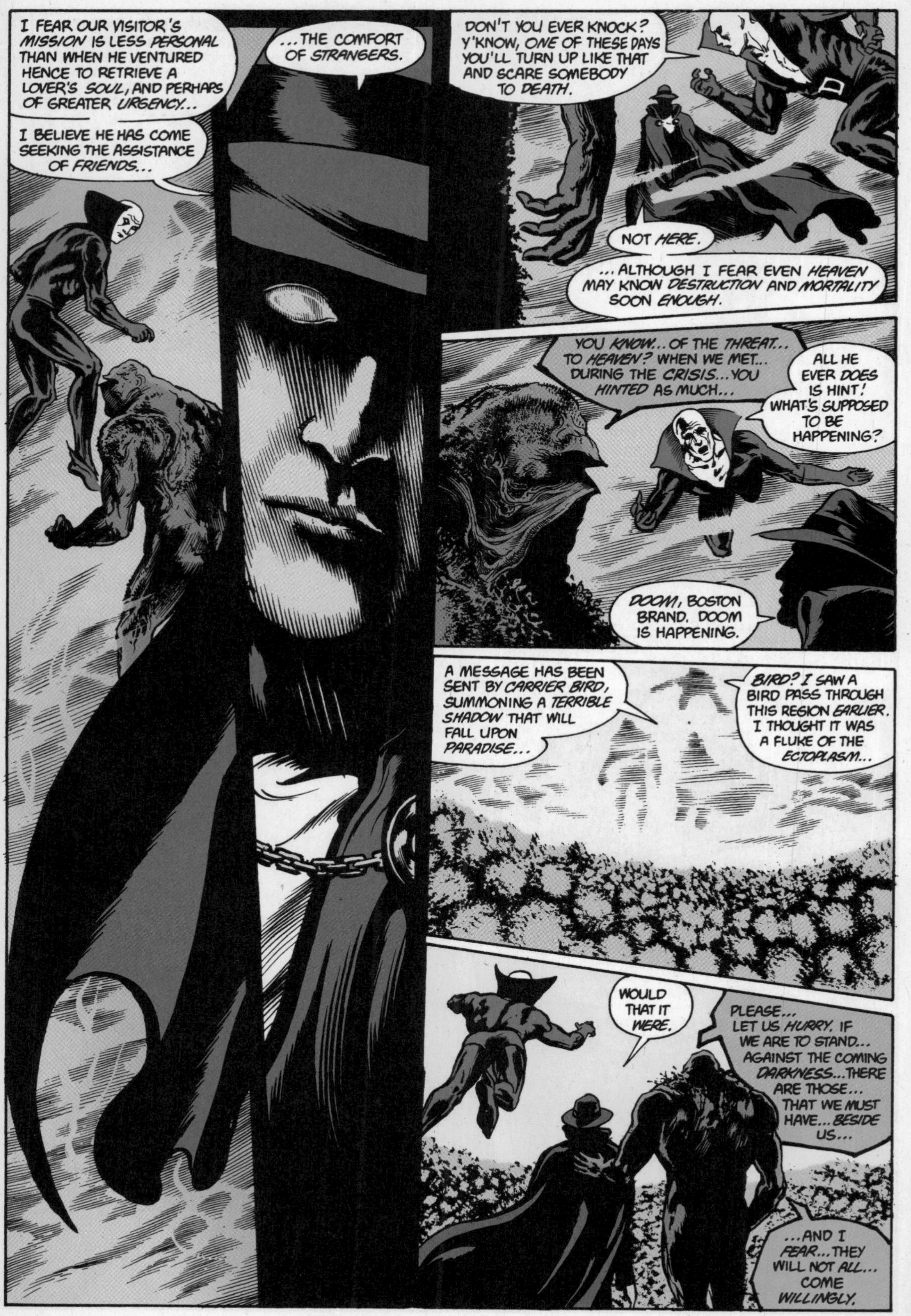
I FEAR OUR VISITOR'S MISSION IS LESS PERSONAL THAN WHEN HE VENTURED HENCE TO RETRIEVE A LOVER'S SOUL, AND PERHAPS OF GREATER URGENCY...
I BELIEVE HE HAS COME SEEKING THE ASSISTANCE OF FRIENDS...
...THE COMFORT OF STRANGERS.
DON'T YOU EVER KNOCK? Y'KNOW, ONE OF THESE DAYS YOU'LL TURN UP LIKE THAT AND SCARE SOMEBODY TO DEATH.
NOT HERE.
...ALTHOUGH I FEAR EVEN HEAVEN MAY KNOW DESTRUCTION AND MORTALITY SOON ENOUGH.
YOU KNOW... OF THE THREAT... TO HEAVEN? WHEN WE MET... DURING THE CRISIS... YOU HINTED AS MUCH...
ALL HE EVER DOES IS HINT! WHAT'S SUPPOSED TO BE HAPPENING?
DOOM, BOSTON BRAND. DOOM IS HAPPENING.
A MESSAGE HAS BEEN SENT BY CARRIER BIRD, SUMMONING A TERRIBLE SHADOW THAT WILL FALL UPON PARADISE...
BIRD? I SAW A BIRD PASS THROUGH THIS REGION EARLIER. I THOUGHT IT WAS A FLUKE OF THE ECTOPLASM...
WOULD THAT IT WERE.
PLEASE... LET US HURRY. IF WE ARE TO STAND... AGAINST THE COMING DARKNESS... THERE ARE THOSE... THAT WE MUST HAVE... BESIDE US...
...AND I FEAR... THEY WILL NOT ALL... COME WILLINGLY.

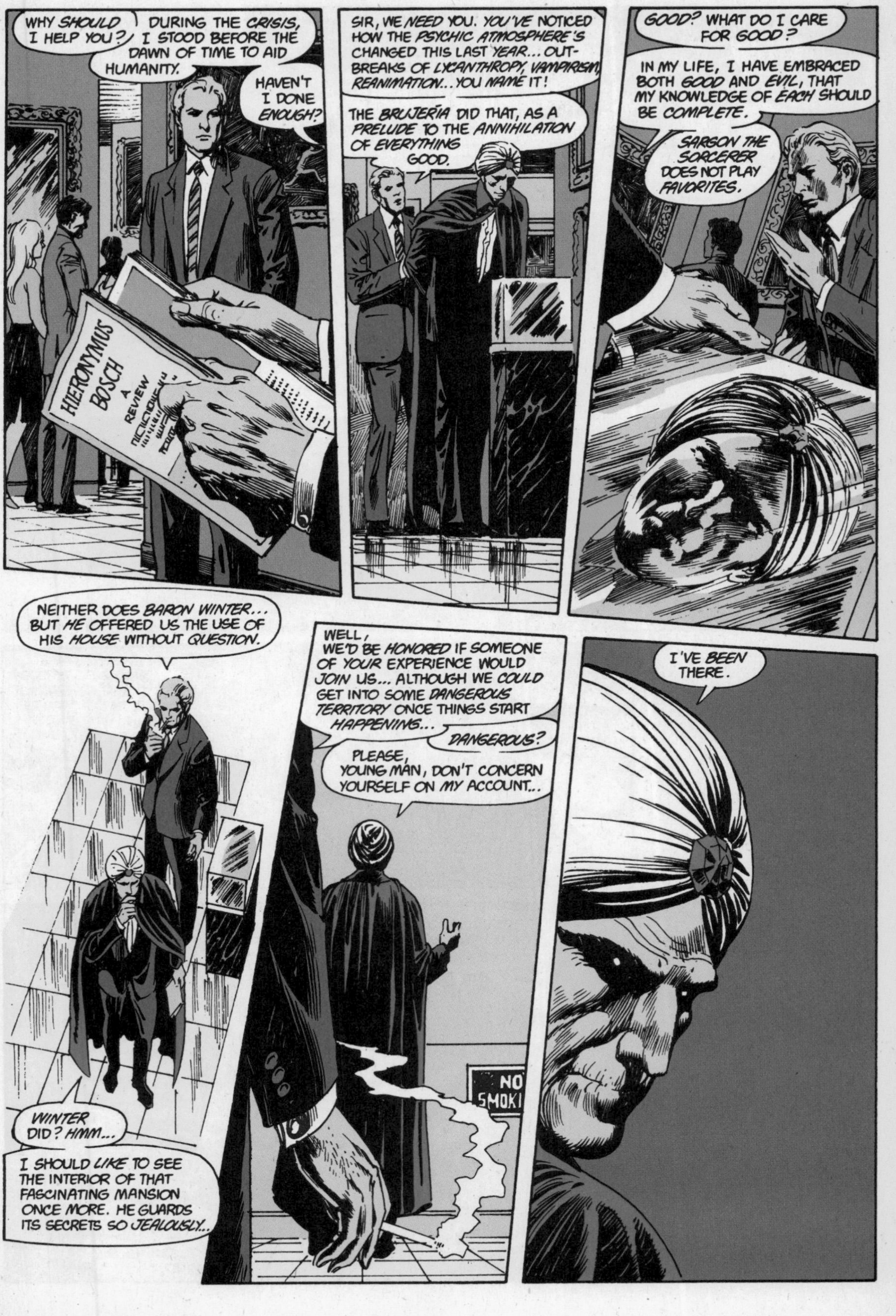
WHY SHOULD I HELP YOU?
DURING THE CRISIS, I STOOD BEFORE THE DAWN OF TIME TO AID HUMANITY.
HAVEN'T I DONE ENOUGH?
HIERONYMUS BOSCH A REVIEW
SIR, WE NEED YOU. YOU'VE NOTICED HOW THE PSYCHIC ATMOSPHERE'S CHANGED THIS LAST YEAR... OUT-BREAKS OF LYCANTHROPY, VAMPIRISM, REANIMATION... YOU NAME IT!
THE BRUJERÍA DID THAT, AS A PRELUDE TO THE ANNIHILATION OF EVERYTHING GOOD.
GOOD? WHAT DO I CARE FOR GOOD?
IN MY LIFE, I HAVE EMBRACED BOTH GOOD AND EVIL, THAT MY KNOWLEDGE OF EACH SHOULD BE COMPLETE.
SARGON THE SORCERER DOES NOT PLAY FAVORITES.
NEITHER DOES BARON WINTER... BUT HE OFFERED US THE USE OF HIS HOUSE WITHOUT QUESTION.
WINTER DID? HMM...
I SHOULD LIKE TO SEE THE INTERIOR OF THAT FASCINATING MANSION ONCE MORE. HE GUARDS ITS SECRETS SO JEALOUSLY...
WELL, WE'D BE HONORED IF SOMEONE OF YOUR EXPERIENCE WOULD JOIN US... ALTHOUGH WE COULD GET INTO SOME DANGEROUS TERRITORY ONCE THINGS START HAPPENING...
DANGEROUS?
PLEASE, YOUNG MAN, DON'T CONCERN YOURSELF ON MY ACCOUNT...
NO SMOKI
I'VE BEEN THERE.

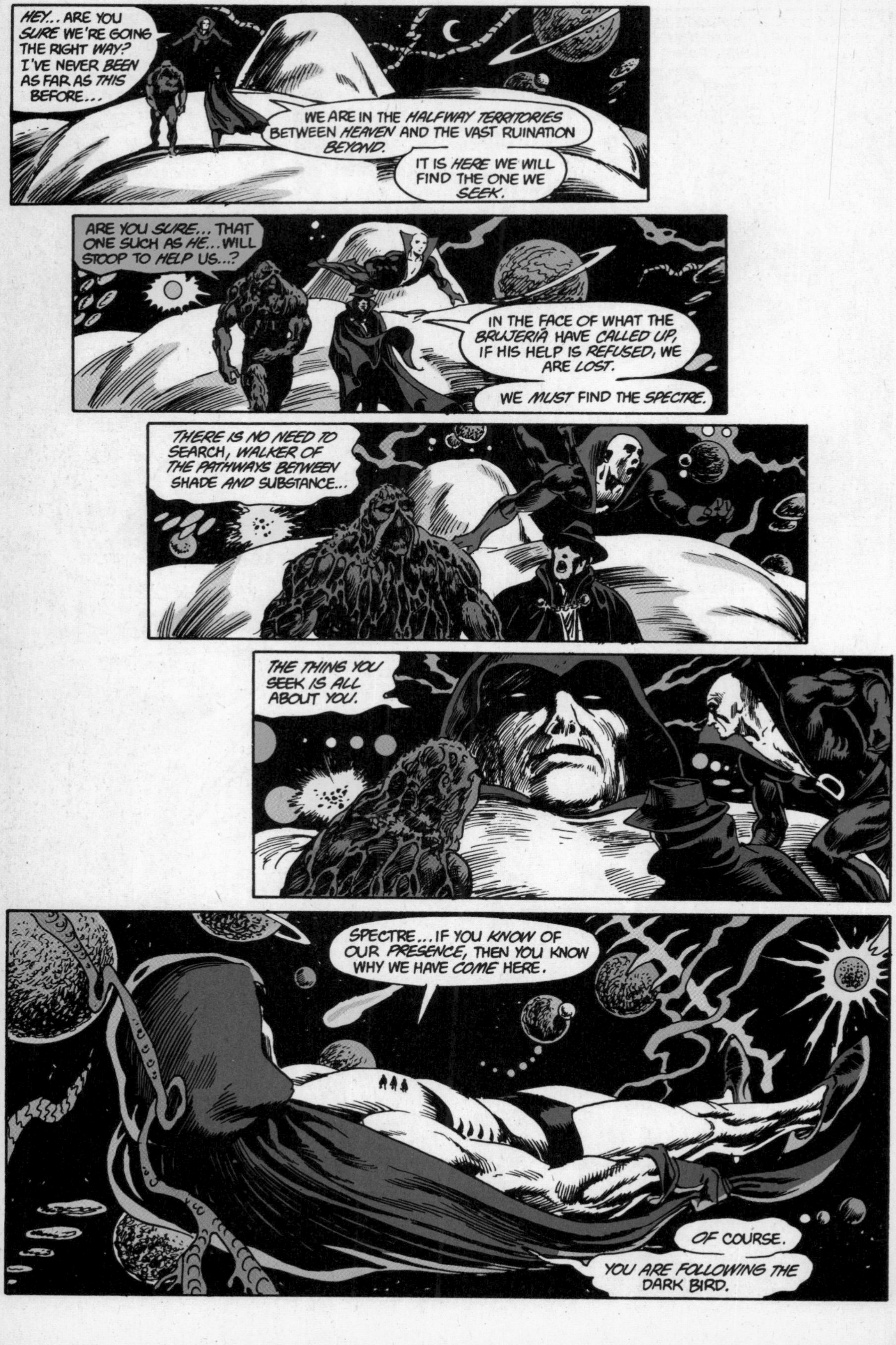
HEY... ARE YOU SURE WE'RE GOING THE RIGHT WAY? I'VE NEVER BEEN AS FAR AS THIS BEFORE...
WE ARE IN THE HALFWAY TERRITORIES BETWEEN HEAVEN AND THE VAST RUINATION BEYOND.
IT IS HERE WE WILL FIND THE ONE WE SEEK.
ARE YOU SURE... THAT ONE SUCH AS HE... WILL STOOP TO HELP US...?
IN THE FACE OF WHAT THE BRUJERIA HAVE CALLED UP, IF HIS HELP IS REFUSED, WE ARE LOST.
WE MUST FIND THE SPECTRE.
THERE IS NO NEED TO SEARCH, WALKER OF THE PATHWAYS BETWEEN SHADE AND SUBSTANCE...
THE THING YOU SEEK IS ALL ABOUT YOU.
SPECTRE... IF YOU KNOW OF OUR PRESENCE, THEN YOU KNOW WHY WE HAVE COME HERE.
OF COURSE.
YOU ARE FOLLOWING THE DARK BIRD.

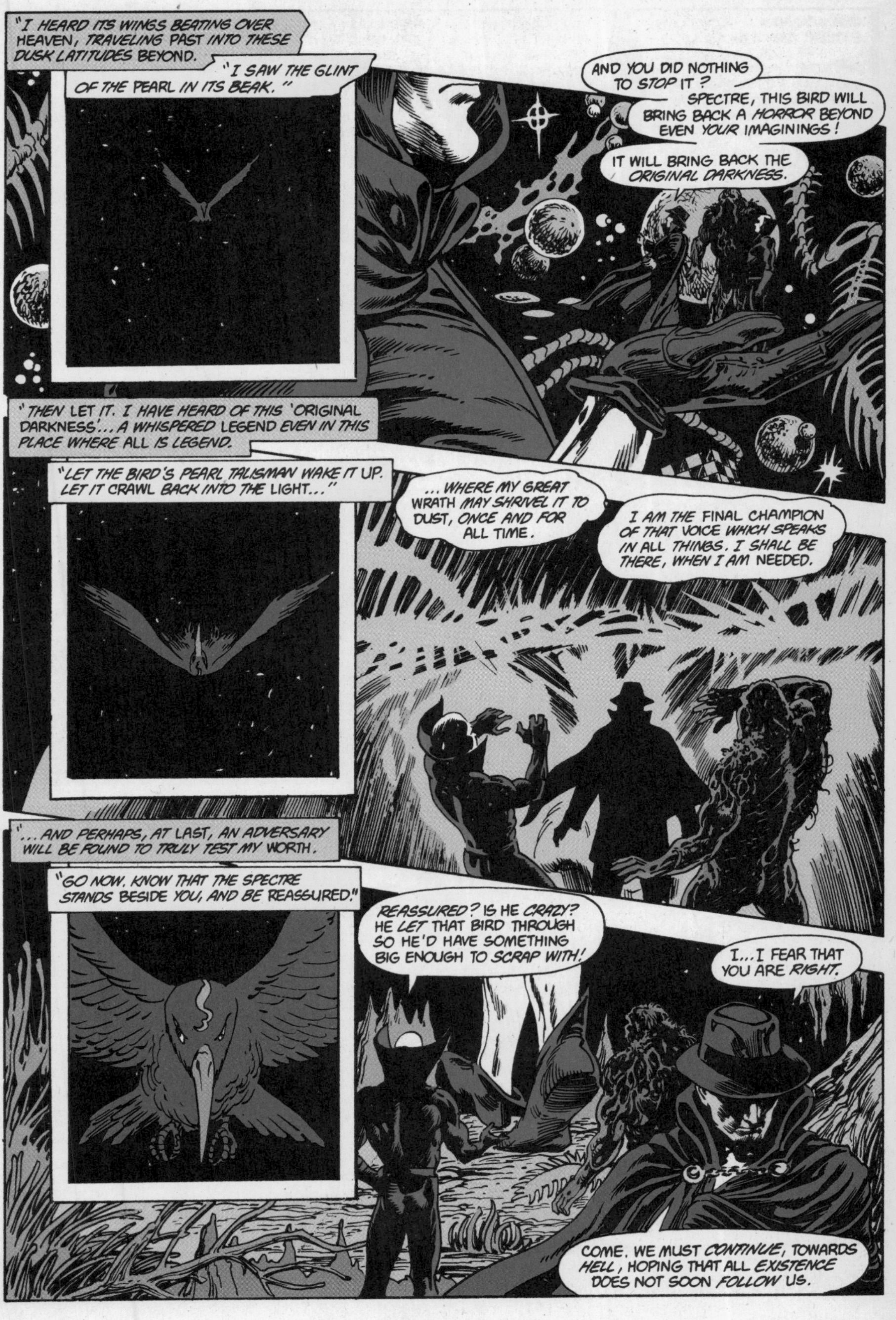
"I HEARD ITS WINGS BEATING OVER HEAVEN, TRAVELING PAST INTO THESE DUSK LATITUDES BEYOND.
"I SAW THE GLINT OF THE PEARL IN ITS BEAK."
AND YOU DID NOTHING TO STOP IT?
SPECTRE, THIS BIRD WILL BRING BACK A HORROR BEYOND EVEN YOUR IMAGININGS!
IT WILL BRING BACK THE ORIGINAL DARKNESS.
"THEN LET IT. I HAVE HEARD OF THIS 'ORIGINAL DARKNESS'... A WHISPERED LEGEND EVEN IN THIS PLACE WHERE ALL IS LEGEND.
"LET THE BIRD'S PEARL TALISMAN WAKE IT UP. LET IT CRAWL BACK INTO THE LIGHT..."
... WHERE MY GREAT WRATH MAY SHRIVEL IT TO DUST, ONCE AND FOR ALL TIME.
I AM THE FINAL CHAMPION OF THAT VOICE WHICH SPEAKS IN ALL THINGS. I SHALL BE THERE, WHEN I AM NEEDED.
"... AND PERHAPS, AT LAST, AN ADVERSARY WILL BE FOUND TO TRULY TEST MY WORTH.
"GO NOW. KNOW THAT THE SPECTRE STANDS BESIDE YOU, AND BE REASSURED."
REASSURED? IS HE CRAZY? HE LET THAT BIRD THROUGH SO HE'D HAVE SOMETHING BIG ENOUGH TO SCRAP WITH!
I... I FEAR THAT YOU ARE RIGHT.
COME. WE MUST CONTINUE, TOWARDS HELL, HOPING THAT ALL EXISTENCE DOES NOT SOON FOLLOW US.

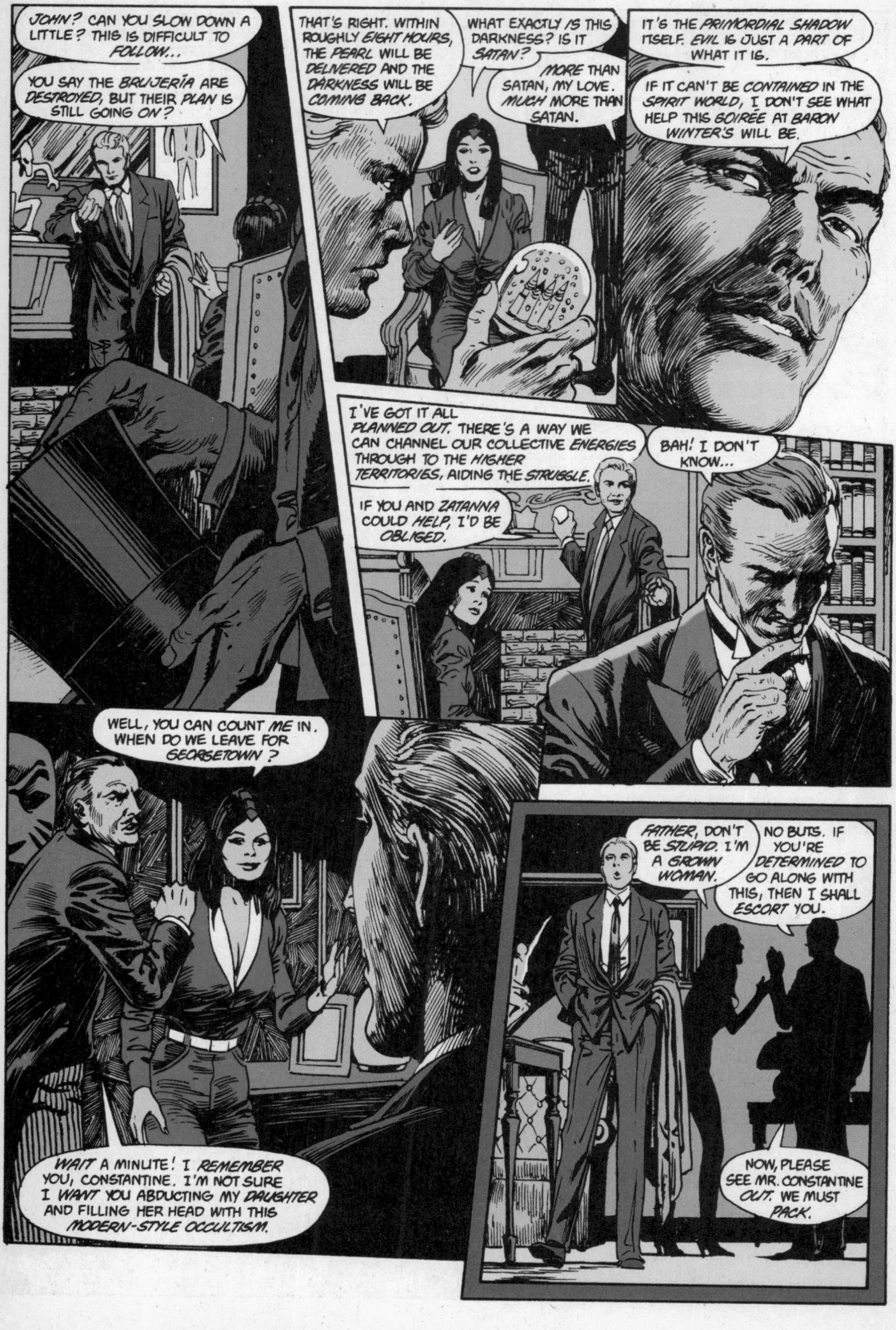
JOHN? CAN YOU SLOW DOWN A LITTLE? THIS IS DIFFICULT TO FOLLOW...
YOU SAY THE BRUJERÍA ARE DESTROYED, BUT THEIR PLAN IS STILL GOING ON?
THAT'S RIGHT. WITHIN ROUGHLY EIGHT HOURS, THE PEARL WILL BE DELIVERED AND THE DARKNESS WILL BE COMING BACK.
WHAT EXACTLY IS THIS DARKNESS? IS IT SATAN?
MORE THAN SATAN, MY LOVE. MUCH MORE THAN SATAN.
IT'S THE PRIMORDIAL SHADOW ITSELF. EVIL IS JUST A PART OF WHAT IT IS.
IF IT CAN'T BE CONTAINED IN THE SPIRIT WORLD, I DON'T SEE WHAT HELP THIS SOIRÉE AT BARON WINTER'S WILL BE.
I'VE GOT IT ALL PLANNED OUT. THERE'S A WAY WE CAN CHANNEL OUR COLLECTIVE ENERGIES THROUGH TO THE HIGHER TERRITORIES, AIDING THE STRUGGLE.
IF YOU AND ZATANNA COULD HELP, I'D BE OBLIGED.
BAH! I DON'T KNOW...
WELL, YOU CAN COUNT ME IN. WHEN DO WE LEAVE FOR GEORGETOWN?
WAIT A MINUTE! I REMEMBER YOU, CONSTANTINE. I'M NOT SURE I WANT YOU ABDUCTING MY DAUGHTER AND FILLING HER HEAD WITH THIS MODERN-STYLE OCCULTISM.
FATHER, DON'T BE STUPID. I'M A GROWN WOMAN.
NO BUTS. IF YOU'RE DETERMINED TO GO ALONG WITH THIS, THEN I SHALL ESCORT YOU.
NOW, PLEASE SEE MR. CONSTANTINE OUT. WE MUST PACK.

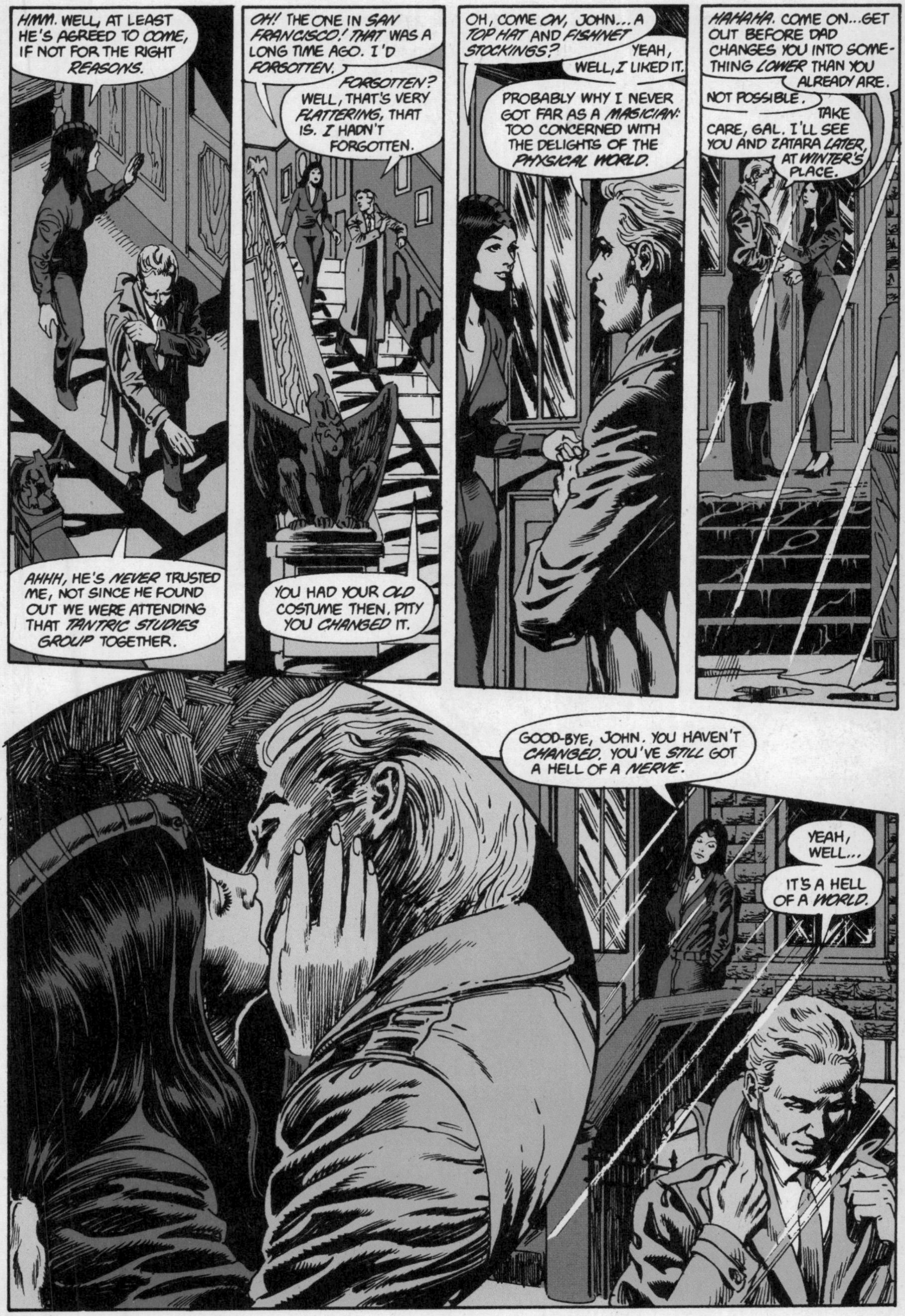
HMM. WELL, AT LEAST HE'S AGREED TO COME, IF NOT FOR THE RIGHT REASONS.
AHHH, HE'S NEVER TRUSTED ME, NOT SINCE HE FOUND OUT WE WERE ATTENDING THAT TANTRIC STUDIES GROUP TOGETHER.
OH! THE ONE IN SAN FRANCISCO! THAT WAS A LONG TIME AGO. I'D FORGOTTEN.
FORGOTTEN? WELL, THAT'S VERY FLATTERING, THAT IS. I HADN'T FORGOTTEN.
YOU HAD YOUR OLD COSTUME THEN. PITY YOU CHANGED IT.
OH, COME ON, JOHN... A TOP HAT AND FISHNET STOCKINGS?
YEAH, WELL, I LIKED IT.
PROBABLY WHY I NEVER GOT FAR AS A MAGICIAN: TOO CONCERNED WITH THE DELIGHTS OF THE PHYSICAL WORLD.
HAHAHA. COME ON...GET OUT BEFORE DAD CHANGES YOU INTO SOMETHING LOWER THAN YOU ALREADY ARE.
NOT POSSIBLE.
TAKE CARE, GAL. I'LL SEE YOU AND ZATARA LATER, AT WINTER'S PLACE.
GOOD-BYE, JOHN. YOU HAVEN'T CHANGED. YOU'VE STILL GOT A HELL OF A NERVE.
YEAH, WELL...
IT'S A HELL OF A WORLD.

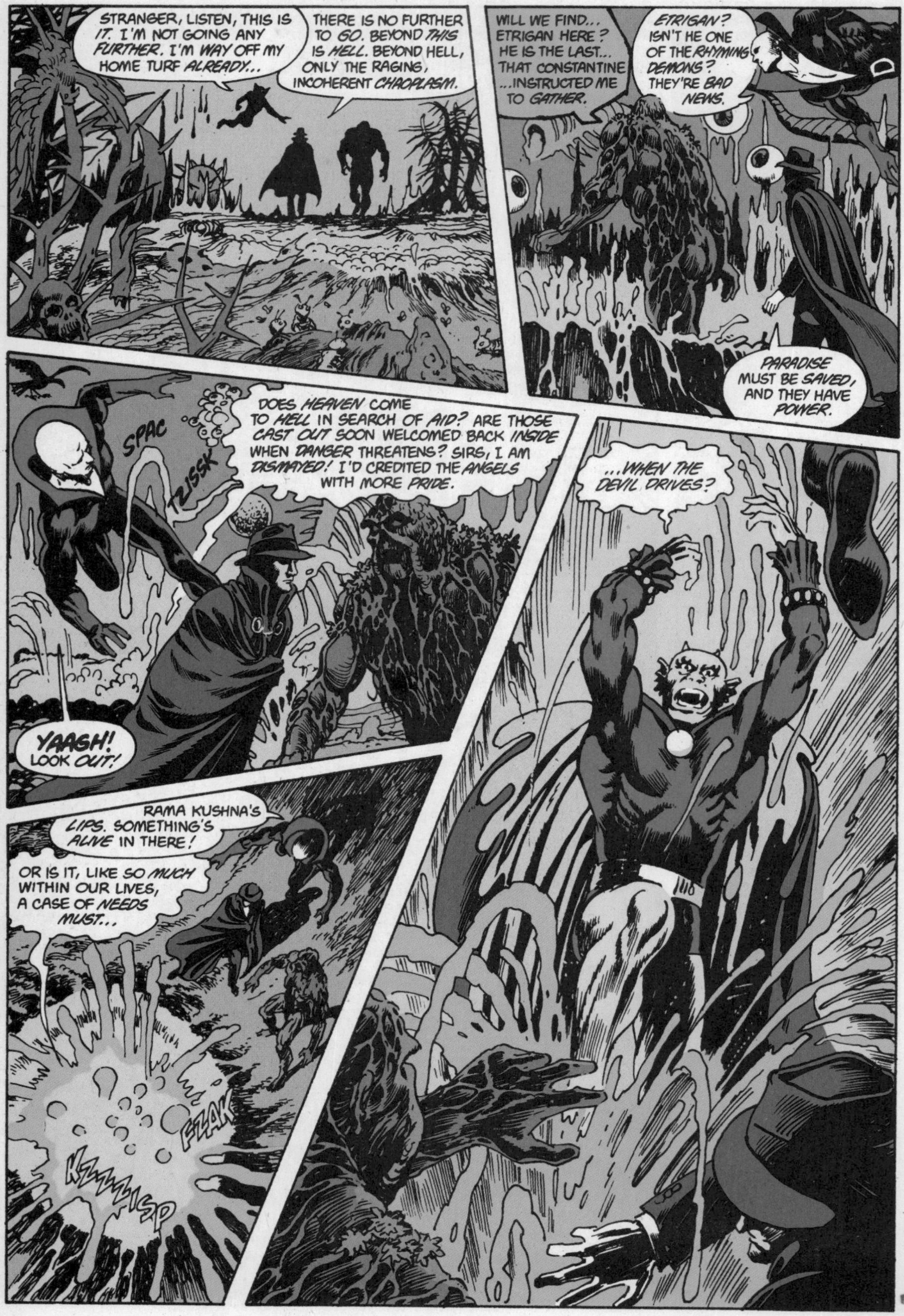
STRANGER, LISTEN, THIS IS IT. I'M NOT GOING ANY FURTHER. I'M WAY OFF MY HOME TURF ALREADY...
THERE IS NO FURTHER TO GO. BEYOND THIS IS HELL. BEYOND HELL, ONLY THE RAGING, INCOHERENT CHAOPLASM.
WILL WE FIND... ETRIGAN HERE? HE IS THE LAST... THAT CONSTANTINE ...INSTRUCTED ME TO GATHER.
ETRIGAN? ISN'T HE ONE OF THE RHYMING DEMONS? THEY'RE BAD NEWS.
PARADISE MUST BE SAVED, AND THEY HAVE POWER.
DOES HEAVEN COME TO HELL IN SEARCH OF AID? ARE THOSE CAST OUT SOON WELCOMED BACK INSIDE WHEN DANGER THREATENS? SIRS, I AM DISMAYED! I'D CREDITED THE ANGELS WITH MORE PRIDE.
SPAC
TZISSK
YAASH! LOOK OUT!
RAMA KUSHNA'S LIPS. SOMETHING'S ALIVE IN THERE!
OR IS IT, LIKE SO MUCH WITHIN OUR LIVES, A CASE OF NEEDS MUST...
FZAK
KZZZZISP
...WHEN THE DEVIL DRIVES?

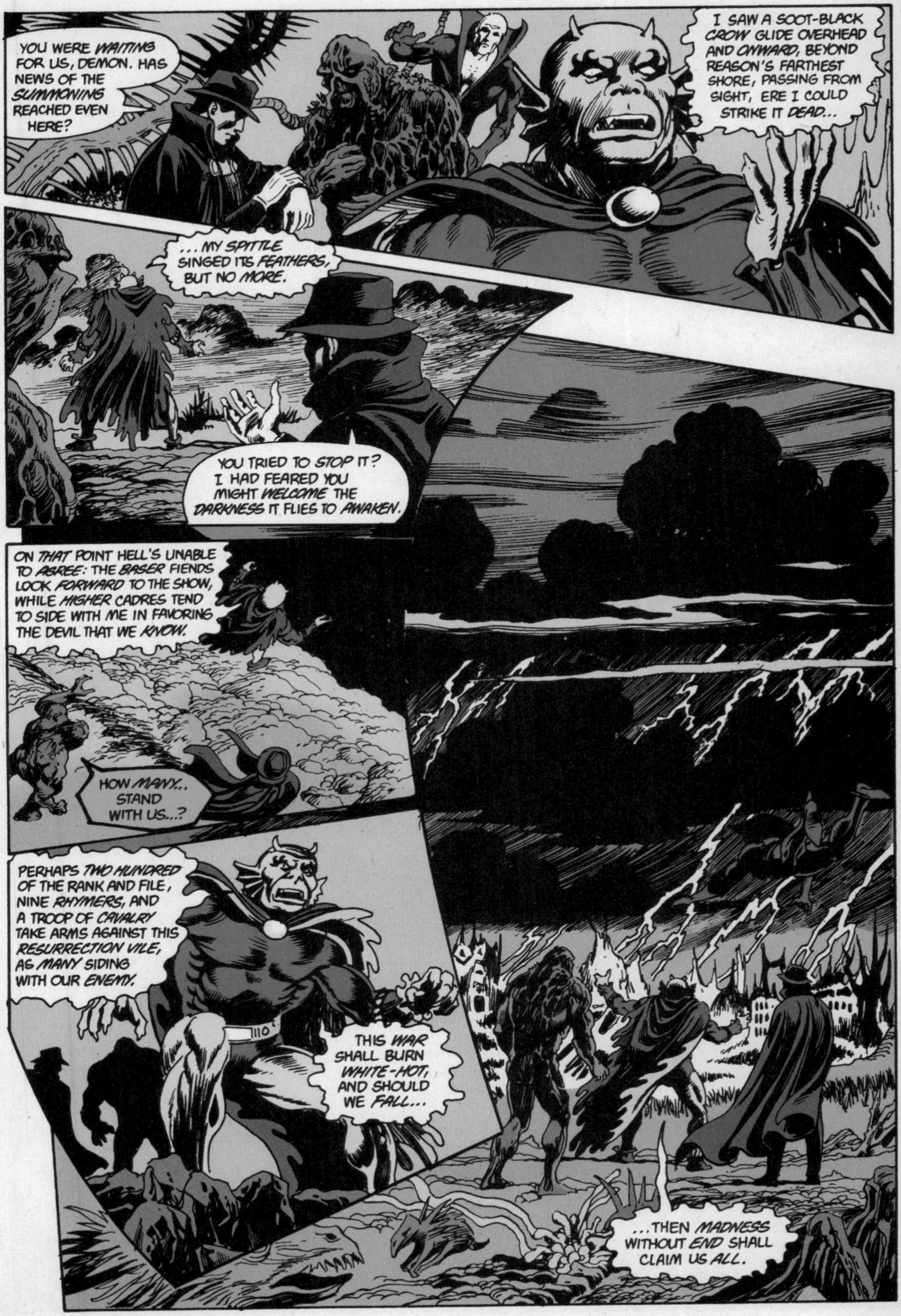
YOU WERE WAITING FOR US, DEMON. HAS NEWS OF THE SUMMONING REACHED EVEN HERE?
I SAW A SOOT-BLACK CROW GLIDE OVERHEAD AND ONWARD, BEYOND REASON'S FARTHEST SHORE, PASSING FROM SIGHT, ERE I COULD STRIKE IT DEAD...
...MY SPITTLE SINGED ITS FEATHERS, BUT NO MORE.
YOU TRIED TO STOP IT? I HAD FEARED YOU MIGHT WELCOME THE DARKNESS IT FLIES TO AWAKEN.
ON THAT POINT HELL'S UNABLE TO AGREE: THE BASER FIENDS LOOK FORWARD TO THE SHOW, WHILE HIGHER CADRES TEND TO SIDE WITH ME IN FAVORING THE DEVIL THAT WE KNOW.
HOW MANY.. STAND WITH US...?
PERHAPS TWO HUNDRED OF THE RANK AND FILE, NINE RHYMERS, AND A TROOP OF CAVALRY TAKE ARMS AGAINST THIS RESURRECTION VILE, AS MANY SIDING WITH OUR ENEMY.
THIS WAR SHALL BURN WHITE-HOT, AND SHOULD WE FALL...
...THEN MADNESS WITHOUT END SHALL CLAIM US ALL.

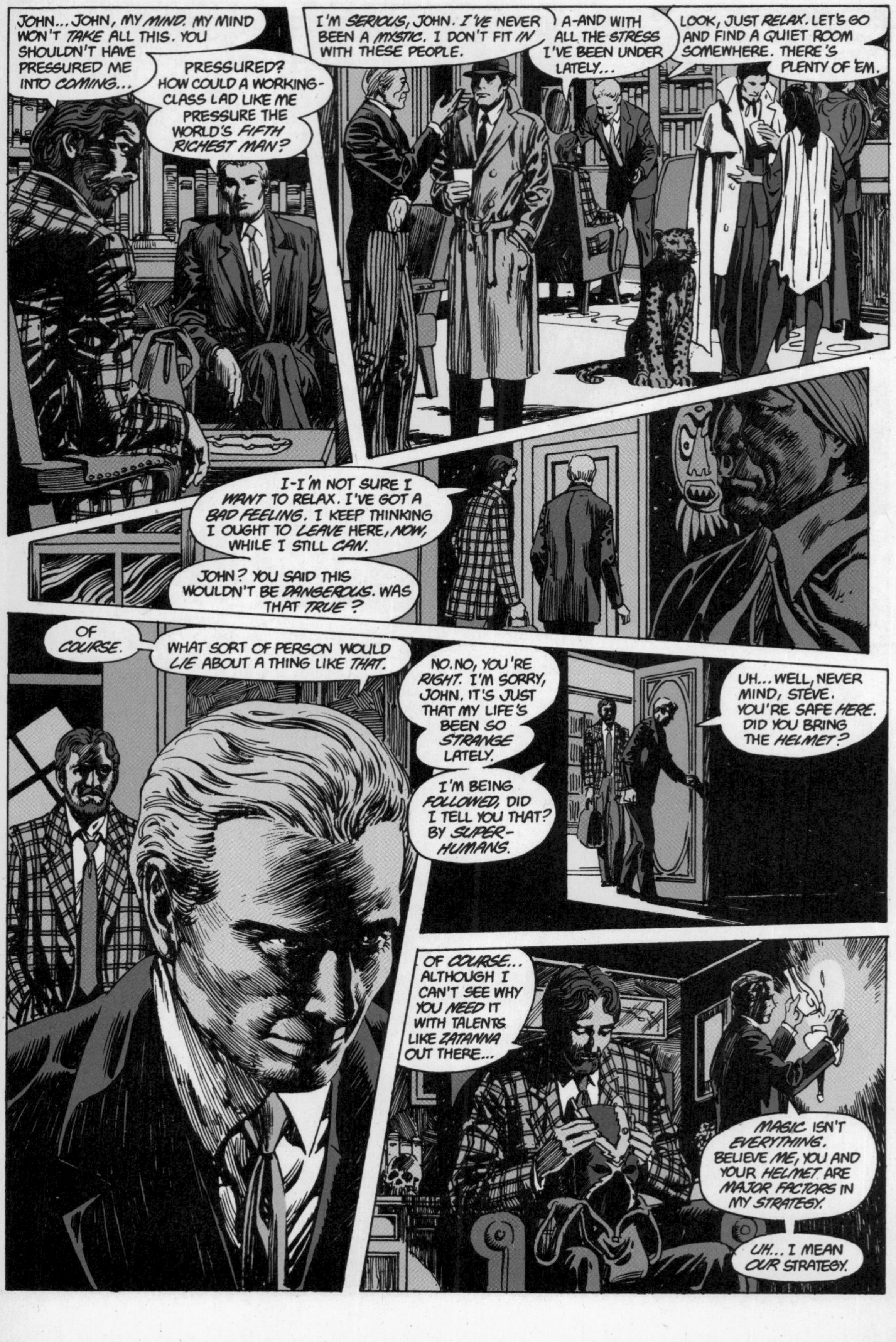
JOHN... JOHN, MY MIND. MY MIND WON'T TAKE ALL THIS. YOU SHOULDN'T HAVE PRESSURED ME INTO COMING...
PRESSURED? HOW COULD A WORKING-CLASS LAD LIKE ME PRESSURE THE WORLD'S FIFTH RICHEST MAN?
I'M SERIOUS, JOHN. I'VE NEVER BEEN A MYSTIC. I DON'T FIT IN WITH THESE PEOPLE.
A-AND WITH ALL THE STRESS I'VE BEEN UNDER LATELY...
LOOK, JUST RELAX. LET'S GO AND FIND A QUIET ROOM SOMEWHERE. THERE'S PLENTY OF 'EM.
I-I'M NOT SURE I WANT TO RELAX. I'VE GOT A BAD FEELING. I KEEP THINKING I OUGHT TO LEAVE HERE, NOW, WHILE I STILL CAN.
JOHN? YOU SAID THIS WOULDN'T BE DANGEROUS. WAS THAT TRUE?
OF COURSE.
WHAT SORT OF PERSON WOULD LIE ABOUT A THING LIKE THAT.
NO. NO, YOU'RE RIGHT. I'M SORRY, JOHN. IT'S JUST THAT MY LIFE'S BEEN SO STRANGE LATELY.
I'M BEING FOLLOWED, DID I TELL YOU THAT? BY SUPER-HUMANS.
UH... WELL, NEVER MIND, STEVE. YOU'RE SAFE HERE. DID YOU BRING THE HELMET?
OF COURSE... ALTHOUGH I CAN'T SEE WHY YOU NEED IT WITH TALENTS LIKE ZATANNA OUT THERE...
MAGIC ISN'T EVERYTHING. BELIEVE ME, YOU AND YOUR HELMET ARE MAJOR FACTORS IN MY STRATEGY.
UH... I MEAN OUR STRATEGY.

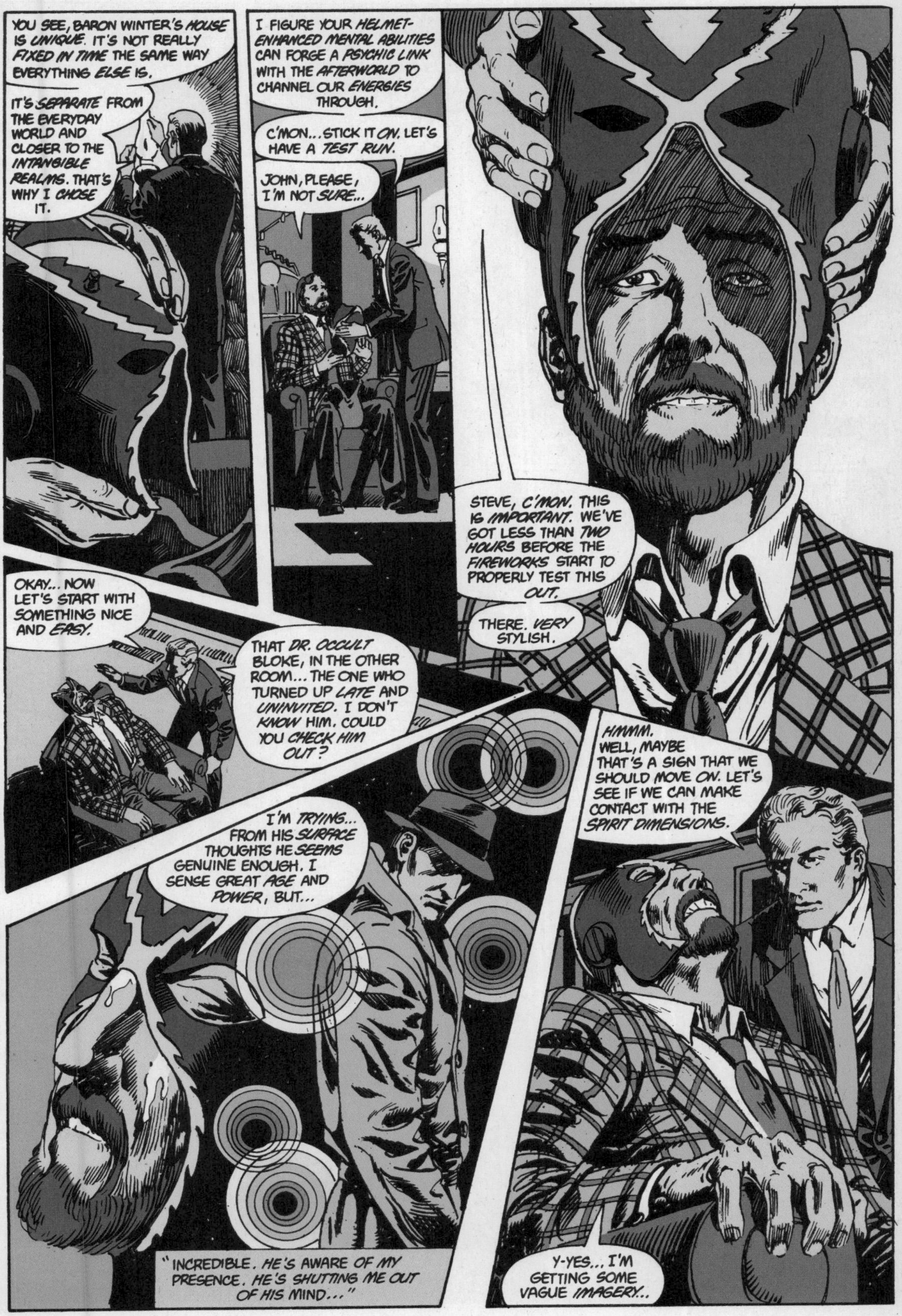
YOU SEE, BARON WINTER'S HOUSE IS UNIQUE. IT'S NOT REALLY FIXED IN TIME THE SAME WAY EVERYTHING ELSE IS.
IT'S SEPARATE FROM THE EVERYDAY WORLD AND CLOSER TO THE INTANGIBLE REALMS. THAT'S WHY I CHOSE IT.
I FIGURE YOUR HELMET-ENHANCED MENTAL ABILITIES CAN FORGE A PSYCHIC LINK WITH THE AFTERWORLD TO CHANNEL OUR ENERGIES THROUGH.
C'MON... STICK IT ON. LET'S HAVE A TEST RUN.
JOHN, PLEASE, I'M NOT SURE...
STEVE, C'MON. THIS IS IMPORTANT. WE'VE GOT LESS THAN TWO HOURS BEFORE THE FIREWORKS START TO PROPERLY TEST THIS OUT.
THERE. VERY STYLISH.
OKAY... NOW LET'S START WITH SOMETHING NICE AND EASY.
THAT DR. OCCULT BLOKE, IN THE OTHER ROOM... THE ONE WHO TURNED UP LATE AND UNINVITED. I DON'T KNOW HIM. COULD YOU CHECK HIM OUT?
I'M TRYING... FROM HIS SURFACE THOUGHTS HE SEEMS GENUINE ENOUGH. I SENSE GREAT AGE AND POWER, BUT...
"INCREDIBLE. HE'S AWARE OF MY PRESENCE. HE'S SHUTTING ME OUT OF HIS MIND..."
HMMM. WELL, MAYBE THAT'S A SIGN THAT WE SHOULD MOVE ON. LET'S SEE IF WE CAN MAKE CONTACT WITH THE SPIRIT DIMENSIONS.
Y-YES... I'M GETTING SOME VAGUE IMAGERY...

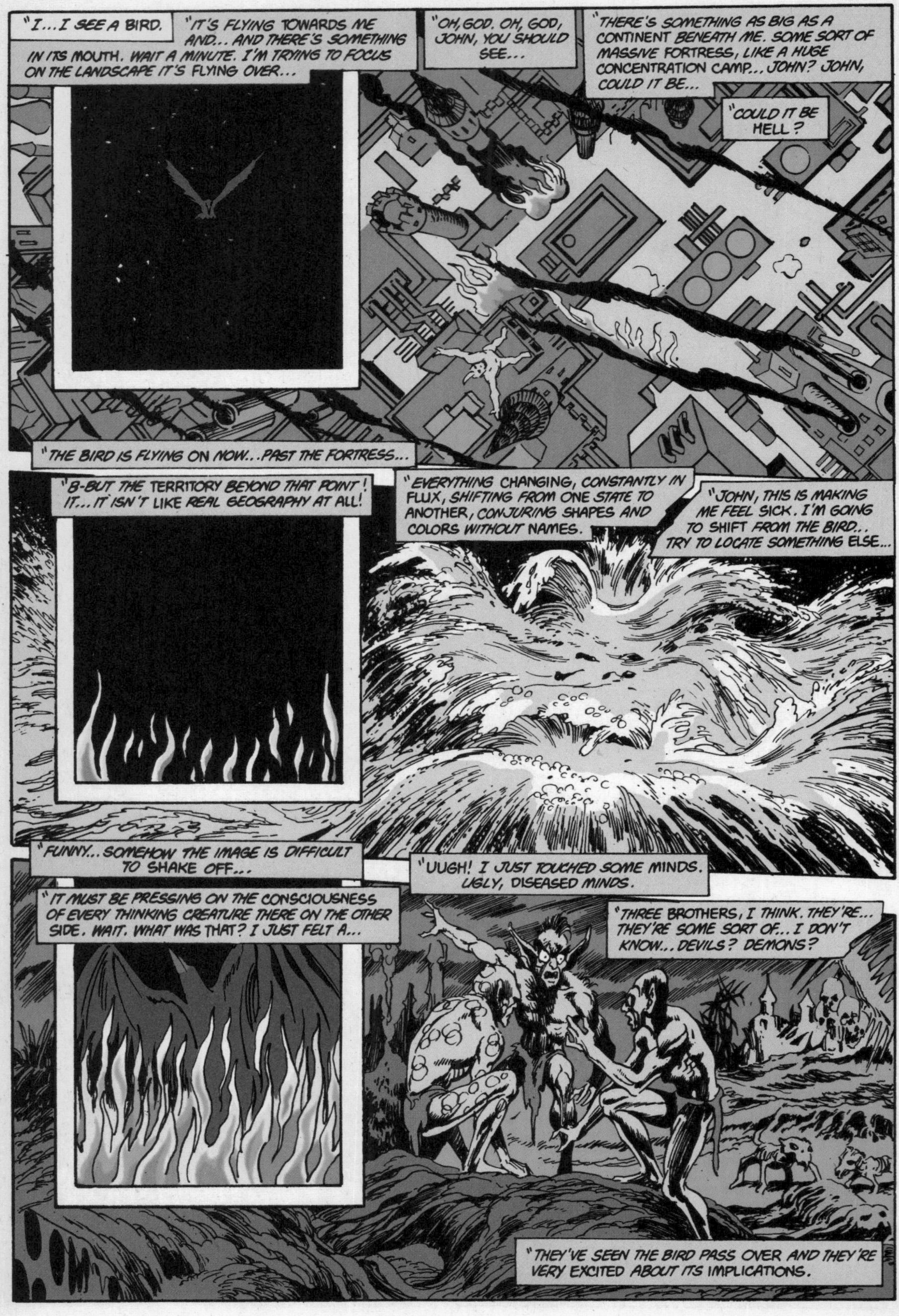
"I... I SEE A BIRD.
"IT'S FLYING TOWARDS ME AND... AND THERE'S SOMETHING IN ITS MOUTH. WAIT A MINUTE. I'M TRYING TO FOCUS ON THE LANDSCAPE IT'S FLYING OVER...
"OH, GOD. OH, GOD, JOHN, YOU SHOULD SEE...
"THERE'S SOMETHING AS BIG AS A CONTINENT BENEATH ME. SOME SORT OF MASSIVE FORTRESS, LIKE A HUGE CONCENTRATION CAMP... JOHN? JOHN, COULD IT BE...
"COULD IT BE HELL?
"THE BIRD IS FLYING ON NOW... PAST THE FORTRESS...
"B-BUT THE TERRITORY BEYOND THAT POINT! IT... IT ISN'T LIKE REAL GEOGRAPHY AT ALL!
"EVERYTHING CHANGING, CONSTANTLY IN FLUX, SHIFTING FROM ONE STATE TO ANOTHER, CONJURING SHAPES AND COLORS WITHOUT NAMES.
"JOHN, THIS IS MAKING ME FEEL SICK. I'M GOING TO SHIFT FROM THE BIRD.. TRY TO LOCATE SOMETHING ELSE...
"FUNNY... SOMEHOW THE IMAGE IS DIFFICULT TO SHAKE OFF...
"IT MUST BE PRESSING ON THE CONSCIOUSNESS OF EVERY THINKING CREATURE THERE ON THE OTHER SIDE. WAIT. WHAT WAS THAT? I JUST FELT A...
"UUGH! I JUST TOUCHED SOME MINDS. UGLY, DISEASED MINDS.
"THREE BROTHERS, I THINK. THEY'RE... THEY'RE SOME SORT OF... I DON'T KNOW... DEVILS? DEMONS?
"THEY'VE SEEN THE BIRD PASS OVER AND THEY'RE VERY EXCITED ABOUT ITS IMPLICATIONS.

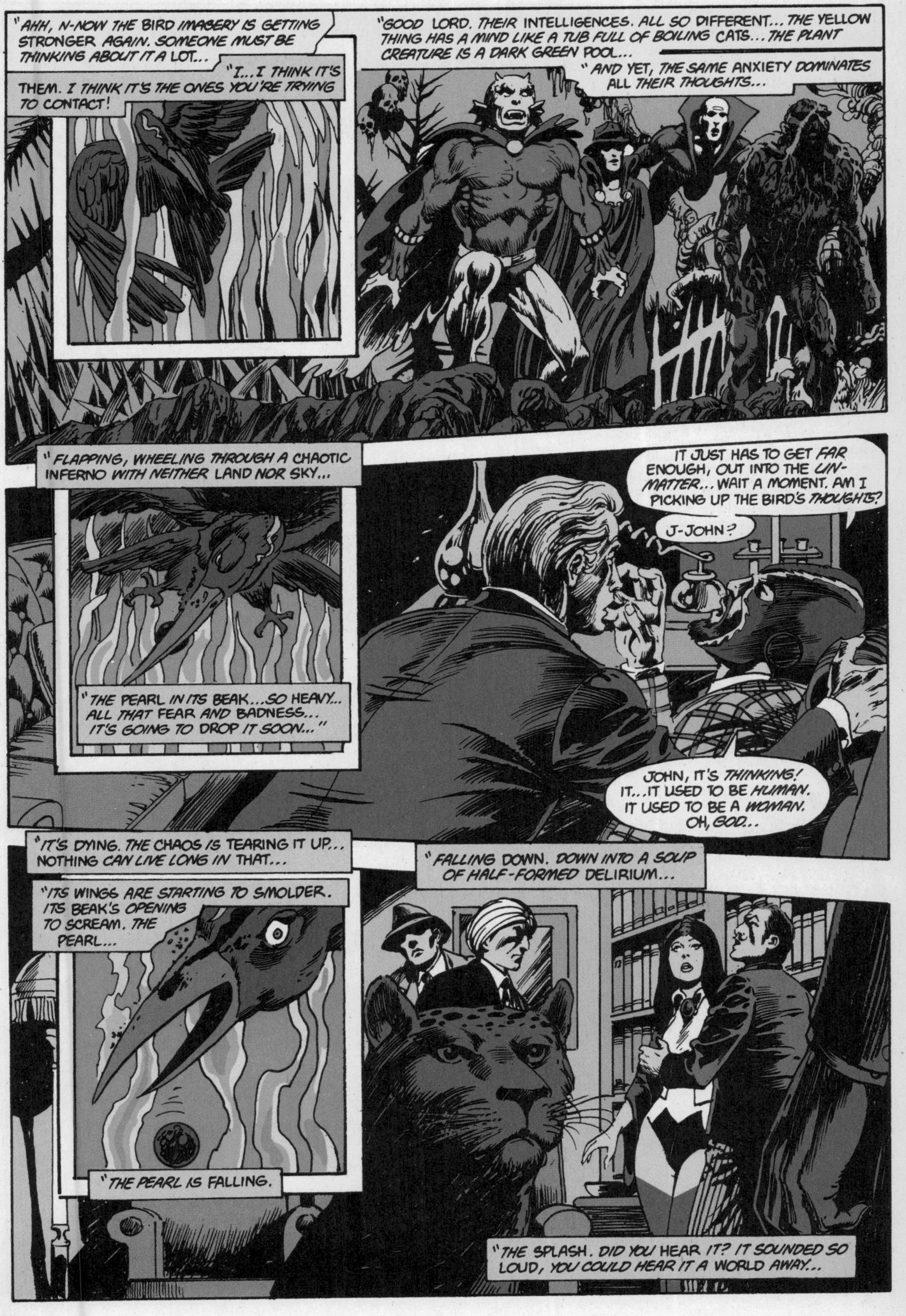
"AHH, N-NOW THE BIRD IMAGERY IS GETTING STRONGER AGAIN. SOMEONE MUST BE THINKING ABOUT IT A LOT...
"I...I THINK IT'S THEM. I THINK IT'S THE ONES YOU'RE TRYING TO CONTACT!
"GOOD LORD. THEIR INTELLIGENCES. ALL SO DIFFERENT... THE YELLOW THING HAS A MIND LIKE A TUB FULL OF BOILING CATS... THE PLANT CREATURE IS A DARK GREEN POOL...
"AND YET, THE SAME ANXIETY DOMINATES ALL THEIR THOUGHTS...
"FLAPPING, WHEELING THROUGH A CHAOTIC INFERNO WITH NEITHER LAND NOR SKY...
"THE PEARL IN ITS BEAK...SO HEAVY... ALL THAT FEAR AND BADNESS... IT'S GOING TO DROP IT SOON..."
IT JUST HAS TO GET FAR ENOUGH, OUT INTO THE UN-MATTER... WAIT A MOMENT. AM I PICKING UP THE BIRD'S THOUGHTS?
J-JOHN?
JOHN, IT'S THINKING! IT...IT USED TO BE HUMAN. IT USED TO BE A WOMAN. OH, GOD...
"IT'S DYING. THE CHAOS IS TEARING IT UP... NOTHING CAN LIVE LONG IN THAT...
"ITS WINGS ARE STARTING TO SMOLDER. ITS BEAK'S OPENING TO SCREAM. THE PEARL...
"THE PEARL IS FALLING.
"FALLING DOWN. DOWN INTO A SOUP OF HALF-FORMED DELIRIUM...
"THE SPLASH. DID YOU HEAR IT? IT SOUNDED SO LOUD, YOU COULD HEAR IT A WORLD AWAY...

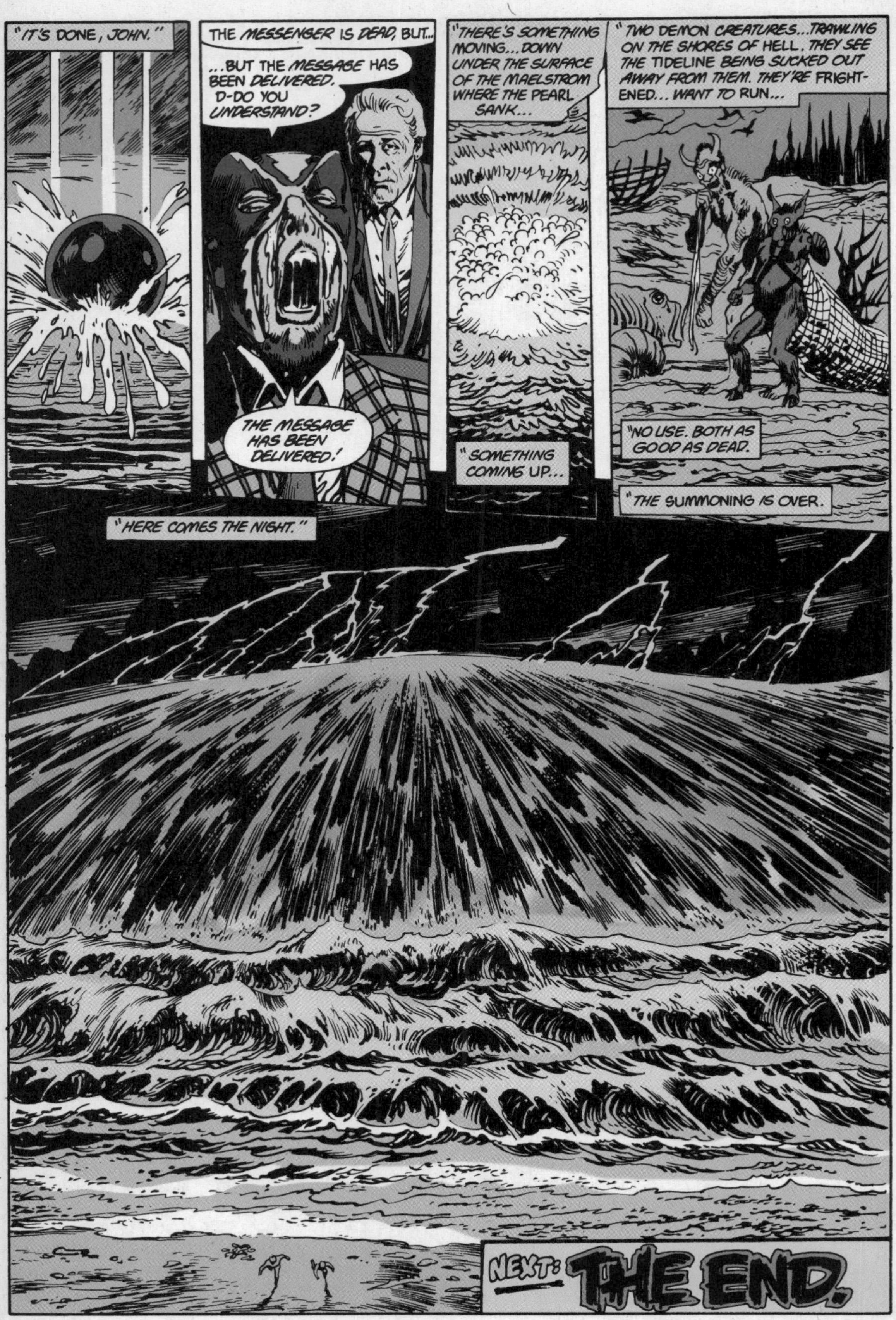
"IT'S DONE, JOHN."
THE MESSENGER IS DEAD, BUT...
...BUT THE MESSAGE HAS BEEN DELIVERED. D-DO YOU UNDERSTAND?
THE MESSAGE HAS BEEN DELIVERED!
"THERE'S SOMETHING MOVING... DOWN UNDER THE SURFACE OF THE MAELSTROM WHERE THE PEARL SANK...
"SOMETHING COMING UP...
"TWO DEMON CREATURES... TRAWLING ON THE SHORES OF HELL. THEY SEE THE TIDELINE BEING SUCKED OUT AWAY FROM THEM. THEY'RE FRIGHTENED... WANT TO RUN...
"NO USE. BOTH AS GOOD AS DEAD.
"THE SUMMONING IS OVER.
"HERE COMES THE NIGHT."
NEXT: THE END.

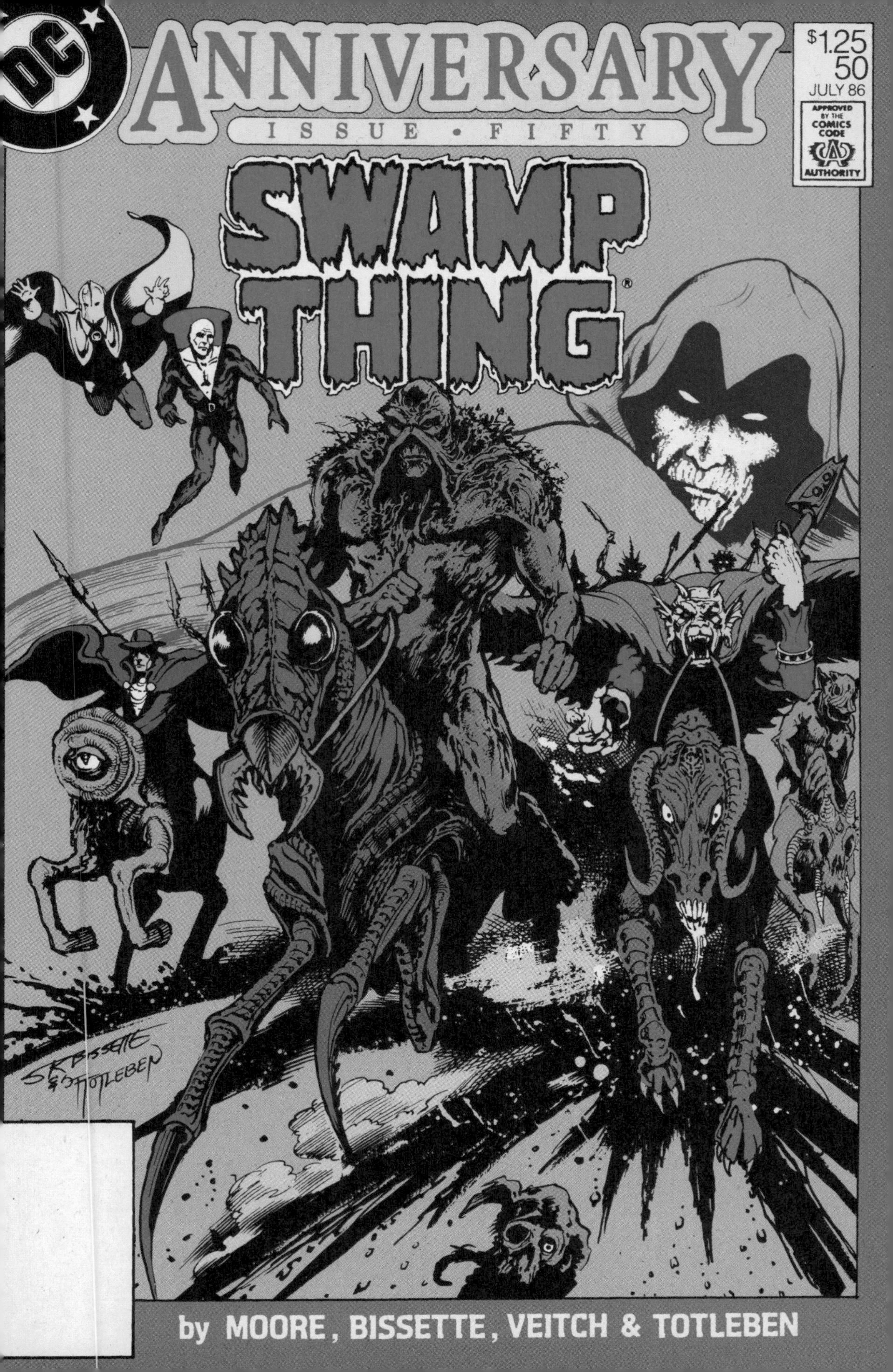
DC
ANNIVERSARY
ISSUE • FIFTY
$1.25
50
JULY 86
APPROVED BY THE COMICS CODE AUTHORITY
SWAMP THING®
S.R. BISSETTE & J. TOTLEBEN
by MOORE, BISSETTE, VEITCH & TOTLEBEN

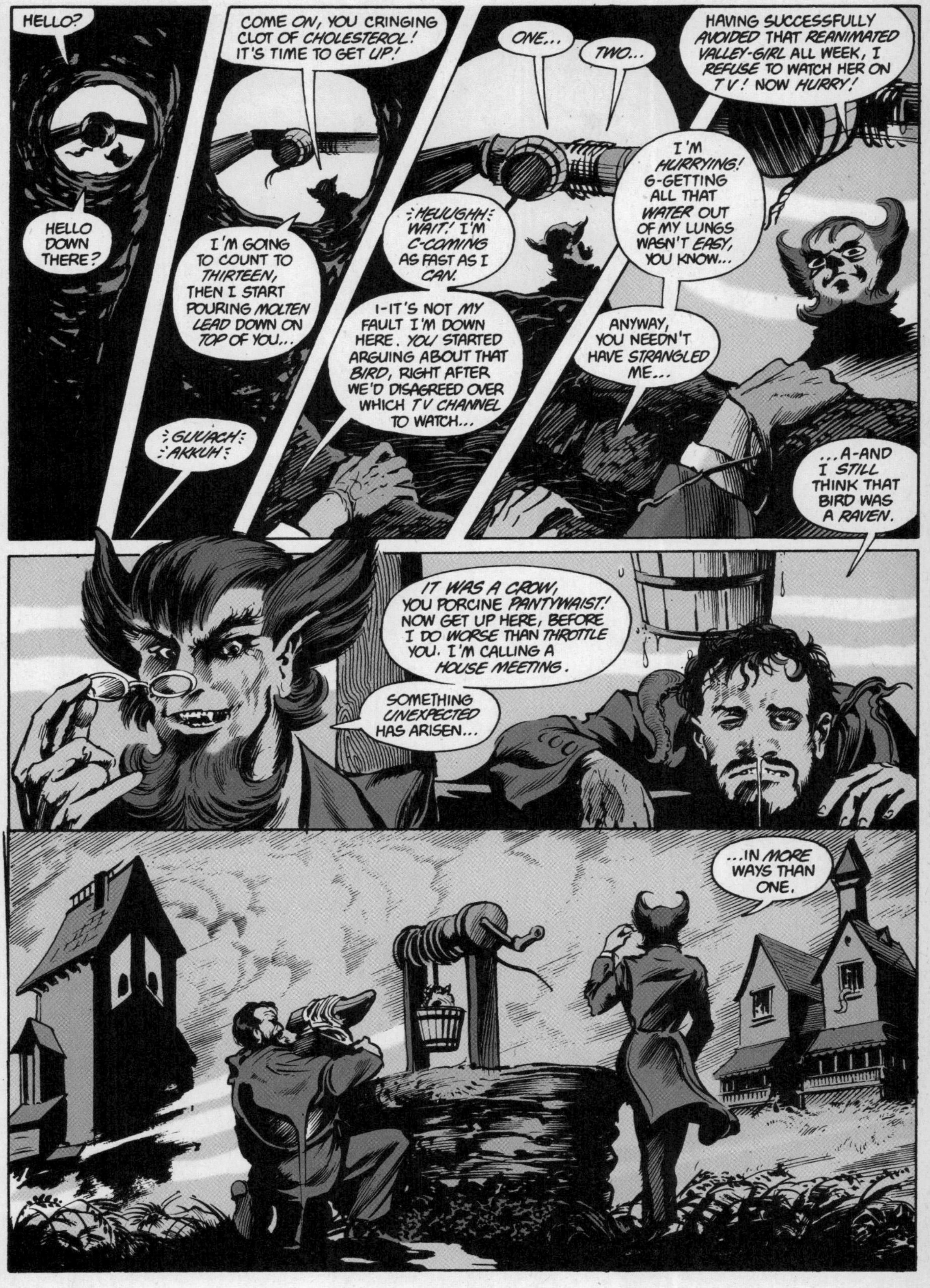
HELLO?
HELLO DOWN THERE?
COME ON, YOU CRINGING CLOT OF CHOLESTEROL! IT'S TIME TO GET UP!
I'M GOING TO COUNT TO THIRTEEN, THEN I START POURING MOLTEN LEAD DOWN ON TOP OF YOU...
GUUACH AKKUH
ONE...
TWO...
HEUUGHH WAIT! I'M C-COMING AS FAST AS I CAN.
I-IT'S NOT MY FAULT I'M DOWN HERE. YOU STARTED ARGUING ABOUT THAT BIRD, RIGHT AFTER WE'D DISAGREED OVER WHICH TV CHANNEL TO WATCH...
HAVING SUCCESSFULLY AVOIDED THAT REANIMATED VALLEY-GIRL ALL WEEK, I REFUSE TO WATCH HER ON TV! NOW HURRY!
I'M HURRYING! G-GETTING ALL THAT WATER OUT OF MY LUNGS WASN'T EASY, YOU KNOW...
ANYWAY, YOU NEEDN'T HAVE STRANGLED ME...
...A-AND I STILL THINK THAT BIRD WAS A RAVEN.
IT WAS A CROW, YOU PORCINE PANTYWAIST! NOW GET UP HERE, BEFORE I DO WORSE THAN THROTTLE YOU. I'M CALLING A HOUSE MEETING.
SOMETHING UNEXPECTED HAS ARISEN...
...IN MORE WAYS THAN ONE.

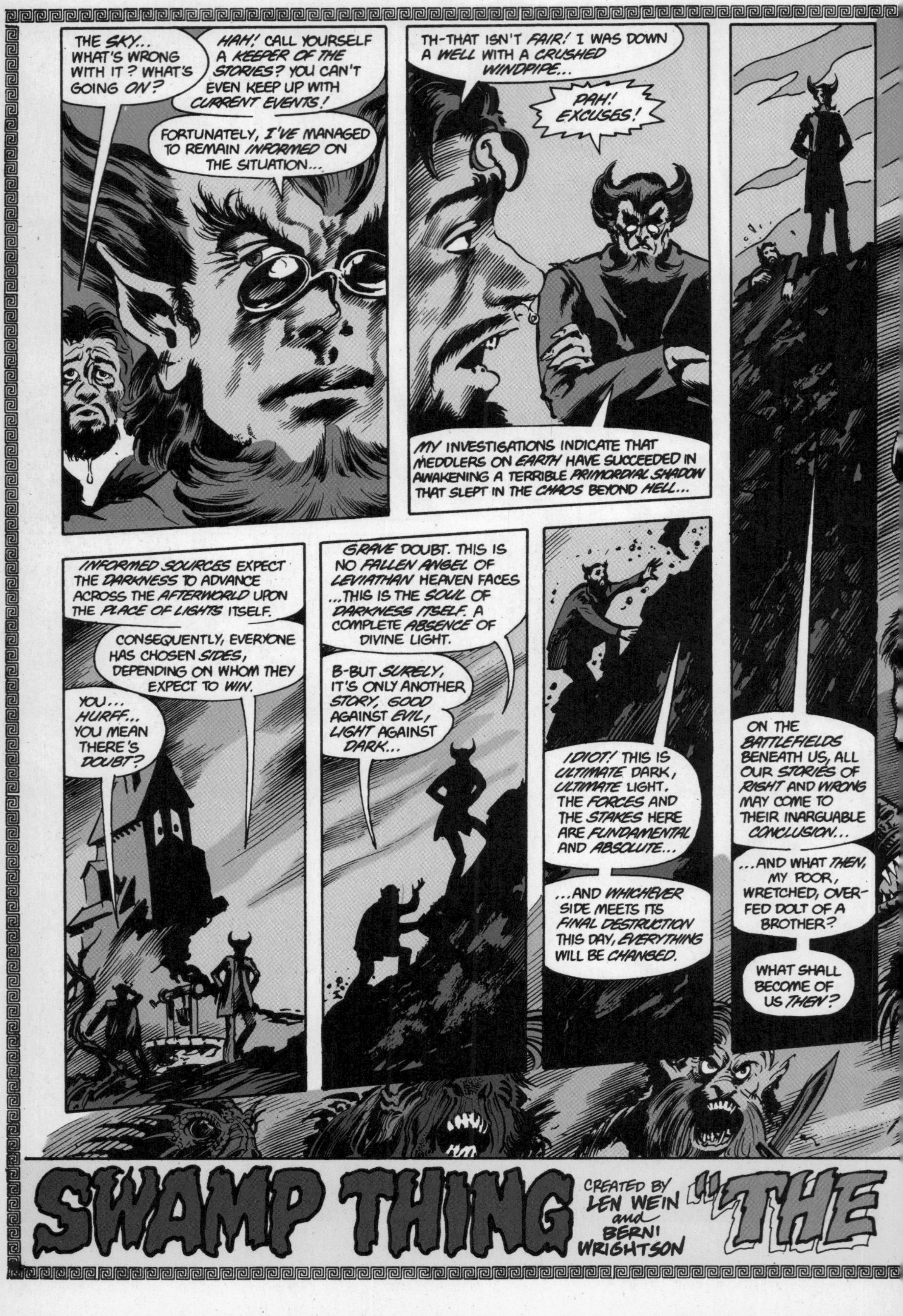
THE SKY... WHAT'S WRONG WITH IT? WHAT'S GOING ON?
HAH! CALL YOURSELF A KEEPER OF THE STORIES? YOU CAN'T EVEN KEEP UP WITH CURRENT EVENTS!
FORTUNATELY, I'VE MANAGED TO REMAIN INFORMED ON THE SITUATION...
TH-THAT ISN'T FAIR! I WAS DOWN A WELL WITH A CRUSHED WINDPIPE...
PAH! EXCUSES!
MY INVESTIGATIONS INDICATE THAT MEDDLERS ON EARTH HAVE SUCCEEDED IN AWAKENING A TERRIBLE PRIMORDIAL SHADOW THAT SLEPT IN THE CHAOS BEYOND HELL...
INFORMED SOURCES EXPECT THE DARKNESS TO ADVANCE ACROSS THE AFTERWORLD UPON THE PLACE OF LIGHTS ITSELF.
CONSEQUENTLY, EVERYONE HAS CHOSEN SIDES, DEPENDING ON WHOM THEY EXPECT TO WIN.
YOU... HURFF... YOU MEAN THERE'S DOUBT?
GRAVE DOUBT. THIS IS NO FALLEN ANGEL OF LEVIATHAN HEAVEN FACES ...THIS IS THE SOUL OF DARKNESS ITSELF. A COMPLETE ABSENCE OF DIVINE LIGHT.
B-BUT SURELY, IT'S ONLY ANOTHER STORY, GOOD AGAINST EVIL, LIGHT AGAINST DARK...
IDIOT! THIS IS ULTIMATE DARK, ULTIMATE LIGHT. THE FORCES AND THE STAKES HERE ARE FUNDAMENTAL AND ABSOLUTE...
...AND WHICHEVER SIDE MEETS ITS FINAL DESTRUCTION THIS DAY, EVERYTHING WILL BE CHANGED.
ON THE BATTLEFIELDS BENEATH US, ALL OUR STORIES OF RIGHT AND WRONG MAY COME TO THEIR INARGUABLE CONCLUSION...
...AND WHAT THEN, MY POOR, WRETCHED, OVER-FED DOLT OF A BROTHER?
WHAT SHALL BECOME OF US THEN?
SWAMP THING
CREATED BY LEN WEIN and BERNI WRIGHTSON
"THE

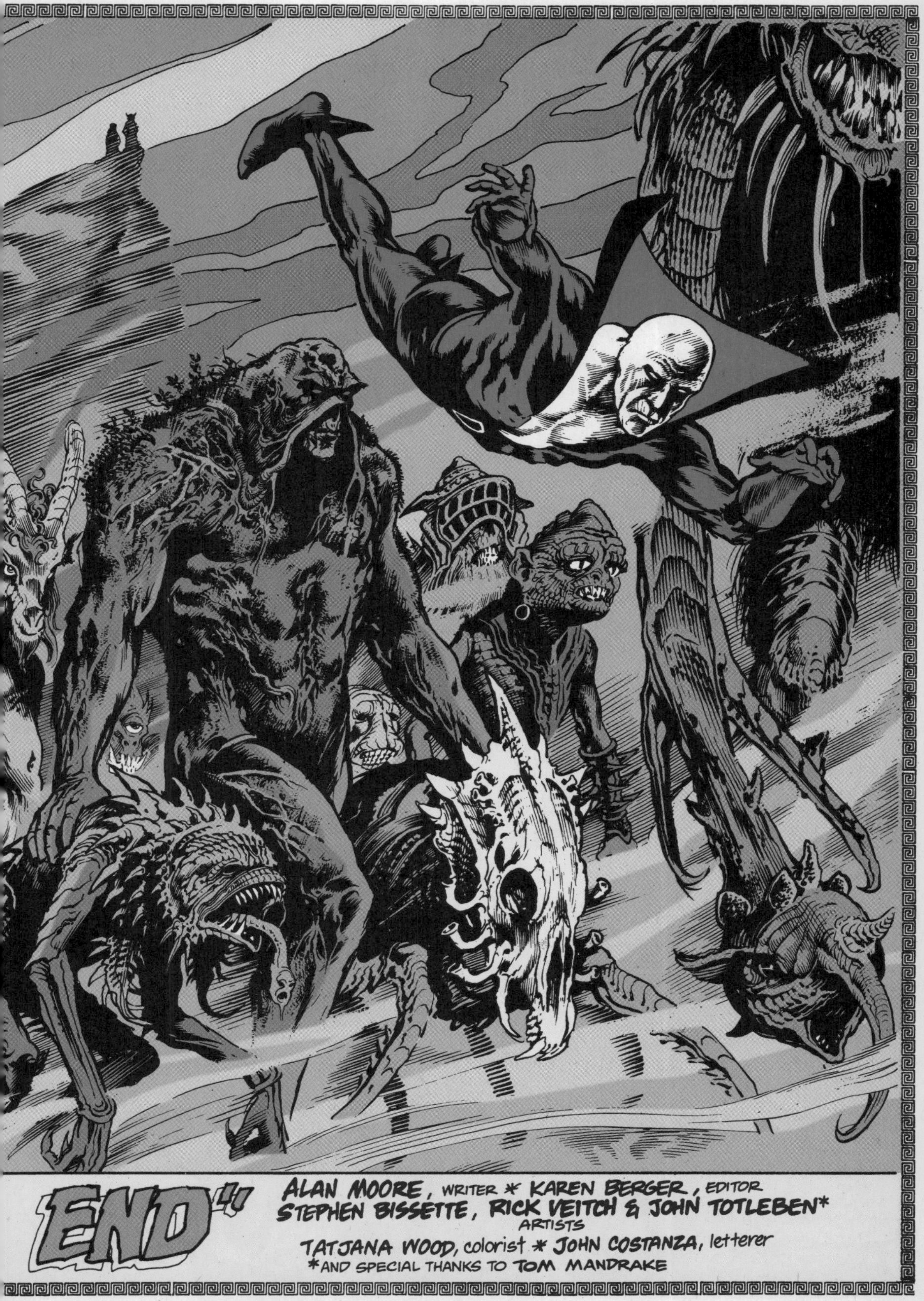
END!!
ALAN MOORE, WRITER * KAREN BERGER, EDITOR
STEPHEN BISSETTE, RICK VEITCH & JOHN TOTLEBEN*
ARTISTS
TATJANA WOOD, colorist * JOHN COSTANZA, letterer
*AND SPECIAL THANKS TO TOM MANDRAKE

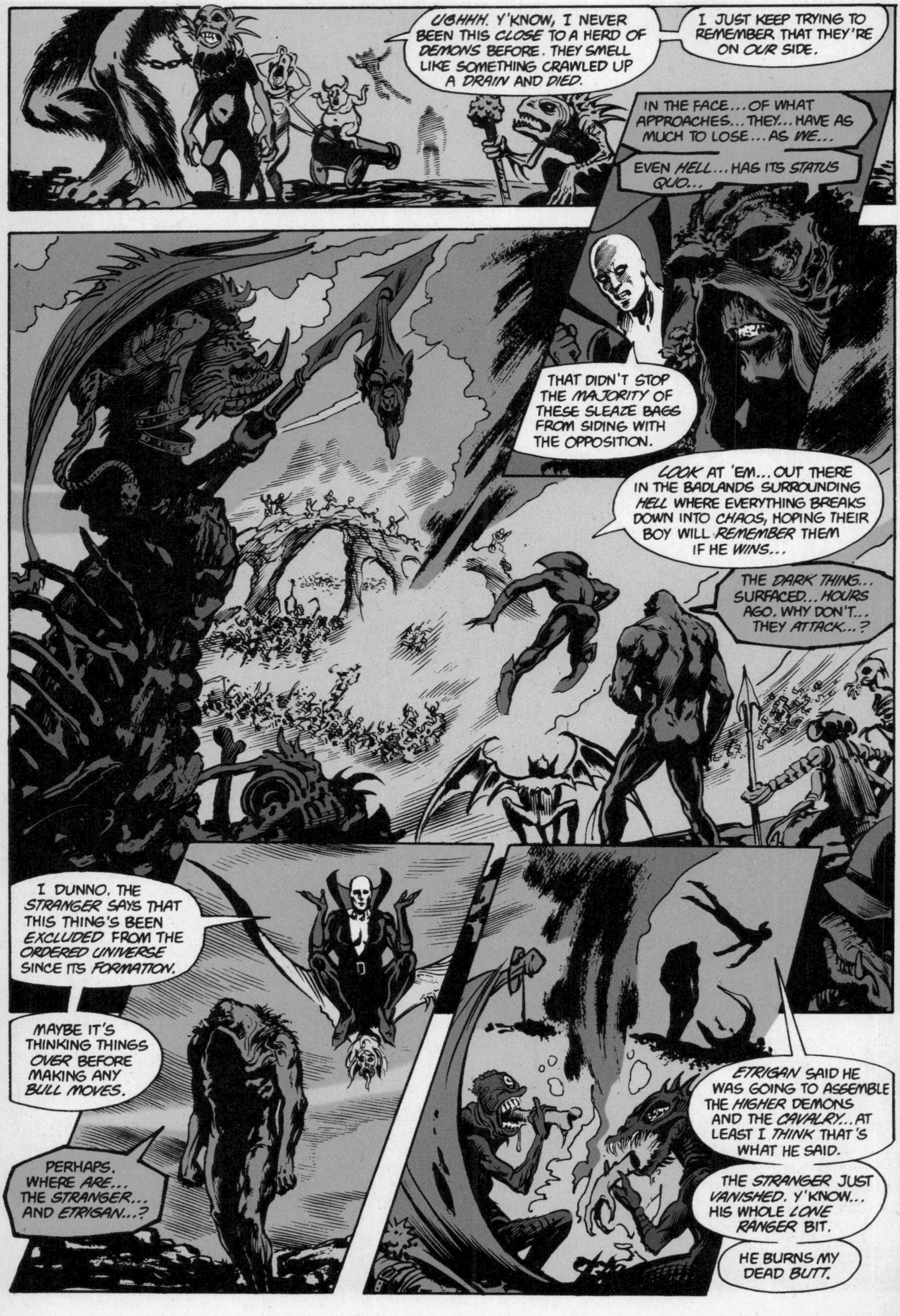
UGHHH. Y'KNOW, I NEVER BEEN THIS CLOSE TO A HERD OF DEMONS BEFORE. THEY SMELL LIKE SOMETHING CRAWLED UP A DRAIN AND DIED.
I JUST KEEP TRYING TO REMEMBER THAT THEY'RE ON OUR SIDE.
IN THE FACE... OF WHAT APPROACHES... THEY... HAVE AS MUCH TO LOSE... AS WE...
EVEN HELL... HAS ITS STATUS QUO...
THAT DIDN'T STOP THE MAJORITY OF THESE SLEAZE BAGS FROM SIDING WITH THE OPPOSITION.
LOOK AT 'EM... OUT THERE IN THE BADLANDS SURROUNDING HELL WHERE EVERYTHING BREAKS DOWN INTO CHAOS, HOPING THEIR BOY WILL REMEMBER THEM IF HE WINS...
THE DARK THING... SURFACED... HOURS AGO. WHY DON'T... THEY ATTACK...?
I DUNNO. THE STRANGER SAYS THAT THIS THING'S BEEN EXCLUDED FROM THE ORDERED UNIVERSE SINCE ITS FORMATION.
MAYBE IT'S THINKING THINGS OVER BEFORE MAKING ANY BULL MOVES.
PERHAPS. WHERE ARE... THE STRANGER... AND ETRIGAN...?
ETRIGAN SAID HE WAS GOING TO ASSEMBLE THE HIGHER DEMONS AND THE CAVALRY... AT LEAST I THINK THAT'S WHAT HE SAID.
THE STRANGER JUST VANISHED. Y'KNOW... HIS WHOLE LONE RANGER BIT.
HE BURNS MY DEAD BUTT.

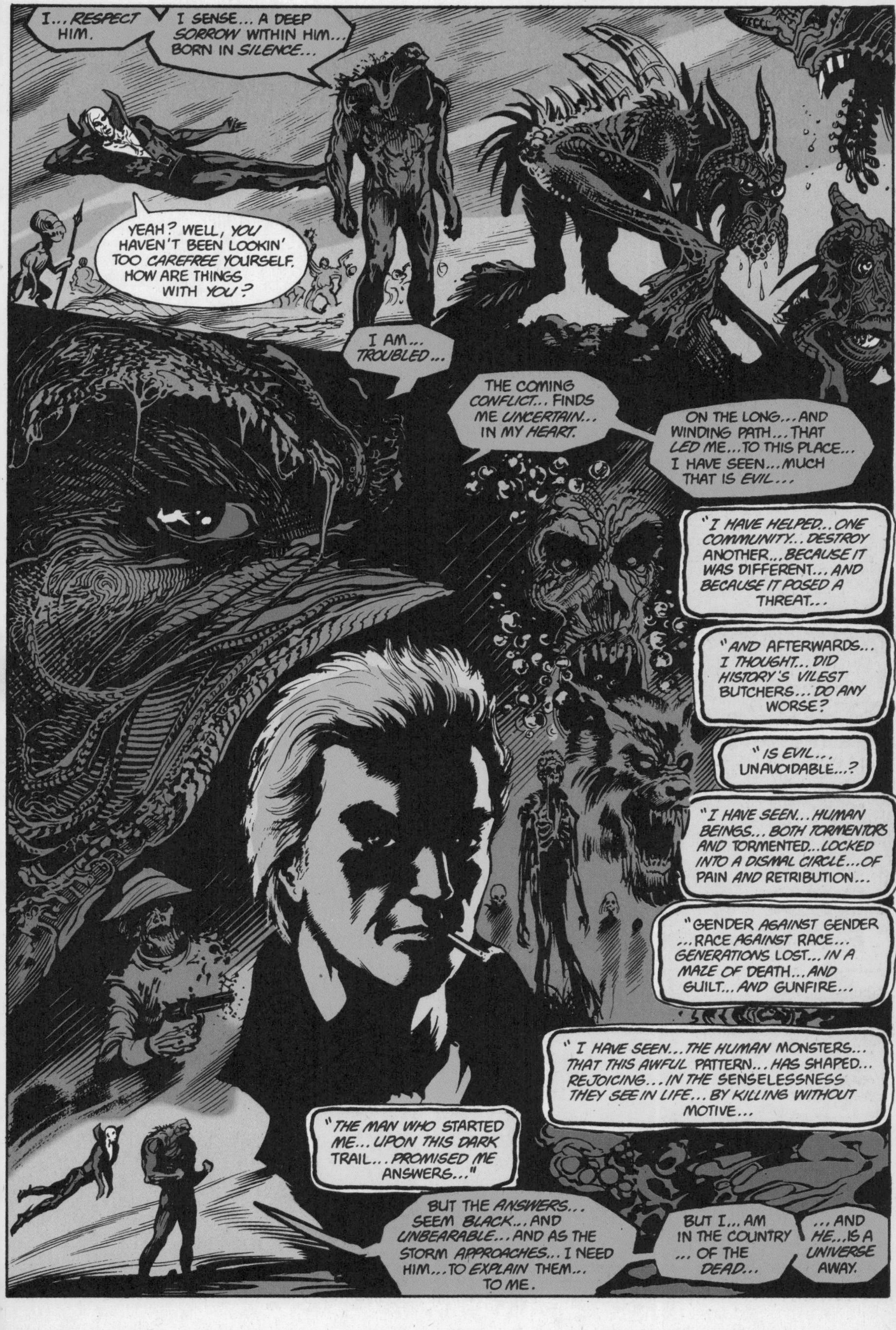
I... RESPECT HIM.
I SENSE... A DEEP SORROW WITHIN HIM... BORN IN SILENCE...
YEAH? WELL, YOU HAVEN'T BEEN LOOKIN' TOO CAREFREE YOURSELF. HOW ARE THINGS WITH YOU?
I AM... TROUBLED...
THE COMING CONFLICT... FINDS ME UNCERTAIN... IN MY HEART.
ON THE LONG... AND WINDING PATH... THAT LED ME... TO THIS PLACE... I HAVE SEEN... MUCH THAT IS EVIL...
"I HAVE HELPED... ONE COMMUNITY... DESTROY ANOTHER... BECAUSE IT WAS DIFFERENT... AND BECAUSE IT POSED A THREAT...
"AND AFTERWARDS... I THOUGHT... DID HISTORY'S VILEST BUTCHERS... DO ANY WORSE?
"IS EVIL... UNAVOIDABLE...?
"I HAVE SEEN... HUMAN BEINGS... BOTH TORMENTORS AND TORMENTED... LOCKED INTO A DISMAL CIRCLE... OF PAIN AND RETRIBUTION...
"GENDER AGAINST GENDER ... RACE AGAINST RACE... GENERATIONS LOST... IN A MAZE OF DEATH... AND GUILT... AND GUNFIRE...
" I HAVE SEEN... THE HUMAN MONSTERS... THAT THIS AWFUL PATTERN... HAS SHAPED... REJOICING... IN THE SENSELESSNESS THEY SEE IN LIFE... BY KILLING WITHOUT MOTIVE...
"THE MAN WHO STARTED ME... UPON THIS DARK TRAIL... PROMISED ME ANSWERS..."
BUT THE ANSWERS... SEEM BLACK... AND UNBEARABLE... AND AS THE STORM APPROACHES... I NEED HIM... TO EXPLAIN THEM... TO ME.
BUT I... AM IN THE COUNTRY ... OF THE DEAD...
... AND HE... IS A UNIVERSE AWAY.

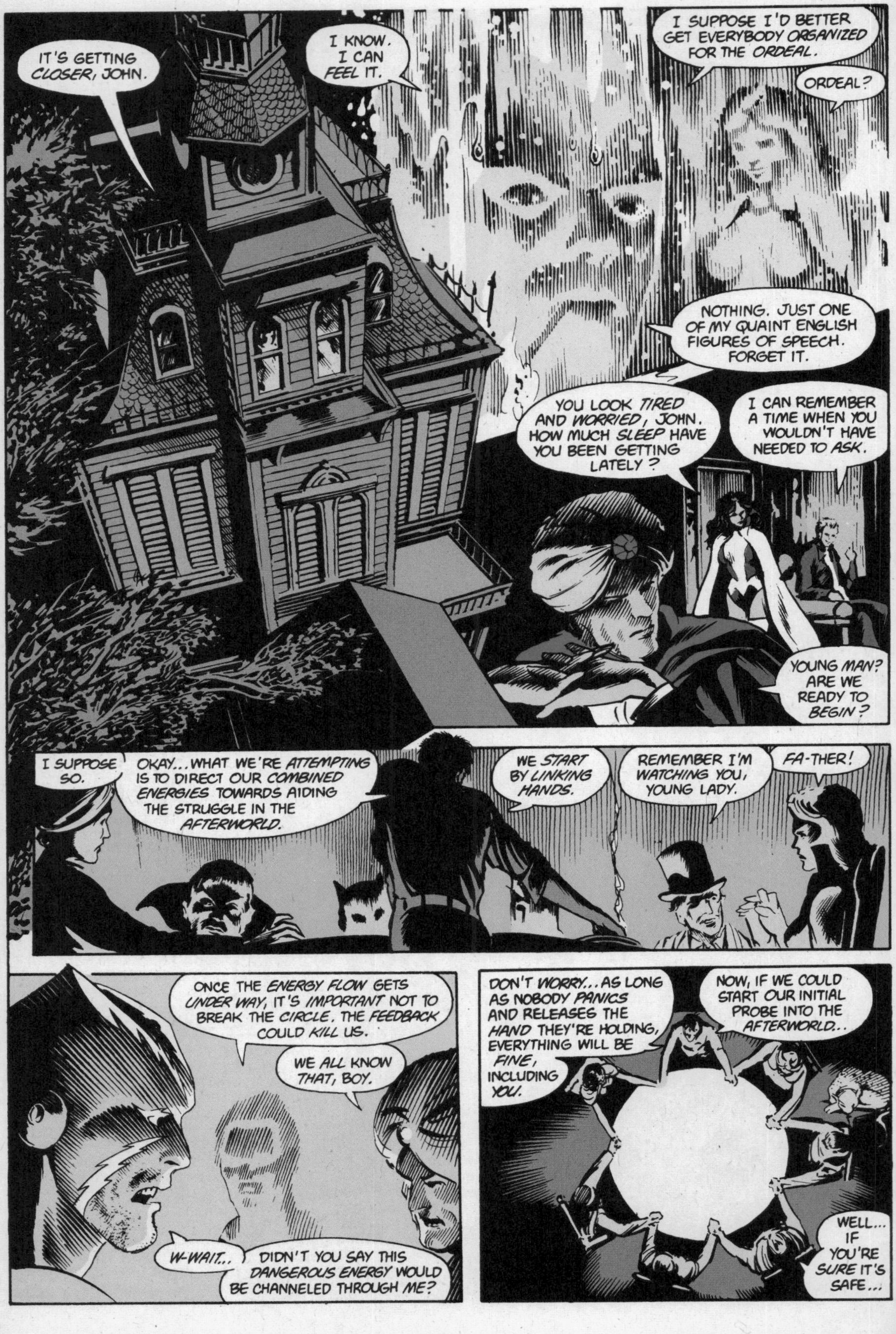
IT'S GETTING CLOSER, JOHN.
I KNOW. I CAN FEEL IT.
I SUPPOSE I'D BETTER GET EVERYBODY ORGANIZED FOR THE ORDEAL.
ORDEAL?
NOTHING. JUST ONE OF MY QUAINT ENGLISH FIGURES OF SPEECH. FORGET IT.
YOU LOOK TIRED AND WORRIED, JOHN. HOW MUCH SLEEP HAVE YOU BEEN GETTING LATELY?
I CAN REMEMBER A TIME WHEN YOU WOULDN'T HAVE NEEDED TO ASK.
YOUNG MAN? ARE WE READY TO BEGIN?
I SUPPOSE SO.
OKAY... WHAT WE'RE ATTEMPTING IS TO DIRECT OUR COMBINED ENERGIES TOWARDS AIDING THE STRUGGLE IN THE AFTERWORLD.
WE START BY LINKING HANDS.
REMEMBER I'M WATCHING YOU, YOUNG LADY.
FA-THER!
ONCE THE ENERGY FLOW GETS UNDER WAY, IT'S IMPORTANT NOT TO BREAK THE CIRCLE. THE FEEDBACK COULD KILL US.
WE ALL KNOW THAT, BOY.
W-WAIT...
DIDN'T YOU SAY THIS DANGEROUS ENERGY WOULD BE CHANNELED THROUGH ME?
DON'T WORRY... AS LONG AS NOBODY PANICS AND RELEASES THE HAND THEY'RE HOLDING, EVERYTHING WILL BE FINE, INCLUDING YOU.
NOW, IF WE COULD START OUR INITIAL PROBE INTO THE AFTERWORLD...
WELL... IF YOU'RE SURE IT'S SAFE...

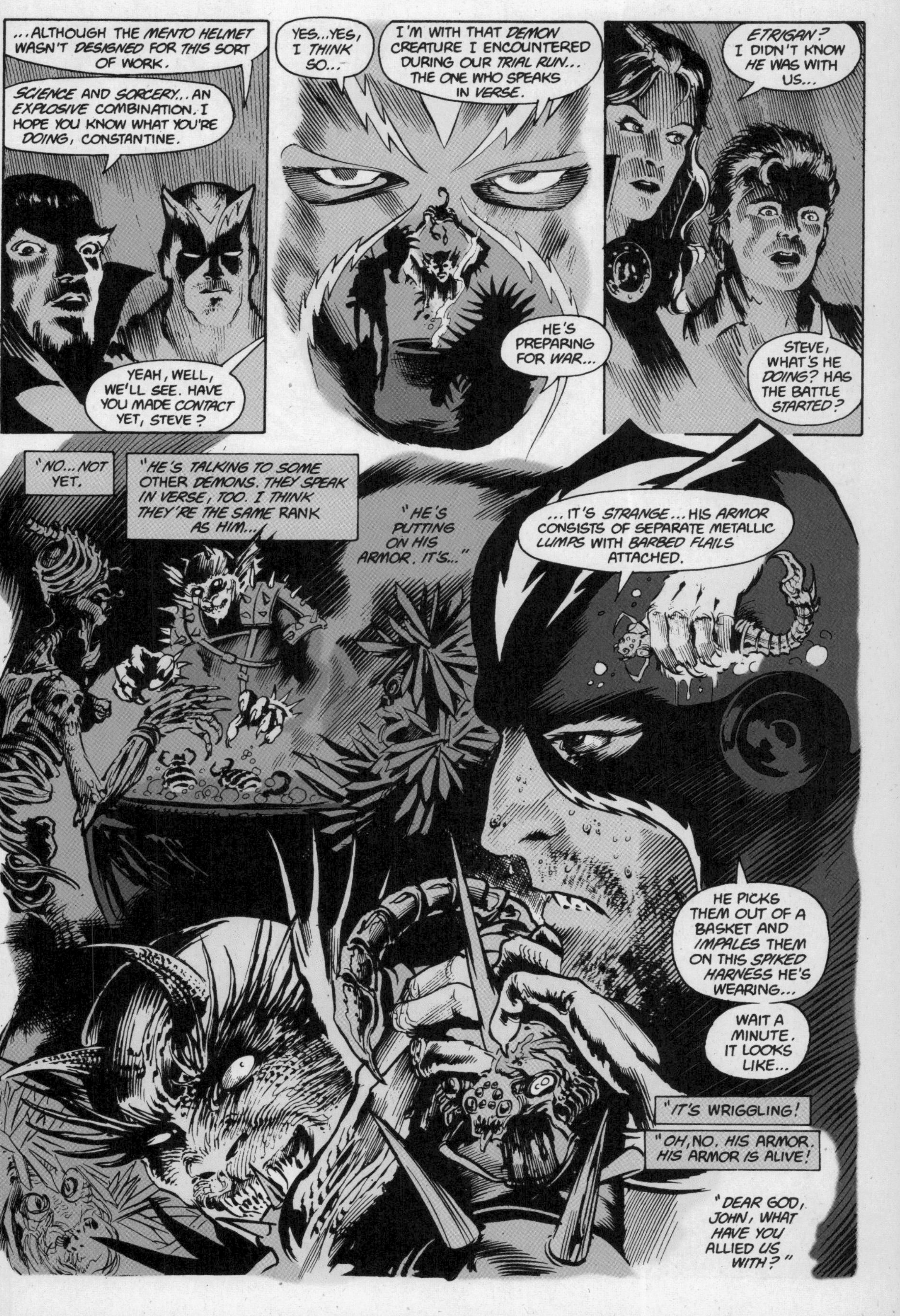
...ALTHOUGH THE MENTO HELMET WASN'T DESIGNED FOR THIS SORT OF WORK.
SCIENCE AND SORCERY... AN EXPLOSIVE COMBINATION. I HOPE YOU KNOW WHAT YOU'RE DOING, CONSTANTINE.
YEAH, WELL, WE'LL SEE. HAVE YOU MADE CONTACT YET, STEVE?
YES...YES, I THINK SO...
I'M WITH THAT DEMON CREATURE I ENCOUNTERED DURING OUR TRIAL RUN... THE ONE WHO SPEAKS IN VERSE.
HE'S PREPARING FOR WAR...
ETRIGAN? I DIDN'T KNOW HE WAS WITH US...
STEVE, WHAT'S HE DOING? HAS THE BATTLE STARTED?
"NO... NOT YET.
"HE'S TALKING TO SOME OTHER DEMONS. THEY SPEAK IN VERSE, TOO. I THINK THEY'RE THE SAME RANK AS HIM...
"HE'S PUTTING ON HIS ARMOR. IT'S..."
...IT'S STRANGE... HIS ARMOR CONSISTS OF SEPARATE METALLIC LUMPS WITH BARBED FLAILS ATTACHED.
HE PICKS THEM OUT OF A BASKET AND IMPALES THEM ON THIS SPIKED HARNESS HE'S WEARING...
WAIT A MINUTE. IT LOOKS LIKE...
"IT'S WRIGGLING!
"OH, NO. HIS ARMOR. HIS ARMOR IS ALIVE!
"DEAR GOD, JOHN, WHAT HAVE YOU ALLIED US WITH?"

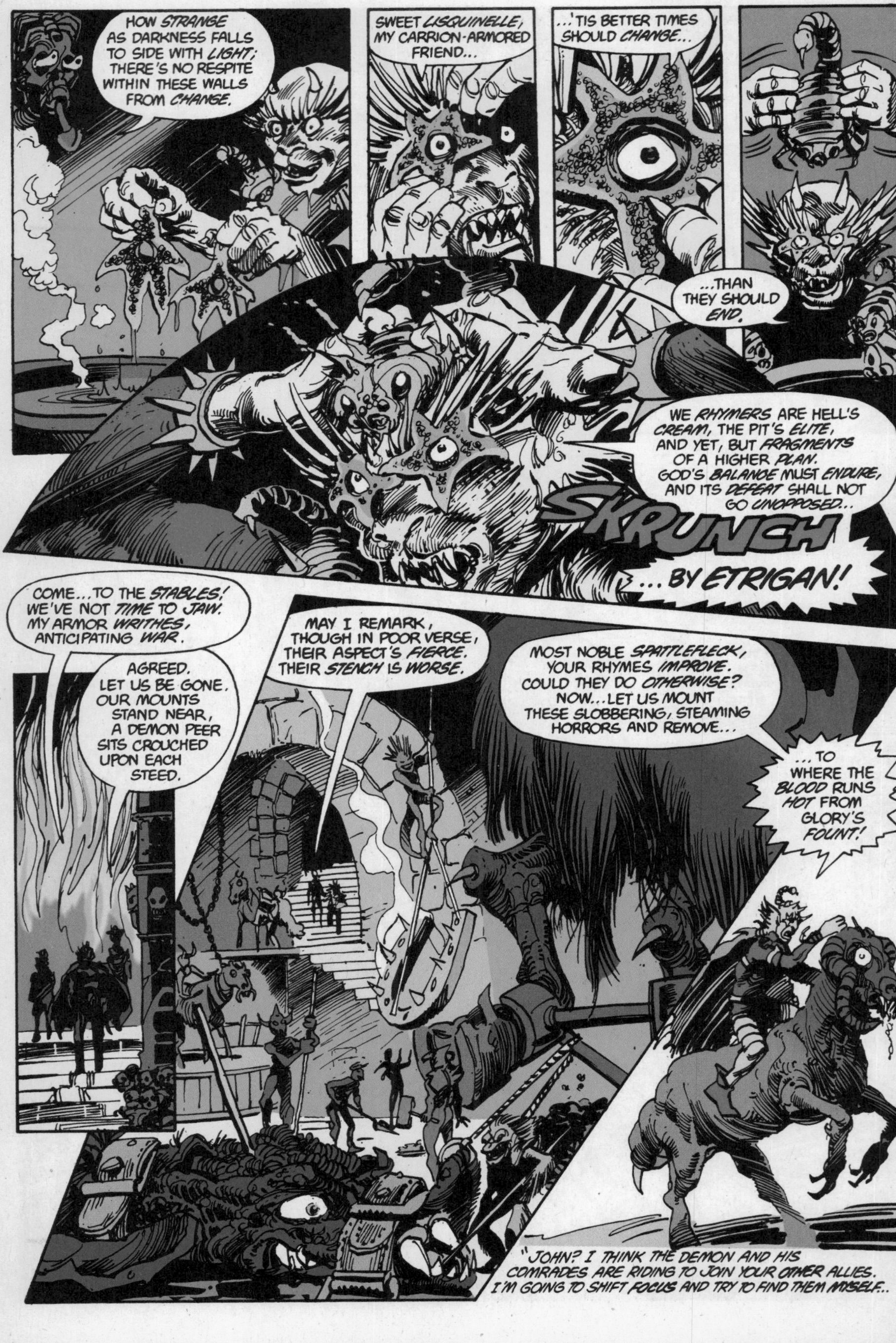
HOW STRANGE AS DARKNESS FALLS TO SIDE WITH LIGHT; THERE'S NO RESPITE WITHIN THESE WALLS FROM CHANGE.
SWEET LISQUINELLE, MY CARRION-ARMORED FRIEND...
...'TIS BETTER TIMES SHOULD CHANGE...
...THAN THEY SHOULD END.
WE RHYMERS ARE HELL'S CREAM, THE PIT'S ELITE, AND YET, BUT FRAGMENTS OF A HIGHER PLAN. GOD'S BALANCE MUST ENDURE, AND ITS DEFEAT SHALL NOT GO UNOPPOSED...
SKRUNCH
...BY ETRIGAN!
COME...TO THE STABLES! WE'VE NOT TIME TO JAW. MY ARMOR WRITHES, ANTICIPATING WAR.
AGREED. LET US BE GONE. OUR MOUNTS STAND NEAR, A DEMON PEER SITS CROUCHED UPON EACH STEED.
MAY I REMARK, THOUGH IN POOR VERSE, THEIR ASPECT'S FIERCE. THEIR STENCH IS WORSE.
MOST NOBLE SPATTLEFLECK, YOUR RHYMES IMPROVE. COULD THEY DO OTHERWISE? NOW...LET US MOUNT THESE SLOBBERING, STEAMING HORRORS AND REMOVE...
...TO WHERE THE BLOOD RUNS HOT FROM GLORY'S FOUNT!
"JOHN? I THINK THE DEMON AND HIS COMRADES ARE RIDING TO JOIN YOUR OTHER ALLIES. I'M GOING TO SHIFT FOCUS AND TRY TO FIND THEM MYSELF...

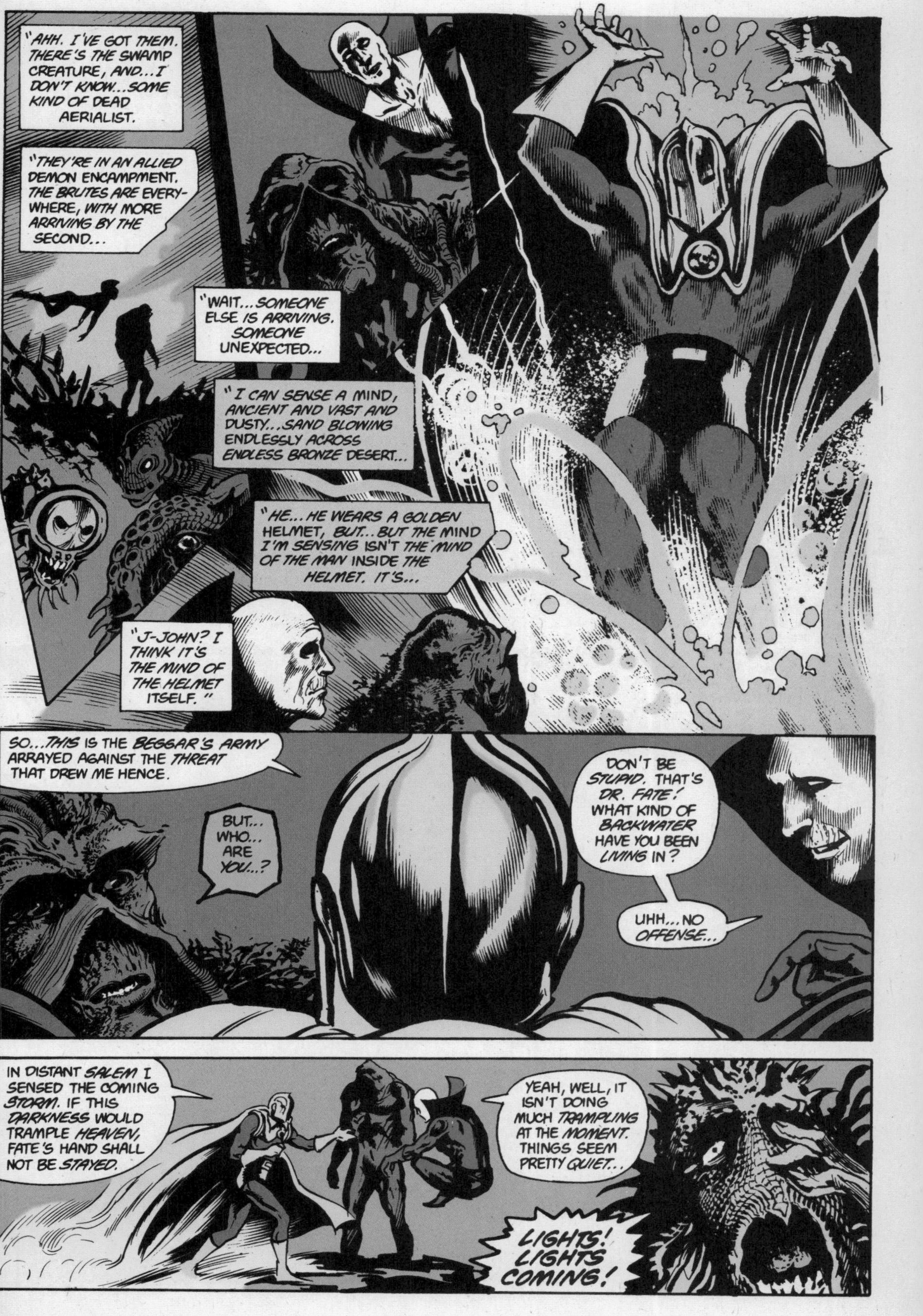
"AHH. I'VE GOT THEM. THERE'S THE SWAMP CREATURE, AND... I DON'T KNOW... SOME KIND OF DEAD AERIALIST.
"THEY'RE IN AN ALLIED DEMON ENCAMPMENT. THE BRUTES ARE EVERYWHERE, WITH MORE ARRIVING BY THE SECOND...
"WAIT... SOMEONE ELSE IS ARRIVING. SOMEONE UNEXPECTED...
"I CAN SENSE A MIND, ANCIENT AND VAST AND DUSTY... SAND BLOWING ENDLESSLY ACROSS ENDLESS BRONZE DESERT...
"HE... HE WEARS A GOLDEN HELMET, BUT... BUT THE MIND I'M SENSING ISN'T THE MIND OF THE MAN INSIDE THE HELMET. IT'S...
"J-JOHN? I THINK IT'S THE MIND OF THE HELMET ITSELF."
SO... THIS IS THE BEGGAR'S ARMY ARRAYED AGAINST THE THREAT THAT DREW ME HENCE.
BUT... WHO... ARE YOU...?
DON'T BE STUPID. THAT'S DR. FATE! WHAT KIND OF BACKWATER HAVE YOU BEEN LIVING IN?
UHH... NO OFFENSE...
IN DISTANT SALEM I SENSED THE COMING STORM. IF THIS DARKNESS WOULD TRAMPLE HEAVEN, FATE'S HAND SHALL NOT BE STAYED.
YEAH, WELL, IT ISN'T DOING MUCH TRAMPLING AT THE MOMENT. THINGS SEEM PRETTY QUIET...
LIGHTS! LIGHTS COMING!

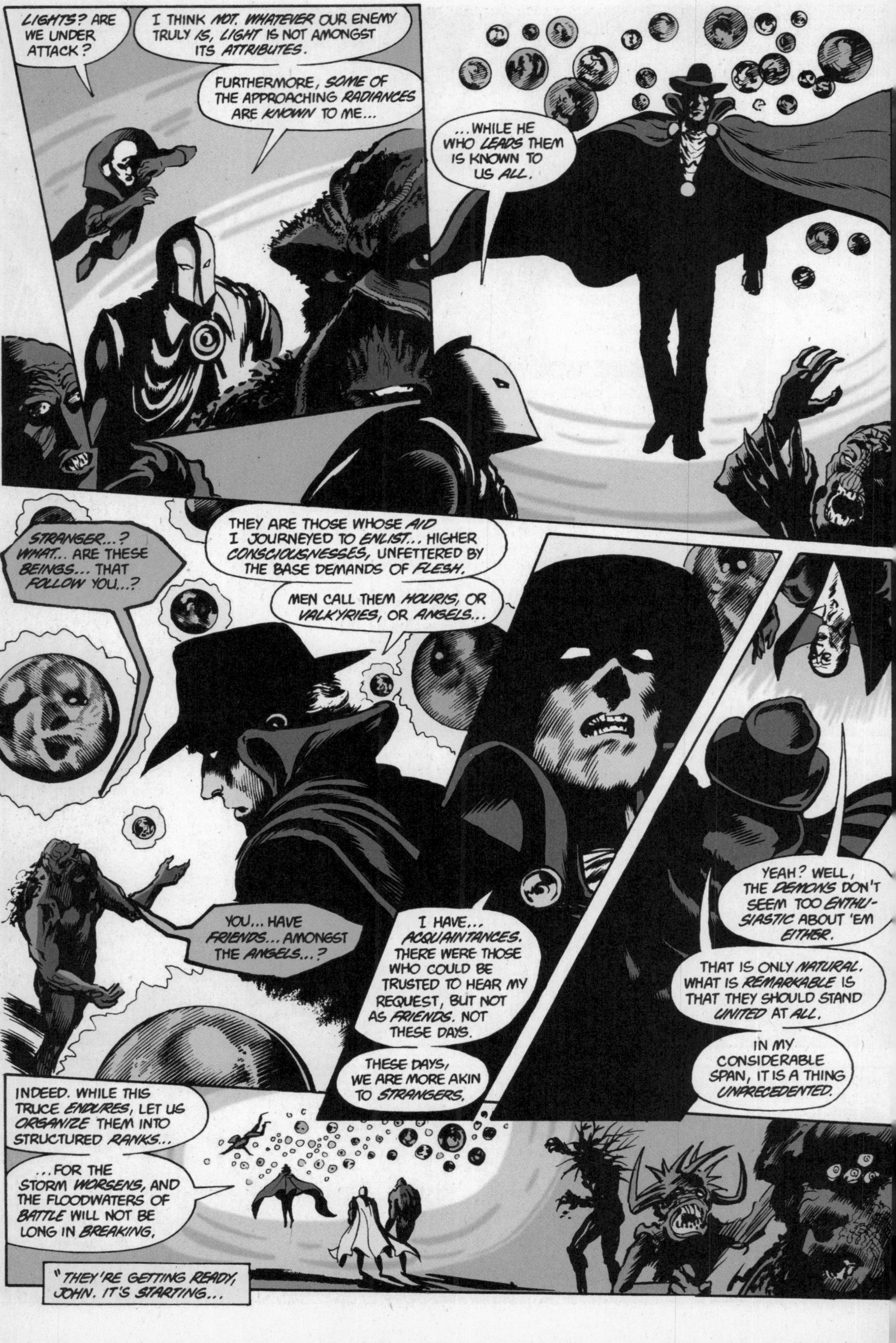
LIGHTS? ARE WE UNDER ATTACK?
I THINK NOT. WHATEVER OUR ENEMY TRULY IS, LIGHT IS NOT AMONGST ITS ATTRIBUTES.
FURTHERMORE, SOME OF THE APPROACHING RADIANCES ARE KNOWN TO ME...
...WHILE HE WHO LEADS THEM IS KNOWN TO US ALL.
STRANGER...? WHAT... ARE THESE BEINGS... THAT FOLLOW YOU...?
THEY ARE THOSE WHOSE AID I JOURNEYED TO ENLIST... HIGHER CONSCIOUSNESSES, UNFETTERED BY THE BASE DEMANDS OF FLESH.
MEN CALL THEM HOURIS, OR VALKYRIES, OR ANGELS...
YOU... HAVE FRIENDS... AMONGST THE ANGELS...?
I HAVE... ACQUAINTANCES. THERE WERE THOSE WHO COULD BE TRUSTED TO HEAR MY REQUEST, BUT NOT AS FRIENDS. NOT THESE DAYS.
THESE DAYS, WE ARE MORE AKIN TO STRANGERS.
YEAH? WELL, THE DEMONS DON'T SEEM TOO ENTHUSIASTIC ABOUT 'EM EITHER.
THAT IS ONLY NATURAL. WHAT IS REMARKABLE IS THAT THEY SHOULD STAND UNITED AT ALL.
IN MY CONSIDERABLE SPAN, IT IS A THING UNPRECEDENTED.
INDEED. WHILE THIS TRUCE ENDURES, LET US ORGANIZE THEM INTO STRUCTURED RANKS...
...FOR THE STORM WORSENS, AND THE FLOODWATERS OF BATTLE WILL NOT BE LONG IN BREAKING.
"THEY'RE GETTING READY, JOHN. IT'S STARTING...

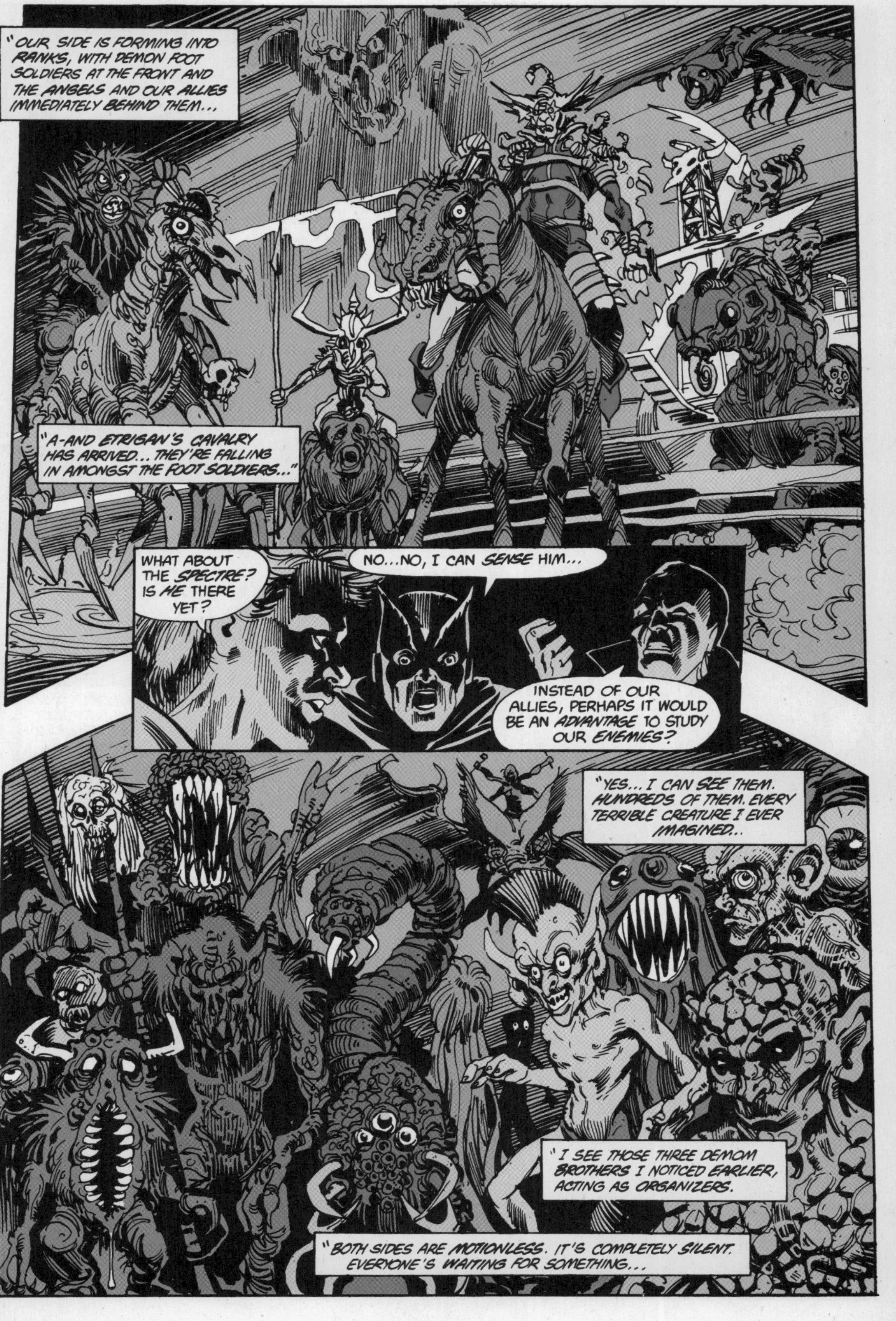
"OUR SIDE IS FORMING INTO RANKS, WITH DEMON FOOT SOLDIERS AT THE FRONT AND THE ANGELS AND OUR ALLIES IMMEDIATELY BEHIND THEM...
"A-AND ETRIGAN'S CAVALRY HAS ARRIVED... THEY'RE FALLING IN AMONGST THE FOOT SOLDIERS..."
WHAT ABOUT THE SPECTRE? IS HE THERE YET?
NO...NO, I CAN SENSE HIM...
INSTEAD OF OUR ALLIES, PERHAPS IT WOULD BE AN ADVANTAGE TO STUDY OUR ENEMIES?
"YES... I CAN SEE THEM. HUNDREDS OF THEM. EVERY TERRIBLE CREATURE I EVER IMAGINED...
"I SEE THOSE THREE DEMOM BROTHERS I NOTICED EARLIER, ACTING AS ORGANIZERS.
"BOTH SIDES ARE MOTIONLESS. IT'S COMPLETELY SILENT. EVERYONE'S WAITING FOR SOMETHING...

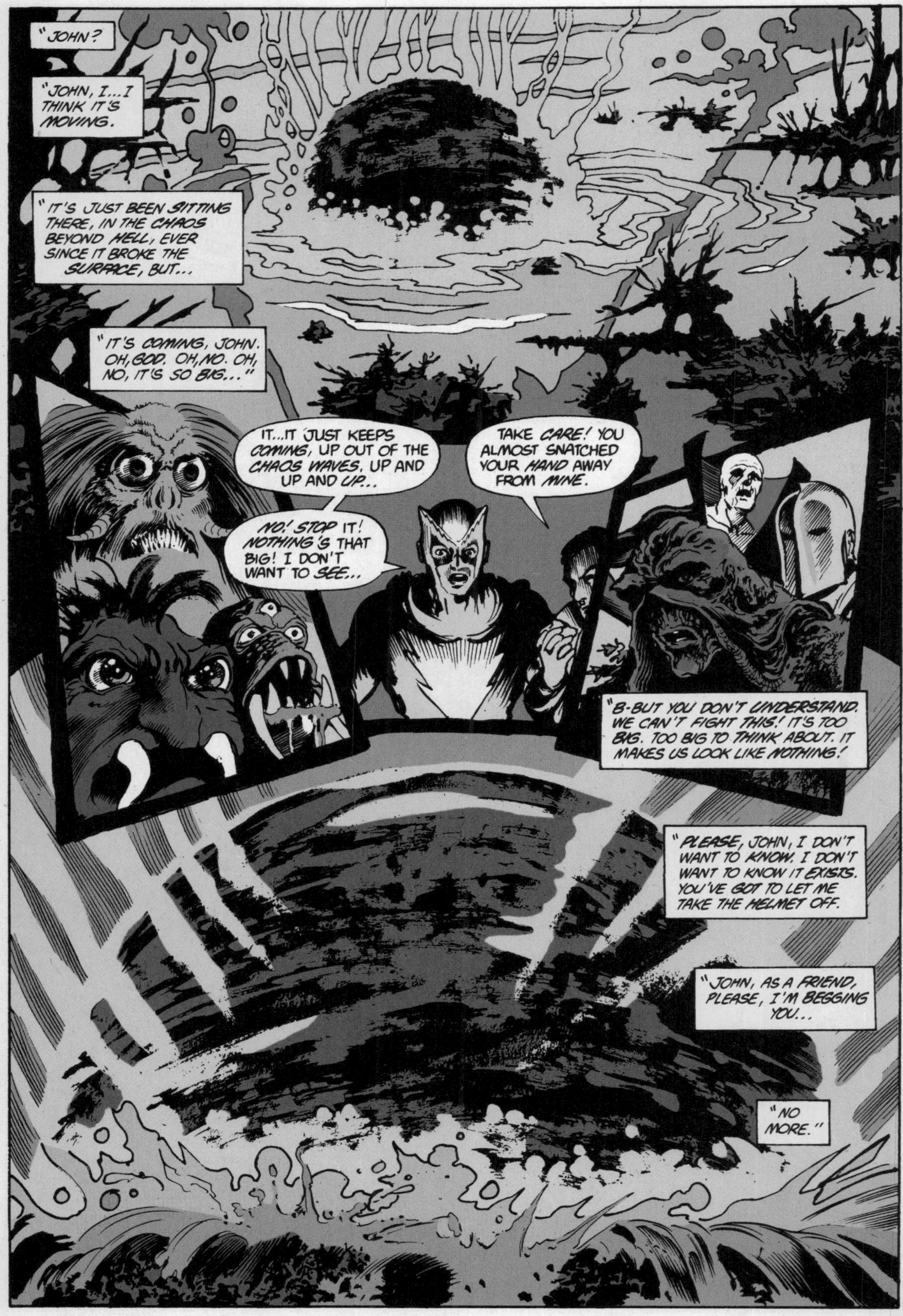
"JOHN?
"JOHN, I...I THINK IT'S MOVING.
"IT'S JUST BEEN SITTING THERE, IN THE CHAOS BEYOND HELL, EVER SINCE IT BROKE THE SURFACE, BUT...
"IT'S COMING, JOHN. OH, GOD. OH, NO. OH, NO, IT'S SO BIG..."
IT...IT JUST KEEPS COMING, UP OUT OF THE CHAOS WAVES, UP AND UP AND UP...
TAKE CARE! YOU ALMOST SNATCHED YOUR HAND AWAY FROM MINE.
NO! STOP IT! NOTHING'S THAT BIG! I DON'T WANT TO SEE...
"B-BUT YOU DON'T UNDERSTAND. WE CAN'T FIGHT THIS! IT'S TOO BIG. TOO BIG TO THINK ABOUT. IT MAKES US LOOK LIKE NOTHING!
"PLEASE, JOHN, I DON'T WANT TO KNOW. I DON'T WANT TO KNOW IT EXISTS. YOU'VE GOT TO LET ME TAKE THE HELMET OFF.
"JOHN, AS A FRIEND, PLEASE, I'M BEGGING YOU...
"NO MORE."

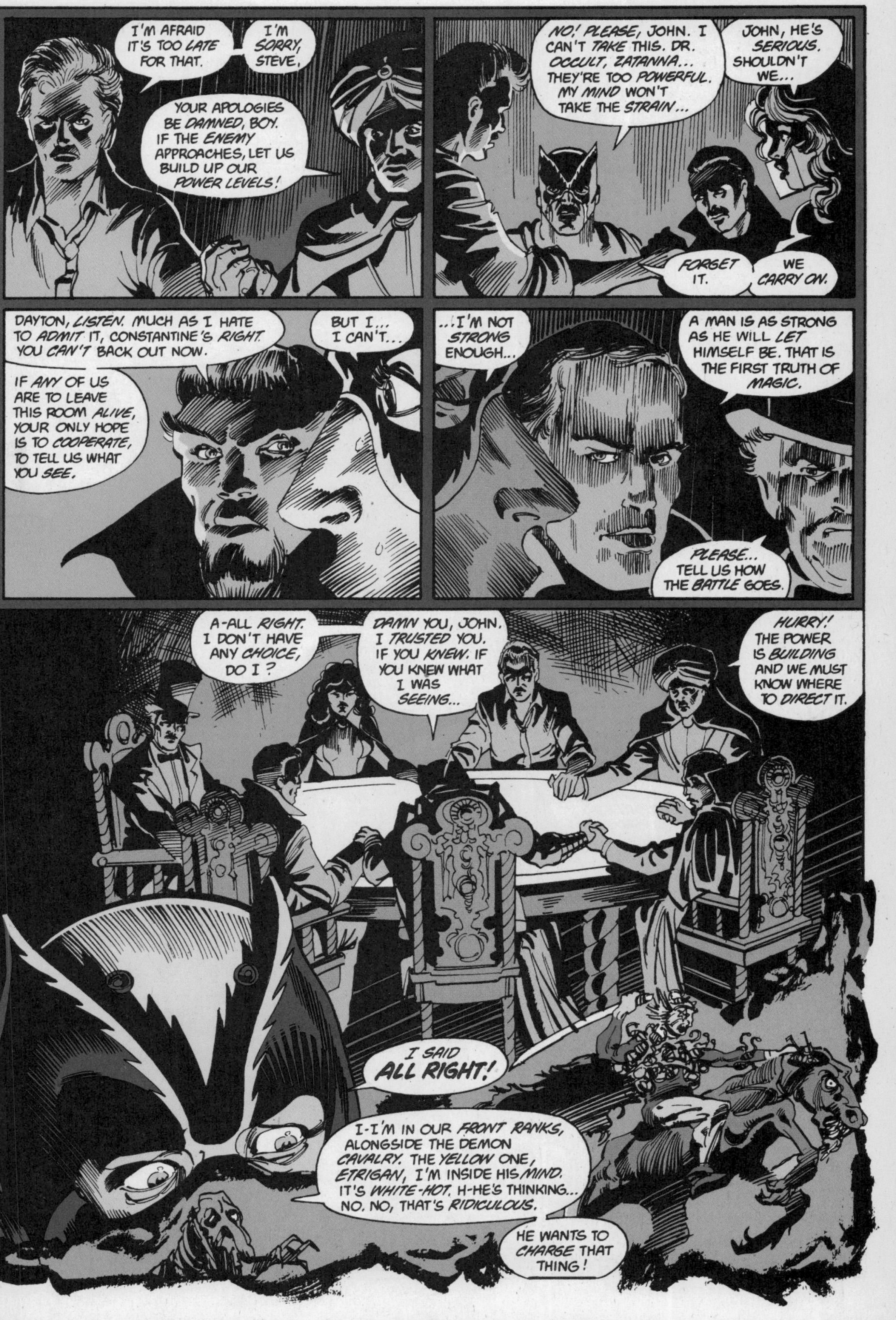
I'M AFRAID IT'S TOO LATE FOR THAT.
I'M SORRY, STEVE.
YOUR APOLOGIES BE DAMNED, BOY. IF THE ENEMY APPROACHES, LET US BUILD UP OUR POWER LEVELS!
NO! PLEASE, JOHN. I CAN'T TAKE THIS. DR. OCCULT, ZATANNA... THEY'RE TOO POWERFUL. MY MIND WON'T TAKE THE STRAIN...
JOHN, HE'S SERIOUS. SHOULDN'T WE...
FORGET IT.
WE CARRY ON.
DAYTON, LISTEN. MUCH AS I HATE TO ADMIT IT, CONSTANTINE'S RIGHT. YOU CAN'T BACK OUT NOW.
IF ANY OF US ARE TO LEAVE THIS ROOM ALIVE, YOUR ONLY HOPE IS TO COOPERATE, TO TELL US WHAT YOU SEE.
BUT I... I CAN'T...
...I'M NOT STRONG ENOUGH...
A MAN IS AS STRONG AS HE WILL LET HIMSELF BE. THAT IS THE FIRST TRUTH OF MAGIC.
PLEASE... TELL US HOW THE BATTLE GOES.
A-ALL RIGHT. I DON'T HAVE ANY CHOICE, DO I?
DAMN YOU, JOHN. I TRUSTED YOU. IF YOU KNEW. IF YOU KNEW WHAT I WAS SEEING...
HURRY! THE POWER IS BUILDING AND WE MUST KNOW WHERE TO DIRECT IT.
I SAID ALL RIGHT!
I-I'M IN OUR FRONT RANKS, ALONGSIDE THE DEMON CAVALRY. THE YELLOW ONE, ETRIGAN, I'M INSIDE HIS MIND. IT'S WHITE-HOT. H-HE'S THINKING... NO. NO, THAT'S RIDICULOUS.
HE WANTS TO CHARGE THAT THING!

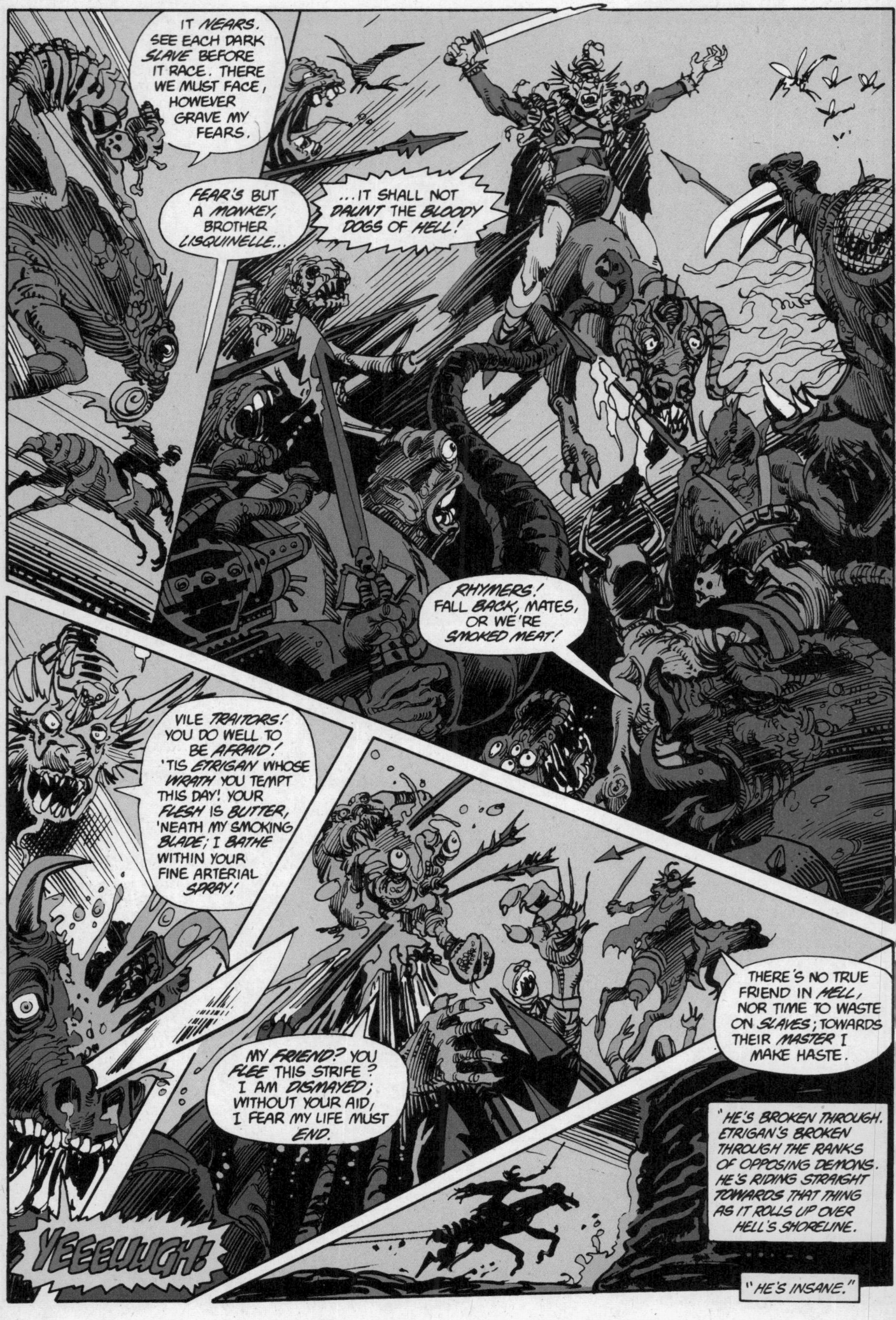
IT NEARS. SEE EACH DARK SLAVE BEFORE IT RACE. THERE WE MUST FACE, HOWEVER GRAVE MY FEARS.
FEAR'S BUT A MONKEY, BROTHER LISQUINELLE...
...IT SHALL NOT DAUNT THE BLOODY DOGS OF HELL!
RHYMERS! FALL BACK, MATES, OR WE'RE SMOKED MEAT!
VILE TRAITORS! YOU DO WELL TO BE AFRAID! 'TIS ETRIGAN WHOSE WRATH YOU TEMPT THIS DAY! YOUR FLESH IS BUTTER, 'NEATH MY SMOKING BLADE; I BATHE WITHIN YOUR FINE ARTERIAL SPRAY!
YEEEUUGH!
MY FRIEND? YOU FLEE THIS STRIFE? I AM DISMAYED; WITHOUT YOUR AID, I FEAR MY LIFE MUST END.
THERE'S NO TRUE FRIEND IN HELL, NOR TIME TO WASTE ON SLAVES; TOWARDS THEIR MASTER I MAKE HASTE.
"HE'S BROKEN THROUGH. ETRIGAN'S BROKEN THROUGH THE RANKS OF OPPOSING DEMONS. HE'S RIDING STRAIGHT TOWARDS THAT THING AS IT ROLLS UP OVER HELL'S SHORELINE.
"HE'S INSANE."

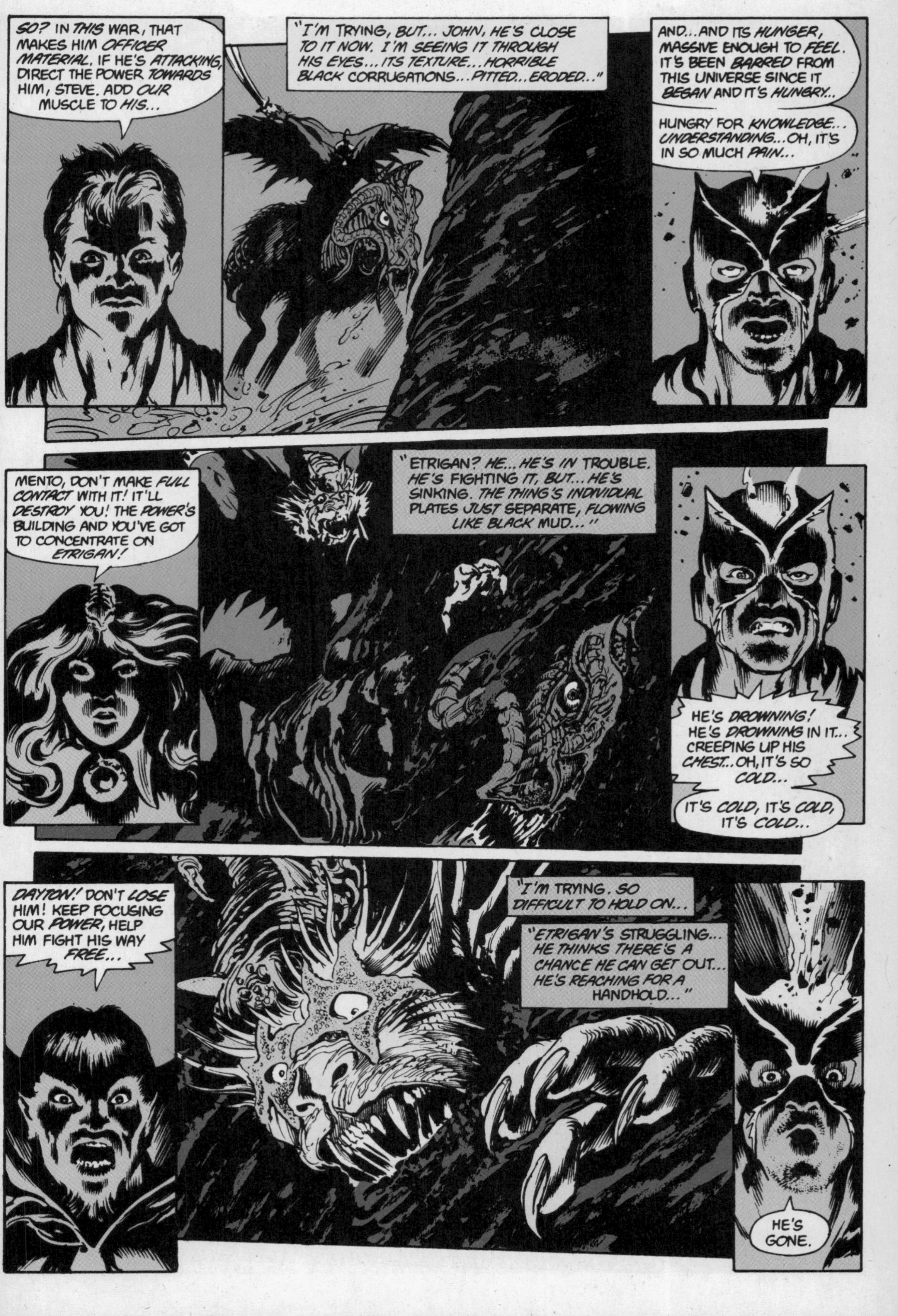
SO? IN THIS WAR, THAT MAKES HIM OFFICER MATERIAL. IF HE'S ATTACKING, DIRECT THE POWER TOWARDS HIM, STEVE. ADD OUR MUSCLE TO HIS...
"I'M TRYING, BUT... JOHN, HE'S CLOSE TO IT NOW. I'M SEEING IT THROUGH HIS EYES... ITS TEXTURE... HORRIBLE BLACK CORRUGATIONS... PITTED... ERODED..."
AND... AND ITS HUNGER, MASSIVE ENOUGH TO FEEL. IT'S BEEN BARRED FROM THIS UNIVERSE SINCE IT BEGAN AND IT'S HUNGRY...
HUNGRY FOR KNOWLEDGE... UNDERSTANDING... OH, IT'S IN SO MUCH PAIN...
MENTO, DON'T MAKE FULL CONTACT WITH IT! IT'LL DESTROY YOU! THE POWER'S BUILDING AND YOU'VE GOT TO CONCENTRATE ON ETRIGAN!
"ETRIGAN? HE... HE'S IN TROUBLE. HE'S FIGHTING IT, BUT... HE'S SINKING. THE THING'S INDIVIDUAL PLATES JUST SEPARATE, FLOWING LIKE BLACK MUD..."
HE'S DROWNING! HE'S DROWNING IN IT... CREEPING UP HIS CHEST... OH, IT'S SO COLD...
IT'S COLD, IT'S COLD, IT'S COLD...
DAYTON! DON'T LOSE HIM! KEEP FOCUSING OUR POWER, HELP HIM FIGHT HIS WAY FREE...
"I'M TRYING. SO DIFFICULT TO HOLD ON...
"ETRIGAN'S STRUGGLING... HE THINKS THERE'S A CHANCE HE CAN GET OUT... HE'S REACHING FOR A HANDHOLD..."
HE'S GONE.

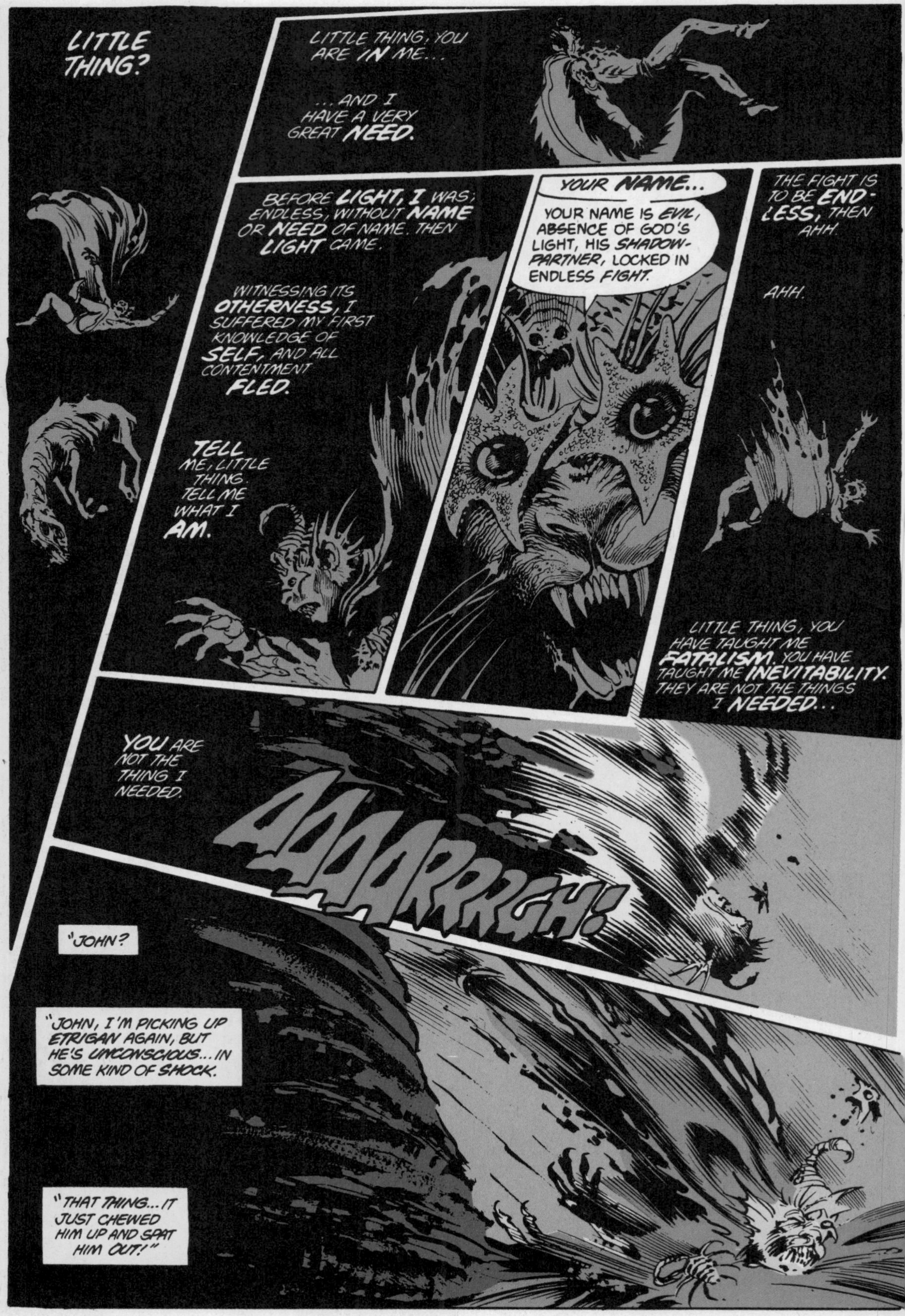
LITTLE THING?
LITTLE THING, YOU ARE IN ME...
...AND I HAVE A VERY GREAT NEED.
BEFORE LIGHT, I WAS; ENDLESS, WITHOUT NAME OR NEED OF NAME. THEN LIGHT CAME.
WITNESSING ITS OTHERNESS, I SUFFERED MY FIRST KNOWLEDGE OF SELF, AND ALL CONTENTMENT FLED.
TELL ME, LITTLE THING. TELL ME WHAT I AM.
YOUR NAME...
YOUR NAME IS EVIL, ABSENCE OF GOD'S LIGHT, HIS SHADOW-PARTNER, LOCKED IN ENDLESS FIGHT.
THE FIGHT IS TO BE END-LESS, THEN AHH.
AHH.
LITTLE THING, YOU HAVE TAUGHT ME FATALISM. YOU HAVE TAUGHT ME INEVITABILITY. THEY ARE NOT THE THINGS I NEEDED...
YOU ARE NOT THE THING I NEEDED.
AAAARRRGH!
"JOHN?
"JOHN, I'M PICKING UP ETRIGAN AGAIN, BUT HE'S UNCONSCIOUS... IN SOME KIND OF SHOCK.
"THAT THING... IT JUST CHEWED HIM UP AND SPAT HIM OUT!"

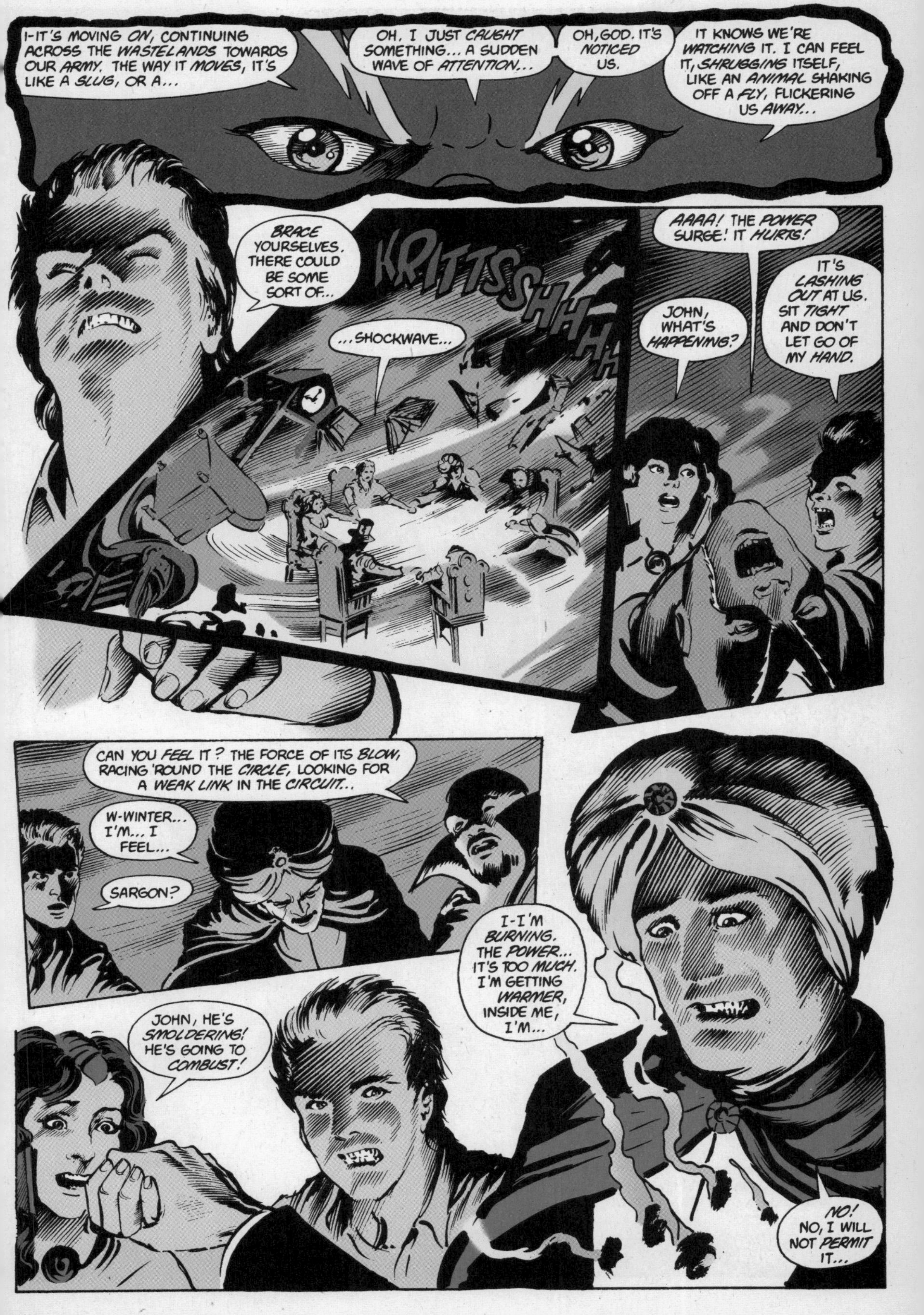
I-IT'S MOVING ON, CONTINUING ACROSS THE WASTELANDS TOWARDS OUR ARMY. THE WAY IT MOVES, IT'S LIKE A SLUG, OR A...
OH, I JUST CAUGHT SOMETHING... A SUDDEN WAVE OF ATTENTION...
OH, GOD. IT'S NOTICED US.
IT KNOWS WE'RE WATCHING IT. I CAN FEEL IT, SHRUGGING ITSELF, LIKE AN ANIMAL SHAKING OFF A FLY, FLICKERING US AWAY...
BRACE YOURSELVES. THERE COULD BE SOME SORT OF...
KRITTSSHHHH
...SHOCKWAVE...
AAAA! THE POWER SURGE! IT HURTS!
JOHN, WHAT'S HAPPENING?
IT'S LASHING OUT AT US. SIT TIGHT AND DON'T LET GO OF MY HAND.
CAN YOU FEEL IT? THE FORCE OF ITS BLOW, RACING 'ROUND THE CIRCLE, LOOKING FOR A WEAK LINK IN THE CIRCUIT...
W-WINTER... I'M... I FEEL...
SARGON?
I-I'M BURNING. THE POWER... IT'S TOO MUCH. I'M GETTING WARMER, INSIDE ME, I'M...
JOHN, HE'S SMOLDERING! HE'S GOING TO COMBUST!
NO! NO, I WILL NOT PERMIT IT...

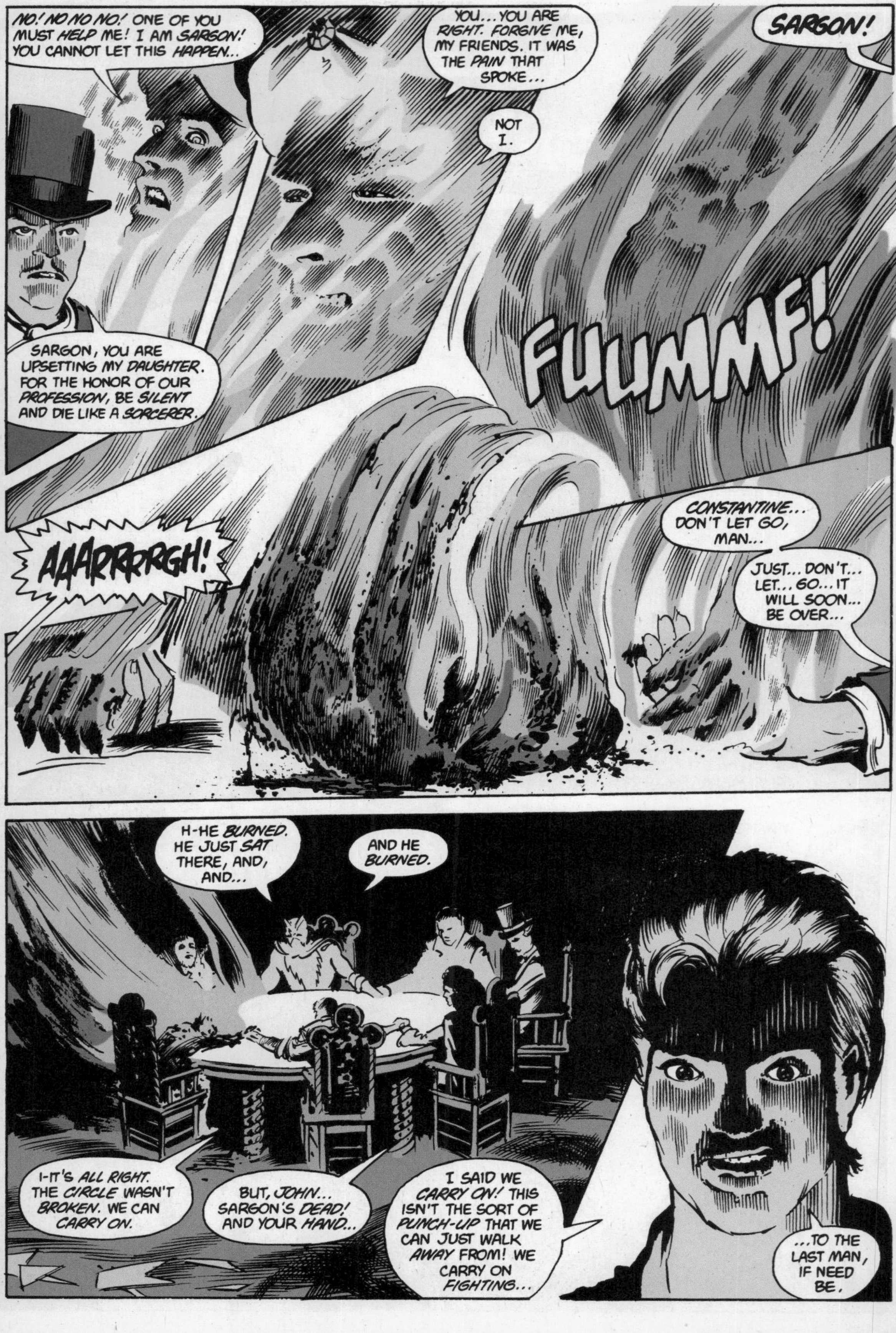
NO! NO NO NO! ONE OF YOU MUST HELP ME! I AM SARGON! YOU CANNOT LET THIS HAPPEN...
SARGON, YOU ARE UPSETTING MY DAUGHTER. FOR THE HONOR OF OUR PROFESSION, BE SILENT AND DIE LIKE A SORCERER.
YOU... YOU ARE RIGHT. FORGIVE ME, MY FRIENDS. IT WAS THE PAIN THAT SPOKE...
NOT I.
SARGON!
FUUMMF!
AAARRRRGH!
CONSTANTINE... DON'T LET GO, MAN...
JUST... DON'T... LET... GO... IT WILL SOON... BE OVER...
H-HE BURNED. HE JUST SAT THERE, AND, AND...
AND HE BURNED.
I-IT'S ALL RIGHT. THE CIRCLE WASN'T BROKEN. WE CAN CARRY ON.
BUT, JOHN... SARGON'S DEAD! AND YOUR HAND...
I SAID WE CARRY ON! THIS ISN'T THE SORT OF PUNCH-UP THAT WE CAN JUST WALK AWAY FROM! WE CARRY ON FIGHTING...
...TO THE LAST MAN, IF NEED BE.

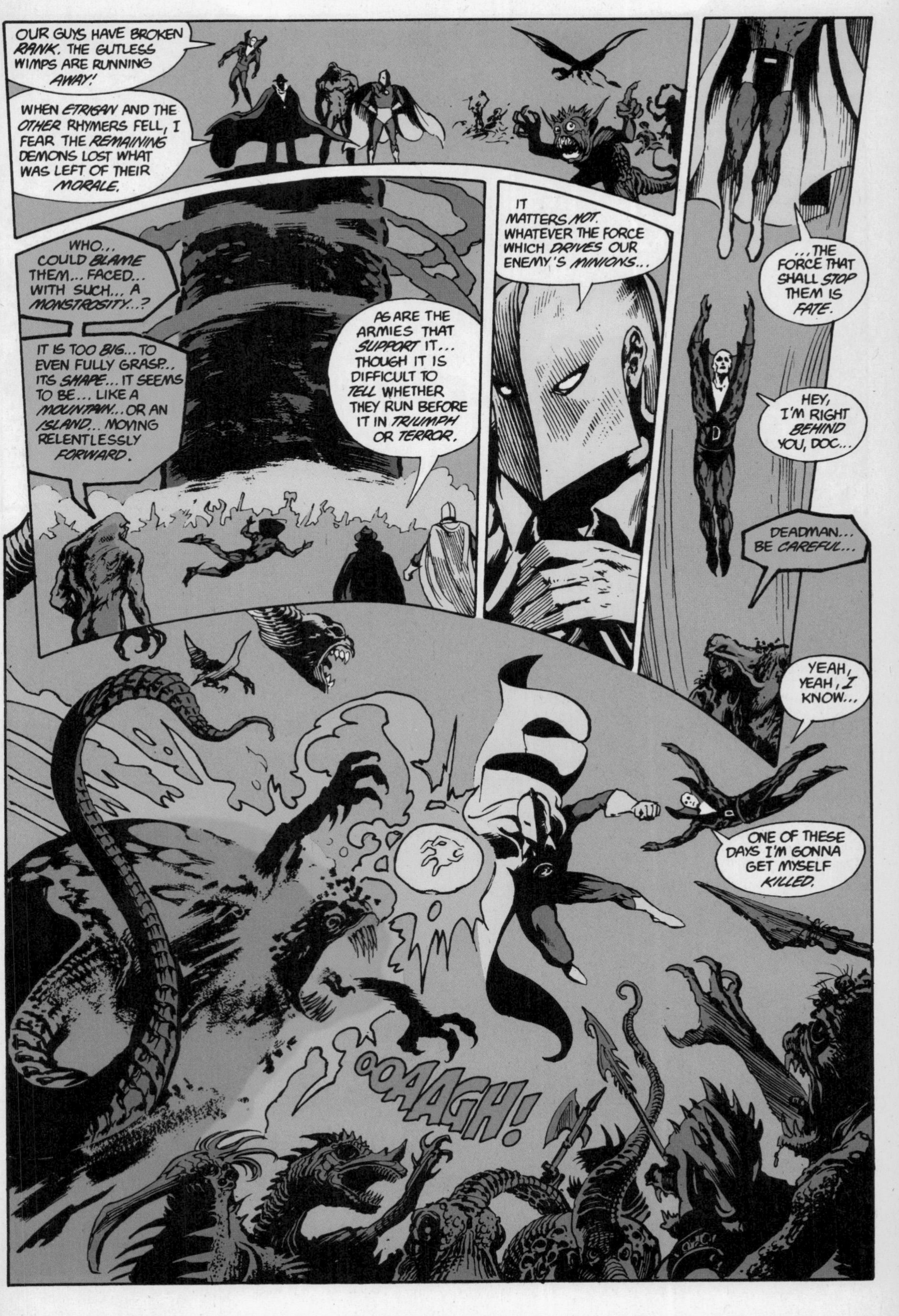
OUR GUYS HAVE BROKEN RANK. THE GUTLESS WIMPS ARE RUNNING AWAY!
WHEN ETRIGAN AND THE OTHER RHYMERS FELL, I FEAR THE REMAINING DEMONS LOST WHAT WAS LEFT OF THEIR MORALE.
WHO... COULD BLAME THEM... FACED... WITH SUCH... A MONSTROSITY...?
IT IS TOO BIG... TO EVEN FULLY GRASP... ITS SHAPE... IT SEEMS TO BE... LIKE A MOUNTAIN... OR AN ISLAND... MOVING RELENTLESSLY FORWARD.
AS ARE THE ARMIES THAT SUPPORT IT... THOUGH IT IS DIFFICULT TO TELL WHETHER THEY RUN BEFORE IT IN TRIUMPH OR TERROR.
IT MATTERS NOT. WHATEVER THE FORCE WHICH DRIVES OUR ENEMY'S MINIONS...
...THE FORCE THAT SHALL STOP THEM IS FATE.
HEY, I'M RIGHT BEHIND YOU, DOC...
DEADMAN... BE CAREFUL...
YEAH, YEAH, I KNOW...
ONE OF THESE DAYS I'M GONNA GET MYSELF KILLED.
OOAAGH!

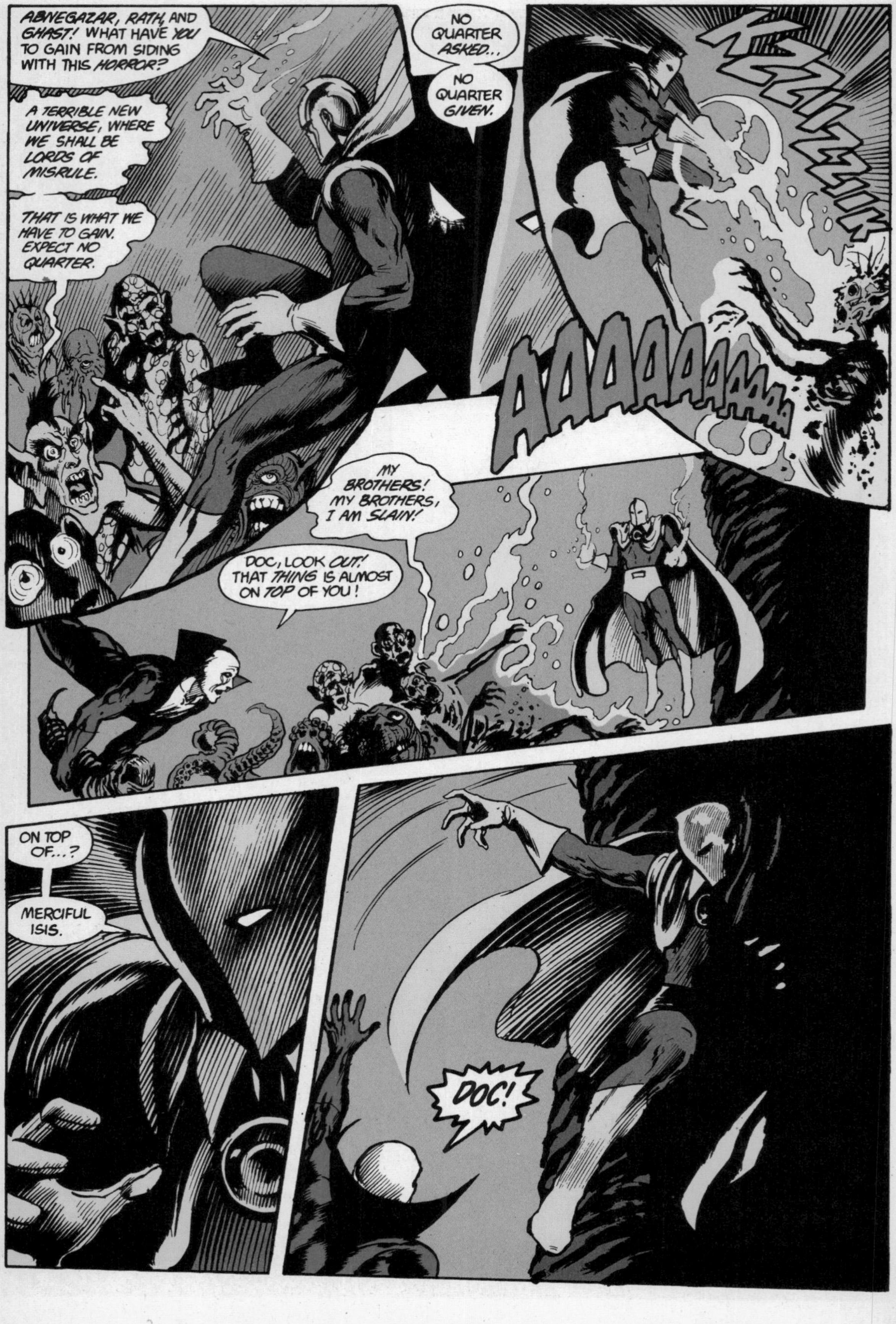
ABNEGAZAR, RATH, AND GHAST! WHAT HAVE YOU TO GAIN FROM SIDING WITH THIS HORROR?
A TERRIBLE NEW UNIVERSE, WHERE WE SHALL BE LORDS OF MISRULE.
THAT IS WHAT WE HAVE TO GAIN. EXPECT NO QUARTER.
NO QUARTER ASKED...
NO QUARTER GIVEN.
KZZZZZZZIIIK
AAAAAAAAAA
MY BROTHERS! MY BROTHERS, I AM SLAIN!
DOC, LOOK OUT! THAT THING IS ALMOST ON TOP OF YOU!
ON TOP OF...?
MERCIFUL ISIS.
DOC!

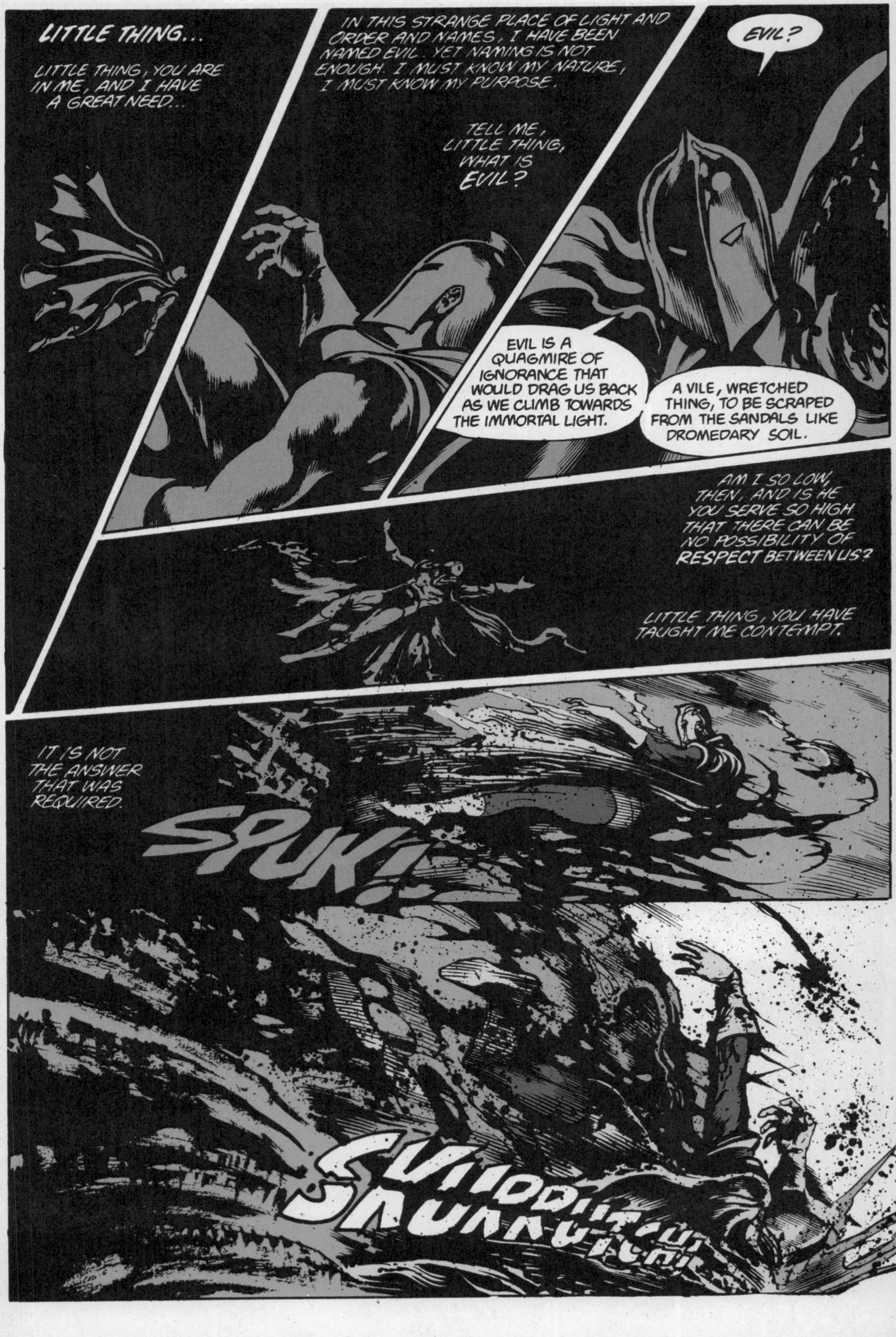
LITTLE THING...
LITTLE THING, YOU ARE IN ME, AND I HAVE A GREAT NEED...
IN THIS STRANGE PLACE OF LIGHT AND ORDER AND NAMES, I HAVE BEEN NAMED EVIL. YET NAMING IS NOT ENOUGH. I MUST KNOW MY NATURE, I MUST KNOW MY PURPOSE.
TELL ME, LITTLE THING, WHAT IS EVIL?
EVIL?
EVIL IS A QUAGMIRE OF IGNORANCE THAT WOULD DRAG US BACK AS WE CLIMB TOWARDS THE IMMORTAL LIGHT.
A VILE, WRETCHED THING, TO BE SCRAPED FROM THE SANDALS LIKE DROMEDARY SOIL.
AM I SO LOW, THEN, AND IS HE YOU SERVE SO HIGH THAT THERE CAN BE NO POSSIBILITY OF RESPECT BETWEEN US?
LITTLE THING, YOU HAVE TAUGHT ME CONTEMPT.
IT IS NOT THE ANSWER THAT WAS REQUIRED.
SPUK!

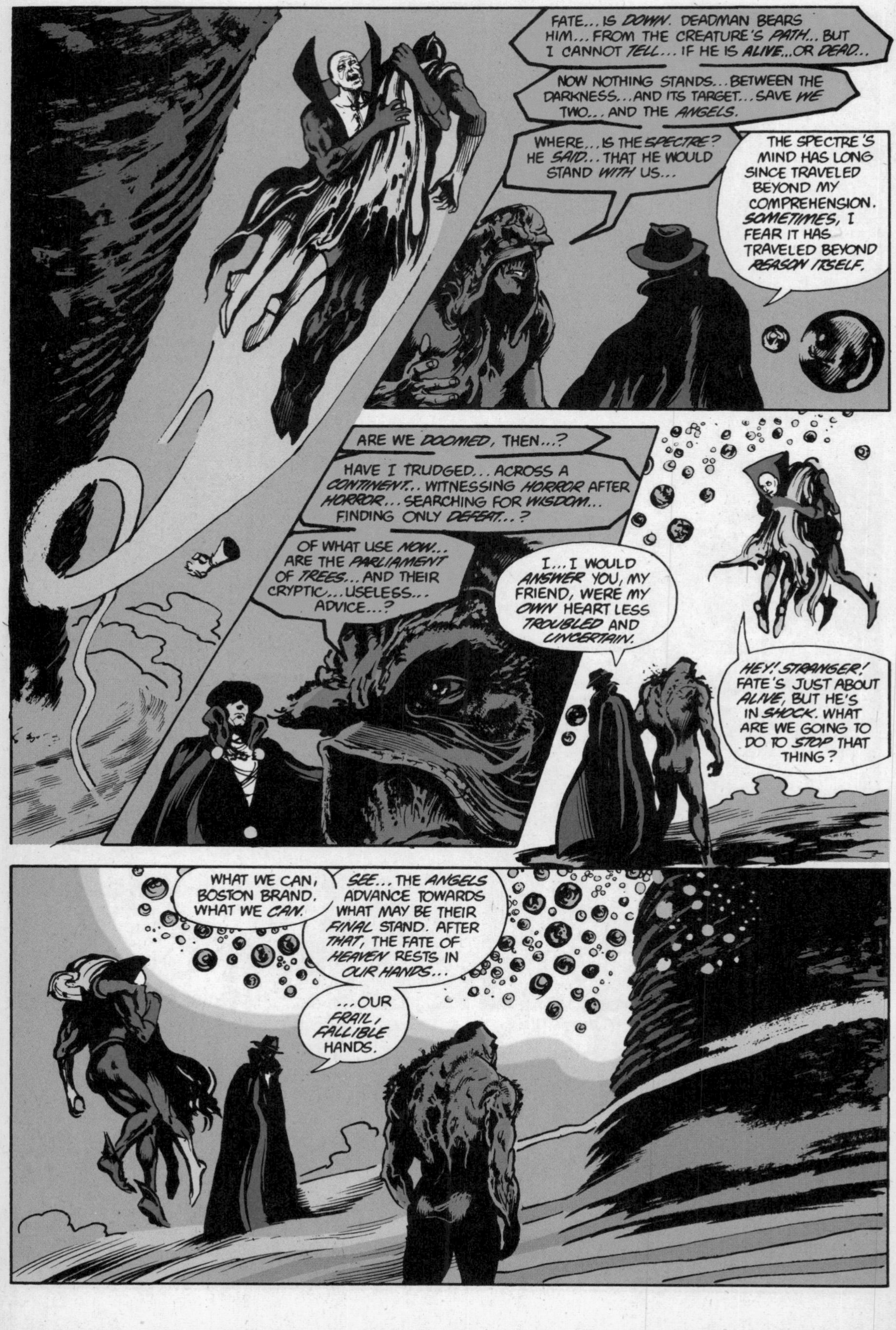
FATE... IS DOWN. DEADMAN BEARS HIM... FROM THE CREATURE'S PATH... BUT I CANNOT TELL... IF HE IS ALIVE...OR DEAD...
NOW NOTHING STANDS... BETWEEN THE DARKNESS... AND ITS TARGET... SAVE WE TWO... AND THE ANGELS.
WHERE... IS THE SPECTRE? HE SAID... THAT HE WOULD STAND WITH US...
THE SPECTRE'S MIND HAS LONG SINCE TRAVELED BEYOND MY COMPREHENSION. SOMETIMES, I FEAR IT HAS TRAVELED BEYOND REASON ITSELF.
ARE WE DOOMED, THEN...?
HAVE I TRUDGED... ACROSS A CONTINENT... WITNESSING HORROR AFTER HORROR... SEARCHING FOR WISDOM... FINDING ONLY DEFEAT...?
OF WHAT USE NOW... ARE THE PARLIAMENT OF TREES... AND THEIR CRYPTIC... USELESS... ADVICE...?
I... I WOULD ANSWER YOU, MY FRIEND, WERE MY OWN HEART LESS TROUBLED AND UNCERTAIN.
HEY! STRANGER! FATE'S JUST ABOUT ALIVE, BUT HE'S IN SHOCK. WHAT ARE WE GOING TO DO TO STOP THAT THING?
WHAT WE CAN, BOSTON BRAND. WHAT WE CAN.
SEE... THE ANGELS ADVANCE TOWARDS WHAT MAY BE THEIR FINAL STAND. AFTER THAT, THE FATE OF HEAVEN RESTS IN OUR HANDS...
...OUR FRAIL, FALLIBLE HANDS.

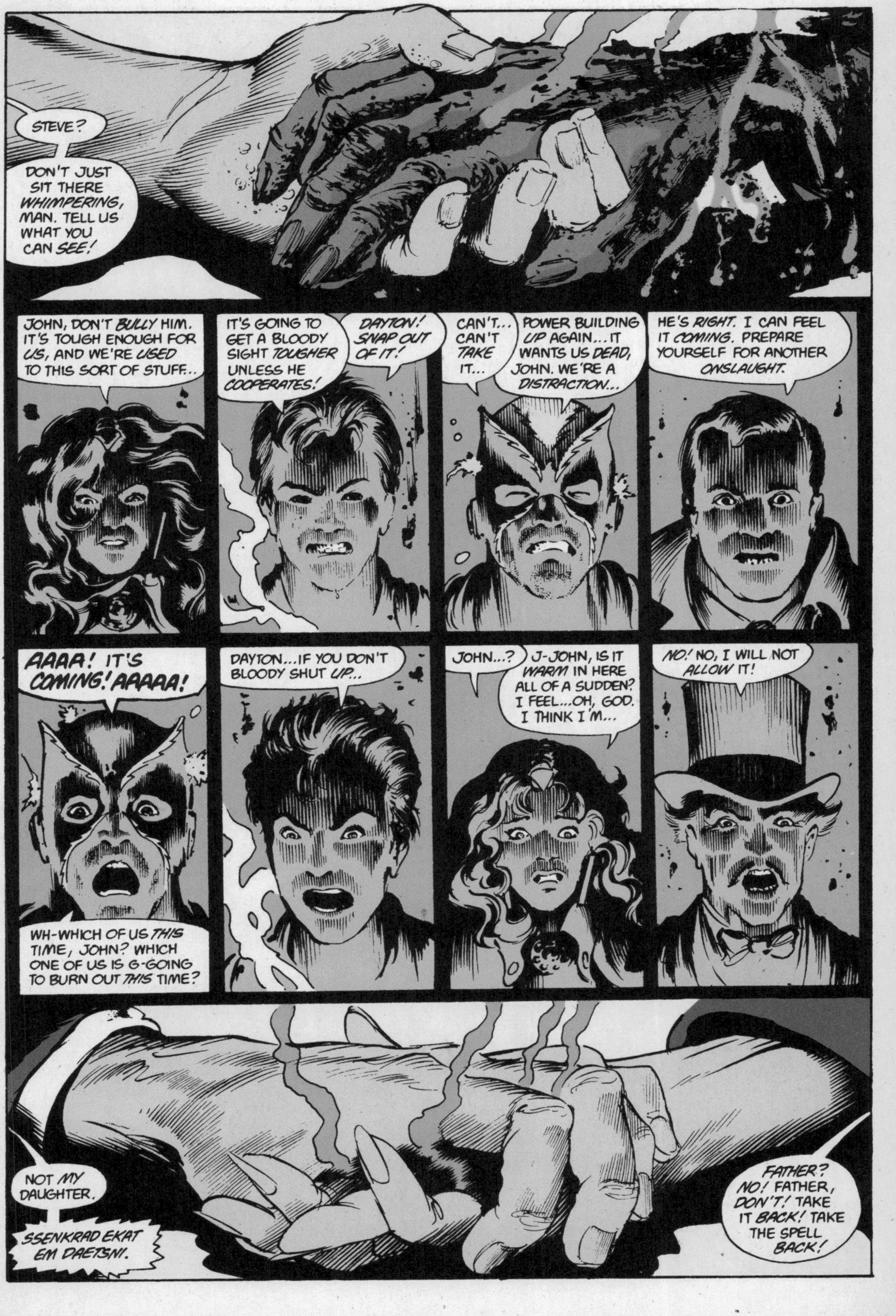
STEVE?
DON'T JUST SIT THERE WHIMPERING, MAN. TELL US WHAT YOU CAN SEE!
JOHN, DON'T BULLY HIM. IT'S TOUGH ENOUGH FOR US, AND WE'RE USED TO THIS SORT OF STUFF...
IT'S GOING TO GET A BLOODY SIGHT TOUGHER UNLESS HE COOPERATES!
DAYTON! SNAP OUT OF IT!
CAN'T... CAN'T TAKE IT...
POWER BUILDING UP AGAIN... IT WANTS US DEAD, JOHN. WE'RE A DISTRACTION...
HE'S RIGHT. I CAN FEEL IT COMING. PREPARE YOURSELF FOR ANOTHER ONSLAUGHT.
AAAA! IT'S COMING! AAAAA!
WH-WHICH OF US THIS TIME, JOHN? WHICH ONE OF US IS G-GOING TO BURN OUT THIS TIME?
DAYTON... IF YOU DON'T BLOODY SHUT UP...
JOHN...?
J-JOHN, IS IT WARM IN HERE ALL OF A SUDDEN? I FEEL... OH, GOD. I THINK I'M...
NO! NO, I WILL NOT ALLOW IT!
NOT MY DAUGHTER.
SSENKRAD EKAT EM DAETSNI.
FATHER? NO! FATHER, DON'T! TAKE IT BACK! TAKE THE SPELL BACK!

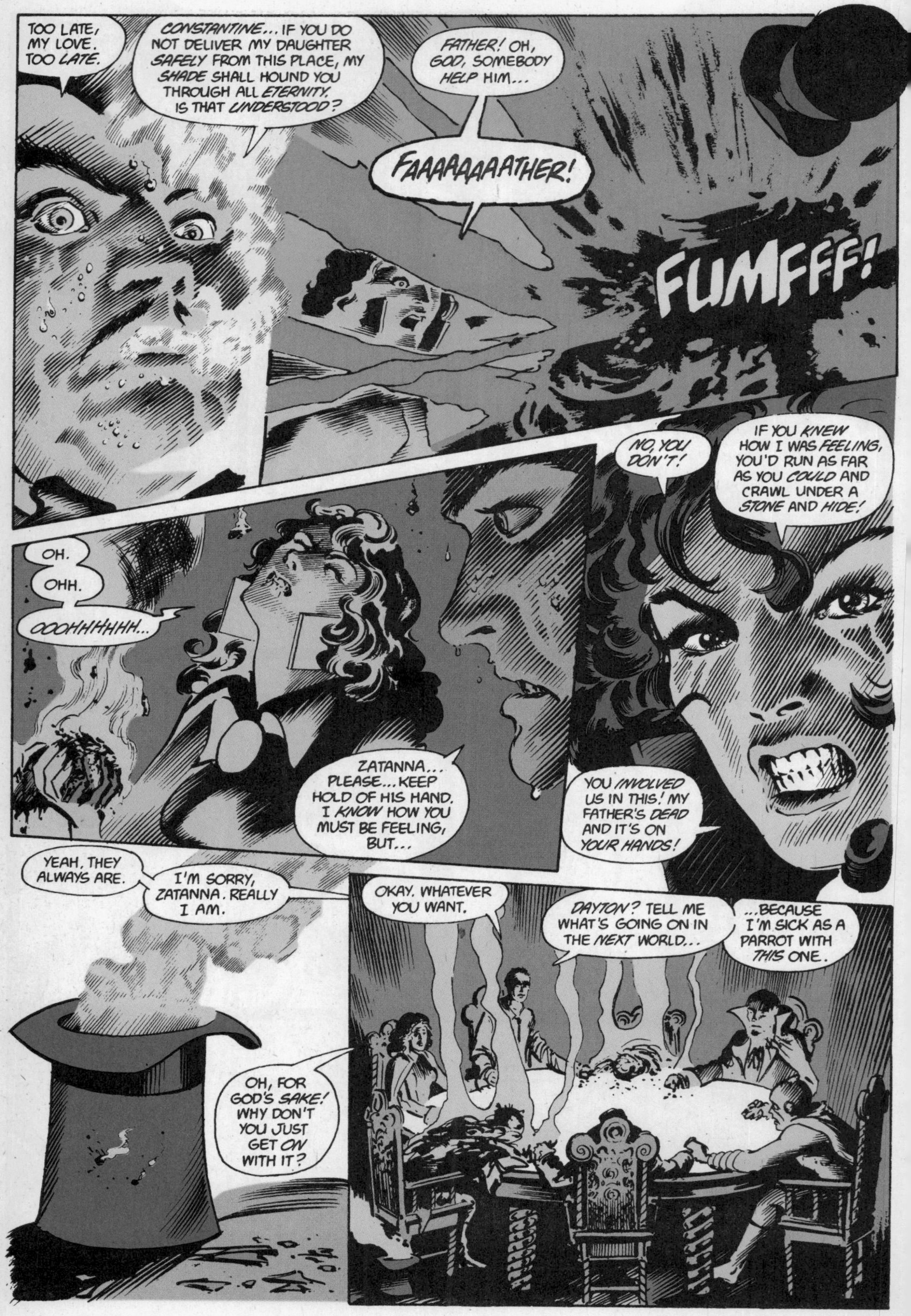
TOO LATE, MY LOVE. TOO LATE.
CONSTANTINE... IF YOU DO NOT DELIVER MY DAUGHTER SAFELY FROM THIS PLACE, MY SHADE SHALL HOUND YOU THROUGH ALL ETERNITY. IS THAT UNDERSTOOD?
FATHER! OH, GOD, SOMEBODY HELP HIM...
FAAAAAAAATHER!
FUMFFF!
OH.
OHH.
OOOHHHHHH...
ZATANNA... PLEASE... KEEP HOLD OF HIS HAND. I KNOW HOW YOU MUST BE FEELING, BUT...
NO, YOU DON'T!
IF YOU KNEW HOW I WAS FEELING, YOU'D RUN AS FAR AS YOU COULD AND CRAWL UNDER A STONE AND HIDE!
YOU INVOLVED US IN THIS! MY FATHER'S DEAD AND IT'S ON YOUR HANDS!
YEAH, THEY ALWAYS ARE.
I'M SORRY, ZATANNA. REALLY I AM.
OH, FOR GOD'S SAKE! WHY DON'T YOU JUST GET ON WITH IT?
OKAY. WHATEVER YOU WANT.
DAYTON? TELL ME WHAT'S GOING ON IN THE NEXT WORLD...
...BECAUSE I'M SICK AS A PARROT WITH THIS ONE.

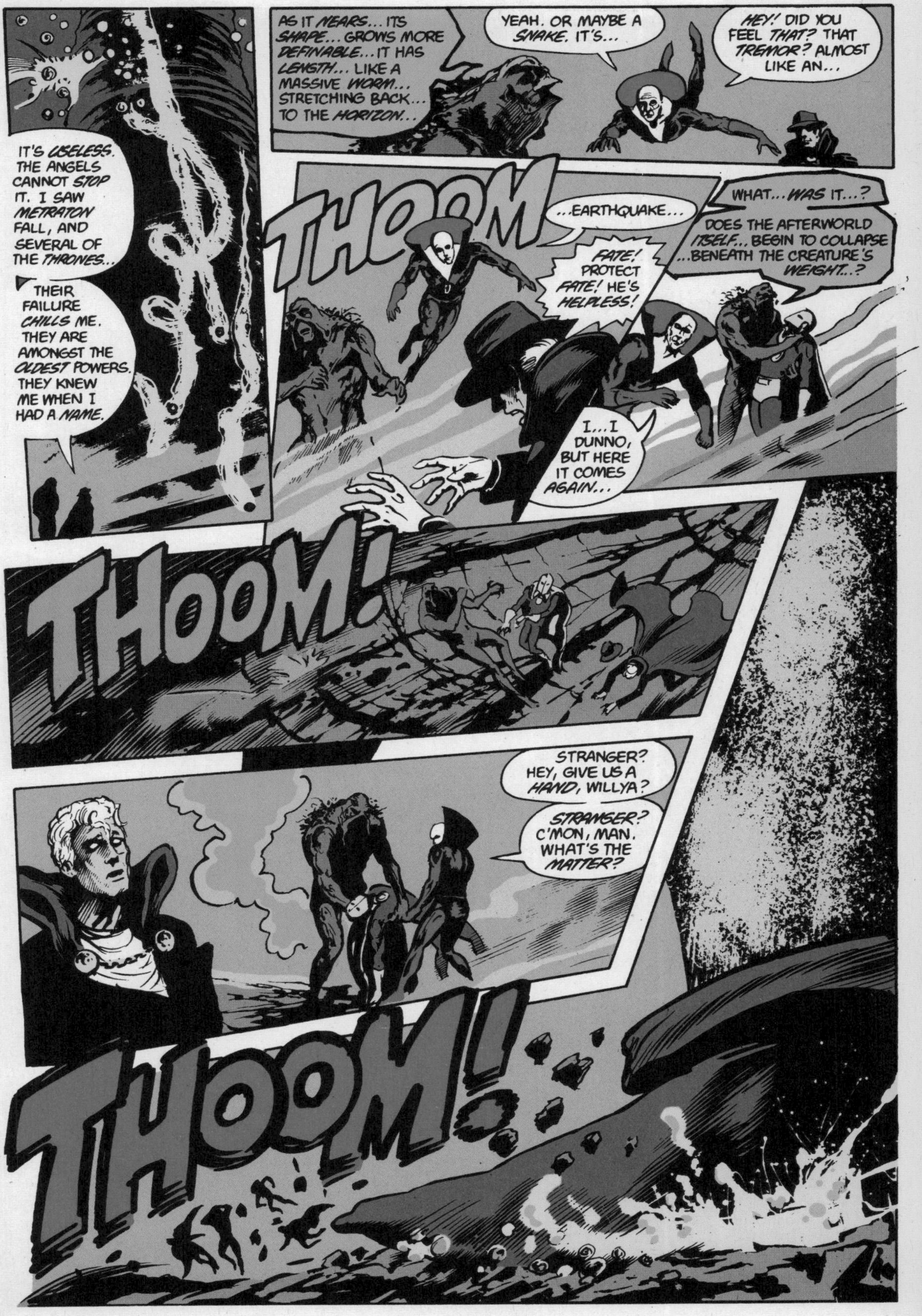
AS IT NEARS... ITS SHAPE... GROWS MORE DEFINABLE... IT HAS LENGTH... LIKE A MASSIVE WORM... STRETCHING BACK... TO THE HORIZON...
YEAH. OR MAYBE A SNAKE. IT'S...
HEY! DID YOU FEEL THAT? THAT TREMOR? ALMOST LIKE AN...
IT'S USELESS. THE ANGELS CANNOT STOP IT. I SAW METRATON FALL, AND SEVERAL OF THE THRONES...
THEIR FAILURE CHILLS ME. THEY ARE AMONGST THE OLDEST POWERS. THEY KNEW ME WHEN I HAD A NAME.
THOOM
...EARTHQUAKE...
WHAT... WAS IT...?
DOES THE AFTERWORLD ITSELF... BEGIN TO COLLAPSE ...BENEATH THE CREATURE'S WEIGHT...?
FATE! PROTECT FATE! HE'S HELPLESS!
I... I DUNNO, BUT HERE IT COMES AGAIN...
THOOM!
STRANGER? HEY, GIVE US A HAND, WILLYA?
STRANGER? C'MON, MAN. WHAT'S THE MATTER?
THOOM!

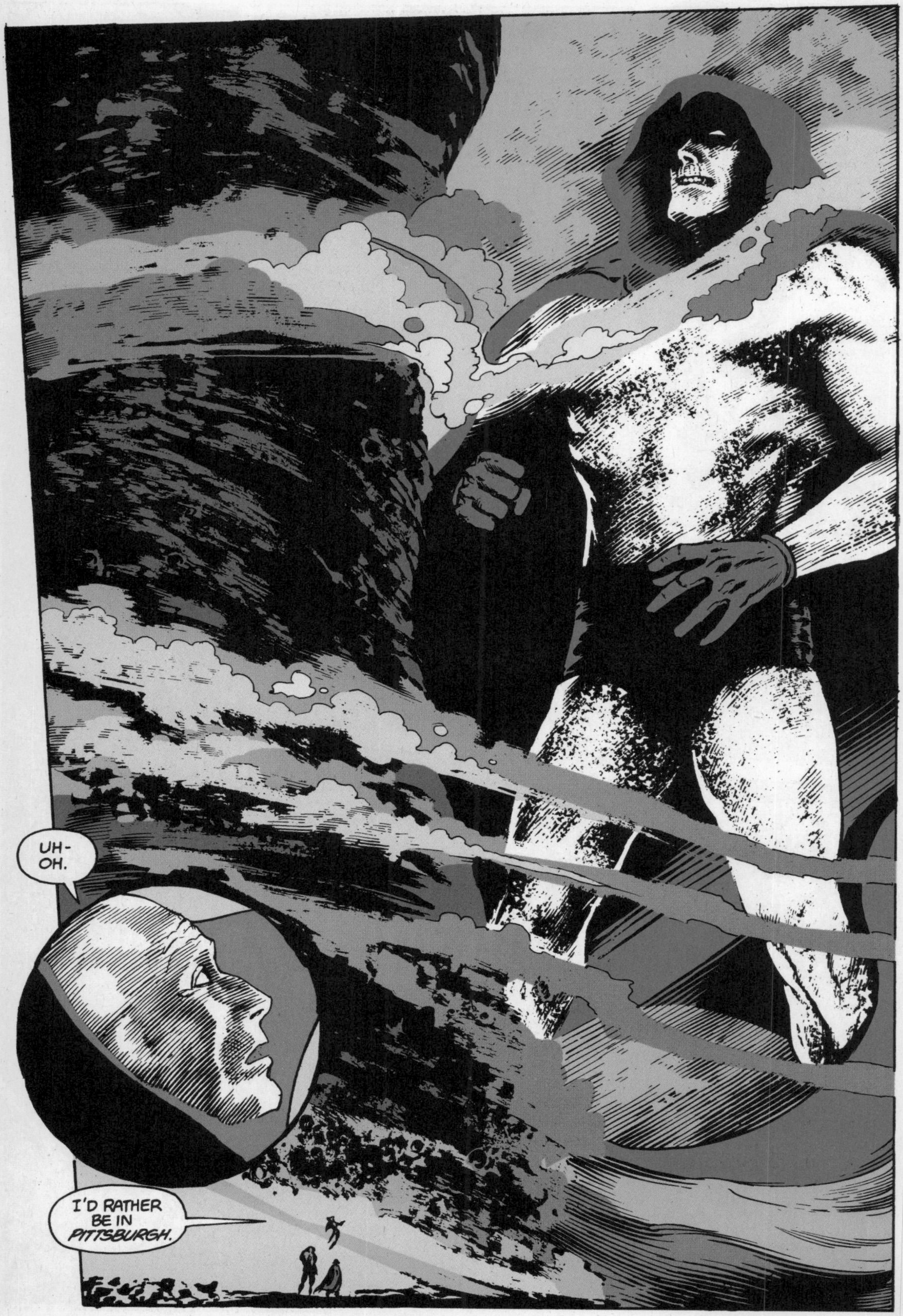
UH-OH.
I'D RATHER BE IN PITTSBURGH.

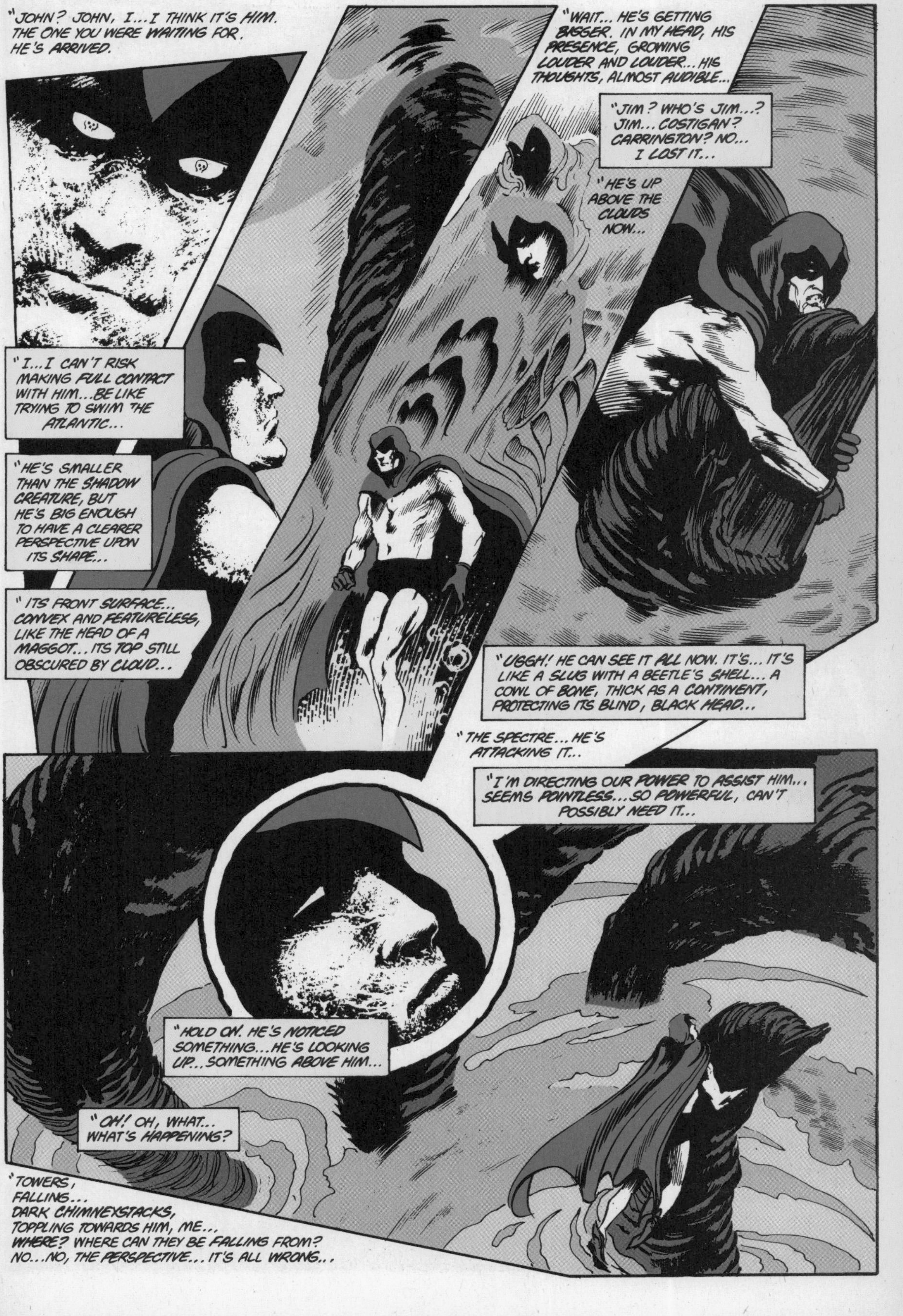
"JOHN? JOHN, I...I THINK IT'S HIM. THE ONE YOU WERE WAITING FOR. HE'S ARRIVED.
"I...I CAN'T RISK MAKING FULL CONTACT WITH HIM...BE LIKE TRYING TO SWIM THE ATLANTIC...
"HE'S SMALLER THAN THE SHADOW CREATURE, BUT HE'S BIG ENOUGH TO HAVE A CLEARER PERSPECTIVE UPON ITS SHAPE...
"ITS FRONT SURFACE... CONVEX AND FEATURELESS, LIKE THE HEAD OF A MAGGOT...ITS TOP STILL OBSCURED BY CLOUD...
"WAIT... HE'S GETTING BIGGER. IN MY HEAD, HIS PRESENCE, GROWING LOUDER AND LOUDER...HIS THOUGHTS, ALMOST AUDIBLE...
"JIM? WHO'S JIM...? JIM... COSTIGAN? CARRINGTON? NO... I LOST IT...
"HE'S UP ABOVE THE CLOUDS NOW...
"UGGH! HE CAN SEE IT ALL NOW. IT'S... IT'S LIKE A SLUG WITH A BEETLE'S SHELL... A COWL OF BONE, THICK AS A CONTINENT, PROTECTING ITS BLIND, BLACK HEAD...
"THE SPECTRE... HE'S ATTACKING IT...
"I'M DIRECTING OUR POWER TO ASSIST HIM... SEEMS POINTLESS...SO POWERFUL, CAN'T POSSIBLY NEED IT...
"HOLD ON. HE'S NOTICED SOMETHING...HE'S LOOKING UP...SOMETHING ABOVE HIM...
"OH! OH, WHAT... WHAT'S HAPPENING?
"TOWERS, FALLING... DARK CHIMNEYSTACKS, TOPPLING TOWARDS HIM, ME... WHERE? WHERE CAN THEY BE FALLING FROM? NO...NO, THE PERSPECTIVE... IT'S ALL WRONG...

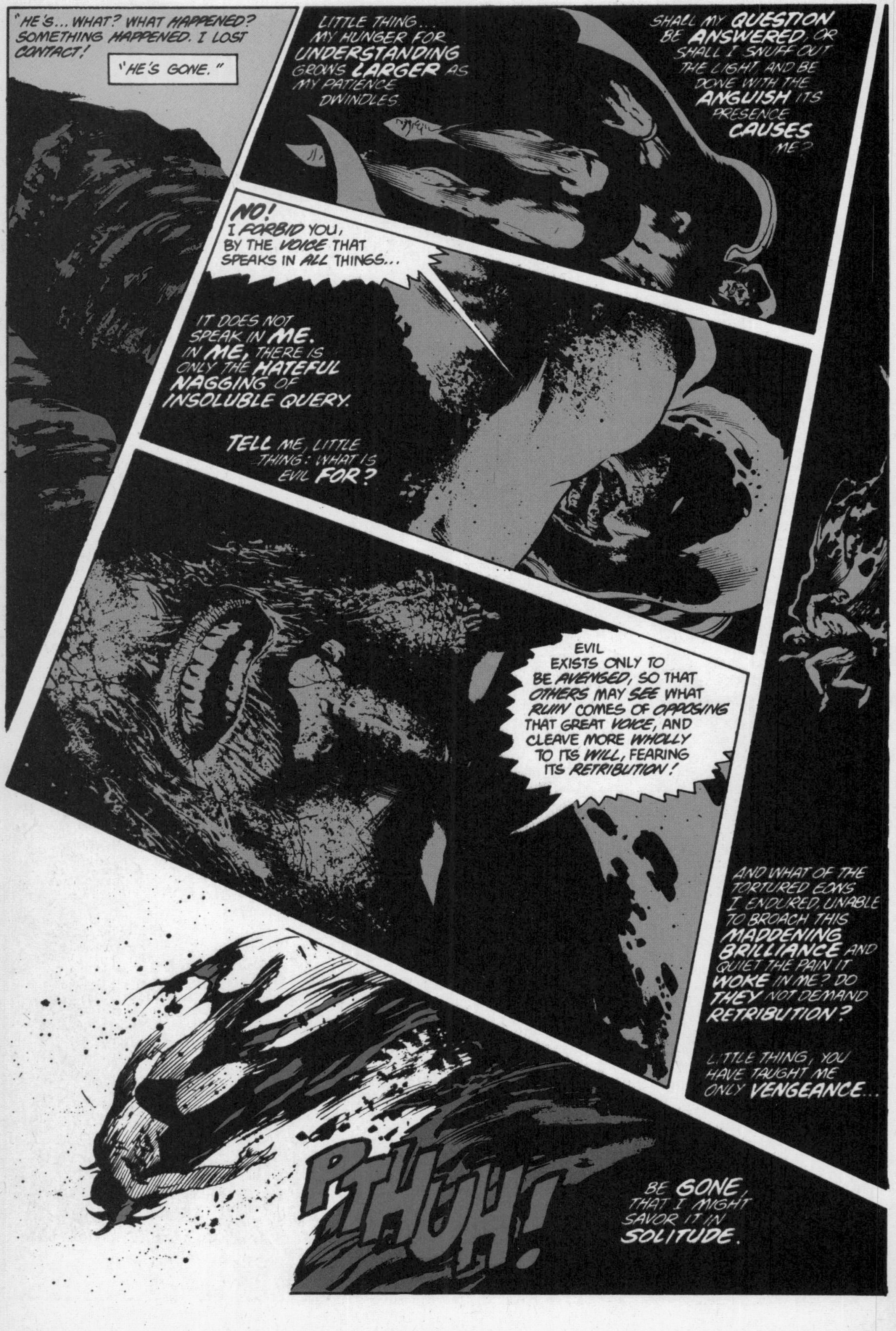
"HE'S... WHAT? WHAT HAPPENED? SOMETHING HAPPENED. I LOST CONTACT!
"HE'S GONE."
LITTLE THING... MY HUNGER FOR UNDERSTANDING GROWS LARGER AS MY PATIENCE DWINDLES.
SHALL MY QUESTION BE ANSWERED, OR SHALL I SNUFF OUT THE LIGHT, AND BE DONE WITH THE ANGUISH ITS PRESENCE CAUSES ME?
NO! I FORBID YOU, BY THE VOICE THAT SPEAKS IN ALL THINGS...
IT DOES NOT SPEAK IN ME. IN ME, THERE IS ONLY THE HATEFUL NAGGING OF INSOLUBLE QUERY.
TELL ME, LITTLE THING: WHAT IS EVIL FOR?
EVIL EXISTS ONLY TO BE AVENGED, SO THAT OTHERS MAY SEE WHAT RUIN COMES OF OPPOSING THAT GREAT VOICE, AND CLEAVE MORE WHOLLY TO ITS WILL, FEARING ITS RETRIBUTION!
AND WHAT OF THE TORTURED EONS I ENDURED, UNABLE TO BROACH THIS MADDENING BRILLIANCE AND QUIET THE PAIN IT WOKE IN ME? DO THEY NOT DEMAND RETRIBUTION?
LITTLE THING, YOU HAVE TAUGHT ME ONLY VENGEANCE...
PTHUH!
BE GONE, THAT I MIGHT SAVOR IT IN SOLITUDE.

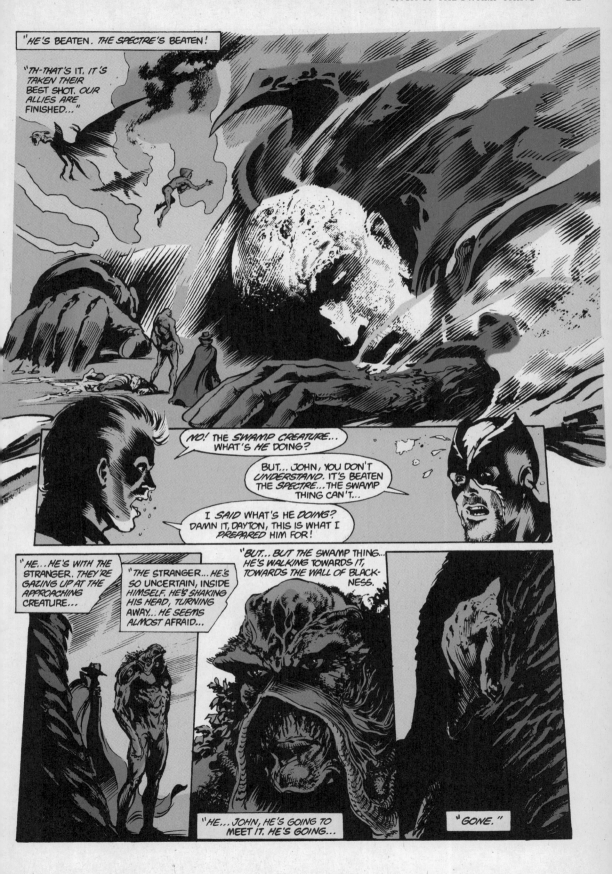

"HE'S BEATEN. THE SPECTRE'S BEATEN!"

"TH-THAT'S IT. IT'S TAKEN THEIR BEST SHOT. OUR ALLIES ARE FINISHED..."

NO! THE SWAMP CREATURE... WHAT'S HE DOING?

BUT... JOHN, YOU DON'T UNDERSTAND. IT'S BEATEN THE SPECTRE...THE SWAMP THING CAN'T...

I SAID WHAT'S HE DOING? DAMN IT, DAYTON, THIS IS WHAT I PREPARED HIM FOR!

"HE...HE'S WITH THE STRANGER. THEY'RE GAZING UP AT THE APPROACHING CREATURE..."

"THE STRANGER... HE'S SO UNCERTAIN, INSIDE HIMSELF. HE'S SHAKING HIS HEAD, TURNING AWAY... HE SEEMS ALMOST AFRAID..."

"BUT...BUT THE SWAMP THING... HE'S WALKING TOWARDS IT, TOWARDS THE WALL OF BLACKNESS."

"HE...JOHN, HE'S GOING TO MEET IT. HE'S GOING..."

"GONE."

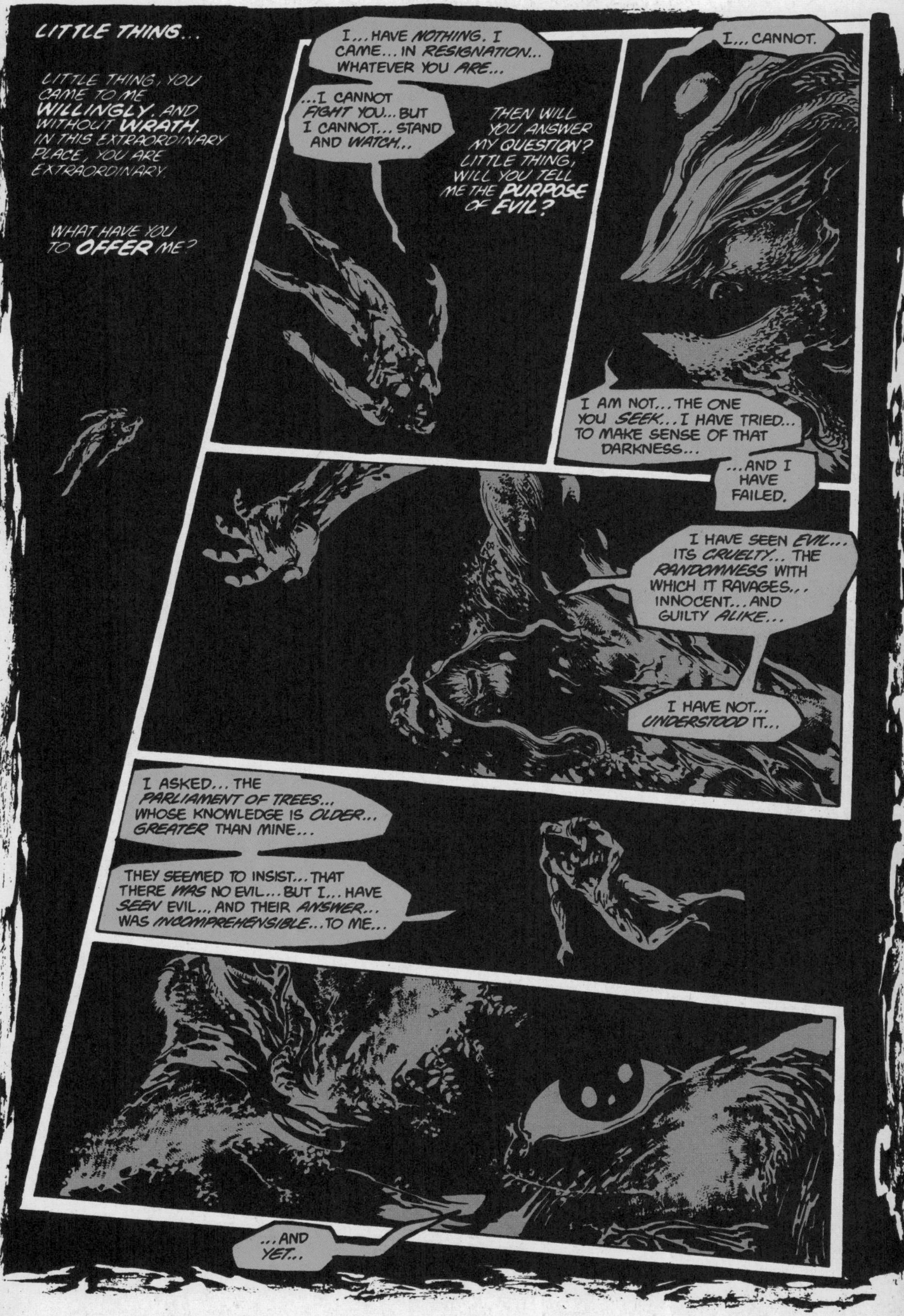
LITTLE THING...
LITTLE THING, YOU CAME TO ME WILLINGLY. AND WITHOUT WRATH. IN THIS EXTRAORDINARY PLACE, YOU ARE EXTRAORDINARY.
WHAT HAVE YOU TO OFFER ME?
I... HAVE NOTHING. I CAME... IN RESIGNATION... WHATEVER YOU ARE...
...I CANNOT FIGHT YOU... BUT I CANNOT... STAND AND WATCH...
THEN WILL YOU ANSWER MY QUESTION? LITTLE THING, WILL YOU TELL ME THE PURPOSE OF EVIL?
I... CANNOT.
I AM NOT... THE ONE YOU SEEK... I HAVE TRIED... TO MAKE SENSE OF THAT DARKNESS...
...AND I HAVE FAILED.
I HAVE SEEN EVIL... ITS CRUELTY... THE RANDOMNESS WITH WHICH IT RAVAGES... INNOCENT... AND GUILTY ALIKE...
I HAVE NOT... UNDERSTOOD IT...
I ASKED... THE PARLIAMENT OF TREES... WHOSE KNOWLEDGE IS OLDER... GREATER THAN MINE...
THEY SEEMED TO INSIST... THAT THERE WAS NO EVIL... BUT I... HAVE SEEN EVIL... AND THEIR ANSWER... WAS INCOMPREHENSIBLE... TO ME...
...AND YET...

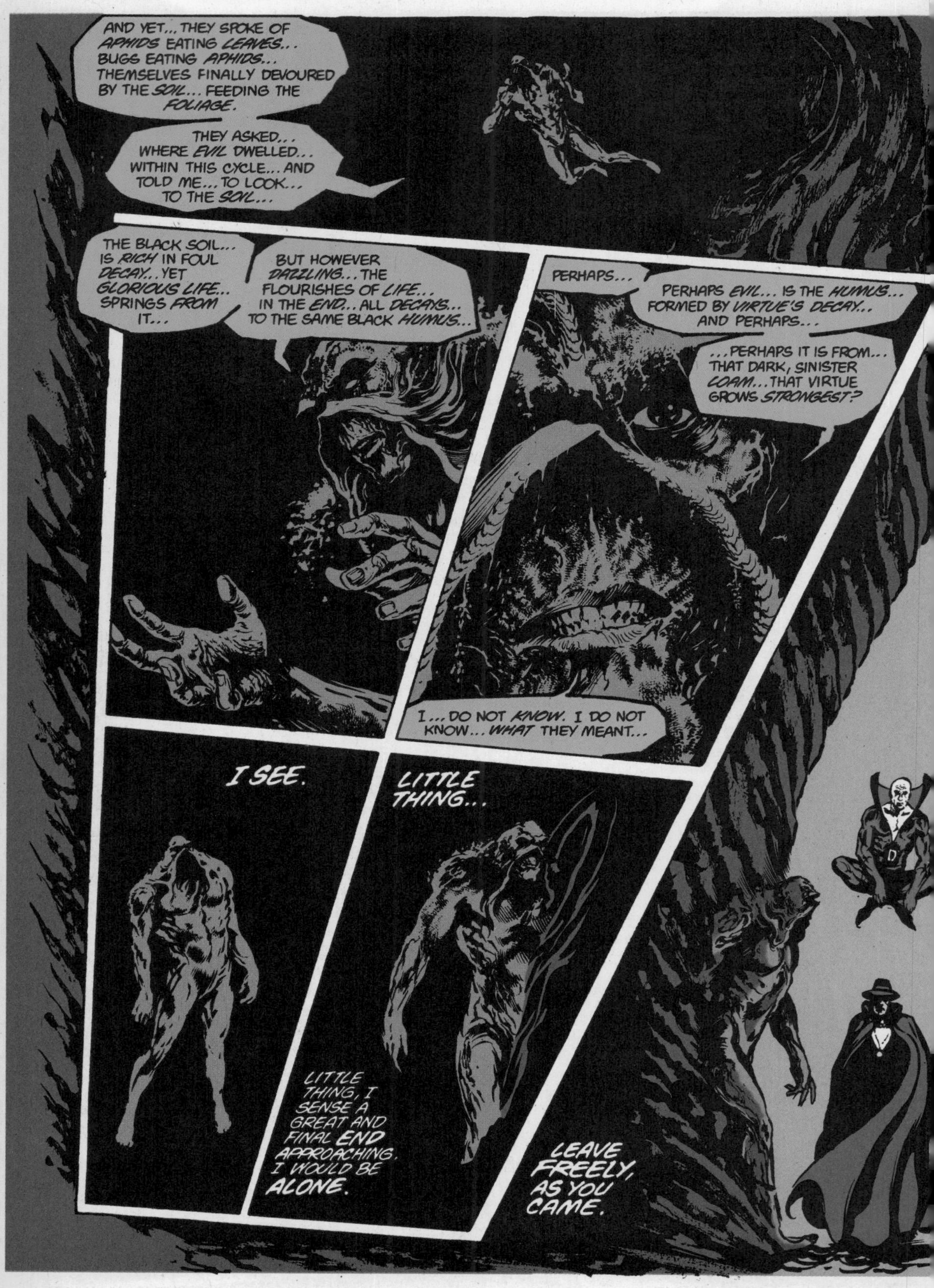
AND YET... THEY SPOKE OF APHIDS EATING LEAVES... BUGS EATING APHIDS... THEMSELVES FINALLY DEVOURED BY THE SOIL... FEEDING THE FOLIAGE.
THEY ASKED... WHERE EVIL DWELLED... WITHIN THIS CYCLE... AND TOLD ME... TO LOOK... TO THE SOIL...
THE BLACK SOIL... IS RICH IN FOUL DECAY... YET GLORIOUS LIFE... SPRINGS FROM IT...
BUT HOWEVER DAZZLING... THE FLOURISHES OF LIFE... IN THE END... ALL DECAYS... TO THE SAME BLACK HUMUS...
PERHAPS...
PERHAPS EVIL... IS THE HUMUS... FORMED BY VIRTUE'S DECAY... AND PERHAPS...
...PERHAPS IT IS FROM... THAT DARK, SINISTER LOAM... THAT VIRTUE GROWS STRONGEST?
I... DO NOT KNOW. I DO NOT KNOW... WHAT THEY MEANT...
I SEE.
LITTLE THING...
LITTLE THING, I SENSE A GREAT AND FINAL END APPROACHING. I WOULD BE ALONE.
LEAVE FREELY, AS YOU CAME.

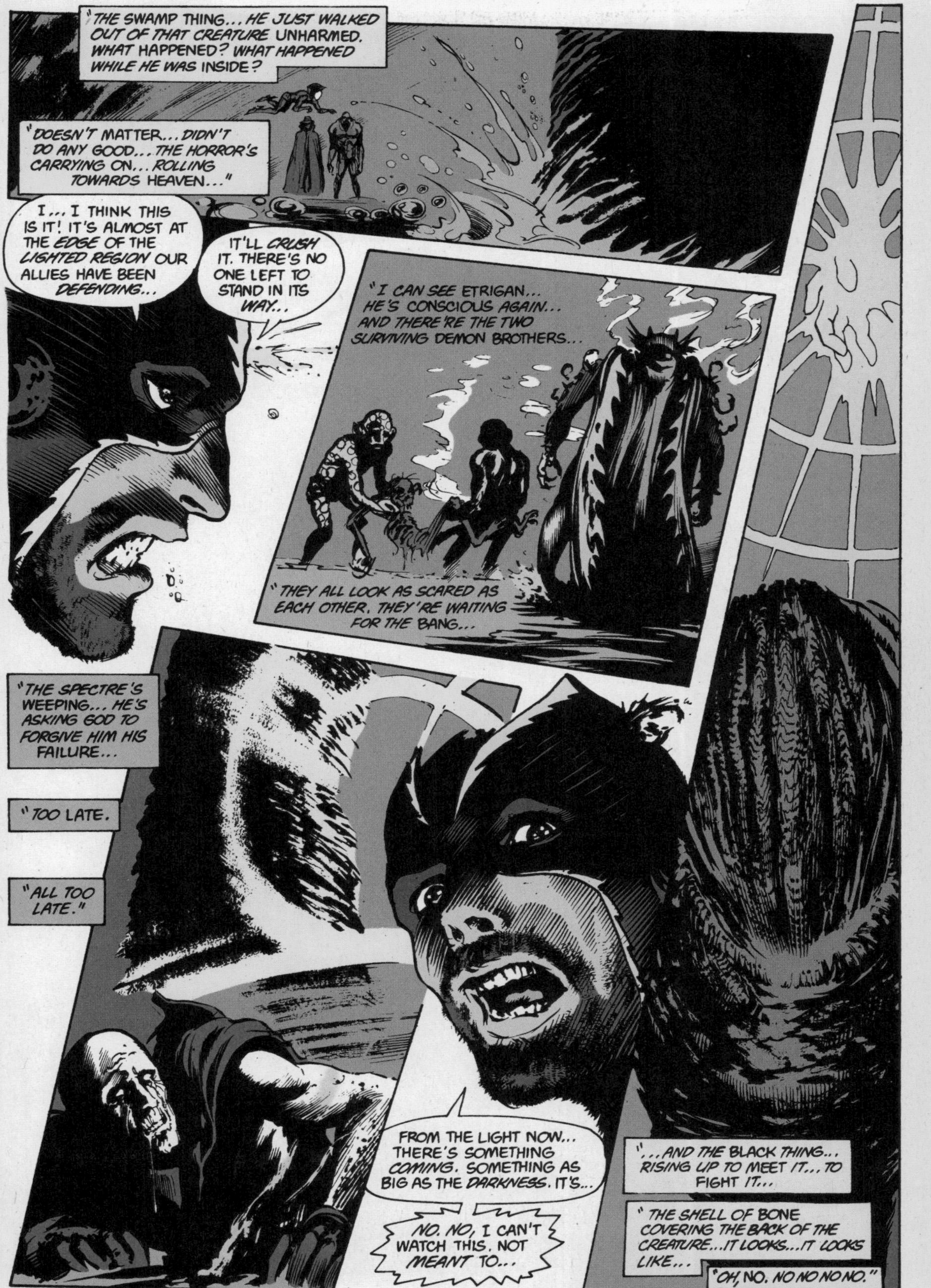
"THE SWAMP THING... HE JUST WALKED OUT OF THAT CREATURE UNHARMED. WHAT HAPPENED? WHAT HAPPENED WHILE HE WAS INSIDE?
"DOESN'T MATTER... DIDN'T DO ANY GOOD... THE HORROR'S CARRYING ON... ROLLING TOWARDS HEAVEN..."
I... I THINK THIS IS IT! IT'S ALMOST AT THE EDGE OF THE LIGHTED REGION OUR ALLIES HAVE BEEN DEFENDING...
IT'LL CRUSH IT. THERE'S NO ONE LEFT TO STAND IN ITS WAY...
"I CAN SEE ETRIGAN... HE'S CONSCIOUS AGAIN... AND THERE'RE THE TWO SURVIVING DEMON BROTHERS...
"THEY ALL LOOK AS SCARED AS EACH OTHER. THEY'RE WAITING FOR THE BANG...
"THE SPECTRE'S WEEPING... HE'S ASKING GOD TO FORGIVE HIM HIS FAILURE...
"TOO LATE.
"ALL TOO LATE."
FROM THE LIGHT NOW... THERE'S SOMETHING COMING. SOMETHING AS BIG AS THE DARKNESS. IT'S...
NO. NO, I CAN'T WATCH THIS. NOT MEANT TO...
"...AND THE BLACK THING... RISING UP TO MEET IT... TO FIGHT IT...
"THE SHELL OF BONE COVERING THE BACK OF THE CREATURE... IT LOOKS... IT LOOKS LIKE...
"OH, NO. NO NO NO NO."

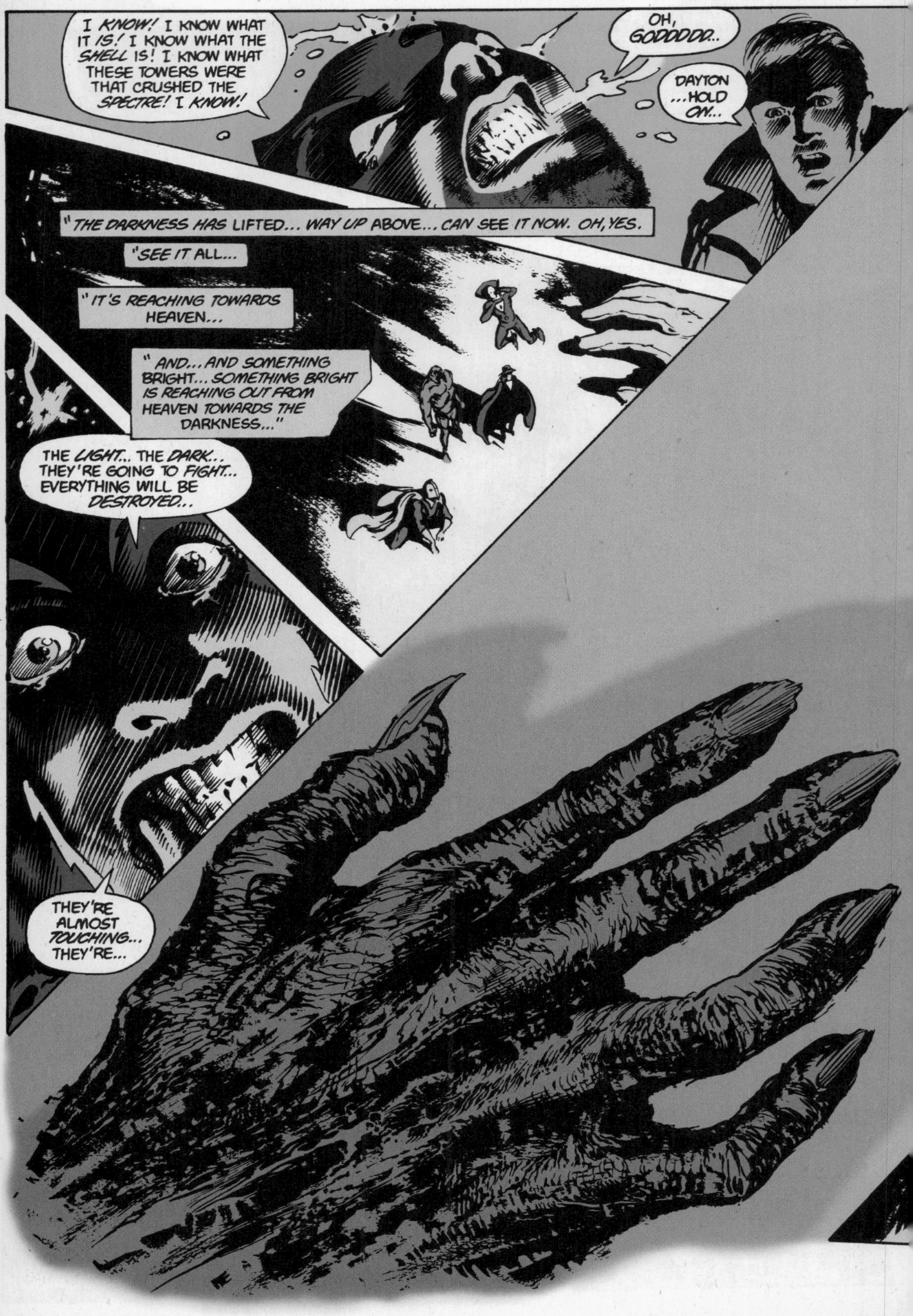
I KNOW! I KNOW WHAT IT IS! I KNOW WHAT THE SHELL IS! I KNOW WHAT THESE TOWERS WERE THAT CRUSHED THE SPECTRE! I KNOW!
OH, GODDDDD...
DAYTON ...HOLD ON...
"THE DARKNESS HAS LIFTED... WAY UP ABOVE... CAN SEE IT NOW. OH, YES.
"SEE IT ALL...
"IT'S REACHING TOWARDS HEAVEN...
"AND... AND SOMETHING BRIGHT... SOMETHING BRIGHT IS REACHING OUT FROM HEAVEN TOWARDS THE DARKNESS..."
THE LIGHT... THE DARK... THEY'RE GOING TO FIGHT... EVERYTHING WILL BE DESTROYED...
THEY'RE ALMOST TOUCHING... THEY'RE...

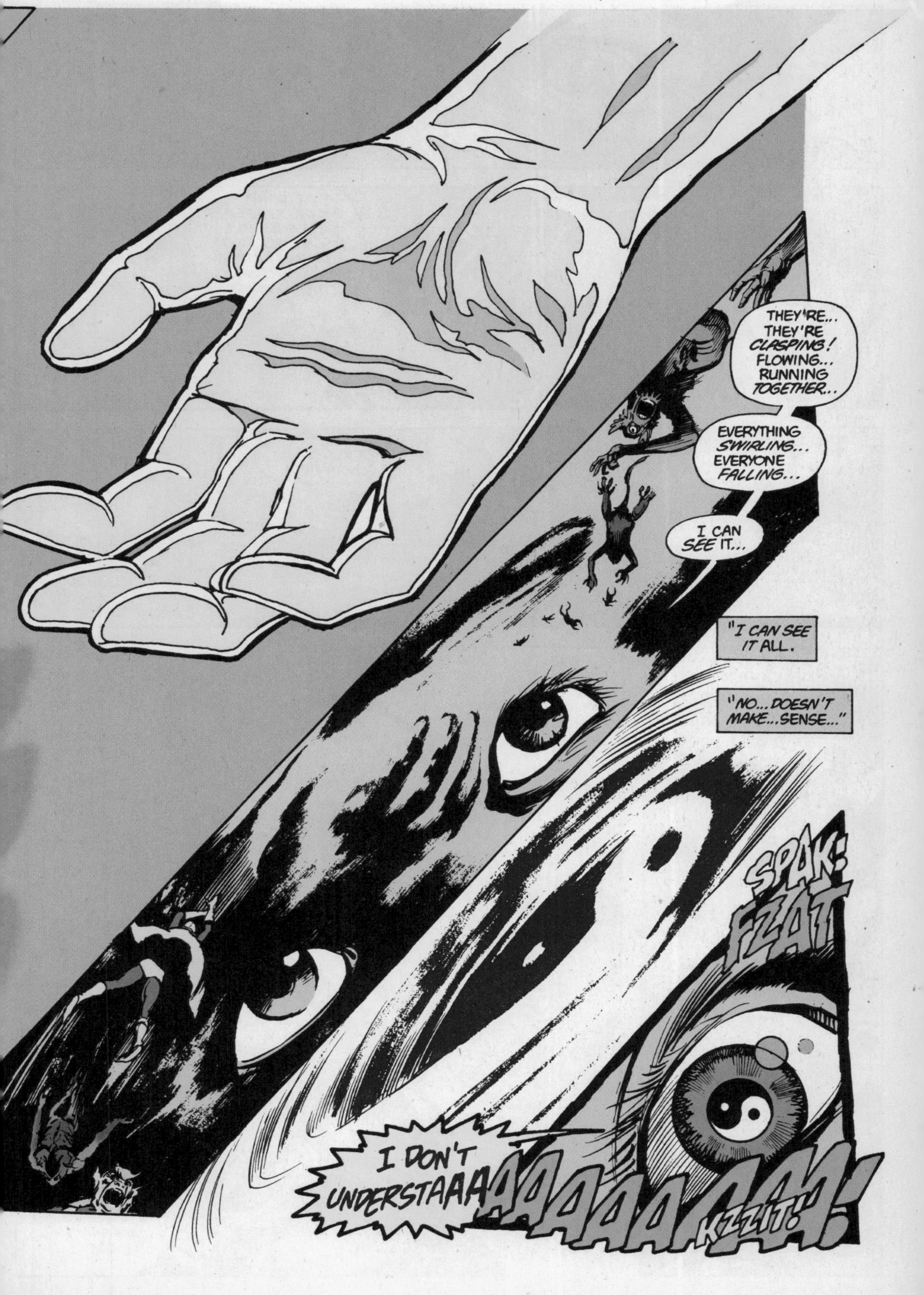
THEY'RE... THEY'RE CLASPING! FLOWING... RUNNING TOGETHER...
EVERYTHING SWIRLING... EVERYONE FALLING...
I CAN SEE IT...
"I CAN SEE IT ALL.
"NO... DOESN'T MAKE... SENSE..."
SPAK! FZAT
I DON'T UNDERSTAAAAAAAAAAAAAM!
KZZIT!

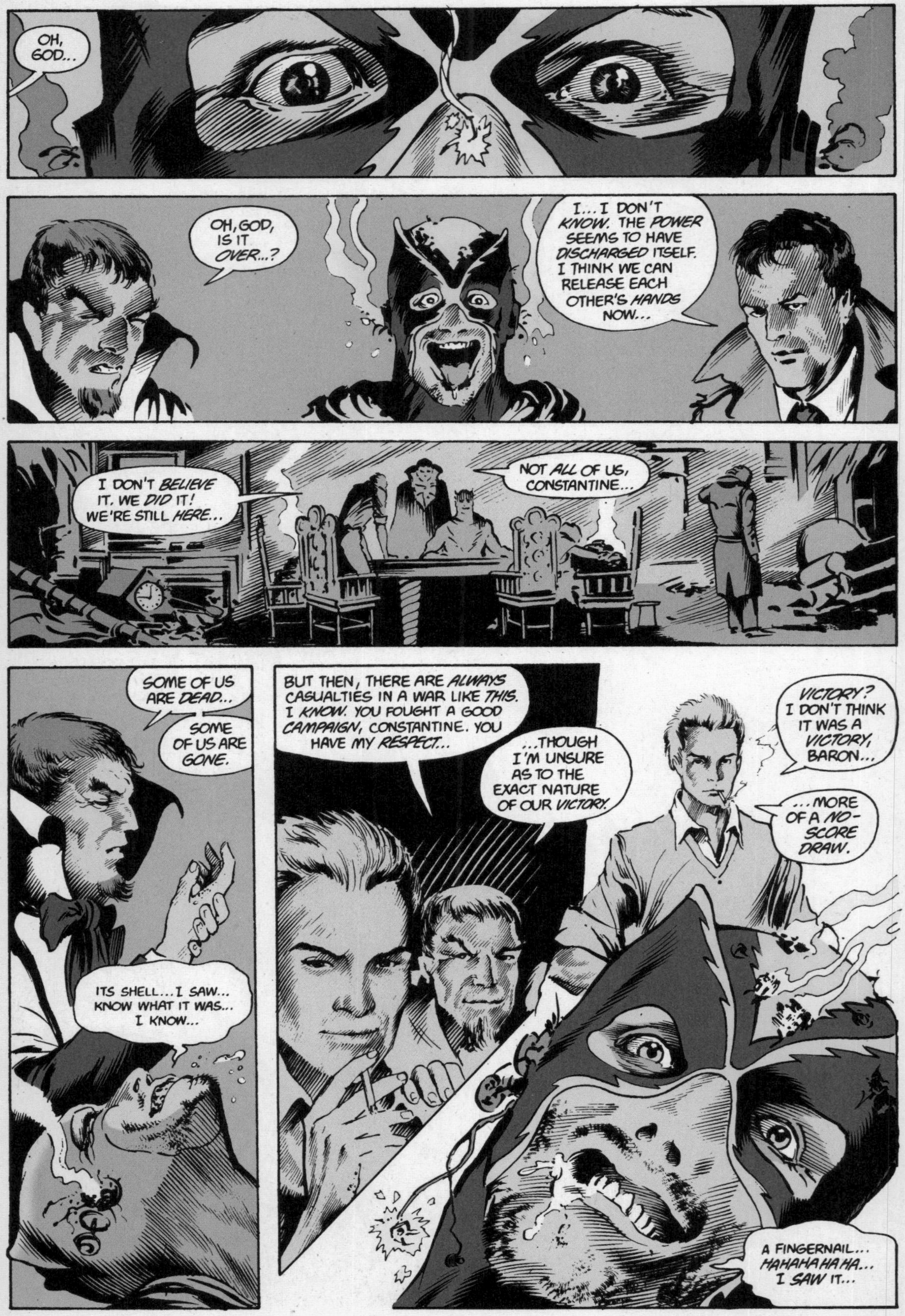
OH, GOD...
OH, GOD, IS IT OVER...?
I... I DON'T KNOW. THE POWER SEEMS TO HAVE DISCHARGED ITSELF. I THINK WE CAN RELEASE EACH OTHER'S HANDS NOW...
I DON'T BELIEVE IT. WE DID IT! WE'RE STILL HERE...
NOT ALL OF US, CONSTANTINE...
SOME OF US ARE DEAD...
SOME OF US ARE GONE.
ITS SHELL... I SAW... KNOW WHAT IT WAS... I KNOW...
BUT THEN, THERE ARE ALWAYS CASUALTIES IN A WAR LIKE THIS. I KNOW. YOU FOUGHT A GOOD CAMPAIGN, CONSTANTINE. YOU HAVE MY RESPECT...
...THOUGH I'M UNSURE AS TO THE EXACT NATURE OF OUR VICTORY.
VICTORY? I DON'T THINK IT WAS A VICTORY, BARON...
...MORE OF A NO-SCORE DRAW.
A FINGERNAIL... HAHAHA HA HA... I SAW IT...

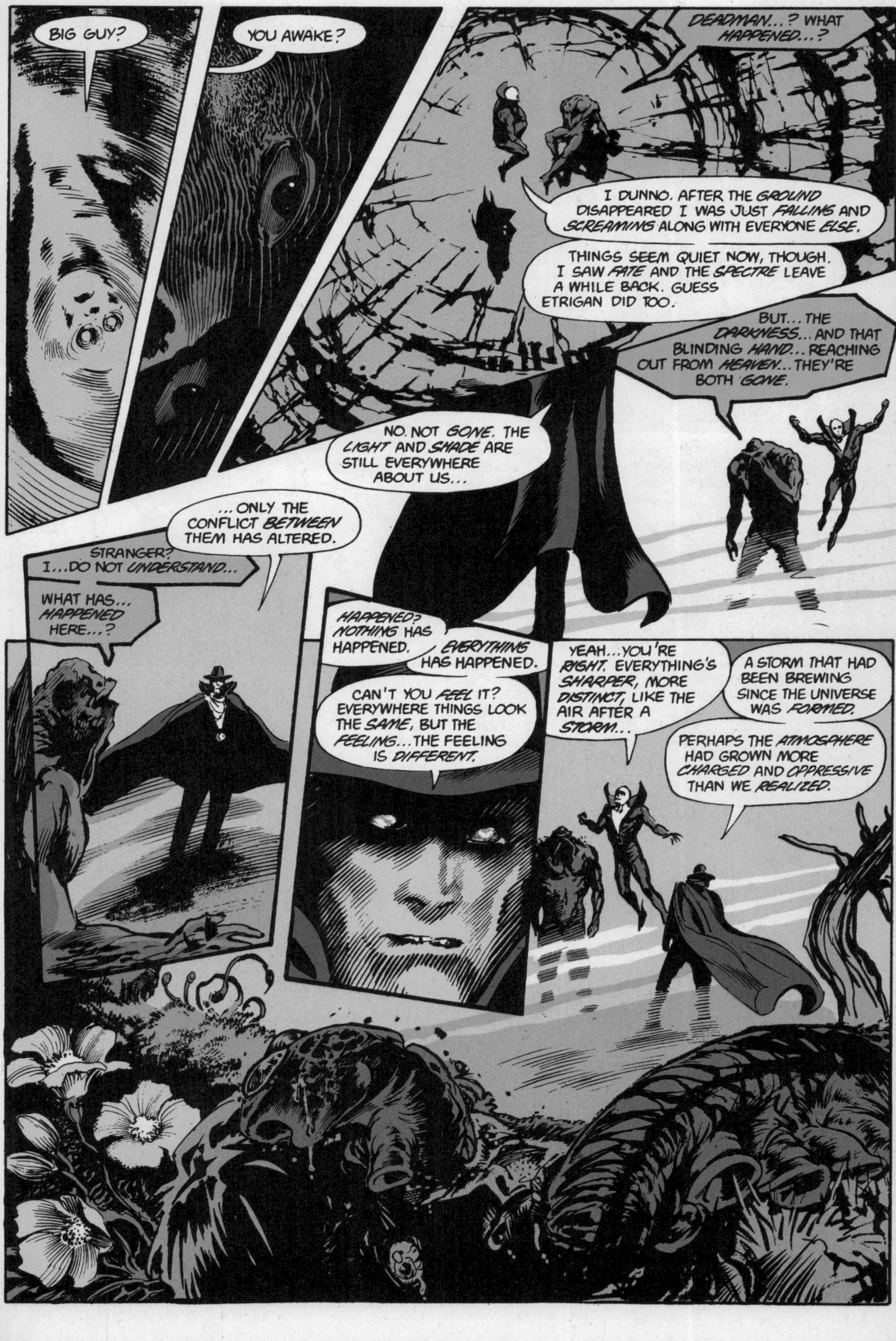
BIG GUY?
YOU AWAKE?
DEADMAN...? WHAT HAPPENED...?
I DUNNO. AFTER THE GROUND DISAPPEARED I WAS JUST FALLING AND SCREAMING ALONG WITH EVERYONE ELSE.
THINGS SEEM QUIET NOW, THOUGH. I SAW FATE AND THE SPECTRE LEAVE A WHILE BACK. GUESS ETRIGAN DID TOO.
BUT... THE DARKNESS... AND THAT BLINDING HAND... REACHING OUT FROM HEAVEN... THEY'RE BOTH GONE.
NO. NOT GONE. THE LIGHT AND SHADE ARE STILL EVERYWHERE ABOUT US...
...ONLY THE CONFLICT BETWEEN THEM HAS ALTERED.
STRANGER? I...DO NOT UNDERSTAND...
WHAT HAS... HAPPENED HERE...?
HAPPENED? NOTHING HAS HAPPENED.
EVERYTHING HAS HAPPENED.
CAN'T YOU FEEL IT? EVERYWHERE THINGS LOOK THE SAME, BUT THE FEELING... THE FEELING IS DIFFERENT.
YEAH...YOU'RE RIGHT. EVERYTHING'S SHARPER, MORE DISTINCT, LIKE THE AIR AFTER A STORM...
A STORM THAT HAD BEEN BREWING SINCE THE UNIVERSE WAS FORMED.
PERHAPS THE ATMOSPHERE HAD GROWN MORE CHARGED AND OPPRESSIVE THAN WE REALIZED.

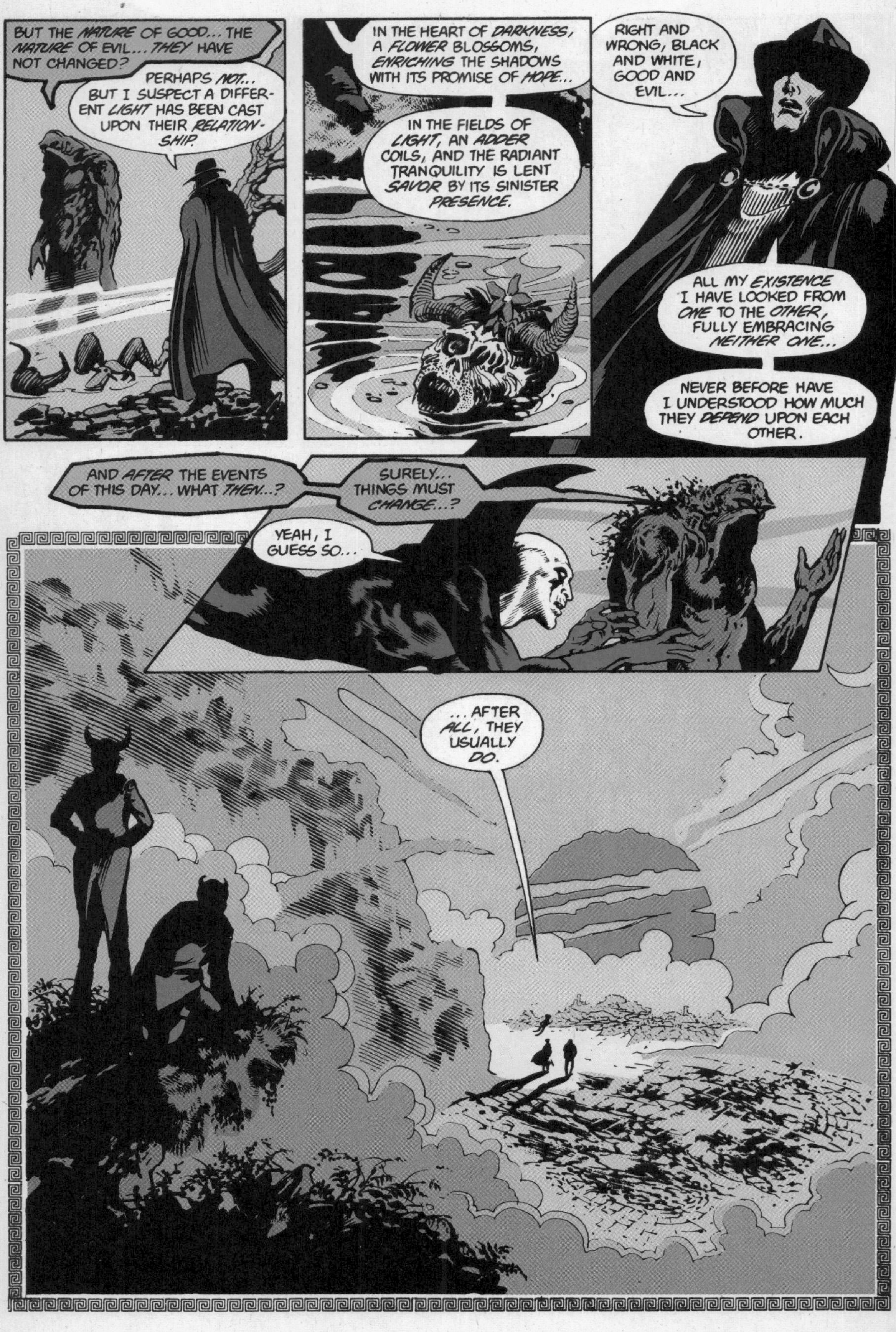
BUT THE NATURE OF GOOD... THE NATURE OF EVIL... THEY HAVE NOT CHANGED?
PERHAPS NOT... BUT I SUSPECT A DIFFERENT LIGHT HAS BEEN CAST UPON THEIR RELATIONSHIP.
IN THE HEART OF DARKNESS, A FLOWER BLOSSOMS, ENRICHING THE SHADOWS WITH ITS PROMISE OF HOPE...
IN THE FIELDS OF LIGHT, AN ADDER COILS, AND THE RADIANT TRANQUILITY IS LENT SAVOR BY ITS SINISTER PRESENCE.
RIGHT AND WRONG, BLACK AND WHITE, GOOD AND EVIL...
ALL MY EXISTENCE I HAVE LOOKED FROM ONE TO THE OTHER, FULLY EMBRACING NEITHER ONE...
NEVER BEFORE HAVE I UNDERSTOOD HOW MUCH THEY DEPEND UPON EACH OTHER.
AND AFTER THE EVENTS OF THIS DAY... WHAT THEN...?
SURELY... THINGS MUST CHANGE...?
YEAH, I GUESS SO...
...AFTER ALL, THEY USUALLY DO.

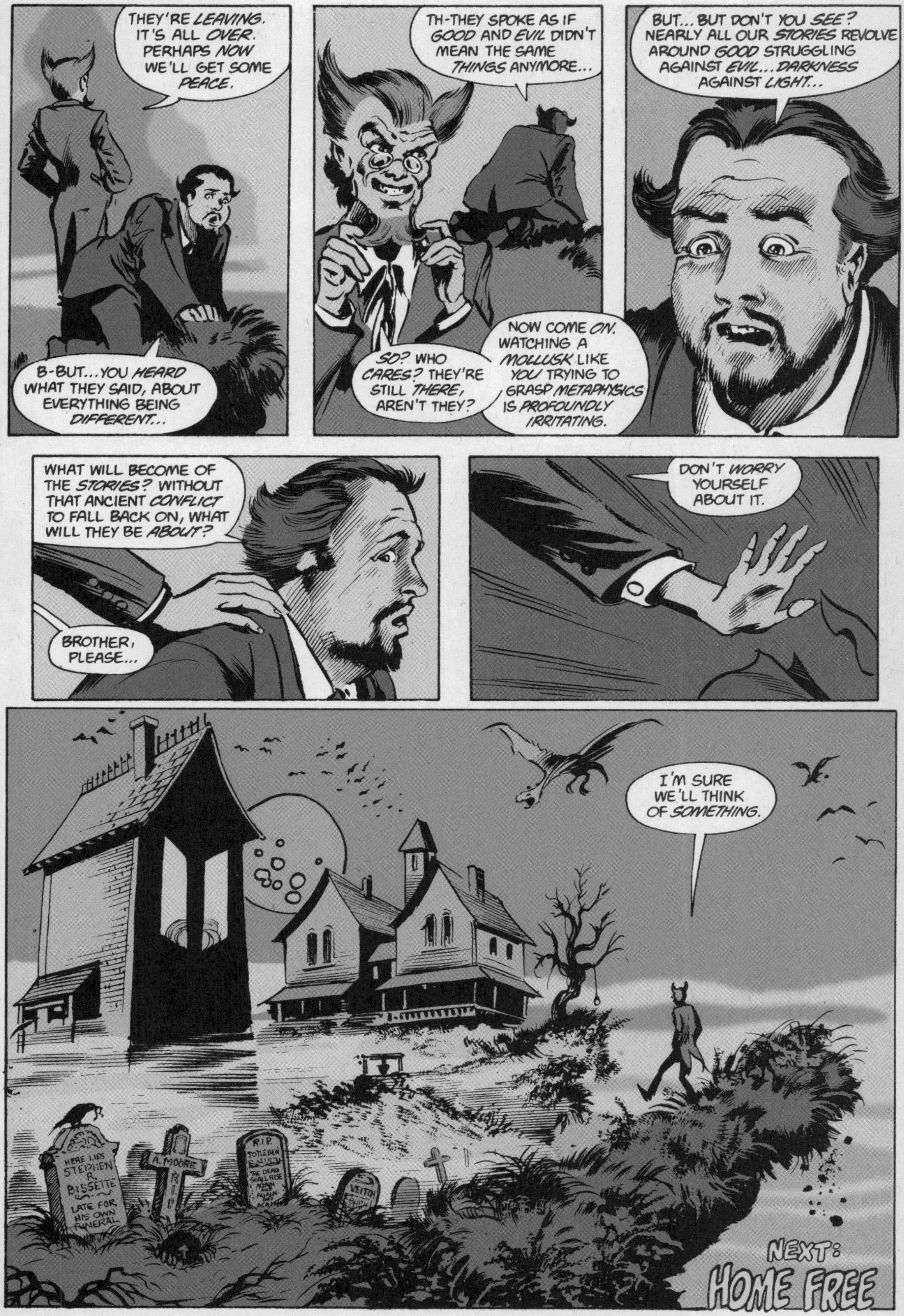
THEY'RE LEAVING. IT'S ALL OVER. PERHAPS NOW WE'LL GET SOME PEACE.
B-BUT... YOU HEARD WHAT THEY SAID, ABOUT EVERYTHING BEING DIFFERENT...
TH-THEY SPOKE AS IF GOOD AND EVIL DIDN'T MEAN THE SAME THINGS ANYMORE...
SO? WHO CARES? THEY'RE STILL THERE, AREN'T THEY?
NOW COME ON. WATCHING A MOLLUSK LIKE YOU TRYING TO GRASP METAPHYSICS IS PROFOUNDLY IRRITATING.
BUT... BUT DON'T YOU SEE? NEARLY ALL OUR STORIES REVOLVE AROUND GOOD STRUGGLING AGAINST EVIL... DARKNESS AGAINST LIGHT...
WHAT WILL BECOME OF THE STORIES? WITHOUT THAT ANCIENT CONFLICT TO FALL BACK ON, WHAT WILL THEY BE ABOUT?
BROTHER, PLEASE...
DON'T WORRY YOURSELF ABOUT IT.
I'M SURE WE'LL THINK OF SOMETHING.
HERE LIES STEPHEN R. BISSETTE LATE FOR HIS OWN FUNERAL
A. MOORE R.I.P.
R.I.P.
VEITCH
NEXT: HOME FREE

This portrait of the Swamp Thing was created by artist John Totleben for the one-shot anthology title *Vertigo Gallery: Dreams & Nightmares*, released in 1995.

ALAN MOORE is perhaps the most acclaimed writer in the graphic story medium, having garnered countless awards for works such as *Watchmen*, *V For Vendetta*, *From Hell*, *Miracleman* and *Swamp Thing*. He is also the mastermind behind the America's Best Comics line, through which he has created (along with many talented illustrators) *The League of Extraordinary Gentlemen*, *Promethea*, *Tom Strong*, *Tomorrow Stories* and *Top 10*. As one of the medium's most important innovators since the early 1980s, Moore has influenced an entire generation of comics creators, and his work continues to inspire an ever-growing audience. He resides in central England.

Following his multi-award-winning tenure on *Swamp Thing*, Joe Kubert School pioneer class graduate **STEPHEN R. BISSETTE** went on to co-found, edit, and co-publish the controversial and Eisner Award-winning horror anthology *Taboo*, collaborate with Alan Moore, Rick Veitch, Chester Brown, Dave Gibbons and John Totleben on the Image series *1963*, and create and self-publish four issues of *S.R. Bissette's Tyrant*. He has also been on the faculty of the Center for Cartoon Studies in White River Junction, Vermont since its opening in 2005. Bissette's film criticism, articles and short fiction have appeared in over two dozen periodicals and anthologies, and his original novella *Aliens: Tribes* won a Bram Stoker Award in 1993. Most recently he penned the short story "Copper" for the zombie anthology *The New Dead*, co-authored *Prince of Stories: The Many Worlds of Neil Gaiman*, and provided characteristically memorable illustrations for *The Vermont Monster Guide*.

After a childhood in Erie, Pennsylvania spent consuming a steady diet of comics, monster magazines and monster movies, **JOHN TOTLEBEN** went to the Joe Kubert School of Cartoon and Graphic Art where he met Stephen Bissette. Together they worked on *Bizarre Adventures* followed by *Swamp Thing*, which they drew for almost three years. Totleben is best known for his illustrative work on Alan Moore's *Miracleman*. His other credits include *1963*, *Vermillion* and *The Dreaming*.

Born on July 8, 1959 in Niagara Falls, **STAN WOCH** attended the Pratt Institute's School of Art and Design from 1977 to 1979 and the Kubert School from 1979 to 1981. His comic book credits include *Swamp Thing*, *World's Finest*, *Teen Titans*, *Airboy*, *Clive Barker's Tapping the Vein*, *Black Orchid*, *The Sandman*, *Hellblazer*, *Robin*, *Batman: Shadow of the Bat*, *Batman: Gotham Adventures* and *Superman Adventures*.

RICK VEITCH worked in the underground comics scene before attending the Joe Kubert School of Cartoon and Graphic Art. After graduating, he worked with Stephen Bissette on *Bizarre Adventures* before creating and illustrating *The One*, the innovative Epic Comics miniseries. In addition to writing and drawing an acclaimed run on *Swamp Thing*, he is the creator/cartoonist of *Brat Pack*, *Maximortal* and the dream-based *Rare Bit Fiends*, and a contributing artist on *1963*. He is also the writer and artist of the miniseries *Greyshirt: Indigo Sunset* from America's Best Comics, and the creator of the critically acclaimed graphic novel *Can't Get No* and the spectacularly satirical series *Army@Love* from Vertigo.

ALFREDO ALCALA's graceful, moody inks helped maintain the style on *Swamp Thing* through many penciller changes. DC first employed Alcala's talents in its horror and war comics such as *Ghosts*, *Unexpected*, and *Weird War Tales*. Later he moved on to titles including *All-Star Squadron*, *Savage Sword of Conan*, *Batman*, *Swamp Thing* and countless others for both DC and Marvel. After a long battle with cancer, Alcala passed away in April, 2000.

RON RANDALL has been working professionally as an illustrator and storyteller for over twenty years. He has worked for all the major American comic publishers, including DC, Marvel, Dark Horse and Image, as well as commercial clients such as Disney, Nike, SeaWorld and Sony.

TOM MANDRAKE has contributed his drawing skills to such titles as *The Spectre*, *Martian Manhunter*, *Batman* and *Swamp Thing* as well as many others. He has illustrated such books as *Aces Abroad* and *GRRM: The George RR Martin Retrospective* and the young adult novel *The Forest King: The Woodlark's Shadow*. Mandrake has also worked as art director for the independent film *Zombie Prom*, which won several awards including Best Comics-Oriented Film and the Judges' Choice Award at the 2006 Comic Con International Independent Film Festival in San Diego.

TATJANA WOOD switched careers from dressmaking to comics coloring in the late 1960s and quickly established herself as one of the top colorists in the field, winning two Shazam awards in the early 1970s.

Over his long and prolific career, **JOHN COSTANZA** has lettered a huge number of comics and has won numerous awards along the way. A cartoonist in his own right, Costanza has also contributed stories and art to a variety of titles, beginning in the late 1960s and continuing right through to the new millennium.